A Guide to the Immigration Act 2016

A Guide to the Immigration Act 2016

First Edition

Alison Harvey
BA (Oxon), MA, Barrister, Legal Director,
Immigration Law Practitioners' Association (ILPA)

and

Zoe Harper
BA (Hons), MSc, Barrister, Legal Officer,
Immigration Law Practitioners' Association (ILPA)

Bloomsbury Professional

Bloomsbury Professional

An imprint of Bloomsbury Publishing Plc

Bloomsbury Professional Ltd	Bloomsbury Publishing Plc
41–43 Boltro Road	50 Bedford Square
Haywards Heath	London
RH16 1BJ	WC1B 3DP
UK	UK

www.bloomsbury.com

BLOOMSBURY and the Diana logo are trademarks of Bloomsbury Publishing Plc

© Bloomsbury Professional Ltd 2017

All rights reserved. No part of this publication may be reproduced or transmitted in any form or by any means, electronic or mechanical, including photocopying, recording, or any information storage or retrieval system, without prior permission in writing from the publishers.

While every care has been taken to ensure the accuracy of this work, no responsibility for loss or damage occasioned to any person acting or refraining from action as a result of any statement in it can be accepted by the authors, editors or publishers.

All UK Government legislation and other public sector information used in the work is Crown Copyright ©. All House of Lords and House of Commons information used in the work is Parliamentary Copyright ©. This information is reused under the terms of the Open Government Licence v3.0 (http://www.nationalarchives.gov.uk/doc/open-government-licence/version/3) except where otherwise stated.

All Eur-lex material used in the work is © European Union, http://eur-lex.europa.eu/, 1998–2017.

British Library Cataloguing-in-Publication Data

A catalogue record for this book is available from the British Library.

ISBN:	PB:	978 1 78451 928 5
	ePDF:	978 1 78451 930 8
	ePub:	978 1 78451 929 2

Typeset by Compuscript Ltd, Shannon
Printed and bound by CPI Group (UK) Ltd, Croydon, CR0 4YY

To find out more about our authors and books visit www.bloomsburyprofessional.com. Here you will find extracts, author information, details of forthcoming events and the option to sign up for our newsletters

Acknowledgements

We are grateful to the MPs and peers of all parties (and of none) and their staff who shared information and documents with us. Thanks also to Andrew Elliott of the Home Office Bill team and his colleagues, who responded patiently to our questions. Our thanks go to James Ewins QC and to Stephen Shaw CBE for opportunities provided to us, with others, to discuss the subject matter of their enquiries both during and subsequent to the publication of their respective reports.

We are grateful to the ILPA members and to the colleagues from other organizations, many of whom are ILPA members, who worked on the Bill and who have attended our ILPA training sessions and our presentations on it for the Association of Visitors to Immigration Detainees, the Council of Scottish Local Authorities (COSLA), Public Law Project and LawWorks. We thank them for their comments and insights.

Particular thanks go to Ronan Toal of Garden Court Chambers who trained alongside us. We thank Emma Smale of Action for Children; Tom Southerden, Steve Symonds, and Lucy Wake of Amnesty International; Emily-Anna Gibbs and Carita Thomas of the Anti Trafficking and Labour Exploitation Unit; Deborah Gellner and Hazel Williams of the Asylum Support Appeals Project; John Cox and Pierre Makhlouf of Bail for Immigration Detainees; Augustus Della Porta of Bates Wells and Braithwaite LLP; Janet Farrell, Jed Pennington and Jane Ryan of Bhatt Murphy Solicitors; Julian Bild; Sonia Routledge of Birnberg Peirce; Howard Mollett of Care International; Lucy Capron of The Children's Society; George Gabriel of Citizens UK; Anita Hurrell of Coram Children's Legal Centre; Helena Brice and Sarah Macfadyen of Crisis; Tamsin Alger and Jerome Phelps of Detention Action; Zubier Yazdani of Deighton Peirce Glynn; Laura Dubinsky and Alasdair Mackenzie of Doughty Street Chambers; Toufique Hossain and Patrick Page of Duncan Lewis Solicitors; Claire Falconer and Caroline Robinson of Focus on Labour Exploitation; Bridget O'Rourke of the Equality and Human Rights Commission; Lucy Gregg and Sile Reynolds of Freedom from Torture; Adrian Berry, Michelle Brewer, Shu Shin Luh, Stephanie Harrison QC and Colin Yeo of Garden Court Chambers; TJ Birdi and Andrew Leak of the Helen Bamber Foundation; Liliana Bird, Jess Mills and Josie Naughton of Help Refugees; Justin Bates, Arden Chambers, and Giles Peaker, Anthony Gold—of the Housing Law Practitioners' Association; Kate Roberts of the Human Trafficking Foundation; JB Louveaux and Angela Patrick of Justice; Saira Grant, Chai Patel and Charlotte Peel of the Joint Council for the Welfare of Immigrants; Catherine Kenny of Kalayaan; Anselm Benedict of the Law Society; Sarah Craig (Glasgow University) of the Law Society of Scotland; Sam Ingham of Laura Devine Solicitors; Jonathan Kingham

Acknowledgements

of LexisNexis; Sam Hawke and Rachel Robinson of Liberty; Raza Hussain QC of Matrix Chambers; Theresa Schleicher of Medical Justice; Sue Lukes of MigrationWorks CIC; Daniel Vincent of the National Aids Trust; Alaa Elaydi of the National Union of Students; Catherine Maclay of Platt and Associates; David Chirico of 1 Pump Court Chambers; Gabrielle Bourke of the Royal College of Midwives; Samir Jeraj and Dr Leander Neckles of the Race Equality Foundation; Karl Pike and Hugo Tristram of the Red Cross; Kamena Dorling and Frances Trevena, Coram Children's Legal Centre and Ilona Pinter, Children's Society—co-chairs of the Refugee Children's Consortium and all members of the Consortium; James Conyers and Paul Hook of Refugee Action; Judith Dennis and Jon Featonby of the Refugee Council; Simon Gordon of the Residential Landlords' Association; Jasbindar Bhatoa and Nicole Masri of Rights of Women; Daniela Reale of Save the Children; Christopher Desira of Seraphus; Deborah Garvie of Shelter; Sue Shutter; Adam O'Boyle of Safe Passage; Mike Kaye of Still Human Still Here; Rosa Crawford of the Trades Union Congress; Sarah Rimmington of UKCISA; Leonard Zulu of UNHCR; Melanie Teff of UNICEF UK; Gemma Lousely and Natasha Walter of Women for Refugee Women.

Our thanks go to Tamara Smith, Parliamentary Officer at ILPA for her support in marshalling this material, to Helen Williams at ILPA for her editorial work, and to Kiran Goss, Harriet Espin-Bradley and Jane Bradford at Bloomsbury Professional.

Contents

Acknowledgements v
Table of Statutes ix
Table of Statutory Instruments xix
Table of Immigration Rules xxi
Table of Cases xxiii
Table of Regional and International Legislation xxvii
Abbreviations xxix

Introduction xxxi

    Commencement xxxi

    Dramatis Personae xxxiii

    Ministerial Statements xxxv

Chapter 1	Part 1—Labour Market and Illegal Working	1
Chapter 2	Part 2—Access to Services	177
Chapter 3	Part 3—Enforcement	237
Chapter 4	Part 4—Appeals	317
Chapter 5	Part 5—Support etc for Certain Categories of Migrant	333
Chapter 6	Part 6—Border Security	413
Chapter 7	Part 7—Language Requirements for Public Sector Workers	451
Chapter 8	Part 8—Fees and Charges—Immigration and Passports, and Civil Registration	467
Chapter 9	Part 9—Miscellaneous and General—Welfare of Children and Final Provisions	481
Appendix	Materials—Whole Act, Parts 1–9	495

Index 519

Table of Statutes

Asylum and Immigration (Treatment of Claimants etc) Act 2004 c 19		Children Act 1989 c 41 – *contd*	
		s.22(4)	5.5
		(5)	5.5
s.9	5.2	22C(7)	5.5
10	5.2	(8)(b)	5.5
14	3.11	23	5.4
(3)	3.4	23A	5.4
36	3.16	23C	5.4–1, 5.4.8
49(3)	9.6	23CA	5.4–8
Banking and Financial Dealings Act 1971 c 80	1.17	23CZA	5.4
		23D	5.4
Births and Deaths Registration Act 1953 c 20		24A	5.4–1, 5.4.8
s.13	8.6	24B	5.4–1, 5.4.8
30–33A	8.6	24D	5.4.8
34A	8.6	105(1)	5.5–8
38A	8.6	Civic Government (Scotland) Act 1982 c 45	2.4
(6)	8.6		
39	8.6	s.13	2.4
39A	8.6	13(3C)	2.4
41	8.6	13A	2.4
Borders, Citizenship and Immigration Act 2009 c 11	9.1	(1)	2.4
		(3)	2.4
s.23	3.3	23(1)	2.4
54A	3.15	Sch.1	2.4
55	4.1, 9.1	Sch.5	2.4
63	9.1	Civil Jurisdiction and Judgments Act 1982 c 27	
British Nationality Act 1981 c 61			
s.50A	5.4.1	s.52(2)	9.6
Care Act 2014 c 23	5.4.1	Civil Partnership Act 2004 c 33	
s.21	5.2	s.29	3.10
Charities Act 2011 c 25		34	8.6
s.1	8.1	152(1)	3.10
Charities Act (Northern Ireland) 2008 c 12		(3)	3.10
		Commissioners for Revenue and Customs Act 2005 c 11	
s.1	8.1	s.7(11)	1.7
Children Act 1989 c 41	5.2.8, 5.4.9.1, 5.6	19	1.7
		(2)	1.7
s.3	5.5	20(9)	1.7
4	5.5	Companies Act 2006 c 26	
5	5.5		
17	5.4.1–7	s.381	8.1

Table of Statutes

Consular Fees Act 1980 c 23	
s.1	8.5
Consular Relations Act 1968 c 18	
Sch.1	8.3
Counter-Terrorism and Security Act 2015 c 6	
s.2	6.2
Courts Act 2003 c 39	
s.98	6.1
Crime and Courts Act 2003 c 22...	1.13
s.54	4.1
Criminal Attempts Act 1981 c 47	
s.1	2.4
Criminal Justice Act 1925 c 86	
s.33	1.29–30
Criminal Justice Act 2003 c 44	
s.154(1)	1.27
281(1)	2.1
(3)(a)	2.1
(5)	2.1, 2.5, 6.2
Criminal Justice Act (Northern Ireland) 1945 c 15	
s.18	1.29–30
Criminal Justice and Immigration Act 2008 c 4	
s.132	3.16
133	3.16
(5)	2.4
134	5.2
135	5.2
Criminal Law Act 1977 c 45	
s.1	2.4
Criminal Law (Consolidation) (Scotland) Act 1995	
s.14A	3.11
24A(7)	3.11
26A(2)	3.11
26B	3.11
(1)	3.11
Criminal Procedure (Scotland) Act 1995 c 39	
s.70	1.29–30
143	1.29–30
Customs and Excise Management Act 1979 c 2	
s.8	6.2
Data Protection Act 1998 c 29	1.7, 1.31
Education Act 1996 c 56	
s.4	3.10
564	8.6

Education Act 1996 c 56 – *contd*	
s.564(4)	8.6
579(1)	3.10
Education Reform Act 1988 c 40	
Sch.6	5.4
Education (Scotland) Act 1980 c 44	
s.135(1)	3.10
Employment Agencies Act 1973 c 35	1.3, 1.11–12, 1.15–16, 1.18–19, 1.23, 1.25–6, 1.33
s.8A	1.3, 1.11–12, 1.14
3A	1.3
8A(2)	1.11
9(4)(b)	1.3, 1.14
9	1.11, 1.31
13	1.11
Employment Rights Act 1996 c 18	
s.191(3)	2.1, 7.2
194(6)	2.1
195(5)	2.1
230	1.3
Energy Act 2004 c 20	3.13
Equality Act 2010 c 15	7.2, 7.5
European Communities Act 1972 c 68	
s.2(2)	8.1
Factories Act 1961 c 34	
s.178	8.6
178(3)	8.6
Finance (No.2) Act 1987 c 51	
s.102	8.5
Fisheries (Northern Ireland) Act 1966 c 17	1.31
Freedom of Information Act 2000 c 36	
Sch.1	1.31
Further and Higher Education Act 1992 c 13	
s.90	3.10
91	3.10
Further and Higher Education (Scotland) Act 2005 asp 6	
s.35	3.10
Gangmasters (Licensing) Act 2004 c 11	1.3, 1.12, 1.14–16, 1.18–19, 1.23, 1.25–6, 1.33
s.1	1.31
(1)	1.13, 1.31
(2)(a)–(c)	1.3

x

Table of Statutes

Gangmasters (Licensing) Act 2004 c 11 – *contd*		Housing (Scotland) Act 2001 asp 10	5.2
s.2	1.31	Hovercraft Act 1968 c 59	
3(5)(b)	1.10	s.1	6.2
3	1.31	Human Rights Act 1998 c 42	9.6
7	1.3	s.1	3.16
8	1.31	6	3.16.3
(1)	1.31	(1)	2.5
13(2)	1.13	Human Trafficking and Exploitation (Criminal Justice and Support for Victims) Act (Northern Ireland) 2015 c 2	
(3)	1.13		
14	1.31		
15	1.3, 1.12, 1.14, 1.31		
16	1.31		
17	1.31	Sch.3	1.31
18	1.12	Immigration Act 1971 c 77	2.3–5, 3.4, 5.4
19	1.31		
(1A)	1.31	Pt.3	3.5
22A	1.13, 1.31	s.3(1)(c)(i)	2.1
(1)(d)	1.13	(6)	3.6
54A(8)	1.31	3C	2.4, 3.17, 4.1
55	1.31	(1)(c)	3.17
58	1.31	(2)(a)	3.17
60	1.31	(3)	4.1
Sch.2	1.31	3D(3)	4.1
Sch.3	1.31	3D	4.1–2
Sch.4	1.31	4	3.17
Government of Wales Act 2006 c 32	7.3–4, 7.7–8	4(1)	1.33.1, 3.17
		(2)	3.1, 6.2
Harbours Act 1964 c 40		5(1)	2.1, 3.6
s.14	3.10	8	6.3
16	6.2	8A	6.3
Harbours, Docks and Piers Clauses Act 1847 c 27		8B	6.3
s.79	3.10, 6.2	(3)	6.3
Health and Safety at Work etc Act 1974 c 37		(4)	6.3
		(5)	6.3
s.18(7)	1.6	11	3.16
19	1.6	18A(1)	3.7
Higher Education Act 2004 c 8		24	2.1, 3.16
s.11	3.10	24A	2.1
21	3.10	24B	2.1–3
House of Commons Disqualification Act 1975 c 24		(2)	2.1
		(3)	2.1
Sch.1	1.31	(3)(a)	2.1
Housing Act 1985 c 68		(3)(b)	2.1
Sch.1	5.2	(9)	2.1
Housing Act 1988 c 50		(10)	2.1
Sch.1	5.2	25	6.2
		25A	6.2
Housing (Scotland) Act 1988 c 43		25B	6.2
Sch.4	5.2	26A	5.2

Table of Statutes

Immigration Act 1971 c 77 – *contd*

s.27	6.1
28	3.16, 6.2
28A	2.2, 6.2
(3)(a)	2.1
28B(5)	2.1
28CA(1)	2.1
28D	3.9
(1A)–(1D)	3.9
(2A)	3.9
(4)	2.1
28FA(1)(a)	2.1
28FB	3.9
28H	3.5
28J	3.9
28K	3.9
(2A)	3.9
(3)	3.9
28L	3.1, 3.9, 3.13
28Q(1)	6.2
(2)	6.2
28ZI	3.5
33	8.3, 8.5
(1)	8.1
34(4)	2.1
36	9.6
78	4.1
281	3.2–3
Sch.1	6.1
Sch.2	1.6, 1.13, 2.1, 2.3, 3.1, 3.13, 3.15–14, 4.3, 6.1–2
Sch.3	3.15–16
Sch.4A	6.2

Immigration Act 2014 c 22   3.17, 8.5

Pt.2	9.6
s.1	3.15
2	3.15
3	3.15
7	3.16.6
15	2.4, 3.2
15(3)	2.4
16	2.4
17	2.4
19	9.1
23	2.3–4, 3.2
24	2.3–4
25	3.2
29	2.3–4
30	2.3–4
44(5)(b)(ii)	2.3

Immigration Act 2014 c 22 – *contd*

s.63	4.1
70	8.1
(2)	8.1
(6)	8.1
70A	8.1
71	4.1, 9.1
74(2)(ja)	8.1
76(6)	9.6
94B	4.1
122(2A)	2.3
Sch.2	3.16.6
Sch.3	5.2, 5.4
Sch.9	3.12, 4.2–3

Immigration and Asylum Act 1999 c 33

Pt.8	3.6
Pt.3	3.16.4
s.2	5.2
2B(2)(c)(ii)	5.2.2
4	3.16.5, 5.1–7
10	3.16
(6)	2.1
20(3)(da)	3.10
20	3.10
20A	3.10
45	5.2
46	5.2
47	5.2
51(3)	3.7
(15)	3.6–7
(16)	3.7
53	3.16, 5.2
69(11)(b)	5.5
82(2)	5.2
93(3B)	5.2
(3D)	5.2
94	5.2
(1)	5.2, 5.4
(2A)	5.2.2
(2B)	5.2
(2B)(a)	5.2
(2C)	5.2
(2D)	5.2–4
(3)	5.2, 5.5
(3A)(b)	5.2.2
(3B)(a)	5.2.2
(3C)	5.2
(3D)(b)	5.2.2
(5)	5.2–9

Table of Statutes

Immigration and Asylum Act 1999 c 33 – *contd*		Immigration, Asylum and Nationality Act 2006 c 13	
s.95	3.16, 5.2–7	s.15	2.3–5, 3.2
(1)	5.2.2	(3)	2.3–5
(3)–(8)	5.2, 5.4	16	2.3–5
(3D)(b)(i)	5.2	17	2.3–5
(5)	5.2.7.1	21	2.2, 2.5
95A	5.1–7	(1)	2.2
(1)	5.2	(1A)	2.1–2
(1)(c)	5.2	(2)(a)(i)	2.2
(2)	5.2.3	22	2.2
(2B)(c)(ii)	5.2	24	3.16
(3)	5.2–4	(a)	2.2
(3A)(a)	5.2	25(b)	2.2
(4)	5.2–5	26	2.2
(5)	5.2.5	28AA(1)	2.2
(8)	5.2.6	35	2.2
96	5.2	43(1)(b)	5.2
(1)	5.2	(2)	5.2
(1A)	5.2.7	(5)	5.2
(2)	5.2	(6)	5.2
97	5.2	(7)	5.2
98	5.2	44	5.2
98A	5.2.8, 5.4	63(3)	9.6
99	5.2	Sch.1	4.2
100	5.2	Intelligence Services Act 1994 c 13	1.7
101	5.2	s.2(2)(a)	1.7
103	5.2	4(2)(a)	1.7
112	5.2	7(11)	1.7
113	5.2	Interpretation Act 1978 c 30	1.12, 1.33, 2.3, 3.4, 5.9, 9.3
114	5.2		
118(1)(b)	5.2	s.7	1.17
122	5.2	Legal Aid, Sentencing and Punishment of Offenders Act 2012 c 10	
125	5.2		
127	5.2		
141	3.12, 3.16, 5.2		
142	3.12	s.9	4.1
143	3.12	Sch.1	4.1, 5.2, 7.1
144A(2)	3.12	Licensing Act 2003 c 17	2.5
147	3.6–7	s.1	2.3
154	3.16	1(6)	2.3
166	3.10, 5.2	3(1)	2.3
(5)	5.2	10	2.3
167	5.2	11	2.3, 2.5
(1)	6.3	13	2.3
170(7)	9.6	(4)	2.3
Sch.1	3.10	16(2A)	2.3
Sch.8	5.2	27(1A)	2.3
Sch.11	3.8	16	2.3
Sch.13	3.16	27	2.3

Table of Statutes

Licensing Act 2003 c 17 – *contd*
s.35 .... 2.5
42 .... 2.3
   (2A) 2.3
   (8) 2.3
44(5) 2.3
   (5)(b)(ii) 2.3
45 .... 2.3
47 .... 2.3
48 .... 2.3
69 .... 2.3
113 .... 2.3
   (2A) 2.3
   (4) 2.3
115 .... 2.3
   (2A) 2.3
120 .... 2.3
   (2)(aa) 2.3
   (5A) 2.3
   (5B) 2.3
122 .... 2.3
123 .... 2.3
124 .... 2.3
   (5A) 2.3
125(3) 2.3
132 .... 2.3
167(1) 2.5
179 .... 2.3
   (1A) 2.3
192 .... 2.3
192A 2.3
193 .... 2.3
   (2) 2.3
194 .... 2.3
Sch.4 .... 2.3
Sch.5 .... 2.3
Sch.6 .... 2.5
Sch.10 .... 2.3
Local Government etc (Scotland) Act 1994 c 39
s.2 .... 1.6, 3.10
Local Government (Miscellaneous Provisions) Act 1976 c 57 .... 2.4
s.23(1) 2.4
51 .... 2.4
   (1ZA) 2.4
53 .... 2.4
   (1) 2.4
   (1)(a) 2.4

Local Government (Miscellaneous Provisions) Act 1976 c 57 – *contd*
s.53(1)(b) 2.4
53A(1)(a) 2.4
   (9) 2.4
   (10) 2.4
   (12) 2.4
55 .... 2.4
   (1A) 2.4
59 .... 2.4
   (1ZA) 2.4
61 .... 2.4
62 .... 2.4
61(1) 2.4
62(1) 2.4
   (4) 2.4
62A(1)(a) 2.4
   (1)(b) 2.4
   (3) 2.4
   (4) 2.4
   (5) 2.4
   (7) 2.4
74(4) 2.4
77 .... 2.4
78B(3) 2.4
79 .... 2.4
79A 2.4
   (3) 2.4
80 .... 2.4
London Hackney Carriages Act 1843 c 86 .... 2.4
s.18 .... 2.4
Magistrates' Courts Act 1980 c 43
Sch.3 .... 1.29–30
Marine Navigation Act 2013 c 23
s.7 .... 6.2
Marriage Act 1949 c 76
s.27 .... 8.6
31 .... 8.6
41 .... 8.6
43D 8.6
51 .... 8.6
57 .... 8.6
63–65A 8.6
71A 8.6
   (9) 8.6
74 .... 8.6
78 .... 8.6
   (1) 8.6

Table of Statutes

Marriage (Registrar General's Licence) Act 1970 c 34	
s.17	8.6
Marriage (Same Sex Couples) Act 2013 c 30	
s.9	8.6
Mental Health Act 1983 c 20	3.14
Merchant Shipping Act 1995 c 21	6.2
Metropolitan Public Carriage Act 1869 c 115	2.4
s.4	2.4
8(7)	2.4
8A(2)	2.4
(4)	2.4
(8)	2.4
(12)	2.4
(14)	2.4
11	2.4
Mineral Workings (Offshore Installations) Act 1971 c 61	
s.1	3.13
Ministers of the Crown Act 1975 c 26	3.15
Modern Slavery Act 2015 c 30	1.3, 1.12, 1.31.1
Pt.2	1.11
s.1	1.3, 6.2
2	1.3, 6.2
3(2)	1.3
4	1.3
11A	1.3, 1.11–12
12	1.11
14	1.3
(1)(b)	1.3
(3)(d)	1.3
(3)(e)	1.3
(3)(i)	1.3
(3)(l)	1.3
15	1.11
19	1.11
(7)	1.11
20	1.11
23	1.11
26	1.11
27	1.3, 1.11
30	1.11
(1)	1.3
(2)	1.3
30A	1.3, 1.11–12

Modern Slavery Act 2015 c 30 – *contd*	
s.33	1.11
34	2.1
39	6.2
43(3)	2.1
45	2.1
52	1.31
53	1.33.1
54A(9)	1.31
60	9.6
(6)	9.6
Sch.2	6.2
Sch.3	1.31
National Assistance Act 1948 c 29	
s.21	5.4.1
National Health Service Act 2006 c 41	
s.25	1.6, 1.31, 3.10
30	1.6, 1.31, 3.10
National Health Service (Consequential Provisions) Act 2006 c 43	
Sch.3	5.2
National Health Service (Scotland) Act 1978 c 29	
s.12A	3.10
National Health Service (Wales) Act 2006 c 42	
s.11	1.6, 1.31, 3.10
18	1.6, 1.31, 3.10
Sch.15	5.2
Nationality, Immigration and Asylum Act 2002 c 41	3.16.4–17
Pt.5A	9.1
s.10A(2)	5.4
16	5.2
18	5.2
(1)	5.2
(1A)	5.2
(3)	5.2, 5.4–1
19(1)(a)	5.2
23	3.16, 5.2
23C(4)(b)	5.4
23CA(4)	5.4
24B(2)(b)	5.4
26	5.2
29	5.2
30	3.16
31(3)	5.2

Table of Statutes

Nationality, Immigration and Asylum Act 2002 c 41 – *contd*	
s.35	5.2
43	5.2
44	5.2
49	5.2
51	5.2
55	5.2
62	3.14–16
67	3.16.1
68	3.16
69	3.16
70	3.16, 5.2
71	3.16, 5.2
78	3.15, 4.1
82	5.5
(1)	4.1, 5.4.9
(2)	5.2, 5.5
(2)(a)(i)	5.2
(2)(a)(ii)	5.2
83	5.4.8.1
92(3)(a)	4.1
94B	4.1
s.96(2)	5.4.9
97	4.1
97A(2C)	4.1
98B	9.1
104	4.2
105	3.6
120(4)(b)	4.2
163(4)	9.6
Sch.3	3.15, 5.2, 5.4.11, 5.6
National Minimum Wage Act 1998 c 39	1.3, 1.12, 1.14–16, 1.18–19, 1.23, 1.25–6, 1.33
s.1	1.3
13	1.3, 1.7, 1.11–12, 1.14
14	1.11
15	1.11, 1.31
(5A)	1.31
19A	1.3
Sch.2	1.11
Natural Environment and Rural Communities Act 2006 c 16	
Sch.7	1.31
Northern Ireland Act 1998 c 47	
s.78(6)	7.3
Northern Ireland Assembly Disqualification Act 1975 c 25	
Sch.1	1.31
Official Secrets Act 1989 c 6	1.1
Parliamentary Commissioner Act 1967 c 13	
Sch.2	1.31
Pensions Act 2004 c 35	
Sch.3	1.31
Places of Worship Registration Act 1855 c 81	
s.5	8.6
Plymouth City Council Act 1975 c iv	2.4
s.2	2.4
1(2)	2.4
2(1)	2.4
2A	2.4
(3)	2.4
(5)	2.4
2B(1)	2.4
(2)	2.4
9	2.4
11(1)	2.4
(1)(a)	2.4
(1)(b)	2.4
11A(1)	2.4
(8)	2.4
(9)	2.4
(10)	2.4
(11)	2.4
12	2.4
13	2.4
13A(8)	2.4
(9)	2.4
13A(11)	2.4
17	2.4
(1A)	2.4
19	2.4
(1)	2.4
20(1)	2.4
20	2.4
20A(1)(a)	2.4
(1)(b)	2.4
(4)	2.4
(5)	2.4
(7)	2.4
37	2.4
Police Act 1996 c 16	
s.101(1)	1.6

Table of Statutes

Police and Criminal Evidence Act 1984 c 60	1.10, 3.13, 3.16
s.10	3.13, 6.2
19	3.3
23	3.13
114A	1.12
114B	1.3, 1.11–12, 1.31
(1)	1.12
(4)(e)	1.12
(9)	1.12
(10)	1.12
(11)	1.12
Police and Fire Reform (Scotland) Act 2012 asp 8	
s.99	6.2
Police Reform Act 2002 c 30	
10	1.31
26C	1.31
26D(1)	1.31
Police Reform and Social Responsibility Act 2011 c 13	
s.109(9)	2.3
(10)	2.3
111(3)	2.3
(5)	2.3
Policing and Crime Act 2017 c3	6.2
Port of London Act 1968 c 32	3.10
Private Hire Vehicles (London) Act 1998 c 34	2.4
s.1(1)	2.4
2(1)	2.4
3	2.4
(3A)	2.4
3A(7)	2.4
(9)	2.4
13	2.4
13A(1)(a)	2.4
(7)	2.4
(8)	2.4
16	2.4
25	2.4
32	2.4
35	2.4
(3)	2.4
(4)	2.4
35A(1)	2.4
(3)	2.4
35B(1)	2.4
(2)	2.4

Proceeds of Crime Act 2002 c 29	2.1
s.14	2.1
70	2.1
92	2.1
218	2.1
412	3.13, 6.2
Protection from Eviction Act 1977 c 43	
s.3A(7A)	5.2
Public Expenditure and Receipts Act 1968 c 14	
Sch.3	8.6
Public Records Act 1958 c 51	
Sch.1	1.31
Public Services Reform (Scotland) Act 2010 asp 8	2.4
Registration of Births, Deaths and Marriages (Scotland) Act 1965 c 49	
s.7	3.10
Registration Service Act 1953 c 37	
16	8.6
19B	8.6
Regulation of Investigatory Powers Act 2000 c 23	1.31
Pt.1	1.7
Sch.1	1.31
Regulatory Enforcement and Sanctions Act 2008 c 13	
Sch.5	1.31
Rehabilitation of Offenders Act 1974 c 53	2.4–5
Rent (Scotland) Act 1984 c 58	
s.23A(5A)	5.2
Reserve Forces Act 1996 c 14	
Pt.11	2.1, 7.2
Road Traffic Act 1960 c 16	
s.1117	2.4
Savings Banks Act 1887 c 40	
s.10	8.6
Scotland Act 1998 c 48	7.3
Security Services Act 1989 c 5	
s.2(2)(a)	1.7
Serious Crime Act 2007 c 27	
Pt.2	1.3, 1.14
Social Security Administration Act 1992 c 5	
s.124	8.6
(5)(a)	8.6

Table of Statutes

Social Services and Well-being (Wales) Act 2014 anaw 4	
s.46	5.2
Special Immigration Appeals Act 1997 c 68	
s.2(2)(a)	4.2
3	3.16
5	3.16
9(3)	9.6
Sch.3	3.16
Superannuation Act 1972 c 11	
Sch.1	1.31
Taxis Act (Northern Ireland) 2008 c 4	2.4
s.1(3)	2.4
2	2.4
(4A)	2.4
2A(8)	2.4
22(6)	2.4
23(2A)	2.4
23A(8)	2.4
26	2.4
32	2.4
34	2.4
56	2.4
s.56A(1)	2.4
Taxis Act (Northern Ireland) 2008 c 4 – *contd*	
(3)	2.4
56B(1)	2.4
(2)(b)	2.4
(3)	2.4
87	2.4
Territorial Waters Jurisdiction Act 1878 c 73	
s.3	6.2
Town Police Clauses Act 1847 c 89	
s.46	2.4
68	2.4
UK Borders Act 2007 c 30	2.1
s.17	5.2
32(5)	3.6
36	3.14–13
(1)	3.15
(3C)	3.16
40	3.10, 5.2
45	3.9
54	3.9
60(4)	9.6
61(2)	2.4, 3.3, 3.6, 3.10–11, 9.3
Welsh Language Act 1993 c 38	7.7

Table of Statutory Instruments

Accession of Croatia (Immigration and Worker Authorisation) Regulations 2013 (SI 2013/1460) 2.1–2

Accession (Immigration and Worker Authorisation) Regulations 2006 SI 2006/3317) 2.1

Agency Workers Regulations 2010 (SI 2010/93) 7.2, 7.4

Agency Workers Regulations (Northern Ireland) 2011 (SR 2011/350) 7.2, 7.4

Asylum Support Regulations 2000 (SI 2000/704) 5.2.2, 5.4.7

Care Leavers (England) Regulations 2010 (SI 2010/2571) . 5.4.12

Criminal Attempts and Conspiracy (Northern Ireland) Order 1983 (SI 1983/1120 (NI 13)) 2.4

Data Protection (Processing of Sensitive Personal Data) Order 2000 (SI 2000/417) 1.7

Detention Centre Rules 2001 (SI 2001/238) 3.14

Education and Libraries (Northern Ireland) Order 1986 (SI 1986/594 (NI 3)) 3.10

Education and Libraries (Northern Ireland) Order 1993 (SI 1993/2810 (NI 12)) 3.10

Education (Student Support) Regulations 2011 (SI 2011/1986) 5.4.10

Employment (Miscellaneous Provisions) (Northern Ireland) Order 1981 (SI 1981/839 (NI 20)) 1.31

Employment Rights (Northern Ireland) Order 1996 (SI 1996/1919 (NI 16)) 2.1, 7.2

Further Education (Northern Ireland) Order 1997 (SI 1997/1772 (NI 15)) 3.10

Health and Personal Social Services (Northern Ireland) Order 1991 (SI 1991/194 (NI 1)) 3.10

Housing (Northern Ireland) Order 1983 (SI 1983/1118 (NI 15)) 5.2

Illegal Working Compliance Order Regulations 2016 (SI 2016/1058) 1.38

Immigration Act 2014 (Commencement No 6) Order 2016 (SI 2016/11) 9.6

Immigration Act 2016 (Commencement No 1) Regulations 2016 (SI 2016/603) 1.1.1.1–2, 1.3–13, 1.25, 2.1, 3.1, 5.3, 5.5–9, 6.2–3, 8.3–6, 9.5

Immigration Act 2016 (Commencement No 2 and Transitional Provisions) Regulations 2016 (SI 2016/1037) 1.14.1, 1.15–24, 1.26–30, 1.37–38, 2.4–6, 3.9, 3.17, 4.1–3, 7.1–9

Immigration Act 2016 (Consequential Amendments) Regulations 2016 (SI 2016/655) 1.1, 1.10, 9.3

Immigration Act 2014 (Current Accounts) (Compliance etc) Regulations 2016 (SI 2016/1073) 2.10

Immigration Act 2016 (Transitional Provision) Regulations 2016 (SI 2016/712) 2.1–2, 9.3

Table of Statutory Instruments

Immigration (Designation of Travel Bans) Order 2000 (SI 2000/2724)	6.3
Immigration (Guidance on Detention of Vulnerable Persons) Regulations 2016 (SI 2016/847)	3.4
Immigration and Nationality (Fees) Regulations 2006 (SI 2006/226)	8.1
Immigration (Residential Accommodation) (Termination of Residential Tenancy Agreements) (Guidance etc) Regulations 2016 (SI 2016/1060)	2.4, 2.5
Immigration (Short-term Holding Facilities) Regulations 2002 (SI 2002/2538)	3.14
Immigration (Variation of Leave) Order 2016 (SI 2016/948)	1.31.1
Judgments Enforcement (Northern Ireland) Order 1981 (SI 1981/226 (NI.6))	6.1
Labour Market Enforcement (Code of Practice on Labour Market Enforcement Undertakings and Orders: Appointed Day) Regulations (2016) (SI 2016/1044)	1.25
London Cab Order 1934 (SO 1934/1346)	2.4
Magistrates' Courts (Northern Ireland) Order 1981 (SI 1981/1675 (NI 26))	1.18, 1.23, 1.29–30
Marriage (Northern Ireland) Order 2003 (SI 2003/413 (NI 3))	3.10
Official Secrets Act 1989 (Prescription) Order 1990 (SI 1990/200)	1.1
Police and Criminal Evidence Act 1984 (Application to immigration officer and designated customs officials in England and Wales) Order 2013 (SI 2013/1542)	3.3
Police and Criminal Evidence (Northern Ireland) Order 1989 (SI 1989/1341 (NI 12))	3.3, 3.13, 6.2
Rehabilitation of Offenders (Northern Ireland) Order 1978 (SI 1978/1908 (NI 27))	2.4–5
Road Traffic (Northern Ireland) Order 1981 (SI 1981/154 (NI 1))	2.8
Road Traffic Offenders (Northern Ireland) Order 1966 (SI 1996/1320 (NI 10))	2.4
Tribunal Procedure (First-tier Tribunal) (Immigration and Asylum Chamber) Rules 2014 (SI 2014/2604 (L 31))	3.16.6
Welsh Language (Wales) Measure 2011 (mccc/2011 nawm 1)	7.7
Working Time Regulations 1998 (SI 1998/1833)	1.6

Table of Immigration Rules

Immigration Rules HC 395.. 3.17, 4.2
Statement of Changes in Immigration Rules HC 474... 1.33.1
Statement of Changes in Immigration Rules HC 532... 9.1
Statement of Changes in Immigration Rules HC 667... 1.33.1

Table of Cases

A

Alabi (CO/1231/2016) 2.3
Alvi, R (Alvi) v Secretary of State for the Home Department [2012] UKSC 33 .... 2.4

B

B, R (B) v Secretary of State for the Home Department (No 2) [2015] EWCA Civ 445; [2016] QB 789; [2015] 3 WLR 1031 .... 3.16.1
Birmingham County Council v Clue [2010] EWCA Civ 460 .... 5.2.2

D

Das v Secretary of State for the Home Department [2014] EWCA Civ 45; 2014] 1 WLR 3538; [2014] ACD 78 .... 3.14
De Souza Ribeiro v France (22689/07) [2012] ECHR 2066 .... 4.1

E

Ehsan, R (Ehsan) v Secretary of State for the Home Department [2016] UKSC 63 .... 3.17
EO, RA, CE, OE, and RAN, R (EO, RA, CE, OE, and RAN) v Secretary of State for the Home Department [2013] EWHC 1236 (Admin); [2013] ACD 116 .... 3.14

G

Gudanaviciene, R (Gudanaviciene) v Director of Legal Aid Casework [2014] EWCA Civ 1622; [2015] 1 WLR 2247; [2015] 3 All ER 827 .... 4.1

H

Hardial Singh, R (Hardial Singh) v Governor of Durham Prison [1984] 1 WLR 704; [1984] 1 All ER 983; [1983] Imm AR 198 .... 3.14
Hirsi Jamaa v Italy (27765/09) (2012) 55 EHRR 21; 33 BHRC 244 .... 6.2
Hottak, R (Hottak) v Secretary of State for Foreign and Commonwealth Affairs [2016] EWCA Civ 438; [2016] 1 WLR 3791; [2016] 3 All ER 935 .... 5.3.2

I

Immigration Law Practitioners' Association, R (Immigration Law Practitioners' Association) v Secretary of State for the Home Department [1997] Imm AR 189 .... 3.17

Table of Cases

Iqbal, R (Iqbal) v Secretary of State for the Home Department [2016] UKSC 63; [2015] EWCA Civ 838; [2016] 1 WLR 582; [2016] 2 All ER 469; [2016] Imm AR 77 .... 3.17

J

Jeunesse v The Netherlands (2016) 60 EHRR 789 .... 9.6
Jones v Wrotham Park Settled Estates [1980] AC 74 .... 2.4

K

Kiarie, R (Kiarie) v Secretary of State for the Home Department [2015] EWCA Civ 1020; [2016] 1 WLR 1961; [2016] 3 All ER 741; [2016] Imm AR 209 .... 4.1
Kebede, R (Kebede) v Newcastle City Council [2013] EWCA Civ 960; [2014] PTSR 82 .... 5.4.10

L

Lim, R (Lim) v Secretary of State for the Home Department [2007] EWCA Civ 77 .... 4.1

M

Medical Justice, R (Medical Justice, JXL, et or) CO/5386/2016, CO/5262/2016, CO/5630/2016, CO/5533/2016, CO/5529/2016, CO/5535/22016, CO/5534/2016, CO/5532/2016, CO/4835/2016 .... 3.14
Mirza, R (Mirza) v Secretary of State for the Home Department [2016] UKSC 63 .... 3.17
MK v Secretary of State for the Home Department [2012] EWHC 1896 (Admin) 5.2.2
MM, R (MM) V Secretary of State for the Home Department [2017] UKSC 10 .... 9.6
MM (Lebanon), R (MM (Lebanon)) v Secretary of State for the Home Department [2014] EWCA Civ 985; [2015] 1 WLR 1073 .... 9.1
Mulumba, R (Mulumba) and First Tier Tribunal (Asylum Support) and the Secretary of State for the Home Department (CO/2114/2014) 5.2.2

N

Nuro v Home Office [2014] EWHC 462 (Admin) 2.1

O

O, R (O) v Barking and Dagenham London Borough Council [2010] EWCA Civ 1101; [2011] 1 WLR 1283; [2011] 2 All ER 337 .... 5.4.8–12

P

Paulet v United Kingdom [2014] ECHR 477 .... 2.1
Paulet v United Kingdom (6219/08) (2015) 61 EHRR 39; [2014] Lloyd's Rep FC 484; 37 BHRC 695; [2014] Crim LR 750 .... 2.1
Pepper v Hart [1992] UKHL 3 .... 3.15

R

Romans (CO/192/2016) 2.3
Ruiz Zambrano v Office National de l'Emploi (ONEm) (C-34/09) EU:C:2011:124; [2011] EUECJ C-34/09; [2012] QB 265; [2012] 2 WLR 886; [2011] ECR I-1177 .... 5.4.12
R v Carter, Kulish and Lyashkov [2006] EWCA Crim 416 .... 2.1

S

Secretary of State for the Home Department v ZAT [2016] EWCA Civ 810 .... 5.3
Shepherd Masimba Kambadzi v Secretary of State for the Home Department [2011] UKSC 23; [2011] 1 WLR 1299; [2011] 4 All ER 975 .... 3.14
Singh v Hammond [1987] 1 WLR 283; [1987] 1 All ER 829 .... 3.1, 6.2
SO, R (SO) v London Borough of Barking and Dagenham [2010] EWCA Civ 1101 .... 5.7.1
SS (Nigeria) [2014] 1 WLR 998 .... 4.1

W

Walumba Lumba & Kadian Mighty v Secretary of State for the Home Department [2011] UKSC 12; [2012] 1 AC 245; [2011] 2 WLR 671; [2011] 4 All ER 1; [2011] UKHRR 437 .... 3.14
Waya, R v Waya [2012] UKSC 51; [2013] 1 AC 294; [2012] 3 WLR 1188; [2013] 1 All ER 889; [2013] 2 Cr App R (S) 20 .... 2.1

Z

ZAT (Article 8 ECHR: Dublin Regulation: Interface: Proportionality), R (on the application of ZAT) v Secretary of State for the Home Department [2016] UKUT 61 (IAC); [2016] Imm AR 655 .... 5.3
ZH (Tanzania) v Secretary of State for the Home Department [2011] UKSC 4 .... 4.1

Table of Regional and International Legislation

Convention concerning Labour Inspection in Industry and Commerce 1947 (ILO 1950) (No.81)
  Art.3(1) 1.13
  Art.3(2) 1.13
Council Directive 2003/9 laying down minimum standards for the reception of asylum seekers 5.2.2
European Convention on Human Rights 1950 .... 3.16.3, 5.2.4, 5.4.1, 6.3
  Art.3 .... 4.1, 5.2.2
  Art.5 .... 3.16.5
  Art.8 .... 4.1, 5.3–1, 9.1
  Art.13 .... 4.1
  Protocol No.1
  Art.1 .... 2.1, 2.5
Regulation 604/2013 on the criteria for determining the Member State responsible for examining an application for international protection by a third-country national or a stateless person (Dublin III Regulation)
  Art.8 .... 5.3
  Art.9 .... 5.3
  Art.11 .... 5.3
United Nations Convention on the Law of the Sea 1982 .... 6.2
United Nations Convention relating to the Status of Refugees 1951 .... 5.2.2, 6.3
  Art.33 .... 6.2
United Nations Convention on the Rights of the Child 1989 .... 4.1
United Nations Convention on Torture 1984 .... 3.14
Vienna Convention on Consular Relations 1963
  Art.5 .... 8.3

Abbreviations

ASBO	Anti-Social Behaviour Order
ATLEU	Anti Trafficking and Labour Exploitation Unit
BCIA 2009	Borders, Citizenship and Immigration Act 2009
BDRA 1953	Births and Deaths Registration Act 1953
CA 1989	Children Act 1989
CG(S)A 1982	Civil Government (Scotland) Act 1982
CL(C)(S)A 1995	Criminal Law (Consolidation) (Scotland) Act 1995
CPS	Crown Prosecution Service
DPA 1998	Data Protection Act 1998
EA 2010	Equality Act 2010
EAA 1973	Employment Agencies Act 1973
ECA 1972	European Communities Act 1972
ECHR	European Convention on Human Rights
EU	European Union
GLA	Gangmasters Licensing Authority
GLAA	Gangmasters and Labour Abuse Authority
GLA 2004	Gangmasters (Licensing) Act 2004
HA 1988	Housing Act 1988
HMRC	Her Majesty's Revenue and Customs
HRA 1998	Human Rights Act 1998
HSE	Health and Safety Executive
IA 1971	Immigration Act 1971
IA 2014	Immigration Act 2014
IA 2016	Immigration Act 2016
IAA 1999	Immigration and Asylum Act 1999
IANA 2006	Immigration, Asylum and Nationality Act 2006
ILPA	Immigration Law Practitioners' Association
JCWI	Joint Council for the Welfare of Immigrants
LA	Local Authority (UK)
LA 2003	Licensing Act 2003

Abbreviations

LASPO 2012	Legal Aid, Sentencing and Punishment of Offenders Act 2012
LG (MP)A 1986	Local Government (Miscellaneous Provisions) Act 1976
LHCA 1843	London Hackney Carriages Act 1843
MoD	Ministry of Defence
MPCA 1869	Metropolitan Public Carriage Act 1869
MW(OI)A 1971	Mineral Workings (Offshore Installations) Act 1971
MSA 2015	Modern Slavery Act 2015
NAA 1948	National Assistance Act 1948
NCA	National Crime Agency
NIAA 2002	Nationality, Immigration and Asylum Act 2002
NGOs	Non-Governmental Organizations
NMW	National Minimum Wage
NMWA 1998	National Minimum Wage Act 1998
OSA 1989	Official Secrets Act 1989
PCCA 1975	Plymouth City Council Act 1975
PACE 1984	Police and Criminal Evidence Act 1984
PAYE	Pay As You Earn
PBS	Points-based system
PSNI	Police Service Northern Ireland
PHV	Private Hire Vehicle
PHV(L)A 1998	Private Hire Vehicles (London) Act 1998
POCA 2002	Proceeds of Crime Act 2002
RA 1977	Rent Act 1977
RSA 1953	Registration Services Act 1953
RTA 1988	Road Traffic Act 1988
SIAC	Special Immigration Appeals Commission
SSHD	Secretary of State for the Home Department
TA (NI) 2008	Taxis Act (Northern Ireland) 2008
TPCA 1847	Town Police Clauses Act 1847
UKBA 2007	UK Borders Act 2007

Introduction

COMMENCEMENT

This commentary is up-to-date as at 2 December 2016 and all references herein to commencement are to commencement as of that date.

The Immigration Act 2016 (IA 2016) became law on 12 May 2016 but the only provisions that came into force on that date were ss 61(3)–(5), and Part 9 Miscellaneous and General. Section 95(4) provided for s 85, pertaining to the immigration skills charge, to come into force on 12 July 2016.

The rest of the Act is commenced by order. Two commencement orders have so far been made. The Immigration Act 2016 (Commencement No 1) Regulations 2016, SI 2016/603 were made on 23 May 2016, bringing certain provisions into force on 31 May 2016 and 12 July 2016. The Immigration Act 2016 (Commencement No 2 and Transitional Provisions) Regulations 2016, SI 2016/1037 were made on 31 October 2016 bringing further provisions into force on 1 November 2016, 21 November 2016, 25 November 2016 and 1 December 2016.

Provisions that came into force on 31 May 2016:

Section 67 Unaccompanied refugee children;

Sections 69–72 Transfer of responsibility for relevant children;

Section 75 Maritime enforcement; and

Schedule 14 Maritime enforcement.

Provisions that came into force on 12 July 2016:

Sections 1–9 Director of Labour Market Enforcement;

Sections 10–13 Gangmasters and Labour Abuse Authority;

Section 25 Code of Practice;

Sections 31–33 Supplementary provision;

Section 34 Offence of illegal working;

Section 35 Offence of employing illegal worker;

Sections 46–53 Powers of immigration officers etc;

Section 55 Supply of information to Secretary of State;

Introduction

Section 56 Detention etc by immigration officers in Scotland;

Section 57 Power to take fingerprints etc. from dependants;

Section 58 Interpretation of Part 3;

Section 59 Guidance on detention of vulnerable persons;

Section 60 Limitation on detention of pregnant women;

Section 76 Persons excluded from the United Kingdom under international obligations;

Section 86 Power to make passport fees regulations;

Section 87 Passport fees regulations: supplemental;

Section 88 Power to charge for passport validation services;

Section 89 Civil registration fees;

Schedule 1 Persons to whom Director etc may disclose information;

Schedule 2 Functions in relation to labour market;

Schedule 3 Consequential and related amendments;

Schedule 9 Duty to supply nationality documents to Secretary of State: persons to whom duty applies; and

Schedule 15 Civil registration fees.

Provisions that came into force on 1 November 2016:

Section 39 Offence of leasing premises (for the purpose of making subordinate legislation only);

Section 40 Eviction (for the purpose of making subordinate legislation only);

Section 45 Bank accounts (for the purpose of making subordinate legislation only); and

Schedule 7 Bank accounts (for the purpose of making subordinate legislation only).

Provisions that came into force on 21 November 2016:

Sections 77–84 Language requirements for public sector workers.

Provisions that came into force on 25 November 2016:

Sections 14–17 Labour market enforcement undertakings;

Sections 18–24 Labour market enforcement orders; and

Introduction

Sections 26–30 Labour market enforcement undertakings and orders: supplementary.

Provisions that came into force on 01 December 2016:

Section 37 Private hire vehicles;

Section 38 Illegal working closure notices and illegal working compliance orders;

Section 39 Offence of leasing premises (for all remaining purposes);

Section 40 Eviction (for all remaining purposes);

Section 41 Order for possession of dwelling house;

Section 54 Amendments to search warrant provisions;

Section 62 Power to cancel leave extended under section 3C of the Immigration Act 1971;

Sections 63–65 Appeals;

Schedule 5 Private hire vehicles;

Schedule 6 Illegal working closure notices and illegal working compliance orders; and

Schedule 8 Amendments to search warrant provisions.

DRAMATIS PERSONAE

The Ministers in charge of the Bill were (titles and offices held as of the date at which they feature):

Lord Ashton of Hyde, Government Whip

Rt Hon Lord Bates, Minister of State, Home Office

Rt Hon James Brokenshire MP, Minister of State for Immigration and Security

Robert Buckland QC, MP, Solicitor General

Lord Keen of Elie, Advocate General for Scotland

Rt Hon Theresa May MP, Home Secretary

The Public Bill Committee was chaired by Peter Bone MP and Albert Owen MP.

Introduction

Other speakers, authors and recipients of letters were the following (titles and offices held as of the date at which they feature):

Lord Alton of Liverpool, cross bench peer

Margaret Burgess MSP, Minister for Housing and Welfare, Scottish Parliament

Rt Hon David Cameron MP, Prime Minister

Robert Goodwill MP, Minister of State for Immigration

Rt Hon Greg Clark MP, Secretary of State for Communities and Local Government

Baroness Fookes, chair, House of Lords' Select Committee on Delegated Powers and Regulatory Reform

Robert Goodwill MP, Minister of State for Immigration

Rt Hon Ben Gummer MP, Minister of State for the Cabinet Office and Paymaster General

Baroness Hamwee, leading on the Bill for the Liberal Democrats

Rt Hon Robert Halfon MP, Minister of State for Apprenticeships and Skills

Rt Hon Matthew Hancock MP, Minister of State for the Cabinet Office and Paymaster General

Rt Hon Harriet Harman MP, chair, Joint Committee on Human Rights

Lord Hope of Craighhead, Conservative back bench peer

Baroness Kennedy of the Shaws, Labour back bench peeress

Carwyn Jones, First Minister, Welsh Assembly

Lord Lang of Monkton, chair, House of Lords' Select Committee on the Constitution

Baroness Lister of Burtersett, Labour back bench peeress

Earl of Listowel, cross bench peer

Gordon Marsden MP, Shadow Minister

Michael Matheson MSP, Cabinet Secretary for Justice, Scottish Government

Rt Hon Nicky Morgan MP, Secretary of State for Education

Stuart McDonald MP, leading on the Bill for the Scottish National Party

Alex Neil MSP, Cabinet Secretary for Social Justice, Communities and Pensioners' Rights, Scottish Government

Lord Ramsbotham, cross-bench peer

Introduction

Lord Rosser, leading on the Bill for the official opposition in the Lords

Sir Keir Starmer MP, KCB, QC, leading on the bill for the official opposition in the Commons

Rt Hon Nicola Sturgeon MSP, First Minister, Scotland

Baroness Williams of Trafford, Junior Minister, Home Office

Humza Yousaf MSP, Minister for Europe and International Development, Scottish Government

Parliamentary select committees scrutinizing the Bill were:

The House of Lords' Select Committee on the Constitution;

The House of Lords' Select Committee on Delegated Powers and Regulatory Reform; and

The Joint Select Committee on Human Rights.

MINISTERIAL STATEMENTS

The commentary includes Ministerial Statements made during the passage of the Act that provide further information about its provisions. Sometimes Ministerial Statements simply provide further information about Home Office plans and illuminate a provision that is otherwise sketchy. Sometimes they constitute assurances constraining how a power may be used, in accordance with the doctrine of *Pepper v Hart* [1992] UKHL 4.

Under *Pepper v Hart* [1992] UKHL 4 the courts can have regard to the parliamentary record only where the legislation on its face is ambiguous.

If the legislation is not ambiguous then even if what it says is not what Ministers intended, no regard can be had to the record. Parliamentarians often forget this. Assurances may, of course, be persuasive politically where the words of the Act do not bind Ministers. They may also be persuasive in representations seeking to hold civil servants and decision-makers to the intentions of the legislature.

Throughout the text, any reference to a section, Part or Schedule refers to a section, Part or Schedule of the Immigration Act 2016 unless otherwise stated.

Part I—Labour Market and Illegal Working

CHAPTER I—LABOUR MARKET

1.1 Chapter 1 of Part 1 of the Immigration Act 2016 (IA 2016) introduces measures aimed at tackling abuse and exploitation in the labour market and at the enforcement of labour market standards. It was highlighted during Parliamentary debates that the provisions in Chapter 2 of Part 1 – introducing a new offence of illegal working – may undermine these aims by making it more difficult for migrants in situations of exploitation to seek help from the authorities out of fear that they may themselves be criminalised.

The proposals for tackling exploitation in the labour market were the subject of a consultation that ran from 13 October 2015 to 7 December 2015[1] in parallel with the passage of the Act through Parliament. The Immigration Law Practitioners' Association (ILPA) responded to the consultation[2] and was among 93 agencies, including statutory organisations, trade bodies, labour providers, trade unions and non-governmental organisations (NGOs) that did so. This meant that the Bill was introduced to Parliament on 17 September 2015 containing draft provisions only in relation to the new role of Director of Labour Market Enforcement[3] with many provisions introduced following the consultation through Government amendments to the Bill, in a 54-page document, for consideration at the first sitting of the House of Lords' Committee, with 100 further Government amendments at report stage, drawing criticism from parliamentarians about the reduced opportunity for scrutiny.

Sections 1–9 in this Part create the new role of Director of Labour Market Enforcement with responsibility for assessing the scale and nature of abuse in the labour market and for developing an annual strategy to tackle this.

Sections 10–13 expand the functions of the Gangmasters Licensing Authority (GLA) and rename it the Gangmasters and Labour Abuse Authority (GLAA) to reflect this change. Its licensing role will be extended to cover more industries and it has been given new PACE-based enforcement powers in England and Wales to prevent, detect and investigate worker exploitation across all labour market sectors.

Sections 14–30 introduce a new regime of Labour Market Enforcement (LME) undertakings and orders, backed up by a criminal offence for

1.1 *A Guide to the Immigration Act 2016*

non-compliance, aimed at deterring the exploitation of workers by employers. This has the effect of introducing custodial penalties for a number of labour market offences, such as non-payment of the National Minimum Wage (NMW), which were previously only punishable with a fine.

On 20 June 2016, the Immigration Act 2016 (Consequential Amendments) Regulations 2016, SI 2016/655 were laid before Parliament coming into force on 12 July 2016. These made amendments to secondary legislation that are consequential to changes made by Part 1. A reference to the 'Director of Labour Market Enforcement' was inserted into Schedule 2 to the Official Secrets Act 1989 (Prescription) Order 1990, SI 1990/200. This prescribes certain persons for the purposes of the Official Secrets Act 1989 (OSA 1989), the effect of which is that those persons who are prescribed become Crown servants for all purposes of the Act. The regulations also amended secondary legislation to replace references to the 'Gangmasters Licensing Authority' with references to the 'Gangmasters and Labour Abuse Authority'.

The need for adequate resourcing for enforcing labour market standards was identified as a concern. Professor Sir David Metcalf of the Migration Advisory Committee told the Public Bill Committee:

> 'I think that successive Governments have put more resources in – certainly into HMRC, but less so with the GLA. One understands the difficulties with the public finances, but we probably do not have sufficient resources. In the low-skilled report, we calculated that you would get an inspection from HMRC once every 250 years and you would get a prosecution once in a million years. Funding remains an issue, particularly for the Gangmasters' Licensing Authority'.[4]

Fears of inadequate resourcing were particularly acute with regard to the GLA. The US State Department *Trafficking in Persons Report 2015* recorded that funding and staffing for the UK's GLA had decreased and recommended that the UK Government increase funds for this agency.[5] The measures in the Act expanding the role of the GLA will place even greater demands on its resources.

---

1 *Tackling exploitation in the labour market: government response consultation document*, Home Office and Department for Business, Innovation and Skills, 13 October 2015. Available at: https://www.gov.uk/government/consultations/labour-market-exploitation-improving-enforcement (accessed 6 November 2016).

2 *ILPA response to Department for Business Innovation and Skills Consultation: Tackling Exploitation in the Labour Market*, ILPA, 7 December 2015. Available at: http://www.ilpa.org.uk/resources.php/31617/ilpa-response-to-department-for-business-innovation-and-skills-consultation-tackling-exploitation-in (accessed 6 November 2016).

3 Immigration Bill, Bill 74 of session 2015–2016. Available at: http://www.publications.parliament.uk/pa/bills/cbill/2015-2016/0074/15074.pdf (accessed 6 November 2016).

4 Public Bill Committee, House of Commons, 20 October 2015, Q37. Available at: http://www.publications.parliament.uk/pa/cm201516/cmpublic/immigration/151020/am/151020s01.pdf (accessed 6 November 2016).
5 *Trafficking in Persons Report 2015, Country Narratives: United Kingdom*, US Department of State. Available at: https://www.state.gov/documents/organization/243562.pdf at p 349 (accessed 6 November 2016).

SECTION 1—DIRECTOR OF LABOUR MARKET ENFORCEMENT

> **Summary**
>
> Establishes the Director of Labour Market Enforcement.

1.1.1

1 Director of Labour Market Enforcement

(1) The Secretary of State must appoint a person as the Director of Labour Market Enforcement (referred to in this Chapter as "the Director").

(2) The Director is to hold office in accordance with the terms of his or her appointment.

(3) The functions of the Director are exercisable on behalf of the Crown.

(4) The Secretary of State must provide the Director with such staff, goods, services, accommodation and other resources as the Secretary of State considers the Director needs for the exercise of his or her functions.

(5) The Secretary of State must—

   (a) pay the Director such expenses, remuneration and allowances, and

   (b) pay or make provision for the payment of such pension to or in respect of the Director,

as may be provided for by or under the terms of the Director's appointment.

Commencement: 12 July 2016, Immigration Act 2014 (Commencement No 1) Regulations 2016, SI 2016/603.

Definitions: 'the Director' Director of Labour Market Enforcement, s 1(1).

Regulations: See also The Immigration Act 2016 (Consequential Amendments) Order 2016, SI 2016/655, made under s 92 of this Act, amending the Official Secrets Act (Prescription) Order 1990, SI 1990/200.

1.1.1 A Guide to the Immigration Act 2016

Devolution: Applies throughout the UK.

This section establishes the new role of Director of Labour Market Enforcement (s 1(1)) and requires the Secretary of State to provide the resources she considers necessary for the Director to carry out their functions, including staff, accommodation and other resources (s 1(4)). Ministers stated that the Director would be appointed by, and jointly accountable to, the Home Secretary and the Secretary of State for Business, Skills and Innovation.[1] The role, functions and activities of the Director are described in later sections.

While the role of the Director encompasses the renamed GLAA, the Employment Agency Standards Inspectorate and the NMW Commission, it does not cover the Health and Safety Executive (HSE) or local authorities. Local authorities have statutory responsibilities for the enforcement of health and safety legislation (mainly in the distribution, retail, office, leisure and catering sectors) and for the rights of children at work.

During the passage of the Act, amendments were proposed to define the role of the Director of Labour Market Enforcement within this section as one focused on protecting workers from exploitation, particularly in view of concerns regarding the wide data-sharing powers that allow the Director to share information with the immigration services, see s 6. Ministers insisted that the primary function of the Director was protecting workers from exploitation rather than enforcing immigration control, however, they resisted amendments to this effect. The Minister in the House of Lords stated:

> 'Concerns have been expressed that the director will get involved in enforcing our immigration laws. I reassure noble Lords that that is not part of the role of the Director of Labour Market Enforcement. I know that there was some discussion about the exchanges in Committee in another place on this, but I am happy to place on record again my remarks in my letter of 8 January:
>
> > "I want to reassure colleagues",
> >
> > following Second Reading, that immigration control,
> >
> > "is not part of the role of the Director of Labour Enforcement. Nowhere in this Bill is the Director given the power or purpose to do that ... they would be acting outside of their statutory powers".
>
> It is useful to get that very clear statement on the record in Committee. Concerns have been expressed that the director will get involved in enforcing our immigration laws, and I want to ensure that that is not the case.'[2]

The Immigration Act 2016 (Consequential Amendments) Regulations 2016, SI 2016/655 inserts a reference to the 'Director of Labour Market Enforcement'

Part 1—Labour Market and Illegal Working **1.2**

into Schedule 2 to the Official Secrets Act 1989 (Prescription) Order 1990 (SI 1990/200). This prescribes certain persons for the purposes of the Official Secrets Act 1989, the effect of which is that those persons who are prescribed become Crown servants for all purposes of the Act.

---

1 Rt Hon Lord Bates, Minister of State, Home Office, Immigration Bill 2015/16, House of Lords Committee, first sitting, *Hansard* HL col 530 (18 January 2016). Available at: http://www.publications.parliament.uk/pa/ld201516/ldhansrd/text/160118-0001.htm#1601184000412 (accessed 6 November 2016).
2 Rt Hon Lord Bates, Minister of State, Home Office, Immigration Bill 2015/16, House of Lords Committee, first sitting, *Hansard* HL, col 543 (18 January 2016). Available at: http://www.publications.parliament.uk/pa/ld201516/ldhansrd/text/160118-0001.htm#1601184000412 (accessed 6 November 2016).

SECTION 2—LABOUR MARKET ENFORCEMENT STRATEGY

Summary

Sets out the requirements for the annual labour market enforcement strategy to be produced by the Director, describing functions and activities in relation to the strategy.

1.2

2 Labour market enforcement strategy

(1) The Director must before the beginning of each financial year prepare a labour market enforcement strategy for that year and submit it to the Secretary of State for approval.

(2) A labour market enforcement strategy (referred to in this Chapter as a "strategy") is a document which—

 (a) sets out the Director's assessment of—

  (i) the scale and nature of non-compliance in the labour market during the year before the one to which the strategy relates, and

  (ii) the likely scale and nature of such non-compliance during the year to which the strategy relates and the following two years,

 (b) contains a proposal for the year to which the strategy relates setting out—

  (i) how labour market enforcement functions should be exercised,

  (ii) the education, training and research activities the Secretary of State, and any other person by whom, or by whose officers,

1.2 A Guide to the Immigration Act 2016

labour market enforcement functions are exercisable, should undertake or facilitate in connection with those functions,

(iii) the information, or descriptions of information, that should be provided to the Director for the purposes of his or her functions by any person by whom, or by whose officers, labour market enforcement functions are exercisable, and

(iv) the form and manner in which, and frequency with which, that information should be provided,

(c) sets out the activities the Director proposes to undertake during the year to which the strategy relates in the exercise of his or her functions under section 8, and

(d) deals with such other matters as the Director considers appropriate.

(3) The proposal mentioned in paragraph (b) of subsection (2) must, in particular, set out how the funding available for the purposes of the functions and activities mentioned in sub-paragraphs (i) and (ii) of that paragraph should be allocated.

(4) The Director may at any time prepare a revised strategy and submit it to the Secretary of State for approval.

(5) The Secretary of State may approve a strategy either with or without modifications (but a modification may not relate to the assessment described in paragraph (a) of subsection (2)).

(6) Any person by whom labour market enforcement functions are exercisable during a year to which a strategy approved under this section relates must, in exercising those functions, have regard to the strategy.

Commencement: 12 July 2016, Immigration Act 2014 (Commencement No 1) Regulations 2016, SI 2016/603.

Definitions:

'the Director' Director of Labour Market Enforcement, s 1(1)

'labour market enforcement functions' s 3(2), see detailed commentary on s 3;

'non-compliance in the labour market' s 3(1), see detailed commentary on s 3;

'strategy' labour market enforcement strategy, s 2(2).

Devolution: Applies throughout the UK.

The Director of Labour Market Enforcement is required to prepare an annual labour market enforcement strategy and submit it to the Secretary of State for approval. The Secretary of State can approve the strategy with or without certain modifications, though the Secretary of State may not modify the assessment made by the Director of the scale and nature of labour market abuses.

The strategy must include an assessment of the scale and nature of non-compliance in the labour market (s 2(a)). Non-compliance in the labour market is defined in s 3 and includes both the commission of labour market offences, as well as breaches of labour market legislation, such as the non-payment of the National minimum wage (NMW) or the breach of gangmaster licensing conditions. See the commentary on s 3 for further details.

The strategy must also include a proposal for how labour market enforcement functions should be exercised (including education, training and research carried out by the relevant enforcers) and, most controversially, how the funding should be allocated. The role of the Director encompasses the renamed Gangmasters and Labour Abuse Authority (GLAA), the Employment Agency Standards Inspectorate and the NMW Commission, and labour market enforcement functions are defined to include the functions of officers acting under legislation applied by these bodies (s 3(2)). Those exercising labour market enforcement functions are required to have regard to the strategy once it is made. The strategy will also set out the activities the Director proposes to undertake during the year, in relation to his or her intelligence hub and other matters.

ILPA and the Anti Trafficking and Labour Exploitation Unit (ATLEU) highlighted the importance of the Director of Labour Market Enforcement monitoring and reporting on the extent to which victims of non-compliance in the labour market are able to access remedies as these have an important restorative function, not only in terms of providing the financial support to promote recovery, but also in terms of providing recognition of abuse and ensuring justice. The Minister in the House of Lords gave the following assurances:

'Similarly, a successful strategy will be based on the evidence of what enforcement has happened in previous years, including what remedies were secured for victims.[1]

... Similarly, as the strategy will set out how the enforcement bodies are to exercise their functions, including seeking remedies for victims, the success of this must be covered by the annual report.'[2]

---

1 Rt Hon Lord Bates, Minister of State, Home Office, Immigration Bill 2015/16, House of Lords Committee, first sitting, *Hansard* col 536 (18 January 2016). Available at: http://www.publications.parliament.uk/pa/ld201516/ldhansrd/text/160118-0001.htm#16011840004I2 (accessed 6 November 2016).
2 Rt Hon Lord Bates, Minister of State, Home Office, Immigration Bill 2015/16, House of Lords Committee, first sitting, *Hansard* col 544 (18 January 2016). Available at: http://www.publications.parliament.uk/pa/ld201516/ldhansrd/text/160118-0001.htm#16011840004I2 (accessed 6 November 2016).

1.3 *A Guide to the Immigration Act 2016*

SECTION 3—NON-COMPLIANCE IN THE LABOUR MARKET ETC: INTERPRETATION

1.3

> **Summary**
>
> Definitions for the purposes of this Part of the Act.

3 Non-compliance in the labour market etc: interpretation

(1) For the purposes of this Chapter each of the following constitutes "non-compliance in the labour market"—

    (a) the commission of a labour market offence;

    (b) failure to comply with the requirement under section 1 of the National Minimum Wage Act 1998 (workers to be paid at least national minimum wage);

    (c) failure to pay any financial penalty required to be paid by a notice of underpayment served under section 19 of that Act (see section 19A of that Act);

    (d) breach of a condition of a licence granted under section 7 of the Gangmasters (Licensing) Act 2004;

    (e) failure to comply with any other requirement imposed by or under any enactment and which is prescribed by regulations made by the Secretary of State.

(2) In this Chapter "labour market enforcement functions" means—

    (a) any function of the Secretary of State in connection with prohibition orders made under section 3A of the Employment Agencies Act 1973,

    (b) any function of an officer acting for the purposes of that Act (see section 8A of that Act),

    (c) any function of an officer acting for the purposes of the National Minimum Wage Act 1998 (see section 13 of that Act),

    (d) any function of the Gangmasters and Labour Abuse Authority conferred by section 1(2)(a) to (c) of the Gangmasters (Licensing) Act 2004,

    (e) any function of an enforcement officer or a compliance officer acting for the purposes of that Act (see section 15 of that Act),

    (f) any function of the Gangmasters and Labour Abuse Authority under Part 2 of the Modern Slavery Act 2015 (slavery and trafficking prevention orders etc),

Part 1—Labour Market and Illegal Working 1.3

(g) any function of an officer of that Authority acting for the purposes of Part 1 or 2 of that Act (see sections 11A and 30A of that Act),

(h) any function of an enforcing authority under this Chapter,

(i) any function an officer has by virtue of section 26, and

(j) any other function prescribed by regulations made by the Secretary of State.

(3) In this section "labour market offence" means—

(a) an offence under the Employment Agencies Act 1973 other than one under section 9(4)(b) of that Act;

(b) an offence under the National Minimum Wage Act 1998;

(c) an offence under the Gangmasters (Licensing) Act 2004;

(d) an offence under section 1 of the Modern Slavery Act 2015;

(e) an offence under section 2 or 4 of that Act—

(i) which is committed in relation to a worker or a person seeking work, or

(ii) which is otherwise committed in circumstances where subsection (2) of section 3 of that Act applies;

(f) an offence under section 30(1) or (2) of that Act which is committed in relation to—

(i) an order which was made on the application of the Gangmasters and Labour Abuse Authority, or

(ii) an order which was made under section 14 of that Act and which falls within subsection (4) below;

(g) an offence under section 27;

(h) any other offence prescribed by regulations made by the Secretary of State;

(i) an offence of attempting or conspiring to commit an offence mentioned in paragraphs (a) to (h);

(j) an offence under Part 2 of the Serious Crime Act 2007 in relation to an offence so mentioned;

(k) an offence of inciting a person to commit an offence so mentioned;

(l) an offence of aiding, abetting, counselling or procuring the commission of an offence so mentioned.

(4) An order made under section 14 of the Modern Slavery Act 2015 falls within this subsection if—

(a) the order was made following—

(i) the conviction of the defendant of an offence mentioned in subsection (3)(d), (e) or (i) to (l), or

1.3 A Guide to the Immigration Act 2016

    (ii) a finding of a kind mentioned in section 14(1)(b) or (c) of that Act in connection with any such offence, and

  (b) the prosecution resulted from an investigation conducted by a labour abuse prevention officer (within the meaning of section 114B of the Police and Criminal Evidence Act 1984).

(5) In this section "worker" has the same meaning as in the Employment Rights Act 1996 (see section 230 of that Act) and the reference to a person seeking work is to be read accordingly.

(6) In this section references to the Gangmasters (Licensing) Act 2004 are references to that Act only so far as it applies in relation to England and Wales and Scotland.

Commencement: 12 July 2016 Immigration Act 2014 (Commencement No 1) Regulations 2016, SI 2016/603.

Regulations: See s 32 which places limitations on the regulations that may be made under this section to ensure they do not encroach on devolved powers. Regulations may be made under:

s 3(1)(e): prescribing requirements imposed by or under any enactment, failure to comply with which is to be treated as 'non-compliance in the labour market';

s 3(1)(j): prescribing functions which are designated 'labour market enforcement functions';

s 3(3)(h): power to make regulations prescribing additional offences which are to be designated 'labour market offences'.

The negative procedure in parliament applies unless the regulations amend or repeal primary legislation (s 93(2)(a)).

Definitions:

'the Director' Director of Labour Market Enforcement, s 1(1);

'Gangmasters' Licensing Act 2004' references to that Act insofar as it applies to England and Wales and Scotland, s 3(6);

'labour market enforcement functions' s 3(2), see detailed commentary below;

'labour market offence' s 3(3), see detailed commentary below;

'non-compliance in the labour market' s 3(1), see detailed commentary below;

'worker' s 3(5) and Employment Rights Act 1996, s 230.

Devolution: Applies throughout the UK except that references to the Gangmasters (Licensing Act) 2004 (GLA 2004) in this section for definitions, non-compliance in the labour market, labour market enforcement functions and labour market offences do not apply in Northern Ireland (s 3(6)).

Restrictions are also placed on regulatory-making powers to ensure they do not encroach on devolved powers (s 32).

This section sets out definitions used in this Chapter of Part I of the Act. Section 3(3) defines a 'labour market offence'. These include offences under:

- the Employment Agencies Act 1973, regulating employment agencies and businesses, such as offences of failing to comply with regulations on the proper conduct of agencies with regards to advertising, keeping records and with the prohibition on charging fees to those seeking employment. The offence under s 9(4)(b) of that Act, relating to limitations on disclosure by those empowered to conduct inspections of employment agencies, is excluded from the definition;
- the National Minimum Wage Act 1998 (NMWA 1998), which includes, for example, offences of refusing or wilfully neglecting to pay the national minimum wage and non-compliance with requirements on record-keeping;
- the GLA 2004, such as offences of operating as a gangmaster, providing labour to the agricultural and shellfish industries, without a licence or in breach of its conditions;
- section 1 of the Modern Slavery Act 2015 (MSA 2015) on holding a person in slavery or servitude or requiring them to perform compulsory or forced labour;
- sections 2 and 4 of the MSA 2015 criminalising human trafficking, limited for the purpose of this Act to where these are committed in relation to a worker or a person seeking work, or where they involve slavery, servitude, compulsory or forced labour;
- subsections 30(1)–(2) of the MSA 2015 regarding breach of a slavery and trafficking prevention order, interim prevention order, risk order or interim risk order, or failure to comply with a requirement to surrender a passport or provide a name and address, limited for the purpose of this Act to where the order or requirement was made on the application of the GLAA or where the order was made following a conviction resulting from an investigation conducted by a labour abuse prevention officer;
- section 27 of the Immigration Act 2016 regarding breach of a labour market enforcement (LME) order.

Labour market offences also include attempting, conspiring, inciting, aiding and abetting etc in relation to those offences (ss 3(3)(i)–(l)). The Secretary of State can add further labour market offences, whether contained in primary or secondary legislation, by regulations (s 3(h)).

1.3 A Guide to the Immigration Act 2016

Non-compliance in the labour market, defined in s 3(1), is broader and includes both the commission of labour market offences as set out above and other breaches of labour market legislation that do not give rise to a criminal offence. These are identified as failure to comply with NMW requirements or with penalties required for underpayment of the NMW under the NMWA 1998; breach of gangmaster licence conditions under the GLA 2004; and any other requirements that may be prescribed by regulations. These all fall within the scope of the Director's duties under s 2 to assess the scale and nature of non-compliance in the labour market and develop a strategy to address these concerns.

Section 3(2) defines 'labour market enforcement functions'. These include the functions of the Employment Agency Standards Inspectorate, Her Majesty's Revenue and Customs (HMRC) NMW team, and the Gangmasters and Labour Abuse Authority (GLAA). These functions therefore fall within the remit of the Director in their role of co-ordinating how labour market functions should be exercised. Other functions may be prescribed by the Secretary of State through regulations.

Section 3(5) defines 'worker' for the purpose of this Chapter in accordance with s 230 of the Employment Rights Act 1996. This differs from the definition used in respect of the offence of illegal working in s 34 in Chapter 2 of this Part and states:

'(3) In this Act 'worker' (except in the phrases 'shop worker' and 'betting worker') means an individual who has entered into or works under (or, where the employment has ceased, worked under)—

a contract of employment, or

any other contract, whether express or implied and (if it is express) whether oral or in writing, whereby the individual undertakes to do or perform personally any work or services for another party to the contract whose status is not by virtue of the contract that of a client or customer of any profession or business undertaking carried on by the individual;

and any reference to a worker's contract shall be construed accordingly.'

Ministers stated that the provision did not redefine 'worker' for the purposes of the Employment Agencies Act 1973, the NMWA 1998 or the GLA 2004, and that the coverage of those Acts continued to apply in the same way, regardless of whether workers had the right to work in the UK.[1] The strategic focus of the Director, however, was envisaged as improving the enforcement of labour market legislation for workers legally in the UK, but the Director could include action that would protect workers more broadly and the Director's remit will include modern slavery offences.[2]

1 Rt Hon Lord Bates, Minister of State, Home Office, Immigration Bill 2015/16, House of Lords Committee, first sitting, *Hansard* col 544 (18 January 2016). Available at: http://www.publications.parliament.uk/pa/ld201516/ldhansrd/text/160118-0001.htm#1601184000412 (accessed 6 November 2016).
2 Rt Hon James Brokenshire MP, Minister for Immigration, Immigration Bill 2015/16 Public Bill Committee, House of Commons, *Hansard* cols 183-4 (27 October 2015). Available at: http://www.publications.parliament.uk/pa/cm201516/cmpublic/immigration/151027/am/151027s01.htm (accessed 6 November 2016).

SECTION 4—ANNUAL AND OTHER REPORTS

1.4

> **Summary**
>
> Provision as to the contents of the Director's annual report and other reports.

4 Annual and other reports

(1) As soon as reasonably practicable after the end of each financial year in respect of which the Secretary of State has approved a strategy under section 2, the Director must submit to the Secretary of State an annual report for that year.

(2) An annual report must include—

 (a) an assessment of the extent to which labour market enforcement functions were exercised, and activities of the kind mentioned in section 2(2)(b)(ii) were carried out, in accordance with the strategy during the year to which the report relates,

 (b) an assessment of the extent to which the strategy had an effect on the scale and nature of non-compliance in the labour market during that year, and

 (c) a statement of the activities the Director undertook during that year in the exercise of his or her functions under section 8.

(3) The Director must submit to the Secretary of State a report dealing with any matter—

 (a) which the Secretary of State has requested the Director to report on, or

 (b) which a strategy approved by the Secretary of State under section 2 states is a matter the Director proposes to report on,

and must do so as soon as reasonably practicable after the request is made or the strategy is approved.

1.5   *A Guide to the Immigration Act 2016*

Commencement: 12 July 2016, Immigration Act 2014 (Commencement No 1) Regulations 2016, SI 2016/603.

Definitions:

'the Director' Director of Labour Market Enforcement, s 1(1);

'labour market enforcement functions' s 3(2), see detailed commentary on s 3;

'strategy' labour market enforcement strategy, s 2(2).

Devolution: Applies throughout the UK.

This section makes provision as to the contents of the Director's annual and other reports. The Director's annual report must include an assessment of the extent to which labour market enforcement functions were exercised, the activities carried out, and their impact on the scale and nature of non-compliance in the labour market. The Director is also required to submit reports on specific matters that may be requested by the Secretary of State as soon as reasonably practicable.

SECTION 5—PUBLICATION OF STRATEGY AND REPORTS

Summary

Requires the Secretary of State to lay the reports before Parliament but permits her to remove material which might be against national security interests, jeopardise the safety of any person in the UK, or prejudice a criminal investigation or prosecution.

1.5

5 Publication of strategy and reports

(1)   The Secretary of State must lay before Parliament—

(a)   any strategy the Secretary of State approves under section 2, and

(b)   any annual or other report the Secretary of State receives under section 4,

and must do so as soon as reasonably practicable after approving the strategy or receiving the report.

(2)   A document laid under subsection (1) must not contain material removed under subsection (3).

(3) The Secretary of State may remove from a document to be laid under subsection (1) any material the publication of which the Secretary of State considers—

    (a) would be against the interests of national security,

    (b) might jeopardise the safety of any person in the United Kingdom, or

    (c) might prejudice the investigation or prosecution of an offence under the law of England and Wales, Scotland or Northern Ireland.

Commencement: 12 July 2016, Immigration Act 2014 (Commencement No 1) Regulations 2016, SI 2016/603.

Regulations: None, but the strategy must be laid before Parliament, s 5(1).

Definitions:

'the Director' Director of Labour Market Enforcement, s 1(1);

'labour market enforcement functions' s 3(2), see detailed commentary on s 3;

'strategy' labour market enforcement strategy, s 2(2).

Devolution: Applies throughout the UK.

The Secretary of State must lay before Parliament as soon as reasonably practicable any strategy which she has approved (she is permitted to require modifications to the strategy but not to its assessment of non-compliance in the labour market, see s 2(5)) or any annual or other report. She can remove any material which would be against the interests of national security, might jeopardise the safety of any person in the UK, or might prejudice the investigation or prosecution of an offence.

SECTION 6—INFORMATION GATEWAYS AND SCHEDULE 1—PERSONS TO WHOM DIRECTOR ETC MAY DISCLOSE INFORMATION

> **Summary**
>
> Creates information gateways through which information may be shared with the Director and through which the Director may share information.

1.6

6 Information gateways

(1) A person may disclose information to the Director or a relevant staff member if the disclosure is made for the purposes of the exercise of any function of the Director.

1.6 A Guide to the Immigration Act 2016

(2) Information obtained by the Director or a relevant staff member in connection with the exercise of any function of the Director may be used by the Director or a relevant staff member in connection with the exercise of any other function of the Director.

(3) The Director or a relevant staff member may disclose information obtained in connection with the exercise of any function of the Director to a specified person if the disclosure is made for the purposes of the exercise of any function of the specified person.

(4) "Specified person" means a person specified in Schedule 1 (persons to whom Director etc may disclose information).

(5) The Secretary of State may by regulations amend Schedule 1.

(6) In this section, "relevant staff member" means a member of staff provided to the Director under section 1(4).

Schedule 1 Persons to whom director etc may disclose information

Authorities with functions in connection with the labour market or the work place etc

The Secretary of State.

HMRC Commissioners.

A person by whom, or by whose officers, labour market enforcement functions are exercisable.

The Health and Safety Executive.

An enforcing authority within the meaning of Part 1 of the Health and Safety at Work etc. Act 1974 (see section 18(7) of that Act).

An inspector appointed by such an enforcing authority (see section 19 of that Act).

An enforcement authority within the meaning of regulation 28 of the Working Time Regulations 1998 (S.I. 1998/1833).

An inspector appointed by such an enforcement authority (see Schedule 3 to those Regulations).

The Low Pay Commission.

The Pensions Regulator.

Law enforcement and border security

A chief officer of police for a police area in England and Wales.

A local policing body within the meaning given by section 101(1) of the Police Act 1996.

The chief constable of the British Transport Police Force.

The chief constable of the Police Service of Scotland.

The Chief Constable of the Police Service of Northern Ireland.

A person appointed as an immigration officer under paragraph 1 of Schedule 2 to the Immigration Act 1971.

Local Government

A county or district council in England.

A London borough council.

The Greater London Authority.

The Common Council of the City of London.

The Council of the Isles of Scilly.

A county or county borough council in Wales.

A council constituted under section 2 of the Local Government etc. (Scotland) Act 1994.

A district council in Northern Ireland.

Health bodies

The Care Quality Commission.

A National Health Service trust established under section 25 of the National Health Service Act 2006 or section 18 of the National Health Service (Wales) Act 2006.

An NHS foundation trust within the meaning given by section 30 of the National Health Service Act 2006.

A Local Health Board established under section 11 of the National Health Service (Wales) Act 2006.

Other

The Independent Anti-slavery Commissioner.

A Northern Ireland department.

Commencement: 12 July 2016, Immigration Act 2014 (Commencement No 1) Regulations 2016, SI 2016/603.

Regulations: May be made under s 6(5) to amend Schedule 1 *Persons to whom the Director may disclose information*. The affirmative procedure must be used (s 93(2)(b)).

Definitions:

'the Director' Director of Labour Market Enforcement, s 1(1);

'relevant staff member' defined in s 6(6) as a staff member provided to the Director under s 1(4);

'specified person' a person specified in Schedule 1 *Persons to whom the Director may disclose information*, s 6(4).

Devolution: Applies throughout the UK.

1.7 *A Guide to the Immigration Act 2016*

The section creates very large information gateways. Any person, including a legal person, such as a firm, organisation or public body, is empowered to disclose information to the Director or a staff member for the exercise of any of the Director's functions. Having obtained the information, the Director can put it to use for any of the relevant functions.

The Director or their staff members are permitted to disclose information received in connection with their functions to any legal person specified in Schedule 1 for the purpose of exercising their functions. These include National Health Service Trusts, Local Health Boards, local councils and, causing particular concern, immigration officers. The Minister in the House of Lords stated that the Director would be acting outside their statutory powers if they got involved in or shared information for immigration control purposes.[1] The commentary on s 1 also discusses this point.

See also s 13 which is in similar terms but creates gateways through which information can be exchanged to and from the Gangmaster and Labour Abuse Authority (GLAA) or a relevant officer.

---

[1] Rt Hon Lord Bates, Minister of State, Home Office, Immigration Bill 2015/16, House of Lords Report Stage, *Hansard* HL col 1300 (9 March 2016). Available at: http://www.publications.parliament.uk/pa/ld201516/ldhansrd/text/160309-0001.htm#16030940000606 (accessed 6 November 2016).

SECTION 7—INFORMATION GATEWAYS: SUPPLEMENTARY

Summary

This section sets out some limits on the information that can be disclosed under s 6.

1.7

7 Information gateways: supplementary

(1) A disclosure of information which is authorised by section 6 does not breach—

    (a) an obligation of confidence owed by the person making the disclosure, or

    (b) any other restriction on the disclosure of information (however imposed).

(2) But nothing in section 6 authorises the making of a disclosure which—

    (a) contravenes the Data Protection Act 1998, or

Part 1—Labour Market and Illegal Working **1.7**

(b) is prohibited by Part 1 of the Regulation of Investigatory Powers Act 2000.

(3) Section 6 does not limit the circumstances in which information may be disclosed apart from that section.

(4) Section 6(1) does not authorise a person serving in an intelligence service to disclose information to the Director or a relevant staff member.

But this does not affect the disclosures which such a person may make in accordance with intelligence service disclosure arrangements.

(5) Intelligence service information may not be disclosed by the Director or a relevant staff member without authorisation from the appropriate service chief.

(6) If the Director or a relevant staff member has disclosed intelligence service information to a person, that person may not further disclose that information without authorisation from the appropriate service chief.

(7) HMRC information may not be disclosed by the Director or a relevant staff member without authorisation from HMRC Commissioners.

(8) If the Director or a relevant staff member has disclosed HMRC information to a person, that person may not further disclose that information without authorisation from HMRC Commissioners.

(9) Subsections (7) and (8) do not apply to national minimum wage information.

(10) If a person contravenes subsection (7) or (8) by disclosing revenue and customs information relating to a person whose identity—

(a) is specified in the disclosure, or

(b) can be deduced from it,

section 19 of the Commissioners for Revenue and Customs Act 2005 (wrongful disclosure) applies in relation to that disclosure as it applies in relation to a disclosure of such information in contravention of section 20(9) of that Act.

(11) In this section—

"appropriate service chief" means—

(a) the Director-General of the Security Service (in the case of information obtained by the Director or a relevant staff member from that Service or a person acting on its behalf);

(b) the Chief of the Secret Intelligence Service (in the case of information so obtained from that Service or a person acting on its behalf);

(c) the Director of GCHQ (in the case of information so obtained from GCHQ or a person acting on its behalf);

"GCHQ" has the same meaning as in the Intelligence Services Act 1994;

1.7 *A Guide to the Immigration Act 2016*

"HMRC information" means information disclosed to the Director or a relevant staff member under section 6 by HMRC Commissioners or a person acting on behalf of HMRC Commissioners;

"intelligence service" means—

(a) the Security Service;

(b) the Secret Intelligence Service;

(c) GCHQ;

"intelligence service disclosure arrangements" means—

(a) arrangements made by the Director-General of the Security Service under section 2(2)(a) of the Security Service Act 1989 about the disclosure of information by that Service,

(b) arrangements made by the Chief of the Intelligence Service under section 2(2)(a) of the Intelligence Services Act 1994 about the disclosure of information by that Service, and

(c) arrangements made by the Director of GCHQ under section 4(2)(a) of that Act about the disclosure of information by GCHQ;

"intelligence service information" means information obtained from an intelligence service or a person acting on behalf of an intelligence service;

"national minimum wage information" means information obtained by an officer in the course of acting—

(a) for the purposes of the National Minimum Wage Act 1998 (see section 13 of that Act), or

(b) by virtue of section 26(2);

"relevant staff member" has the same meaning as in section 6;

"revenue and customs information relating to a person" has the meaning given in section 19(2) of the Commissioners for Revenue and Customs Act 2005.

Commencement: 12 July 2016, Immigration Act 2014 (Commencement No 1) Regulations 2016, SI 2016/603.

Regulations: May be made under s 6(5) to amend Schedule 1 *Persons to whom the Director may disclose information.* The affirmative procedure must be used (s 93(2)(b)).

Definitions:

'appropriate service chief' Director-General of the Security Service, Chief of the Secret Intelligence Service, Director of GCHQ, regarding information from their body and including relevant staff members from the organisation or a person acting on their behalf, s 7(11);

'the Director' Director of Labour Market Enforcement, s 1(1);

Part 1—Labour Market and Illegal Working 1.7

'GCHQ' Intelligence Services Act 1994, s 7(11);

'HMRC information' information disclosed to the Director by Her Majesty's Revenue and Customs (HMRC) commissioners or a person acting on their behalf, s 7(11);

'intelligence service' the Security Service, Secret Intelligence Service or GCHQ, s 7(11);

'intelligence service disclosure arrangements' arrangements made by the Director-General of the Security Service, the Chief of the Intelligence Service or Director of GCHQ about the disclosure of information by their respective bodies, s 7(11);

'intelligence service information' information obtained from the intelligence service or a person acting on their behalf, s 7(11);

'national minimum wage information' information from an officer acting for the purposes of the National Minimum Wage Act 1998 or taking action following failure to comply with a labour market enforcement undertaking or order, s 7(11);

'relevant staff member' a member of staff provided to the Director under s 1(4); s 7(11), s 6(6);

'revenue and customs information relating to a person' as under s (19(2) of the Commissioners for Revenue and Customs Act 2005, s 7(11)

Devolution: Applies throughout the UK.

This section provides that a disclosure authorised by s 6 does not breach an obligation of confidence, or any other restriction, however imposed. There are restrictions on sharing information, however, where to do so would breach the Data Protection Act 1998 (DPA 1998) or if it is prohibited by Part I of the Regulation of Investigatory Powers Act 2000 which concerns intercept evidence (s 7(1)).

The DPA 1998 provides that data must be processed in accordance with eight principles under which information must be (Schedule 1, Part 1, s 4):

- fairly and lawfully processed;
- processed only for specified purposes;
- adequate, relevant and not excessive;
- accurate and up-to-date;
- not kept for longer than is necessary;
- processed in line with individuals' rights;
- secure;

1.7 *A Guide to the Immigration Act 2016*

- not transferred outside the European Economic Area (EEA) unless that country or territory ensures an adequate level of protection.

Sensitive personal data, defined (s 2) as data on:

- racial or ethnic origin;
- political opinions;
- religion;
- membership of a trade union;
- physical or mental health or condition;
- sexual life;

may be shared without consent where further specified conditions are met, including:[1]

- where it is in the substantial public interest;
- where it is necessary for the prevention or detection of any unlawful act;
- where the discharge of any function designed for protecting members of the public against dishonesty, malpractice, or other seriously improper conduct by, or the unfitness or incompetence of, any person (whether alleged or established); or mismanagement in the administration of, or failures in services provided by, any body or association;
- where it is shared with a view to the publication by any person and the data controller reasonably believes that such publication would be in the public interest;
- where it is necessary for the discharge of any function which is designed for the provision of confidential counselling, advice, support, or any other service;
- where it is necessary for the exercise of any functions conferred on a constable by any rule of law.

The DPA 1998 gives individuals rights to know what data is held about them; but these do not in any way narrow information gateways.

There are limitations on the information that those working with the intelligence services may disclose. HMRC information may be disclosed with authorization at the requisite level.

---

[1] Data Protection (Processing of Sensitive Personal Data) Order 2000, SI 2000/417.

SECTION 8—INFORMATION HUB

> **Summary**
>
> Gives the staff of the Director of Labour Market Enforcement powers to request information that they consider would facilitate the exercise of the Director's functions from those exercising labour market enforcement functions and within the timeframe they require.

1.8

8 Information hub

(1) The Director must gather, store, process, analyse and disseminate information relating to non-compliance in the labour market.

(2) The Director may request any person by whom, or by whose officers, labour market enforcement functions are exercisable to provide the Director with any non-compliance information specified or of a description specified in the request.

(3) "Non-compliance information" means information relating to non-compliance in the labour market which the Director considers would facilitate the exercise of any of his or her functions.

(4) A person by whom, or by whose officers, labour market enforcement functions are exercisable may request the Director to provide the person, or an officer of the person, with any enforcement information specified or of a description specified in the request.

(5) "Enforcement information" means information which the person making the request considers would facilitate the exercise of any labour market enforcement function of the person or of an officer of the person.

(6) A person who receives a request under this section must respond to it in writing within a reasonable period.

Commencement: 12 July 2016, Immigration Act 2014 (Commencement No 1) Regulations 2016, SI 2016/603.

Definitions:

'the Director' Director of Labour Market Enforcement, s 1(1);

'enforcement information' information considered to facilitate the exercise of any labour market enforcement function by the person requesting it, s 8(5);

'labour market enforcement functions' s 3(2), see detailed commentary on s 3;

1.9 *A Guide to the Immigration Act 2016*

'non-compliance information' information relating to non-compliance in the labour market which the Director considers would facilitate the exercise of their functions, s 8(3).

Devolution: Applies throughout the UK.

This section gives the staff of the Director of Labour Market Enforcement powers to request information that they consider would facilitate the exercise of the Director's functions from those exercising labour market enforcement functions and within the timeframe they require.

SECTION 9—RESTRICTION ON EXERCISING FUNCTIONS IN RELATION TO INDIVIDUAL CASES

> **Summary**
>
> Prevents the Director from exercising any function, or making any recommendation in an individual case, but individual cases can be considered and conclusions drawn from them in the context of considering a general issue.

1.9

9 Restriction on exercising functions in relation to individual cases

(1) The Director must not in exercising any function make any recommendation in relation to an individual case.

(2) Subsection (1) does not prevent the Director considering individual cases and drawing conclusions about them for the purpose of, or in the context of, considering a general issue.

Commencement: 12 July 2016, Immigration Act 2014 (Commencement No 1) Regulations 2016, SI 2016/603.

Definitions: 'the Director' Director of Labour Market Enforcement, s 1(1).

Devolution: Applies throughout the UK.

The section prevents the Director from exercising any function or making any recommendation in an individual case, but individual cases can be considered and conclusions drawn from them in the context of considering a general issue. This is comparable to the position of the Children's Commissioners for England and Wales.

GANGMASTERS AND LABOUR ABUSE AUTHORITY

SECTION 10—RENAMING OF GANGMASTERS AND LABOUR ABUSE AUTHORITY

> **Summary**
>
> Renames the Gangmasters Licensing Authority to become the 'Gangmasters and Labour Abuse Authority' in reflection of its broadened remit, and effects consequent changes to other legislation.

1.10

10 Renaming of Gangmasters Licensing Authority

(1) The Gangmasters Licensing Authority is renamed the Gangmasters and Labour Abuse Authority.

(2) In any enactment passed before the day on which this section comes into force, and in any instrument or other document made before that day, references to the Gangmasters Licensing Authority are to be read, in relation to any time on or after that day, as references to the Gangmasters and Labour Abuse Authority.

Commencement: 12 July 2016, Immigration Act 2014 (Commencement No 1) Regulations 2016, SI 2016/603.

Regulations: See the Immigration Act 2016 (Consequential Amendments) Regulations 2016, SI 2016/655, made under s 92 of this Act, which replaces references to 'Gangmasters Licensing Authority' with references to 'Gangmasters and Labour Abuse Authority' in secondary legislation.

Devolution: Applies throughout the UK.

The section renames the Gangmasters Licensing Authority (GLA) the 'Gangmasters and Labour Abuse Authority' (GLAA) to reflect an expansion of its functions under the Act.

The GLAA currently licences those supplying workers to the agricultural and shellfish industries. Its licensing role will be expanded to cover other industries that will be set out in regulations made under s 3(5)(b) of the Gangmasters Licensing Act 2004, as amended by Schedule 3, para 17. The Secretary of State is required to consult with the GLAA and the Director of Labour Market Enforcement before making regulations under this provision.

1.11 A Guide to the Immigration Act 2016

New functions are conferred on the GLAA under s 11 and Schedule 2 so that labour abuse prevention officers may investigate breaches of the National Minimum Wage (NMW) and the national living wage and breaches by employment agencies where they are in connection with labour market exploitation. Under s 13, they may also be given powers under the Police and Criminal Evidence Act 1984 (PACE 1984) to arrest suspects, to enter premises where they believe labour market offending is taking place and to search for and seize evidence.

SECTION 11—FUNCTIONS IN RELATION TO LABOUR MARKET AND SCHEDULE 2—FUNCTIONS IN RELATION TO LABOUR MARKET

> **Summary**
>
> Provides new investigative functions for the Gangmasters and Labour Abuse Authority (GLAA) and empowers the Secretary of State to confer other functions on the GLAA and its officers.

1.11

11 Functions in relation to labour market

(1) Schedule 2 (functions in relation to labour market) has effect.

(2) The Secretary of State may by regulations confer other functions on the Gangmasters and Labour Abuse Authority or its officers.'

Schedule 2

Functions in relation to labour market

Employment Agencies Act 1973 (c. 35)

1 The Employment Agencies Act 1973 is amended as follows.

2 Before section 9 insert—

"8A Appointment of officers

(1) The Secretary of State may—

(a) appoint officers to act for the purposes of this Act, and

(b) instead of or in addition to appointing any officers under this section, arrange with any relevant authority for officers of that authority to act for those purposes.

Part 1—Labour Market and Illegal Working **1.11**

- (2) The following are relevant authorities—
  - (a) any Minister of the Crown or government department;
  - (b) any body performing functions on behalf of the Crown;
  - (c) the Gangmasters and Labour Abuse Authority."

3(1) Section 9 (inspection) is amended as follows.

(2) Before subsection (1) insert—

"(A1) This section does not apply to an officer acting for the purposes of this Act in relation to England and Wales if the officer is a labour abuse prevention officer within the meaning of section 114B of the Police and Criminal Evidence Act 1984 (PACE powers for labour abuse prevention officers)."

(3) In subsection (1), for "duly authorised in that behalf by the Secretary of State" substitute " acting for the purposes of this Act ".

(4) In subsection (4)(a), in each of sub-paragraphs (ii) and (iii), for "or servant appointed by, or person exercising functions on behalf of, the Secretary of State" substitute " acting for the purposes of this Act, ".

National Minimum Wage Act 1998 (c. 39)

4 The National Minimum Wage Act 1998 is amended as follows.

5 In section 13 (appointment of officers for enforcement)—

(a) in subsection (1)(b), for the words from "Minister of the Crown" to "body shall" substitute " relevant authority for officers of that authority to";

(b) after subsection (1) insert—

"(1A) The following are relevant authorities—
  - (a) any Minister of the Crown or government department;
  - (b) any body performing functions on behalf of the Crown;
  - (c) the Gangmasters and Labour Abuse Authority."

6 In section 14 (powers of officers) before subsection (1) insert—

"(A1) This section does not apply to an officer acting for the purposes of this Act in relation to England and Wales if the officer is a labour abuse prevention officer within the meaning of section 114B of the Police and Criminal Evidence Act 1984 (PACE powers for labour abuse prevention officers)."

7 In section 15 (information obtained by officers)—

(a) in subsection (3)(b), after "any" insert "eligible";

(b) in subsection (4)(a), after "to any" insert "eligible";

(c) in subsection (8), for the words from " "relevant" to "body which", substitute "eligible relevant authority" means any relevant authority within the meaning given by section 13(1A) which".

1.11 *A Guide to the Immigration Act 2016*

Modern Slavery Act 2015 (c.30)

8   The Modern Slavery Act 2015 is amended as follows.

9   Before section 12 (but after the italic heading before it) insert—

"11A Enforcement by Gangmasters and Labour Abuse Authority

(1) The Secretary of State may make arrangements with the Gangmasters and Labour Abuse Authority for officers of the Authority to act for the purposes of this Part in taking action in circumstances in which it appears that an offence under this Part which is a labour market offence (within the meaning of section 3 of the Immigration Act 2016) has been, is being or may be committed.

(2) For provision about the powers of such an officer who is acting for the purposes of this Part, see section 114B of the Police and Criminal Evidence Act 1984 (PACE powers for labour abuse prevention officers)."

10(1) Section 15 (slavery and trafficking prevention orders on application) is amended as follows.

(2) In subsection (1)—

(a) omit the "or" after paragraph (b);

(b) after paragraph (c) insert ", or

(d) the Gangmasters and Labour Abuse Authority."

(3) In subsection (7)—

(a) for "or the Director General", in the first place it occurs, substitute ", the Director General or the Gangmasters and Labour Abuse Authority";

(b) for "or the Director General", in the second place it occurs, substitute ", the Director General or the Authority ".

(4) In subsection (8)(b)—

(a) for "or the Director General", in the first place it occurs, substitute ", the Director General or the Gangmasters and Labour Abuse Authority ";

(b) for "or the Director General", in the second place it occurs, substitute ", the Director General or the Authority".

11   In section 19(7) (requirement to provide name and address)—

(a) for "or an immigration officer" substitute ", an immigration officer or the Gangmasters and Labour Abuse Authority ";

(b) for "or the officer" substitute ", the officer or the Authority ".

Part 1—Labour Market and Illegal Working **1.11**

12(1) Section 20 (variation, renewal and discharge) is amended as follows.

(2) In subsection (2), after paragraph (f) insert—

"(g) where the order was made on an application under section 15 by the Gangmasters and Labour Abuse Authority, the Authority."

(3) In subsection (9)—

(a) for "or the Director General", in the first place it occurs, substitute ", the Director General or the Gangmasters and Labour Abuse Authority ";

(b) for "or the Director General", in the second and third places it occurs, substitute ", the Director General or the Authority ".

13(1) Section 23 (slavery and trafficking risk orders) is amended as follows.

(2) In subsection (1)—

(a) omit the "or" after paragraph (b);

(b) after paragraph (c) insert ", or

(d) the Gangmasters and Labour Abuse Authority."

(3) In subsection (6)—

(a) for "or the Director General", in the first place it occurs, substitute ", the Director General or the Gangmasters and Labour Abuse Authority ";

(b) for "or the Director General", in the second place it occurs, substitute ", the Director General or the Authority ".

(4) In subsection (7)(b)—

(a) for "or the Director General" substitute ", the Director General or the Gangmasters and Labour Abuse Authority ";

(b) for "or Director General" substitute ", the Director General or the Authority ".

14 In section 26(7) (requirement to provide name and address)—

(a) for "or an immigration officer" substitute ", an immigration officer or the Gangmasters and Labour Abuse Authority ";

(b) for "or the officer" substitute ", the officer or the Authority ".

15(1) Section 27 (variation, renewal and discharge) is amended as follows

(2) In subsection (2), after paragraph (f) insert—

"(g) where the order was made on an application by the Gangmasters and Labour Abuse Authority, the Authority."

1.11 *A Guide to the Immigration Act 2016*

(3) In subsection (7)—

(a) for "or the Director General" in the first place it occurs, substitute ", the Director General or the Gangmasters and Labour Abuse Authority";

(b) for "or the Director General" in the second and third places it occurs, substitute ", the Director General or the Authority".

16 After section 30 (offences) insert—

"30A Enforcement by Gangmasters and Labour Abuse Authority

(1) The Secretary of State may make arrangements with the Gangmasters and Labour Abuse Authority for officers of the Authority to act for the purposes of this Part in taking action in circumstances in which it appears that an offence under this Part which is a labour market offence (within the meaning of section 3 of the Immigration Act 2016) has been, is being or may be committed.

(2) For provision about the powers of such an officer who is acting for the purposes of this Part, see section 114B of the Police and Criminal Evidence Act 1984 (PACE powers for labour abuse prevention officers)."

17 In section 33 (guidance), in subsection (1) for "and the Director General of the National Crime Agency" substitute ", the Director General of the National Crime Agency and the Gangmasters and Labour Abuse Authority".

Commencement: 12 July 2016, Immigration Act 2014 (Commencement No 1) Regulations 2016, SI 2016/603.

Amends: The Employment Agencies Act 1973 (EAA 1973), inserting a new s 8A *Appointment of Officers* and amending s 9 *Inspection* (Schedule 2, para 2);

The National Minimum Wage Act 1998 (NMWA 1998), amending s 13 *Appointment of officers for enforcement* (Schedule 2, para 5), s 14 *Powers of officers* (Schedule 2, para 6), s 15 *Information obtained by officers* (Schedule 2, para 7);

The Modern Slavery Act 2015 (MSA 2015), inserting new s 11A *Enforcement by Gangmaster and Labour Abuse Authority* (Schedule 2, para 9) and new s 30A *Enforcement by Gangmaster and Labour Abuse Authority* (Schedule 2, para 16), amending s 15 *Slavery and Trafficking Prevention Orders* (Schedule 2, para 10), s 19 *Requirement to provide name and address* (Schedule 2, para 11), s 20 *Variation, renewal and discharge* (Schedule 2, para 12), s 23 *Slavery and Trafficking Risk Orders* (Schedule 2, para 13), s 26 *Requirement to provide name and address* (Schedule 2, para 14), s 27 *Variation, renewal and discharge* (Schedule 2, para 15) and s 33 *Guidance* (Schedule 2, para 17).

Regulations: To confer other functions on the Gangmasters and Labour Abuse Authority (GLAA) or its officers, s 11(2). These are subject to the negative procedure unless the regulations repeal primary legislation when the affirmative procedure is required (s 93(2)(c)). See also s 32 which places limitations on the regulations that may be made under this section to ensure they do not encroach on devolved powers.

Definitions:

'Gangmasters and Labour Abuse Authority' s 10(1);

'relevant authorities' any Minister of the Crown or Government department, any body performing functions on behalf of the Crown or the GLAA, in new s 8A(2) *Appointment of officers* of the EAA 1973 (Schedule 2, para 2) and amended s 13 *Appointment of officers for enforcement* of the NMWA 1998 (Schedule 2, para 5).

Devolution: Applies throughout the UK, but restrictions are placed on regulatory-making powers to ensure they do not encroach on devolved powers (s 32).

Section 11 introduces Schedule 2 and creates the regulation-making powers. The EAA 1973 and the NMWA 1998 are amended by Schedule 2 to include the GLAA as a 'relevant authority' under those Acts. This has the effect of enabling the GLAA to, *inter alia*, investigate breaches of the national minimum wage and the national living wage and investigate breaches by employment agencies where they are in connection with labour market exploitation. Amendments to the MSA 2015 under Schedule 2 also enable the GLAA to apply to the courts for slavery and trafficking orders under Part 2 of the MSA 2015. The Secretary of State is empowered to confer additional functions on the GLAA by regulations (s 11(2)).

SECTION 12—PACE POWERS IN ENGLAND AND WALES FOR LABOUR ABUSE PREVENTION OFFICERS

Summary

Gives the Gangmasters and Labour Abuse Authority PACE-related investigative and enforcement powers in England and Wales.

1.12

12 PACE powers in England and Wales for labour abuse prevention officers

(1) After section 114A of the Police and Criminal Evidence Act 1984 insert—

"114B Application of Act to labour abuse prevention officers

(1) The Secretary of State may by regulations apply any provision of this Act which relates to investigations of offences conducted by police officers to investigations of labour market offences conducted by labour abuse prevention officers.

(2) The regulations may apply provisions of this Act with any modifications specified in the regulations.

(3) In this section "labour abuse prevention officer" means an officer of the Gangmasters and Labour Abuse Authority who—

    (a) falls within subsection (4), and

    (b) is authorised (whether generally or specifically) by the Secretary of State for the purposes of this section.

(4) An officer of the Gangmasters and Labour Abuse Authority falls within this subsection if he or she is—

    (a) acting for the purposes of the Employment Agencies Act 1973 (see section 8A of that Act),

    (b) acting for the purposes of the National Minimum Wage Act 1998 (see section 13 of that Act),

    (c) acting for the purposes of the Gangmasters (Licensing) Act 2004 as an enforcement officer within the meaning of section 15 of that Act,

    (d) acting for the purposes of Part 1 or 2 of the Modern Slavery Act 2015 (see sections 11A and 30A of that Act), or

    (e) acting for any other purpose prescribed in regulations made by the Secretary of State.

(5) The investigations for the purposes of which provisions of this Act may be applied by regulations under this section include investigations of offences committed, or suspected of having been committed, before the coming into force of the regulations or of this section.

(6) Regulations under this section are to be made by statutory instrument.

(7) Regulations under this section may make—

    (a) different provision for different purposes;

    (b) provision which applies generally or for particular purposes;

    (c) incidental, supplementary, consequential, transitional or transitory provision or savings.

(8) Regulations under subsection (4)(e) may, in particular, make such provision amending, repealing or revoking any enactment as the Secretary of State considers appropriate in consequence of any provision made by the regulations.

(9) A statutory instrument containing regulations under subsection (4)(e) may not be made unless a draft of the instrument has been laid before, and approved by a resolution of, each House of Parliament.

(10) Any other statutory instrument containing regulations under this section is subject to annulment in pursuance of a resolution of either House of Parliament.

Part 1—Labour Market and Illegal Working **1.12**

(11) In this section—

"enactment" includes an enactment contained in subordinate legislation within the meaning of the Interpretation Act 1978;

"labour market offence" has the meaning given in section 3 of the Immigration Act 2016."

(12) In section 18 of the Gangmasters (Licensing) Act 2004 (obstruction of officers), in subsection (1)(a), after "this Act" insert "or functions conferred by virtue of section 114B of the Police and Criminal Evidence Act 1984 (application of that Act to Authority officers)".

Commencement: 12 July 2016, Immigration Act 2014 (Commencement No 1) Regulations 2016, SI 2016/603.

Amends: The Police and Criminal Evidence Act 1984 (PACE 1984), inserting a new section 114B *Application of Act to labour abuse prevention officers* (s 12(1)).

Regulations: s 12(1) inserts new s 114B of the PACE 1984. Regulations may be made under s 114B(1), subject to the negative procedure in parliament (s 114B(10), to apply any provision of PACE to labour abuse prevention officers conducting investigations of labour market offences for the purposes of the Employment Agencies Act 1973 (EAA 1973), the National Minimum Wage Act 1998 (NMWA 1998), the Gangmasters (Licensing) Act 2004 (GLA 2004) or Part 1 or 2 of the Modern Slavery Act 2015 (MSA 2015). These purposes may be extended by regulations that may be made under s 114B(4)(e), subject to the affirmative procedure in parliament (s 114B(9)).

Definitions:

'enactment' includes enactments contained in subordinate legislation within the meaning of the Interpretation Act 1978, new s 114B(11) PACE 1984 inserted by s 12(1);

'labour market offence' s 3(3), see detailed commentary on s 3.

Devolution: Applies only in England and Wales.

The Secretary of State can designate trained labour abuse prevention officers with powers under the PACE 1984. These may only be used in relation to labour market offences under the EAA 1973, the NMWA 1998, the GLA 2004, Part 1 and Part 2 of the MSA 2016 and breaches of the new labour market enforcement orders and undertakings under the Immigration Act 2016. The Secretary of State can make regulations to extend the provisions under which labour abuse prevention officers may conduct investigations under PACE provisions.

The powers are similar to those of HMRC and immigration enforcement officers and include powers to arrest suspects, enter premises where they believe labour market offending is taking place and to search for and seize evidence.

SECTION 13—RELATIONSHIP WITH OTHER AGENCIES AND REQUESTS FOR ASSISTANCE

> **Summary**
>
> A formal statutory mechanism for the Gangmasters and Labour Abuse Authority to request assistance from the National Crime Agency, the police or immigration enforcement, and *vice versa* for those agencies to ask for the assistance of the GLAA.

1.13

13 Relationship with other agencies: requests for assistance

(1) The Gangmasters (Licensing) Act 2004 is amended as follows.

(2) Before section 23 (but after the italic heading before it) insert—

"**22A Relationship with other agencies: requests for assistance**

(1) The Authority may request any of the following to provide assistance to the Authority or any of its officers—

　　(a) a chief officer of police for a police area in England and Wales;

　　(b) the Director General of the National Crime Agency;

　　(c) a person appointed as an immigration officer under paragraph 1 of Schedule 2 to the Immigration Act 1971;

　　(d) any other person prescribed or of a prescribed description.

(2) The Authority may make a request under subsection (1) only if it considers that the assistance would facilitate the exercise of any function by the Authority or any of its officers.

(3) Any of the following persons may request the Authority to provide assistance to the person—

　　(a) a chief officer of police for a police area in England and Wales;

　　(b) a person appointed as an immigration officer under paragraph 1 of Schedule 2 to the Immigration Act 1971;

　　(c) any other person prescribed or of a prescribed description.

(4) A person may make a request under subsection (3) only if the person considers that the assistance would facilitate the exercise by the person of any function.

(5) A request under this section must—

　　(a) set out what assistance is being requested, and

(b) explain how the assistance would facilitate the exercise of the function.

(6) A person who receives a request under this section must respond to it in writing within a reasonable period.

(7) Regulations under this section must not make provision which would be—

(a) within the legislative competence of the Scottish Parliament if contained in an Act of that Parliament,

(b) within the legislative competence of the National Assembly for Wales if contained in an Act of that Assembly, or

(c) within the legislative competence of the Northern Ireland Assembly if contained in an Act of that Assembly made without the consent of the Secretary of State."

(8) In section 25 (regulations, rules and orders), in subsection (5)—

(a) omit the "or" at the end of paragraph (a);

(b) at the end insert ", or

(c) section 22A(1)(d) or (3)(c) (regulations regarding persons whom the Authority may request to provide assistance and who may request assistance from Authority)."

Commencement: 12 July 2016, Immigration Act 2014 (Commencement No 1) Regulations 2016, SI 2016/603.

Amends: Gangmasters Licensing Act 2004 (GLA 2004), inserting new s 22A *Relationship with other agencies, requests for assistance* (s 13(2)) and amending s 25 *Rules, regulations and orders* (s 13(3)).

Regulations: May be made under new s 22A(1)(d) of the GLA 2004, inserted by s 13(2), to prescribe persons or descriptions of persons from whom the Gangmasters and Labour Abuse Authority (GLAA) may request assistance. Regulations are subject to limitations ensuring that they do not encroach on devolved powers (new 22A(1)(d) of that Act) and are made subject to the affirmative procedure in Parliament (s 25(5) of that Act).

Definitions:

'the Authority' the GLAA, s 1(1) of the GLA 2004 read with s 10(1) of the Immigration Act 2016.

Devolution: Applies throughout the UK.

The section inserts new s 22A *Relationship with other agencies: requests for assistance* into the GLA 2004 creating a formal statutory mechanism for the GLAA to request assistance from the National Crime Agency (NCA), the

1.13 *A Guide to the Immigration Act 2016*

police or an immigration officer. A request for assistance may only be made by the GLAA where this would facilitate the exercise of its functions or those of its officers.

In the same way, police and immigration officers may request assistance from the GLAA where this would facilitate the exercise of their functions.

In both cases, a request for assistance must set out the assistance sought and how it would assist the relevant functions. A written response to a request must be given and within a reasonable period of time.

The Secretary of State may include through regulations other bodies in the lists of those that may give or receive requests for assistance under these powers. These regulations are subject to limitations so that the Secretary of State may not add bodies where their powers are reserved, so as not to encroach on the authority of the devolved administrations.

The Crime and Courts Act 2003 provides the NCA with powers to ask for assistance and the GLAA falls within the scope of that power.

The ability for immigration officers to seek the assistance of the GLAA in carrying out their functions was a controversial provision. On the relationship between the GLAA and immigration enforcement, the Minister in the House of Lords stated:

> 'It is entirely possible that the GLAA will become aware of a situation involving gangmasters that also involves illegal working and the employment of illegal workers. In such circumstances, it is vital that a defined partnership exists to enable the exchange of information while ensuring that roles remain distinct. This already happens and we are taking the opportunity to formulate how that relationship works. This is part of what I referred to earlier. Often – we are told by the prosecuting authorities – when someone is guilty of an offence in one area, they are an offender in multiple areas.'[1]

The provision gave rise to concerns that it creates the potential for joint labour inspection and immigration operations that could discourage victims of labour exploitation who have an insecure immigration status from coming forward. Joint inspections have been criticised by the Special Rapporteur on the Human Rights of Migrants for this reason.[2] The GLAA could, however, decline a request for assistance if to do so would undermine its protective role and duties towards victims of labour exploitation. The International Labour Organization Labour Inspection Convention 1947 (No 81), ratified by the UK in 1949, identifies the function of labour inspection as securing the enforcement of legal provisions relating to conditions of work and the protection of workers, providing advice and information to employees and workers on complying with the provisions, and highlighting abuses not covered in law.[3] It states that any additional duties should not prejudice in any way the authority and impartiality which are necessary to inspectors in their relations with employers and workers.[4]

---

1   Rt Hon Lord Bates, Minister of State, Home Office, Immigration Bill 2015/16, House of Lords Committee, first sitting, *Hansard* HL col 580 (18 January 2016). Available at: http://www.publications.parliament.uk/pa/ld201516/ldhansrd/text/160118-0001.htm#1601184000412 (accessed 6 November 2016).
2   *Report of the Special Rapporteur on the human rights of migrants, François Crépeau, Labour exploitation of migrants*, A/HRC/26/35, 3 April 2014. Available at: http://www.ohchr.org/Documents/Issues/SRMigrants/A.HRC.26.35.pdf (accessed 6 November 2016).
3   Article 3(1) International Labour Office Labour Inspection Convention 1947 (No 81). Available at: http://www.ilo.org/dyn/normlex/en/f?p=NORMLEXPUB:12100:0::NO::P12100_INSTRUMENT_ID:312226 (accessed 6 November 2016).
4   Article 3(2) ibid (accessed 6 November 2016).

LABOUR MARKET ENFORCEMENT UNDERTAKINGS

1.14   These provisions create a new regime of labour market enforcement (LME) undertakings and orders, backed up by a criminal offence for non-compliance. They may be considered a sort of Anti-Social Behaviour Order (ASBO) for employers. The effect is to introduce custodial penalties for a number of labour market offences that were previously only punishable with a fine.

The enforcement bodies will be able to seek a LME undertaking where they believe a trigger offence under specified labour market legislation has been or is being committed. The undertaking includes measures aimed at preventing or reducing the risk of committing further labour market offences and any other requirements. An undertaking may remain in place for up to two years.

Where a business refuses to give an undertaking within a specified period or where the undertaking is breached, an enforcement body may apply to the court for a LME order. A court can also make an order of its own motion following conviction for a 'trigger offence'. Where a business fails to comply with an order, a criminal offence is committed, the maximum penalty for which is two years imprisonment and/or a fine on conviction on indictment, or twelve months imprisonment and/or a fine on summary conviction. Provision is made to appeal against, vary or discharge an order; and to empower the enforcing authorities to operate the new regime.

1.14.1   *A Guide to the Immigration Act 2016*

SECTION 14—POWER TO REQUEST A LABOUR MARKET ENFORCEMENT UNDERTAKING

> **Summary**
>
> Power for an enforcing authority to invite a person to give a labour market enforcement undertaking.

1.14.1
14 Power to request LME undertaking

(1) This section applies where an enforcing authority believes that a person has committed, or is committing, a trigger offence.

(2) An enforcing authority may give a notice to the person—

   (a) identifying the trigger offence which the authority believes has been or is being committed;

   (b) giving the authority's reasons for the belief;

   (c) inviting the person to give the authority a labour market enforcement undertaking in the form attached to the notice.

(3) A labour market enforcement undertaking (an "LME undertaking") is an undertaking by the person giving it (the "subject") to comply with any prohibitions, restrictions and requirements set out in the undertaking (as to which see section 15).

(4) "Trigger offence" means—

   (a) an offence under the Employment Agencies Act 1973 other than one under section 9(4)(b) of that Act;

   (b) an offence under the National Minimum Wage Act 1998;

   (c) an offence under the Gangmasters (Licensing) Act 2004;

   (d) any other offence prescribed by regulations made by the Secretary of State;

   (e) an offence of attempting or conspiring to commit an offence mentioned in paragraphs (a) to (d);

   (f) an offence under Part 2 of the Serious Crime Act 2007 in relation to an offence so mentioned;

   (g) an offence of inciting a person to commit an offence so mentioned;

   (h) an offence of aiding, abetting, counselling or procuring the commission of an offence so mentioned.

(5) "Enforcing authority"—

   (a) in relation to a trigger offence under the Employment Agencies Act 1973, means the Secretary of State or any authority whose officers are acting for the purposes of that Act (see section 8A of that Act);

Part 1—Labour Market and Illegal Working **1.14.1**

(b) in relation to a trigger offence under the National Minimum Wage Act 1998, means the Secretary of State or any authority whose officers are acting for the purposes of that Act (see section 13 of that Act);

(c) in relation to a trigger offence under the Gangmasters (Licensing) Act 2004, means the Secretary of State or any authority whose officers are acting as enforcement officers for the purposes of that Act (see section 15 of that Act);

(d) in relation to an offence which is a trigger offence by virtue of subsection (4)(d) (including an offence mentioned in subsection (4)(e) to (h) in connection with such an offence), has the meaning prescribed in regulations made by the Secretary of State.

(6) In subsection (5), a reference to an offence under an Act includes a reference to an offence mentioned in subsection (4)(e) to (h) in connection with such an offence.

(7) In this section references to the Gangmasters (Licensing) Act 2004 are references to that Act only so far as it applies in relation to England and Wales and Scotland.

Commencement: 25 November 2016, The Immigration Act 2016 (Commencement No 2 and Transitional Provisions) Regulations 2016, SI 2016/1037.

Regulations: Prescribing additional offences as trigger offences (s 14(4)). The affirmative procedure is required (s 93(d)). See also s 32 which places limitations on the regulations that may be made under this section to ensure they do not encroach on devolved powers.

Definitions:

'enforcing authority' the Secretary of State or any authority whose officers are acting for the purposes of the Employment Agencies Act 1973 (EAA 1973), the National Minimum Wage Act 1998 (NMWA 1998), the Gangmasters Licensing Act 2004 (GLA 2004), or in connection with offences that may be prescribed, s 14(5);

'Gangmasters Licensing Act 2004' the Act only insofar as it applies in England and Wales and Scotland;

'labour market enforcement undertaking'/'LME undertaking' an undertaking by the person giving it to comply with prohibitions, restrictions and requirements set out in the undertaking, s 14(3);

'subject' a person giving a labour market enforcement undertaking, s 14(3);

'trigger offence' s 14(4).

Devolution: Applies throughout the UK, though references to the GLA 2004 in this section do not apply in Northern Ireland (s 3(6)). Restrictions are

1.14.1 *A Guide to the Immigration Act 2016*

also placed on regulatory-making powers to ensure they do not encroach on devolved powers (s 32).

This section gives powers to enforcing authorities to seek a LME undertaking by issuing a notice to a person they believe has committed or is committing a 'trigger offence'.

'Trigger offences' are defined as offences under the EAA 1973 (except the offence under s 9(4)(b) of that Act relating to limitations on disclosure by those empowered to conduct inspections of employment agencies); offences under the NMWA 1998 and offences under the GLA 2004. The commentary on s 3 above provides some examples of the types of offences that may be committed under these Acts. The definition includes attempting or conspiring to commit an offence under these Acts as well as aiding, abetting etc. Further offences may be included as 'trigger' offences by the Secretary of State through regulations.

The enforcing authorities are defined as either the Secretary of State or the authority whose officers have powers to act under the relevant Act. As discussed above, under s 2 and Schedule 11, the GLAA is empowered to act for the purpose of all these provisions. The Employment Agency Standards Inspectorate and the HMRC National Minimum Wage team will be able to seek LME undertakings and orders under their respective remits.

The notice issued by the enforcing authority identifies the trigger offence, provides reasons why the authority believes it has been, or is being committed and invites the person to give the authority a LME undertaking in the form attached to the notice. The undertaking is to comply with any prescribed measures set out in the document that the enforcing authority considers just and reasonable to prevent, or reduce the person's risk of not complying with their obligations under labour market legislation, and/or to publicise the fact that an undertaking is being made (see also s 15 and commentary). Section 16 makes provision in relation to the duration of any undertaking and further provisions in relation to issuing the notice are set out in s 17.

SECTION 15—MEASURES IN LABOUR MARKET ENFORCEMENT UNDERTAKINGS

> **Summary**
>
> Defines the scope of the measures an enforcing authority may include in a labour market enforcement (LME) undertaking.

1.15

15 Measures in LME undertakings

(1) An LME undertaking may include a prohibition, restriction or requirement (each a "measure") if, and only if—

    (a) the measure falls within subsection (2) or (3) (or both), and

    (b) the enforcing authority considers that the measure is just and reasonable.

(2) A measure falls within this subsection if it is for the purpose of—

    (a) preventing or reducing the risk of the subject not complying with any requirement imposed by or under the relevant enactment, or

    (b) bringing to the attention of persons likely to be interested in the matter—

        (i) the existence of the LME undertaking,

        (ii) the circumstances in which it was given, and

        (iii) any action taken (or not taken) by the subject in order to comply with the undertaking.

(3) A measure falls within this subsection if it is prescribed, or is of a description prescribed, in regulations made by the Secretary of State.

(4) The enforcing authority must not—

    (a) invite the subject to give an LME undertaking, or

    (b) agree to the form of an undertaking,

unless the authority believes that at least one measure in the undertaking is necessary for the purpose mentioned in subsection (5).

(5) That purpose is preventing or reducing the risk of the subject—

    (a) committing a further trigger offence under the relevant enactment, or

    (b) continuing to commit the trigger offence.

(6) An LME undertaking must set out how each measure included for the purpose mentioned in subsection (2)(a) is expected to achieve that purpose.

(7) In this section, the "relevant enactment" means the enactment under which the enforcing authority believes the trigger offence concerned has been or is being committed.

Commencement: 25 November 2016, The Immigration Act 2016 (Commencement No 2 and Transitional Provisions) Regulations 2016, SI 2016/1037.

Regulations: Prescribing additional 'measures' which may be included in labour market enforcement (LME) undertakings, additional to those set out in s 15(2), (s 15(3)).

Definitions:

'enforcing authority' the Secretary of State or any authority whose officers are acting for the purposes of the Employment Agencies Act 1973, the National Minimum Wage Act 1998, the Gangmasters Licensing Act 2004, or in connection with offences that may be prescribed, s 14(5);

'labour market enforcement undertaking'/'LME Undertaking' an undertaking by the person giving it to comply with prohibitions, restrictions and requirements set out in the undertaking, s 14(3);

'measure' a prohibition, restriction or requirement, s 15(1);

'relevant enactment' the enactment under which the enforcing authority believes the trigger offence has been or is being committed, s 15(7);

'subject' a person giving a labour market enforcement undertaking, s 14(3);

'trigger offence' see s 14(4).

The section defines the scope of the measures that an enforcing authority may include in an undertaking. A prohibition, restriction or requirement may only be included in an undertaking if the enforcing authority considers that the measure is just and reasonable for the purpose of preventing or reducing the risk of non-compliance with employment legislation or for publicising the undertaking made, and any actions the person has taken or failed to take under the undertaking. The authority must set out how any measure aimed at preventing or reducing the risk of non-compliance with labour legislation is expected to achieve that purpose. By operation of s 15(4), at least one of the measures within the undertaking must be aimed at preventing or reducing the risk of the individual committing or continuing to commit a further 'trigger offence'.

Examples of the types of measures that might be used were not discussed during the passage of the Act through parliament. It will be difficult for a court to assess compliance with an undertaking or an order if the measures prescribed are qualitative in nature or poorly defined. Types of measures are discussed in the Code of Practice issued to enforcing authorities: see commentary on s 25.

SECTION 16—DURATION

Summary

Provides for a labour market enforcement (LME) undertaking to last for up to two years, for the circumstances in which a person can be released from an undertaking and for those who should be informed of such release.

1.16

16 Duration

(1) An LME undertaking has effect from when it is accepted by the enforcing authority or from the later time specified in it for this purpose.

(2) An LME undertaking has effect for the period specified in it but the maximum period for which an undertaking may have effect is 2 years.

(3) The enforcing authority may release the subject from an LME undertaking.

(4) The enforcing authority must release the subject from an LME undertaking if at any time during the period for which it has effect the authority believes that no measure in it is necessary for the purpose mentioned in section 15(5).

(5) If the enforcing authority releases the subject from an LME undertaking it must take such steps as it considers appropriate to bring that fact to the attention of—

  (a) the subject;

  (b) any other persons likely to be interested in the matter.

Commencement: 25 November 2016, The Immigration Act 2016 (Commencement No 2 and Transitional Provisions) Regulations 2016, SI 2016/1037.

Definitions:

'enforcing authority' the Secretary of State or any authority whose officers are acting for the purposes of the Employment Agencies Act 1973, the National Minimum Wage Act 1998, the Gangmasters Licensing Act 2004, or in connection with offences that may be prescribed, s 14(5);

'labour market enforcement undertaking'/'LME Undertaking' an undertaking by the person giving it to comply with prohibitions, restrictions and requirements set out in the undertaking, s 14(3);

'measure' a prohibition, restriction or requirement, s 15(1);

'subject' a person giving a labour market enforcement undertaking, s 14(3);

'trigger offence' s 14(4).

Devolution: Applies throughout the UK.

A LME undertaking takes effect from when it is accepted by an enforcing authority and lasts for the period specified within it, which may be up to two years.

The enforcing authority may release a person from their undertaking by advising the person or any other persons likely to be interested in the matter.

1.17 *A Guide to the Immigration Act 2016*

The enforcing authority is required to release a person from their undertaking if it believes, at any time during the period it is in effect, that there are no measures, or no longer any measures, which comply with the requirements in s 15 above.

SECTION 17—FURTHER PROVISION ABOUT GIVING NOTICE UNDER SECTION 14

> **Summary**
> Describes how notice of an invitation to make an undertaking shall be given and deals with deemed service.

1.17

17 Further provision about giving notice under section 14

(1) A notice may be given under section 14 to a person by—

    (a) delivering it to the person,

    (b) leaving it at the person's proper address,

    (c) sending it by post to the person at that address, or

    (d) subject to subsection (6), sending it to the person by electronic means.

(2) A notice to a body corporate may be given to any officer of that body.

(3) A notice to a partnership may be given to any partner.

(4) A notice to an unincorporated association (other than a partnership) may be given to any member of the governing body of the association.

(5) For the purposes of this section and of section 7 of the Interpretation Act 1978 (service of documents by post) in its application to this section, the proper address of a person is the person's last known address (whether of the person's residence or of a place where the person carries on business or is employed) and also—

    (a) in the case of a body corporate or an officer of the body, the address of the body's registered or principal office in the United Kingdom;

    (b) in the case of a partnership or a partner, the address of the principal office of the partnership in the United Kingdom;

    (c) in the case of an unincorporated association (other than a partnership) or a member of its governing body, the principal office of the association in the United Kingdom.

(6) A notice may be sent to a person by electronic means only if—

    (a) the person has indicated that notices under section 14 may be given to the person by being sent to an electronic address and in an electronic form specified for that purpose, and

    (b) the notice is sent to that address in that form.

(7) A notice sent to a person by electronic means is, unless the contrary is proved, to be treated as having been given on the working day immediately following the day on which it was sent.

(8) In this section—

"electronic address" means any number or address used for the purposes of sending or receiving documents or information by electronic means;

"officer", in relation to a body corporate, means a director, manager, secretary or other similar officer of the body;

"working day" means a day other than a Saturday, a Sunday, Christmas Day, Good Friday or a bank holiday under the Banking and Financial Dealings Act 1971 in any part of the United Kingdom.

Commencement: 25 November 2016, The Immigration Act 2016 (Commencement No 2 and Transitional Provisions) Regulations 2016, SI 2016/1037.

Definitions:

'electronic address' any number or address used for the purposes of sending or receiving documents or information by electronic means, s 17(8);

'officer' in relation to a body corporate means a director, manager, secretary or similar officer of the body, s 17(8);

'proper address of a person' s 17(5);

'working day' a day other than a Saturday, Sunday, Christmas Day, Good Friday or a bank holiday under the Banking and Financial Dealings Act 1971 in any part of the UK, s 17(8).

Devolution: Applies throughout the UK.

Further provision is made about the nature of notices that give an invitation to make a labour market undertaking (LME) undertaking.

A notice may be given to a person by delivering it to them, leaving it at their proper address or posting it to their proper address. This is the person's last known address, whether this is their residence or a place from where they carry out business or are employed.

Persons include legal persons such as corporate bodies and partnerships, with unincorporated associations treated as such under s 29(1). For corporate bodies or their officers, the notice may be given to any officer of that body and may also be sent to the address of the body's registered or principal office in the UK. Similarly, a notice may be sent to any partner of a partnership and the address of the principal office of the partnership in the UK may be used for service. A notice may be given to any member of the governing body of an unincorporated association and the address for service may include the principal office of the association in the UK.

A notice may also be sent electronically where the person has indicated that this may be done and it is sent electronically in the correct form. A notice sent electronically is treated as having been given on the working day immediately following the day on which it was sent.

LABOUR MARKET ENFORCEMENT ORDERS

SECTION 18—POWER TO MAKE A LABOUR MARKET ENFORCEMENT ORDER ON APPLICATION

> **Summary**
>
> Power for a court to make a labour market enforcement (LME) order on application by an enforcing authority.

1.18

18 Power to make LME order on application

(1) The appropriate court may, on an application by an enforcing authority under section 19, make a labour market enforcement order against a person if the court—

   (a) is satisfied, on the balance of probabilities, that the person has committed, or is committing, a trigger offence, and

   (b) considers that it is just and reasonable to make the order.

(2) A labour market enforcement order (an "LME order") is an order which—

   (a) prohibits or restricts the person against whom it is made ("the respondent") from doing anything set out in the order;

   (b) requires the respondent to do anything set out in the order.

See section 21.

Part 1—Labour Market and Illegal Working **1.18**

(3) In this section "the appropriate court"—

    (a) where the conduct constituting the trigger offence took or is taking place primarily in England and Wales, means a magistrates' court;

    (b) where that conduct took or is taking place primarily in Scotland, means the sheriff;

    (c) where that conduct took or is taking place primarily in Northern Ireland, means a court of summary jurisdiction.

(4) An application for an LME order under this section is—

    (a) in England and Wales, to be made by complaint;

    (b) in Northern Ireland, to be made by complaint under Part 8 of the Magistrates' Courts (Northern Ireland) Order 1981 (S.I. 1981/1675 (N.I. 26)).

Commencement: 25 November 2016, The Immigration Act 2016 (Commencement No 2 and Transitional Provisions) Regulations 2016, SI 2016/1037.

Definitions:

'appropriate court' magistrates' court (England and Wales), sheriff court (Scotland) or court of summary jurisdiction (Northern Ireland), s 18(3);

'enforcing authority' the Secretary of State or any authority whose officers are acting for the purposes of the Employment Agencies Act 1973, the National Minimum Wage Act 1998, the Gangmasters Licensing Act 2004, or in connection with offences that may be prescribed, s 14(5);

'labour market enforcement undertaking'/'LME Undertaking' an undertaking by the person giving it to comply with prohibitions, restrictions and requirements set out in the undertaking, s 14(3);

'labour market enforcement order'/'LME order' an order which prohibits or restricts the person against whom it is made from doing anything set out in the order or requires them to do something set out in the order, s 18(2);

'respondent' person against whom a labour market enforcement order is made, s 18(2);

Devolution: Applies throughout the UK. See courts to which an application can be made, s 18(3).

The court may make a LME order on application by an enforcing authority. It must be satisfied on the balance of probabilities that the person against whom the order is made is committing, or has committed, a trigger offence and that it is just and reasonable to make the order. The court will be a magistrates' court in England and Wales, a sheriff court in Scotland or a court of summary jurisdiction in Northern Ireland.

1.19 *A Guide to the Immigration Act 2016*

SECTION 19—APPLICATIONS

> **Summary**
>
> Sets out the requirements for an enforcing authority to make an application for a labour market enforcement (LME) order.

1.19

19 Applications

(1) An enforcing authority may apply for an LME order to be made under section 18 against a person (the "proposed respondent") if—

 (a) the authority has served a notice on the proposed respondent under section 14, and

 (b) the proposed respondent—

  (i) refuses to give an LME undertaking, or

  (ii) otherwise fails, before the end of the negotiation period, to give an LME undertaking in the form attached to the notice or in such other form as may be agreed with the enforcing authority.

(2) An enforcing authority may also apply for an LME order if the proposed respondent—

 (a) has given an LME undertaking to the enforcing authority, and

 (b) has failed to comply with the undertaking.

(3) In subsection (1) "the negotiation period" means—

 (a) the period of 14 days beginning with the day after that on which the notice mentioned in paragraph (a) of that subsection was given, or

 (b) such longer period as may be agreed between the enforcing authority and the proposed respondent.

Commencement: 25 November 2016, The Immigration Act 2016 (Commencement No 2 and Transitional Provisions) Regulations 2016, SI 2016/1037.

Definitions:

'enforcing authority' the Secretary of State or any authority whose officers are acting for the purposes of the Employment Agencies Act 1973, the National Minimum Wage Act 1998, the Gangmasters Licensing Act 2004, or in connection with offences that may be prescribed, s 14(5);

Part 1—Labour Market and Illegal Working **1.20**

'labour market enforcement undertaking'/'LME Undertaking' an undertaking by the person giving it to comply with prohibitions, restrictions and requirements set out in the undertaking, s 14(3);

'labour market enforcement order' / 'LME order' an order which prohibits or restricts the person against whom it is made from doing anything set out in the order or requires them to do something set out in the order, s 18(2);

'negotiation period' period of 14 days from the day after the notice was given or any longer period agreed between the enforcing authority and the respondent, s 19(3);

'proposed respondent', person against whom an enforcing authorities applies for a labour market enforcement order, s 19(1);

Devolution: Applies throughout the UK. See courts to which an application may be made (s 18(3)) and the method by which an application may be made (s 18(4)).

An application for an order can be made by an enforcing authority when a person has refused to give an undertaking within a period of 14 days, or longer if agreed or, having given one, has failed to comply with it.

SECTION 20—POWER TO MAKE A LABOUR MARKET ENFORCEMENT ORDER ON CONVICTION

Summary
Empowers a court to make a labour market enforcement (LME) order of its own motion following conviction for a 'trigger offence'.

1.20

20 Power to make LME order on conviction

(1) This section applies where a court deals with a person in respect of a conviction for a trigger offence.

(2) The court may make an LME order against the person if the court considers it is just and reasonable to do so.

(3) An LME order must not be made under this section except—

    (a) in addition to a sentence imposed in respect of the offence concerned, or

    (b) in addition to an order discharging the person conditionally or, in Scotland, discharging the person absolutely.

Commencement: 25 November 2016, The Immigration Act 2016 (Commencement No 2 and Transitional Provisions) Regulations 2016, SI 2016/1037.

Definitions:

'labour market enforcement order' / 'LME order' an order which prohibits or restricts the person against whom it is made from doing anything set out in the order or requires them to do something set out in the order, s 18(2);

'trigger offence' s 14(4).

Devolution: Applies throughout the UK.

A court may make a LME order of its own motion following the conviction of a person for a 'trigger offence' if the court considers it just and reasonable to do so. A LME order may only be made in addition to a sentence imposed in respect of the offence concerned or in addition to a conditional discharge or, in Scotland, in addition to an absolute discharge.

SECTION 21—MEASURES IN LABOUR MARKET ENFORCEMENT ORDERS

> **Summary**
>
> Describes the measures a labour market enforcement (LME) order can contain.

1.21

21 Measures in LME orders

(1) An LME order may include a prohibition, restriction or requirement (each a "measure") if, and only if, the measure falls within subsection (2) or (3) (or both).

(2) A measure falls within this subsection if it is for the purpose of—

    (a) preventing or reducing the risk of the respondent not complying with any requirement imposed by or under the relevant enactment, or

    (b) bringing to the attention of persons likely to be interested in the matter—

        (i) the existence of the LME order,

        (ii) the circumstances in which it was made, and

        (iii) any action taken (or not taken) by the respondent in order to comply with the order.

(3) A measure falls within this subsection if it is prescribed, or is of a description prescribed, in regulations made by the Secretary of State.

Part 1—Labour Market and Illegal Working **1.21**

(4) Where an LME order includes a measure for the purpose mentioned in subsection (2)(a), the order must set out how the measure is expected to achieve that purpose.

(5) In this section the "relevant enactment" means the enactment under which the trigger offence concerned has been or is being committed.

Commencement: 25 November 2016, The Immigration Act 2016 (Commencement No 2 and Transitional Provisions) Regulations 2016, SI 2016/1037.

Regulations: Describing additional measures which can be contained in a labour market enforcement (LME) order, s 21(3).

Definitions:

'labour market enforcement order'/'LME order' an order which prohibits or restricts the person against whom it is made from doing anything set out in the order or requires them to do something set out in the order, s 18(2);

'measure' a prohibition, restriction or requirement, s 21(1);

'relevant enactment' the enactment under which the trigger offence concerned has been committed, s 21(5);

'trigger offence' s 14(4).

Devolution: Applies throughout the UK.

The section defines the scope of the measures that may be included in a LME order. A prohibition, restriction or requirement may only be included in an order if it is for the purpose of preventing, or reducing the risk of non-compliance with employment legislation or for publicising the undertaking made and any actions the person has taken or failed to take under the undertaking. They can also be ancillary measures such as telling third parties of the existence of the order. If a measure is included for the purpose of preventing or reducing the risk of non-compliance, the order must set out how the measure is expected to achieve that purpose.

Unlike s 15, which defines the scope of measures within undertakings, there is no requirement that at least one of the measures be aimed at preventing or reducing the risk of the person committing or continuing to commit a further 'trigger offence'.

Examples of the types of measures that might be included were not discussed during the passage of the Act through Parliament. It will be difficult for a court to assess compliance with an undertaking or an order if the measures prescribed are qualitative in nature or poorly defined. Types of measures are discussed in the code of practice issued to enforcing authorities: see commentary on s 25.

1.22　*A Guide to the Immigration Act 2016*

SECTION 22—FURTHER PROVISION ABOUT LABOUR MARKET ENFORCEMENT ORDERS

> **Summary**
>
> Specifies that an order may not be made against someone under 18 years or last for more than two years and makes provision for the court to release a person from an undertaking or discharge other orders.

1.22

22 Further provision about LME orders

(1) An LME order has effect for the period specified in it but the maximum period for which an order may have effect is 2 years.

(2) An LME order may not be made against an individual who is under 18.

(3) If a court makes an LME order, the court may also—

　(a) release the respondent from any LME undertaking given in relation to the trigger offence concerned;

　(b) discharge any other LME order which is in force against the respondent and which was made by the court or any other court in the same part of the United Kingdom as the court.

Commencement: 25 November 2016, The Immigration Act 2016 (Commencement No 2 and Transitional Provisions) Regulations 2016, SI 2016/1037.

Definitions:

'labour market enforcement order'/'LME order' an order which prohibits or restricts the person against whom it is made from doing anything set out in the order or requires them to do something set out in the order, s 18(2);

'trigger offence' s 14(4).

Devolution: Applies throughout the UK.

The section makes further provision about LME orders. An order cannot be made against a person under the age of 18 years. An order must be made for a specified period and for no longer than a period of two years.

The court is empowered to release a person from any LME undertaking given in relation to the trigger offence concerned. It may also discharge any other LME order which is in force against a person and which was made by the court or any other court in the same part of the UK as the court. This suggests that a person may be subject to more than one LME order at any time.

SECTION 23—VARIATION AND DISCHARGE

> **Summary**
>
> Makes provision for the variation or discharge of a labour market enforcement (LME) order.

1.23

23 Variation and discharge

(1) The appropriate court may by order vary or discharge an LME order—

    (a) on the application of the respondent;

    (b) if the order was made under section 18, on the application of the enforcing authority who applied for the order;

    (c) if the order was made under section 20, on the application of the enforcing authority whose officer conducted the investigation which resulted in the prosecution of the respondent for the trigger offence.

(2) In this section "the appropriate court"—

    (a) in relation to an LME order made in England and Wales (whether made under section 18 or 20), means a magistrates' court;

    (b) in relation to such an order made in Scotland, means the sheriff;

    (c) in relation to such an order made in Northern Ireland, means a court of summary jurisdiction.

(3) An application for an order under this section is—

    (a) if made to a magistrates' court in England and Wales, to be made by complaint;

    (b) if made to a court of summary jurisdiction in Northern Ireland, to be made by complaint under Part 8 of the Magistrates' Courts (Northern Ireland) Order 1981 (S.I. 1981/1675 (N.I. 26)).

Commencement: 25 November 2016, The Immigration Act 2016 (Commencement No 2 and Transitional Provisions) Regulations 2016, SI 2016/1037.

Definitions:

'appropriate court' magistrates' court (England and Wales), sheriff court (Scotland), court of summary jurisdiction (Northern Ireland), s 23(2);

'enforcing authority' the Secretary of State or any authority whose officers are acting for the purposes of the Employment Agencies Act 1973, the National Minimum Wage Act 1998, the Gangmasters Licensing Act 2004, or in connection with offences that may be prescribed, s 14(5);

1.24 A Guide to the Immigration Act 2016

'labour market enforcement order'/'LME order' an order which prohibits or restricts the person against whom it is made from doing anything set out in the order or requires them to do something set out in the order, s 18(2);

'respondent' person against whom a labour market enforcement order is made, s 18(2), s 33;

'trigger offence' s 14(4).

Devolution: Applies throughout the UK.

A person can apply for the variation or discharge of an order made against them but an enforcing authority can also apply for variation or discharge of the order. Applications are to the same courts as in s 18.

SECTION 24—APPEALS

Summary

Provides for an appeal against the making of a labour market enforcement (LME) order or of a decision not to vary or discharge such an order by the person against whom the order was made.

1.24

24 Appeals

(1) A respondent may appeal against—

    (a) the making of an LME order under section 18;

    (b) the making of, or refusal to make, an order under section 23.

(2) An appeal under subsection (1) is to be made—

    (a) where the order was made or refused by a magistrates' court in England and Wales, to the Crown Court;

    (b) where the order was made or refused by the sheriff, to the Sheriff Appeal Court;

    (c) where the order was made or refused by a court of summary jurisdiction in Northern Ireland, to a county court.

(3) On an appeal under subsection (1) the court hearing the appeal may make such orders as may be necessary to give effect to its determination of the appeal, and may also make such incidental or consequential orders as appear to it to be just and reasonable.

(4) An LME order that has been varied by virtue of subsection (3) remains an order of the court that first made it for the purposes of section 23.

(5) A respondent may appeal against the making of an LME order under section 20 as if the order were a sentence passed on the respondent for the trigger offence.

Commencement: 25 November 2016, The Immigration Act 2016 (Commencement No 2 and Transitional Provisions) Regulations 2016, SI 2016/1037.

Definitions:

'labour market enforcement order'/'LME order' an order which prohibits or restricts the person against whom it is made from doing anything set out in the order or requires them to do something set out in the order, s 18(2);

'trigger offence' s 14(4);

Devolution: Applies throughout UK. See courts to which an appeal can be made, s 24(2).

An appeal may be brought against the making of a LME order or against a decision not to vary or discharge an order by the person against whom the order was made.

If the order was made or refused by a magistrates' court in England and Wales, the appeal is to the Crown Court. If the order was made or refused by a sheriff court in Scotland then the appeal is to the Sheriff Appeal Court. An order made or refused by a court of summary jurisdiction in Northern Ireland may be appealed to a county court.

LME ORDERS AND UNDERTAKINGS: SUPPLEMENTARY

SECTION 25—CODE OF PRACTICE

Summary

Provides for a code of practice to be issued giving guidance to the enforcing authorities about the exercise of functions under ss 14–23 and to which the enforcing authorities must have regard.

1.25

25 Code of practice

(1) The Secretary of State must issue a code of practice giving guidance to enforcing authorities about the exercise of their functions under sections 14 to 23.

(2) The Secretary of State may revise the code from time to time.

(3) The code and any revised code—

   (a) must not be issued unless a draft has been laid before Parliament, and

   (b) comes into force on such day as the Secretary of State appoints by regulations.

(4) The Secretary of State must publish the code and any revised code.

(5) An enforcing authority must have regard to the current version of the code in exercising its functions under sections 14 to 23.

Commencement: 12 July 2016, Immigration Act 2014 (Commencement No 1) Regulations 2016, SI 2016/603.

Regulations: The Labour Market Enforcement (Code of Practice on Labour Market Enforcement Undertakings and Orders: Appointed Day) Regulations 2016, SI 2016/1044, made under s 25(3)(b) appointing a day on which the code of practice shall come into force.

Definitions:

'enforcing authority' the Secretary of State or any authority whose officers are acting for the purposes of the Employment Agencies Act 1973, the National Minimum Wage Act 1998, the Gangmasters Licensing Act 2004, or in connection with offences that may be prescribed, s 14(5);

Devolution: Applies throughout the UK.

The section provides that the Secretary of State must issue a code of practice giving guidance to enforcing authorities about the exercise of their functions under ss 14–23 with regard to labour market enforcement (LME) undertakings and orders.

The code of practice and any revision must be laid before Parliament and published. It is brought into force on a day that the Secretary of State appoints in regulations. The draft code of practice was laid in draft before Parliament on 31 October 2016 and published in its final version on 29 November 2016.[1] It was brought into force on 25 November 2016 through The Labour Market Enforcement (Code of Practice on Labour Market Enforcement Undertakings and Orders: Appointed Day) Regulations 2016, SI 2016/1044.

Part 1—Labour Market and Illegal Working 1.26

Enforcing authorities are required to have regard to the current version of the code in exercising their functions under ss 14–23.

---

1   Home Office and Department for Business, Energy and Industrial Strategy, Code of Practice on Labour Market Enforcement Undertakings and Orders, 29 November 2016 at: https://www.gov.uk/government/publications/labour-market-enforcement-undertakings-and-orders-code-of-practice (accessed 1 December 2016).

SECTION 26—INVESTIGATIVE FUNCTIONS

Summary

Gives the enforcing authorities investigatory powers with respect to labour market enforcement (LME) undertakings or orders relating to offences under the Acts that they are charged with enforcing.

1.26

26 Investigative functions

(1)   An officer acting for the purposes of the Employment Agencies Act 1973—

   (a)   may also act for the purposes of taking action where it appears that a person has failed to comply with an LME undertaking or an LME order where the trigger offence to which the undertaking or order relates is an offence under that Act, and

   (b)   in doing so, has the same powers and duties as he or she has when acting for the purposes of that Act.

(2)   An officer acting for the purposes of the National Minimum Wage Act 1998—

   (a)   may also act for the purposes of taking action where it appears that a person has failed to comply with an LME undertaking or an LME order where the trigger offence to which the undertaking or order relates is an offence under that Act, and

   (b)   in doing so, has the same powers and duties as he or she has when acting for the purposes of that Act.

(3)   An officer acting as an enforcement officer for the purposes of the Gangmasters (Licensing) Act 2004—

   (a)   may also act for the purposes of taking action where it appears that a person has failed to comply with an LME undertaking or an LME order where the trigger offence to which the undertaking or order relates is an offence under that Act, and

   (b)   in doing so, has the same powers and duties as he or she has when acting as an enforcement officer for the purposes of that Act.

1.26 *A Guide to the Immigration Act 2016*

(4) In this section references to the Gangmasters (Licensing) Act 2004 are references to that Act only so far as it applies in relation to England and Wales and Scotland.

Commencement: 25 November 2016, The Immigration Act 2016 (Commencement No 2 and Transitional Provisions) Regulations 2016, SI 2016/1037.

Definitions:

'Gangmasters Licensing Act 2004' the Act only insofar as it applies in England and Wales and Scotland;

'enforcing authority' the Secretary of State or any authority whose officers are acting for the purposes of the Employment Agencies Act 1973, the National Minimum Wage Act 1998, the Gangmasters Licensing Act 2004 (but not in relation to Northern Ireland), or in connection with offences that may be prescribed, s 14(5);

'labour market enforcement order'/'LME order' an order which prohibits or restricts the person against whom it is made from doing anything set out in the order or requires them to do something set out in the order, s 18(2);

'labour market enforcement undertaking'/'LME Undertaking' an undertaking by the person giving it to comply with prohibitions, restrictions and requirements set out in the undertaking, s 14(3);

Devolution: Applies throughout the UK but an officer acting as an enforcement officer for the purposes of the Gangmasters (Licensing) Act 2004 is only empowered to act where it appears that a person has failed to comply with a LME undertaking or order in relation to England, Wales or Scotland.

The section gives the enforcing authorities investigatory powers with respect to labour market undertakings or orders relating to offences under the Acts which they are charged with enforcing.

An officer acting as an enforcement officer for the purposes of the Gangmasters (Licensing) Act 2004 is only empowered to act, however, where it appears that a person has failed to comply with a LME undertaking or order in relation to England, Wales or Scotland.

SECTION 27—OFFENCE

Summary

Makes it a criminal offence to fail, without reasonable excuse, to comply with a labour market enforcement (LME) order.

1.27

27 Offence

(1) A person against whom an LME order is made commits an offence if the person, without reasonable excuse, fails to comply with the order.

(2) A person guilty of an offence under this section is liable—

   (a) on conviction on indictment, to imprisonment for a term not exceeding 2 years, to a fine or to both;

   (b) on summary conviction in England and Wales, to imprisonment for a term not exceeding 12 months, to a fine or to both;

   (c) on summary conviction in Scotland, to imprisonment for a term not exceeding 12 months, to a fine not exceeding the statutory maximum or to both;

   (d) on summary conviction in Northern Ireland, to imprisonment for a term not exceeding 6 months, to a fine not exceeding the statutory maximum or to both.

(3) In relation to an offence committed before the commencement of section 154(1) of the Criminal Justice Act 2003, the reference in subsection (2)(b) to 12 months is to be read as a reference to 6 months.

Commencement: 25 November 2016, The Immigration Act 2016 (Commencement No 2 and Transitional Provisions) Regulations 2016, SI 2016/1037.

Definitions:

'labour market enforcement order'/'LME order' an order which prohibits or restricts the person against whom it is made from doing anything set out in the order or requires them to do something set out in the order, s 18(2);

12 months in s 27(2)(b) to be read as 6 months in relation to an offence committed in England and Wales before the coming into effect of s 154(1) of the Criminal Justice Act 2003.

Criminal offence: s 27(1).

Devolution: Applies throughout the UK. The maximum sentence on summary conviction is lower in Northern Ireland than in England, Wales and Scotland.

The section makes it a criminal offence to fail, without reasonable excuse, to comply with a LME order.

The maximum penalty is two years imprisonment and/or a fine following conviction on indictment. On summary conviction in England, Wales and Scotland, the maximum penalty is 12 months imprisonment and/or a fine which, in Scotland, must not exceed the statutory maximum. The maximum sentence on summary conviction is lower in Northern Ireland where it is six months imprisonment and/or a fine not exceeding the statutory maximum.

SECTION 28—OFFENCES BY BODIES CORPORATE

Summary

Provides for both a body corporate and a consenting, complicit or neglectful officer of that body to be guilty of the offence of breaching a labour market enforcement (LME) order.

1.28

28 Offences by bodies corporate

(1) If an offence under section 27 committed by a body corporate is proved—

   (a) to have been committed with the consent or connivance of an officer of the body, or

   (b) to be attributable to any neglect on the part of such an officer,

   the officer, as well as the body corporate, is guilty of the offence and liable to be proceeded against and punished accordingly.

(2) In subsection (1) "officer", in relation to a body corporate, means—

   (a) a director, manager, secretary or other similar officer of the body;

   (b) a person purporting to act in any such capacity.

(3) If the affairs of a body corporate are managed by its members, subsection (1) applies in relation to the acts and defaults of a member in connection with the member's functions of management as if the member were a director of the body corporate.

Commencement: 25 November 2016, The Immigration Act 2016 (Commencement No 2 and Transitional Provisions) Regulations 2016, SI 2016/1037.

Definitions:

'officer' in relation to a body corporate means a director, manager, secretary or similar officer of the body or anyone purporting to act in such a capacity, s 28(2).

Devolution: Applies throughout the UK.

The section provides that both a body corporate and an officer of that body who has consented to, been complicit in, or whose neglect contributed to, the breach of a labour market enforcement (LME) order may be guilty of an offence and subject to proceedings and punishment accordingly.

SECTION 29—APPLICATION TO UNINCORPORATED ASSOCIATIONS

Summary

Provides for an unincorporated association to be treated as a legal person and for both the association and a consenting, complicit or neglectful officer of that association to be guilty of the offence of breaching a labour market enforcement (LME) order.

1.29

29 Application to unincorporated associations

(1) In a case falling within subsection (2), an unincorporated association is to be treated as a legal person for the purposes of sections 14 to 27.

(2) A case falls within this subsection if it relates to a trigger offence for which it is possible to bring proceedings against an unincorporated association in the name of the association.

(3) Proceedings for an offence under section 27 alleged to have been committed by an unincorporated association may be brought against the association in the name of the association.

(4) For the purposes of such proceedings—

    (a) rules of court relating to the service of documents have effect as if the association were a body corporate, and

    (b) the following provisions apply as they apply in relation to a body corporate—

        (i) section 33 of the Criminal Justice Act 1925 and Schedule 3 to the Magistrates' Courts Act 1980;

        (ii) sections 70 and 143 of the Criminal Procedure (Scotland) Act 1995;

        (iii) section 18 of the Criminal Justice Act (Northern Ireland) 1945 (c. 15 (N.I.)) and Schedule 4 to the Magistrates' Courts (Northern Ireland) Order 1981 (S.I. 1981/1675 (N.I. 26)).

1.29 *A Guide to the Immigration Act 2016*

(5) A fine imposed on the association on its conviction of an offence is to be paid out of the funds of the association.

(6) If an offence under section 27 committed by an unincorporated association is proved—

(a) to have been committed with the consent or connivance of an officer of the association, or

(b) to be attributable to any neglect on the part of such an officer,

the officer, as well as the association, is guilty of the offence and liable to be proceeded against and punished accordingly.

(7) In subsection (6) "officer", in relation to any association, means—

(a) an officer of the association or a member of its governing body;

(b) a person purporting to act in such a capacity.

Commencement: 25 November 2016, The Immigration Act 2016 (Commencement No 2 and Transitional Provisions) Regulations 2016, SI 2016/1037.

Definitions:

'officer' in relation to any association means an officer of the association or member of its governing body or a person purporting to act in such a capacity, s 29(7);

'trigger offence' s 14(4).

Devolution: Applies throughout the UK.

Section 29(1) provides for unincorporated associations to be treated as legal persons for the purposes of ss 14–27 dealing with labour market enforcement (LME) orders and undertakings for a trigger offence where proceedings may be brought against the association in the name of the association. It also makes provision for rules and proceedings of court to apply as if the unincorporated association was a body corporate.

Both the unincorporated association and an officer of the association or a member of its governing body who has consented, been complicit in, or whose neglect contributed to, the breach of a LME order may be guilty of an offence and subject to proceedings and punishment accordingly.

Section 29(5) provides that a fine imposed on the association on its conviction of an offence must be paid out of the funds of the association.

SECTION 30—APPLICATION TO PARTNERSHIPS

> **Summary**
>
> Provides for a partnership not regarded as a legal person to be treated as such in relation to the breach of a labour market enforcement (LME) order and for a partner to be guilty where they consented to, were complicit in or whose negligence contributed to an offence by another partner.

1.30

30 Application to partnerships

(1) If an offence under section 27 committed by a partner of a partnership which is not regarded as a legal person is shown—

 (a) to have been committed with the consent or connivance of another partner, or

 (b) to be attributable to any neglect on the part of another partner,

 that other partner, as well as the first-mentioned partner, is guilty of the offence and liable to be proceeded against and punished accordingly.

(2) Proceedings for an offence under section 27 alleged to have been committed by a partnership which is regarded as a legal person may be brought against the partnership in the firm name.

(3) For the purposes of such proceedings—

 (a) rules of court relating to the service of documents have effect as if the partnership were a body corporate, and

 (b) the following provisions apply as they apply in relation to a body corporate—

  (i) section 33 of the Criminal Justice Act 1925 and Schedule 3 to the Magistrates' Courts Act 1980;

  (ii) sections 70 and 143 of the Criminal Procedure (Scotland) Act 1995;

  (iii) section 18 of the Criminal Justice Act (Northern Ireland) 1945 (c. 15 (N.I.)) and Schedule 4 to the Magistrates' Courts (Northern Ireland) Order 1981 (S.I. 1981/1675 (N.I. 26)).

(4) A fine imposed on a partnership on its conviction of an offence is to be paid out of the funds of the partnership.

1.30 *A Guide to the Immigration Act 2016*

(5) If an offence under section 27 committed by a partnership is proved—

    (a) to have been committed with the consent or connivance of a partner, or

    (b) to be attributable to any neglect on the part of a partner,

the partner, as well as the partnership, is guilty of the offence and liable to be proceeded against and punished accordingly.

(6) In subsections (1) and (5) "partner" includes a person purporting to act as a partner.

(7) For the purposes of this section a partnership is, or is not, "regarded as a legal person" if it is, or is not, so regarded under the law of the country or territory under which it was formed.

Commencement: 25 November 2016, The Immigration Act 2016 (Commencement No 2 and Transitional Provisions) Regulations 2016, SI 2016/1037.

Definitions:

'partner' in s 30(1) and s 30(5) includes a person purporting to act as a partner, s 30(6);

'regarded as a legal person' whether a partnership is regarded as a legal person depends upon the law of the country or territory under which it was formed, s 30(7).

Devolution: Applies throughout the UK.

Section 30(1) provides that partnerships that are not regarded as legal persons (because they were not legal persons under the law of the country or territory in which they were formed) are to be treated as such for the purposes of an offence under s 27 regarding breach of a labour market enforcement (LME) order.

A partner (or a person purporting to act as such) will be guilty where they consented to, were complicit in, or whose negligence contributed to the offence of breaching a LME order by another partner.

Under s 30(3), the rules of court and court proceedings apply as if the partnership was a body corporate.

SUPPLEMENTARY PROVISION

SECTION 31—CONSEQUENTIAL AND RELATED AMENDMENTS AND SCHEDULE 3—CONSEQUENTIAL AND RELATED AMENDMENTS

> **Summary**
> Amends existing legislation to refer to the renamed Gangmasters and Labour Abuse Authority (GLAA), to allow its licensing role to be widened to other industries, incorporate references to LME undertakings and orders, and to establish and govern the powers of the enforcing authorities.

1.31

31 Consequential and related amendments

Schedule 3 (consequential and related amendments) has effect.

Schedule 3
Consequential and related amendments

Public Records Act 1958 (c. 51)

1   In the Public Records Act 1958, in Schedule 1 (definition of public records), in Part 2 of the Table at the end of paragraph 3 (other establishments and organisations), for "Gangmasters Licensing Authority" substitute " Gangmasters and Labour Abuse Authority ".

Parliamentary Commissioner Act 1967 (c. 13)

2   In the Parliamentary Commissioner Act 1967, in Schedule 2 (departments etc subject to investigation)—

   (a)   at the appropriate place insert " Director of Labour Market Enforcement ";

   (b)   for "Gangmasters Licensing Authority" substitute " Gangmasters and Labour Abuse Authority ".

Superannuation Act 1972 (c. 11)

3   In the Superannuation Act 1972, in Schedule 1 (kinds of employment to which that Act applies)—

   (a)   under the heading "Other bodies", for "Gangmasters Licensing Authority" substitute " Gangmasters and Labour Abuse Authority ";

1.31 *A Guide to the Immigration Act 2016*

  (b) under the heading "Offices", at the appropriate place insert " Director of Labour Market Enforcement ".

Employment Agencies Act 1973 (c. 35)

4(1) Section 9 of the Employment Agencies Act 1973 (inspection) is amended as follows.

 (2) In subsection (4)—

  (a) in paragraph (a), for the words before sub-paragraph (i) substitute " No information to which this subsection applies shall be disclosed except— ";

  (b) at the end of paragraph (a) insert "; or

   (vii) to an officer acting by virtue of section 26 of the Immigration Act 2016 (investigative functions in connection with labour market enforcement undertakings and orders); or

   (viii) to an officer acting for the purposes of Part 2 of the Employment (Miscellaneous Provisions) (Northern Ireland) Order 1981 for any purpose relating to that Part; or

   (ix) to the Pensions Regulator for the purposes of the exercise of any function of the Regulator; or

   (x) to the Care Quality Commission for the purposes of the exercise of any function of the Commission."

 (3) After subsection (4) insert—

  "(5) Subsection (4) applies to—

  (a) information obtained in the course of exercising the powers conferred by this section,

  (b) information obtained pursuant to section 15(5A) of the National Minimum Wage Act 1998, and

  (c) information obtained in the course of exercising powers by virtue of section 26(1) of the Immigration Act 2016 (investigative functions in connection with labour market enforcement undertakings and orders)."

House of Commons Disqualification Act 1975 (c. 24)

5 In the House of Commons Disqualification Act 1975, in Schedule 1 (offices disqualifying for membership)—

  (a) in Part 2 (bodies of which all members are disqualified), for "Gangmasters Licensing Authority" substitute " Gangmasters and Labour Abuse Authority ";

  (b) in Part 3 (other disqualifying offices), at the appropriate place insert " Director of Labour Market Enforcement ".

Part 1—Labour Market and Illegal Working **1.31**

Northern Ireland Assembly Disqualification Act 1975 (c. 25)

6   In the Northern Ireland Assembly Disqualification Act 1975, in Schedule 1 (offices disqualifying for membership)—

   (a)   in Part 2 (bodies of which all members are disqualified), for "Gangmasters Licensing Authority" substitute " Gangmasters and Labour Abuse Authority ";

   (b)   in Part 3 (other disqualifying offices), at the appropriate place insert " Director of Labour Market Enforcement ".

National Minimum Wage Act 1998 (c. 39)

7(1)   Section 15 of the National Minimum Wage Act 1998 (information obtained by officers) is amended as follows.

   (2)   In subsection (1)—

      (a)   after "to" insert "—(a)";

      (b)   at the end insert ", and

         (b)   any information obtained by an officer acting by virtue of section 26(2) of the Immigration Act 2016 (investigative functions in connection with labour market enforcement undertakings and orders)."

   (3)   After subsection (5B) insert—

   "(5C) Information to which this section applies—

      (a)   may be supplied by, or with the authorisation of, the Secretary of State to an officer acting by virtue of section 26 of the Immigration Act 2016 (investigative functions in connection with labour market enforcement undertakings and orders); and

      (b)   may be used by an officer so acting for any purpose for which the officer is so acting."

Regulation of Investigatory Powers Act 2000 (c. 23)

8   In the Regulation of Investigatory Powers Act 2000, in Schedule 1 (relevant public authorities), in Part 1 (relevant authorities for purposes of sections 28 and 29 of that Act) in paragraph 20E for "Gangmasters Licensing Authority" substitute " Gangmasters and Labour Abuse Authority ".

Freedom of Information Act 2000 (c. 36)

9   In the Freedom of Information Act 2000, in Schedule 1 (public authorities), in Part 6 (other public bodies and offices: general)—

   (a)   at the appropriate place insert " Director of Labour Market Enforcement ";

   (b)   for "Gangmasters Licensing Authority" substitute " Gangmasters and Labour Abuse Authority ".

1.31 *A Guide to the Immigration Act 2016*

Police Reform Act 2002 (c. 30)

10 The Police Reform Act 2002 is amended as follows.

11 In section 10 (general functions of the Independent Police Complaints Commission)—

   (a) in subsection (1), after paragraph (g) insert—

   "(ga) to carry out such corresponding functions in relation to officers of the Gangmasters and Labour Abuse Authority in their capacity as labour abuse prevention officers (see section 114B of the Police and Criminal Evidence Act 1984 (PACE powers for labour abuse prevention officers)).";

   (b) in subsection (3), after paragraph (bc) insert—

   "(bd) any regulations under section 26D of this Act (labour abuse prevention officers);".

12 After section 26C insert—

"26D Labour abuse prevention officers

   (1) The Secretary of State may make regulations conferring functions on the Commission in relation to the exercise of functions by officers of the Gangmasters and Labour Abuse Authority (the "Authority") in their capacity as labour abuse prevention officers (see section 114B of the Police and Criminal Evidence Act 1984 (PACE powers for labour abuse prevention officers)).

   (2) Regulations under this section may, in particular—

   (a) apply (with or without modifications), or make provision similar to, any provision of or made under this Part;

   (b) make provision for payment by the Authority to, or in respect of, the Commission.

   (3) The Commission and the Parliamentary Commissioner for Administration may jointly investigate a matter in relation to which—

   (a) the Commission has functions by virtue of this section, and

   (b) the Parliamentary Commissioner for Administration has functions by virtue of the Parliamentary Commissioner Act 1967.

   (4) An officer of the Authority may disclose information to the Commission, or to a person acting on the Commission's behalf, for the purposes of the exercise by the Commission, or by any person acting on the Commission's behalf, of an Authority complaints function.

   (5) The Commission and the Parliamentary Commissioner for Administration may disclose information to each other for the purposes of the exercise of a function—

   (a) by virtue of this section, or

Part 1—Labour Market and Illegal Working **1.31**

   (b) under the Parliamentary Commissioner Act 1967.

 (6) Regulations under this section may, in particular, make—

   (a) further provision about the disclosure of information under subsection (4) or (5);

   (b) provision about the further disclosure of information that has been so disclosed.

 (7) In this section "Authority complaints function" means a function in relation to the exercise of functions by officers of the Authority."

Gangmasters (Licensing) Act 2004 (c. 11)

13 The Gangmasters (Licensing) Act 2004 is amended as follows.

14 In the italic heading before section 1, for "Gangmasters Licensing Authority" substitute " Gangmasters and Labour Abuse Authority ".

15 In section 1 (Gangmasters Licensing Authority)—

   (a) in the heading, for "Gangmasters Licensing Authority" substitute " Gangmasters and Labour Abuse Authority ";

   (b) for subsection (1) substitute—

    "(1) The body known as the Gangmasters Licensing Authority is to continue to exist and is to be known as the Gangmasters and Labour Abuse Authority (in this Act referred to as "the Authority").";

   (c) after subsection (3) insert—

    "(3A) When carrying out functions during a year to which a labour market enforcement strategy approved under section 2 of the Immigration Act 2016 relates, the Authority and its officers must carry out those functions in accordance with the strategy."

16 In section 2 (directions etc by the Secretary of State), in subsection (2) after "the Authority" insert " and the Director of Labour Market Enforcement ".

17 In section 3 (work to which Act applies)—

   (a) in subsection (5)(b), for the words from "the following nature" to the end substitute " a prescribed description as being work to which this Act applies ";

   (b) after subsection (5) insert—

    "(6) The Secretary of State must consult the Authority and the Director of Labour Market Enforcement before making regulations under subsection (5)."

18 In section 8 (general power of Authority to make rules)—

   (a) in subsection (1), after "may" insert " with the approval of the Secretary of State ";

   (b) omit subsection (3).

1.31 *A Guide to the Immigration Act 2016*

19 In section 14 (offences: supplementary provisions) after subsection (2) insert—

"(2A) Subsections (1) and (2) do not apply to an enforcement officer who is acting for the purposes of this Act in relation to England and Wales if the officer is a labour abuse prevention officer within the meaning of section 114B of the Police and Criminal Evidence Act 1984 (PACE powers for labour abuse prevention officers)."

20 In section 15 (enforcement and compliance officers) after subsection (6) insert—

"(6A) Subsections (5) and (6) do not apply to an enforcement officer who is acting for the purposes of this Act in relation to England and Wales if the officer is a labour abuse prevention officer within the meaning of section 114B of the Police and Criminal Evidence Act 1984 (PACE powers for labour abuse prevention officers)."

21 In section 16 (powers of officers) before subsection (1) insert—

"(A1) This section does not apply to an enforcement officer who is acting for the purposes of this Act in relation to England and Wales if the officer is a labour abuse prevention officer within the meaning of section 114B of the Police and Criminal Evidence Act 1984 (PACE powers for labour abuse prevention officers)."

22 In section 17 (entry by warrant) before subsection (1) insert—

"(A1) This section does not apply to an enforcement officer who is acting for the purposes of this Act in relation to England and Wales if the officer is a labour abuse prevention officer within the meaning of section 114B of the Police and Criminal Evidence Act 1984 (PACE powers for labour abuse prevention officers)."

23(1) Section 19 (information relating to gangmasters) is amended as follows.

(2) In subsection (1)—

   (a) for the words before paragraph (a) substitute " Information to which this subsection applies— ";

   (b) for paragraph (a) substitute—

      "(a) may be supplied to any person for use for the purposes of, or for any purpose connected with, the exercise of functions under this Act,

      (aa) may be supplied to any person by whom, or by whose officers, labour market enforcement functions are exercisable for the purposes of, or for any purpose connected with, the exercise of such functions, and".

(3) After subsection (1) insert—

"(1A) Subsection (1) applies to—

   (a) information held by any person for the purposes of, or for any purpose connected with, the exercise of functions under this Act, and

Part 1—Labour Market and Illegal Working 1.31

- (b) information held by any officer acting by virtue of section 26(3) of the Immigration Act 2016 (investigative functions in connection with labour market enforcement undertakings and orders).

(1B) In subsection (1) "labour market enforcement functions" has the same meaning as in Chapter 1 of Part 1 of the Immigration Act 2016 (see section 3 of that Act)."

(4) In subsection (2)—

- (a) omit "relating to the operations of a person acting as a gangmaster";
- (b) for "(1)(b)" substitute " (1)(aa) or (b) ".

24(1) Schedule 2 (application of Act to Northern Ireland) is amended as follows.

(2) In the italic heading before paragraph 3, for "Gangmasters Licensing Authority" substitute " Gangmasters and Labour Abuse Authority ".

(3) In paragraph 6—

- (a) after "work in Northern Ireland," insert "—(a)";
- (b) at the end insert ", and
    - (b) the requirement under subsection (2) of that section to consult the Director of Labour Market Enforcement is to be ignored."

(4) In paragraph 7, for paragraph (b) substitute—

"(b) paragraph (b) is to be read as if for "work of a prescribed description as being work to which this Act applies" there were substituted "work of the following nature as being work to which this Act applies—

- (i) the gathering (by any manner) of wild creatures, or wild plants, of a prescribed description and the processing and packaging of anything so gathered, and
- (ii) the harvesting of fish from a fish farm (within the meaning of the Fisheries Act (NI) 1966 (c 17 (NI))."

(5) In paragraph 10, for sub-paragraph (2) substitute—

"(2) Section 8(1) as it applies in relation to Northern Ireland licences is to be read as if the words "with the approval of the Secretary of State" were omitted.

(3) The Authority must consult the relevant Northern Ireland department before making any Northern Ireland rules about fees."

(6) After paragraph 16 insert—

"Section 19: Information relating to gangmasters

16A(1) Section 19 as it applies in relation to Northern Ireland functions is to be read as if—

- (a) paragraph (aa) of subsection (1) (and the reference to it in subsection (2)) were omitted,

1.31 *A Guide to the Immigration Act 2016*

> > (b) subsections (1A)(b) and (1B) were omitted, and
> >
> > (c) in subsection (2), after "Information" there were inserted the words " relating to the operations of a person acting as a gangmaster ".
> >
> > (2) In this paragraph "Northern Ireland functions" means functions under this Act in connection with persons acting as gangmasters in Northern Ireland or persons acting as gangmasters in relation to work in Northern Ireland.
>
> *Section 22A: Relationship with other agencies: requests for assistance*
>
> 16B Section 22A does not apply in relation to the Authority's functions in connection with persons acting as gangmasters in Northern Ireland or persons acting as gangmasters in relation to work in Northern Ireland."

Pensions Act 2004 (c. 35)

25 In the Pensions Act 2004, in Schedule 3 (certain permitted disclosures of restricted information held by the Pensions Regulator), at the end of the table insert—

> "Director of Labour Market Enforcement or a member of staff provided to the Director under section 1(4) of the Immigration Act 2016. Any of the Director's functions."

Natural Environment and Rural Communities Act 2006 (c. 16)

26 In the Natural Environment and Rural Communities Act 2006, in Schedule 7 (designated bodies), in paragraph 13, for "Gangmasters' Licensing Authority" substitute " Gangmasters and Labour Abuse Authority ".

Regulatory Enforcement and Sanctions Act 2008 (c. 13)

27 In the Regulatory Enforcement and Sanctions Act 2008, in Schedule 5 (designated regulators), for "Gangmasters Licensing Authority" substitute " Gangmasters and Labour Abuse Authority ".

Modern Slavery Act 2015 (c. 30)

28 The Modern Slavery Act 2015 is amended as follows.

29 In section 52 (duty to notify Secretary of State about suspected victims of slavery or human trafficking), in subsection (5)(k), for "Gangmasters Licensing Authority" substitute " Gangmasters and Labour Abuse Authority ".

30 At the beginning of Part 7, after the italic heading "Miscellaneous" insert—

"54A Gangmasters and Labour Abuse Authority: information gateways

> (1) A specified person may disclose information to the Gangmasters and Labour Abuse Authority (the "Authority") or a relevant officer if the disclosure is made for the purposes of the exercise of any function of the Authority or the officer under this Act.

Part 1—Labour Market and Illegal Working   1.31

(2) Information obtained by the Authority or a relevant officer in connection with the exercise of any function of the Authority or the officer under this Act may be used by the Authority or the officer in connection with the exercise of any other such function of the Authority or the officer.

(3) The Authority or a relevant officer may disclose to a specified person information obtained in connection with the exercise of any function of the Authority or the officer under this Act if the disclosure is made for the purposes of the exercise of any function of the specified person.

(4) A disclosure of information which is authorised by this section does not breach—

   (a) an obligation of confidence owed by the person making the disclosure, or

   (b) any other restriction on the disclosure of information (however imposed).

(5) But nothing in this section authorises the making of a disclosure which—

   (a) contravenes the Data Protection Act 1998, or

   (b) is prohibited by Part 1 of the Regulation of Investigatory Powers Act 2000.

(6) This section does not limit the circumstances in which information may be disclosed apart from this section.

(7) "Specified person" means a person specified in Schedule 4A (information gateways: specified persons).

(8) The Secretary of State may by regulations amend Schedule 4A.

(9) In this section, "relevant officer" means an officer of the Authority who is acting for the purposes of Part 1 or 2 of this Act (see sections 11A and 30A)."

31 Omit section 55 (review of Gangmasters Licensing Authority).

32 In section 58 (regulations), in subsection (4), after paragraph (j) insert—

"(ja) regulations under section 54A(8) (power to amend Schedule 4A);".

33 In section 60 (extent)—

   (a) in subsection (1), after "section 53)" insert " and section 54A, and Schedule 4A, in Part 7 ";

   (b) in subsection (3), after "and 7" insert " (except for section 54A and Schedule 4A) ".

34 In Schedule 3 (public authorities under duty to co-operate with the Independent Anti-slavery Commissioner), for "Gangmasters Licensing Authority" substitute " Gangmasters and Labour Abuse Authority ".

1.31 *A Guide to the Immigration Act 2016*

35 After Schedule 4 insert—

Schedule 4A
Information gateways: specified persons

Authorities with functions in connection with the labour market etc

The Secretary of State.

A person by whom, or by whose officers, labour market enforcement functions (within the meaning given by section 3 of the Immigration Act 2016) are exercisable.

Law enforcement and border security

A chief officer of police for a police area in England and Wales.

The chief constable of the British Transport Police Force.

An immigration officer.

Local government

A county council in England or Wales.

A county borough council in Wales.

A district council in England.

A London borough council.

The Greater London Authority.

The Common Council of the City of London.

The Council of the Isles of Scilly.

Health bodies

A National Health Service trust established under section 25 of the National Health Service Act 2006 or section 18 of the National Health Service (Wales) Act 2006.

An NHS foundation trust within the meaning given by section 30 of the National Health Service Act 2006.

A Local Health Board established under section 11 of the National Health Service (Wales) Act 2006.

Other

The Independent Anti-slavery Commissioner."

Human Trafficking and Exploitation (Criminal Justice and Support for Victims) Act (Northern Ireland) 2015 (c. 2) (N.I.)

36 In the Human Trafficking and Exploitation (Criminal Justice and Support for Victims) Act (Northern Ireland) 2015, in Schedule 3 (slavery and trafficking prevention orders), in Part 3 (supplementary) in paragraph 18(7)(e), for "Gangmasters Licensing Authority" substitute " Gangmasters and Labour Abuse Authority ".

Part 1—Labour Market and Illegal Working **1.31**

Commencement: 12 July 2016, Immigration Act 2014 (Commencement No 1) Regulations 2016, SI 2016/603.

Amends: See Schedule 3 for full list of amendments.

Definitions:

'the Authority' the Gangmasters and Labour Abuse Authority (GLAA), Police Reform Act 2002 s 26D(1) (Schedule 3, para 12), Gangmasters Licensing Act 2004 (GLA 2004) s1(1) (Schedule 3, para 15)

'information to which this subsection applies' GLA 2004, s 19(1A) *Information relating to gangmasters* (Schedule 3, para 23);

'Northern Ireland functions' GLA 2004, Schedule 2 *Application of the Act to Northern Ireland,* para 16(2);

'relevant officer' an officer of the GLAA who is acting for the purposes of Part 1 or Part 2 of the Modern Slavery Act 2015 (MSA 2015), s 54A(9) *Gangmasters and Labour Abuse Authority: information gateways* of the MSA 2015 (Schedule 3, para 30);

'specified person' a person specified in Schedule 4A *Information gateways: specified persons* of the MSA 2015 (Schedule 3, para 30).

Devolution: Applies throughout the UK.

Section 31 introduces Schedule 3 which amends a wide range of legislation to refer to the renamed GLAA. Section 3(5)(b) of the GLAA is amended by Schedule 3 para 17 to enable its licensing role to be expanded to cover other industries. These will be set out in regulations made under this section by the Secretary of State.

The Schedule also makes amendments to incorporate references to labour market enforcement (LME) undertakings and orders, and to establish and govern the powers of the enforcing authorities.

SECTION 32—REGULATIONS UNDER CHAPTER 1

Summary

Places limitations on the regulations that can be made under ss 3, 11 or 14 to ensure that they do not encroach on devolved powers.

32 Regulations under Chapter 1

(1) Regulations under section 3 or 14 must not prescribe a requirement, function or offence if provision imposing the requirement, conferring the function or creating the offence falls within subsection (3).

(2) Regulations under section 11 must not confer a function if provision doing so falls within subsection (3).

(3) Provision falls within this subsection if—

   (a) it would be within the legislative competence of the Scottish Parliament if contained in an Act of that Parliament,

   (b) it would be within the legislative competence of the National Assembly for Wales if contained in an Act of that Assembly, or

   (c) it would be within the legislative competence of the Northern Ireland Assembly if contained in an Act of that Assembly made without the consent of the Secretary of State.

(4) Regulations under section 3, 11 or 14 may make such provision amending, repealing or revoking any provision of any enactment, including this Chapter, as the Secretary of State considers appropriate in consequence of the regulations.

Commencement: 12 July 2016, Immigration Act 2014 (Commencement No 1) Regulations 2016, SI 2016/603.

Regulations: No freestanding regulations but relates to regulations made under ss 3, 11 and 14.

Devolution: Devolution is the subject matter of the section.

This section places limitations on the regulations that may be made under s 3, 11 or 14. These deal with non-compliance in the labour market, functions in relation to the labour market, and powers to request labour market enforcement (LME) undertakings. Regulations under these sections must not make provision that would fall within the competence of the Scottish Parliament if contained within an Act of that Parliament, or of the National Assembly for Wales if contained within an Act of that Assembly, or of the Northern Ireland Assembly if contained within an Act of that Assembly made without the consent of the Secretary of State. This is to ensure that they do not encroach on devolved powers.

The Rt Hon Lord Bates, Minister of State for the Home Office explained with regard to the role of the Director of Labour Market Enforcement:

> 'The requirement to consult Scottish and Northern Irish Ministers in Amendment 3 brings me to the territorial extent of this role. Employment

law is broadly reserved as the UK operating as a single labour market brings great benefits to workers and employers. Therefore, the Director's remit will be UK-wide. However, there are parts of the remit where the policy is not reserved. To deal with this, we are legislating to ensure that the Director can set the strategy to enforce labour market legislation only to the extent that it already applies and is reserved'.[1]

---

[1] Rt Hon Lord Bates, Minister of State, Home Office, Immigration Bill 2015/16, House of Lords Committee, first sitting, *Hansard* HL col 544 (18 January 2016). Accessed at: http://www.publications.parliament.uk/pa/ld201516/ldhansrd/text/160118-0001.htm#1601184000412 (6 November 2016)

SECTION 33—INTERPRETATION OF CHAPTER 1

Summary

Definitions for the purposes of Chapter 1.

1.33

33 Interpretation of Chapter 1

In this Chapter—

"the Director" has the meaning given by section 1;

"enactment" includes—

- (a) an enactment contained in subordinate legislation within the meaning of the Interpretation Act 1978;

- (b) an enactment contained in, or in an instrument made under, an Act of the Scottish Parliament;

- (c) an enactment contained in, or in an instrument made under, a Measure or Act of the National Assembly for Wales;

- (d) an enactment contained in, or in an instrument made under, Northern Ireland legislation;

"enforcing authority" has the meaning given by section 14;

"financial year" means a period of 12 months ending with 31 March;

"HMRC Commissioners" means the Commissioners for Her Majesty's Revenue and Customs;

"labour market enforcement functions" has the meaning given by section 3;

"LME order" has the meaning given by section 18;

"LME undertaking" has the meaning given by section 14;

1.33 *A Guide to the Immigration Act 2016*

"non-compliance in the labour market" has the meaning given by section 3;

"the respondent" has the meaning given by section 18;

"strategy" has the meaning given by section 2;

"subject" has the meaning given by section 14;

"trigger offence" has the meaning given by section 14.

Commencement: 12 July 2016, Immigration Act 2014 (Commencement No 1) Regulations 2016, SI 2016/603.

Definitions:

'the Director' Director of Labour Market Enforcement, s 1;

'enactment' includes enactments contained in subordinate legislation and those made under an Act of the Scottish Parliament, a Measure or Act of the National Assembly for Wales or Northern Ireland legislation, s 33;

'enforcing authority' the Secretary of State or any authority whose officers are acting for the purposes of the Employment Agencies Act 1973, the National Minimum Wage Act 1998, the Gangmasters Licensing Act 2004, or in connection with offences that may be prescribed, s 14(5);

'financial year' a period of 12 months ending with 31 March, s 33;

'HMRC Commissioners' Commissioners of Her Majesty's Revenue and Customs, s 33;

'labour market enforcement functions' s 3;

'labour market enforcement order'/'LME order' an order which prohibits or restricts the person against whom it is made from doing anything set out in the order or requires them to do something set out in the order, s 18;

'labour market enforcement undertaking'/'LME Undertaking' an undertaking by the person giving it to comply with prohibitions, restrictions and requirements set out in the undertaking, s 14;

'non-compliance in the labour market' s 3;

'the respondent' person against whom a labour market enforcement order is made, s 18;

'strategy' labour market enforcement strategy, s 2;

'subject' person giving an undertaking, s 14;

'trigger offence' s 14.

Devolution: Applies throughout the UK.

This section contains definitions for the purpose of Chapter 1, as above.

Other legislative provisions: overseas domestic workers

1.33.1 The Parliamentary debates on Part 1 of the Act dealing with labour exploitation provided the opportunity to consider amendments to address the protection available to overseas domestic workers who suffer abuse at the hands of their employers.

Under para 159A of the Immigration Rules, leave may be granted for entry as a domestic worker in a private household, for a period of six months only, where the individual has worked for their employer for a period of one year and will be working for that employer in the UK. This changed the position of domestic workers who, until 2012, had been able to change employers and extend their leave. The ability to change employers and extend their leave had acted as an important protection for overseas domestic workers against trafficking, slavery and exploitation.

Concerns about the change in position were highlighted during the debates on the Modern Slavery Act 2015 (MSA 2015) and led to the Government making provision for overseas domestic workers at s 53 of that Act. This section requires that the Immigration Rules make provision for migrant domestic workers recognized as victims of trafficking or slavery. The rules must allow for further leave to be granted for the purpose of working as a domestic worker in a private household for a period of no less than six months (if a maximum is set) and for the ability to change employer to be permitted during that leave.

The amendments made to the Immigration Rules in consequence by the Statement of Changes in Immigration Rules HC 474[1] that came into effect from 15 October 2015, were the most restrictive possible implementation of s 53 of the MSA 2015. Overseas domestic workers who were recognised as having been trafficked or enslaved could have leave extended for up to six months, but leave could be given in increments of less than six months. The worker had no recourse to public funds during this period and was permitted to work only as a domestic worker. The provisions provided little incentive to domestic workers to leave situations of abuse, and they risked destitution if they failed to find gainful employment for such a short period.

The concerns highlighted during the Parliamentary debates on the Modern Slavery Act 2015 led to the Government commissioning an independent review of the overseas domestic worker route with the intention that the Government implement the review's recommendations.[2] The *Independent Review of the Overseas Domestic Worker Visa* by James Ewins[3] (now QC)

1.33.1 *A Guide to the Immigration Act 2016*

was published by the Government during the course of the Immigration Act 2016 debates. Amendments were tabled seeking to give effect to the recommendations of the review and, in particular, to ensure that all overseas domestic workers were able to change employer, and remain in the UK for up to two and a half years. Mr Ewins QC wrote:

> 'the underlying rationale of a right to change employer is to give the overseas domestic worker a safe way out of an abusive situation, of which safe re-employment is an essential part.... to make the right to change employer effective in practice, the duration of any extensions must be of sufficient length to give the overseas domestic worker both sufficient incentive and reasonable prospects of finding such alternative employment.'[4]

The amendments succeeded in the House of Lords, but were defeated in the House of Commons. The Government agreed that workers should be allowed to change employer, but only within the currency of the six-month visa. The paradigm is very much 'rescue' rather than 'empowerment'. The Lords did not insist on its amendment when the Bill came back from the Commons.

The Government agreed to make a further change to address the difficulty raised that overseas domestic workers may not readily be able to secure alternative employment as a domestic worker, even when they are referred into the national referral mechanism, if their permission to work ends when the six-month period of their admission expires. The Government committed to use powers to grant, vary or refuse leave under s 4(1) of the Immigration Act 1971 to ensure that when an overseas domestic worker has been referred into the national referral mechanism during their initial six-month stay, their permission to take employment will continue while their case is assessed, and without the worker having to make an application.

This was brought into effect from 6 October 2016 by the Immigration (Variation of Leave) Order 2016, SI 2016/948 that provides that where a 'competent authority' determines that it has 'reasonable grounds' to believe that a person who has been granted limited leave to enter the UK as an overseas domestic worker, or a private servant in a diplomatic household, is a victim of modern slavery, the person's leave is extended until 28 days after the competent authority notifies the person of its conclusive decision as to whether or not the person is such a victim.

In the most recent change to the Immigration Rules, in effect from 24 November 2016 following the Statement of Changes in Immigration Rules HC 667,[5] the Government will allow those domestic workers, whether in a private or a diplomatic household, who have been found to be victims of trafficking or slavery (through a positive conclusive grounds decision under the national referral mechanism) to apply to stay in the UK for up to two years. As previously they will be able to work during this period, but only as a domestic worker in a private or diplomatic household, and they cannot have 'recourse to public funds': ie any state benefits or housing. Applications have to be made within 28 days of getting the positive 'conclusive grounds' decision or, if another type of application is pending, within 28 days of the decision on that application.

From 24 November 2016, not only those currently working as domestic workers or with leave in this category (which they are applying to extend) can apply but also those who had been domestic workers and were then given leave outside the Immigration Rules as a survivor of trafficking or slavery will be able to apply for this two-year grant of leave.

This right is in addition to the right of any domestic worker who is found to have been enslaved or trafficked to apply for leave as a trafficked person which, if granted, permits them to work in any job (including as a domestic worker) and does permit them to have recourse to public funds. Such leave is normally granted for between 12 and 30 months.

---

1 Statement of Changes in Immigration Rules HC 474, 17 September 2015. Available at: https://www.gov.uk/government/publications/statement-of-changes-to-the-immigration-rules-hc437-17-september-2015 (accessed 6 November 2016).
2 Karen Bradley MP, *Modern Slavery Bill 2015*, House of Lords' Committee, *Hansard* HC, col 650 (17 March 2015). Available at: http://www.publications.parliament.uk/pa/cm201415/cmhansrd/cm150317/debtext/150317-0001.htm (accessed 6 November 2016).
3 James Ewins, *Independent Review of the Overseas Domestic Worker Visa*, 6 November 2015 (published 17 December 2015) https://www.gov.uk/government/uploads/system/uploads/attachment_data/file/486532/ODWV_Review_-_Final_Report__6_11_15_.pdf (accessed 6 November 2016).
4 Ibid, para 101.
5 Statement of Changes in Immigration Rules HC 667, 3 November 2016. Available at: https://www.gov.uk/government/publications/statement-of-changes-to-the-immigration-rules-hc667-3-november-2016 (accessed 1 December 2016).

CHAPTER 2—ILLEGAL WORKING

OFFENCES

SECTION 34—OFFENCE OF ILLEGAL WORKING

Summary

Creates a new criminal offence of working while knowing or having reasonable cause to believe that a person is disqualified from working because of their immigration status.

1.34

34 Offence of illegal working

(1) The Immigration Act 1971 is amended as follows.

(2) In section 3(1)(c)(i) (power to grant limited leave to enter or remain in the United Kingdom subject to condition restricting employment or occupation) for "employment" substitute " work ".

(3) After section 24A insert—

"24B Illegal working

(1) A person ("P") who is subject to immigration control commits an offence if—

    (a) P works at a time when P is disqualified from working by reason of P's immigration status, and

    (b) at that time P knows or has reasonable cause to believe that P is disqualified from working by reason of P's immigration status.

(2) For the purposes of subsection (1) a person is disqualified from working by reason of the person's immigration status if—

    (a) the person has not been granted leave to enter or remain in the United Kingdom, or

    (b) the person's leave to enter or remain in the United Kingdom—

        (i) is invalid,

        (ii) has ceased to have effect (whether by reason of curtailment, revocation, cancellation, passage of time or otherwise), or

        (iii) is subject to a condition preventing the person from doing work of that kind.

(3) A person who is guilty of an offence under subsection (1) is liable on summary conviction—

    (a) in England and Wales, to imprisonment for a term not exceeding 51 weeks or a fine, or both,

    (b) in Scotland or Northern Ireland, to imprisonment for a term not exceeding 6 months or a fine not exceeding level 5 on the standard scale, or both.

(4) In relation to an offence committed before section 281(5) of the Criminal Justice Act 2003 comes into force, the reference in subsection (3)(a) to 51 weeks is to be read as a reference to 6 months.

(5) If a person is convicted of an offence under subsection (1) in England and Wales, the prosecutor must consider whether to ask the court to commit the person to the Crown Court under section 70 of the

Proceeds of Crime Act 2002 (committal with view to confiscation order being considered).

(6) If a person is convicted of an offence under subsection (1) in Scotland, the prosecutor must consider whether to ask the court to act under section 92 of the Proceeds of Crime Act 2002 (making of confiscation order).

(7) If a person is convicted of an offence under subsection (1) in Northern Ireland, the prosecutor must consider whether to ask the court to commit the person to the Crown Court under section 218 of the Proceeds of Crime Act 2002 (committal with view to confiscation order being considered).

(8) The reference in subsection (1) to a person who is subject to immigration control is to a person who under this Act requires leave to enter or remain in the United Kingdom.

(9) Where a person is on immigration bail within the meaning of Part 1 of Schedule 10 to the Immigration Act 2016—

  (a) the person is to be treated for the purposes of subsection (2) as if the person had been granted leave to enter the United Kingdom, but

  (b) any condition as to the person's work in the United Kingdom to which the person's immigration bail is subject is to be treated for those purposes as a condition of leave.

(10) The reference in subsection (1) to a person working is to that person working—

  (a) under a contract of employment,

  (b) under a contract of apprenticeship,

  (c) under a contract personally to do work,

  (d) under or for the purposes of a contract for services,

  (e) for a purpose related to a contract to sell goods,

  (f) as a constable,

  (g) in the course of Crown employment,

  (h) as a relevant member of the House of Commons staff, or

  (i) as a relevant member of the House of Lords staff.

(11) In subsection (10)—

"contract to sell goods" means a contract by which a person acting in the course of a trade, business, craft or profession transfers or agrees to transfer the property in goods to another person (and for this purpose "goods" means any tangible moveable items);

1.34 *A Guide to the Immigration Act 2016*

"Crown employment"—

(a) in relation to England and Wales and Scotland, has the meaning given by section 191(3) of the Employment Rights Act 1996;

(b) in relation to Northern Ireland, has the meaning given by Article 236(3) of the Employment Rights (Northern Ireland) Order 1996 (SI 1996/1919 (NI 16));

"relevant member of the House of Commons staff" has the meaning given by section 195(5) of the Employment Rights Act 1996;

"relevant member of the House of Lords staff" has the meaning given by section 194(6) of the Employment Rights Act 1996.

(12) Subsection (1) does not apply to—

(a) service as a member of the naval, military or air forces of the Crown, or

(b) employment by an association established for the purposes of Part 11 of the Reserve Forces Act 1996.

(13) In this section "contract" means a contract whether express or implied and, if express, whether oral or in writing."

(4) In section 28A(3)(a) (arrest without warrant) after "section" insert " 24B, ".

(5) In section 28B(5) (search and arrest by warrant: relevant offences) after "24A," insert " 24B, ".

(6) In section 28CA(1) (business premises: entry to arrest) after paragraph (b) insert—

"(ba) for an offence under section 24B,".

(7) In section 28D(4) (entry and search of premises: relevant offences) after "24A," insert " 24B, ".

(8) In section 28FA(1)(a) (search for personnel records: offences to which section applies) for "or 24A(1)" substitute ", 24A(1) or 24B(1) ".

Commencement: 12 July 2016, Immigration Act 2014 (Commencement No 1) Regulations 2016, SI 2016/603. See further the Immigration Act 2016 (Transitional Provision) Regulations 2016 SI 2016/712 which provide, pending the coming into force of s 61 and Schedule 10 *Immigration Bail,* for a person at large in the United Kingdom by virtue of para 21(1) of Schedule 2 to the Immigration Act 1971 to be treated for the purposes of new s 24B(2) of the Immigration Act 1971 as if the person had been granted leave to enter the United Kingdom, with any restriction as to employment imposed under para 21(2) treated for those purposes as a condition of leave. As a result, a person on temporary admission or bail with permission to work is not caught by the new offence.

Part 1—Labour Market and Illegal Working **1.34**

Amends: Immigration Act 1971 (IA 1971), s 3(1)(c)(i) substituting 'work' for 'employment' and inserts a new s 24B *Illegal working* into that Act.

Regulations: See the Immigration Act 2016 (Transitional Provision) Regulations 2016, SI 2016/712.

Definitions:

'contract' express or implied, oral or in writing, s 34(13);

'contract to sell goods' s 34(11) for the purposes of s 34(10);

'Crown employment' s 34(11) for the purposes of s 34(10);

'relevant member of the House of Commons staff' s 34(11) for the purposes of s 34(10);

'relevant member of the House of Lords staff' s 34(11) for the purposes of s 34(10);

'working' see 24B(10), IA1971 inserted by s 34(3), references to a person working are to working under a contract of employment, of apprenticeship, or personally to do work under or for the purposes of a contract for services, for a purpose related to a contract to sell goods, as a constable, in the course of Crown employment or as a relevant member of House of Commons' or Lords' staff.

Offences: IA 1971 s 24B Illegal working (s 34(3)).

Devolution: Applies throughout UK. Maximum penalty on summary conviction is lower (six months as opposed to 21 weeks) in Scotland (s 24B(3)). Different criminal provisions apply in different jurisdictions.

New s 24B of the IA 1971, inserted by this section, introduces a new offence making it a crime for a person to work while knowing or having reasonable cause to believe that they are disqualified from working because of their immigration status. The offence covers both those found working whilst living unlawfully in the UK and those found working in breach of the conditions of their leave in the UK. The *mens rea* element is the product of the parliamentary process. In the Bill as presented to Parliament, this was a strict liability offence.[1] Under new s s 24B(2) of the IA 1971, as inserted by s 34(3), a person's immigration status means that they do not have the right to work if:

- they require but have not been granted leave to enter or remain in the UK ('immigration bail' as set out in s 61 and Schedule 10 is treated as though it were a grant of leave to enter, and the conditions attached to it as if they were conditions of leave, see new s 24B(9) of the IA 1971, as inserted by IA 2016, s 34(3) and, pending the coming into force of those provisions, see the Immigration Act 2016 (Transitional Provision) Regulations 2016, SI 2016/712 discussed below);

1.34 *A Guide to the Immigration Act 2016*

- their leave is invalid: a deportation order, or notice of intention to remove a person, or a family member of a person being removed, invalidates leave;[2]
- their leave has been curtailed, revoked, cancelled, has run out, or otherwise ceased to be valid;
- a condition of their leave prevents them from doing the work in question (IA 1971 s 24B(9) as inserted by s 34(3) of this Act).

The new offence will remain a 'summary only' offence but will carry increased sentencing powers of 51 weeks in England and Wales.

It is already a criminal offence, under IA 1971, s 24, to enter the UK without leave when leave is required, to overstay or to breach a condition of leave, such as working when work is prohibited. Thus all those who may face prosecution under this section can be prosecuted already under existing immigration offences.

The Minister, the Rt Hon Lord Bates, said in his letter following Lords' second reading[3] that the introduction of the new offence would align the position of those found to be working whilst living in the UK without leave with that of persons found to be working in breach of the conditions of their lawful stay. The rationale given for introducing a new criminal offence of illegal working was the potential to seize earnings through confiscation orders made under the Proceeds of Crime Act 2002 (POCA 2002).[4] In the letter, the Minister stated:

> '[T]he new offence will provide us with a firmer basis for using Proceeds of Crime Act seizure powers – which apply only in cases where the cash involved exceeds £1,000. To be clear, the Government already uses Proceeds of Crime Act powers in relation to those committing immigration offences under existing provisions in the UK Borders Act 2007. In 2014–15, the courts approved the forfeiture of cash totalling £542,668 seized by immigration officers. Following criminal convictions for immigration-related offences courts ordered the confiscation of assets totalling £966,024. We expect that in-country seizure could double with the use of the extended powers enabled by the new illegal working offence.'

The Minister said that the Government can confiscate relevant sums from those who work in breach of the terms of their existing stay under the POCA 2002 but cannot do so for those working in the UK illegally, and said that the Government was, therefore, seeking to close this gap.[5] Statistics provided by the Government, however, indicate that the POCA 2002 is not typically used to confiscate earnings from those found to be working in breach of conditions of their lawful stay.[6]

Part 1—Labour Market and Illegal Working **1.34**

It is unlikely to be proportionate for prosecutors to seek a confiscation order under the POCA 2002 for working illegally in the UK. The Crown Prosecution Service (CPS) guidance *Proceeds of Crime*[7] says that prosecutors should prioritise the recovery of assets from serious organized crime and serious economic crime. The guidance sets out that: 'If a financial investigation has revealed that a suspect has few or no realisable assets, then it may not be a proportionate use of resources to pursue confiscation'.[8] Confiscation orders under the POCA 2002 can, even without the new offence, be brought in specific cases where fraud or deception has been used in relation to illegal working, for example, where an individual has deceived their employer as to their entitlement to work in the UK.[9]

A confiscation order must be proportionate to the aim of the legislation, that is to recover the financial benefit that the offender has obtained from the criminal conduct, not further to punish the offender, or to act as a deterrent.[10] If the confiscation order is not proportionate then it will be a violation of the right to peaceful enjoyment of property under Article 1 of Protocol No 1 to the European Convention on Human Rights (ECHR).[11]

The Government cited[12] the case of *Nuro v the Home Office* [2014] EWHC 462 (Admin) as an example of a case in which it was held that, in the absence of a specific criminal offence, it was not possible to obtain a confiscation order to seize earnings from a self-employed handyperson working without leave. The case pre-dates the judgment and discussion of proportionality in *Paulet v UK*[13] and may not survive *Paulet*.

Proceedings brought under the POCA 2002 are often lengthy. They normally take place after sentencing by a criminal court and require the setting down of a timetable, with delays often in excess of six months after sentencing date. POCA 2002, s 14 allows for the postponement of POCA proceedings for up to two years, more in exceptional circumstances, from the date of conviction.

Provision as to the use of the POCA 2002 is made in ss 24B(5)–(7) of the IA 1971, as inserted by s 34(3).

The offence is not, as has been suggested[14] a new departure. The Accession of Croatia (Immigration and Worker Authorisation) Regulations 2013[15] and the Accession (Immigration and Worker Authorisation) Regulations 2006[16] created criminal offences for Croatian, Romanian and Bulgarian nationals working without authorisation in the UK, and for those employing them in breach of the regulations.

In an answer to a Parliamentary question, the Minister, the Rt Hon James Brokenshire MP, provided data on prosecutions under the Accession (Immigration and Worker Authorisation) Regulations 2006 which showed that since they came into force on 1 January 2007, there had been three

1.34 *A Guide to the Immigration Act 2016*

prosecutions under regulation 12 (the offence committed by employers) and no prosecutions under regulation 13 (the offence committed by employees). During the same period, 491 fixed penalty notices were issued to employees who breached the regulations.[17]

In the same written answer, the Minister stated that the Home Office had no record of any fixed penalty notices issued to Croatian nationals working in breach of the Accession of Croatia (Immigration and Worker Authorisation) Regulations 2013[18] and that the Home Office had not issued any civil penalties to employers in respect of breaches of those regulations.[19] EEA nationals do not have 'leave' to be in the UK and thus the range of offences with which they can be charged is much narrower than is the case for a third country national. Thus, it is easier to see how an offence of illegal working might fill a gap in cases of EEA nationals than in cases of third country nationals, and it would be anticipated that the offence would be used proportionally more frequently for EEA nationals than for third country nationals.

The Minister, the Rt Hon James Brokenshire MP said at Commons' report:

> 'The Government would not want to prosecute those who have been forced to travel here and exploited for the profit of others, which goes to the heart of the matter. That is why the offence is not aimed at the victims of modern slavery. The statutory defence in section 45 of the Modern Slavery Act 2015 will apply'.[20]

Work is broadly defined (IA 1971, s 24B(10) as inserted by s 34(3)). References to a person 'working' are to a person working under a contract of employment; of apprenticeship; or personally to do work under, or for the purposes of, a contract for services; for a purpose related to a contract to sell goods; as a constable; in the course of crown employment; or as a relevant member of House of Commons' or Lords' staff.[21] Section 34(2) substitutes the word 'work' for 'employment' in s 3(1)(c)(i) of the IA 1971, which deals with conditions that can be imposed on a grant of limited leave to remain. Thus conditions could be imposed on a grant of leave prohibiting self-employment, and a person could face prosecution for breaching those conditions.

Broad as this definition is, it does not encompass voluntary work. That was put beyond all doubt by a debate on an amendment that would have removed voluntary work from the ambit of the offence. The Rt Hon Lord Bates said in reply 'we believe that this is unnecessary because someone undertaking genuine voluntary work would not be working under the purposes of a contract. Therefore, genuine voluntary work is not caught by new Section 24B(9), introduced by Clause 8, and it therefore falls outside the ambit of the offence.'[22]

The section makes provision for powers of search and arrest in relation to the offence.[23]

The maximum penalty in England and Wales is 51 weeks imprisonment and an unlimited fine.[24] In Scotland and Northern Ireland, the maximum period of imprisonment is six months and the maximum fine is level 5.[25] As described above, in theory at least, proceeds of crime may be confiscated.

Section 34 came into force on 12 July 2016 as did the changes to the offence of employing an illegal worker (s 35). Section 24B(9) of the IA 1971 inserted by s 34(3) ensures that those on immigration bail within the meaning of Schedule 10, Part 1, who have permission to work, are not committing a criminal offence and, by operation of that section, nor is their employer.[26] However, Schedule 10, Part 1 was not in force when ss 34–35 came into force and no commencement order has to date (17 February 2017) been made in respect of it. The transitional provisions pertaining to the transition from temporary admission to immigration bail can be found at para 13 of Schedule 10.

The commencement of s 34 and of s 35 without the commencement of Schedule 10 would have left a person on temporary admission who works in the position of committing a criminal offence by so doing, regardless of whether they had permission so to do. ILPA raised this with the Home Office[27] when the commencement order[28] was published and received a reply that 'we intend to make transitional provisions which will have the effect that, until the immigration bail provisions are commenced, the reference to immigration bail in the new illegal working offence should be read as temporary admission release from detention'.[29]

The Immigration Act 2016 (Transitional Provision) Regulations 2016, SI 2016/712 were laid on 5 July 2016. They provide:

'Offence of illegal working: transitional provision

2. Where a person is at large in the United Kingdom by virtue of paragraph 21(1) of Schedule 2 to the Immigration Act 1971 (temporary admission or release from detention) –

   (a) the person is to be treated for the purposes of section 24B(2) of the Immigration Act 1971(c) as if the person had been granted leave to enter the United Kingdom, but

   (b) any restriction as to employment imposed under paragraph 21(2) is to be treated for those purposes as a condition of leave.'

A person at large under para 21(1) of Schedule 2 to the IA 1971 is a person who is liable to detention and, under para 16(1), (1A) or (2) of the IA 1971, is temporarily admitted on the written authority of an immigration officer.

The order therefore sought to remedy the problem identified by treating those granted temporary admission by an immigration officer in the same way as if they had leave to enter for the purposes of s 34. A person on

1.34 *A Guide to the Immigration Act 2016*

temporary admission with permission to work is not caught by the offence as a result. Persons granted bail by the First-tier Tribunal pending the coming into force of Schedule 10 to this Act, would still be caught by the illegal working offence as the wording of the patch does not cover those detained under paras 16(1), (1A) or (2) of the IA 1971 and granted bail by the tribunal.

The question of permission to work for persons seeking asylum was the subject of amendments tabled during the passage of the Act.[30] These would have placed an obligation on the Secretary of State (SSHD) to make immigration rules to give persons seeking asylum permission to work if they had been waiting for more than six months, nine months in a later version of the amendment,[31] for their application for asylum to be decided by the Home Office, or had waited more than six months for a decision on whether to treat their further submissions as a fresh claim for asylum. The SSHD would have had to make rules to grant permission on terms no less favourable than the terms on which permission is given to recognised refugees, which is currently that they are not restricted as to the employment they can undertake.

The Minister, the Rt Hon James Brokenshire MP, responded to an amendment on the point[32] at Commons' report, 'We do not consider this to be sensible', and said that the Government considered that existing policies giving permission to work, in occupations on the shortage occupation list only, when an initial application for asylum (exclusive of appeals) has been outstanding for 12 months, strike the right balance.[33]

An amendment providing for persons seeking asylum to be able to work in any job if their claim was not determined within the Home Office target time of six months was pressed to a vote and carried in the Lords,[34] but was defeated when the Bill returned to the Commons.[35]

On ping-pong, the Lords produced a revised version, providing for permission to work after nine months,[36] but this was not pressed to a vote. This was due to the lack of support from the Labour party, which had supported the amendment at an earlier stage but indicated that it was reviewing its policy on the matter.[37]

---

1 Bill 74 session 2015–2016, clause 8.
2 IA 1971 s 5(1) and Immigration and Asylum Act 1999 (IAA 1999) s 10(6).
3 Rt Hon Lord Bates to Lord Rosser, *Issues raised at second reading*, 8 January 2016. Lord Green of Dedington and the Rt Hon Lord Bates make reference to this letter in the debate at *Hansard* HL cols 622 and 626 (18 Jan 2016).
4 Ibid.
5 *Hansard*, HL col 626 (18 January 2016).
6 Lord Bates, *Hansard* Written Answer HL5290, *Home Office Immigration: Proceeds of Crime*, 2 February 2016. Available at: http://www.parliament.uk/business/publications/

written-questions-answers-statements/written-question/Lords/2016-01-20/HL5290/ (accessed 9 November 2016).
7 *Proceeds of Crime*, CPS. Available at: http://www.cps.gov.uk/legal/p_to_r/proceeds_of_crime_act_guidance/ (accessed 9 November 2016).
8 Ibid.
9 See *R v Carter, Kulish and Lyashkov* [2006] EWCA Crim 416; *R v Paulet* [2009] EWCA Crim 1573.
10 *R v Waya* [2012] UKSC 5.
11 See the discussion in *Paulet v UK* [2014] ECHR 477 (13 May 2014).
12 Rt Hon Lord Bates, Written Answer HL 5291, 28 January 2016. Available at: http://www.parliament.uk/business/publications/written-questions-answers-statements/written-question/Lords/2016-01-20/HL5291 (accessed 9 November 2016).
13 *Paulet v UK* [2014] ECHR 477 (13 May 2014).
14 Prime Minister's speech of 21 May 2015. Available at: https://www.gov.uk/government/speeches/pm-speech-on-immigration (accessed 9 November 2016).
15 Accession of Croatia (Immigration and Worker Authorisation) Regulations 2013, SI 2014/1460, regs 11–18.
16 Accession (Immigration and Worker Authorisation) Regulations 2006 SI 2006/3317, regs 12–13.
17 Rt Hon James Brokenshire MP, Written Answer 12752, *Worker Registration Scheme*, 21 October 2015.
18 Accession of Croatia (Immigration and Worker Authorisation) Regulations 2013, SI 2014/1460, regs 11–18.
19 Ibid.
20 *Hansard*, HL, col 208 (1 December 2015).
21 IA 1971, s 24B(10), as inserted by IA 2016, s 34(3).
22 Lords' Report, Amendment 57, *Hansard*, HL, col 624 (9 March 2016).
23 IA 1971, s 34(4)–(8) amending IA 1971 ss 28A–28B, 28CA, 28D and 28FA.
24 Section 24B(3)(a) of IA 1971 as inserted by s 34(3).
25 £5000, s 24B(3)(b) of IA 1971 as inserted by s 34(3).
26 See s 21(1A) of the Immigration, Asylum and Nationality Act 2006 (IANA 2006) inserted by s 35.
27 Email of Alison Harvey, Legal Director, ILPA to Sally Weston, Immigration and Border Policy Directorate, Home Office, 2 June 2016 at 12.33pm.
28 Immigration Act 2016 (Commencement No 1) Regulations 2016, SI 2016/603 (C 44).
29 Philippa Rouse, Head of Illegal Migration, Identity Security and Enforcement, Immigration and Border Policy Directorate (IBPD), Home Office to Alison Harvey, Legal Director ILPA, by email, 3 June 2016 at 12.30pm.
30 Amendment 228 debated in the Public Bill Committee, 13th sitting (morning), *Hansard* cols 460–463 (10 November 2016); Amendment 2 debated at Commons' Report *Hansard*, HC cols 227–246 (1 December 2016); Amendment 134 debated in Lords' Committee *Hansard*, HL col 850–851 (20 January 2016); Amendment 57 Lords' Report Immigration Bill *Hansard* HL cols 1320–1336.
31 Amendment 59B, debated at Ping-Pong, *Hansard* HL Vol 771 (26 April 2016).
32 Amendment 2.
33 *Hansard* HC, col 227 (1 December 2016).
34 Amendment 57 *Hansard* HL col 1336, division, amendment carried by 280 votes to 195.
35 Debate on Lords amendment 59, *Hansard*, HC, Vol 608. Lords' amendment disagreed, 303 votes to 60.
36 Amendment 59B, debated *Hansard* HL Vol 771 (26 April 2016).
37 Lord Rosser, 'we are currently reviewing this issue as part of a wider policy review and consequently we will not be supporting the Motion sending the matter back again to the Commons – albeit now saying nine months rather than six months.' *Hansard* HL Vol 771 (26 April 2016).

SECTION 35—OFFENCE OF EMPLOYING ILLEGAL WORKER

> **Summary**
>
> Expands the offence under the Immigration, Asylum and Nationality Act 2006 (IANA 2006) s 21 *Offence* of knowingly employing an illegal worker so that the test is no longer 'knowingly' employing such a worker but employing such a worker when the employer has reasonable cause to believe that they are disqualified from working because of their immigration status.

1.35

35 Offence of employing illegal worker

(1) Section 21 of the Immigration, Asylum and Nationality Act 2006 (offence of knowingly employing illegal worker) is amended in accordance with subsections (2) to (4).

(2) In subsection (1) for the words from "an adult" to the end of the subsection substitute " disqualified from employment by reason of the employee's immigration status. "

(3) After subsection (1) insert—

"(1A) A person commits an offence if the person—

    (a) employs another person ("the employee") who is disqualified from employment by reason of the employee's immigration status, and

    (b) has reasonable cause to believe that the employee is disqualified from employment by reason of the employee's immigration status.

(1B) For the purposes of subsections (1) and (1A) a person is disqualified from employment by reason of the person's immigration status if the person is an adult subject to immigration control and—

    (a) the person has not been granted leave to enter or remain in the United Kingdom, or

    (b) the person's leave to enter or remain in the United Kingdom—

        (i) is invalid,

        (ii) has ceased to have effect (whether by reason of curtailment, revocation, cancellation, passage of time or otherwise), or

        (iii) is subject to a condition preventing the person from accepting the employment."

(4) In subsection (2)(a)(i) (maximum term of imprisonment for conviction of offence on indictment) for "two" substitute " five ".

(5) Section 22 of the Immigration, Asylum and Nationality Act 2006 (offences by bodies corporate etc) is amended in accordance with subsections (6) and (7).

(6) After subsection (1) insert—

"(1A) For the purposes of section 21(1A) a body (whether corporate or not) shall be treated as having reasonable cause to believe a fact about an employee if a person who has responsibility within the body for an aspect of the employment has reasonable cause to believe that fact."

(7) In each of subsections (2) and (4) after "21(1)" insert " or (1A) ".

(8) In section 24(a) of the Immigration, Asylum and Nationality Act 2006 (immigration bail) for "21(1)" substitute " 21(1B) ".

(9) In section 28A of the Immigration Act 1971 (arrest without warrant)—

(a) after subsection (9A) insert—

"(9B) An immigration officer may arrest without warrant a person who, or whom the immigration officer has reasonable grounds for suspecting—

(a) has committed or attempted to commit an offence under section 21(1) or (1A) of the Immigration, Asylum and Nationality Act 2006 (employment of illegal worker etc), or

(b) is committing or attempting to commit that offence.",

(b) in subsection (10) for "and (5)" substitute ", (5) and (9B) ", and

(c) in subsection (11) for "and (5)" substitute ", (5) and (9B) ".

(10) In section 28AA(1) of that Act (arrest with warrant) for paragraphs (a) and (b) substitute " section 24(1)(d) ".

Commencement: 12 July 2016, Immigration Act 2014 (Commencement No 1) Regulations 2016, SI 2016/603.

Amends: Immigration, Asylum and Nationality Act 2006 (IANA 2006), s 21 *Offence* and s 22 *Offence: bodies corporate* & c.

Regulations: See the Immigration Act 2016 (Transitional Provision) Regulations 2016, SI 2016/712.

Definitions:

'the employee' a person employed by another person;

A reference to *employment* is to employment under a contract of service or apprenticeship, whether express or implied and whether oral or written, (IANA 2006, s 25(b)).

Devolution: Applies throughout UK.

1.35 *A Guide to the Immigration Act 2016*

Offences: expanded criminal offence of employing a person without permission to work, Immigration, Asylum and Nationality Act 2006, s 21, amended by s 35(1)–(4).

Section 35 broadens the existing offence under s 21 of the Immigration, Asylum and Nationality Act (IANA 2006) of employing a person without permission to work so that as well as catching those who knowingly employ such a person it catches employers who have reasonable cause to believe that the worker had no right to take the employment. The reason for this was stated to be to capture those who deliberately do not check a worker's documents so that they can at most be liable for a civil penalty, rather than a criminal offence.[1] The offence encompasses a wider swathe of employers.

The offence is only committed where the employee does not have the right to work. It is thus not committed by an employer who erroneously believes that their employee does not have the right to work.

The offence is committed when the employer employs someone who does not have permission to work. This covers a contract of service or apprenticeship, whether express or implied, and whether oral or written (IANA 2006, s 25(b)) but is not as broad as the definition of work used in s 24B of the Immigration Act 1971 (IA 1971) as inserted by s 34 of this Act.

While the threshold for commission of the offence is lowered, the maximum penalty is raised, from two to five years.[2] Amendments to change the test to one of recklessness were resisted by the Government.[3]

---

1   Public Bill Committee 6th sitting (afternoon) *Hansard,* HC, col 222 (27 October 2015).
2   IANA 2006 s 21(2)(a)(i) as amended by s 35(4).
3   House of Commons' Report, amendment 33.

ILLEGAL WORKING IN LICENSED PREMISES

SECTION 36—LICENCING ACT 2003: AMENDMENTS RELATING TO ILLEGAL WORKING AND SCHEDULE 4—LICENCING ACT 2003: AMENDMENTS RELATING TO ILLEGAL WORKING

Summary

Makes it a requirement for the grant of a personal or premises licence that the licensee has the right to work in the UK. The Secretary of State (SSHD) is incorporated into the licensing regime.

1.36

36 Licensing Act 2003: amendments relating to illegal working

(1) Schedule 4 (Licensing Act 2003: amendments relating to illegal working) has effect.

(2) The Secretary of State may by regulations make provision which—

    (a) has a similar effect to the amendments made by Schedule 4, and

    (b) applies in relation to Scotland or Northern Ireland.

(3) Regulations under subsection (2) may—

    (a) amend, repeal or revoke any enactment;

    (b) confer functions on any person.

(4) Regulations under subsection (2) may not confer functions on—

    (a) the Scottish Ministers,

    (b) the First Minister and deputy First Minister in Northern Ireland,

    (c) a Northern Ireland Minister, or

    (d) a Northern Ireland department.

(5) In this section "enactment" includes—

    (a) an enactment contained in subordinate legislation within the meaning of the Interpretation Act 1978;

    (b) an enactment contained in, or in an instrument made under, an Act of the Scottish Parliament;

    (c) an enactment contained in, or in an instrument made under, Northern Ireland legislation.'

Schedule 4

Licencing Act 2003: Amendments relating to illegal working

Part 1

Entitlement to work in the United Kingdom

1   After section 192 of the Licensing Act 2003 insert—

"192A Entitlement to work in the United Kingdom

(1) For the purposes of this Act an individual is entitled to work in the United Kingdom if—

    (a) the individual does not under the Immigration Act 1971 require leave to enter or remain in the United Kingdom, or

    (b) the individual has been granted such leave and the leave—

        (i) is not invalid,

1.36 *A Guide to the Immigration Act 2016*

> > (ii) has not ceased to have effect (whether by reason of curtailment, revocation, cancellation, passage of time or otherwise), and
> >
> > (iii) is not subject to a condition preventing the individual from doing work relating to the carrying on of a licensable activity within section 1(1)(a) or (d).
>
> (2) Where an individual is on immigration bail within the meaning of Part 1 of Schedule 10 to the Immigration Act 2016—
>
> > (a) the individual is to be treated for the purposes of subsection (1) as if the individual had been granted leave to enter the United Kingdom, but
> >
> > (b) any condition as to the individual's work in the United Kingdom to which the individual's immigration bail is subject is to be treated for those purposes as a condition of leave."

Part 2

Premises licences

2 Part 3 of the Licensing Act 2003 (premises licences) is amended as follows.

3 In section 13(4) (meaning of "responsible authority"), after paragraph (h) insert—

> "(ha)where the premises (not being a vessel) are being, or are proposed to be, used for a licensable activity within section 1(1)(a) or (d), the Secretary of State,".

4(1) Section 16 (applicant for premises licence) is amended as follows.

(2) In subsection (1), at the beginning insert " Subject to subsections (2) and (2A), ".

(3) In subsection (2), omit "But".

(4) After subsection (2) insert—

> "(2A) An individual who is resident in the United Kingdom may not apply for a premises licence authorising premises to be used for a licensable activity within section 1(1)(a) or (d) unless the individual is entitled to work in the United Kingdom."

5 In section 27 (death, incapacity, insolvency etc of licence holder), after subsection (1) insert—

> "(1A) A premises licence that authorises premises to be used for a licensable activity within section 1(1)(a) or (d) also lapses if the holder of the licence ceases to be entitled to work in the United Kingdom at a time when the holder of the licence is resident in the United Kingdom (or becomes so resident without being entitled to work in the United Kingdom)."

6(1) Section 42 (application for transfer of premises licence) is amended as follows.

(2) After subsection (2) insert—

"(2A) Where the applicant is an individual who is resident in the United Kingdom and the premises licence authorises premises to be used for a licensable activity within section 1(1)(a) or (d) he must also be entitled to work in the United Kingdom."

(3) After subsection (5) insert—

"(5ZA) Where the premises licence authorises premises to be used for a licensable activity within section 1(1)(a) or (d), the relevant person must also give notice of the application to the Secretary of State."

(4) In subsection (5A), for "subsection (5)" substitute " subsections (5) and (5ZA) ".

(5) After subsection (7) insert—

"(8) Where the Secretary of State is given notice under subsection (5ZA) and is satisfied that the exceptional circumstances of the case are such that granting the application would be prejudicial to the prevention of illegal working in licensed premises, the Secretary of State must give the relevant licensing authority a notice stating the reasons for being so satisfied.

(9) The Secretary of State must give that notice within the period of 14 days beginning with the day on which the Secretary of State is notified of the application under subsection (5ZA)."

7(1) Section 44(5) (determination of transfer application) is amended as follows.

(2) In the words before paragraph (a), after "section 42(6)" insert " or (8) ".

(3) In paragraph (a), for "chief officer of police" substitute " person ".

(4) For paragraph (b) substitute—

"(b) having regard to the notice—

(i) where the notice is given under section 42(6), reject the application if it considers it appropriate for the promotion of the crime prevention objective to do so, or

(ii) where the notice is given under section 42(8), reject the application if it considers it appropriate for the prevention of illegal working in licensed premises to do so."

8(1) Section 45 (notification of determination under section 44) is amended as follows.

(2) In subsection (2)—

(a) after "that section" insert " or the Secretary of State gave a notice under subsection (8) of that section ";

1.36 *A Guide to the Immigration Act 2016*

   (b) for "(and it" substitute " (which, in either case, ".

 (3) After subsection (2) insert—

   "(2A) Where the Secretary of State gave a notice under subsection (8) of section 42 (which was not withdrawn), the notice under subsection (1) of this section must also be given to the Secretary of State."

9(1) Section 47 (interim authority notice following death etc of licence holder) is amended as follows.

 (2) In subsection (1)—

   (a) after "or (c)" insert " or (1A) ";

   (b) after "holder" insert " or change of immigration status ".

 (3) In subsection (3), after "subject to" insert " subsection (3A) and ".

 (4) After subsection (3) insert—

   "(3A) Where the premises licence authorises premises to be used for a licensable activity within section 1(1)(a) or (d), a person falling within subsection (2)(a) or (b) who is an individual who is resident in the United Kingdom may give an interim authority notice only if the person is entitled to work in the United Kingdom."

 (5) In subsection (7), after paragraph (a) insert—

   "(aa) where the premises licence authorises premises to be used for a licensable activity within section 1(1)(a) or (d), at the end of the initial 28 day period unless before that time the person who gave the interim authority notice has given a copy of the notice to the Secretary of State;".

 (6) In subsection (7A)—

   (a) in paragraph (a), for "subsection (7)(a) does" substitute " paragraphs (a) and (aa) of subsection (7) do ";

   (b) in paragraph (b), at the end insert " and, where the premises licence authorises premises to be used for a licensable activity within section 1(1)(a) or (d), to the Secretary of State. "

10(1) Section 48 (cancellation of interim authority notice following police objections) is amended as follows.

 (2) In the heading, omit "police".

 (3) In subsection (1), for "This section" substitute " Subsection (2) ".

 (4) After subsection (2) insert—

   "(2A) Subsection (2B) applies where—

    (a) an interim authority notice by a person ("the relevant person") is given in accordance with section 47,

    (b) the Secretary of State is given a copy of the interim authority notice before the end of the initial 28 day period (within the meaning of that section), and

Part 1—Labour Market and Illegal Working **1.36**

      (c)   the Secretary of State is satisfied that the exceptional circumstances of the case are such that a failure to cancel the interim authority notice would be prejudicial to the prevention of illegal working in licensed premises.

  (2B)   The Secretary of State must before the end of the second working day following receipt of the copy of the interim authority notice give the relevant licensing authority a notice stating why the Secretary of State is so satisfied."

(5)   In subsection (3)—

    (a)   in the words before paragraph (a), for "by the chief officer of police" substitute " under subsection (2) or (2B) ";

    (b)   in paragraph (a), for "chief officer of police" substitute " person who gave the notice ";

    (c)   for paragraph (b) substitute—

        "(b)   having regard to the notice—

            (i)   where the notice is given under subsection (2), cancel the interim authority notice if it considers it appropriate for the promotion of the crime prevention objective to do so, or

            (ii)   where the notice is given under subsection (2B), cancel the interim authority notice if it considers it appropriate for the prevention of illegal working in licensed premises to do so."

(6)   After subsection (5) insert—

  "(5A)   Where an interim authority notice is cancelled under subsection (3)(b)(ii), the licensing authority must also give a copy of the notice under subsection (4) to the Secretary of State."

11   In section 50 (reinstatement of licence on transfer following death etc of holder), in subsection (3), for "(who, in the case of an individual, is aged 18 or over)" substitute " (and who would, where applicable, satisfy subsections (2) and (2A) of section 42) ".

Part 3

Personal licences

12   Part 6 of the Licensing Act 2003 (personal licences) is amended as follows.

13(1)   Section 113 (meaning of "relevant offence" and "foreign offence") is amended as follows.

  (2)   In the heading, for "and "foreign offence"" substitute ", "immigration offence", "foreign offence" and "immigration penalty"".

  (3)   After subsection (2) insert—

  "(2A)   In this Part "immigration offence" means—

        (a)   an offence referred to in paragraph 7A of Schedule 4, or

(b) an offence listed in paragraph 24 or 25 of Schedule 4 that is committed in relation to an offence referred to in paragraph 7A of that Schedule."

(4) At the end insert—

"(4) In this Part "immigration penalty" means a penalty under—

(a) section 15 of the Immigration, Asylum and Nationality Act 2006 ("the 2006 Act"), or

(b) section 23 of the Immigration Act 2014 ("the 2014 Act").

(5) For the purposes of this Part a person to whom a penalty notice under section 15 of the 2006 Act has been given is not to be treated as having been required to pay an immigration penalty if—

(a) the person is excused payment by virtue of section 15(3) of that Act, or

(b) the penalty is cancelled by virtue of section 16 or 17 of that Act.

(6) For the purposes of this Part a person to whom a penalty notice under section 15 of the 2006 Act has been given is not to be treated as having been required to pay an immigration penalty until such time as—

(a) the period for giving a notice of objection under section 16 of that Act has expired and the Secretary of State has considered any notice given within that period, and

(b) if a notice of objection was given within that period, the period for appealing under section 17 of that Act has expired and any appeal brought within that period has been finally determined, abandoned or withdrawn.

(7) For the purposes of this Part a person to whom a penalty notice under section 23 of the 2014 Act has been given is not to be treated as having been required to pay an immigration penalty if—

(a) the person is excused payment by virtue of section 24 of that Act, or

(b) the penalty is cancelled by virtue of section 29 or 30 of that Act.

(8) For the purposes of this Part a person to whom a penalty notice under section 23 of the 2014 Act has been given is not to be treated as having been required to pay an immigration penalty until such time as—

(a) the period for giving a notice of objection under section 29 of that Act has expired and the Secretary of State has considered any notice given within that period, and

(b) if a notice of objection was given within that period, the period for appealing under section 30 of that Act has expired and any appeal brought within that period has been finally determined, abandoned or withdrawn."

14(1) Section 115 (period of validity of personal licence) is amended as follows.

(2) In subsection (2), after "subsections" insert " (2A), ".

Part 1—Labour Market and Illegal Working   **1.36**

(3) After subsection (2) insert—

"(2A) A personal licence ceases to have effect if the holder of the licence ceases to be entitled to work in the United Kingdom."

15(1) Section 120 (determination of application for grant) is amended as follows.

(2) In subsection (2)—

(a) after paragraph (a) insert—

"(aa)he is entitled to work in the United Kingdom,";

(b) in paragraph (d), at the end insert " or required to pay an immigration penalty ".

(3) In subsection (3), for "paragraph (a), (b) or (c)" substitute " any of paragraphs (a) to (c) ".

(4) In subsection (4), for "(a), (b) and (c)" substitute " (a) to (c) ".

(5) In subsection (5)—

(a) omit the "and" at the end of paragraph (a);

(b) at the end of paragraph (b) insert "and

(c) the applicant having been required to pay any immigration penalty,".

(6) After subsection (5) insert—

"(5A) If it appears to the authority that the applicant meets the conditions in paragraphs (a) to (c) of subsection (2) but fails to meet the condition in paragraph (d) of that subsection by virtue of having been—

(a) convicted of an immigration offence,

(b) convicted of a foreign offence that the authority considers to be comparable to an immigration offence, or

(c) required to pay an immigration penalty,

the authority must give the Secretary of State a notice to that effect.

(5B) Where, having regard to—

(a) any conviction of the applicant for an immigration offence,

(b) any conviction of the applicant for a foreign offence which the Secretary of State considers to be comparable to an immigration offence, and

(c) the applicant having been required to pay any immigration penalty,

the Secretary of State is satisfied that granting the licence would be prejudicial to the prevention of illegal working in licensed premises, the Secretary of State must, within the period of 14 days beginning with the day the Secretary of State received the notice under subsection (5A), give the authority a notice stating the reasons for being so satisfied (an "immigration objection notice")."

1.36   A Guide to the Immigration Act 2016

(7) In subsection (6), for "is given within that period (or the notice is withdrawn)" substitute " or immigration objection notice is given within the period of 14 days referred to in subsection (5) or (5B) (as the case may be), or any such notice given is withdrawn, ".

(8) In subsection (7)—

  (a) in the words before paragraph (a), for "In any other case," substitute " Where an objection notice or an immigration objection notice is given within the period of 14 days referred to in subsection (5) or (5B) (as the case may be), and not withdrawn, ";

  (b) in paragraph (a)—

   (i) omit "objection";

   (ii) for "chief officer of police" substitute " person who gave the notice ";

  (c) for paragraph (b) substitute—

   "(b) having regard to the notice, must—

    (i) where the notice is an objection notice, reject the application if it considers it appropriate for the promotion of the crime prevention objective to do so, or

    (ii) where the notice is an immigration objection notice, reject the application if it considers it appropriate for the prevention of illegal working in licensed premises to do so."

(9) After subsection (7) insert—

  "(7A) An application that is not rejected by the authority under subsection (7)(b) must be granted by it."

16(1) Section 122 (notification of determinations) is amended as follows.

(2) In subsection (1)—

  (a) after "objection notice" insert " or the Secretary of State gave an immigration objection notice ";

  (b) after "(which" insert ", in either case, ".

(3) After subsection (2) insert—

  "(2A) Where the Secretary of State gave an immigration objection notice (which was not withdrawn) the notice under subsection (1)(a) or (2), as the case may be, must also be given to the Secretary of State."

(4) In subsection (3), in the definition of "objection notice", for "has" substitute " and "immigration objection notice" have ".

17(1) Section 123 (duty to notify licensing authority of convictions during application period) is amended as follows.

(2) In the heading, after "convictions" insert " etc ".

(3) In subsection (1)—

(a) after "application period" insert ", or is required to pay an immigration penalty during that period ";

(b) after "conviction" insert " or the requirement to pay (as the case may be) ".

18(1) Section 124 (convictions coming to light after grant) is amended as follows.

(2) In subsection (1)—

(a) for "("the offender")" substitute " ("the licence holder") ";

(b) at the end insert " or was required during that period to pay an immigration penalty ".

(3) In subsection (3)—

(a) in paragraph (a)—

(i) for "applicant" substitute " licence holder ";

(ii) for ", and" substitute " which occurred before the end of the application period, ";

(b) in paragraph (b), after "relevant offence" insert " and which occurred before the end of the application period ";

(c) at the end of paragraph (b) insert "and

(c) the licence holder having been required before the end of the application period to pay any immigration penalty,";

(d) in the words after paragraph (b), omit "which occurred before the end of the application period,".

(4) After subsection (3) insert—

"(3A) Where the licence holder was (during the application period)—

(a) convicted of an immigration offence,

(b) convicted of a foreign offence that the licensing authority considers to be comparable to an immigration offence, or

(c) required to pay an immigration penalty,

the authority must give the Secretary of State a notice to that effect.

(3B) Where, having regard to—

(a) any conviction of the licence holder for an immigration offence which occurred before the end of the application period,

(b) any conviction of the licence holder for a foreign offence which the Secretary of State considers to be comparable to an immigration offence and which occurred before the end of the application period, and

(c) the licence holder having been required before the end of the application period to pay any immigration penalty,

the Secretary of State is satisfied that continuation of the licence would be prejudicial to the prevention of illegal working in licensed premises, the Secretary of State must, within the period of 14 days beginning with the day the Secretary of State received the notice under subsection (3A), give the authority a notice stating the reasons for being so satisfied (an "immigration objection notice")."

(5) In subsection (4)—

   (a) in the words before paragraph (a), for "is given within that period" substitute " or an immigration objection notice is given within the period of 14 days referred to in subsection (3) or (3B), as the case may be, ";

   (b) in paragraph (a)—

      (i) omit "objection";

      (ii) for "holder of the licence, the chief officer of police" substitute " licence holder, the person who gave the notice ";

   (c) in paragraph (b), for the words from "revoke" to the end of the paragraph substitute "—

      (i) where the notice is an objection notice, revoke the licence if it considers it appropriate for the promotion of the crime prevention objective to do so, or

      (ii) where the notice is an immigration objection notice, revoke the licence if it considers it appropriate for the prevention of illegal working in licensed premises to do so."

(6) After subsection (5) insert—

   "(5A) Where the authority revokes or decides not to revoke a licence under subsection (4)(b)(ii) it must also notify the Secretary of State of the decision and its reasons for making it."

19(1) Section 125(3) (form of personal licence) is amended as follows.

(2) For "of each" substitute "of—

   (a) each".

(3) At the end insert—

   "(b) each immigration penalty that the holder has been required to pay and the date of each notice by which such a penalty was imposed."

20(1) Section 132 (licence holder's duty to notify licensing authority of convictions) is amended as follows.

(2) In the heading, after "convictions" insert " etc ".

Part 1—Labour Market and Illegal Working **1.36**

(3) After subsection (2) insert—

"(2A) Subsection (2B) applies where the holder of a personal licence is required to pay an immigration penalty.

(2B) The holder must, as soon as reasonably practicable after being required to pay the penalty, give the relevant licensing authority a notice containing details of the penalty, including the date of the notice by which the penalty was imposed."

(4) In subsection (3), after "(2)" insert " or (2B) ".

21 In Schedule 4 (personal licence: relevant offences), after paragraph 7 insert—

"7A An offence under any of the Immigration Acts."

Part 4

Rights of entry

22(1) Section 179 of the Licensing Act 2003 (rights of entry to investigate licensable activities) is amended as follows.

(2) After subsection (1) insert—

"(1A) Where an immigration officer has reason to believe that any premises are being used for a licensable activity within section 1(1)(a) or (d), the officer may enter the premises with a view to seeing whether an offence under any of the Immigration Acts is being committed in connection with the carrying on of the activity."

(3) In subsection (2)—

(a) after "authorised person" insert " or an immigration officer ";

(b) for "the power", in the first place it occurs, substitute " a power ".

(4) In subsection (3), for "the power" substitute " a power ".

(5) In subsection (4), after "authorised person" insert " or an immigration officer ".

(6) In subsection (6)—

(a) omit "and" at the end of the definition of "authorisation";

(b) at the end of the subsection insert—

""immigration officer" means a person appointed as an immigration officer under paragraph 1 of Schedule 2 to the Immigration Act 1971."

Part 5

Appeals

23 Schedule 5 to the Licensing Act 2003 (appeals) is amended as follows.

24(1) Paragraph 6 (transfer of licence) is amended as follows.

(2) In sub-paragraph (1)—

(a) after "42(6)" insert " or the Secretary of State gave a notice under section 42(8) ";

(b) after "(which" insert " , in either case, ".

(3) In sub-paragraph (2), after "police" insert " or the Secretary of State, as the case may be, ".

25(1) Paragraph 7 (interim authority notice) is amended as follows.

(2) In sub-paragraph (1)(b)—

(a) after "48(2)" insert " or the Secretary of State gives a notice under section 48(2B) ";

(b) after "(which" insert " , in either case, ".

(3) In sub-paragraph (3), for "the notice under that subsection," substitute " the interim authority notice under section 48(3) after the giving of a notice by a chief officer of police under section 48(2), ".

(4) After sub-paragraph (3) insert—

"(3A) Where the relevant licensing authority decides not to cancel the interim authority notice under section 48(3) after the giving of a notice by the Secretary of State under section 48(2B), the Secretary of State may appeal against that decision."

26 In paragraph 9 (general provision about appeals under Part 1 of Schedule 5), in sub-paragraph (4), after "paragraph 7(3)" insert " or (3A) ".

27(1) Paragraph 17 (personal licences) is amended as follows.

(2) In sub-paragraph (2)—

(a) for "section 120(7)" substitute " 120(7A) after the giving of a notice under section 120(5) ";

(b) for "objection notice (within the meaning of section 120(5))" substitute " notice ".

(3) After sub-paragraph (2) insert—

"(2A) Where a licensing authority grants an application for a personal licence under section 120(7A) after the giving of a notice under section 120(5B), the Secretary of State may appeal against that decision."

(4) After sub-paragraph (5) insert—

"(5A) Where in a case to which section 124 applies—

(a) the Secretary of State gives a notice under subsection (3B) of that section (and does not later withdraw it), and

Part 1—Labour Market and Illegal Working **1.36**

  (b) the licensing authority decides not to revoke the licence,

  the Secretary of State may appeal against the decision."

(5) In sub-paragraph (8), for "(2), (3) or (5)" substitute " (2), (2A), (5) or (5A) ".

28 At the end insert—

Part 4

Questions about leave to enter or remain in the UK

19 On an appeal under this Schedule, a magistrates' court is not entitled to entertain any question as to whether—

 (a) an individual should be, or should have been, granted leave to enter or remain in the United Kingdom, or

 (b) an individual has, after the date of the decision being appealed against, been granted leave to enter or remain in the United Kingdom."

Part 6

General

29 In section 10 of the Licensing Act 2003, (sub-delegation of functions by licensing committee etc), in subsection (4)(a), in sub-paragraphs (v), (vi) and (x), omit "police".

30(1) Section 193 of the Licensing Act 2003 (other definitions) is amended as follows.

 (2) The existing text becomes subsection (1).

 (3) After that subsection insert—

  "(2) For the purposes of references in this Act to the prevention of illegal working in licensed premises, a person is working illegally if by doing that work at that time the person is committing an offence under section 24B of the Immigration Act 1971."

31 In section 194 of the Licensing Act 2003 (index of defined expressions), insert the following entries at the appropriate places—

"entitled to work in the United Kingdom section 192A"

"immigration offence section 113"

"immigration penalty (and required to pay, in relation to an immigration penalty) section 113"

"working illegally, in relation to the prevention of illegal working in licensed premises section 193"

32 In the Police Reform and Social Responsibility Act 2011, omit sections 109(9) and (10) and 111(3) and (5).

Part 7

Transitional provision

33 The amendments of sections 13, 16, 42, 47 and 120 of the Licensing Act 2003 made by paragraphs 3, 4, 6, 9 and 15 respectively of this Schedule do not apply in relation to applications made, or interim authority notices given, before the coming into force of the respective paragraph.

34 The amendment of section 27 of the Licensing Act 2003 made by paragraph 5 of this Schedule does not apply in relation to a premises licence granted pursuant to an application made before the coming into force of that paragraph.

35 The amendments of section 115 of the Licensing Act 2003 made by paragraph 14 of this Schedule do not apply in relation to a personal licence granted pursuant to an application made before the coming into force of that paragraph.

36 The amendment of Schedule 4 to the Licensing Act 2003 made by paragraph 21 of this Schedule applies on and after the coming into force of that paragraph in relation to—

(a) personal licences granted before, on or after the coming into force of that paragraph, and

(b) offences committed before, on or after the coming into force of that paragraph.

Commencement: Not yet in force.

Amends: The Licensing Act 2003 (LA 2003). See Schedule 4 for full details.

Orders and Regulations: Power to make regulations with 'similar effect' to those made by Schedule 4 to apply in relation to Scotland or Northern Ireland. Affirmative procedure (s 93(e)).

Definitions:

'crime prevention objective' LA 2003, s 193;

An individual is *entitled to work in the UK* for the purposes of the LA 2003 if the individual does not require leave under the immigration Act 1971 (IA 1971) or has valid leave under the Act which has not ceased to have effect and is not subject to a condition prohibiting work. Those on immigration bail are to be treated as though they had been granted leave, LA 2003, s 192A, as inserted by Schedule 4 para 1;

'Immigration Acts' UK Borders Act 2007, s 61(2);

'immigration bail' Immigration Act 2016 (IA 2016), Schedule 10, Part 1 (LA 2003, s 192 as inserted by Schedule 4, para 1);

'immigration offence' for the purposes of Part 6 of the LA 2003, s 113(2A) of that Act (Schedule 4 para 13);

'immigration officer' LA 2003, s 179: 'a person appointed as an immigration officer under para 1 of Schedule 2 to the IA 1971';

'immigration penalty' for the purposes of Part 6 of the LA 2003, s 113(4) of that Act (Schedule 4, para 13);

'interim authority notice' LA 2003, s 47;

'licensable activity' LA 2003, s 1;

'licensed premises' LA 2003, s 193;

'licensing authority' LA 2003, s 3(1);

'penalty notice' see Immigration, Asylum and Nationality Act 2006 (IANA 2006), s 15 where this is explained rather than defined;

'personal licence' LA 2003, s 111(1);

'premises' LA 2003, s 193: any place and includes a vehicle, vessel or moveable structure;

'premises licence' LA 2003, s 11;

'relevant licensing authority' LA 2003, for the purposes of Part 3, s 12; for the purposes of Part 4, s 68;

'responsible authority' LA 2003 for the purposes of Part 3, s 13(4) (amended by Schedule 4, para 3); for the purposes of Part 4, s 69;

premises are 'used' for a licensable activity if that activity is carried on on or from the premises, (LA 2003), s 1(6);

'vessel' LA 2003, s 193: includes a ship, boat, raft or other apparatus constructed or adapted for floating on water;

'working illegally in the UK' for the purposes of the LA 2003, LA 2003 s 193(2) (Schedule 4, Part 6, para 30(3)

'enactment' s 36(5), includes subordinate legislation and legislation made, or made under, legislation made by the Scottish parliament or an enactment or instrument made under Northern Ireland legislation.

Offences: None, contrast s 37 and Schedule 5 below.

Devolution: Regulation-making powers allowing similar provision to be made in Scotland and Northern Ireland (s 36(2)). Regulations can amend not only Acts of the Scottish Parliament or Northern Ireland legislation, but also Acts of the UK Parliament (and subordinate legislation made under them) (s 36(3) and (5)). They may confer function on the Scottish Ministers, on the First Minister and Deputy Minister in Northern Ireland or on a Northern Ireland Department (s 36(4)).

Subsection 36(1) gives effect to Schedule 1, where the changes to the licensing framework are set out. It will be a requirement for a personal or

1.36 *A Guide to the Immigration Act 2016*

premises licence that the licensee has the right to work in the UK (Licensing Act 2003: for a premises licence, new s 16(2A), for a transfer of premises licence, new s 42(2A), for a personal licence, s 120(2)(aa)). A licence will lapse when the holder ceases to be entitled to work in the UK (LA 2003: for a premises licence, new s 27(1A), for a personal licence, s 115(2A)).

The SSHD will be added to the list of responsible authorities under the LA 2003 (see s 13 and 69 of that Act) so that she must be notified before a premises licence is issued or transferred. She can intervene where she is satisfied that the exceptional circumstances of the case are such that the issue of a licence would be prejudicial to the prevention of illegal working in licensed premises (LA 2003, s 42(8)). She can object to the grant of the licence and this is to be taken into account by the licencing authority which must reject the application for a licence 'if it considers it appropriate for the prevention of illegal working ... to do so' (LA 2003, s 44(5)(b)(ii)). Thus the decision remains with the licencing authority. The SSHD can, however, appeal against a grant of a licence, or a refusal to cancel a licence, despite her objection.[1]

If an applicant for a personal licence has been convicted of an immigration offence, or is required to pay a civil penalty in an immigration matter,[2] then the SSHD must be notified of the application (LA 2003 new s 120(5A)). She can give an 'immigration objection notice' if satisfied that granting the licence would be prejudicial to the prevention of illegal working (new s 120(5B)). Contrast s 42(8); here there is no requirement of exceptional circumstances. Her notice can be taken into account by the licencing authority. It must reject the application 'if it considers it appropriate for the prevention of illegal working ... to do so'.[3] If it grants the application it must give the SSHD its written reasons for so doing.[4]

Where an immigration officer 'has reasonable grounds to believe that any premises are being used for a licensable activity' there is a new power for the immigration officer to enter the premises 'with a view to seeing whether an offence under any of the Immigration Acts is being committed in connection with the carrying on of the activity' (LA 2003, s 179(1A)).

It is not only the sale of alcohol which requires a licence. So does, for example, the sale of hot food or drink between 11.00pm and 5.00am (see LA 2003, s 11).

The provisions apply only to England and Wales but portmanteau provisions would allow the SSHD to extend them to Scotland and Northern Ireland by regulation and the Explanatory Memorandum to the Bill records the view that a legislative consent motion would not be required for this.[5] The Rt Hon James Brokenshire MP stated in a letter to Michael Matheson MSP on 9 February 2016 that Scots legislation is complex, and was also being amended, and that these were the reasons for using secondary legislation; to allow the UK Government extra time to draft the regulations. He indicated in that letter that the Scottish Government officials and lawyers had commented on draft provisions. See further the discussion of devolution in the notes to s 37 below.

See Schedule 6, para 9(6) which places a court making an illegal working compliance order in relation to premises in England and Wales in respect of which a premises licence is in force under an obligation to notify the relevant licensing authority that the order has been made.

---

1 LA 2003, Schedule 5, paras 7(3A) and 17(2A) inserted by Schedule 5, paras 25 and 27 respectively.
2 Employing a person not allowed to work under s 15 of IANA 2006 or, renting property to a person not allowed to rent under s 23 of the IA 2014: LA 2003, s 113(4) inserted by Schedule 4, para 13.
3 Schedule 5, para 7 inserting new subs 44(5)b)(ii) into LA 2003. The text of the IA 2016 goes awry here, referring to paragraphs rather than subsections.
4 Schedule 5, para 16 inserting a new subs 122(2A) and para 18 inserting a new subs 124(5A) into LA 2003.
5 See Annex B. Available at: http://www.publications.parliament.uk/pa/bills/lbill/2015-2016/0079/en/15079en.pdf (accessed 9 November 2016). See Amendments 47–50, and 52–53, at Lords' Report, opposing the extension of the provisions to Scotland.

ILLEGAL WORKING IN RELATION TO PRIVATE HIRE VEHICLES ETC

SECTION 37—PRIVATE HIRE VEHICLES ETC AND SCHEDULE 5—PRIVATE HIRE VEHICLES ETC

> **Summary**
>
> Provision similar to the licencing regime described in s 36, but in respect of the licenced hackney carriage and private hire vehicles.

1.37

37 Private hire vehicles etc

Schedule 5 (private hire vehicles etc) has effect.

Schedule 5
Private hire vehicles etc

London Hackney Carriages Act 1843 (c. 86)

1.37 *A Guide to the Immigration Act 2016*

1(1) Section 18 of the London Hackney Carriages Act 1843 (licences and badges to be delivered up on the discontinuance of licences) is amended as follows.

(2) At the beginning insert " (1) ".

(3) At the end of subsection (1) insert—

"(2) Subsection (1) does not require the delivery of a licence and badge on the expiry of the licence if the licence was granted in accordance with section 8A(2) or (4) of the Metropolitan Public Carriage Act 1869 (but see section 8A(6) of that Act)."

Metropolitan Public Carriage Act 1869 (c. 115)

2 The Metropolitan Public Carriage Act 1869 is amended as follows.

3 In section 8(7) (driver's licence to be in force for three years unless suspended or revoked) for "A" substitute " Subject to section 8A, a ".

4 After section 8 insert—

"8A Drivers' licences for persons subject to immigration control

(1) Subsection (2) applies if—

(a) a licence under section 8 is to be granted to a person who has been granted leave to enter or remain in the United Kingdom for a limited period ("the leave period"),

(b) the person's leave has not been extended by virtue of section 3C of the Immigration Act 1971 (continuation of leave pending variation decision), and

(c) apart from subsection (2), the period for which the licence would have been in force would have ended after the end of the leave period.

(2) Transport for London must grant the licence for a period which ends at or before the end of the leave period.

(3) Subsection (4) applies if—

(a) a licence under section 8 is to be granted to a person who has been granted leave to enter or remain in the United Kingdom for a limited period, and

(b) the person's leave has been extended by virtue of section 3C of the Immigration Act 1971 (continuation of leave pending variation decision).

(4) Transport for London must grant the licence for a period that does not exceed six months.

(5) A licence under section 8 ceases to be in force if the person to whom it was granted becomes disqualified by reason of the person's immigration status from driving a hackney carriage.

(6) If a licence granted in accordance with subsection (2) or (4) expires, the person to whom it was granted must, within the period of

Part 1—Labour Market and Illegal Working **1.37**

7 days beginning with the day after that on which it expired, return to Transport for London—

(a) the licence,

(b) the person's copy of the licence (if any), and

(c) the person's driver's badge.

(7) If subsection (5) applies to a licence, the person to whom it was granted must, within the period of 7 days beginning with the day after the day on which the person first became disqualified, return to Transport for London—

(a) the licence,

(b) the person's copy of the licence (if any), and

(c) the person's driver's badge.

(8) A person who, without reasonable excuse, contravenes subsection (6) or (7) is guilty of an offence and liable on summary conviction—

(a) to a fine not exceeding level 3 on the standard scale, and

(b) in the case of a continuing offence, to a fine not exceeding ten pounds for each day during which an offence continues after conviction.

(9) The Secretary of State may by regulations made by statutory instrument amend the amount for the time being specified in subsection (8)(b).

(10) Regulations under subsection (9) may make transitional, transitory or saving provision.

(11) A statutory instrument containing regulations under subsection (9) may not be made unless a draft of the instrument has been laid before, and approved by a resolution of, each House of Parliament.

(12) For the purposes of this section a person is disqualified by reason of the person's immigration status from driving a hackney carriage if the person is subject to immigration control and—

(a) the person has not been granted leave to enter or remain in the United Kingdom, or

(b) the person's leave to enter or remain in the United Kingdom—

(i) is invalid,

(ii) has ceased to have effect (whether by reason of curtailment, revocation, cancellation, passage of time or otherwise), or

(iii) subject to a condition preventing the person from driving a hackney carriage.

1.37 *A Guide to the Immigration Act 2016*

(13) Where a person is on immigration bail within the meaning of Part 1 of Schedule 10 to the Immigration Act 2016—

(a) the person is to be treated for the purposes of this section as if the person had been granted leave to enter the United Kingdom, but

(b) any condition as to the person's work in the United Kingdom to which the person's immigration bail is subject is to be treated for those purposes as a condition of leave.

(14) For the purposes of this section a person is subject to immigration control if under the Immigration Act 1971 the person requires leave to enter or remain in the United Kingdom."

Plymouth City Council Act 1975 (c. xx)

5   The Plymouth City Council Act 1975 is amended as follows.

6   After section 2 insert—

"2A Persons disqualified by reason of immigration status

(1) For the purposes of this Act a person is disqualified by reason of the person's immigration status from carrying on a licensable activity if the person is subject to immigration control and—

(a) the person has not been granted leave to enter or remain in the United Kingdom, or

(b) the person's leave to enter or remain in the United Kingdom—

(i) is invalid,

(ii) has ceased to have effect (whether by reason of curtailment, revocation, cancellation, passage of time or otherwise), or

(iii) is subject to a condition preventing the person from carrying on the licensable activity.

(2) Where a person is on immigration bail within the meaning of Part 1 of Schedule 10 to the Immigration Act 2016—

(a) the person is to be treated for the purposes of this Act as if the person had been granted leave to enter the United Kingdom, but

(b) any condition as to the person's work in the United Kingdom to which the person's immigration bail is subject is to be treated for those purposes as a condition of leave.

(3) For the purposes of this section a person is subject to immigration control if under the Immigration Act 1971 the person requires leave to enter or remain in the United Kingdom.

Part 1—Labour Market and Illegal Working **1.37**

(4) For the purposes of this section a person carries on a licensable activity if the person—

    (a) drives a private hire vehicle,

    (b) operates a private hire vehicle, or

    (c) drives a hackney carriage.

2B Immigration offences and immigration penalties

(1) In this Act "immigration offence" means—

    (a) an offence under any of the Immigration Acts,

    (b) an offence under section 1 of the Criminal Attempts Act 1981 of attempting to commit an offence within paragraph (a), or

    (c) an offence under section 1 of the Criminal Law Act 1977 of conspiracy to commit an offence within paragraph (a).

(2) In this Act "immigration penalty" means a penalty under—

    (a) section 15 of the Immigration, Asylum and Nationality Act 2006 ("the 2006 Act"), or

    (b) section 23 of the Immigration Act 2014 ("the 2014 Act").

(3) For the purposes of this Act a person to whom a penalty notice under section 15 of the 2006 Act has been given is not to be treated as having been required to pay an immigration penalty if—

    (a) the person is excused payment by virtue of section 15(3) of that Act, or

    (b) the penalty is cancelled by virtue of section 16 or 17 of that Act.

(4) For the purposes of this Act a person to whom a penalty notice under section 15 of the 2006 Act has been given is not to be treated as having been required to pay an immigration penalty until such time as—

    (a) the period for giving a notice of objection under section 16 of that Act has expired and the Secretary of State has considered any notice given within that period, and

    (b) if a notice of objection was given within that period, the period for appealing under section 17 of that Act has expired and any appeal brought within that period has been finally determined, abandoned or withdrawn.

(5) For the purposes of this Act a person to whom a penalty notice under section 23 of the 2014 Act has been given is not to be treated as having been required to pay an immigration penalty if—

    (a) the person is excused payment by virtue of section 24 of that Act, or

(b) the penalty is cancelled by virtue of section 29 or 30 of that Act.

(6) For the purposes of this Act a person to whom a penalty notice under section 23 of the 2014 Act has been given is not to be treated as having been required to pay an immigration penalty until such time as—

(a) the period for giving a notice of objection under section 29 of that Act has expired and the Secretary of State has considered any notice given within that period, and

(b) if a notice of objection was given within that period, the period for appealing under section 30 of that Act has expired and any appeal brought within that period has been finally determined, abandoned or withdrawn."

7(1) Section 9 (licensing of drivers of private hire vehicles) is amended as follows.

(2) In subsection (1)—

(a) in paragraph (a) after "satisfied" insert " —(i) ", and

(b) for the "or" at the end of paragraph (a) substitute "and

(ii) that the applicant is not disqualified by reason of the applicant's immigration status from driving a private hire vehicle; or".

(3) After subsection (1) insert—

"(1A) In determining for the purposes of subsection (1) whether an applicant is disqualified by reason of the applicant's immigration status from driving a private hire vehicle, the Council must have regard to any guidance issued by the Secretary of State."

8 In section 11(1) (drivers' licences for hackney carriages and private hire vehicles)—

(a) in paragraph (a) for "Every" substitute " Subject to section 11A, every ", and

(b) in paragraph (b) after "1889," insert " but subject to section 11A, ".

9 After section 11 insert—

"11A Drivers' licences for persons subject to immigration control

(1) Subsection (2) applies if—

(a) a licence within section 11(1)(a) or (b) is to be granted to a person who has been granted leave to enter or remain in the United Kingdom for a limited period ("the leave period"),

(b) the person's leave has not been extended by virtue of section 3C of the Immigration Act 1971 (continuation of leave pending variation decision), and

Part 1—Labour Market and Illegal Working **1.37**

(c) apart from subsection (2), the period for which the licence would have been in force would have ended after the end of the leave period.

(2) The Council must specify a period in the licence as the period for which it remains in force; and that period must end at or before the end of the leave period.

(3) Subsection (4) applies if—

(a) a licence within section 11(1)(a) or (b) is to be granted to a person who has been granted leave to enter or remain in the United Kingdom for a limited period, and

(b) the person's leave has been extended by virtue of section 3C of the Immigration Act 1971 (continuation of leave pending variation decision).

(4) The Council must specify a period in the licence as the period for which it remains in force; and that period must not exceed six months.

(5) A licence within section 11(1)(a) ceases to be in force if the person to whom it was granted becomes disqualified by reason of the person's immigration status from driving a private hire vehicle.

(6) A licence within section 11(1)(b) ceases to be in force if the person to whom it was granted becomes disqualified by reason of the person's immigration status from driving a hackney carriage.

(7) If a licence granted in accordance with subsection (2) or (4) expires, the person to whom it was granted must, within the period of 7 days beginning with the day after that on which it expired, return the licence and the person's driver's badge to the Council.

(8) If subsection (5) or (6) applies to a licence, the person to whom it was granted must, within the period of 7 days beginning with the day after the day on which the person first became disqualified, return the licence and the person's driver's badge to the Council.

(9) A person who, without reasonable excuse, contravenes subsection (7) or (8) is guilty of an offence and liable on summary conviction—

(a) to a fine not exceeding level 3 on the standard scale, and

(b) in the case of a continuing offence, to a fine not exceeding ten pounds for each day during which an offence continues after conviction.

(10) The Secretary of State may by regulations made by statutory instrument amend the amount for the time being specified in subsection (9)(b).

(11) Regulations under subsection (10) may make transitional, transitory or saving provision.

1.37 *A Guide to the Immigration Act 2016*

(12) A statutory instrument containing regulations under subsection (10) may not be made unless a draft of the instrument has been laid before, and approved by a resolution of, each House of Parliament."

10(1) Section 13 (licensing of operators of private hire vehicles) is amended as follows.

(2) In subsection (1)—

(a) after "satisfied" insert " —(a) ", and

(b) at the end of paragraph (a) insert "; and

(c) if the applicant is an individual, that the applicant is not disqualified by reason of the applicant's immigration status from operating a private hire vehicle."

(3) After subsection (1) insert—

"(1A) In determining for the purposes of subsection (1) whether an applicant is disqualified by reason of the applicant's immigration status from operating a private hire vehicle, the Council must have regard to any guidance issued by the Secretary of State."

(4) In subsection (2) for "Every" substitute " Subject to section 13A, every ".

11 After section 13 insert—

"13A Operators' licences for persons subject to immigration control

(1) Subsection (2) applies if—

(a) a licence under section 13 is to be granted to a person who has been granted leave to enter or remain in the United Kingdom for a limited period ("the leave period"),

(b) the person's leave has not been extended by virtue of section 3C of the Immigration Act 1971 (continuation of leave pending variation decision), and

(c) apart from subsection (2), the period for which the licence would have been in force would have ended after the end of the leave period.

(2) The Council must specify a period in the licence as the period for which it remains in force; and that period must end at or before the end of the leave period.

(3) Subsection (4) applies if—

(a) a licence under section 13 is to be granted to a person who has been granted leave to enter or remain in the United Kingdom for a limited period, and

(b) the person's leave has been extended by virtue of section 3C of the Immigration Act 1971 (continuation of leave pending variation decision).

Part 1—Labour Market and Illegal Working **1.37**

(4) The Council must specify a period in the licence as the period for which it remains in force; and that period must not exceed six months.

(5) A licence under section 13 ceases to be in force if the person to whom it was granted becomes disqualified by reason of the person's immigration status from operating a private hire vehicle.

(6) If a licence granted in accordance with subsection (2) or (4) expires, the person to whom it was granted must, within the period of 7 days beginning with the day after that on which it expired, return the licence to the Council.

(7) If subsection (5) applies to a licence, the person to whom it was granted must, within the period of 7 days beginning with the day after the day on which the person first became disqualified, return it to the Council.

(8) A person who, without reasonable excuse, contravenes subsection (6) or (7) is guilty of an offence and liable on summary conviction—

 (a) to a fine not exceeding level 3 on the standard scale, and

 (b) in the case of a continuing offence, to a fine not exceeding ten pounds for each day during which an offence continues after conviction.

(9) The Secretary of State may by regulations made by statutory instrument amend the amount for the time being specified in subsection (8)(b).

(10) Regulations under subsection (9) may make transitional, transitory or saving provision.

(11) A statutory instrument containing regulations under subsection (9) may not be made unless a draft of the instrument has been laid before, and approved by a resolution of, each House of Parliament."

12(1) Section 17 (qualification for drivers of hackney carriages) is amended as follows.

 (2) In subsection (1)—

 (a) in paragraph (a) after "satisfied" insert " —(i) ", and

 (b) for the "or" at the end of paragraph (a) substitute "and

 (ii) that the applicant is not disqualified by reason of the applicant's immigration status from driving a hackney carriage; or".

 (3) After subsection (1) insert—

 "(1A) In determining for the purposes of subsection (1) whether an applicant is disqualified by reason of the applicant's immigration status from driving a hackney carriage, the Council must have regard to any guidance issued by the Secretary of State."

1.37 *A Guide to the Immigration Act 2016*

13(1) Section 19 (suspension and revocation of drivers' licences) is amended as follows.

(2) In subsection (1) before the "or" at the end of paragraph (a) insert—

"(aa) that he has since the grant of the licence been convicted of an immigration offence or required to pay an immigration penalty;".

(3) After subsection (1) insert—

"(1A) Subsection (1)(aa) does not apply if—

(a) in a case where the driver has been convicted of an immigration offence, the conviction is a spent conviction within the meaning of the Rehabilitation of Offenders Act 1974, or

(b) in a case where the driver has been required to pay an immigration penalty—

(i) more than three years have elapsed since the date on which the penalty was imposed, and

(ii) the amount of the penalty has been paid in full."

(4) After subsection (2) insert—

"(2A) The requirement in subsection (2)(a) to return a driver's badge does not apply in a case where section 20A applies (but see subsection (2) of that section)."

14(1) Section 20 (suspension and revocation of operators' licences) is amended as follows.

(2) In subsection (1) before the "or" at the end of paragraph (c) insert—

"(ca) that the operator has since the grant of the licence been convicted of an immigration offence or required to pay an immigration penalty;".

(3) After subsection (1) insert—

"(1A) Subsection (1)(ca) does not apply if—

(a) in a case where the operator has been convicted of an immigration offence, the conviction is a spent conviction within the meaning of the Rehabilitation of Offenders Act 1974, or

(b) in a case where the operator has been required to pay an immigration penalty—

(i) more than three years have elapsed since the date on which the penalty was imposed, and

(ii) the amount of the penalty has been paid in full."

Part 1—Labour Market and Illegal Working **1.37**

15   After section 20 insert—

"20A Return of licences suspended or revoked on immigration grounds

(1) Subsection (2) applies if—

(a) under section 19 the Council suspend, revoke or refuse to renew the licence of a driver of a hackney carriage or a private hire vehicle on the ground mentioned in subsection (1)(aa) of that section, or

(b) under section 20 the Council suspend, revoke or refuse to renew an operator's licence on the ground mentioned in subsection (1)(ca) of that section.

(2) The person to whom the licence was granted must, within the period of 7 days beginning with the relevant day, return to the Council—

(a) the licence, and

(b) in the case of a licence of a driver of a hackney carriage or a private hire vehicle, the person's driver's badge.

(3) In subsection (2) "the relevant day" means—

(a) where the licence is suspended or revoked, the day on which the suspension or revocation takes effect;

(b) where the Council refuse to renew the licence, the day on which the licence expires as a result of the failure to renew it.

(4) A person who, without reasonable excuse, contravenes subsection (2) is guilty of an offence and liable on summary conviction—

(a) to a fine not exceeding level 3 on the standard scale, and

(b) in the case of a continuing offence, to a fine not exceeding ten pounds for each day during which an offence continues after conviction.

(5) The Secretary of State may by regulations made by statutory instrument amend the amount for the time being specified in subsection (4)(b).

(6) Regulations under subsection (5) may make transitional, transitory or saving provision.

(7) A statutory instrument containing regulations under subsection (5) may not be made unless a draft of the instrument has been laid before, and approved by a resolution of, each House of Parliament."

16 In section 37 (appeals) after subsection (2) insert—

"(3) On an appeal under this Act or an appeal under section 302 of the Act of 1936 as applied by this section, the court is not entitled to entertain any question as to whether—

(a) a person should be, or should have been, granted leave to enter or remain in the United Kingdom, or

(b) a person has, after the date of the decision being appealed against, been granted leave to enter or remain in the United Kingdom."

Local Government (Miscellaneous Provisions) Act 1976 (c. 57)

17 The Local Government (Miscellaneous Provisions) Act 1976 is amended as follows.

18(1) Section 51 (licensing of drivers of private hire vehicles) is amended as follows.

(2) In subsection (1)—

(a) in paragraph (a) after "satisfied" insert " —(i) ", and

(b) for the "or" at the end of paragraph (a) substitute "and

(ii) that the applicant is not disqualified by reason of the applicant's immigration status from driving a private hire vehicle; or".

(3) After subsection (1) insert—

"(1ZA) In determining for the purposes of subsection (1) whether an applicant is disqualified by reason of the applicant's immigration status from driving a private hire vehicle, a district council must have regard to any guidance issued by the Secretary of State."

19 In section 53(1) (drivers' licences for hackney carriages and private hire vehicles)—

(a) in paragraph (a) for "Every" substitute " Subject to section 53A, every ", and

(b) in paragraph (b) after "1889," insert " but subject to section 53A, ".

20 After section 53 insert—

"53A Drivers' licences for persons subject to immigration control

(1) Subsection (2) applies if—

(a) a licence within section 53(1)(a) or (b) is to be granted to a person who has been granted leave to enter or remain in the United Kingdom for a limited period ("the leave period")

(b) the person's leave has not been extended by virtue of section 3C of the Immigration Act 1971 (continuation of leave pending variation decision); and

(c) apart from subsection (2), the period for which the licence would have been in force would have ended after the end of the leave period.

(2) The district council which grants the licence must specify a period in the licence as the period for which it remains in force; and that period must end at or before the end of the leave period.

(3) Subsection (4) applies if—

(a) a licence within section 53(1)(a) or (b) is to be granted to a person who has been granted leave to enter or remain in the United Kingdom for a limited period; and

(b) the person's leave has been extended by virtue of section 3C of the Immigration Act 1971 (continuation of leave pending variation decision).

(4) The district council which grants the licence must specify a period in the licence as the period for which it remains in force; and that period must not exceed six months.

(5) A licence within section 53(1)(a) ceases to be in force if the person to whom it was granted becomes disqualified by reason of the person's immigration status from driving a private hire vehicle.

(6) A licence within section 53(1)(b) ceases to be in force if the person to whom it was granted becomes disqualified by reason of the person's immigration status from driving a hackney carriage.

(7) If a licence granted in accordance with subsection (2) or (4) expires, the person to whom it was granted must, within the period of 7 days beginning with the day after that on which it expired, return the licence and the person's driver's badge to the district council which granted the licence.

(8) If subsection (5) or (6) applies to a licence, the person to whom it was granted must, within the period of 7 days beginning with the day after the day on which the person first became disqualified, return the licence and the person's driver's badge to the district council which granted the licence.

(9) A person who, without reasonable excuse, contravenes subsection (7) or (8) is guilty of an offence and liable on summary conviction—

(a) to a fine not exceeding level 3 on the standard scale; and

(b) in the case of a continuing offence, to a fine not exceeding ten pounds for each day during which an offence continues after conviction.

(10) The Secretary of State may by regulations made by statutory instrument amend the amount for the time being specified in subsection (9)(b).

(11) Regulations under subsection (10) may make transitional, transitory or saving provision.

1.37 *A Guide to the Immigration Act 2016*

- (12) A statutory instrument containing regulations under subsection (10) may not be made unless a draft of the instrument has been laid before, and approved by a resolution of, each House of Parliament."

21(1) Section 55 (licensing of operators of private hire vehicles) is amended as follows.

(2) In subsection (1)—

- (a) after "satisfied" insert " —(a) ", and
- (b) at the end of paragraph (a) insert "; and
- (c) if the applicant is an individual, that the applicant is not disqualified by reason of the applicant's immigration status from operating a private hire vehicle."

(3) After subsection (1) insert—

"(1A) In determining for the purposes of subsection (1) whether an applicant is disqualified by reason of the applicant's immigration status from operating a private hire vehicle, a district council must have regard to any guidance issued by the Secretary of State."

(4) In subsection (2) for "Every" substitute " Subject to section 55ZA, every ".

22 After section 55 insert—

"55ZA Operators' licences for persons subject to immigration control

(1) Subsection (2) applies if—

- (a) a licence under section 55 is to be granted to a person who has been granted leave to enter or remain in the United Kingdom for a limited period ("the leave period");
- (b) the person's leave has not been extended by virtue of section 3C of the Immigration Act 1971 (continuation of leave pending variation decision); and
- (c) apart from subsection (2), the period for which the licence would have been in force would have ended after the end of the leave period.

(2) The district council which grants the licence must specify a period in the licence as the period for which it remains in force; and that period must end at or before the end of the leave period.

(3) Subsection (4) applies if—

- (a) a licence under section 55 is to be granted to a person who has been granted leave to enter or remain in the United Kingdom for a limited period; and
- (b) the person's leave has been extended by virtue of section 3C of the Immigration Act 1971 (continuation of leave pending variation decision).

(4) The district council which grants the licence must specify a period in the licence as the period for which it remains in force; and that period must not exceed six months.

(5) A licence under section 55 ceases to be in force if the person to whom it was granted becomes disqualified by reason of the person's immigration status from operating a private hire vehicle.

(6) If a licence granted in accordance with subsection (2) or (4) expires, the person to whom it was granted must, within the period of 7 days beginning with the day after that on which it expired, return the licence to the district council which granted the licence.

(7) If subsection (5) applies to a licence, the person to whom it was granted must, within the period of 7 days beginning with the day after the day on which the person first became disqualified, return it to the district council which granted the licence.

(8) A person who, without reasonable excuse, contravenes subsection (6) or (7) is guilty of an offence and liable on summary conviction—

(a) to a fine not exceeding level 3 on the standard scale; and

(b) in the case of a continuing offence, to a fine not exceeding ten pounds for each day during which an offence continues after conviction.

(9) The Secretary of State may by regulations made by statutory instrument amend the amount for the time being specified in subsection (8)(b).

(10) Regulations under subsection (9) may make transitional, transitory or saving provision.

(11) A statutory instrument containing regulations under subsection (9) may not be made unless a draft of the instrument has been laid before, and approved by a resolution of, each House of Parliament."

23(1) Section 59 (qualification for drivers of hackney carriages) is amended as follows.

(1) In subsection (1)—

(a) in paragraph (a) after "satisfied" insert " —(i) ", and

(b) for the "or" at the end of paragraph (a) substitute "and

(i) that the applicant is not disqualified by reason of the applicant's immigration status from driving a hackney carriage; or".

(2) After subsection (1) insert—

"(1ZA) In determining for the purposes of subsection (1) whether an applicant is disqualified by reason of the applicant's immigration status from driving a hackney carriage, a district council must have regard to any guidance issued by the Secretary of State."

1.37 *A Guide to the Immigration Act 2016*

24(1) Section 61 (suspension and revocation of drivers' licences) is amended as follows.

(2) In subsection (1) before the "or" at the end of paragraph (a) insert—

"(aa)that he has since the grant of the licence been convicted of an immigration offence or required to pay an immigration penalty;".

(3) After subsection (1) insert—

"(1A) Subsection (1)(aa) does not apply if—

- (a) in a case where the driver has been convicted of an immigration offence, the conviction is a spent conviction within the meaning of the Rehabilitation of Offenders Act 1974, or
- (b) in a case where the driver has been required to pay an immigration penalty—
    - (i) more than three years have elapsed since the date on which the penalty was imposed, and
    - (ii) the amount of the penalty has been paid in full."

(3) After subsection (2) insert—

"(2ZA) The requirement in subsection (2)(a) to return a driver's badge does not apply in a case where section 62A applies (but see subsection (2) of that section).

25(1) Section 62 (suspension and revocation of operators' licences) is amended as follows.

(2) In subsection (1) before the "or" at the end of paragraph (c) insert—

"(ca)that the operator has since the grant of the licence been convicted of an immigration offence or required to pay an immigration penalty;".

(3) After subsection (1) insert—

"(1A) Subsection (1)(ca) does not apply if—

- (a) in a case where the operator has been convicted of an immigration offence, the conviction is a spent conviction within the meaning of the Rehabilitation of Offenders Act 1974, or
- (b) in a case where the operator has been required to pay an immigration penalty—
    - (i) more than three years have elapsed since the date on which the penalty was imposed, and
    - (ii) the amount of the penalty has been paid in full."

26 After section 62 insert—

"62 Return of licences suspended or revoked on immigration grounds

(1) Subsection (2) applies if—

- (a) under section 61 a district council suspend, revoke or refuse to renew the licence of a driver of a hackney carriage or a private

Part 1—Labour Market and Illegal Working **1.37**

hire vehicle on the ground mentioned in subsection (1)(aa) of that section, or

(b) under section 62 a district council suspend, revoke or refuse to renew an operator's licence on the ground mentioned in subsection (1)(ca) of that section.

(2) The person to whom the licence was granted must, within the period of 7 days beginning with the relevant day, return to the district council—

(a) the licence, and

(b) in the case of a licence of a driver of a hackney carriage or a private hire vehicle, the person's driver's badge.

(3) In subsection (2) "the relevant day" means—

(a) where the licence is suspended or revoked, the day on which the suspension or revocation takes effect;

(b) where the district council refuse to renew the licence, the day on which the licence expires as a result of the failure to renew it.

(4) A person who, without reasonable excuse, contravenes subsection (2) is guilty of an offence and liable on summary conviction—

(a) to a fine not exceeding level 3 on the standard scale, and

(b) in the case of a continuing offence, to a fine not exceeding ten pounds for each day during which an offence continues after conviction.

(5) The Secretary of State may by regulations made by statutory instrument amend the amount for the time being specified in subsection (4)(b).

(6) Regulations under subsection (5) may make transitional, transitory or saving provision.

(7) A statutory instrument containing regulations under subsection (5) may not be made unless a draft of the instrument has been laid before, and approved by a resolution of, each House of Parliament."

27 In section 77 (appeals) after subsection (3) insert—

"(4) On an appeal under this Part of this Act or an appeal under section 302 of the Act of 1936 as applied by this section, the court is not entitled to entertain any question as to whether—

(a) a person should be, or should have been, granted leave to enter or remain in the United Kingdom; or

(b) a person has, after the date of the decision being appealed against, been granted leave to enter or remain in the United Kingdom."

1.37 *A Guide to the Immigration Act 2016*

28 After section 79 insert—

"79A Persons disqualified by reason of immigration status

(1) For the purposes of this Part of this Act a person is disqualified by reason of the person's immigration status from carrying on a licensable activity if the person is subject to immigration control and—

    (a) the person has not been granted leave to enter or remain in the United Kingdom; or

    (b) the person's leave to enter or remain in the United Kingdom—

        (i) is invalid;

        (ii) has ceased to have effect (whether by reason of curtailment, revocation, cancellation, passage of time or otherwise); or

        (iii) is subject to a condition preventing the person from carrying on the licensable activity.

(2) Where a person is on immigration bail within the meaning of Part 1 of Schedule 10 to the Immigration Act 2016—

    (a) the person is to be treated for the purposes of this Part of this Act as if the person had been granted leave to enter the United Kingdom; but

    (b) any condition as to the person's work in the United Kingdom to which the person's immigration bail is subject is to be treated for those purposes as a condition of leave.

(3) For the purposes of this section a person is subject to immigration control if under the Immigration Act 1971 the person requires leave to enter or remain in the United Kingdom.

(4) For the purposes of this section a person carries on a licensable activity if the person—

    (a) drives a private hire vehicle;

    (b) operates a private hire vehicle; or

    (c) drives a hackney carriage.

79B Immigration offences and immigration penalties

(1) In this Part of this Act "immigration offence" means—

    (a) an offence under any of the Immigration Acts;

    (b) an offence under section 1 of the Criminal Attempts Act 1981 of attempting to commit an offence within paragraph (a); or

    (c) an offence under section 1 of the Criminal Law Act 1977 of conspiracy to commit an offence within paragraph (a).

Part 1—Labour Market and Illegal Working **1.37**

(2) In this Part of this Act "immigration penalty" means a penalty under—

    (a) section 15 of the Immigration, Asylum and Nationality Act 2006 ("the 2006 Act"); or

    (b) section 23 of the Immigration Act 2014 ("the 2014 Act").

(3) For the purposes of this Part of this Act a person to whom a penalty notice under section 15 of the 2006 Act has been given is not to be treated as having been required to pay an immigration penalty if—

    (a) the person is excused payment by virtue of section 15(3) of that Act; or

    (b) the penalty is cancelled by virtue of section 16 or 17 of that Act.

(4) For the purposes of this Part of this Act a person to whom a penalty notice under section 15 of the 2006 Act has been given is not to be treated as having been required to pay an immigration penalty until such time as—

    (a) the period for giving a notice of objection under section 16 of that Act has expired and the Secretary of State has considered any notice given within that period; and

    (b) if a notice of objection was given within that period, the period for appealing under section 17 of that Act has expired and any appeal brought within that period has been finally determined, abandoned or withdrawn.

(5) For the purposes of this Part of this Act a person to whom a penalty notice under section 23 of the 2014 Act has been given is not to be treated as having been required to pay an immigration penalty if—

    (a) the person is excused payment by virtue of section 24 of that Act; or

    (b) the penalty is cancelled by virtue of section 29 or 30 of that Act.

(6) For the purposes of this Part of this Act a person to whom a penalty notice under section 23 of the 2014 Act has been given is not to be treated as having been required to pay an immigration penalty until such time as—

    (a) the period for giving a notice of objection under section 29 of that Act has expired and the Secretary of State has considered any notice given within that period; and

    (b) if a notice of objection was given within that period, the period for appealing under section 30 of that Act has expired and any appeal brought within that period has been finally determined, abandoned or withdrawn."

1.37 *A Guide to the Immigration Act 2016*

Civic Government (Scotland) Act 1982 (c. 45)

29   The Civic Government (Scotland) Act 1982 is amended as follows.

30   In section 13 (taxi and private hire car driving licences) after subsection (3) insert—

"(3A)   A licensing authority shall not grant a licence to any person under this section unless the authority is satisfied that the person is not disqualified by reason of the person's immigration status from driving a taxi or private hire car.

(3B)   Section 13A makes provision for the purposes of subsection (3A) about the circumstances in which a person is disqualified by reason of the person's immigration status from driving a taxi or private hire car.

(3C)   In determining for the purposes of subsection (3A) whether a person is disqualified by reason of the person's immigration status from driving a taxi or private hire car, a licensing authority must have regard to any guidance issued by the Secretary of State."

31   After section 13 insert—

"13A Persons disqualified by reason of immigration status

(1)   For the purposes of section 13(3A) a person is disqualified by reason of the person's immigration status from driving a taxi or private hire car if the person is subject to immigration control and—

(a)   the person has not been granted leave to enter or remain in the United Kingdom, or

(b)   the person's leave to enter or remain in the United Kingdom—

(i)   is invalid,

(ii)   has ceased to have effect (whether by reason of curtailment, revocation, cancellation, passage of time or otherwise), or

(iii)   is subject to a condition preventing the person from driving a taxi or private hire car.

(2)   Where a person is on immigration bail within the meaning of Part 1 of Schedule 10 to the Immigration Act 2016—

(a)   the person is to be treated for the purposes of this section as if the person had been granted leave to enter the United Kingdom, but

(b)   any condition as to the person's work in the United Kingdom to which the person's immigration bail is subject is to be treated for those purposes as a condition of leave

(3)   For the purposes of this section a person is subject to immigration control if under the Immigration Act 1971 the person requires leave to enter or remain in the United Kingdom."

Part 1—Labour Market and Illegal Working **1.37**

32(1) Schedule 1 (licensing – further provisions as to the general system) is amended as follows.

(2) In paragraph 8 (duration of licences) in sub-paragraph (8) after "paragraphs" insert " 8A and ".

(3) After paragraph 8 insert—

"Taxi etc driving licences for persons subject to immigration control

8A(1) Sub-paragraph (2) applies if—

(a) a taxi driver's licence or private hire car driver's licence is to be granted to a person who has been granted leave to enter or remain in the United Kingdom for a limited period ("the leave period"),

(b) the person's leave has not been extended by virtue of section 3C of the Immigration Act 1971 (continuation of leave pending variation decision), and

(c) apart from sub-paragraph (2), the period for which the licence would have had effect would have ended after the end of the leave period.

(2) The licensing authority which grants the licence must specify a period in the licence as the period for which it has effect; and that period must end at or before the end of the leave period.

(3) Sub-paragraph (4) applies if—

(a) a taxi driver's licence or private hire car driver's licence is to be granted to a person who has been granted leave to enter or remain in the United Kingdom for a limited period, and

(b) the person's leave has been extended by virtue of section 3C of the Immigration Act 1971 (continuation of leave pending variation decision).

(4) The licensing authority which grants the licence must specify a period in the licence as the period for which it has effect; and that period must not exceed six months.

(5) A taxi driver's licence or private hire car driver's licence ceases to have effect if the person to whom it was granted becomes disqualified by reason of the person's immigration status from driving a taxi or private hire car.

(6) Section 13A (persons disqualified by reason of immigration status) applies for the purposes of sub-paragraph (5) as it applies for the purposes of section 13(3A).

(7) If a licence granted in accordance with sub-paragraph (2) or (4) expires, the person to whom it was granted must, within the period of 7 days beginning with the day after that on which it expired, return the licence to the licensing authority.

1.37 *A Guide to the Immigration Act 2016*

(8) If sub-paragraph (5) applies to a licence, the person to whom it was granted must, within the period of 7 days beginning with the day after the day on which the person first became disqualified, return the licence to the licensing authority which granted the licence.

(9) A person who, without reasonable excuse, contravenes sub-paragraph (7) or (8) is guilty of an offence and liable on summary conviction to a fine not exceeding level 3 on the standard scale.

(10) This paragraph applies in relation to the renewal of a licence as it applies in relation to the grant of a licence."

(4) In paragraph 11 (suspension and revocation of licences) after sub-paragraph (2) insert—

"(2A) A licensing authority may order the suspension or revocation of a taxi driver's licence or a private hire car driver's licence if the holder of the licence has, since its grant, been convicted of an immigration offence or required to pay an immigration penalty (see paragraph 20).

(2B) Sub-paragraph (2A) does not apply if—

(a) in a case where the holder of the licence has been convicted of an immigration offence, the conviction is a spent conviction within the meaning of the Rehabilitation of Offenders Act 1974, or

(b) in a case where the holder of the licence has been required to pay an immigration penalty—

(i) more than three years have elapsed since the date on which the penalty was imposed, and

(ii) the amount of the penalty has been paid in full."

(5) In paragraph 18 (appeals) after sub-paragraph (8) insert—

"(8A) On an appeal under this paragraph relating to a taxi driver's licence or a private hire car driver's licence, the sheriff is not entitled to entertain any question as to whether—

(a) a person should be, or should have been, granted leave to enter or remain in the United Kingdom, or

(b) a person has, after the date of the decision being appealed against, been granted leave to enter or remain in the United Kingdom."

(6) After paragraph 19 insert—

"20(1) In this Schedule "immigration offence" means an offence under any of the Immigration Acts.

(2) In this Schedule "immigration penalty" means a penalty under—

(a) section 15 of the Immigration, Asylum and Nationality Act 2006 ("the 2006 Act"), or

(b) section 23 of the Immigration Act 2014 ("the 2014 Act").

Part 1—Labour Market and Illegal Working **1.37**

(3) For the purposes of this Schedule a person to whom a penalty notice under section 15 of the 2006 Act has been given is not to be treated as having been required to pay an immigration penalty if—

(a) the person is excused payment by virtue of section 15(3) of that Act, or

(b) the penalty is cancelled by virtue of section 16 or 17 of that Act.

(4) For the purposes of this Schedule a person to whom a penalty notice under section 15 of the 2006 Act has been given is not to be treated as having been required to pay an immigration penalty until such time as—

(a) the period for giving a notice of objection under section 16 of that Act has expired and the Secretary of State has considered any notice given within that period, and

(b) if a notice of objection was given within that period, the period for appealing under section 17 of that Act has expired and any appeal brought within that period has been finally determined, abandoned or withdrawn.

(5) For the purposes of this Schedule a person to whom a penalty notice under section 23 of the 2014 Act has been given is not to be treated as having been required to pay an immigration penalty if—

(a) the person is excused payment by virtue of section 24 of that Act, or

(b) the penalty is cancelled by virtue of section 29 or 30 of that Act.

(6) For the purposes of this Schedule a person to whom a penalty notice under section 23 of the 2014 Act has been given is not to be treated as having been required to pay an immigration penalty until such time as—

(a) the period for giving a notice of objection under section 29 of that Act has expired and the Secretary of State has considered any notice given within that period, and

(b) if a notice of objection was given within that period, the period for appealing under section 30 of that Act has expired and any appeal brought within that period has been finally determined, abandoned or withdrawn."

Road Traffic Offenders (Northern Ireland) Order 1996 (SI 1996/1320 (NI 10))

33(1) Part 1 of Schedule 1 to the Road Traffic Offenders (Northern Ireland) Order 1996 (SI 1996/1320 (NI 10)) is amended as follows.

(2) After the entry relating to section 1(3) of the Taxis Act (Northern Ireland) 2008 insert—

"Section 2A(8) Failing to return an operator's licence Summarily Level 3 on the standard scale".

(3) After the entry relating to section 22(6) of the Taxis Act (Northern Ireland) 2008 insert—

"Section 23A(8) Failing to return an operator's licence Summarily Level 3 on the standard scale".

Private Hire Vehicles (London) Act 1998 (c. 34)

34 The Private Hire Vehicles (London) Act 1998 is amended as follows.

35 In section 1(1) (meaning of "private hire vehicle" etc)—

    (a) omit the "and" at the end of paragraph (a), and

    (b) at the end of paragraph (b) insert "; and

        (c) operate", in relation to a private hire vehicle, means to make provision for the invitation or acceptance of, or to accept, private hire bookings in relation to the vehicle."

36(1) Section 3 (London operator's licences) is amended as follows.

  (2) In subsection (3) for the "and" at the end of paragraph (a) substitute—

    "(aa) if the applicant is an individual, the applicant is not disqualified by reason of the applicant's immigration status from operating a private hire vehicle; and".

  (3) After subsection (3) insert—

    "(3A) In determining for the purposes of subsection (3) whether an applicant is disqualified by reason of the applicant's immigration status from operating a private hire vehicle, the licensing authority must have regard to any guidance issued by the Secretary of State."

  (4) In subsection (5) for "A" substitute " Subject to section 3A, a ".

37 After section 3 insert—

"3A London PHV operator's licences for persons subject to immigration control

    (1) Subsection (2) applies if—

        (a) a London PHV operator's licence is to be granted to a person who has been granted leave to enter or remain in the United Kingdom for a limited period ("the leave period");

        (b) the person's leave has not been extended by virtue of section 3C of the Immigration Act 1971 (continuation of leave pending variation decision); and

        (c) apart from subsection (2), the period for which the licence would have been granted would have ended after the end of the leave period.

    (2) The licence must be granted for a period which ends at or before the end of the leave period.

Part 1—Labour Market and Illegal Working **1.37**

(3) Subsection (4) applies if—

(a) a London PHV operator's licence is to be granted to a person who has been granted leave to enter or remain in the United Kingdom for a limited period; and

(b) the person's leave has been extended by virtue of section 3C of the Immigration Act 1971 (continuation of leave pending variation decision).

(4) The licence must be granted for a period which does not exceed six months.

(5) A London PHV operator's licence ceases to be in force if the person to whom it was granted becomes disqualified by reason of the person's immigration status from operating a private hire vehicle.

(6) If subsection (5) applies to a licence, the person to whom it was granted must, within the period of 7 days beginning with the day after the day on which the person first became disqualified, return it to the licensing authority.

(7) A person who, without reasonable excuse, contravenes subsection (6) is guilty of an offence and liable on summary conviction—

(a) to a fine not exceeding level 3 on the standard scale; and

(b) in the case of a continuing offence, to a fine not exceeding ten pounds for each day during which an offence continues after conviction.

(4) The Secretary of State may by regulations amend the amount for the time being specified in subsection (7)(b)."

38(1) Section 13 (London PHV driver's licences) is amended as follows.

(2) In subsection (2) for the "and" at the end of paragraph (a) substitute—

"(aa) the applicant is not disqualified by reason of the applicant's immigration status from driving a private hire vehicle; and".

(3) After subsection (2) insert—

"(2A) In determining for the purposes of subsection (2) whether an applicant is disqualified by reason of the applicant's immigration status from driving a private hire vehicle, the licensing authority must have regard to any guidance issued by the Secretary of State."

(4) In subsection (5) at the beginning of paragraph (c) insert "subject to section 13A,".

39 After section 13 insert—

"13A London PHV driver's licences for persons subject to immigration control

(1) Subsection (2) applies if—

(a) a London PHV driver's licence is to be granted to a person who has been granted leave to enter or remain in the United Kingdom for a limited period ("the leave period");

(b) the person's leave has not been extended by virtue of section 3C of the Immigration Act 1971 (continuation of leave pending variation decision); and

(c) apart from subsection (2), the period for which the licence would have been granted would have ended after the end of the leave period.

(2) The licence must be granted for a period which ends at or before the end of the leave period.

(3) Subsection (4) applies if—

(a) a London PHV driver's licence is to be granted to a person who has been granted leave to enter or remain in the United Kingdom for a limited period; and

(b) the person's leave has been extended by virtue of section 3C of the Immigration Act 1971 (continuation of leave pending variation decision).

(4) The licence must be granted for a period which does not exceed six months.

(5) A London PHV driver's licence ceases to be in force if the person to whom it was granted becomes disqualified by reason of the person's immigration status from driving a private hire vehicle.

(6) If subsection (5) applies to a licence, the person to whom it was granted must, within the period of 7 days beginning with the day after the day on which the person first became disqualified, return the licence and the person's driver's badge to the licensing authority.

(7) A person who, without reasonable excuse, contravenes subsection (6) is guilty of an offence and liable on summary conviction—

(a) to a fine not exceeding level 3 on the standard scale; and

(b) in the case of a continuing offence, to a fine not exceeding ten pounds for each day during which an offence continues after conviction.

(8) The Secretary of State may by regulations amend the amount for the time being specified in subsection (7)(b)."

40(1) Section 16 (power to suspend or revoke licences) is amended as follows.

(2) In subsection (2) before the "or" at the end of paragraph (a) insert—

"(aa) the licence holder has, since the grant of the licence, been convicted of an immigration offence or required to pay an immigration penalty;".

(3) After subsection (2) insert—

"(2A) Subsection (2)(aa) does not apply if—

(a) in a case where the licence holder has been convicted of an immigration offence, the conviction is a spent conviction

Part 1—Labour Market and Illegal Working **1.37**

within the meaning of the Rehabilitation of Offenders Act 1974, or

 (b) in a case where the licence holder has been required to pay an immigration penalty—

  (i) more than three years have elapsed since the date on which the penalty was imposed, and

  (ii) the amount of the penalty has been paid in full."

(4) In subsection (4) at the end of paragraph (a) insert—

"(aa) the licence holder has, since the grant of the licence, been convicted of an immigration offence or required to pay an immigration penalty;".

(5) After subsection (4) insert—

"(5) Subsection (4)(aa) does not apply if—

 (a) in a case where the licence holder has been convicted of an immigration offence, the conviction is a spent conviction within the meaning of the Rehabilitation of Offenders Act 1974, or

 (b) in a case where the licence holder has been required to pay an immigration penalty—

  (i) more than three years have elapsed since the date on which the penalty was imposed, and

  (ii) the amount of the penalty has been paid in full."

41 In section 25 (appeals) after subsection (7) insert—

"(8) On an appeal under this Act to the magistrates' court or the Crown Court, the court is not entitled to entertain any question as to whether—

 (a) a person should be, or should have been, granted leave to enter or remain in the United Kingdom; or

 (b) a person has, after the date of the decision being appealed against, been granted leave to enter or remain in the United Kingdom."

42(1) Section 32 (regulations) is amended as follows.

(2) In subsection (1) after "other than section" in the first place those words appear insert " 3A(8), 13A(8) or ".

(3) After subsection (2) insert—

"(2A) The power to make regulations conferred on the Secretary of State by section 3A(8) or 13A(8) is exercisable by statutory instrument.

(2B) A statutory instrument containing regulations under either of those sections may not be made unless a draft of the instrument has been laid before, and approved by a resolution of, each House of Parliament."

(4) In subsection (4) after "made under section" insert " 3A(8), 13A(8) or ".

43   After section 35 insert—

"35A Persons disqualified by reason of immigration status

(1) For the purposes of this Act a person is disqualified by reason of the person's immigration status from carrying on a licensable activity if the person is subject to immigration control and—

   (a) the person has not been granted leave to enter or remain in the United Kingdom; or

   (b) the person's leave to enter or remain in the United Kingdom—

      (i) is invalid;

      (ii) has ceased to have effect (whether by reason of curtailment, revocation, cancellation, passage of time or otherwise); or

      (iii) Is subject to a condition preventing the person from carrying on the licensable activity.

(2) Where a person is on immigration bail within the meaning of Part 1 of Schedule 10 to the Immigration Act 2016—

   (a) the person is to be treated for the purposes of this Act as if the person had been granted leave to enter the United Kingdom; but

   (b) any condition as to the person's work in the United Kingdom to which the person's immigration bail is subject is to be treated for those purposes as a condition of leave.

(3) For the purposes of this section a person is subject to immigration control if under the Immigration Act 1971 the person requires leave to enter or remain in the United Kingdom.

(4) For the purposes of this section a person carries on a licensable activity if the person—

   (a) operates a private hire vehicle; or

   (b) drives a private hire vehicle.

35B Immigration offences and immigration penalties

(1) In this Act "immigration offence" means—

   (a) an offence under any of the Immigration Acts;

   (b) an offence under section 1 of the Criminal Attempts Act 1981 of attempting to commit an offence within paragraph (a); or

   (c) an offence under section 1 of the Criminal Law Act 1977 of conspiracy to commit an offence within paragraph (a).

Part 1—Labour Market and Illegal Working 1.37

(2) In this Act "immigration penalty" means a penalty under—

(a) section 15 of the Immigration, Asylum and Nationality Act 2006 ("the 2006 Act"), or

(b) section 23 of the Immigration Act 2014 ("the 2014 Act").

(3) For the purposes of this Act a person to whom a penalty notice under section 15 of the 2006 Act has been given is not to be treated as having been required to pay an immigration penalty if—

(a) the person is excused payment by virtue of section 15(3) of that Act; or

(b) the penalty is cancelled by virtue of section 16 or 17 of that Act.

(4) For the purposes of this Act a person to whom a penalty notice under section 15 of the 2006 Act has been given is not to be treated as having been required to pay an immigration penalty until such time as—

(a) the period for giving a notice of objection under section 16 of that Act has expired and the Secretary of State has considered any notice given within that period; and

(b) if a notice of objection was given within that period, the period for appealing under section 17 of that Act has expired and any appeal brought within that period has been finally determined, abandoned or withdrawn.

(5) For the purposes of this Act a person to whom a penalty notice under section 23 of the 2014 Act has been given is not to be treated as having been required to pay an immigration penalty if—

(a) the person is excused payment by virtue of section 24 of that Act; or

(b) the penalty is cancelled by virtue of section 29 or 30 of that Act.

(6) For the purposes of this Act a person to whom a penalty notice under section 23 of the 2014 Act has been given is not to be treated as having been required to pay an immigration penalty until such time as—

(a) the period for giving a notice of objection under section 29 of that Act has expired and the Secretary of State has considered any notice given within that period; and

(b) if a notice of objection was given within that period, the period for appealing under section 30 of that Act has expired and any appeal brought within that period has been finally determined, abandoned or withdrawn."

44 In section 36 (interpretation) at the appropriate place insert—

""operate" has the meaning given in section 1(1);".

1.37 *A Guide to the Immigration Act 2016*

Taxis Act (Northern Ireland) 2008 (c. 4)

    45   The Taxis Act (Northern Ireland) 2008 is amended as follows.

    46(1)   Section 2 (operator's licences) is amended as follows.

      (2)   In subsection (4) for the "and" at the end of paragraph (a) substitute—

          "(aa) if the applicant is an individual, the applicant is not disqualified by reason of the applicant's immigration status from operating a taxi service; and".

      (3)   After subsection (4) insert—

          "(4A) In determining for the purposes of subsection (4) whether an applicant is disqualified by reason of the applicant's immigration status from operating a taxi service, the Department must have regard to any guidance issued by the Secretary of State."

      (4)   In subsection (7) for "An" substitute " Subject to section 2A, an ".

    47   After section 2 insert—

"2A Operator's licences for persons subject to immigration control

      (1)   Subsection (2) applies if—

          (a) an operator's licence is to be granted to a person who has been granted leave to enter or remain in the United Kingdom for a limited period ("the leave period"),

          (b) the person's leave has not been extended by virtue of section 3C of the Immigration Act 1971 (continuation of leave pending variation decision), and

          (c) apart from subsection (2), the period for which the licence would have been granted would have ended after the end of the leave period.

      (2)   The licence must be granted for a period which ends at or before the end of the leave period.

      (3)   Subsection (4) applies if—

          (a) an operator's licence is to be granted to a person who has been granted leave to enter or remain in the United Kingdom for a limited period, and

          (b) the person's leave has been extended by virtue of section 3C of the Immigration Act 1971 (continuation of leave pending variation decision).

      (4)   The licence must be granted for a period which does not exceed six months.

      (5)   An operator's licence ceases to be in force if the person to whom it was granted becomes disqualified by reason of the person's immigration status from operating a taxi service.

Part 1—Labour Market and Illegal Working **1.37**

(6) If a licence granted in accordance with subsection (2) or (4) expires, the person to whom it was granted must, within the period of 7 days beginning with the day after that on which it expired, return it to the Department.

(7) If subsection (5) applies to a licence, the person to whom it was granted must, within the period of 7 days beginning with the day after the day on which the person first became disqualified, return it to the Department.

(8) A person who, without reasonable excuse, contravenes subsection (6) or (7) is guilty of an offence."

48(1) Section 23 (taxi driver's licences) is amended as follows.

(2) In subsection (2) after paragraph (a) insert—

"(aa) the applicant is not disqualified by reason of the applicant's immigration status from driving a taxi;".

(3) After subsection (2) insert—

"(2A) In determining for the purposes of subsection (2) whether an applicant is disqualified by reason of the applicant's immigration status from driving a taxi, the Department must have regard to any guidance issued by the Secretary of State."

(4) In subsection (8) for "A" substitute " Subject to section 23A, a ".

49 After section 23 insert—

"23A Taxi driver's licences for persons subject to immigration control

(1) Subsection (2) applies if—

(a) a taxi driver's licence is to be granted to a person who has been granted leave to enter or remain in the United Kingdom for a limited period ("the leave period"),

(b) the person's leave has not been extended by virtue of section 3C of the Immigration Act 1971 (continuation of leave pending variation decision), and

(c) apart from subsection (2), the period for which the licence would have been granted would have ended after the end of the leave period.

(2) The licence must be granted for a period which ends at or before the end of the leave period.

(3) Subsection (4) applies if—

(a) a taxi driver's licence is to be granted to a person who has been granted leave to enter or remain in the United Kingdom for a limited period, and

(b) the person's leave has been extended by virtue of section 3C of the Immigration Act 1971 (continuation of leave pending variation decision).

1.37 *A Guide to the Immigration Act 2016*

    (4)   The licence must be granted for a period which does not exceed six months.

    (5)   A taxi driver's licence ceases to be in force if the person to whom it was granted becomes disqualified by reason of the person's immigration status from driving a taxi.

    (6)   If a licence granted in accordance with subsection (2) or (4) expires, the person to whom it was granted must, within the period of 7 days beginning with the day after that on which it expired, return to the Department—

        (a)   the licence,

        (b)   the person's driver's badge, and

        (c)   any other evidence of identification which the Department has issued under section 24.

    (7)   If subsection (5) applies to a licence, the person to whom it was granted must, within the period of 7 days beginning with the day after the day on which the person first became disqualified, return to the Department—

        (a)   the licence,

        (b)   the person's driver's badge, and

        (c)   any other evidence of identification which the Department has issued under section 24.

    (8)   A person who, without reasonable excuse, contravenes subsection (6) or (7) is guilty of an offence."

50(1)   Section 26 (power to suspend, revoke or curtail licences) is amended as follows.

    (2)   In subsection (2) before the "or" at the end of paragraph (a) insert—

    "(aa)   the licence holder has, since the grant of the licence, been convicted of an immigration offence or required to pay an immigration penalty;".

    (3)   After subsection (2) insert—

    "(2A)   Subsection (2)(aa) does not apply if—

        (a)   in a case where the licence holder has been convicted of an immigration offence, the conviction is a spent conviction within the meaning of the Rehabilitation of Offenders (Northern Ireland) Order 1978 (SI 1978/1908 (NI 27)), or

        (b)   in a case where the licence holder has been required to pay an immigration penalty—

            (i)   more than three years have elapsed since the date on which the penalty was imposed, and

            (ii)   the amount of the penalty has been paid in full."

(4) In subsection (6) before the "or" at the end of paragraph (a) insert—

    "(aa) the licence holder has, since the grant of the licence, been convicted of an immigration offence or required to pay an immigration penalty;".

(5) After subsection (6) insert—

    "(7) Subsection (6)(aa) does not apply if—

        (a) in a case where the licence holder has been convicted of an immigration offence, the conviction is a spent conviction within the meaning of the Rehabilitation of Offenders (Northern Ireland) Order 1978 (SI 1978/1908 (NI 27)), or

        (b) in a case where the licence holder has been required to pay an immigration penalty—

            (i) more than three years have elapsed since the date on which the penalty was imposed, and

            (ii) the amount of the penalty has been paid in full."

51   In section 32 (return of licences etc) after subsection (5) insert—

    "(5A) Subsection (4) does not apply if the licence was granted in accordance with section 2A(2) or (4) or 23A(2) or (4) (but see sections 2A(6) and 23A(6))."

52   In section 34 (appeals) after subsection (5) insert—

    "(6) On any appeal, the court is not entitled to entertain any question as to whether—

        (a) a person should be, or should have been, granted leave to enter or remain in the United Kingdom, or

        (b) a person has, after the date of the decision being appealed against, been granted leave to enter or remain in the United Kingdom."

53   After section 56 insert—

"56A Persons disqualified by reason of immigration status

(1) For the purposes of this Act a person is disqualified by reason of the person's immigration status from carrying on a licensable activity if the person is subject to immigration control and—

    (a) the person has not been granted leave to enter or remain in the United Kingdom, or

    (b) the person's leave to enter or remain in the United Kingdom—

        (i) is invalid,

        (ii) has ceased to have effect (whether by reason of curtailment, revocation, cancellation, passage of time or otherwise), or

        (iii) is subject to a condition preventing the person from carrying on the licensable activity.

(2) Where a person is on immigration bail within the meaning of Part 1 of Schedule 10 to the Immigration Act 2016—

(a) the person is to be treated for the purposes of this Part as if the person had been granted leave to enter the United Kingdom, but

(b) any condition as to the person's work in the United Kingdom to which the person's immigration bail is subject is to be treated for those purposes as a condition of leave.

(3) For the purposes of this section a person is subject to immigration control if under the Immigration Act 1971 the person requires leave to enter or remain in the United Kingdom.

(4) For the purposes of this section a person carries on a licensable activity if the person—

(a) operates a taxi service, or

(b) drives a taxi.

56B Immigration offences and immigration penalties

(1) In this Act "immigration offence" means—

(a) an offence under any of the Immigration Acts,

(b) an offence under Article 3 of the Criminal Attempts and Conspiracy (Northern Ireland) Order 1983 (SI 1983/1120 (NI 13)) of attempting to commit an offence within paragraph (a), or

(c) an offence under Article 9 of that Order of conspiracy to commit an offence within paragraph (a).

(2) In subsection (1)(a)—

(a) "the Immigration Acts" has the meaning given by section 61(2) of the UK Borders Act 2007, and

(b) the reference to an offence under any of the Immigration Acts includes an offence under section 133(5) of the Criminal Justice and Immigration Act 2008 (breach of condition imposed on designated person).

(3) In this Act "immigration penalty" means a penalty under—

(a) section 15 of the Immigration, Asylum and Nationality Act 2006 ("the 2006 Act"), or

(b) section 23 of the Immigration Act 2014 ("the 2014 Act").

(4) For the purposes of this Act a person to whom a penalty notice under section 15 of the 2006 Act has been given is not to be treated as having been required to pay an immigration penalty if—

(a) the person is excused payment by virtue of section 15(3) of that Act, or

Part 1—Labour Market and Illegal Working   1.37

(b)   the penalty is cancelled by virtue of section 16 or 17 of that Act.

(5)   For the purposes of this Act a person to whom a penalty notice under section 15 of the 2006 Act has been given is not to be treated as having been required to pay an immigration penalty until such time as—

(a)   the period for giving a notice of objection under section 16 of that Act has expired and the Secretary of State has considered any notice given within that period, and

(b)   if a notice of objection was given within that period, the period for appealing under section 17 of that Act has expired and any appeal brought within that period has been finally determined, abandoned or withdrawn.

(6)   For the purposes of this Act a person to whom a penalty notice under section 23 of the 2014 Act has been given is not to be treated as having been required to pay an immigration penalty if—

(a)   the person is excused payment by virtue of section 24 of that Act, or

(b)   the penalty is cancelled by virtue of section 29 or 30 of that Act.

(7)   For the purposes of this Act a person to whom a penalty notice under section 23 of the 2014 Act has been given is not to be treated as having been required to pay an immigration penalty until such time as—

(a)   the period for giving a notice of objection under section 29 of that Act has expired and the Secretary of State has considered any notice given within that period, and

(b)   if a notice of objection was given within that period, the period for appealing under section 30 of that Act has expired and any appeal brought within that period has been finally determined, abandoned or withdrawn."

Transitional provision

54(1)   Subject to sub-paragraph (2), an amendment made by any of paragraphs 3, 4, 7 to 12, 18 to 23, 30, 32(2) and (3), 36 to 39 and 46 to 49 does not apply in relation to an application for a licence made before the coming into force of that paragraph or a licence granted in response to such an application.

(2)   Sub-paragraph (1) does not prevent an amendment made by any of those paragraphs from applying in relation to—

(a)   an application for the renewal of a licence where that licence was granted before the coming into force of that paragraph, or

(b)   a licence renewed in response to such an application.

1.37 *A Guide to the Immigration Act 2016*

55(1) Subject to sub-paragraphs (2) and (3), an amendment made by any of paragraphs 13, 14, 24, 25, 32(4), 40 and 50 applies in relation to a licence granted before or after the coming into force of that paragraph.

(2) An amendment made by any of those paragraphs applies in relation to a conviction for an immigration offence only if the person in question has been convicted of that offence after the coming into force of that paragraph in respect of the person's conduct after that time.

(3) An amendment made by any of those paragraphs applies in relation to a requirement to pay an immigration penalty only if the person in question has been required to pay the penalty after the coming into force of that paragraph in respect of the person's conduct after that time.

56(1) Section 19(1) of the Plymouth City Council Act 1975 has effect in relation to the licence of a driver of a hackney carriage or private hire vehicle granted before the coming into force of paragraph 13 as if before the "or" at the end of paragraph (a) there were inserted—

"(ab) in the case of a refusal to renew a licence, that he is disqualified by reason of his immigration status from driving a hackney carriage or a private hire vehicle;".

(2) Section 20A(1)(a) of that Act has effect in relation to such a licence as if after "subsection (1)(aa)" there were inserted " or (ab) ".

(3) Section 20(1) of that Act has effect in relation to an operator's licence granted before the coming into force of paragraph 14 as if before the "or" at the end of paragraph (c) there were inserted—

"(cb) in the case of a refusal to renew a licence, that the operator is disqualified by reason of the operator's immigration status from operating a private hire vehicle;".

(4) Section 20A(1)(b) of that Act has effect in relation to such a licence as if after "subsection (1)(ca)" there were inserted " or (cb) ".

(5) Section 61(1) of the Local Government (Miscellaneous Provisions) Act 1976 has effect in relation to the licence of a driver of a hackney carriage or private hire vehicle granted before the coming into force of paragraph 24 as if before the "or" at the end of paragraph (a) there were inserted—

"(ab) in the case of a refusal to renew a licence, that he is disqualified by reason of his immigration status from driving a hackney carriage or a private hire vehicle;".

(6) Section 62A(1)(a) of that Act has effect in relation to such a licence as if after "subsection (1)(aa)" there were inserted " or (ab) ".

(7) Section 62(1) of that Act has effect in relation to an operator's licence granted before the coming into force of paragraph 25 as if before the "or" at the end of paragraph (c) there were inserted—

"(cb) in the case of a refusal to renew a licence, that the operator is disqualified by reason of the operator's immigration status from operating a private hire vehicle;".

Part 1—Labour Market and Illegal Working **1.37**

(8) Section 62A(1)(b) of that Act has effect in relation to such a licence as if after "subsection (1)(ca)" there were inserted " or (cb) ".

(9) Subsections (3A) to (3C) of section 13 of the Civic Government (Scotland) Act 1982 apply in relation to an application for the renewal of a taxi driver's or private hire car driver's licence granted before the coming into force of paragraph 30 as they apply in relation to an application for the grant of such a licence made after that time.

Commencement: 1 December 2016, The Immigration Act 2016 (Commencement No 2 and Transitional Provisions) Regulations 2016, SI 2016/1037. Pending the coming into force of s 61 and Schedule 10 *Immigration Bail*, transitional provision is made in SI 2016/1037 that when a person is on temporary admission or release from detention by virtue of para 21(1) of Schedule 2 to the Immigration Act 1971 (IA 1971), that person is to be treated for the purposes of s 8A of the Metropolitan Public Carriage Act 1869 (MPCA 1869); of the Plymouth City Council Act 1975 (PCCA 1975); of Part 2 of the Local Government (Miscellaneous Provisions) Act 1976 (LG(MP)A 1976), s 13A of the Civic Government (Scotland) Act 1982 (CG(S)A 1982); the Private Hire Vehicles (London) Act 1998 (PHV(L)A 1998) and Part 6 of the Taxis Act (Northern Ireland) 2008 (TA(NI) 2008) as if the person had been granted leave to enter the UK. Any restriction on employment imposed under para 21(2) of Schedule 2 to the IA 1971 is to be treated as a condition of leave.

Amends: London Hackney Carriages Act 1843 (LHCA 1843); MPCA 1869; PCCA 1975; LG(MP)A 1976; CG(S)A 1982; PHV(L)A 1998; TA(NI) 2008, as set out in Schedule 5.

Orders and Regulations: To amend the amount of the fine payable by a person who is guilty of an offence under the MPCA 1869 s 8A(8), MPCA 1869 s 8A(9). Such regulations are subject to the affirmative procedure in parliament, MPCA 1869 s 11 (Schedule 5, para 4); to amend the amount of the fine payable by a person who is guilty of an offence under the PCCA 1975, s 11A(9), PCCA 1975, s 11A(10). Such regulations are subject to the affirmative procedure in parliament, PCCA 1975, s 11A(11) (Schedule 5, para 9); to amend the amount of the fine payable by a person who is guilty of an offence under the PCCA 1975, s 13A(8), PCCA 1975, s 13A(9). Such regulations are subject to the affirmative procedure in parliament, PCCA 1975, s 13A(11) (Schedule 5, para 11); to amend the amount of the fine payable by a person who is guilty of an offence under the PCCA 1975, s 20A(4), PCCA 1975, s 20A(5). Such regulations are subject to the affirmative procedure in parliament, PCCA 1975, s 20A(7) (Schedule 5, para 15). To amend the amount of the fine payable by a person who is guilty of an offence under the LG(MP)A 1976, s 53A(9), LG(MP)A 1976, s 53A(10). Such regulations are subject to the affirmative procedure in parliament, LG(MP)A 1976, s 53A(12) (Schedule 5, para 20); to amend the amount of the fine payable by a person who is guilty of an offence under the LG(MP)A 1976, s 62A(4), LG(MP)A 1976,

1.37 *A Guide to the Immigration Act 2016*

s 62A(4), s 62A(5). Such regulations are subject to the affirmative procedure in parliament, LG(MP)A 1976, s 62A(7) (Schedule 5, para 26). To amend the amount of a fine payable under s 3A(7) of the PHV(L)A 1998, PHV(L)A 1998, s 3A(9) (Schedule 5, para 37). Such regulations are subject to the affirmative procedure in parliament, PHV(L)A 1998, s 32 (Schedule 5, para 42(3)); to amend the amount of a fine payable under s 13A(7) of the PHV(L)A 1998, PHV(L)A 1998, s 13A(8) (Schedule 5, para 39). Such regulations are subject to the affirmative procedure in parliament, PHV(L)A 1998, s 32 (Schedule 5, para 42(3)).

Guidance: Regard must be had to guidance issued by the Secretary of State to assist in determining whether a person is disqualified from driving by reason of their immigration status: PCCA 1975, s 17(1A) (Schedule 5 paragraph 12); LG(MP)A 1976, s 51(1ZA) (Schedule 5, para 18), s 55(1A) (Schedule 5, para 22) and s 59(1ZA) (Schedule 5, para 23); CG(S)A 1982, s 13(3C) (Schedule 5, para 30); PHV(L)A 1998, s 3(3A) (Schedule 5, para 36); TA(NI) 2008, s 2(4A) (Schedule 5, para 46(3)); PHV(L)A 1998, s 13A(7) (Schedule 5, para 39); TA(NI) 2008, s 23(2A) (Schedule 5, para 48). The Guidance issued is: *Guidance for licensing authorities to prevent illegal working in the taxi and private hire sector in England and Wales*, Home Office, 1 December 2016, available at: https://www.gov.uk/government/publications/licensing-authority-guide-to-right-to-work-checks; *Guidance for licensing authorities in Scotland to prevent illegal working in the taxi and private hire car sector*, Home Office, 1 December 2016. Available at: https://www.gov.uk/government/uploads/system/uploads/attachment_data/file/574067/Guidance-for-licensing-authorities-to-prevent-illegal-working-in-the-taxi-and-private-hire-car-sector-in-Scotland.pdf and *Guidance for the department for infrastructure to prevent illegal working in the taxi sector in Northern Ireland*, Home Office, 1 December 2016. Available at: https://www.gov.uk/government/uploads/system/uploads/attachment_data/file/574123/Guidance-for-licensing-authorities-to-prevent-illegal-working-in-the-taxi-and-private-hire-car-sector-in-Northern-Ireland.pdf

Definitions: To *carry on a licensable activity* for the purposes of the PCCA 1975, PCCA 1975, s 2A(5) (Schedule 5, para 6).

'the Council' for the purposes of the PCCA 1975, PCCA 1975, s 2(1);

Of when a person is *disqualified by reason of the person's immigration status*:

- from driving a hackney carriage for the purposes of s 8A of the MPCA 1869, MPCA 1869, s 8A(12) (Schedule 5, para 4);
- from carrying on a licensable activity for the purposes of the PCCA 1975, PCCA 1975, s 2A (Schedule 5, para 4);
- from carrying on a licensable activity for the purposes of Part II of the LG(MP)A 1976, s 79A;

- from driving a taxi or private hire vehicle for the purposes of the CG(S)A; CG(S)A, s13A(1);
- from carrying on a licensable activity for the purposes of the PHV(L)A 1998, PHV(L)A 1998, s35A(1);
- from carrying on a licensable activity for the purposes of the TA(NI) 2008, TA(NI) 2008, s 56A(1) (Schedule 5, para 53);

'driver's badge' in relation to the driver of a hackney carriage, any badge issued by the Council under bye-laws made under s 68 of the Town Police Clauses Act 1947 (TPCA 1947); in relation to the driver of a private hire vehicle, any badge issued under s 12 of the PCCA 1975, PCCA 1975, s 1(2); for the purposes of the LG(MP)A 1976, LG(MP)A 1976, s 80;

'driver's licence' for the purposes of the PCCA 1975, PCCA 1975, s 1(2): in relation to the driver of a hackney carriage, a licence under s 46 of the TPCA 1847 and, in relation to a private hire vehicle, a licence under the PCCA 1975, s 9; for the purposes of the LG(MP)A 1976, LG(MP)A 1976, s 80;

'hackney carriage' MPCA 1869, s 4; for the purposes of the PCCA 1975, PCCA 1975, s 2(1), specifying that the meaning is as in the TPCA 1847 but does not include a public service vehicle for which see s 117 of the Road Traffic Act 1960; LG(MP)A 1976, s 80;

'immigration offence' for the purposes of the PCCA 1975, PCCA 1975, s 2B(1) (Schedule 5, para 6); for the purposes of the LG(MP)A 1976, LG(MP)A 1976, s 80; for the purposes of the PHV(L)A 1998, PHV(L)A 1998, s 35B(1) (Schedule 5, para 43); for the purposes of the TA(NI) 2008, TA(NI) 2008, s 56B(1) (Schedule 5, para 53);

'Immigration Acts' UK Borders Act 2007, s 61(2);

'immigration penalty' for the purposes of the PCCA 1975, PCCA 1975, s 2B(2) (Schedule 5, para 6). For the circumstances in which a person is to be treated as having been required to pay a penalty see s 2B(3)–(6) of the 1975 Act; for the purposes of Schedule 1 to the CG(S)A 1982, CG(S)A 1982, Schedule 1, para 20(1) (Schedule 5, para 32); for the purposes of Schedule 1 to the CG(S)A 1982, CG(S)A 1982, Schedule 1, para 20(2) (Schedule 5, para 32); for the purposes of the PHV(L)A 1998, PHV(L)A 1998, s 35B(2) (Schedule 5, para 43);

'leave period' for the purposes of the PCCA 1975, PCCA 1975, s 11A(1) (Schedule 5, para 6); for the purposes of the LG(MP)A 1976, LG(MP)A 1976, s 53A(1)(a) (Schedule 5, para 20); PHV(L)A 1998, s 13A(1)(a) (Schedule 5, para 39); for the purposes of the TA(NI) 2008, TA(NI) 2008, s 56B(3);

'licensable activity' for the purposes of s 78(4) of the LG(MP)A 1976, LG(MP)A 1976, s 74(4) (Schedule 5, para 28); for the purposes of the PHV(L)A 1998, s 35, PHV(L)A 1998, s 35(4) (Schedule 5, para 43);

1.37 *A Guide to the Immigration Act 2016*

'London PHV operator's licence' PHV(L)A 1998, s 2(1);

A reference to *an offence under any of the Immigration Acts* for the purposes of the TA(NI) 2008 includes an offence under s 133(5) of the Criminal Justice and Immigration Act 2008, TA(NI) 2008, s 56B(2)(b);

'operate' for the purposes of the PHV(L)A 1998, PHV(L)A 1998, s1(1). See the Explanatory Notes to the Act at para 416, which explain that the definition is added because the word 'operate' is subsequently used in other amendments made to the Act;

'operator's licence' PCCA 1975, s 1(2): a licence under s 13 of that Act; LG(MP)A 1976, s 80; TA(NI) 2008 s 87;

'private hire vehicle' PCCA 1975, s 2(1); LG(MP)A 1976, s 80; CG(S)A s 23(1); PHV(L)A 1998, s 1(1) (see Schedule 5, para 35);

'relevant day' LG(MP)A 1976, s 62A(3);

'spent conviction' Rehabilitation of Offenders Act 1974;

'subject to immigration control' for the purposes of the PCCA 1975, PCCA 1975, s 2A(3) (Schedule 5, para 6); for the purposes of s 78B of the LG(MP)A 1976, the LG(MP)A 1976, s 78B(3) (Schedule 5, para 28); for the purposes of s 13A of the CG(S)A 1982, CG(S)A 1982, s 13A(3) (Schedule 5, para 31); for the purposes of the PHV(L)A 1998, s 35, PHV(L)A 1998, s 35(3) (Schedule 5, para 43); 'subject to immigration control' for the purposes of the MPCA 1969 s 8A, MPCA 1969 s 8A(14) (Schedule 5, para 4); for the purposes of the PCCA 1975 s 2A, PCCA 1975, s 2A(3) (Schedule 5, para 6); for the purposes of the LG(MP)A 1976, Part II, LG(MP)A 1976, s 79A(3) (Schedule 5, para 28); for the purposes of the CG(S)A 1982 s 13A, the CG(S)A 1982, s 13A(3) (Schedule 5, para 31); for the purposes of the PHV(L)A 1998, PHV(L)A 1998, s 35A(3) (Schedule 5, para 43); for the purposes of the TA(NI) s 56A, TA(NI) 2008, s 56A(3), (Schedule 5, para 53);

'taxi' CG(S)A 1982, s 23(1); TA(NI)2008, s 87;

'taxi driver's licence' TA(NI)2008 s 87;

Offences: Failure to return a licence which has expired or which ceases to be in force because the driver has been disqualified, to Transport for London, MPCA 1869 s 8A(8) (Schedule 5, para 4); failure to return a driver's licence which has expired or which ceases to be in force because the driver has been disqualified, to Plymouth City Council, PCCA 1975, s 11A(9) (Schedule 5, para 9); failure to return an operator's licence which has expired or which ceases to be in force because the operator has been disqualified, to Plymouth City Council, PCCA 1975, s 11A(8) (Schedule 5, para 11); failure to return a licence suspended or revoked on immigration grounds, PCCA 1975, s 20A(4) (Schedule 5, para 15); failure to return a driver's licence and badge when a licence has expired or ceased to be in force because the driver has been

Part 1—Labour Market and Illegal Working **1.37**

disqualified, LG(MP)A 1976, s 53A(9) (Schedule 5, para 20); failure to return a driver's licence and badge when a licence has been suspended or revoked on immigration grounds, LG(MP)A 1976 s 62(4) (Schedule 5, para 26); CG(S)A 1982, Schedule 1, para 8A(9) (Schedule 1, para 32); PHV(L)A 1998, s 3A(7) (Schedule 5, para, 37); PHV(L)A 1998, s 13A(7) (Schedule, 5 para 39); TA(NI) 2008, s 2A(8) (Schedule 5, para 47); failure to return a driver's licence and badge when a licence has expired or ceased to be in force because the driver has been disqualified TA(NI) 2008, s 23A(8) (Schedule 5, para 49).

Devolution: Extends across the whole of the UK with different provisions for different areas, including the City of Plymouth which has its own licensing regime.

The Bill was amended in the Public Bill Committee, without debate but with a vote,[1] to make provision, akin to that made in s 36, to make immigration status relevant to the licencing regime for private hire vehicles. At that stage, provision as to England, in the form of amendments to the MPCA 1869, the LG(MP)A 1976 and the PHV(L)A 1998 was set out on the face of the Bill, and there was power to make regulations for Scotland and Northern Ireland.[2]

The House of Lords Select Committee on the Constitution, in its seventh report of the session[3] invited the House of Lords to consider whether the differential legislative approaches adopted in respect of England and other parts of the UK in, inter alia, these provisions, and the difference in the degree of scrutiny that this implied, were appropriate. The Committee had invited the Government to justify its view that legislative consent motions from the devolved administrations were not required. The Committee said:

'15. The power to make regulations that have "a similar effect to" provisions contained in the Immigration Bill is vague. In its Delegated Powers Memorandum, the Government seeks to make the case for the use of secondary legislation in this context in the following way:

"In order to make the provisions relating to private hire etc. licensing effective in Scotland and Northern Ireland it will be necessary to make some detailed modifications of Scottish and Northern Ireland legislation. Also there are specific provisions in both Scotland and Northern Ireland which may require consequential amendments to make the scheme effective. This will require detailed input from the devolved administrations, which might itself be consequential on Parliament's views on the amendments relating to England and Wales. It is considered appropriate for the changes for Scotland and Northern Ireland to be made in secondary legislation, therefore, once Parliament has approved the main concept of the scheme with reference to the existing amendments suggested to private hire etc. licensing legislation."

1.37 *A Guide to the Immigration Act 2016*

16. It is not clear why, given that primary legislation has been deemed to be appropriate in England or England and Wales, secondary legislation is considered to be appropriate in Northern Ireland and Scotland (and, where relevant, Wales).'

While the approach of using secondary legislation for Scotland and Northern Ireland was preserved for s 36 it was perhaps harder to justify in the case of these provisions, which had been introduced during the passage of the Bill. The Rt Hon Lord Bates wrote to Lord Rosser on 12 January 2016 to introduce amendments to put the private hire licensing regime for the whole of the UK onto the face of the Bill. By that time the Government had realised that the picture was more complex than it had previously appreciated and that the City of Plymouth had its own licensing regime for private hire vehicles.

The provisions made for England and Wales were tidied up at the same time to ensure that the new criminal offence of not returning a lapsed licence applied equally to licences which had been revoked or had expired, and that the daily fine imposed when a licence was not returned could be amended by Parliament, by regulations subject to the affirmative procedure. This is now the case for all the private hire licensing regimes covered by the Bill.

The Rt Hon Lord Bates, introducing the amended provisions on 20 January 2016,[4] stated that the Government had worked with the Governments of Scotland and Northern Ireland to bring forward these amendments. In the event, in such a crowded timetable, the provisions received scant parliamentary scrutiny despite the number of new criminal offences which they introduce.

A person with no leave, or whose leave does not entitle them to work, may not be granted a private hire licence, be it a driver or operator's licence. Immigration bail will be treated as leave for these purposes. As to those with leave, a private hire licence must not be granted for a longer period than that for which a person has leave to remain. Those with leave extended by s 3C of the Immigration Act 1971 may be granted a licence for a maximum of six months. The check must be repeated at the time of each subsequent application to renew or extend a licence.

The Home Office guidance[5] is a simplified version of the right to work guidance issued for use by employers.[6] The checklist at Annex B to each set of guidance gives quite a detailed description of signs that a document is false.[7]

A list of documents that can be used to prove permission to work is set out in Annex A to each set of guidance. The guidance considers in some detail the situation of persons in the Tier 1 entrepreneur category; Tier 2; Tier 4 (students);[8] persons seeking asylum; EEA nationals and their third country family members. The guidance on EEA nationals is arguably misleading as it gives the impression that restrictions may extend more broadly than Croatian nationals.[9] It appears unlikely that a licensing authority would feel confident to issue a licence to a self-sufficient, or third country family member of, an EEA national given that they are asked to verify whether the individual has comprehensive sickness insurance, not to mention to consider documents such as marriage certificates establishing the relationship with the EEA national. The guidance states that a person's having comprehensive sickness insurance can be established by seeing a private medical insurance policy, a European Health Insurance Card or an S1, S2 or S3 form.[10] It does not indicate that, as set out on the Home Office form EEA(QP), a European Health Insurance Card can only be used as evidence of comprehensive sickness insurance if an individual makes a declaration that they do not intend to stay in the UK permanently.

Where, for example, a person has 3C leave[11] the guidance states that the licensing authority should get in touch with the Home Office's Evidence and Enquiry Unit for confirmation that the person has permission to work. It is suggested in the guidance that this will only be necessary where a licensing authority is confronted with a certificate of application or is satisfied that a person has leave extended by s 3C. The guidance provides that nonetheless it will be for the licensing authority to decide whether to issue a licence to such a person (for a maximum of six months), raising the spectre that licensing authorities will be reluctant to issue a licence in these circumstances.

An email address is provided in the guidance which licencing authorities can use to report a person who presents false documents to them to the Home Office. This the guidance encourages them to do. Licensing authorities are expressly asked, although they do not have to do so, to provide information to the Home Office in cases in which they refuse, suspend or revoke a licence on immigration grounds, so that action can be taken against the person. Licensing authorities will need to consider carefully their policies and whether they consider that they have the necessary consents to share this information. Licensing authorities are reminded in the guidance that s 55 of this Act has expanded the information gateways in s 20 of the Immigration and Asylum Act 1999. Reference is also made to s 20A of the 1999 Act inserted by s 55.[12] See notes to that section.

In turn, it appears to be envisaged that the Home Office provide information to the licensing authorities. Each set of guidance states 'We may provide you with information, or you may obtain information from other sources, which will cause you to wish to suspend or revoke a licence on the basis that the licence holder's immigration status has changed on or after 1 December 2016'. It is suggested in the guidance that in such circumstances the licensing authority may wish to consider whether the 'fit and proper person' test for the granting of a licence is met.

1.37 *A Guide to the Immigration Act 2016*

Where a licence holder's leave comes to an end, their licence automatically lapses. They must return their licence and their driver's badge to the licensing authority. A person who fails to do so within seven days, without reasonable cause, will be committing an offence and, on summary conviction, is liable to a fine and, in the case of a continuing offence, a daily fine for each day they fail to return the documents after conviction.

A person's being convicted of an immigration offence, or being required to pay a civil penalty under immigration laws, is grounds for suspending and revoking a licence. In those circumstances too, failure to return the licence is a criminal offence and a daily fine is payable after the first seven days.

The licensing authority must have regard to any guidance issued by the SSHD in making a decision about someone's immigration status.

While it is possible to appeal against the refusal or revocation of a licence, the court or Sheriff hearing that appeal is not entitled to consider whether the appellant should be granted leave, or has been granted leave subsequent to the decision being appealed.

The SSHD has power to increase the fines by regulations subject to the affirmative procedure. The Rt Hon Lord Bates in his letter of 12 January to Lord Rosser described the reason for this power as being 'to reflect changes in the value of money'. This power does not extend to fines in respect of Northern Ireland or Scotland. The Home Office said in its 12 January 2016 memorandum to the Delegated Powers Committee, 'Equivalent provision has not been made for Scotland and Northern Ireland because it was deemed preferable for the taxi and private hire provisions to remain consistent with other Scottish and Northern Irish licensing provisions'.[13]

Footnote 1 to the guidance states that outside London, these provisions also apply to pedi-cabs by virtue of being 'hackney carriages'. No source is given. For the meaning of 'hackney carriage' the LG(MP)A 1976 at s 80 adopts the definition in the TPCA 1847. That Act provides at s 38:

'38 What to be hackney carriages. Proviso as to stage coaches.

> Every wheeled carriage, whatever may be its form or construction, used in standing or plying for hire in any street within the prescribed distance, and every carriage standing upon any street within the prescribed distance, having thereon any numbered plate required by this or the special Act to be fixed upon a hackney carriage, or having thereon any plate resembling or intended to resemble any such plate as aforesaid, shall be deemed to be a hackney carriage within the meaning of this Act; and in all proceedings at law or otherwise

the term "hackney carriage" shall be sufficient to describe any such carriage:

Provision always, that no stage coach used for the purpose of standing or plying for passengers to be carried for hire at separate fares, and duly licensed for that purpose, and having thereon the proper numbered plates required by law to be placed on such stage coaches, shall be deemed to be a hackney carriage within the meaning of this Act.'

In respect of the MPCA 1869, the Explanatory Notes to the Bill provided that:

'The changes made to the 1869 Act are slightly different to those made to the Local Government (Miscellaneous Provisions) Act 1976 and the Private Hire Vehicles (London) Act 1998. This is because part of the taxi licencing regime in London is governed by secondary legislation rather than primary legislation (the London Cab Order 1934). The intention is that this order will be amended in line with these provisions.'[14]

This is repeated in the Home Office guidance which states that Transport for London will amend the London Cab Order 1934.[15] The guidance further identifies that the provisions also do not apply to booking offices in Scotland and states that the Civic Government (Scotland) Act 1982 (Licencing of Booking Offices) Order 2009[16] 'will be amended by a consequential Order made under the 2016 Act'.[17] Whether this is accurate appears questionable. The Order is a Scottish statutory instrument and to extend the provisions to booking offices in Scotland will require its amendment by the Scottish parliament. Section 92 *Transitional and Consequential Provision* of the Act gives the SSHD power to make transitional and consequential provision but does not confer similar powers on the Scottish Parliament. Nor does Schedule 5 confer such powers. Until an order is made, the provisions do not apply in respect of booking office applications in Scotland.

Paragraphs 54–56 of Schedule 5 make transitional provision so that the amendments, once in force, do not have retrospective effect. They do not prevent persons without lawful immigration status who already hold a licence from continuing to doing so.

Further transitional provision was made on commencement: the Immigration Act 2016 (Commencement No 2 and Transitional Provisions) Regulations 2016, SI 2016/1037 provide that pending the coming into force of s 61 and Schedule 10 *Immigration Bail*, when a person is on temporary admission or release from detention by virtue of para 21(1) of Schedule 2 to the IA 1971, that person is to be treated for the purposes of the Acts amended by Schedule 5 as if the person had been granted leave to enter the UK and any restriction

1.37 *A Guide to the Immigration Act 2016*

on their employment imposed under para 21(2) of Schedule 2 to the 1971 Act treated as a condition of leave. This mirrors the effect of the Immigration Act 2016 (Transitional Provision) Regulations 2016 (SI 2016/712) in respect of s 34. See the notes thereto and see also s 38 and Schedule 6 below.

---

1 Public Bill Committee, fifteenth sitting (morning) *Hansard* col 553, (17 November 2015).
2 See HC Bill 96, clause 11 and Schedule 2.
3 HL Select Committee on the Constitution, *Immigration Bill*, seventh report of session 2015–2016, HL Paper 75.
4 *Hansard* HL, col 798 (20 January 2016). *Guidance for licensing authorities to prevent illegal working in the taxi and private hire sector in England and Wales*, Home Office, 1 December 2016, at: https://www.gov.uk/government/publications/licensing-authority-guide-to-right-to-work-checks; *Guidance for licensing authorities in Scotland to prevent illegal working in the taxi and private hire car sector*, Home Office, 1 December 2016, at: https://www.gov.uk/government/uploads/system/uploads/attachment_data/file/574067/Guidance-for-licensing-authorities-to-prevent-illegal-working-in-the-taxi-and-private-hire-car-sector-in-Scotland.pdf and *Guidance for the department for infrastructure to prevent illegal working in the taxi sector in Northern Ireland*, Home Office, 1 December 2016, at: https://www.gov.uk/government/uploads/system/uploads/attachment_data/file/574123/Guidance-for-licensing-authorities-to-prevent-illegal-working-in-the-taxi-and-private-hire-car-sector-in-Northern-Ireland.pdf (accessed 14 December 2016).
5 *An employer's guide to acceptable right to work documents*, Home Office, May 2015 at: https://www.gov.uk/government/uploads/system/uploads/attachment_data/file/441957/employers_guide_to_acceptable_right_to_work_documents_v5.pdf (accessed 14 December 2016). A link to this is provided in the *Guidance for licencing authorities to prevent illegal working in the taxi and private hire sector in England and Wales* at p14. See also *An employer's guide to right to work checks*, Home Office, 12 July 2016. Available at: https://www.gov.uk/government/uploads/system/uploads/attachment_data/file/571001/Employer_s_guide_to_right_to_work_checks.pdf (accessed 14 December 2016).
6 Resembling the presentation *Guidance on examining identity documents*, National Document Fraud Unit, Home Office, 12 July 2016. Available at: https://www.gov.uk/government/publications/recognising-fraudulent-identity-documents (accessed 14 December 2016).
7 *Immigration Bill: supplementary delegated powers memorandum by the Home Office* (12 January 2016), para 58.
8 Students are restricted as to the number of hours per week they are permitted to work.
9 Who are in any event permitted to work as self-employed persons without restriction, see *Guidance for employers on preventing illegal working in the UK: Croatian nationals*, Home Office, July 2013. Available at: https://www.gov.uk/government/uploads/system/uploads/attachment_data/file/257339/guidance-croation.pdf (accessed 14 December 2016).
10 Form S1 is a certificate of entitlement to healthcare for persons who do not live in the country where they are insured. Examples are given on the Europa website, at: http://europa.eu/youreurope/citizens/work/social-security-forms/index_en.htm (accessed 14 December 2016). For example, posted workers, crossborder workers, pensioners, civil servants and their dependants. The S2 is an authorisation to obtain planned health treatment in another EU or EFTA country. The S3 is a certificate of entitlement to health care in a former country of employment. The Europa website gives the example of retired crossborder workers.
11 Under IA 1971, s 3C.
12 Para 395.
13 SI 2016/1346.
14 SI 2009/145.
15 *Guidance for licensing authorities in Scotland to prevent illegal working in the taxi and private hire car sector*, op cit, fn 4 therein.
16 SSI 2009/145.
17 *Guidance for licensing authorities in Scotland to prevent illegal working in the taxi and private hire car sector*, op cit, at 1.1.

ILLEGAL WORKING NOTICES AND ORDERS

SECTION 38—ILLEGAL WORKING CLOSURE NOTICES AND ILLEGAL WORKING COMPLIANCE ORDERS, AND SCHEDULE 6—ILLEGAL WORKING CLOSURE NOTICES AND ILLEGAL WORKING COMPLIANCE ORDERS

> **Summary**
>
> These provisions set up a new regime of illegal working closure notices and illegal working compliance orders. Immigration officers are given powers to issue notices to close premises where an employer at the premises is employing persons without permission to work, if certain conditions, pertaining to past compliance, are met. The officer is then required to apply to a court for an illegal working compliance order extending the period for which the premises will be closed.

1.38

38 Illegal working closure notices and illegal working compliance orders

Schedule 6 (illegal working closure notices and illegal working compliance orders) has effect.

Schedule 6

Illegal working closure notices and illegal working compliance orders

Illegal working closure notices

1(1)　An immigration officer of at least the rank of chief immigration officer may issue an illegal working closure notice in respect of premises if satisfied on reasonable grounds that the conditions in sub-paragraphs (3) and (6) are met.

(2)　An illegal working closure notice is a notice which prohibits, for a period specified in the notice—

　　(a)　access to the premises other than by a person who habitually lives on the premises, except where authorised in writing by an immigration officer;

　　(b)　paid or voluntary work being performed on the premises, except where so authorised.

1.38 *A Guide to the Immigration Act 2016*

(3) The condition in this sub-paragraph is that an employer operating at the premises is employing a person over the age of 16 and subject to immigration control—

   (a) who has not been granted leave to enter or remain in the United Kingdom, or

   (b) whose leave to enter or remain in the United Kingdom—

      (i) is invalid,

      (ii) has ceased to have effect (whether by reason of curtailment, revocation, cancellation, passage of time or otherwise), or

      (iii) is subject to a condition preventing the person from accepting the employment.

(4) Where a person is on immigration bail within the meaning of Part 1 of Schedule 10—

   (a) the person is to be treated for the purposes of sub-paragraph (3) as if the person had been granted leave to enter the United Kingdom, but

   (b) any condition as to the person's work in the United Kingdom to which the person's immigration bail is subject is to be treated for those purposes as a condition of leave.

(5) A person falling within sub-paragraph (3) is referred to in this Schedule as an "illegal worker".

(6) The condition in this sub-paragraph is that the employer, or a connected person in relation to the employer—

   (a) has been convicted of an offence under section 21 of the Immigration, Asylum and Nationality Act 2006 ("the 2006 Act"),

   (b) has, during the period of three years ending with the date on which the illegal working closure notice is issued, been required to pay a penalty under section 15 of the 2006 Act, or

   (c) has at any time been required to pay such a penalty and failed to pay it.

(7) Sub-paragraph (6)(a) does not apply in relation to a conviction which is a spent conviction for the purposes of the Rehabilitation of Offenders Act 1974 or the Rehabilitation of Offenders (Northern Ireland) Order 1978 (S.I. 1978/1908 (N.I. 27)).

(8) For the purposes of sub-paragraph (6)(b) and (c)—

   (a) a person to whom a penalty notice under section 15 of the 2006 Act has been given is not to be treated as having been required to pay the penalty if—

      (i) the person is excused payment by virtue of section 15(3) of that Act, or

Part 1—Labour Market and Illegal Working **1.38**

- (ii) the penalty is cancelled by virtue of section 16 or 17 of that Act;

(b) a person to whom such a notice has been given is not to be treated as having been required to pay the penalty until such time as—

- (i) the period for giving a notice of objection under section 16 of the 2006 Act has expired and the Secretary of State has considered any notice given within that period, and
- (ii) if a notice of objection was given within that period, the period for appealing under section 17 of that Act has expired and any appeal brought within that period has been finally determined, abandoned or withdrawn.

(9) For the purposes of sub-paragraph (6), a person is a connected person in relation to an employer if—

(a) where the employer is a body corporate, the person is—

- (i) a director, manager or secretary of the body corporate,
- (ii) purporting to act as a director, manager or secretary of the body corporate, or
- (iii) if the affairs of the body corporate are managed by its members, a member of the body corporate;

(b) where the employer is a partnership (whether or not a limited partnership), the person is a partner or purporting to act as a partner;

(c) where the employer is an individual, the person is—

- (i) a body corporate of which the individual has at any time been a director, manager or secretary,
- (ii) a body corporate in relation to which the individual has at any time purported to act as a director, manager or secretary,
- (iii) body corporate whose affairs are managed by its members and the individual has at any time been a member of the body corporate,
- (iv) a partnership (whether or not a limited partnership) in which the individual has at any time been a partner or in relation to which the individual has at any time purported to act as a partner.

(10) An illegal working closure notice may not be issued if the employer shows in relation to the employment of each illegal worker that if a penalty notice were given under section 15 of the 2006 Act the employer would be excused under subsection (3) of that section from paying the penalty.

(11) An illegal working closure notice may be issued only if reasonable efforts have been made to inform—

(a) people who live on the premises (whether habitually or not), and

1.38 *A Guide to the Immigration Act 2016*

       (b)   any person who has an interest in the premises,

that the notice is going to be issued.

(12)   Before issuing an illegal working closure notice the immigration officer must ensure that any person the officer thinks appropriate has been consulted.

(13)   The Secretary of State may by regulations amend sub-paragraph (1) to change the rank specified in that sub-paragraph.

2(1)   An illegal working closure notice must—

       (a)   identify the premises;

       (b)   explain the effect of the notice;

       (c)   state that failure to comply with the notice is an offence;

       (d)   state that an application will be made under paragraph 5 for an illegal working compliance order;

       (e)   specify when and where the application will be heard;

       (f)   explain the effect of an illegal working compliance order.

(2)   The maximum period that may be specified in an illegal working closure notice is 24 hours unless sub-paragraph (3) applies.

(3)   The maximum period is 48 hours if the notice is issued by an immigration officer of at least the rank of immigration inspector.

(4)   In calculating when the period of 48 hours ends, Christmas Day is to be disregarded.

(5)   The period specified in an illegal working closure notice to which sub-paragraph (3) does not apply may be extended by up to 24 hours if an extension notice is issued by an officer of at least the rank of immigration inspector.

(6)   An extension notice is a notice which—

       (a)   identifies the illegal working closure notice to which it relates, and

       (b)   specifies the period of the extension.

(7)   The Secretary of State may by regulations amend sub-paragraph (3) or sub-paragraph (5) to change the rank specified in that sub-paragraph.

Cancellation of illegal working closure notices

3(1)   An immigration officer may by the issue of a cancellation notice cancel an illegal working closure notice if—

       (a)   the immigration officer considers that the condition in paragraph 1(3) or (6) is not met, or

       (b)   the employer shows in relation to the employment of each illegal worker that if a penalty notice were given under section 15 of the

Part 1—Labour Market and Illegal Working **1.38**

2006 Act the employer would be excused under subsection (3) of that section from paying the penalty.

(2) A cancellation notice may be issued only—

    (a) by an immigration officer of at least the rank of the immigration officer who issued the illegal working closure notice, or

    (b) where the illegal working closure notice has been extended by an extension notice, by an immigration officer of at least the rank of the immigration officer who issued the extension notice.

Service of notices

4(1) A notice under paragraph 1, 2 or 3 must be served by an immigration officer.

(2) The immigration officer must if possible—

    (a) fix a copy of the notice to at least one prominent place on the premises,

    (b) fix a copy of the notice to each normal means of access to the premises,

    (c) fix a copy of the notice to any outbuildings that appear to the immigration officer to be used with or as part of the premises,

    (d) give a copy of the notice to at least one person who appears to the immigration officer to have control of or responsibility for the premises,

    (e) give a copy of the notice to the people who live on the premises and to any person who does not live there but was informed (under paragraph 1(11)) that the notice was going to be issued.

(3) If the immigration officer reasonably believes, at the time of serving the notice, that there are persons occupying another part of the building or other structure in which the premises are situated whose access to that part will be impeded if an illegal working compliance order is made under paragraph 5, the immigration officer must also if possible serve the notice on those persons.

(4) The immigration officer may enter any premises, using reasonable force if necessary, for the purposes of complying with sub-paragraph (2)(a).

Illegal working compliance orders

5(1) Whenever an illegal working closure notice is issued an application must be made to the court for an illegal working compliance order (unless the notice has been cancelled under paragraph 3).

(2) An application for an illegal working compliance order must be made by an immigration officer.

(3) The application must be heard by the court not later than 48 hours after service of the illegal working closure notice.

(4) In calculating when the period of 48 hours ends, Christmas Day is to be disregarded.

1.38 *A Guide to the Immigration Act 2016*

(5) The court may make an illegal working compliance order in respect of premises if it is satisfied, on the balance of probabilities—

   (a) that the conditions in paragraph 1(3) and (6) are met, and

   (b) that it is necessary to make the illegal working compliance order to prevent an employer operating at the premises from employing an illegal worker.

(6) An illegal working compliance order may—

   (a) prohibit or restrict access to the premises;

   (b) require a person specified in the order to carry out, at such times as may be so specified, such checks relating to the right to work as may be prescribed by the Secretary of State in regulations;

   (c) require a person specified in the order to produce to an immigration officer, at such times and such places as may be so specified, such documents relating to the right to work as may be prescribed by the Secretary of State in regulations;

   (d) specify the times at which and the circumstances in which an immigration officer may enter the premises to carry out such investigations or inspections as may be specified in the order;

   (e) make such other provision as the court considers appropriate.

(7) Different provisions in an illegal working compliance order may have effect for different periods.

(8) The maximum period for which an illegal working compliance order or any provision in it may have effect is 12 months.

(9) Provision included in an illegal working compliance order which prohibits or restricts access may make such provision—

   (a) in relation to all persons, all persons except those specified, or all persons except those of a specified description;

   (b) having effect at all times, or at all times except those specified;

   (c) having effect in all circumstances, or in all circumstances except those specified.

(10) An illegal working compliance order, or any provision of it, may—

   (a) be made in respect of the whole or any part of the premises;

   (b) include provision about access to a part of the building or structure of which the premises form part.

(11) The court must notify the relevant licensing authority if it makes an illegal working compliance order in relation to premises in England and Wales in respect of which a premises licence is in force.

Part 1—Labour Market and Illegal Working **1.38**

Illegal working compliance orders: adjournment of hearing

6(1) This paragraph applies where an application has been made under paragraph 5 for an illegal working compliance order.

(2) The court may adjourn the hearing of the application for a period of not more than 14 days to enable any person who has an interest in the premises to show why an illegal working compliance order should not be made.

(3) If the court adjourns the hearing it may order that the illegal working closure notice continues in force until the end of the period of adjournment.

Extension of illegal working compliance orders

7(1) An immigration officer may apply to the court for an extension (or further extension) of the period for which any provision of an illegal working compliance order is in force.

(2) The court may grant an application under this paragraph only if it is satisfied, on the balance of probabilities, that it is necessary to grant it to prevent an employer operating at the premises from employing an illegal worker.

(3) Where an application is made under this section, the court may issue a summons directed to—

    (a) any person on whom the illegal working closure notice was served under paragraph 4, or

    (b) any other person who appears to the court to have an interest in the premises,

requiring the person to appear before the court to respond to the application.

(4) If a summons is issued, a notice stating the date, time and place of the hearing of the application must be served on the persons to whom the summons is directed.

(5) No application may be granted under this paragraph such that an illegal working compliance order, or any provision in it—

    (a) is extended for a period exceeding 6 months, or

    (b) is in force for a period exceeding 24 months in total.

Variation or discharge of illegal working compliance orders

8(1) An application may be made to the court under this paragraph—

    (a) by an immigration officer for an illegal working compliance order to be varied or discharged,

    (b) by a person on whom the illegal working closure notice was served under paragraph 4, or by any other person who has an interest in the premises, for an illegal working compliance order to be varied or discharged.

1.38 *A Guide to the Immigration Act 2016*

(2) Where an application is made under this paragraph, the court may issue a summons directed to—

(a) an immigration officer,

(b) any person on whom the illegal working closure notice was served under paragraph 4, or

(c) any other person who appears to the court to have an interest in the premises,

requiring the person to appear before the court to respond to the application.

(3) If a summons is issued, a notice stating the date, time and place of the hearing of the application must be served on the persons to whom the summons is directed.

(4) The court may not discharge an illegal working compliance order unless it is satisfied, on the balance of probabilities, that it is no longer necessary to prevent an employer operating at the premises from employing an illegal worker.

Notice and orders: appeals

9(1) An appeal against a decision—

(a) to make, extend or vary an illegal working compliance order;

(b) not to discharge an illegal working compliance order;

(c) to order that an illegal working closure notice continues in force,

may be made by a person on whom the illegal working closure notice was served under paragraph 4, or any other person who has an interest in the premises.

(2) An appeal against a decision—

(a) not to make an illegal working compliance order;

(b) not to extend a provision of an illegal working compliance order, or not to vary such an order, made on the application of an immigration officer;

(c) to vary or discharge an illegal working compliance order;

(d) not to order that an illegal working closure notice continues in force,

may be made by an immigration officer.

(3) An appeal under this paragraph—

(a) if it is in relation to premises in England and Wales or Northern Ireland, is to the Crown Court,

(b) if it is in relation to premises in Scotland, is to the sheriff appeal court.

(4) An appeal under this paragraph must be made within the period of 21 days beginning with the date of the decision to which it relates.

Part 1—Labour Market and Illegal Working **1.38**

(5) On an appeal under this paragraph the court may make whatever order it thinks appropriate.

(6) The court must notify the relevant licensing authority if it makes an illegal working compliance order in relation to premises in England and Wales in respect of which a premises licence is in force.

Notices and orders: enforcement

10(1) Where access to premises is prohibited or restricted by virtue of an illegal working closure notice or an illegal working compliance order an immigration officer or a constable may enter the premises and do anything necessary to secure the premises against entry.

(2) A person acting under sub-paragraph (1) may use reasonable force.

(3) An immigration officer or a constable, together with any person acting under that person's supervision, may also enter such premises to carry out essential maintenance or repairs.

Notices and orders: offences

11(1) A person who without reasonable excuse remains on or enters premises in contravention of an illegal working closure notice commits an offence.

(2) A person who without reasonable excuse contravenes an illegal working compliance order commits an offence.

(3) A person who without reasonable excuse obstructs a person acting under paragraph 4 or paragraph 10 commits an offence.

(4) A person guilty of an offence under this paragraph is liable on summary conviction—

(a) in England and Wales, to imprisonment for a term not exceeding 51 weeks, to a fine or to both;

(b) in Scotland, to imprisonment for a term not exceeding 12 months, to a fine not exceeding level 5 on the standard scale or to both;

(c) in Northern Ireland, to imprisonment for a term not exceeding 6 months, to a fine not exceeding level 5 on the standard scale or to both.

(5) In relation to an offence committed before section 281(5) of the Criminal Justice Act 2003 comes into force, the reference in sub-paragraph (4)(a) to 51 weeks is to be read as a reference to 6 months.

Access to other premises

12(1) Where—

(a) access to premises is prohibited or restricted by a provision of an illegal working compliance order,

(b) those premises are part of a building or structure, and

(c) there is another part of that building or structure that is not subject to the prohibition or restriction,

an occupier or owner of that other part may apply to the court for an order under this paragraph.

(2) Notice of an application under this paragraph must be given to—

(a) whatever immigration officer the court thinks appropriate;

(b) each person on whom the illegal working closure notice was served under paragraph 4,

(c) any other person who has an interest in the premises.

(3) On an application under this paragraph the court may make whatever order it thinks appropriate in relation to access to any part of the building or structure mentioned in sub-paragraph (1).

(4) For the purposes of sub-paragraph (3), it does not matter whether provision has been made under paragraph 5(10)(b).

Reimbursement of costs

13(1) Where the Secretary of State incurs expenditure for the purpose of clearing, securing or maintaining premises in respect of which an illegal working compliance order is in force, the Secretary of State may apply to the court for an order under this paragraph.

(2) On an application under this paragraph the court may make whatever order it thinks appropriate for the reimbursement (in full or in part) by the owner or occupier of the premises of the expenditure mentioned in sub-paragraph (1).

(3) An application for an order under this paragraph may not be heard unless it is made before the end of the period of 3 months starting with the day on which the illegal working compliance order ceases to have effect.

(4) An order under this paragraph may be made only against a person who has been served with the application for the order.

Exemption from liability

14(1) Each of the following—

(a) the Secretary of State,

(b) an immigration officer,

(c) a police officer,

(d) the chief officer of police under whose direction or control a police officer acts,

is not liable for damages in proceedings for judicial review or the tort of negligence or misfeasance in public office, arising out of anything done or omitted to be done by the person in the exercise or purposed exercise of a power under this Schedule.

Part 1—Labour Market and Illegal Working **1.38**

(2) Sub-paragraph (1) does not apply to an act or omission shown to have been in bad faith.

(3) Sub-paragraph (1) does not apply so as to prevent an award of damages made in respect of an act or omission on the ground that the act or omission was unlawful by virtue of section 6(1) of the Human Rights Act 1998.

(4) This paragraph does not affect any other exemption from liability (whether at common law or otherwise).

Compensation

15(1) A person who claims to have incurred financial loss in consequence of an illegal working closure notice, other than one cancelled under paragraph 3(1)(b), may apply to the court for compensation.

(2) An application under this paragraph may not be heard unless it is made before the end of the period of 3 months starting with the day on which the notice ceases to have effect.

(3) On an application under this paragraph the court may order the payment of compensation out of money provided by Parliament if it is satisfied—

    (a) that at the time the notice was issued, the condition in paragraph 1(3) or (6) was not met;

    (b) that the applicant has incurred financial loss in consequence of the notice; and

    (c) that having regard to all the circumstances it is appropriate to order payment of compensation in respect of that loss.

Guidance

16(1) The Secretary of State may issue guidance about the exercise of functions under this Schedule.

(2) The Secretary of State may revise any guidance issued under this paragraph.

(3) Before issuing or revising guidance under this paragraph the Secretary of State must consult—

    (a) persons whom the Secretary of State considers to represent the views of immigration officers and of chief officers of police, and

    (b) such other persons as the Secretary of State considers appropriate.

(4) The Secretary of State must arrange for any guidance issued or revised under this paragraph to be published.

Interpretation

17(1) In this Schedule—

"court", except where the context otherwise requires, means—

    (a) in relation to premises in England and Wales or Northern Ireland, the magistrates' court;

1.38 A Guide to the Immigration Act 2016

      (b)   in relation to premises in Scotland, the sheriff court;

"owner" in relation to premises, means—

      (a)   a person (other than a mortgagee not in possession) entitled to dispose of the fee simple of the premises, whether in possession or in reversion;

      (b)   a person who holds or is entitled to the rents and profits of the premises under a lease that (when granted) was for a term of not less than 3 years;

"person who has an interest", in relation to premises, includes—

      (a)   the owner;

      (b)   any person with control of or responsibility for the premises;

      (c)   any person who otherwise occupies the premises;

"premises" includes—

      (a)   any land, vehicle, vessel or other place (whether enclosed or not);

      (b)   any outbuildings that are, or are used as, part of premises;

"premises licence" has the meaning given by section 11 of the Licensing Act 2003;

"relevant licensing authority" has the meaning given by section 12 of that Act.

(2)   In this Schedule—

      (a)   a reference to employment is to employment under a contract of service or apprenticeship, whether express or implied and whether oral or written;

      (b)   a person is subject to immigration control if under the Immigration Act 1971 the person requires leave to enter or remain in the United Kingdom.

Amendment of Licensing Act 2003

18   After section 167(1) of the Licensing Act 2003 insert—

"(1A) This section also applies where a court has made an illegal working compliance order under Schedule 6 to the Immigration Act 2016 and the relevant licensing authority has accordingly received a notice under that Schedule."

Commencement: 1 December 2016, The Immigration Act 2016 (Commencement No 2 and Transitional Provisions) Regulations 2016, SI 2016/1037. Pending the coming into force of s 61 and Schedule 10 *Immigration Bail*, transitional provision is made in SI 2016/1037 that when a person is on temporary admission or release from detention by virtue of paragraph 21(1) of Schedule 2 to the IA 1971, that person is to be treated for the purposes of para 1(3) of Schedule 6 to this Act as if the person had been granted leave to enter the UK. Any restriction on employment imposed under paragraph 21(2) of Schedule 2 to the 1971 Act is to be treated as a condition of leave. The effect of this is that the person employing them does not, by so doing, fulfil a condition under para 1(1) of Schedule 6 to this Act for the imposition of an illegal working closure notice.

Amends: Licensing Act 2003, inserting a new subs 167(1A).

Orders and Regulations: Subparas 5(6)(b) and 5(6)(c) of Schedule 6 provide for the Secretary of State to prescribe right to work checks and the production of documents relating to the right to work. The Illegal Working Compliance Order Regulations 2016, SI 2016/1058 have been made and came into effect on 1 December 2016. Sub-para (13) permits the Secretary of State to amend the minimum rank of immigration officer able to issue the closure notice (Schedule 6, para 13). These regulations are subject to the affirmative procedure (s 93(1)(l)). The Secretary of State can also amend the minimum rank of immigration officer who can extend the period of closure for up to 24 hours (Schedule 6, para 2(7)). These regulations are also subject to the affirmative procedure (s 93(1)(m)).

Guidance: The Secretary of State has power to issue guidance about the exercise of functions under Schedule 5 (Schedule 5, para 16(1)) and issued *Illegal working closure notices and compliance orders: Guidance for frontline professionals*, on 1 December 2016, available at: https://www.gov.uk/government/publications/illegal-working-closure-notice-and-compliance-orders

Definitions:

'connected person' in relation to an employer for the purposes of Schedule 6, para 6, Schedule 6, para 9;

'court' Schedule 6, para 17(1);

A reference to *employment* in the schedule is to employment under a contract of service or apprenticeship whether express or implied, oral or written (Schedule 6, para 17(2)(a));

'extension notice' Schedule 6, para 2(6);

'illegal working closure notice' a notice prohibiting access to premises, other than by a person who habitually lives on them except where authorised in writing by an immigration officer, and prohibiting paid or voluntary work on the premises except when so authorised, Schedule 6, para 1(2));

'immigration bail' Schedule 10, Part 1;

'illegal worker' a person falling within the definition in Schedule 3, para 3: over 16, without valid leave or with leave subject to a condition preventing employment. Persons on immigration bail are treated as though they had been

1.38 *A Guide to the Immigration Act 2016*

granted leave (Schedule 3, para 4). See the note on 'Commencement' above and the text below for details of transitional provisions;

'owner' Schedule 6, para 17(1);

'person who has an interest' Schedule 6, para 17(1);

'premises': includes land, vehicles, vessels or any 'other place', includes outbuildings, Schedule 6, para 17(1);

'premises licence' Licensing Act 2003 (LA 2003), s 11 (Schedule 6, para 17(1));

'relevant licensing authority' LA 2003, s 11 (Schedule 6, para 17(1));

'spent conviction' Rehabilitation of Offenders Act 1974;

A person is *'subject to immigration control'* if, under the Immigration Act 1971, the person requires leave to enter or remain in the United Kingdom (Schedule 6, para 17(2)(b)).

Offences: Schedule 6, para 11(1), committed by a person who without reasonable excuse remains on or enters premises in contravention of an illegal working closure notice. Schedule 6, para 11(2), committed by a person who, without reasonable excuse, contravenes an illegal working compliance order. Schedule 6, para 11(3), committed by a person who, without reasonable excuse, obstructs a person serving or enforcing a notice.

Devolution: Applies throughout UK.

The provisions give immigration officers of the rank of Chief Immigration Officer or above powers to close an employer's premises where 'satisfied on reasonable grounds' that the employer is employing an 'illegal worker' as defined and that the employer or a person connected to them has been required to pay a civil penalty in the last three years; has an outstanding civil penalty (from any date); has been convicted of the offence of knowingly employing an 'illegal worker'; or (under the amendments effected by s 35 of this Act) of the offence of employing a person whom they have reasonable cause to believe is not entitled to work (Schedule 6, para 1(6)). Spent convictions are not taken into account.

The officer closes the premises by issuing an illegal working closure notice. The effect of such a notice is that entry to the premises is prohibited, as is paid or voluntary work on the premises (Schedule 6, para 1(2)). The closure notice does not apply to a person who lives on the premises or who is authorised in writing by an immigration officer to access the premises. The initial closure can be for up to 48 hours (Schedule 6 para 2(3)). The immigration officer must then apply to the magistrates' or sheriff court which can extend this for up to 14 days to give the court time to decide on the application for an illegal working compliance order (Schedule 6, para 5).

An illegal working compliance order can prohibit or restrict access to the premises for up to two years (12 months with a possibility of extension under Schedule 6, para 7). The order may prohibit or restrict access for all persons, for all persons except those specified, or for all persons except those of a specified description. It may have effect at all times and in all circumstances or specify exceptions (Schedule 6, para 5(9)). The court must be satisfied on the balance of probabilities of the same matters of which the officer had to be satisfied in issuing the closure notice. The court issuing an order must also be satisfied that the order is necessary to prevent the employer from employing an illegal worker.

Illegal working closure notices and compliance orders are thus a form of anti-social behaviour order for employers. They are civil orders backed by a criminal offence, committed by a person who contravenes them (Schedule 6 para 11).

Guidance issued under Schedule 6 para 16(1): *Illegal working closure notices and compliance orders: Guidance for frontline professionals*[1] states that the statutory requirements set the lowest threshold for issuing a notice but that:

'The intention is to use a closure notice in the most serious cases, where previous civil penalties and convictions have failed to change employer behaviour and, usually, where a significant proportion of workers on the premises at the time of the visit are illegal.... In practice, a closure notice would generally be served ... where a high proportion of the workforce encountered is working illegally and where it is considered that this course of action is required to prevent continuing illegal working. As a matter of policy, it would also be used as a tool to provide an appropriate response where such behaviour has been combined with "phoenixism". This is where a business has closed to evade sanctions, re-opened in a new identity and continued with the non compliant activity.'

The guidance makes clear that in addition to the issue of the notice, consideration will also be given to civil penalties or prosecution for illegal working and other immigration offences.

A notice may not be issued where the employer can show that they have complied with prescribed requirements so that they have an excuse under s 15(3) of the Immigration and Nationality Act 2006 for employing the worker.

The guidance states that no more than three calendar days should elapse between an illegal working operation and the service of the closure notice. The notice can close the premises for a maximum of 48 hours (Schedule 6 para 2(3)). See also para 2(2). The guidance provides that, if it will not be possible to apply to the court for a compliance order within the statutory

1.38 *A Guide to the Immigration Act 2016*

maximum of 48 hours, then an immigration officer should not serve the closure notice but should serve a notice of intention to issue an illegal working closure notice instead.[2]

The court must hear the application for an illegal working compliance order no later than 48 hours after service of the closure notice (Schedule 6, para 5(3)). This excludes Christmas Day (Schedule 6, para 5(4)). The compliance order may be made in respect of the whole or part of the premises and may include provision about access to a part of the building or structure of which the premises forms a part (Schedule 6, para 5(10)). The court may issue a summons directed to any person on whom the closure notice was served or any person who appears to the court to have an interest in the premises, requiring that person to appear before the court to respond to the application (Schedule 6, para 7(3)).

The compliance order may require a person specified in the order to carry out, at such times as may be specified, right to work checks prescribed in the Illegal Working Compliance Order Regulations 2016;[3] to produce right to work documents as prescribed in those regulations; to specify the times at which, and the circumstances in which, an immigration officer may enter the premises to carry out investigations or inspections specified in the order, and may make such other provision as the court considers appropriate. Pro forma of the relevant notices are annexed to the regulations. The Home Office guidance states that an immigration officer:

> 'will usually only request that the court orders the continued prohibited or restricted access to the premises (a) where it is considered that to continue business activity from that location would probably involve the use of illegal workers and where other measures, such as imposing right to work checks, are unlikely to prevent this.'

Where an illegal working compliance order requires a person to carry out checks relating to the right to work in accordance with the regulations, the person must either see documents[4] which demonstrate that the employee has a right to work, as set out in Schedule 1 to the Illegal Working Compliance Order Regulations 2016, or must obtain a positive verification notice from the Home Office employer checking service[5] confirming this right. It is specified that nothing permits the employer to retain documents produced by an employee for the purposes of the regulations for longer than is necessary to comply with their obligations to produce documents to an immigration officer.[6] These obligations[7] pertain to producing copies of the documents not the originals.

The guidance provides that:

> 'an immigration officer will normally request that the court orders the employer to undertake right to work checks on all employees employed

on or out of these premises, and for follow-up compliance inspections by an immigration officer to take place. These inspection visits will not require a separate warrant. The immigration officer will request to be given access to the premises during the usual operating hours, or any other time they have reasonable grounds for believing that work is being carried out at the premises, and specify the frequency of visits.'[8]

The guidance makes suggestions as to terms an immigration officer might ask to be included in the order. These include for copies of right to work documents to be held on the premises or for checks and inspections to include other premises within the ownership of the same employer. The legal basis for such a request is not spelt out, and is unclear.

The person on whom the closure notice was served, or any other person who has an interest in the premises, can appeal against the decision to make, extend, vary or not to discharge the order and an immigration officer can appeal against a decision not to make or vary an order, or against a decision to vary or discharge it, or not to order that it continue in force (Schedule 6, para 9). Where the premises are in England, Wales and Northern Ireland, the appeal is to the Crown Court. In Scotland, the appeal is to the Sheriff Appeal Court (Schedule 6, para 9(3)). An appeal must be made within 21 days of the date of decision (Schedule 6, para 9(3)).

In a tie-in with s 36 of, and Schedule 4 to, this Act, where a court makes an illegal working compliance order for premises in respect of which there is a licence to sell alcohol or late night refreshments in England and Wales, it must notify the relevant licensing authority (Schedule 6, para 9(6)). The licensing authority must review the licence in accordance with the LA 2003, s 167(1) (Schedule 6, para 18). The guidance provides that an immigration officer should inform the court where the premises in England and Wales are licensed (under the LA 2003) and provide information necessary for the court to notify the relevant licensing authority if it makes an illegal working compliance order.

A person who, without reasonable excuse, remains on, or enters, premises in contravention of a notice or order commits an offence (Schedule 6, paras 11(1)–(2)) as does a person who without reasonable excuse obstructs an immigration officer entering premises to serve or to enforce a notice (Schedule 6, para 11(3)). A person who is guilty of this offence is liable on summary conviction, in England and Wales, to imprisonment for a term not exceeding six months, to a fine, or both; in Scotland, to imprisonment for a term not exceeding 12 months, to a fine not exceeding level five on the standard scale, or to both; and in Northern Ireland, to imprisonment for a term not exceeding six months, to a fine not exceeding level five on the standard scale, or to both (Schedule 9, para 11(4)).[9]

1.38 *A Guide to the Immigration Act 2016*

The guidance states that 'Arrest for the offence of breaching a notice or order will generally be by a constable' and that where an inspection is undertaken by a Criminal Financial Investigations officer, in England and Wales, they may effect an arrest for breach of a compliance order using the Police and Criminal Evidence Act 1984 (Application to immigration officers and designated customs officials in England and Wales) Order 2013'.[10]

Under a compliance order, an immigration officer or constable may enter the premises, using reasonable force, to do what is necessary to secure them against entry and may enter the premises, with persons acting under their supervision, to carry out essential maintenance or repairs (Schedule 6, para 10).

An immigration officer, the person on whom the closure notice was served or any person with an interest in the premises can apply to the court to vary, to extend, or to further extend, a compliance order (Schedule 6, para 8). Upon such application the compliance order cannot be extended for more than six months, or so that the compliance order is in force for a total period that exceeds 24 months (Schedule 6, para 7). The court may not discharge an order unless it is satisfied, on the balance of probabilities, that the order is no longer necessary to prevent an employer operating at the premises from employing an illegal worker (Schedule 6, para 8(4)).

The guidance states:

> 'If the business changes ownership it will be necessary to review the compliance order. The order will not be affected where the legal entity remains the same. Depending on the terms of the order, a new employer will probably wish to apply to the court to vary or discharge the order. Immigration officers may ask for the court to impose a requirement on the employer to inform them that they are operating from another premises.'[11]

The Secretary of State (SSHD), immigration officers, police officers, or the chief police officer under whose control a police officer acts, are immune from liability for damages in judicial review proceedings, negligence or misfeasance in public office for anything done in the exercise of powers under the schedule, unless they have acted in bad faith, or the suit is for damages for breaches of human rights (Schedule 6, para 14). It is anticipated that challenges under the Human Rights Act 1998, s 6(1) will thus be based on Article 1 of Protocol 1 to the ECHR which protects the right to peaceful enjoyment of possessions.

The SSHD may make an application for reimbursement of costs in relation to clearing, securing or maintaining premises subject to a compliance order within three months of the notice ceasing to have effect (Schedule 6, para 13). If the court orders such reimbursement it may do so in full or in part (Schedule 6, para 13(2)).

A person who claims to have suffered financial loss as a result of an illegal working closure notice may apply to the court for compensation within three months of the notice ceasing to have effect (Schedule 6, para 15). The court can order compensation if, at the time when the order was applied, the test for its application was not met (Schedule 6, para 15(3)(a)) and, having regard to all the circumstances, the court considers it appropriate to order the payment of compensation in respect of loss incurred (Schedule 6, para 15(3)(a)).

Pending the coming into force of s 61 and Schedule 10 *Immigration Bail*, the Immigration Act 2016 (Commencement No 2 and Transitional Provisions) Regulations 2016, SI 2016/1037 provide that when a person is on temporary admission or release from detention by virtue of para 21(1) of Schedule 2 to the Immigration Act 1971, that person is to be treated for the purposes of para 1(3) of Schedule 6 to this Act as if the person had been granted leave to enter the UK. Any restriction on employment imposed under para 21(2) of Schedule 2 to the 1971 Act is to be treated as a condition of leave. The effect of this is that the person employing them does not, by so doing, fulfil a condition under para 1(1) of Schedule 6 to this Act for the imposition of an illegal working closure notice. These provisions mirror the effect of the Immigration Act 2016 (Transitional Provision) Regulations 2016, SI 2016/712 in respect of s 34 and of the Immigration Act 2016 (Commencement No 2 and Transitional Provisions) Regulations 2016, SI 2016/1037 in respect of s 37 and Schedule 5.

---

1 *Illegal working closure notices and compliance orders: Guidance for frontline professionals*, 1 December 2016. Available at: https://www.gov.uk/government/publications/illegal-working-closure-notice-and-compliance-orders at 3 (accessed 22 December 2016).
2 The form of the notice is at Annex A to the guidance.
3 SI 2016/1058.
4 SI 2016/1058, reg 4.
5 SI 2016/1058, reg 5.
6 SI 2016/1058, reg 10.
7 SI 2016/1058, regs 6 and 8.
8 *Illegal working closure notices and compliance orders: Guidance for frontline professionals*, op. cit.
9 See also Schedule 11, para 11(5) in respect of offences committed before the coming into force of s 281(5) of the Criminal Justice Act 2003.
10 SI 2013/1052.
11 *Illegal working closure notices and compliance orders: Guidance for frontline professionals*, op. cit.

Part 2—Access to Services

RESIDENTIAL TENANCIES

The Immigration Act 2014

2.1 The 'right to rent' scheme, introduced under the Immigration Act 2014 (IA 2014) requires landlords and landladies to check immigration status documents and not rent to people disqualified from renting by their immigration status and who are subject to the scheme. The scheme was originally piloted in the West Midlands and extended across England on 1 February 2016.[1] The Government intends to extend the scheme to the whole of the UK but has not yet done so.[2]

Nobody is disqualified from occupying premises unless they are doing so under a 'residential tenancy agreement' as defined by the IA 2014, s 20. These are tenancies (or leases, licences, sub-leases, sub-tenancies or agreements for the same s 20(3)) granting a right of occupation of premises for residential use (s 20(2)(a)). The scheme therefore covers paying lodgers as well as those renting from landlords or landladies more formally. The scheme only applies where a person is living in the property as their only or main home (s 20(4)) and so does not apply to holiday lets. The agreement must involve the payment of any sum in the nature of rent, whether at a market rate or not (s 20(2)(b), s 20(5)) in order to fall within the scheme. Situations where a person is living in someone's home or residential property without paying rent are therefore not included within the right to rent scheme.

Certain types of residential tenancy agreements are excluded from the scheme (IA 2014, s 20(2)). These are set out in Schedule 3 to the IA 2014 and, in brief, include those granting rights of occupation in social housing (paras 1–2), a care home (para 3), a hospital or hospice (para 4), other accommodation relating to healthcare provision (para 5), a hostel or refuge (para 6), accommodation from or involving local authorities (para 7), accommodation provided by virtue of immigration provisions (para 8), a mobile home (para 9), tied accommodation (para 10), specific types of student accommodation (paras 11–12), or under a long lease (para 13).

The scheme is only applied to adult tenants (see s 22(1)). Thus, the immigration status of a child will not be the cause of any liability of any landlord or landlady for a civil penalty.

2.1 A Guide to the Immigration Act 2016

IA 2014, s 21 sets out when a person is disqualified from occupying premises under a residential tenancy agreement. A person is disqualified if they are not a 'relevant national' (s 21(1)(a)) and do not have a 'right to rent in relation to the premises' (s 21(1)(b)). A 'relevant national' is defined as a British citizen, EEA or Swiss national (s 21(5)). A person does not have a right to rent in relation to specific premises if they require leave to enter or remain but do not have it (s 21(2)(a)), or if their leave is subject to a condition preventing them from occupying the premises (s 21(2)(b)).

Section 21(4) identifies those with a 'limited right to rent'. These are persons who have been granted leave to enter or remain in the UK for a limited period (s 21(4)(a)) or those who are not relevant nationals and are entitled to enter or remain in the UK by virtue of an enforceable EU right or of any provision made under s 2(2) of the European Communities Act 1972 (ECA 1972) (s 21(4)(b)). Whereas EEA nationals are not affected directly by the right to rent scheme, their non-EEA family members may be, having only a limited right to rent.

Under IA 2014, s 21(3) the Secretary of State (SSHD) is empowered to grant someone permission to rent despite the application of s 21(2). Home Office guidance on the right to rent indicates the circumstances in which the SSHD will normally grant permission to rent.[3] These include cases of asylum seekers with an outstanding application or appeal, judicial review, or further submissions; individuals with an outstanding application or appeal on medical grounds under Article 3 of the European Convention on Human Rights (ECHR); those granted bail by an immigration tribunal or the courts; those for whom a decision has been made that there are reasonable grounds to believe they are a victim of modern slavery and those with an outstanding application for discretionary leave following recognition as a victim of modern slavery; families co-operating with the Home Office family returns process; those complying with the Home Office process for voluntary departure; and, exceptionally, in other circumstances where it would assist the Home Office better to progress their case; where the migrant is considered vulnerable, or unable to make their own decisions; or where not to grant permission to rent would breach human rights. Individuals granted permission to rent may face difficulties being able to rent in practice because of the approach adopted by the Home Office to confirming their permission to rent.

During the passage of the IA 2016, the Government resisted amendments that would have made provision for persons seeking asylum who have sufficient funds to rent privately and therefore do not need or qualify for Home Office asylum support accommodation. Because they are on temporary admission, or on 'immigration bail' when Schedule 10 of the IA 2016 comes into force, they have no right to rent under the IA 2014. Immigration bail is not treated as leave to enter for the purposes of these provisions, in contrast with the provisions on illegal working in ss 34–35. Though the Home Office grants permission to rent under IA 2014, s 21(3), the current Home Office approach is that the landlord or landlady should ring the helpline, at which point they will be told that they can rent to the person seeking asylum. This is unsatisfactory: a landlord or landlady is unlikely to pick up the phone in these circumstances.

Landlords and landladies must not rent to a person disqualified to rent (IA 2014, s 22(1)) and may face a civil penalty if they do so (s 23(1)) of up to £3000 (s 23(2)). They must therefore check immigration status documents to ensure they do not rent to a person who is disqualified from renting and must conduct further checks at a later date where a person only has a limited right to rent to ensure that they continue to have the right to rent.

The statutory scheme refers to 'pre-grant contravention' and 'post-grant contravention' (see IA 2014, s 22(10)). This is intended to distinguish between cases where a landlord or landlady grants a right to occupy the relevant premises to someone who requires but does not have leave at the time of renting and cases where they rent to a person who did have leave at the time of renting but later ceases to have leave.

Where the landlord or landlady responsible for the premises changes, liability for any contravention of the provisions will fall upon the landlord or landlady at the time of the contravention: the original landlord or landlady in the case of the pre-grant contravention and whoever is the landlord or landlady when the contravention occurs in a post-grant contravention (s 23(3)). For other legal purposes, ie those not part of this civil penalty scheme, contraventions of the scheme do not have the effect of invalidating or rendering unenforceable the agreement into which the relevant parties have entered (s 22(9)).

The scheme is not to be applied to tenancy agreements existing when the 2014 Act came into effect for the particular area. This follows from subsections 22(4)–(5) of that Act, each of which makes provision as to when there is a contravention for the purposes of the scheme. In each case the issue is 'disqualification' or having a 'limited right to rent' under the scheme at the time of entry into the relevant tenancy agreement.

The Home Office published an evaluation of the operation of the right to rent scheme in the West Midlands' pilot areas.[4] The Minister described this as 'extensive'[5] but the report identifies that sample sizes were low in some areas and that findings should be seen as indicative rather than definitive.[6] Only 68 tenants were interviewed and 88 per cent of these were students. The Minister suggested that the evaluation found 'no hard evidence of discrimination',[7]

2.1 A Guide to the Immigration Act 2016

but it reported that a higher proportion of black and minority ethnic 'mystery shoppers' were asked to provide more information during rental enquiries[8] and recorded comments from landlords and landladies in focus groups indicating potential for discrimination.[9] The Joint Council for the Welfare of Immigrants (JCWI) conducted its own evaluation.[10] It found that landlords or landladies found the checks and the *Code of Practice for Landlords* and the *Code of Practice on Avoiding Discrimination* confusing and difficult to understand and undertook checks incorrectly. JCWI found evidence that landlords and landladies are prepared to discriminate against those with complicated immigration statuses who cannot immediately provide documents. The Residential Landlords Association and the Scottish Federation of Housing Associations both expressed concerns that the provisions would result in direct and indirect discrimination.[11]

Under the IA 2014, landlords and landladies and their agents risked fines of up to £3,000 per tenant. The IA 2016 moves the scheme onto a new footing: one backed by criminal sanctions and creating new powers of eviction. The extent of the scheme under the IA 2016 mirrors that under the 2014 Act: the same premises are exempt.

---

1 IA 2014 (Commencement No. 6) Order 2016, SI 2016/11 (C.2).
2 See for example, *Immigration Act 2016: Factsheet – Residential Tenancies (sections 39–42)*, Home Office, July 2016, available at: https://www.gov.uk/government/publications/immigration-bill-part-2-access-to-services (accessed 14 December 2016).
3 *A short guide on right to rent*, Home Office, 14 June 2016 at https://www.gov.uk/government/publications/landlords-right-to-rent-checks-guide (accessed 14 December 2016).
4 *Evaluation of right to rent scheme, Full evaluation report of phase one*, Research report 83, Home Office, 20 October 2015. Available at: https://www.gov.uk/government/publications/evaluation-of-the-right-to-rent-scheme (accessed 14 December 2016).
5 Rt Hon James Brokenshire MP, Immigration Bill 2015/16, House of Commons Report Stage, *Hansard* Col 207 (1 Decemer 2015). Available at: http://www.publications.parliament.uk/pa/cm201516/cmhansrd/cm151201/debtext/151201-0002.htm (accessed 14 December 2016).
6 Home Office, *Evaluation of right to rent scheme*, above, at p 11.
7 Ibid.
8 Home Office, *Evaluation of right to rent scheme*, above, at p 23.
9 Home Office, *Evaluation of right to rent scheme*, above, at p 24.
10 *'No passport equals no home': An Independent evaluation of the right to rent scheme*, Joint Council for the Welfare of Immigrants, 3 September 2015. Available at: https://www.jcwi.org.uk/sites/jcwi/files/documets/No%20Passport%20Equals%20No%20Home%20Right%20to%20Rent%20Independent%20Evaluation_0.pdf (accessed 14 December 2016).
11 See, for example, the oral evidence of the Residential Landlords Association to the House of Commons, Immigration Bill, Public Bill Committee, 2nd sitting (afternoon), *Hansard* cols 37–88 (20 October 2015). Available at: http://www.publications.parliament.uk/pa/cm201516/cmpublic/immigration/151020/pm/151020s01.htm (accessed 14 December 2016) and the written evidence of the Scottish Federation of Housing Associations to the Public Bill Committee, IB06. Available at: http://www.publications.parliament.uk/pa/cm201516/cmpublic/immigration/memo/ib06.htm (accessed 14 December 2016).

Commencement and transitional provisions

2.2 The new criminal offences under IA 2014, s 33A(1)–(6) inserted by s 39, and the new routes to eviction under new ss 33D–33E of that Act, inserted by s 40, apply whether the tenancy was entered into before or after the sections come into force: what matters is that after the sections come into force the tenant does not have a right to rent and that the person renting knows or has reasonable cause to believe that they do not. The offences contained in the new IA 2014, s 33A(10)–(11) which apply to landlords and landladies, and s 33B, which applies to agents, will only apply in relation to a contravention of the right to rent scheme which occurs after these measures come into force. The protection is illusory for landladies and landlords because those who escape prosecution under s 33A(10)–(11) will be liable to prosecution under s 33A(1)–(6) and s 33. It is, however, of some comfort to agents who will only be caught by their actions after the Act comes into effect.

The provisions on eviction must be read with those on offences. A landlord or landlady who receives notification from the SSHD that the tenant has no right to rent, not only can move to evict but arguably will have to do so, since they run the risk of being prosecuted for the criminal offence if they do not.

Other legislative measures: eligibility for housing and homelessness services

2.3 Changes to the Immigration Rules had produced the unintended consequence that certain young people and households with children given leave to remain in the UK permitting recourse to public funds were made ineligible for local authority housing and homelessness services.

The problem arose because the Allocation of Housing and Homelessness (Eligibility) (England) Regulations 2006, SI 2006/1294 and similar regulations in Wales, Scotland and Northern Ireland, identifying who is eligible for housing and homelessness services, had not kept pace with changes to the Immigration Rules. The regulations identify those granted leave to remain 'outside the rules', or 'discretionary leave', with recourse to public funds among the categories of eligibility for housing and homelessness services. However, since the Supreme Court ruled in *Alvi*[1] that the Home Office should limit its use of discretionary policies for granting leave and that leave should generally be given within the Rules, the Home Office began bringing a range of cases within the Rules. These included unaccompanied children, now granted 'UASC leave' under para 352ZC of the Immigration Rules if there are no adequate arrangements for their care and reception in their country of origin, those granted leave to remain on the basis of their rights to private or family life under the ECHR, Article 8 and others. This had the consequence, however, that they no longer fell within the classes

2.3 *A Guide to the Immigration Act 2016*

of cases covered by the housing and homelessness regulations, leaving many children, young people and families ineligible for housing and homelessness assistance even though they were able to claim public funds.

It was accepted that there had been an oversight and understood in 2013 that the Department for Communities and Local Government (DCLG) would bring forward an amendment to put it right. The problem was not addressed even though the eligibility regulations were later amended. Nor was it addressed when the Welsh Government made regulations under the new Housing (Wales) Act 2014.

During debates on an amendment sponsored by ILPA, the Government committed to drawing up new regulations. Shelter was consulted on these. The parties in the High Court judicial review claims of *Alabi* (CO/1231/2016) and *Romans* (CO/192/2016), challenging the provisions of SI 2006/1294, agreed to extend the stays in these cases until 30 September 2016, by consent orders filed on 3 August 2016, when it became clear that the DCLG would need more time to draft the regulations.

The Allocation of Housing and Homelessness (Eligibility) (England) (Amendment) Regulations 2016, SI 2016/965 were subsequently laid before parliament on 3 October 2016 and came into force in England on 30 October 2016. They include a new category of eligibility for local housing and homelessness services for those granted limited leave to remain under para 276BE(1), para 276DG or Appendix FM of the Immigration Rules on private or family life grounds under ECHR, Article 8 and who do not have a condition on their leave preventing them from having recourse to public funds. The Joint Committee on Human Rights has identified a minor grammatical error in the drafting in the regulation that the DCLG has stated it will correct as soon as possible.[2] Meanwhile courts should read words into legislation to remedy drafting errors if necessary.[3]

The new regulations do not make provision for unaccompanied minors granted 'UASC leave' under the Immigration Rules, para 352ZC. Nor do they make provision for stateless persons granted limited leave to remain under the Immigration Rules, para 403.

The construction of the regulations is narrower than that proposed by ILPA and others, who had advocated that the regulations identify instead those granted limited leave to remain who do not have a condition on their leave preventing them from having recourse to public funds. The broader formulation was proposed to cover those groups who were previously granted discretionary leave to enter or remain with recourse to public funds and to prevent the housing regulations having to be changed each time there was a change to the specific immigration categories and so avoid problems arising in the future where the housing regulations are unable to keep pace with changes in the Immigration Rules.

Whilst the amended regulations resolve the position of children, young people and families granted leave to remain on the basis of their rights to private and family life in the UK, problems remain with the drafting adopted by the DCLG which does not frame the regulations broadly and does not make all those granted limited leave, who have no restrictions on access to public funds, eligible for housing and homelessness assistance.

There is now a need for the devolved administrations to amend the regulations in Wales, Scotland and Northern Ireland.

---

1 R (Alvi) v Secretary of State for the Home Department [2012] UKSC 33.
2 Thirteenth Report of Session, 2016–17, HL Paper 68, Joint Committee on Human Rights, 18 November 2016. Available at: http://www.publications.parliament.uk/pa/jt201617/jtselect/jtstatin/68/68.pdf (accessed 1 December 2016).
3 Jones v Wrotham Park Settled Estates [1980] AC 74.

SECTION 39—OFFENCE OF LEASING PREMISES

Summary

Makes it a criminal offence to rent property to an adult whom the landlady or landlord or the agent knows, or has reasonable cause to believe, is disqualified from renting as a result of their immigration status. There is a defence for a landlady or landlord who has taken reasonable steps to end the tenancy within a reasonable period of time.

2.4

39 Offence of leasing premises

(1) The Immigration Act 2014 is amended in accordance with subsections (2) to (5).

(2) After section 33 insert—

"**Offences**

33A Offences: landlords

(1) The landlord under a residential tenancy agreement which relates to premises in England commits an offence if the first and second conditions are met.

2.4 *A Guide to the Immigration Act 2016*

(2) The first condition is that the premises are occupied by an adult who is disqualified as a result of their immigration status from occupying premises under a residential tenancy agreement.

(3) The second condition is that the landlord knows or has reasonable cause to believe that the premises are occupied by an adult who is disqualified as a result of their immigration status from occupying premises under a residential tenancy agreement.

(4) But unless subsection (5) applies the landlord does not commit an offence under subsection (1) if—

  (a) the premises are located in an area in relation to which section 22 is in force,

  (b) the adult mentioned in subsections (2) and (3) is a limited right occupier, and

  (c) the eligibility period in relation to that occupier has not expired.

(5) This subsection applies if the Secretary of State has given a notice in writing to the landlord which—

  (a) identifies the adult mentioned in subsections (2) and (3), and

  (b) states that the adult is disqualified as a result of their immigration status from occupying premises under a residential tenancy agreement.

(6) It is a defence for a person charged with an offence under subsection (1) to prove that—

  (a) the person has taken reasonable steps to terminate the residential tenancy agreement, and

  (b) the person has taken such steps within a reasonable period beginning with the time when the person first knew or had reasonable cause to believe that the premises were occupied by the adult mentioned in subsections (2) and (3).

(7) In determining whether subsection (6)(a) or (b) applies to a person, the court must have regard to any guidance which, at the time in question, had been issued by the Secretary of State for the purposes of that subsection and was in force at that time.

(8) Guidance issued for the purposes of subsection (6)—

  (a) must be laid before Parliament in draft before being issued, and

  (b) comes into force in accordance with regulations made by the Secretary of State.

Part 2—Access to Services **2.4**

(9) Section 22(9) applies for the purposes of subsection (1) as it applies for the purposes of that section.

(10) A person commits an offence if—

    (a) there has been a post-grant contravention in relation to a residential tenancy agreement which relates to premises in England,

    (b) the person is the responsible landlord in relation to the post-grant contravention,

    (c) the person knows or has reasonable cause to believe that there has been a post-grant contravention in relation to the agreement, and

    (d) none of paragraphs (a), (b) and (c) of section 24(6) applies in relation to the post-grant contravention.

(11) Subsection (10) applies whether or not the landlord is given a notice under section 23 in respect of the contravention.

33B Offences: agents

(1) Subsection (2) applies to an agent who is responsible for a landlord's contravention of section 22 in relation to premises in England.

(2) The agent commits an offence if the agent—

    (a) knew or had reasonable cause to believe that the landlord would contravene section 22 by entering into the residential tenancy agreement in question,

    (b) had sufficient opportunity to notify the landlord of that fact before the landlord entered into the agreement, but

    (c) did not do so.

(3) Subsection (4) applies where—

    (a) a landlord contravenes section 22 in relation to a residential tenancy agreement relating to premises in England,

    (b) the contravention is a post-grant contravention, and

    (c) a person acting as the landlord's agent ("the agent") is responsible for the post-grant contravention.

(4) The agent commits an offence if—

    (a) the agent knows or has reasonable cause to believe that there has been a post-grant contravention in relation to the agreement, and

2.4 *A Guide to the Immigration Act 2016*

        (b)   neither of paragraphs (a) and (b) of section 26(6) applies in relation to the post-grant contravention.

(5) Subsection (4) applies whether or not the agent is given a notice under section 25 in respect of the contravention.

33C Offences: penalties etc

(1) A person who is guilty of an offence under section 33A or 33B is liable—

        (a)   on conviction on indictment, to imprisonment for a term not exceeding five years, to a fine or to both;

        (b)   on summary conviction, to imprisonment for a term not exceeding 12 months, to a fine or to both.

(2) In the application of this section in relation to an offence committed before the coming into force of section 154(1) of the Criminal Justice Act 2003 the reference in subsection (1)(b) to 12 months is to be read as a reference to 6 months.

(3) If an offence under section 33A or 33B is committed by a body corporate with the consent or connivance of an officer of the body, the officer, as well as the body, is to be treated as having committed the offence.

(4) In subsection (3) a reference to an officer of a body includes a reference to—

        (a)   a director, manager or secretary,

        (b)   a person purporting to act as a director, manager or secretary, and

        (c)   if the affairs of the body are managed by its members, a member.

(5) Where an offence under section 33A or 33B is committed by a partnership (whether or not a limited partnership) subsection (3) has effect, but as if a reference to an officer of the body were a reference to—

        (a)   a partner, and

        (b)   a person purporting to act as a partner.

(6) An offence under section 33A or 33B is to be treated as—

        (a)   a relevant offence for the purposes of sections 28B and 28D of the Immigration Act 1971 (search, entry and arrest), and

        (b)   an offence under Part 3 of that Act (criminal proceedings) for the purposes of sections 28E, 28G and 28H of that Act (search after arrest)."

(3) In section 35 (transitional provision) after subsection (3) insert—

"(4) References in this section to this Chapter do not include sections 33A to 33E (offences and eviction).

Part 2—Access to Services **2.4**

(5) Sections 33A to 33C apply in relation to a residential tenancy agreement entered into before or after the coming into force of section 39 of the Immigration Act 2016 (which inserted those sections into this Act).

(6) But sections 33A(10) and (11) and 33B apply only in relation to a contravention of section 22 which occurs after the coming into force of section 39 of the Immigration Act 2016."

(4) In section 36 (Crown application) at the end insert "or the landlord for the purposes of section 33A."

(5) In section 37(4)(a) (provisions in which references to the landlord are to any of them)—

  (a) omit the "and" at the end of sub-paragraph (ii), and

  (b) at the end of sub-paragraph (iii) insert—

   "(iv) section 33A,".

(6) In section 28A of the Immigration Act 1971 (arrest without warrant)—

  (a) after subsection (9B) insert—

   "(9C) An immigration officer may arrest without warrant a person who, or whom the immigration officer has reasonable grounds for suspecting—

   (a) has committed or attempted to commit an offence under section 33A or 33B of the Immigration Act 2014 (offences relating to residential tenancies), or

   (b) is committing or attempting to commit that offence.",

  (b) in subsection (10) for "and (9B)" substitute ", (9B) and (9C)", and

  (c) in subsection (11) for "and (9B)" substitute ", (9B) and (9C)".

Commencement: In force from 1 November 2016 for the purpose of making subordinate legislation only, fully in force from 1 December 2016, The Immigration Act 2016 (Commencement No 2 and Transitional Provisions) Regulations 2016, SI 2016/1037.

Amends: Immigration Act 2014 (IA 2014) inserting a new s 33A *Offences: landlords;* 33B *Offences: agents;* 33C *Offences: penalties* etc. Also amends ss 35 and 37 of that Act. Amends the Immigration Act 1971 (IA 1971), s 28A. Amends the Protection from Eviction Act 1977, s 3A *Excluded tenancies and licences* and the Housing Act 1988, s 5 *Security of tenure*.

Regulations: Made under IA 2014, s 33A(8) to bring into force guidance made under IA 2014, s 33A(7) (both provisions inserted by s 39(2)): The Immigration (Residential Accommodation) (Termination of Residential Tenancy Agreements) (Guidance etc.) Regulations 2016, SI 2016/1060.

2.4 A Guide to the Immigration Act 2016

Guidance: Made under IA 2014, s 33A(7), laid before Parliament and brought into force through regulations made under s 33A(8): Guidance on taking reasonable steps to end a residential tenancy agreement within a reasonable time frame, Home Office, 1 December 2016.

Definitions: *(Not all terms appear in the section but an understanding of all is necessary for a full understanding of the section)*

'adult' a person who has attained the age of 18 years, IA 2014, s 37(1);

'agent' IA 2014, s 33B(3)(c), inserted by s 39;

'building' for the purposes of Schedule 3 to the IA 2014 includes a part of a building, see para 14 thereof;

'care home' an establishment that is a care home for the purposes of the Care Standards Act 2000; accommodation that is provided as a care home service within the meaning of Part 5 of the Public Services Reform (Scotland) Act 2010; an establishment that is a residential care home or a nursing home for the purposes of the Health and Personal Social Services (Quality, Improvement and Regulation) (Northern Ireland) Order 2003 (SI 2003/431 (NI 9)); see Immigration Act 2014, Schedule 3, para 3;

'eligibility period' Immigration Act 2014, s 27, s 37(1);

'excluded agreement' means any agreement of a description for the time being specified in Schedule 3 to the IA 2014 (s 20(6) IA 2014);

'hospital' National Health Service Act 2006, s 275; National Health Service (Wales) Act 2006, s 206; National Health Service (Scotland) Act 1978, s 108; Health and Personal Social Services (Northern Ireland) Order 1972 (S.I. 1972/1265 (N.I. 14)), Article 2(2); see IA 2014 Schedule 3, para 4;

'hospice' an establishment other than a hospital whose primary function is the provision of palliative care to persons resident there who are suffering from a progressive disease in its final stages, IA 2014, Schedule 3, para 4;

'hostel' means a building used for providing, to persons generally or to a class of persons, residential accommodation otherwise than in separate and self-contained premises, and board or facilities for the preparation of food adequate to the needs of those persons (or both); and which is managed by a registered housing association, or not operated on a commercial basis or its costs of operation are provided wholly or in part by a government department or agency, or by a local authority, or it is managed by a voluntary organisation or charity, IA 2014, Schedule 3, para 6;

'landlord' IA 2014, s 20(3);

'limited right occupier' IA 2014, s 24(9);

'limited right to rent' right to rent of a person who has been granted leave to enter or remain in the United Kingdom for a limited period, or is not a

Part 2—Access to Services 2.4

relevant national and is entitled to enter or remain in the United Kingdom by virtue of an enforceable EU right or of any provision made under section 2(2) of the European Communities Act 1972, IA 2014, s 21(4);

'long lease' a lease which is a long lease for the purposes of Chapter 1 of Part 1 of the Leasehold Reform, Housing and Urban Development Act 1993 or which, in the case of a shared ownership lease (within the meaning given by section 7(7) of that Act), would be such a lease if the tenant's total share (within the meaning given by that section) were 100 per cent; the meaning given by section 9(2) of the Land Registration (Scotland) Act 2012. An agreement does not grant a right of occupation for a term of seven years or more if the agreement can be terminated at the option of a party before the end of seven years from the commencement of the term, IA 2014, Schedule 3, para 13;

'mobile home' see the Mobile Homes Act 1983, IA 2014, Schedule 3, para 9;

'occupy', occupy as only or main residence, IA 2014, s 37(1);

'post-grant contravention' IA 2014, s 22(10), s 37(1);

'premises' IA 2014, s 37(1);

'refuge' means a building which is managed by a registered housing association, or not operated on a commercial basis or its costs of operation are provided wholly or in part by a Government department or agency, or by a local authority, or it is managed by a voluntary organisation or charity; and is used wholly or mainly for providing accommodation to persons who have been subject to any incident, or pattern of incidents, of controlling, coercive or threatening behaviour, physical violence, abuse of any other description (whether physical or mental in nature), or threats of any such violence or abuse, IA 2014, Schedule 3, para 6;

'relevant national' a British citizen, a national of another EEA State, or a national of Switzerland, IA 2014, s 21(5);

'rent' any sum paid in the nature of rent, Immigration Act 2014, s 20(5);

'residential tenancy agreement', agreement granting a right of occupation for residential use, for a rent, whether or not a market rent, that is not an excluded agreement, IA 2014, s 20(2);

'residential use' IA 2014 s 20(4): an agreement grants a right of occupation of premises 'for residential use' if, under the agreement, one or more adults have the right to occupy the premises as their only or main residence (whether or not the premises may also be used for other purposes);

'social housing' means, in respect of accommodation, excluded from the right to rent scheme, accommodation provided to a person by virtue of Part 2 of the Housing Act 1985, Part 6 or 7 of the Housing Act 1996, Part 1 or 2 of the

2.4 A Guide to the Immigration Act 2016

Housing (Scotland) Act 1987, Chapter 4 of Part 2 of the Housing (Northern Ireland) Order 1981, Part 2 of the Housing (Northern Ireland) Order 1988, SI 1988/1990, IA 2014, Schedule 3, para 1 (and see Schedule 3, para 2, for important qualifications);

'student accommodation' accommodation provided under an agreement that grants a right of occupation in a building which is used wholly or mainly for the accommodation of students; and is owned or managed by an institution within the meaning of para 5 of Schedule 1 to the Local Government Finance Act 1992, or a body that is specified in regulations made under Article 42(2A) of the Rates (Northern Ireland) Order 1977, SI 1977/2157, or a body established for charitable purposes only or accommodation provided under an agreement that grants a right of occupation in a building which is used wholly or mainly for the accommodation of students and is a hall of residence. In these definitions the meaning of 'student' is found in para 4 of Schedule 1 to the Local Government Finance Act 1992 and in relation to Northern Ireland, means a person who satisfies such conditions as to education or training as may be specified in regulations made under Article 42(2A) of the Rates (Northern Ireland) Order 1977, SI 1977/2157. Immigration Act 2014, Schedule 3, para 11;

'tenancy' includes any lease, licence, sub-lease or sub-tenancy and an agreement for any of those things, IA 2014, s 20(3);

'tenant' IA 2014, s 20(3);

'tied accommodation' means accommodation that is provided by an employer to an employee in connection with a contract of employment, or by a body providing training in a trade, profession or vocation to an individual in connection with that training, where 'employer' and 'employee' have the same meanings as in the Employment Rights Act 1996 (see section 230 of that Act), IA 2014, Schedule 3, para 10.

Devolution: Applies to England only. Can be extended to Wales, Scotland and Northern Ireland by regulations, see s 42.

Offences: s 33A(1), s 33A (10), s 33B(2) and s 33B (4) of the IA 2014 (inserted by s 39(1)).

This section creates four new criminal offences, two that can be committed by landlords and landladies, and two that can be committed by their agents. Where there is more than one landlord or landlady, references are to both (s 39(5)). The offences are inserted into the IA 2014 by s 39(1) and committed when a person does not have a right to rent and the landlord, landlady or agent knows or has reasonable cause to believe that a person does not have a right to rent. They carry a maximum five-year prison sentence (new s 33C, IA 1971).

The provisions came into force on 1 November 2016 for the purpose of making subordinate legislation only and were then brought fully into force on 1 December 2016.[1]

New s 33A of the IA 2014 creates two new offences relating to landlord or landladies. The first offence is committed if a landlord or landlady under a residential tenancy agreement knows or has reasonable grounds to believe that the premises are occupied by an adult disqualified from renting as a result of their immigration status (ss 33A(1)–(5)). This applies where any adult is occupying the premises, regardless of whether the adult is a tenant under, or is named in, the agreement. Subsections 33A(4)–(5) provide that, in areas where the right to rent scheme is in force, the landlord or landlady is not guilty of an offence under s 33A(1) if the adult has a limited right to rent (as defined at IA 2014, s 21(4)) and the eligibility period (as defined at IA 2014, s 27) of the occupier has not expired, unless the SSHD has given a written notice to the landlord or landlady which states that the adult is disqualified as a result of their immigration status from occupying premises under a residential tenancy agreement. New s 33A(9) provides that IA 2014, s 22(9) applies to this new offence and therefore that the commission of an offence will not impact on a landlord or landlady or tenant's ability to enforce any provision of the residential tenancy agreement, displacing the *ex turpi causa* principle in these cases.

A defence is available to a landlord or landlady who has taken reasonable steps to end the tenancy within a reasonable period of time (new s 33A(6)). The courts must have regard to any statutory guidance issued by the SSHD in determining whether the defence applies (new s 33A(7)). Statutory guidance for the purpose of new s 33A(6) was laid before Parliament in draft on 4 November 2016 and was brought into force on 1 December 2016 through The Immigration (Residential Accommodation) (Termination of Residential Tenancy Agreements) (Guidance etc) Regulations 2016, SI 2016/1060, as required by new s 33A(8). The finalised version of the guidance was published on 1 December 2016.[2]

The second offence (new s 33A(10)) relates to a post-grant contravention. A post-grant contravention is committed if the tenant had a limited right to rent when they entered into the residential tenancy agreement, they become a person disqualified from renting (as their leave to remain in the UK expires) during the course of the tenancy, the tenant's eligibility period (as defined at IA 2014, s 27) has expired, the tenant continues to occupy the property and the landlord or landlady knows, or has reasonable cause to believe, this has happened. The eligibility period is defined in the Immigration (Residential Accommodation) (Prescribed Requirements and Codes of Practice) Order 2014, SI 2014/2874 as amended. It is the longer of either one calendar year from the point that a right to rent check was last conducted or in line with the validity of any immigration

2.4 *A Guide to the Immigration Act 2016*

leave or validity period of specific documents. An offence is not committed where the landlord or landlady has conducted the appropriate checks and the eligibility period for occupier with a limited right to rent has not expired. In the case of a contravention, an offence is not committed if the landlord or landlady has notified the Secretary of State of the contravention as soon as reasonably practicable or if their agent is responsible for the contravention. The offence applies whether or not the landlord or landlady has been issued with a civil penalty notice under IA 2014, s 23 (s 33A(8)).

Section 33B is concerned with two offences relating to agents. Subsections 33B(1)–(2) provide that an agent is guilty of an offence if the agent carries out the right to rent checks on behalf of the landlord or landlady (under IA 2014, s 25), knows or has reasonable cause to believe that the landlord or landlady will be authorising someone disqualified from renting to occupy the property if he or she enters into the tenancy agreement and has sufficient opportunity to notify the landlord or landlady beforehand, but does not do so. There is no parallel defence available to agents similar to that under new s 33A(6) for landladies and landlords.

Sections 33B(3)–(4) provide that an agent commits an offence if the agent carries out the right to rent checks on behalf of the landlord or landlady (under IA 2014, s 25), a tenant's leave to remain in the UK expires during the course of the tenancy, having been valid at the time the tenancy was entered into, the tenant's eligibility period has expired, the tenant continues to occupy the property and the agent knows or has reasonable cause to believe this has happened but does not notify the landlord as soon as reasonably practicable. The agent does not commit an offence if they notify the SSHD and the landlord of the contravention as soon as reasonably practicable (s 33B(4)(b)). Section 33B(5) specifies that the agent is guilty of an offence whether or not the agent has been issued with a civil penalty notice under s 25.

Under the IA 2014, it sufficed for a landlord or landlady to conduct periodic checks on a tenant's immigration status. They were then protected from a civil penalty until the end of the eligibility period and when the next check was due, even if the tenant's status changed. Whilst this applies for the criminal offence under new s 33A(10) for post-grant contraventions for landlords or landladies, it will now be the case that if the Secretary of State gives notice in writing to the landlord or landlady that the person has no right to rent, they will face a criminal penalty if they continue to rent to the tenant even though the next check is not yet due unless they take reasonable steps to end the tenancy within a reasonable period. The Minister said during the Report stage of the Bill in the House of Commons:

> 'These offences are not designed to catch out a landlord who has made a genuine mistake, and it is difficult to foresee a situation in which it would be in the public interest to pursue a prosecution against a landlord making reasonable efforts to remove illegal migrants from their property'[3]

Part 2—Access to Services **2.4**

The SSHD has issued statutory guidance identifying the steps and periods of time considered reasonable for ending a tenancy for the purpose of new s 33A(6) (see above) to which the courts must have regard when considering whether the landlord or landlady has committed an offence (new s 33A(7)).

Landlords, landladies or agents face a maximum five-year prison sentence and/or a fine if convicted on indictment or a maximum 12-month prison term and/or a fine if convicted and sentenced by a magistrates' court (new s 33C).

Both the officer of a body corporate and a body corporate are liable for the offence where it is committed by the body corporate with the consent or complicit involvement of an officer of the body (new s 33C(3)). The same applies for individuals who are, or purport to act as, partners where the offence is committed by the partnership (new s 33C(5)). The reference to an officer of a body corporate includes a director, manager or secretary, or person purporting to act as such or, if the affairs of a body are managed by its members, a member (new s 33C(4)).

Section 33C(6) permits immigration officers to use powers provided under the IA 1971 in relation to these offences, including powers to enter and search premises and powers to search persons. Section 39(6) amends s 28A of Part III of the 1971 Act by inserting new s 28A(9C) which provides that an immigration officer may arrest without warrant a person who, or whom the immigration officer has reasonable grounds for suspecting, has committed one of these offences (IA 1971, s 28A(9C) inserted by new IA 2014, s 33C(6)).

---

1 The Immigration Act 2016 (Commencement No 2 and Transitional Provisions) Regulations 2016, SI 2016/1037.
2 *Immigration Act 2014: Guidance on taking reasonable steps to end a residential tenancy agreement within a reasonable time frame*, Home Office, 1 December 2016. Available at: https://www.gov.uk/government/publications/ending-a-residential-tenancy-agreement (accessed 1 December 2016).
3 House of Commons, Immigration Bill 2015/16 Report stage, *Hansard* col 208 (1 December 2015). Available at: http://www.publications.parliament.uk/pa/cm201516/cmhansrd/cm151201/debtext/151201-0002.htm#15120141000002 (accessed 1 December 2016).

SECTION 40—EVICTION

Summary
Provides landlords and landladies with new powers to evict persons with no right to rent. Failure to do so will render them liable to prosecution.

2.5 *A Guide to the Immigration Act 2016*

2.5

40 Eviction

(1) The Immigration Act 2014 is amended in accordance with subsections (2) to (4).

(2) After section 33C (inserted by section 39) insert—

"*Eviction*

33D Termination of agreement where all occupiers disqualified

(1) The landlord under a residential tenancy agreement relating to premises in England may terminate the agreement in accordance with this section if the condition in subsection (2) is met.

(2) The condition is that the Secretary of State has given one or more notices in writing to the landlord which, taken together,—

(a) identify the occupier of the premises or (if there is more than one occupier) all of them, and

(b) state that the occupier or occupiers are disqualified as a result of their immigration status from occupying premises under a residential tenancy agreement.

(3) The landlord may terminate the residential tenancy agreement by giving notice in writing and in the prescribed form to the tenant or, in the case of a joint tenancy, all of the tenants specifying the date on which the agreement comes to an end.

(4) That date must not be earlier than the end of the period of 28 days beginning with the day specified in the notice as the day on which it is given.

(5) The notice may be given—

(a) by delivering it to the tenant or tenants,

(b) by leaving it at the premises,

(c) by sending it by post to the tenant or tenants at the address of the premises, or

(d) in any other prescribed manner.

(6) The notice is to be treated as a notice to quit in a case where a notice to quit would otherwise be required to bring the residential tenancy agreement to an end.

(7) The notice is enforceable as if it were an order of the High Court.

(8) In this section "occupier", in relation to premises to which a residential tenancy agreement applies, means—

(a) a tenant,

(b) a person who, under the agreement, otherwise has the right to occupy the premises and is named in the agreement, and

(c) any other person who the landlord knows is occupying the premises.

33E Other procedures for ending agreement

(1) It is an implied term of a residential tenancy agreement to which this subsection applies that the landlord may terminate the tenancy if the premises to which it relates are occupied by an adult who is disqualified as a result of their immigration status from occupying premises under a residential tenancy agreement.

(2) Subsection (1) applies to a residential tenancy agreement relating to premises in England if—

(a) it is a tenancy or sub-tenancy or an agreement for a tenancy or sub-tenancy, but

(b) it is not a protected or statutory tenancy within the meaning of the Rent Act 1977 or an assured tenancy within the meaning of the Housing Act 1988.

(3) For provision relating to a residential tenancy agreement which is a protected or statutory tenancy where a tenant or occupier is disqualified as a result of their immigration status from occupying premises under a residential tenancy agreement, see Case 10A in Part 1 of Schedule 15 to the Rent Act 1977.

(4) For provision relating to a residential tenancy agreement which is an assured tenancy where a tenant or occupier is disqualified as a result of their immigration status from occupying premises under a residential tenancy agreement, see Ground 7B in Part 1 of Schedule 2 to the Housing Act 1988."

(3) In section 35 (transitional provision) after subsection (6) (inserted by section 39(3)) insert—

"(7) Sections 33D and 33E apply in relation to a residential tenancy agreement entered into before or after the coming into force of section 40 of the Immigration Act 2016 (which inserted those sections into this Act)."

(4) In section 37(4)(a) (provisions in which references to the landlord are to any of them) after sub-paragraph (iv) (inserted by section 39(5)(b)) insert—

"(v) section 33D, and

(vi) section 33E,".

(5) In section 3A of the Protection from Eviction Act 1977 (excluded tenancies and licences) after subsection (7C) insert—

"(7D) A tenancy or licence is excluded if—

(a) it is a residential tenancy agreement within the meaning of Chapter 1 of Part 3 of the Immigration Act 2014, and

(b) the condition in section 33D(2) of that Act is met in relation to that agreement."

2.5 *A Guide to the Immigration Act 2016*

(6) In section 5 of the Housing Act 1988 (security of tenure)—

    (a) in subsection (1) omit the "or" at the end of paragraph (b) and at the end of paragraph (c) insert ", or

        (d) in the case of an assured tenancy—

            (i) which is a residential tenancy agreement within the meaning of Chapter 1 of Part 3 of the Immigration Act 2014, and

            (ii) in relation to which the condition in section 33D(2) of that Act is met,

        giving a notice in accordance with that section,", and

    (b) in subsection (2) omit the "or" at the end of paragraph (a) and at the end of paragraph (b) insert ", or

    (c) the giving of a notice under section 33D of the Immigration Act 2014,".

(7) The amendments made by subsections (5) and (6) apply in relation to a tenancy or (in the case of subsection (5)) a licence entered into before or after the coming into force of this section.

Commencement: In force from 1 November 2016 for the purpose of making subordinate legislation only, fully in force from 1 December 2016, the Immigration Act 2016 (Commencement No 2 and Transitional Provisions) Regulations 2016, SI 2016/1037.

Amends: Immigration Act 2014 (IA 2014), inserting a new s 33D *Termination of agreement where all occupiers disqualified;* s 33E *Other procedures for ending agreement.* Also amends ss 35 and 36 of that Act. Amends s 3A *Excluded tenancies and licences* of the Protection from Eviction Act 1977 (s 40(5)) and amends s 5 *Security of Tenure* of the Housing Act 1988 (s 40(6)).

Regulations: Section 33D(3) of the IA 2014 inserted by s 40(2) makes provision for the landlord/landlady's notice to the tenant to be in the prescribed form. The Immigration (Residential Accommodation) (Termination of Residential Tenancy Agreements) (Guidance etc) Regulations 2016, SI 2016/1060 came into force on 1 December 2016.

Definitions:

'adult' a person who has attained the age of 18 years, IA 2014, s 37(1);

'assured tenancy' Housing Act 1988, s 1;

'eligibility period' IA 2014, s 27, s 37(1);

'landlord' IA 2014, s 20(3);

'occupier' means a tenant, a person named in the residential tenancy agreement with the right to occupy the premises or any other person the landlord knows is occupying the premises, s 33D(8) of the IA 2014 (s 40(2);

'occupy' means occupy as only or main residence, IA 2014, s 37(1);

'post-grant contravention' IA 2014, s 22(10), s 37(1);

'premises' IA 2014, s 37(1);

'protected tenancy' Rent Act 1977, s 1;

'residential tenancy agreement' an agreement granting a right of occupation for residential use, for a rent, whether or not a market rent, that is not an excluded agreement, IA 2014, s 20(2);

'statutory tenancy' Rent Act 1977, s 2;

'tenancy' IA 2014, s 20(3);

'tenant' IA 2014, s 20(3).

Devolution: Applies to England only. Can be extended to Wales, Scotland and Northern Ireland by regulations, see s 42.

This section inserts provisions into the IA 2014 that give landlords and landladies new powers to end a residential tenancy agreement and evict persons occupying their premises where they are disqualified from renting under IA 2014.[1]

New section 33D of the IA 2014, inserted by this section, makes provision for a landlord or landlady to terminate a residential tenancy agreement where the Secretary of State has given written notice to the landlord that all the occupiers are disqualified from occupying premises, either through one notice or through separate notices about different occupants taken together. An occupier is defined as a tenant, a person named in the tenancy agreement, and any other person who the landlord knows is occupying the premises.

The landlord or landlady may terminate the tenancy by giving written notice to the tenant(s) either by delivering it to them, leaving it at the premises, sending it by post to the tenant(s) at the address of the premises, or in any other prescribed manner. This must give at least 28 days' notice of the tenancy agreement ending, starting from the day in which the notice is given. See new s 33D(3) of the IA 2011.

The notice given by the landlord or landlady must be in the prescribed form (new s 33D(3)). This is prescribed in the schedule to the Immigration (Residential Accommodation) (Termination of Residential Tenancy Agreements) (Guidance etc) Regulations 2016, SI 2016/1060. This provides a copy of the form of notice that must be used by a landlord or landlady and also requires that they attach a copy of the Landlord Notice issued by the Secretary of State. The eviction notice is not valid unless the Landlord Notice or Landlord Notices (if there are more than one) are attached. It is important that the Landlord Notice is

2.5 *A Guide to the Immigration Act 2016*

attached as it provides the tenant with an opportunity to contact the Home Office to correct any Home Office errors or address any problems relating to their immigration status.

The landlord or landlady's written notice is 'enforceable as if it were an order of the High Court'. This is unprecedented in housing law. In many civil penalty schemes, including the right to rent scheme, provision is made in this way for a fine to be enforced as if it were a debt due under a court order. It means that the sum of money owed cannot be disputed and steps may be taken to secure the amount owed. There is a significant difference between enforcing a fine under a statutory scheme in this way and having a notice to quit accommodation given by a private individual so enforced.

There will be no need for a landlord or landlady to seek an order for possession and they can use 'self-help' to recover possession, that is, personally turn up and put occupiers and their possessions onto the street or call on, and pay, a High Court Enforcement Officer, previously called a High Court Sheriff, to do so. The Landlord Notice, set out in the schedule to the Immigration (Residential Accommodation) (Termination of Residential Tenancy Agreements) (Guidance etc) Regulations 2016, SI 2016/1060, states that landlords, or anyone acting for them, may not use violence, threats of violence, or manhandle an occupier to gain entry to or recover possession of the premises. They are not permitted to harass occupiers or withdraw services from the premises in order to encourage them to leave. The landlord may not forcibly gain entry to premises whilst there is someone opposed to the entry present on the premises. These actions would constitute a criminal offence.

Section 3A of the Protection from Eviction Act 1977 is amended to exclude from its protection tenancies to which these provisions apply (s 40(5)) and a notice can bring an assured tenancy under the Housing Act 1988 s 5 (security of tenure) to an end (s 40(6)). See also commentary on s 41 on the new mandatory ground for awarding an order of possession.

The Minister was pressed on these matters during the Report stage of the Bill in the House of Commons and suggested that there were safeguards in place:

> 'safeguards already exist. The Secretary of State will serve notices only where she is satisfied that the migrant is here unlawfully and only after taking the migrant's circumstances into consideration. Should there be recognised barriers to illegal migrants leaving the UK that are not of their own making, these will be taken into account'.[2]

It was acknowledged that the provisions also applied to families with children, who would be subject to the same summary eviction processes where the Secretary of State had issued a notice to the landlord or landlady identifying them as disqualified persons. The Minister stated, 'In serving a notice in respect of a child, the Home Office will have regard to its duty to safeguard and promote the rights of children'.[3]

During a later debate, he stated further:

'It is important to underline that because the Home Office will not invoke the eviction process or serve notices until a full consideration of family circumstances has been undertaken ....Although the families will be given warnings throughout the eviction process that it may be invoked, they will be encouraged to make a case on why these measures are not appropriate to them.

The Home Office will consider the circumstances of each member of the family. Eviction will generally be inappropriate where there are existing medical conditions or specific care needs evident, and eviction may mean that a local authority is placed under a duty to remedy the loss of accommodation. There will also be cases where invoking eviction is considered inappropriate. These will be cases where the family involved is considered to have recognised barriers to returning home. These instances can include no viable route of return to their home country, difficulties in securing travel documents or in ensuring that their home country will accept the family's return, and medical or health conditions that make it difficult for a family to return home'.[4]

The eviction of children and families under these provisions is likely to have an impact on children's social services, housing and homelessness departments as local authorities will have duties to house families to promote and safeguard the welfare of children.

New section 33E makes provision for landlords or landladies (in England) to evict in other circumstances where an adult occupant is a disqualified person. These include, for example, circumstances where one or more of the occupants are disqualified persons but other adult members of the household are not disqualified from renting. Under section 33E(1), it becomes an implied term of the residential tenancy agreement that the landlord may terminate the tenancy if the premises are occupied by an adult who is disqualified from doing so as a result of their immigration status. This allows the landlord to pursue eviction under the normal legal routes even if it was not set out in the tenancy agreement.

In sections 33D–33E, where two or more persons jointly constitute the landlord or landlady both of them have the powers under these sections (s 40(4)). An eviction under sections 33D–33E can also take place in respect of a tenancy or licence that was entered into before or after these provisions came into force (s 40(3), s 40(7)).

2.6 *A Guide to the Immigration Act 2016*

1 For a briefing on the housing provisions and eviction powers, see the written evidence submitted by the Housing Law Practitioners Association to the Immigration Bill 2015/16 Public Bill Committee, House of Commons, IB 15, 27 October 2015. Available at: http://www.publications.parliament.uk/pa/cm201516/cmpublic/immigration/memo/ib18.htm (accessed 14 December 2016).
2 Rt Hon James Brokenshire MP, Minister for Immigration, Immigration Bill 2015/16 Report stage, House of Commons, 1 December 2015, *Hansard* col 208. Available at: http://www.publications.parliament.uk/pa/cm201516/cmhansrd/cm151201/debtext/151201-0002.htm#15120141000002 (accessed 14 December 2016).
3 Rt Hon James Brokenshire MP, Minister for Immigration, Immigration Bill 2015/16 Public Bill Committee, House of Commons, 7th sitting, 29 October 2015, *Hansard* Col 278. Available at: http://www.publications.parliament.uk/pa/cm201516/cmpublic/immigration/151029/am/151029s01.htm (accessed 14 December 2016).
4 Rt Hon James Brokenshire MP, Minister for Immigration, Immigration Bill 2015/16 Public Bill Committee, House of Commons, 9th sitting, 3 November 2015, *Hansard* Col 292. Available at: http://www.publications.parliament.uk/pa/cm201516/cmpublic/immigration/151103/am/151103s01.htm (accessed 14 December 2016).

SECTION 41—ORDER FOR POSSESSION OF DWELLING-HOUSE

> **Summary**
>
> Provides for a new mandatory ground for a landlord or landlady to obtain possession of a property following receipt of notification from the Secretary of State that an occupant is a disqualified person.

2.6

41 Order for possession of dwelling-house

(1) The Housing Act 1988 is amended in accordance with subsections (2) to (5).

(2) In Part 1 of Schedule 2 (assured tenancies: grounds on which court must order possession) after Ground 7A insert—

"Ground 7B

Both of the following conditions are met in relation to a dwelling house in England.

Condition 1 is that the Secretary of State has given a notice in writing to the landlord or, in the case of joint landlords, one or more of them which identifies—

(a) the tenant or, in the case of joint tenants, one or more of them, or

(b) one or more other persons aged 18 or over who are occupying the dwelling-house,

as a person or persons disqualified as a result of their immigration status from occupying the dwelling-house under the tenancy.

Condition 2 is that the person or persons named in the notice—

(a) fall within paragraph (a) or (b) of condition 1, and

(b) are disqualified as a result of their immigration status from occupying the dwelling-house under the tenancy.

For the purposes of this ground a person ("P") is disqualified as a result of their immigration status from occupying the dwelling-house under the tenancy if—

(a) P is not a relevant national, and

(b) P does not have a right to rent in relation to the dwelling-house.

P does not have a right to rent in relation to the dwelling-house if—

(a) P requires leave to enter or remain in the United Kingdom but does not have it, or

(b) P's leave to enter or remain in the United Kingdom is subject to a condition preventing P from occupying the dwelling-house.

But P is to be treated as having a right to rent in relation to a dwelling-house if the Secretary of State has granted P permission for the purposes of this ground to occupy a dwelling-house under an assured tenancy.

In this ground "relevant national" means—

(a) a British citizen,

(b) a national of an EEA State other than the United Kingdom, or

(c) a national of Switzerland."

(3) In section 7 (orders for possession)—

(a) in subsection (3) after "subsections (5A) and (6)" insert "and section 10A",

(b) in subsection (5A)(a) for "and 7A" substitute ", 7A and 7B",

(c) in subsection (6)(a) after "Ground 7A" insert ", Ground 7B", and

(d) after subsection (6A) insert—

"(6B) The requirement in subsection (6)(b) that would otherwise apply to an order for possession of a dwelling-house let on an

2.6 *A Guide to the Immigration Act 2016*

assured fixed term tenancy does not apply where the ground for possession is Ground 7B in Part 1 of Schedule 2 to this Act."

(4) In section 8(5) (cases where court may not dispense with notice of proceedings for possession) after "Ground 7A" insert ", 7B".

(5) After section 10 insert—

"10A Power to order transfer of tenancy in certain cases

(1) This section applies on an application for an order for possession of a dwelling-house let on an assured tenancy if the court is satisfied that—

(a) Ground 7B in Schedule 2 is established,

(b) no other ground in that Schedule is established, or one or more grounds in Part 2 of that Schedule are established but it is not reasonable to make an order for possession on that ground or those grounds,

(c) the tenancy is a joint tenancy, and

(d) one or more of the tenants is a qualifying tenant.

(2) In subsection (1)(d) "qualifying tenant" means a person who (within the meaning of Ground 7B) is not disqualified as a result of the person's immigration status from occupying the dwelling-house under the tenancy.

(3) The court may, instead of making an order for possession, order that the tenant's interest under the tenancy is to be transferred so that it is held—

(a) if there is one qualifying tenant, by the qualifying tenant as sole tenant, or

(b) if there is more than one qualifying tenant, by all of them as joint tenants.

(4) The effect of an order under this section is that, from the time the order takes effect, the qualifying tenant or tenants—

(a) are entitled to performance of the landlord's covenants under the tenancy, and

(b) are liable to perform the tenant's covenants under the tenancy.

(5) The effect of an order under this section is that, from the time it takes effect, any other person who was a tenant under the tenancy before the order took effect—

(a) ceases to be entitled to performance of the landlord's covenants under the tenancy, or

(b) ceases to be liable to perform the tenant's covenants under the tenancy.

Part 2—Access to Services **2.6**

(6) Subsection (5) does not remove any right or liability of the person which accrued before the order took effect.

(7) An order under this section does not operate to create a new tenancy as between the landlord and the qualifying tenant or tenants.

(8) In particular, if the tenancy is a fixed term tenancy, the term comes to an end at the same time as if the order had not been made."

(6) In Part 1 of Schedule 15 to the Rent Act 1977 (grounds for possession of dwelling-houses let on or subject to protected or statutory tenancies) after Case 10 insert—

"Case 10A

Both of the following conditions are met in relation to a dwelling-house in England.

Condition 1 is that the Secretary of State has given a notice in writing to the landlord or, in the case of joint landlords, one or more of them which identifies—

(a) the tenant or, in the case of joint tenants, one or more of them, or

(b) one or more other persons aged 18 or over who are occupying the dwelling-house,

as a person or persons disqualified asv a result of their immigration status from occupying the dwelling-house under the tenancy.

Condition 2 is that the person or persons named in the notice—

(a) fall within paragraph (a) or (b) of condition 1, and

(b) are disqualified as a result of their immigration status from occupying the dwelling-house under the tenancy.

For the purposes of this case a person ("P") is disqualified as a result of their immigration status from occupying the dwelling-house under the tenancy if—

(a) P is not a relevant national, and

(b) P does not have a right to rent in relation to the dwelling-house.

P does not have a right to rent in relation to the dwelling-house if—

(a) P requires leave to enter or remain in the United Kingdom but does not have it, or

(b) P's leave to enter or remain in the United Kingdom is subject to a condition preventing P from occupying the dwelling-house.

But P is to be treated as having a right to rent in relation to a dwelling-house if the Secretary of State has granted P permission for the

2.6 *A Guide to the Immigration Act 2016*

purposes of this case to occupy a dwelling-house which is for the time being let on a protected tenancy or subject to a statutory tenancy.

In this case "relevant national" means—

(a) a British citizen,

(b) a national of an EEA State other than the United Kingdom, or

(c) a national of Switzerland."

(7) The amendments made by this section apply in relation to a tenancy entered into before or after the coming into force of this section.

Commencement: 1 December 2016, the Immigration Act 2016 (Commencement No. 2 and Transitional Provisions) Regulations 2016, SI 2016/1037.

Amends: Housing Act 1988 (HA 1988), inserting a new s 10A *Power to order transfer of tenancy in certain cases,* a new ground 7B into Part I of Schedule 2 *Assured Tenancies grounds on which a court must order possession* and amending s 7 *Orders for possession* and s 8 *Cases where a court may not dispense with notice of proceedings for possession*. Amends the Rent Act 1977 (RA 1977), Schedule 15 Part I *Grounds for possession of dwelling houses let on or subject to protected or statutory tenancies,* inserting a new case 10A *Termination of agreement where all occupiers disqualified,* s 33E *Other procedures for ending agreement.* Also amends s 35 and 36 of that Act.

Definitions:

'assured tenancy' HA 1988, s 1;

'dwelling-house' a house or part of a house, HA 1988, s 45(1) and see RA 1977, s 1 to the same effect;

'fixed term tenancy' any tenancy other than a periodic tenancy, HA 1988, s 45(1);

'landlord' RA 1977, 152(1); includes any person from time-to-time deriving title under the original landlord and also includes, in relation to a dwelling-house, any person other than a tenant who is, or but for the existence of an assured tenancy would be, entitled to possession of the dwelling-house;

'let' includes 'sub-let', HA 1988, s 45(1);

'qualifying tenant' a person who is not disqualified as a result of their immigration status from occupying a dwelling-house under the tenancy, HA 1988, s 10A(2);

'relevant national' a British citizen, another EEA national or a Swiss national, HA 1988, Schedule 2 Part I *Ground 7B* (s 41(2)) and RA 1977 Schedule 15 Part I, *Case 10A;*

'residential tenancy agreement' an agreement granting a right of occupation for residential use, for a rent, whether or not a market rent, that is not an excluded agreement, Immigration Act 2014, s 20(2);

'tenancy' includes a sub-tenancy, RA 1977, s 152(1); includes a sub-tenancy and an agreement for a tenancy or sub-tenancy, HA 1988, s 45(1);

'tenant' includes a statutory tenant, a sub-tenant and any person deriving title under the original tenant or sub-tenant, RA 1977, s 152(1); includes a sub-tenant and any person deriving title under the original tenant or sub-tenant, HA 1988, s 45(1);

Devolution: Applies to England only. Can be extended to Wales, Scotland and Northern Ireland by regulations, see s 42.

The section amends the RA 1977 and the HA 1988 to provide for a new mandatory ground for a landlord or landlady to obtain possession of a property following receipt of notification from the Secretary of State (SSHD) that an occupant is a disqualified person. Landlords and landladies can rely on this mandatory ground of possession where the SSHD has given notice in writing that a tenant, tenants or adult occupiers who are occupying the property under the tenancy are disqualified from occupying the property as a result of their immigration status. The mandatory ground for eviction only applies where the landlord has received a Landlord Notice from the SSHD in respect of the qualified person.

The landlord or landlady may choose to transfer the tenancy to other qualified tenants occupying the property without going to court. To evict the tenants, the landlord or landlady may serve a notice seeking possession. If the tenants do not wish to vacate the property, the landlord or landlady can seek possession from the courts. Under the amended provisions of the RA 1977 and the HA 1988, the court will be obliged to issue an order for possession. The court has a power to order that the interest in the property of the tenants who are disqualified be transferred to joint tenants who are not disqualified. If there are no other tenants to whom the tenancy can be transferred, the court has no discretion and must order possession under the mandatory ground.

The amendments apply to all tenancies, whether entered into before or after the coming into force of the section.

The Minister gave as the rationale for the provisions:

> 'The mandatory ground for possession recognises that the Home Office notice is a clear statement of immigration status; it is not necessary or helpful for a court to enter into its own additional assessment of the reasonableness of making a possession order, which would be the effect of making this a discretionary ground.'[1]

2.7 *A Guide to the Immigration Act 2016*

This does not, however, address all the circumstances with which courts may be presented. For example, the court may be satisfied of the immigration status of the person facing eviction but conclude that because of the person's circumstances, for example a baby or children in the family, pregnancy, old age, disability or infirmity, that eviction is not appropriate. The courts would be prevented from making an order they considered appropriate in these circumstances. The Minister suggested that the safeguard would be the Home Office not serving a notice in cases where eviction would not be appropriate.[2]

---

1 Rt Hon James Brokenshire MP, Minister for Immigration, Immigration Bill 2015/16 Public Bill Committee, House of Commons, 29 October 2015, *Hansard* Col 263. Available at: http://www.publications.parliament.uk/pa/cm201516/cmpublic/immigration/151029/pm/151029s01.htm (accessed 14 December 2016).
2 Ibid, *Hansard* col 278.

SECTION 42—EXTENSION TO WALES, SCOTLAND AND NORTHERN IRELAND

> **Summary**
>
> Provides for the Secretary of State to make, through regulations, such provision as she considers appropriate to enable ss 39–41, or provision that has a similar effect, to apply in Wales, Scotland or Northern Ireland.

2.7

42 Extension to Wales, Scotland and Northern Ireland

(1) The Secretary of State may by regulations make such provision as the Secretary of State considers appropriate for enabling any of the residential tenancies provisions to apply in relation to Wales, Scotland or Northern Ireland.

(2) The Secretary of State may by regulations make provision which—

  (a) has a similar effect to any of the residential tenancies provisions, and

  (b) applies in relation to Wales, Scotland or Northern Ireland.

(3) Regulations under subsection (1) or (2) may—

  (a) amend, repeal or revoke any enactment;

  (b) confer functions on any person.

Part 2—Access to Services **2.7**

(4) Regulations under subsection (1) or (2) may not confer functions on—

  (a) the Welsh Ministers,

  (b) the Scottish Ministers,

  (c) the First Minister and deputy First Minister in Northern Ireland,

  (d) a Northern Ireland Minister, or

  (e) a Northern Ireland department.

(5) In this section—

  "enactment" includes—

  (a) an enactment contained in subordinate legislation within the meaning of the Interpretation Act 1978;

  (b) an enactment contained in, or in an instrument made under, an Act or Measure of the National Assembly for Wales;

  (c) an enactment contained in, or in an instrument made under, an Act of the Scottish Parliament;

  (d) an enactment contained in, or in an instrument made under, Northern Ireland legislation;

  "the residential tenancies provisions" means sections 39 to 41 and the amendments made by those sections.

Commencement: Not yet in force.

Definitions:

'enactment' includes subordinate legislation; legislation made, or made under legislation by the Scottish parliament or the National Assembly for Wales; an enactment contained in, or an instrument made under Northern Ireland legislation;

'the residential tenancies provisions' ss 39–41 and the amendments they effect.

Devolution: Regulation-making powers allowing similar provision to be made in Wales, Scotland and Northern Ireland. Regulations can amend not only Acts of the Scottish Parliament or Northern Ireland or Welsh legislation, but also Acts of the UK Parliament (and subordinate legislation made under them).

The section provides a power for the Secretary of State to make, through regulations, such provision as she considers appropriate to enable ss 39–41, or provision that has a similar effect, to apply in Wales, Scotland or Northern Ireland. The right to rent provisions of the Immigration Act 2014 (IA 2014)

2.7 A Guide to the Immigration Act 2016

can be made subject to geographical limitations by regulations so there is no difficulty in extending the 'extent' section of IA 2014.

The extension of the provisions through secondary legislation means that they are not subject to the same detailed scrutiny by Parliament as the provisions for England and Wales. If the measures made in secondary legislation are found to be incompatible with the UK's obligations under the Human Rights Act 1998, they may be struck down rather than simply declared incompatible as is the case for primary legislation.

The Explanatory Notes to the Bill record the Government's view that a legislative consent motion would not be required for any extension.[1]

Anne McLaughlin MP of the Scottish National Party stated that, 'the Minister refused a meeting with the Scottish Government Minister for Housing and Welfare, who has significant concerns not just at a policy level but at an implementation level.'[2]

Although immigration is a reserved matter the right to rent scheme impacts upon areas within the competence of the devolved administrations including matters pertaining to housing, social welfare, town and country planning and economic development.

---

[1] Immigration Bill Explanatory Notes, Bill 79 2015-16-EN (as brought from the House of Commons), 2 December 2015. Available at: http://www.publications.parliament.uk/pa/bills/lbill/2015-2016/0079/en/15079en.pdf, annex B (accessed 14 December 2016).

[2] Anne McLaughlin MP, Immigration Bill 2015/16 Public Bill Committee, House of Commons, 3 November 2015, *Hansard* Col 301. Available at: http://www.publications.parliament.uk/pa/cm201516/cmpublic/immigration/151103/am/151103s01.htm#15110342000216 (accessed 14 December 2016).

DRIVING

SECTION 43—POWERS TO CARRY OUT SEARCHES RELATING TO DRIVING LICENCES

> **Summary**
>
> Creates powers to enable police, immigration officers and other persons (unspecified) authorised by the Secretary of State to enter premises to search for and seize driving licences and to search persons and premises for these.

2.8

43 Powers to carry out searches relating to driving licences

(1) Schedule 2 to the Immigration Act 1971 (administrative provisions as to control of entry etc) is amended in accordance with subsections (2) and (3).

(2) After paragraph 25C insert—

"Entry of premises to search for driving licence

25CA(1) An authorised officer may exercise the powers in this section if the officer has reasonable grounds for believing that a person—

(a) is in possession of a driving licence, and

(b) is not lawfully resident in the United Kingdom.

(2) The authorised officer may enter and search any premises—

(a) occupied or controlled by the person, or

(b) in which the person was when the person was encountered by the officer,

for the driving licence.

(3) The power conferred by sub-paragraph (2) may be exercised—

(a) only if the authorised officer has reasonable grounds for believing that the driving licence is on the premises,

(b) only to the extent that it is reasonably required for the purpose of discovering the driving licence, and

(c) unless the authorised officer is a constable, only if a senior officer has authorised its exercise in writing.

(4) Sub-paragraph (3)(c) does not apply where it is not reasonably practicable for the authorised officer to obtain the authorisation of a senior officer before exercising the power.

(5) An authorised officer who has conducted a search in reliance on sub-paragraph (4) must inform a senior officer as soon as is practicable.

(6) The senior officer authorising a search, or who is informed of one under sub-paragraph (5), must make a record in writing of the grounds for the search.

(7) In this paragraph and paragraphs 25CB and 25CC—

"authorised officer" means—

(a) an immigration officer,

(b) a constable, or

(c) a person of a kind authorised for the purposes of this paragraph and paragraphs 25CB and 25CC by the Secretary of State;

2.8   *A Guide to the Immigration Act 2016*

"driving licence"—

(a) means a licence to drive a motor vehicle granted under Part 3 of the Road Traffic Act 1988 or Part II of the Road Traffic (Northern Ireland) Order 1981 (SI 1981/154 (NI 1)), and

(b) includes a licence of that kind which has been revoked;

"senior officer" means—

(a) in relation to an authorised officer who is an immigration officer, an immigration officer not below the rank of chief immigration officer;

(b) in relation to an authorised officer other than an immigration officer, a person of a kind designated by the Secretary of State for the purposes of this paragraph in relation to an authorised officer of that kind.

(8) For the purposes of this paragraph and paragraphs 25CB and 25CC a person is not lawfully resident in the United Kingdom if the person requires leave to enter or remain in the United Kingdom but does not have it.

Searching persons for driving licences

25CB(1) An authorised officer may exercise the powers in this section if the officer has reasonable grounds for believing that a person—

(a) is in possession of a driving licence, and

(b) is not lawfully resident in the United Kingdom.

(2) The authorised officer may search the person for the driving licence.

(3) The power conferred by sub-paragraph (2) may be exercised—

(a) only if the authorised officer has reasonable grounds for believing that the driving licence may be concealed on the person, and

(b) only to the extent that it is reasonably required for the purpose of discovering the driving licence.

(4) An intimate search may not be carried out under sub-paragraph (2).

(5) In sub-paragraph (4) "intimate search" has the same meaning as in section 28H(11).

Seizure and retention of driving licence

25CC(1) If an authorised officer who is exercising a power to search a person or premises finds a driving licence to which this sub-paragraph applies in the course of the search, the officer may seize and retain the licence.

(2) Sub-paragraph (1) applies to a driving licence if—

    (a) the authorised officer finds the licence in the possession of a person who the authorised officer has reasonable grounds for believing is not lawfully resident in the United Kingdom, or

    (b) the authorised officer has reasonable grounds for believing that the holder of the licence is not lawfully resident in the United Kingdom.

(3) A driving licence seized under sub-paragraph (1) must, as soon as practicable, be given to—

    (a) the Secretary of State, in the case of a licence granted by the Secretary of State, or

    (b) the Department for Infrastructure for Northern Ireland, in the case of a licence granted by the Department.

(4) A person who is in possession of a driving licence by virtue of sub-paragraph (3) must retain it if—

    (a) it has not been revoked,

    (b) it has been revoked but the time limit for an appeal against revocation of the licence has not expired, or

    (c) it has been revoked, such an appeal has been brought but the appeal has not been determined.

(5) A driving licence which is required to be retained under sub-paragraph (4) must be retained—

    (a) until a decision is taken not to revoke it, or

    (b) if it has been or is subsequently revoked—

        (i) until the time limit for an appeal against revocation of the licence expires without an appeal being brought, or

        (ii) until such an appeal is determined.

(6) A driving licence which is in the possession of a person by virtue of sub-paragraph (3) but which is not required to be retained under sub-paragraphs (4) and (5) must be returned to the holder if—

    (a) a decision is taken not to revoke the licence, or

    (b) an appeal against revocation of the licence is determined in favour of the holder.

(7) Otherwise the driving licence may be dealt with in such manner as that person thinks fit.

2.8 *A Guide to the Immigration Act 2016*

        (8)   Neither the Secretary of State nor the Department for Infrastructure for Northern Ireland is obliged to re-issue a licence which has been seized and retained under this paragraph.

        (9)   References in this paragraph to an appeal against the revocation of a licence are to—

            (a)   an appeal under section 100 of the Road Traffic Act 1988, in the case of a licence granted by the Secretary of State, or

            (b)   an appeal under Article 16 of the Road Traffic (Northern Ireland) Order 1981 (SI 1981/154 (NI 1)), in the case of a licence granted by the Department for Infrastructure for Northern Ireland.

        (10)   References in this paragraph to the holder of a driving licence, in relation to a licence that has been revoked, include the person who was the holder of the licence before it was revoked."

(3)   In paragraph 25D(8) (access and copying: meaning of seized material) at the end insert "other than a driving licence seized under paragraph 25CC."

(4)   In section 146(2) of the Immigration and Asylum Act 1999 (use of reasonable force) after paragraph (a) insert—

    "(aa)   paragraph 25CA, 25CB or 25CC of Schedule 2 to the 1971 Act (powers to search for and seize driving licences),".

(5)   In the period (if any) between the coming into force of subsection (2) and the coming into force of the Departments Act (Northern Ireland) 2016, references to the Department for Infrastructure for Northern Ireland in paragraph 25CC(3)(b), (8) and (9)(b) of Schedule 2 to the Immigration Act 1971 (as inserted by subsection (2)) are to be read as references to the Department of the Environment for Northern Ireland.

Commencement: Not yet in force.

Amends: Immigration Act 1971 (IA 1971), Schedule 2 *Administrative provisions as to control of entry etc*, inserting new paragraphs 25CA *Entry of premises to search for driving licences*, 25CB *Searching persons for driving licences* and 25CC *Seizure and retention of driving licences*, and amending paragraph 25D. Amends s 146(2) of the Immigration and Asylum Act 1999 (s 43(4)) on the use of reasonable force so that reasonable force can be used in respect of these new powers of entry, search and seizure.

Regulations: the Secretary of State (SSHD) may designate kinds of persons authorised to carry out entry, search and seizure under these provisions, paragraph 25CA(7). No constraints are placed on these powers.

Definitions:

'authorised officer' an immigration officer, constable, or person of a kind authorised by the SSHD in regulations, paragraph 25CA(7);

'driving licence' licence granted under the Road Traffic Act 1988 or Road Traffic (Northern Ireland) Order 1981, SI 1981/154 drive a motor vehicle including a licence which has been revoked;

'premises' England and Wales: Police and Criminal Evidence Act 1984, s 23 *Meaning of 'premises' etc* includes any place and, in particular, includes any vehicle, vessel, aircraft or hovercraft; any offshore installation ('offshore installation' has the meaning given to it by s 1 of the Mineral Workings (Offshore Installations) Act 1971); any renewable energy installation ('renewable energy installation' has the same meaning as in Chapter 2 of Part 2 of the Energy Act 2004); any tent or movable structure. Northern Ireland: Police and Criminal Evidence (Northern Ireland) Order 1989, SI 1989/1341 (N 12) ditto, see Article 25. Scotland: as in s 412 of the Proceeds of Crime Act 2002, including any vehicle, vessel, aircraft or hovercraft, any offshore installation within the meaning given to it by s 1 of the Mineral Workings (Offshore Installations) Act 1971 and any tent or moveable structure. See IA 1971, s 28L.

Devolution: Applies throughout the UK.

Sections 46–47 of IA 2014 put onto the statute book a policy introduced on 25 March 2010,[1] under which those who are not lawfully in the UK are not entitled to be granted a UK driving licence. Section 46 amended the Road Traffic Act 1988 (RTA 1988) to include a residence requirement under s 97A making normal and lawful residence in the UK a requirement for the grant of a driving licence. A person is not normally and lawfully resident for this purpose if they require leave to enter or remain in the UK but do not have it (s 97A(2) of the RTA 1988). Section 47 of the IA 1971 amended s 99 of the RTA 1988 to provide powers for driving licences to be revoked and to require licences to be surrendered if it appears that the person is not lawfully resident in the UK. Failure to surrender the licence was also made an offence under this section. Amendments were made to the Road Traffic (Northern Ireland) Order 1981, SI 1981/154 NI 1 with the same effect.

New para 25CA of Schedule 2 to the IA 1971, inserted by s 43(2), gives immigration and police officers power to enter premises to search for a driving licence in the possession of a person whom they reasonably believe is not lawfully resident in the UK. New para 25CB gives them power to search a person whom they have reasonable grounds for believing is in possession of a driving licence and who is not lawfully resident in the UK.

In both cases, the test is one of reasonable grounds for believing rather than knowledge that a person is in possession of a driving licence and not lawfully resident in the UK. The Explanatory notes to the Bill stated with regards to the power to search premises, 'For example, an authorised officer would have reasonable grounds to use this power when immigration enforcement apprehends an immigration offender who tells the officers that they have a driving licence.'[2]

2.8 *A Guide to the Immigration Act 2016*

An example of when reasonable suspicion might give rise to search a person for a driving licence was given by the Minister in the House of Lords, 'Reasonable suspicion may occur where a vehicle has been stopped for a suspected driving offence, the police have checked the circumstances of the driver, as appropriate, and those checks have revealed a match against a Home Office record.'[3]

Premises owned or occupied by the person can be searched, but so can the premises in which they were encountered, either with or without prior authorisation from a senior officer. There is an obligation to return driving licences seized only where it is decided not to revoke the licence or the person wins their appeal against revocation of the licence. Normal powers to have access to and copy seized material do not apply. The Explanatory Notes to the Bill stated that this is so that a person cannot make use of a photocopy as a form of identification to enable a settled life,[4] but there are questions about whether there can be a fair appeal when a person cannot examine the evidence held against them.

Once a licence has been seized it must be given either to the SSHD (in practice this will be passed to the Driver and Vehicle Licensing Agency, an executive agency of the Department for Transport), or to the Department of the Environment for Northern Ireland, depending upon who granted the licence. Provision is made to ensure that a driving licence is returned to the holder should the holder successfully appeal against revocation.

The new powers will be piloted by the police in Kent and West Yorkshire and will be brought into force in those areas initially, following the collection of baseline data. There will then be a public consultation on the draft guidance to be issued to police and immigration officers on the use of the powers.[5]

---

1 Paul Clark MP, Parliamentary Under-Secretary of State for Transport, Ministerial Statement: UK Driving Licences (Migrants), 25 March 2010, *Hansard* col 70WS. Available at: http://www.publications.parliament.uk/pa/cm200910/cmhansrd/cm100325/wmstext/100325m0005.htm#10032542000410 (accessed 14 December 2016).

2 Immigration Bill Explanatory Notes, Bill 79 2015-16-EN (as brought from the House of Commons), 2 December 2015. Available at: http://www.publications.parliament.uk/pa/bills/lbill/2015-2016/0079/en/15079en.pdf, para 127 (accessed 14 December 2016).

3 Rt Hon Lord Bates, Minister of State, Home Office, Immigration Bill 2015/16, House of Lords Committee, 3rd sitting, 1 February 2016, *Hansard* col 1597. Available at: http://www.publications.parliament.uk/pa/ld201516/ldhansrd/text/160201-0001.htm#16020190000478 (accessed 14 December 2016).

4 Immigration Bill Explanatory Notes, Bill 79 2015-16-EN (as brought from the House of Commons), 2 December 2015. Available at: http://www.publications.parliament.uk/pa/bills/lbill/2015-2016/0079/en/15079en.pdf, para 129 (accessed 14 December 2016).

5 Baroness Williams of Trafford, Minister of State for the Home Office to Lord Rosser, Pilot of the powers to search for and seize UK driving licences held by illegal immigrants, 14 February 2017. Available at: http://data.parliament.uk/DepositedPapers/Files/DEP2017-0136/Williams_to_Lord_RosserUK_driving_licences_held_illegal_migrants.pdf (accessed 1 March 2017).

SECTION 44—OFFENCE OF DRIVING WHEN UNLAWFULLY IN THE UNITED KINGDOM

> **Summary**
>
> Creates a new criminal offence of driving while not lawfully resident in the UK at a time when a person knows or has reasonable cause to believe that they are not lawfully resident.

2.9

44 Offence of driving when unlawfully in the United Kingdom

(1) The Immigration Act 1971 is amended in accordance with subsections (2) to (6).

(2) Before section 25 insert—

"24C Driving when unlawfully in the United Kingdom

(1) A person commits an offence if—

(a) the person drives a motor vehicle on a road or other public place at a time when the person is not lawfully resident in the United Kingdom, and

(b) at that time the person knows or has reasonable cause to believe that the person is not lawfully resident in the United Kingdom.

(2) A person who is guilty of an offence under subsection (1) is liable on summary conviction—

(a) in England and Wales, to imprisonment for a term not exceeding 51 weeks, to a fine or to both;

(b) in Scotland or Northern Ireland, to imprisonment for a term not exceeding 6 months, to a fine not exceeding level 5 on the standard scale or to both.

(3) In relation to an offence committed before section 281(5) of the Criminal Justice Act 2003 comes into force, the reference in subsection (2)(a) to 51 weeks is to be read as a reference to 6 months.

(4) In this section "motor vehicle" and "road"—

(a) in relation to England and Wales and Scotland, have the same meanings as in the Road Traffic Act 1988;

(b) in relation to Northern Ireland, have the same meanings as in the Road Traffic (Northern Ireland) Order 1995 (SI 1995/2994 (NI 18)).

(5) For the purposes of this section a person is not lawfully resident in the United Kingdom if the person requires leave to enter or remain in the United Kingdom but does not have it.

24D Detention of motor vehicles

(1) If a person ("P") has been arrested for an offence under section 24C committed in England and Wales or Northern Ireland, a senior officer or a constable may detain a relevant vehicle.

(2) Subject to regulations under subsection (8), a vehicle detained under subsection (1) must be released—

(a) when a decision is taken not to charge P with the offence, or

(b) if P is charged with the offence—

(i) when P is acquitted, the charge against P is dismissed or the proceedings are discontinued, or

(ii) if P is convicted, when the court decides not to order forfeiture of the vehicle.

(3) If a person ("P") has been arrested for an offence under section 24C committed in Scotland, a senior officer or a constable may detain a relevant vehicle.

(4) Subject to regulations under subsection (8) a vehicle detained under subsection (3) must be released—

(a) when a decision is taken not to institute criminal proceedings against P for the offence, or

(b) if criminal proceedings are instituted against P for the offence—

(i) when P is acquitted or, under section 147 of the Criminal Procedure (Scotland) Act 1995, liberated or the trial diet is deserted simpliciter, or

(ii) if P is convicted, when the court decides not to order forfeiture of the vehicle.

(5) For the purposes of subsection (4) criminal proceedings are instituted against a person ("P") at whichever is the earliest of P's first appearance before the sheriff or the service on P of a complaint.

(6) A power in subsection (1) or (3) may be exercised by a senior officer or constable at any place at which the senior officer or constable is lawfully present.

(7) A vehicle is a relevant vehicle in relation to P if the officer or constable concerned has reasonable grounds for believing it was used in the commission by P of an offence under section 24C.

(8) The Secretary of State may by regulations make provision about the release of a vehicle detained under subsection (1) or (3).

(9) Regulations under subsection (8) may in particular make provision—

(a) for the release of a vehicle before the time mentioned in subsection (2) or (4);

(b) about the procedure by which a person may seek to have a vehicle released before or after that time;

(c) about the persons to whom a vehicle may or must be released before or after that time;

(d) prescribing conditions to be met before a vehicle may be released before or after that time (including a condition requiring the payment of costs in relation to detention of the vehicle and any application for its release);

(e) as to the destination of payments made in compliance with such a condition;

(f) enabling a person specified in the regulations to waive compliance with such a condition;

(g) as to the disposal of a vehicle in a case where such a condition is not met;

(h) as to the destination of the proceeds arising from the disposal of a vehicle in such a case.

(10) Regulations under subsection (8)—

(a) are to be made by statutory instrument;

(b) may make different provision for different cases;

(c) may make incidental, supplementary, consequential, transitional, transitory or saving provision.

(11) A statutory instrument containing regulations under subsection (8) is subject to annulment in pursuance of a resolution of either House of Parliament.

(12) In this section "senior officer" means an immigration officer not below the rank of chief immigration officer.

24E Powers to enter premises to detain motor vehicle

(1) A senior officer or a constable may enter and search any premises for the purposes of detaining a vehicle under section 24D.

2.9 *A Guide to the Immigration Act 2016*

(2) The power in subsection (1) may be exercised—

  (a) only to the extent that it is reasonably required for that purpose, and

  (b) only if the senior officer or constable knows that a vehicle which may be detained under section 24D is to be found on the premises.

(3) The power in subsection (1) may be exercised—

  (a) by a senior officer ("S") only if S produces identification showing that S is an immigration officer (whether or not S is asked to do so);

  (b) by a constable ("C") only if C produces identification showing that C is a constable (whether or not C is asked to do so).

(4) Subsection (5) applies if, on an application by a senior officer or constable, a justice of the peace is satisfied that there are reasonable grounds for suspecting that a vehicle which may be detained under section 24D may be found on premises mentioned in subsection (6).

(5) The justice of the peace may issue a warrant authorising any senior officer or constable to enter, if need be by force, the premises for the purpose of searching for and detaining the vehicle.

(6) The premises referred to in subsection (4) are—

  (a) one or more sets of premises specified in the application, or

  (b) subject to subsection (10), any premises occupied or controlled by a person specified in the application, including such sets of premises as are so specified (in which case the application is for an "all premises warrant").

(7) If the application is for an all premises warrant, the justice of the peace must also be satisfied—

  (a) that there are reasonable grounds for believing that it is necessary to search premises occupied or controlled by the person in question which are not specified in the application in order to find the vehicle, and

  (b) that it is not reasonably practicable to specify in the application all the premises which the person occupies or controls and which might need to be searched.

(8) Subject to subsection (10), the warrant may authorise entry to and search of premises on more than one occasion if, on the application, the justice of the peace is satisfied that it is necessary to authorise multiple entries in order to achieve the purpose for which the justice issues the warrant.

(9) If it authorises multiple entries, the number of entries authorised may be unlimited, or limited to a maximum.

(10) A justice of the peace in Scotland may not issue—

    (a) an all premises warrant under this section, or

    (b) a warrant under this section authorising multiple entries.

(11) In the application of this section to Scotland, references to a justice of the peace are to be read as references to the sheriff or a justice of the peace.

(12) In this section "senior officer" means an immigration officer not below the rank of chief immigration officer.

24F Orders following conviction of offence under section 24C

(1) If a person is convicted of an offence under section 24C, the court may order the forfeiture of the vehicle used in the commission of the offence.

(2) Where a person who claims to have an interest in the vehicle applies to the court to make representations on the question of forfeiture, the court may not make an order under this section in respect of the vehicle unless the person has been given an opportunity to make representations.

(3) For the purposes of subsection (2) the persons who have an interest in a vehicle include—

    (a) a person who owns it,

    (b) the person in whose name the vehicle is registered under the Vehicle Excise and Registration Act 1994, and

    (c) a person who is in possession of it under a hire purchase agreement (or, in the case of a detained vehicle, was in possession of it under a hire purchase agreement immediately before its detention).

(4) The Secretary of State may by regulations make provision about—

    (a) the disposal of a vehicle forfeited under this section;

    (b) the destination of the proceeds arising from the disposal of such a vehicle.

(5) Regulations under subsection (4)—

    (a) are to be made by statutory instrument;

    (b) may make different provision for different cases;

    (c) may make incidental, supplementary, consequential, transitional, transitory or saving provision.

(6) A statutory instrument containing regulations under subsection (4) is subject to annulment in pursuance of a resolution of either House of Parliament."

(3) In section 28A(3)(a) (arrest without warrant) before "25" insert "24C,".

2.9 *A Guide to the Immigration Act 2016*

(4) In section 28B(5) (search and arrest by warrant: relevant offences) before "26A" insert "24C,".

(5) In section 28CA(1) (business premises: entry to arrest) for the "or" at the end of paragraph (b) substitute—

"(bb) for an offence under section 24C, or"

(6) In section 28D(4) (entry and search of premises: relevant offences) before "25" insert "24C,".

(7) In section 16(2A)(b) of the Police and Criminal Evidence Act 1984 (powers of persons accompanying constables in execution of warrants) after "seizure" insert "or detention".

(8) In Article 18(2A)(b) of the Police and Criminal Evidence (Northern Ireland) Order 1989 (SI 1989/1341 (NI 12)) (powers of persons accompanying constables in execution of warrants) after "seizure" insert "or detention".

(9) In section 146(2) of the Immigration and Asylum Act 1999 (use of reasonable force) before paragraph (a) insert—

"(za) section 24E(1) (powers to enter premises to detain motor vehicle) of the 1971 Act,".

Commencement: Not yet in force.

Amends: Immigration Act 1971 (IA 1971), Schedule 2 *Administrative provisions as to control of entry etc*, inserting new s 24C *Driving when unlawfully in the United Kingdom*, 24D *Detention of motor vehicles*, 24E *Powers to enter premises to detain a motor vehicle*, 24F *Orders following conviction of offence under section 24C*, and amends ss 28A, 28B, 28CA, 28D. Amends s 16(2A) *Powers of persons accompanying constables in the execution of warrants* of the Police and Criminal Evidence Act 1984 and Article 18(2A) *Powers of Persons accompanying constables in execution of warrants* of the Police and Criminal Evidence (Northern Ireland) Order 1989 (SI 1989/1341 (NI 12)). Amends s 146 *Use of reasonable force* of the Immigration and Asylum Act 1999.

Regulations: About the provision for release of a vehicle (s 44(2) inserting s 24D(8) IA 1971 and subject to the negative procedure (s 44(2) inserting IA 1971, s 24D(11)). About the disposal of the vehicle and what is to be done with the proceeds of the same (s 44(2) inserting IA 1971, s 24F(5)), also subject to the negative procedure (s 44(2) inserting IA 1971, s 24F(6)).

Guidance: Commitment given in parliament to issue (non-statutory) guidance to police and immigration officers on the use of stop and search powers for the new offence under IA 1971, s 24C of driving while unlawfully in the UK.

Definitions:

'motor vehicle' means, subject to s 20 of the Chronically Sick and Disabled Persons Act 1970 (which makes special provision about invalid carriages, within the meaning of that Act), a mechanically propelled vehicle intended or adapted for use on roads, Road Traffic Act 1988, s 185 (England, Wales, Scotland); a mechanically propelled vehicle (not being a tramcar or other vehicle running on permanent rails or a trolley vehicle) which is intended or adapted for use on roads, Road Traffic (Northern Ireland) Order 1995, SI 1995/2994, Article 3 subject to Article 6 (which makes provision, *inter alia*, for lawnmowers) (Northern Ireland); s 44(2) inserting s 24D(4) Immigration Act 1971;

'road' in relation to England and Wales, means any highway and any other road to which the public has access, and includes bridges over which a road passes, and in relation to Scotland, means any road within the meaning of the Roads (Scotland) Act 1984 and any other way to which the public has access, and includes bridges over which a road passes, Road Traffic Act 1988, s 192 (England, Wales and Scotland); 'road' includes a public road and any street, carriageway, highway or roadway to which the public has access Road Traffic (Northern Ireland) Order 1995, SI 1995/2994 (NI18)) (Northern Ireland); s 44(2) inserting s 24C(4) IA 1971);

'person not lawfully resident in the United Kingdom' person who requires leave to enter or remain and does not have it (s 44(2) inserting s 24C(4) IA 1971);

'senior officer' a person not below the rank of chief immigration officer (s 44(2) inserting s 24D(12) IA 1971).

Offence: IA 1971, s 24C *Driving when unlawfully in the United Kingdom* inserted by s 44(20).

Devolution: Applies throughout the UK. Specific provisions relating to the powers of the courts in the devolved areas.

The section creates a new offence (under new s 24C of the IA 1971) of driving whilst not lawfully resident in the UK. A person is defined as not being lawfully resident where they require leave to enter the UK but do not have it. The offence has the intended effect of preventing those without leave in the UK from driving where they have a valid foreign-issued licence as well as where they are no longer entitled to a UK driving licence.[1] The offence is only committed if, at the time of the offence, the person knows or has reasonable cause to believe that they are not lawfully resident in the UK. The provision had originally been drafted as a strict liability offence but was amended by the Government for Report stage in the House of Lords following sustained opposition to a strict liability offence during the consideration of the provision by Parliament:

> 'I believe that we are of one mind in our intention to ensure that migrants are not prosecuted for this offence where they hold a genuine and reasonable belief that they are in the UK legally. The Government have been persuaded that it would be appropriate to place further safeguards on the face of the statute. These amendments introduce a *mens rea* element so that an illegal migrant will only commit the offence of driving while illegally present if they knew or had reasonable cause to believe they were in the UK illegally.

2.9   *A Guide to the Immigration Act 2016*

This will protect those who genuinely and reasonably believed they were here in the UK lawfully, while ensuring that other migrants cannot seek to avoid prosecution by avoiding contact with the Home Office and/or their legal representatives, in order to establish the necessary doubt as to whether they could reasonably be expected to have known they were required to leave the UK'.[2]

A person guilty of this offence will be liable on summary conviction to imprisonment of up to 51 weeks and/or a fine in England and Wales, or to imprisonment of up to 6 months and/or a fine not exceeding level 5 on the standard scale in Scotland or Northern Ireland.

Under powers in Part 3 of the IA 1971 where the provision is inserted, immigration officers may arrest, without a warrant, a person who has committed, or who they have reasonable grounds for suspecting has committed, the offence. A justice of the peace (or a sheriff or justice of the peace in Scotland) may issue a warrant permitting an immigration officer or constable to enter premises to search for and arrest a person suspected of committing the new driving offence and a constable or immigration officer may enter and search business premises for the purpose of arresting a person suspected of committing the offence. A justice of the peace (or a sheriff or justice of the peace in Scotland) may issue a warrant permitting an immigration officer to enter and search premises, where there are reasonable grounds for believing that material may be found on those premises that relate to the offence.

There was considerable concern expressed in Parliament, including from Baroness Lawrence of Clarendon, about the creation of the offence and the use of stop and search powers in relation to it with regard to the impact on community cohesion and race relations. The Government made the following statements, including a commitment to consult on and issue guidance to police and immigration officers:

> 'we intend the police to use these powers reactively after they have already stopped a vehicle for an objective reason – I will come back to that particular use of words, as the noble Lord, Lord Alton, asked me to – such as a driving offence. I emphasise that these powers will not be used by the police to stop vehicles simply to check the immigration status of the driver. That is an important distinction between the roles and responsibilities of the police and of immigration enforcement. It is one that we recognise should be maintained. Thirdly, these powers must be used proportionately. To that end, we have put in place safeguards against misuse.
>
> Finally, I reiterate that the Government are absolutely clear that no one should be stopped, under existing police powers, on the basis of their race or ethnicity. This would be unlawful ...
>
> We have listened carefully to the concerns raised about these clauses. In response, the Home Office will go further. We will issue guidance to police

and immigration officers on the operation of these powers and we will consult publicly on that draft guidance. This consultation will take place before implementation. It will raise awareness and provide an important gateway through which communities will be able to consider and comment on, among other things, appropriate safeguards.'[3]

The government has since stated that the new search powers will be piloted by the police in Kent and West Yorkshire and will be brought into force in those areas initially, following the collection of baseline data. There will be an evaluation of the pilot, then the public consultation will take place on the draft guidance to be issued to police and immigration officers on the use of these powers.[4]

When a person is arrested for this new offence, s 24D of the IA 1971 creates a new power to impound the vehicle used in the commission of the offence until a decision is made as to whether to charge the person (or a decision to institute proceedings in Scotland) and then while proceedings are ongoing. That the vehicle is not owned by the person driving it does not necessarily mean that it will be returned; this will be a matter for regulations. Vehicles owned by the person suspected of not having leave and vehicles owned by others that the person has driven may both be impounded. The regulations may also make provision for the disposal of vehicles where conditions for releasing of the vehicle are not met.

New s 24E of the IA 1971 provides the police and immigration officers with the power to enter premises in order to detain a relevant vehicle. This power can be exercised without a warrant if the relevant officer knows the vehicle is on the premises, or with a warrant if a justice of the peace is satisfied that there are reasonable grounds for suspecting that the vehicle is on the premises.

Under IA 1971, s 24F inserted by this section, if a person is convicted of an offence under IA 1971, s 24C, the court may order forfeiture of the relevant vehicle. Forfeiture orders cannot be made unless any person with an interest in the vehicle, who has applied to the court to make representations against forfeiture, has been allowed to present these to the court.

---

1 Rt Hon Lord Bates, Minister of State, Home Office, Immigration Bill 2015/6 House of Lords Report Stage, 2nd sitting, 15 March 2016, *Hansard* Col 1771. Available at: http://www.publications.parliament.uk/pa/ld201516/ldhansrd/text/160315-0001.htm#16031556000351 (accessed 14 December 2016).
2 Rt Hon Lord Bates, Minister of State, Home Office, Immigration Bill 2015/6 House of Lords Report Stage, 2nd sitting, 15 March 2016, *Hansard* Col 1770. Available at: http://www.publications.parliament.uk/pa/ld201516/ldhansrd/text/160315-0001.htm#16031556000351 (accessed 14 December 2016).
3 Ibid, *Hansard* HL col 1771.
4 Baroness Williams of Trafford, Minister of State for the Home Office to Lord Rosser, Pilot of the powers to search for and seize UK driving licences held by illegal immigrants, 14 February 2017. Available at: http://data.parliament.uk/DepositedPapers/Files/DEP2017-0136/Williams_to_Lord_RosserUK_driving_licences_held_illegal_migrants.pdf (accessed 1 March 2017).

BANK ACCOUNTS

SECTION 45—BANK ACCOUNTS AND SCHEDULE 7—BANK ACCOUNTS

> **Summary**
>
> Requires banks and building societies periodically to check the immigration status of current account holders and to notify the Home Office if a person does not have the correct legal status. The Secretary of State will then either apply for a court order freezing the disqualified person's account or accounts, or require the bank or building society to close the account or accounts as soon as possible. There is a right of appeal against a freezing order.

2.10

45 Bank accounts

(1) Schedule 7 (bank accounts) has effect.

(2) Before the end of the period mentioned in subsection (3), the Secretary of State must—

    (a) review the operation of sections 40A to 40G of the Immigration Act 2014 (inserted by Schedule 7),

    (b) prepare a report of the review, and

    (c) lay a copy of the report before Parliament.

(3) The period referred to in subsection (2) is the period of 5 years beginning with the day on which Schedule 7 comes fully into force.'

'Schedule 7

Bank accounts

1   The Immigration Act 2014 is amended as follows.

2   After section 40 (prohibition on opening current accounts for disqualified persons) insert—

"40A Requirement to carry out immigration checks in relation to current accounts

(1) A bank or building society must, at such times or with such frequency as is specified in regulations made by the Treasury, carry out an immigration check in relation to each current account held with it that is not an excluded account.

Part 2—Access to Services **2.10**

(2) For the purposes of this section carrying out an "immigration check" in relation to a current account means checking whether, according to information supplied by the Secretary of State to a specified anti-fraud organisation or a specified data-matching authority, the account is operated by or for a disqualified person.

(3) A "disqualified person" is a person

    (a) who is in the United Kingdom,

    (b) who requires leave to enter or remain in the United Kingdom but does not have it, and

    (c) for whom the Secretary of State considers that a current account should not be provided by a bank or building society.

(4) A current account is an excluded account for the purposes of subsection (1) if the account is operated by or for a person or body of a description specified in regulations made by the Treasury.

(5) An account is operated by or for a person or body if the person or body is an account holder or a signatory or identified as a beneficiary in relation to the account.

(6) A bank or building society must—

    (a) make arrangements with a specified anti-fraud organisation or a specified data-matching authority for the purpose of enabling the bank or building society to carry out immigration checks in relation to current accounts, and

    (b) pay any reasonable fee required to be paid under those arrangements.

(7) In this section "specified anti-fraud organisation" and "specified data-matching authority" have the same meaning as in section 40(3)(a).

40B Requirement to notify existence of current accounts for disqualified persons

(1) This section applies where, as a result of an immigration check carried out under section 40A, a bank or building society identifies a current account that is operated by or for a person who the bank or building society believes to be a disqualified person.

(2) Where this section applies, the bank or building society (as the case may be) must as soon as reasonably practicable—

    (a) notify the Secretary of State that a current account held with it is operated by or for a person who it believes to be a disqualified person, and

    (b) provide the Secretary of State with such other information as may be prescribed.

(3) A notification made, or information provided, under subsection (2) must be made or provided in the prescribed form and manner.

(4) In subsections (2) and (3) "prescribed" means prescribed in regulations made by the Treasury.

(5) Regulations under subsection (2) may (in particular) require the provision of information relating to any accounts held with the bank or building society that are operated by or for the person who is believed to be a disqualified person.

40C Action to be taken by Secretary of State following section 40B notification

(1) Where the Secretary of State receives a notification from a bank or building society under section 40B(2) in relation to a person, the Secretary of State must check whether the person is a disqualified person.

(2) If the Secretary of State determines that the person is a disqualified person, the Secretary of State may apply under section 40D for a freezing order in respect of one or more of the accounts held with the bank or building society that are operated by or for the disqualified person.

(3) If the Secretary of State decides not to apply for a freezing order under subsection (2), or decides to apply for a freezing order in respect of one or more but not all of the accounts held with the bank or building society that are operated by or for the disqualified person, the Secretary of State must notify the bank or building society that it is subject to the duty in section 40G(2) in relation to the disqualified person.

(4) A notification made under subsection (3) must contain the prescribed information and be made in the prescribed form and manner.

(5) In subsection (4) "prescribed" means prescribed in regulations made by the Treasury.

(6) If the Secretary of State determines that the person is not a disqualified person, the Secretary of State must notify the bank or building society accordingly.

40D Freezing orders

(1) On an application by the Secretary of State under section 40C(2), the court may make a freezing order in respect of any account specified in the application.

(2) A freezing order in respect of an account is an order that prohibits each person and body by or for whom the account is operated from making withdrawals or payments from the account.

(3) A freezing order may be made subject to exceptions.

(4) An exception may (in particular)—

(a) make provision for the disqualified person to meet his or her reasonable living expenses and reasonable legal expenses;

(b) allow another person or body by or for whom the account is operated to make withdrawals or payments from the account.

(5) An application for a freezing order may be made without notice.

(6) The court may vary or discharge a freezing order made in respect of an account (whether made under this section or on an appeal under section 40E) on an application made by—

(a) the Secretary of State, or

(b) a person or body by or for whom the account is operated.

(7) If the Secretary of State applies for a freezing order in respect of an account and the order is not made, or the order is made but subsequently discharged, the Secretary of State must notify the bank or building society that it is subject to the duty in section 40G(2) in relation to the disqualified person.

(8) A notification made under subsection (7) must contain the information and be in the form and manner prescribed in regulations made under subsection (4) of section 40C for the purposes of subsection (3) of that section.

(9) In this section—

"the court" means—

(a) in England and Wales, a magistrates' court;

(b) in Scotland, the sheriff;

(c) in Northern Ireland, a court of summary jurisdiction;

"the disqualified person" means the person who, following a check under section 40C(1), was determined to be a disqualified person, resulting in the application for the freezing order.

40E Freezing orders: appeals

(1) An appeal may be made to the relevant appeal court against a decision of a court under section 40D.

(2) The right of appeal under subsection (1) is exercisable by—

(a) the Secretary of State, and

(b) if the decision relates to a freezing order that is in force in respect of an account, a person or body by or for whom the account is operated.

(3) On an appeal under this section the relevant appeal court may make—

(a) whatever orders are necessary to give effect to its determination of the appeal;

(b) whatever incidental or consequential orders appear to it to be just.

2.10 A Guide to the Immigration Act 2016

(4) In this section "the relevant appeal court" means—

    (a) the Crown Court, where the decision appealed against is a decision of a magistrates' court;

    (b) the Sheriff Appeal Court, where the decision appealed against is a decision of the sheriff;

    (c) a county court, where the decision appealed against is a decision of a court of summary jurisdiction.

40F Freezing orders: code of practice

(1) The Secretary of State must issue a code of practice—

    (a) specifying the factors that the Secretary of State will consider when deciding whether to apply for a freezing order under section 40C(2),

    (b) outlining the arrangements for keeping a freezing order under review for the purpose of deciding whether to apply under section 40D(6) for its variation or discharge, and

    (c) specifying the factors that the Secretary of State will consider when deciding whether to make such an application.

(2) The Secretary of State must from time to time review the code and may revise and re-issue it following a review.

(3) The code (or revised code)—

    (a) may not be issued unless a draft has been laid before Parliament, and

    (b) comes into force in accordance with provision contained in regulations made by the Secretary of State.

40G Closure of accounts not subject to freezing order

(1) This section applies where—

    (a) a bank or building society makes a notification under section 40B(2) in relation to a person,

    (b) the person is determined by the Secretary of State (following a check under section 40C(1)) to be a disqualified person, and

    (c) the bank or building society receives a notification under section 40C(3) or 40D(7) in relation to the disqualified person.

(2) Where this section applies the bank or building society must as soon as reasonably practicable close each account held with it that—

    (a) in the case of a notification under section 40C(3), is operated by or for the disqualified person and is not the subject of an application for a freezing order;

    (b) in the case of a notification under section 40D(7), is operated by or for the disqualified person and in respect of which a freezing order is not in force.

(3) The bank or building society may delay closing an account which it would otherwise be required to close under subsection (2) if at the time at which it would otherwise be required to close it—

    (a) the account is overdrawn, or

    (b) where the account is operated by or for the disqualified person and one or more bodies or other persons, the bank or building society considers that closing the account would significantly adversely affect the interests of any of those other bodies or persons.

(4) Where subsection (3) applies, closure of the account may be delayed for such period as is reasonable (but not indefinitely).

(5) If an account falling within subsection (2) is operated by or for the disqualified person and one or more bodies or other persons, the bank or building society is to be treated as having complied with that subsection in relation to that account if, as soon as reasonably practicable, it takes all such steps as are necessary to prevent the account from being operated by or for the disqualified person (instead of closing the account).

(6) Where the bank or building society closes an account in compliance with this section, it must tell each person or body by or for whom the account is operated, if it may lawfully do so, why it has closed the account.

(7) Where the bank or building society prevents an account from being operated by or for the disqualified person by virtue of subsection (5), it must tell each person or body by or for whom the account is operated, if it may lawfully do so, why it has prevented the account from being operated by or for the disqualified person.

(8) The bank or building society must provide the Secretary of State with information about the steps that it has taken to comply with this section.

(9) Information provided under subsection (8) must be provided in the prescribed form and manner and at the prescribed times or with the prescribed frequency.

(10) In subsection (9) "prescribed" means prescribed in regulations made by the Treasury.

40H Sections 40A to 40G: interpretation

(1) This section applies for the purposes of sections 40A to 40G.

(2) "Account" includes a financial product by means of which a payment may be made.

(3) "Freezing order" has the meaning given by section 40D(2).

(4) "Disqualified person" has the meaning given by section 40A(3).

(5) References to an account being operated by or for a person or body are to be read in accordance with section 40A(5)."

2.10 *A Guide to the Immigration Act 2016*

3(1) Section 41 (regulation by Financial Conduct Authority) is amended as follows.

(2) In subsection (1), at the end insert "and the requirements imposed on them by sections 40A, 40B and 40G".

(3) In subsection (2)(a), at the end insert "or immigration checks under section 40A".

4 In section 42 (meaning of "bank" and "building society"), in subsections (1) and (5), for "and 41" substitute "to 41".

5(1) Section 43 (power to amend) is amended as follows.

(2) In subsection (1)(b), after "40(1)" insert "or the requirement in section 40A(1)".

(3) In subsection (1)(c), for "that section" substitute "section 40 or 40A".

6 In section 74 (orders and regulations), in subsection (2) (statutory instruments to which the affirmative resolution procedure applies), after paragraph (b) insert—

"(ba) regulations under section 40A(4);

(bb) regulations under section 40B;".

7(1) Section 18 of the Civil Jurisdiction and Judgments Act 1982 (enforcement of UK judgments in other parts of UK) is amended as follows.

(2) In subsection (3), for "subsection (4)" substitute "subsections (4) and (4ZA)".

(3) After subsection (4) insert—

"(4ZA) This section applies to a freezing order made under section 40D of the Immigration Act 2014 by a magistrates' court in England and Wales or a court of summary jurisdiction in Northern Ireland."

Commencement: Not yet in force (see note below on commencement).

Amends: Schedule 7 to the Immigration Act 2014 (IA 2014), inserting ss 40A to 40G and amending s 41 *Regulation by the Financial Conduct Authority*, s 42 *Meaning of 'bank' and 'building society'*, s 43 *Power to amend* and s 74 *Orders and Regulations*. Amends s 18 *Enforcement of UK judgments in other parts of the UK* of the Civil Jurisdiction and Judgments Act 1982.

Regulations: Made under:

s 40A(1) by the Treasury to specify the times or frequency with which a bank or building society must carry out immigration checks on each current account that is not excluded;

s 40A(4) by the Treasury to specify accounts excluded from immigration checks;

s 40B(2) by the Treasury to specify the information provided by banks or building societies to the Secretary of State (SSHD) when notifying her that an account is operated by a disqualified person;

s 40B(3) by the Treasury to specify the form and manner in which information must be provided y banks or building societies to the SSHD when notifying her that an account is operated by disqualified person;

s 40C(4) by the Treasury to specify the information included and the form and manner of the notification by the SSHD to a bank or building society of their duty to close an account if she chooses not to make a freezing order;

s 40D(8) by the Treasury to specify the information included and the form and manner of the notification by the SSHD to a bank or building society of their duty to close an account if she applies for a freezing order and this is not made;

s 40F(3)(b) by the SSHD to bring into force the code of practice on freezing orders;

s 40G(9) by the Treasury to specify the form, manner and the times or frequency in which banks or building societies must provide information to the SSHD about the steps it has taken to comply with closing appropriate accounts.

Powers inserted into the IA 2014 by the Immigration Act 2016 (IA 2016), Schedule 7, para 2. Regulations made under ss 40A(4) and 40B are subject to the affirmative procedure, IA 2014, s 74(ba).

The Treasury has laid draft regulations before Parliament under IA 2014, ss 40A(1), 40C(4) and 40G(9): The Immigration 2014 (Current Accounts) (Compliance etc.) Regulations 2016, SI 2016/1073.

Guidance: The SSHD must issue a code of practice specifying the factors that she will consider when deciding to apply for a freezing order; the arrangements for keeping an order under review and the factors relevant to deciding whether to apply to vary or discharge the order (IA 2014, s 40F). The Code and any revisions must be laid before parliament and come into effect in accordance with regulations made by the Secretary of State which are subject to the negative procedure.

Definitions:

'account' a financial product by means of which a payment may be made, IA 2014, s 40H(2) inserted by Schedule 7, para 2; references to *an account being operated by or for a person or body* refer to a person or body who is an account holder, signatory or identified beneficiary, IA 2014, ss 40A(5) and 40H(4) inserted by Schedule 7, para 2;

2.10 *A Guide to the Immigration Act 2016*

'the court' for the purposes of IA 2014, s 40D *Freezing orders*: a magistrates' court (England and Wales), sheriff's court (Scotland) or court of summary jurisdiction (Northern Ireland), IA 2014, s 40D(9);

'disqualified person' for the purpose of IA 2014, s 40A: a person in the UK who requires leave to enter or remain but does not have it and for whom the Secretary of State considers that a bank account should not be provided (s 40A(3) inserted by Schedule 7, para 2). For the purpose of s 40D: a person who, following a check under s 40C(1), was determined to be a disqualified person resulting in the application for the freezing order (IA 2014, s 40D(9) inserted by Schedule 7, para 2);

'freezing order' order prohibiting each person or body by or for whom an account is operated from making withdrawals or payments from the account, IA 2014, s 40D(2);

'prescribed' for the purposes of IA 2014, s 40B *Requirement to notify existence of current accounts for disqualified persons*' and 40G *Closure of accounts not subject to a freezing order* means prescribed in regulations made by the Treasury, IA 2014, new ss 40B(4) and 40G(9) inserted by Schedule 7, para 2;

'relevant appeal court' Crown Court (England and Wales), Sheriff appeal court (Scotland) or county court (Northern Ireland), IA 2014, s 40E(4) inserted by Schedule 7, para 2;

'status check' as IA 2014, s 40(3)(a), checking with a specified anti-fraud organisation or a specified data-matching authority whether, according to information supplied to that organisation or authority by the SSHD, the person is disqualified;

'specified anti-fraud organisation' IA 2014, s 40(3)(a) read with s 40(4), any unincorporated association, body corporate or other person which enables or facilitates any sharing of information to prevent fraud or a particular kind of fraud or which has any of these functions as its purpose or one or more of its purposes. Currently the specified organisations are Call Credit Information Group Limited, BAE Systems Applied Intelligence Limited, Dun and Bradstreet Limited, Equifax Limited and Synectics Solutions Limited; see the Serious Crime Act 2007 (Specified Anti-fraud Organisations) Order, SI 2014/1608;

'specified data-matching organisation' IA 2014, s 40(3)(a) read with s 40(4).

Devolution: Applies throughout the UK. See Schedule 7, para 7 amending s 18 of the Civil Jurisdiction and Judgments Act 1982 so that freezing orders can be enforced in other parts of the UK.

Under IA 2014, ss 40–43 banks and building societies are prohibited from opening current accounts for people within the UK who would require leave to enter or remain but do not have it. The new provisions of the IA 2016 take this further by introducing provisions that will require banks and building societies to periodically check the immigration status of current account holders and to notify the Home Office if a person does not have the correct legal status. The SSHD will then either apply for a court order freezing the disqualified person's account or accounts, or will notify the bank or building society that it is under a duty to close the account as soon as reasonably practicable.

Both sets of provisions form part of measures aimed at creating a 'hostile environment' for migrants living and working in the UK illegally, in this case by making it more difficult for migrants to do so through restricting access to banking services.[1] The 2016 Act provisions are not yet in force, but the Home Secretary, Amber Rudd MP, stated in her speech to the Conservative Party conference of 4 October 2016 that they would be applied by banks from autumn 2017.[2] The Treasury laid The Immigration 2014 (Current Accounts) (Compliance etc) Regulations 2016, SI 2016/1073 in draft before Parliament on 8 November 2016. These state that the regulations will come into force on 30 October 2017. They also state that banks or building societies must carry out the relevant checks during each quarter of the year beginning with the quarter commencing on 1 January 2018.

Section 45 of the IA 2016 introduces Schedule 7 and makes provision for the SSHD to review the operation of the new provisions within five years and lay a report before Parliament. All the detail is in the Schedule, para 2 of which inserts new provisions into IA 2014.

Under new s 40A(2) of IA 2014, inserted by Schedule 7, para 2, a person is disqualified from operating a current bank account if they are in the UK, would require leave to enter or remain in the UK but do not have it, and for whom the SSHD considers that a current account should not be provided by a bank or building society. This mirrors the definition of a person disqualified from opening a bank account under ss 40(2) and 40(3)(b) of IA 2014.

The banks will check the details of current account holders against information notified by the Home Office to an anti-fraud organisation (currently CIFAS) or by a specified data-matching authority to identify whether, according to information supplied by the SSHD, the person is a disqualified person.

Under new s 40B(2) of the IA 2014, the bank or building society must notify the SSHD as soon as practicable if it finds, through its checks, that an account is being operated by or for a person whom the bank believes is a disqualified person. New s 40C sets out the action that is then taken by the SSHD, who may either apply for a freezing order (s 40C(2)) to be issued by a court under s 40D or may instead notify the bank or building society of its duty under s 40G(2) to close the person's current account.

A freezing order may be issued by a magistrates' court (England and Wales), sheriff court (Scotland) or a court of summary jurisdiction (Northern Ireland) on application by the SSHD, either with or without notice to the disqualified person. A freezing order has the effect of preventing a person or body from making withdrawals or payments from their account, though exceptions may be made, for example, to allow the disqualified person to meet their reasonable living expenses and reasonable legal expenses or to allow another holder or beneficiary of the account to make withdrawals or payments. The court may vary or discharge an order on the application of either the SSHD or of the account holder, signatory or beneficiary.

There is a right of appeal, under IA 2014, s 40E, to the Crown Court (England and Wales), Sheriff Appeal Court (Scotland) or a county court (Northern Ireland) against an order to freeze a current bank account. The court is empowered to make any orders necessary to give effect to the appeal and any incidental or consequential orders it considers just. The court is therefore able to award compensation in favour of the person whose account was frozen, where appropriate.

Under IA 2014, s 40F, the Home Office is required to issue a code of practice on the factors it will take into account when deciding whether to apply for a freezing order and on its arrangements for keeping orders under review. The Home Office has indicated that it would notify the bank of their duty to close an account in routine cases in order to disrupt the person's ability to remain in the UK and encourage them to leave voluntarily but it would use its power to apply for a freezing order in 'hard-to-remove cases with significant funds to leverage co-operation with the removal process'.[3] The Government's impact assessment of the banking provisions states, 'In addition, in a very limited number of cases, the power to freeze significant sums held in the illegal migrant's account/s will create a powerful incentive to agree to voluntary departure and secure the release of frozen funds once the illegal migrant has returned to their country of origin'.[4]

Where the Home Office notifies the bank or building society of its duty to close a person's account, it must do so as soon as reasonably practicable (IA 2014, s 40G(2)). The bank or building society may, however, delay closing the account where the account is withdrawn or where it is a joint account and closing the account would significantly adversely affect the interests of the other account holder or beneficiary (IA 2014, s 40(3)).

Concerns were raised in the House of Common with regard to the position of individuals whose current account was closed by their bank in error.[5] The Solicitor General, Robert Buckland QC committed to address the concerns in writing and subsequently wrote to Albert Owen MP outlining safeguards to prevent this occurring.[6] He stated that the Home Office will conduct further

Part 2—Access to Services   **2.10**

checks on being notified by a bank that a person may be disqualified from operating a bank account:

> 'Under the new provisions the Home Office will be notified by banks when they believe an account holder is a disqualified person. It will then carry out a further thorough check before the bank will be required to take any action to close an account. The bank will be notified if circumstances have changed and the person is no longer disqualified. This double check will act as a further safeguard to make sure that the bank acts on the most up to date information'.[7]

People will be informed by their bank of the reason their account is subject to closure in order to provide an opportunity to address the inaccuracy:

> 'Individuals whose accounts are subject to closure will be informed by their bank of the reason why, provided that it is lawful to do so. If, despite all the checks, a person still considers they are lawfully present and that incorrect information has been provided, they will be given the information they need to contact the Home Office swiftly so that an error can be rectified'.[8]

The Solicitor General repeated the further assurance given in this correspondence that, 'If an account is closed, any credit balance will not be withheld from the individual but returned to them by the bank in the normal way'[9] during the debates in the House of Commons.[10]

Those whose account is closed in error based on inaccurate or out-of-date information held on Home Office databases will face a high level of disruption: their current account may have been used, for example, to receive their salary, pay their rent or mortgage or pay other important bills. The measures restricting access to bank accounts are therefore likely to have an even greater impact on people who have not breached any immigration provisions than those seen previously.

---

1   Home Office, *Immigration Act 2016 Factsheet – Banks* (Section 45), July 2016. Available at: https://www.gov.uk/government/uploads/system/uploads/attachment_data/file/537220/Immigration_Act_-_Part_2_-_Bank_Accounts.pdf (accessed 14 December 2016).
2   Amber Rudd MP, Home Secretary, Speech to Conservative Party Conference 2016, 4 October 2016. Available at: http://press.conservatives.com/post/151334637685/rudd-speech-to-conservative-party-conference-2016 (accessed 14 December 2016).
3   *Immigration Act 2016 Factsheet – Banks* (Section 45), Home Office, July 2016. Available at: https://www.gov.uk/government/uploads/system/uploads/attachment_data/file/537220/Immigration_Act_-_Part_2_-_Bank_Accounts.pdf (accessed 14 December 2016).
4   *Immigration Bill: tackling existing current accounts held by illegal migrants, impact assessment No RPC15-HMT-3042*, HM Treasury, 3 August 2015. Available at: https://www.gov.uk/government/uploads/system/uploads/attachment_data/file/462233/Immigration_Bill_bank_accounts_impact_assessment.pdf (accessed 14 December 2016).
5   Immigration Bill 2015/16 Public Bill Committee, House of Commons 9th sitting (morning), *Hansard* cols 316-317 3 November 2016. Available at: http://www.publications.parliament.uk/pa/cm201516/cmpublic/immigration/151103/am/151103s01.htm (accessed 14 December

235

2.10 *A Guide to the Immigration Act 2016*

2016). Also 10th sitting (afternoon), *Hansard* col 321 (3 November 2016). Available at: http://www.publications.parliament.uk/pa/cm201516/cmpublic/immigration/151103/pm/151103s01.htm (accessed 14 December 2016).
6 *Immigration Bill – Measures on bank accounts*, Robert Buckland QC MP, Solicitor General to Albert Owen MP, chair, Public Bill Committee, 4 November 2015. Available at: http://www.publications.parliament.uk/pa/cm201516/cmpublic/immigration/memo/ib37.pdf (accessed 14 December 2016).
7 Ibid.
8 Ibid.
9 *Immigration Bill – Measures on bank accounts*, Robert Buckland QC MP, Solicitor General to Albert Owen MP, chair, Public Bill Committee, 4 November 2015. Available at: http://www.publications.parliament.uk/pa/cm201516/cmpublic/immigration/memo/ib37.pdf (accessed 14 December 2016).
10 Immigration Bill 2015/16 Public Bill Committee, House of Commons, 10th sitting (morning), *Hansard* col 323, 3 November 2016. Available at: http://www.publications.parliament.uk/pa/cm201516/cmpublic/immigration/151103/pm/151103s01.htm (accessed 14 December 2016).

Part 3—Enforcement

POWERS OF IMMIGRATION OFFICERS ETC

SECTION 46—POWERS IN CONNECTION WITH EXAMINATION, DETENTION AND REMOVAL

> **Summary**
>
> New powers to question persons with lawful leave. Powers for officers lawfully on premises to search for, seize and retain documents, without a warrant.

3.1

46 Powers in connection with examination, detention and removal

(1) Schedule 2 to the Immigration Act 1971 (administrative provisions as to control on entry etc) is amended as follows.

(2) In paragraph 2(1) (examination by immigration officers) at the end of paragraph (c) insert "; and

    (d) whether, if he has been given leave which is still in force, his leave should be curtailed."

(3) After paragraph 15 insert—

"15A Search of premises in connection with removal

    (1) This paragraph applies if—

        (a) an immigration officer is lawfully on any premises, and

        (b) a person who is liable to be detained under paragraph 16(2) is on the premises.

    (2) The immigration officer may search the premises for documents which—

        (a) relate to the person, and

        (b) may be evidence for a ground on which the person's leave to enter or remain in the United Kingdom may be curtailed.

3.1 *A Guide to the Immigration Act 2016*

        (3)   The power may be exercised—

                (a)   only if the immigration officer has reasonable grounds for believing there are documents within sub-paragraph (2) on the premises, and

                (b)   only to the extent that it is reasonably required for the purpose of discovering such documents.

        (4)   An immigration officer searching premises under this paragraph may seize any document the officer finds which the officer has reasonable grounds for believing is a document within sub-paragraph (2).

        (5)   Sub-paragraph (6) applies where—

                (a)   an immigration officer is searching premises under this paragraph, and

                (b)   any document the officer has reasonable grounds for believing is a document within sub-paragraph (2) is stored in any electronic form and is accessible from the premises.

        (6)   The immigration officer may require the document to be produced in a form in which it can be taken away and in which it is visible and legible or from which it can readily be produced in a visible and legible form.

        (7)   If a requirement under sub-paragraph (6) is not complied with or a document to which that sub-paragraph applies cannot be produced in a form of the kind mentioned in that sub-paragraph, the immigration officer may seize the device or medium on which it is stored.

        (8)   But sub-paragraphs (4) to (7) do not apply to a document which the immigration officer has reasonable grounds for believing is an item subject to legal privilege.

        (9)   An immigration officer may retain a document seized under this paragraph while—

                (a)   the person to whom the document relates is liable to be detained under paragraph 16(2), and

                (b)   the document falls within sub-paragraph (2)(b).

        (10)   But a document may not be retained for the purpose mentioned in sub-paragraph (9) if a photograph or copy would be sufficient for that purpose."

    (4)   In paragraph 25A (entry and search of premises where person arrested or detained under Schedule 2)—

        (a)   after sub-paragraph (7) insert—

            "(7A)   Sub-paragraph (7B) applies where—

Part 3—Enforcement **3.1**

- (a) an officer is searching premises under this paragraph, and
- (b) any document the officer has reasonable grounds for believing is a relevant document is stored in any electronic form and is accessible from the premises.

(7B) The officer may require the document to be produced in a form in which it can be taken away and in which it is visible and legible or from which it can readily be produced in a visible and legible form.

(7C) If a requirement under sub-paragraph (7B) is not complied with or a document to which that sub-paragraph applies cannot be produced in a form of the kind mentioned in that sub-paragraph, the officer may seize the device or medium on which it is stored.",

(b) in sub-paragraph (8) for "sub-paragraph (7)(a) does" substitute " sub-paragraphs (7) to (7C) do ", and

(c) in sub-paragraph (8A) for "sub-paragraph (7)" substitute " this paragraph ".

(5) In paragraph 25B (search of person arrested under Schedule 2) after sub-paragraph (8) insert—

"(8A) Sub-paragraph (8B) applies where—

- (a) an officer is searching a person under this paragraph, and
- (b) any document the officer has reasonable grounds for believing is a document within sub-paragraph (3)(b) is stored in any electronic form on a device or medium found on the person.

(8B) The officer may require the document to be produced in a form in which it can be taken away and in which it is visible and legible or from which it can readily be produced in a visible and legible form.

(8C) If a requirement under sub-paragraph (8B) is not complied with or a document to which that sub-paragraph applies cannot be produced in a form of the kind mentioned in that sub-paragraph, the officer may seize the device or medium on which it is stored.

(8D) Sub-paragraphs (8B) and (8C) do not apply to a document which the officer has reasonable grounds for believing is an item subject to legal privilege."

Commencement: 12 July 2016, Immigration Act 2014 (Commencement No 1) Regulations 2016, SI 2016/603.

3.1 *A Guide to the Immigration Act 2016*

Amends: Immigration Act 1971 (IA 1971), Schedule 2 *Administrative provisions as to control on entry* inserting new para 15A *Search of premises in connection with removal* and amending paras 2, 25A and 25B.

Guidance: *Search and Seizure*, v3, Home Office, Removals, enforcement and detention: general guidance, 16 December 2016. Available at: https://www.gov.uk/government/uploads/system/uploads/attachment_data/file/578886/Search-and-seizure_v3.pdf (accessed 22 December 2016).

Definitions:

'legal privilege' IA 1971, s 28L, see s 58;

'premises' IA 197, 1 s 28L, see s 58.

Devolution: Applies throughout the UK.

This section provides new powers to question persons with lawful leave and new powers for officers lawfully on premises to search for, seize and retain documents, without a warrant.

The Explanatory Notes to the Act[1] explain the new powers to question persons with lawful leave, amendments to para 2 of Schedule 2 to the IA 1971, as being 'so that it is clear that examination by an immigration officer can happen where a person has leave'. In short, the power is at large, for there does not appear to be any requirement that there be any reason to think that the person's leave should be curtailed, merely that the examination will assist the officer in satisfying her/himself that this is the case.

The breadth of the power is all the greater given the way in which the Home Office interprets examination in para 2(1) of Schedule 2 to the IA 1971 where reference is made to the examination of persons 'who have arrived in the UK'. This was a matter canvassed during the passage of the Act.[2] The Enforcement Instructions and Guidance, Chapter 31.10, as available until 7 October 2016,[3] relied on *Singh v Hammond* [1987] 1 WLR 283, where it was held:

'An examination, I would hold, can properly be conducted by an immigration officer away from the place of entry and on a later date after the person the subject of the examination has already entered, if the immigration officer has some information in his possession which causes him to inquire whether the person being examined is a British citizen and if not, whether he may enter the United Kingdom without leave, and if not, which is the relevant question in this case, whether he should have been given leave and on what conditions.'

Part 3—Enforcement **3.1**

The text is now repeated in the Home Office instruction on enforcement interviews.[4] If this interpretation is correct then, provided the person has entered the UK at some point, there will be a power under the IA 1971, s 2(1)(d) as inserted by this section, to examine them to see if their leave should be curtailed. It is suggested that *Singh v Hammond* is not correctly decided. Schedule 2 is concerned with the examination of persons arriving in or leaving the UK (see the IA 1971 s 4(2)) and, read in context, the paragraph appears concerned with the port of entry. The concerns surfaced during the passage of the Act[5] during the discussions of the *Maritime Enforcement* provisions of Part 6, see the notes to those provisions below.

Paragraph 2(1) of Schedule 2 to the IA 1971 must be read with para 16(2) which provides a power to detain a person to be examined under para 2 pending that examination. It thus appears to provide a power to detain persons with leave pending examination into the question of whether their leave should be curtailed.

The other change effected by this section is the insertion of new para 15A of Schedule 2 to the 1971 Act. This gives immigration officers who are already lawfully on premises a power to search for documents that relate to a person liable to detention, and that will assist in removing the person from the UK. The power arises where there are reasonable grounds for believing that there are such documents on the premises and to the extent that a search is reasonably required to discover them. Documents, including electronic documents, that may be evidence of grounds for curtailing a person's leave, can be seized and retained but documents that benefit from legal privilege, such as solicitor-client correspondence, are excluded (para 15A(8)). Original documents will not be retained if a photograph or copy is sufficient. Where an electronic document cannot be copied, the device on which it is stored may be taken away.

---

1 Para 255.
2 Public Bill Committee 10th sitting (afternoon), *Hansard* cols 327–328 (3 November 2015).
3 Chapter 31 *Enforcement Visits* was withdrawn on 7 October 2016.
4 Home Office General Instructions, Immigration Removal, Enforcement and Detention, *Enforcement Interviews*, v1.0, 12 July 2016. Reference is made to the case in the Home Office General Instructions, Immigration Removal, Enforcement and Detention, *Operational enforcement visits* v 2, 19 January 2017.
5 Public Bill Committee, 10th sitting (afternoon) *Hansard*, cols 327–328 (3 November 2016).

SECTION 47 SEARCH OF PREMISES IN CONNECTION WITH IMPOSITION OF CIVIL PENALTY

3.2

> **Summary**
>
> Powers for officers lawfully on premises to search for, seize and retain documents 'which might be of assistance in determining' whether a person is liable to the imposition of a civil penalty for employing a person without permission to work or leasing property to a person with no right to rent.

47 Search of premises in connection with imposition of civil penalty

(1) This section applies if an immigration officer is lawfully on any premises.

(2) The immigration officer may search the premises for documents which might be of assistance in determining whether a person is liable to the imposition of a penalty under—

　　(a) section 15 of the Immigration, Asylum and Nationality Act 2006 (penalty for employing illegal worker etc), or

　　(b) section 23 or 25 of the Immigration Act 2014 (penalty for leasing premises to disqualified person etc).

(3) The power may be exercised—

　　(a) only if the immigration officer has reasonable grounds for believing there are documents within subsection (2) on the premises, and

　　(b) only to the extent that it is reasonably required for the purpose of discovering such documents.

(4) An immigration officer searching premises under this section may seize any document the officer finds which the officer has reasonable grounds for believing is a document within subsection (2).

(5) Subsection (6) applies where—

　　(a) an immigration officer is searching premises under this section, and

　　(b) any document the officer has reasonable grounds for believing is a document within subsection (2) is stored in any electronic form and is accessible from the premises.

(6) The immigration officer may require the document to be produced in a form in which it can be taken away and in which it is visible and legible or from which it can readily be produced in a visible and legible form.

Part 3—Enforcement   **3.2**

(7) If a requirement under subsection (6) is not complied with or a document to which that subsection applies cannot be produced in a form of the kind mentioned in that subsection, the immigration officer may seize the device or medium on which it is stored.

(8) But subsections (4) to (7) do not apply to a document or item which the immigration officer has reasonable grounds for believing is an item subject to legal privilege.

(9) An immigration officer may retain a document or item seized under this section while the officer has reasonable grounds for believing that the document may be required—

(a) for the purposes of determining whether a person is liable to the imposition of a penalty under a provision mentioned in subsection (2),

(b) for the purposes of any objection relating to the imposition of such a penalty, or

(c) for the purposes of any appeal or other legal proceedings relating to the imposition of such a penalty.

(10) But a document or item may not be retained for a purpose mentioned in subsection (9) if a photograph or copy would be sufficient for that purpose.

(11) Section 28I of the Immigration Act 1971 (seized material: access and copying) applies to a document seized and retained under this section as it applies to anything seized and retained under Part 3 of that Act.

Commencement: 12 July 2016, Immigration Act 2014 (Commencement No 1) Regulations 2016, SI 2016/603.

Definitions:

'legal privilege' see s 58;

'premises' see s 58.

Guidance: *Search and Seizure*, v3, Home Office, Removals, enforcement and detention, general guidance, 16 December 2016. Available at: https://www.gov.uk/government/uploads/system/uploads/attachment_data/file/578886/Search-and-seizure_v3.pdf

Devolution: Applies throughout the UK.

This section gives immigration officers who are already lawfully on premises a power to search, without a warrant, for documents which might assist in determining whether a person is liable to a civil penalty for employing a person without permission to work (Immigration Act 2014 (IA 2014), s 15), or for leasing premises to a person with no right to rent (IA 2014, ss 23 and 25), where there are reasonable grounds for believing that there are such documents on the premises and to the extent to which a search is reasonably required to discover them. There is no requirement of a hint that the person

3.3 A Guide to the Immigration Act 2016

is so liable, only that the documents will assist in determining whether they are or not. It appears to be a power to check the documents of a landlady or landlord against whom no suspicions are entertained.

Documents, including electronic documents, can be seized and retained but documents that benefit from legal privilege, such as solicitor-client correspondence, are excluded (s 47(8)). Original documents may not be retained if a photograph or copy is sufficient. Where an electronic document cannot be copied, the device on which it is stored may be taken away. An employer or landlady/landlord has the right to access documents that have been seized, and to copy them, but if there are reasonable grounds to believe that this access would jeopardize an investigation against the employer or landlady/landlord, or the functions of an immigration officer, access will be denied.

It is striking that this section, and ss 48 and 51 which follow, do not amend the Immigration Act 1971 but sit outside it, increasing the confusion as to powers of search.

SECTION 48—SEIZURE AND RETENTION IN RELATION TO OFFENCES

> **Summary**
>
> Gives immigration officers who are already lawfully on premises, a power to seize and retain anything they find in the course of exercising a function under the Immigration Acts if they have reasonable grounds for believing that it has been obtained in consequence of the commission of an offence or is evidence of a criminal offence.

3.3

48 Seizure and retention in relation to offences

(1) This section applies if an immigration officer is lawfully on any premises.

(2) The immigration officer may seize anything which the officer finds in the course of exercising a function under the Immigration Acts if the officer has reasonable grounds for believing—

    (a) that it has been obtained in consequence of the commission of an offence, and

    (b) that it is necessary to seize it in order to prevent it being concealed, lost, damaged, altered or destroyed.

Part 3—Enforcement **3.3**

(3) The immigration officer may seize anything which the officer finds in the course of exercising a function under the Immigration Acts if the officer has reasonable grounds for believing—

    (a) that it is evidence in relation to an offence, and

    (b) that it is necessary to seize it in order to prevent the evidence being concealed, lost, altered or destroyed.

(4) The immigration officer may require any information which is stored in any electronic form and is accessible from the premises to be produced if the officer has reasonable grounds for believing—

    (a) that—

        (i) it is evidence in relation to an offence, or

        (ii) it has been obtained in consequence of the commission of an offence, and

    (b) that it is necessary to seize it in order to prevent it being concealed, lost, tampered with or destroyed.

(5) The reference in subsection (4) to information which is stored in any electronic form being produced is to such information being produced in a form—

    (a) in which it can be taken away, and

    (b) in which it is visible and legible or from which it can readily be produced in a visible and legible form.

(6) This section does not authorise an immigration officer to seize an item which the officer has reasonable grounds for believing is an item subject to legal privilege.

(7) Anything seized by an immigration officer under this section which relates to an immigration offence may be retained so long as is necessary in all the circumstances and in particular—

    (a) may be retained, except as provided for by subsection (8)—

        (i) for use as evidence at a trial for an offence, or

        (ii) for forensic examination or for investigation in connection with an offence, and

    (b) may be retained in order to establish its lawful owner, where there are reasonable grounds for believing that it has been obtained in consequence of the commission of an offence.

(8) Nothing may be retained for a purpose mentioned in subsection (7)(a) if a photograph or copy would be sufficient for that purpose.

(9) Section 28I of the Immigration Act 1971 (seized material: access and copying) applies to anything seized and retained under this section which relates to an immigration offence as it applies to anything seized and retained by an immigration officer under Part 3 of that Act.

3.3 *A Guide to the Immigration Act 2016*

(10) This section does not apply in relation to anything which may be seized by an immigration officer under—

(a) section 19 of the Police and Criminal Evidence Act 1984 as applied by an order under section 23 of the Borders, Citizenship and Immigration Act 2009, or

(b) Article 21 of the Police and Criminal Evidence (Northern Ireland) Order 1989 (SI 1989/1341 (NI 12) as applied by that section.

(11) In this section and section 49 "immigration offence" means an offence which relates to an immigration or nationality matter.

Commencement: 12 July 2016, Immigration Act 2014 (Commencement No 1) Regulations 2016, SI 2016/603.

Definitions:

'Immigration Acts' UK Borders Act 2007, s 61(2) (see s 91(5)).

'immigration offence' an offence which relates to an immigration or nationality matter, s 48(11);

'legal privilege', see s 58;

'premises' see s 58.

Guidance: *Search and Seizure*, v3, Home Office, Removals, enforcement and detention, general guidance, 16 December 2016. Available at: https://www.gov.uk/government/uploads/system/uploads/attachment_data/file/578886/Search-and-seizure_v3.pdf

Devolution: Applies throughout the UK. See s 48(10)(b) in respect of the Police and Criminal Evidence (Northern Ireland) Order 1989, SI 1989/1341.

Prior to the commencement of this section, when immigration officers in England and Wales searched premises for immigration purposes, for example, to check the immigration status of a person, they could only seize evidence of a non-immigration crime if they were trained criminal investigators and thus able to rely on Police and Criminal Evidence Act 1984 (PACE 1984), s 19, as applied by the Police and Criminal Evidence Act (Application to immigration officers and designated customs officials in England and Wales) Order 2013 (SI 2013/1542) or the Police and Criminal Evidence (Northern Ireland) Order 1989 (SI 1989/1341). Otherwise, they had to call for assistance from the police when they discovered evidence of a non-immigration crime.

This section gives immigration officers who are already lawfully on premises, power to seize and retain anything they find 'in the course of exercising a function under the Immigration Acts' if they have reasonable grounds for believing that it has been obtained 'in consequence of the commission of an offence' or that it is evidence in relation to an offence and that it is necessary to seize it to prevent its being concealed, lost, damaged altered or destroyed.

The section does not apply to anything that could be seized under s 19 of PACE 1984 as applied by SI 2013/1542 and SI 1989/1341 so it appears that the trained criminal investigators will continue to use that section rather than the new powers.

Documents, including electronic documents, can be seized and retained but documents that benefit from legal privilege, such as solicitor–client correspondence, are excluded (s 48(6)).

An employer or landlady/landlord can access documents that have been seized and copy them, but where there are reasonable grounds to believe that this access would jeopardize an investigation, access will be denied.

The powers of seizure and retention relate to any offence, not just an immigration offence, but specific provision is made as to the period for which anything seized which relates to an immigration offence can be retained. It can be held 'so long as is necessary in all the circumstances'. It is specified that it can be retained for use as evidence at trial; for examination or investigation; or to establish the lawful owner of the property, but this is an illustrative not an exhaustive list.

See further below s 49.

SECTION 49—DUTY TO PASS ON ITEMS SEIZED UNDER SECTION 48

> **Summary**
>
> Places an immigration officer under a duty to pass on items seized under s 48 as soon as reasonably practicable or, if no investigating authority will accept them, to return them to the person from whom they were seized or the place from they were seized or taken away.

3.4

49 Duty to pass on items seized under section 48

(1) This section applies if an immigration officer exercises—

    (a) the power under section 48 to seize or take away an item on the basis that the item or information contained in it has been obtained in

3.4 *A Guide to the Immigration Act 2016*

consequence of the commission of, or is evidence in relation to, an offence other than an immigration offence (a "relevant offence"), or

(b) a power to that effect in Part 3 of the Immigration Act 1971 as applied by section 14(3) of the Asylum and Immigration (Treatment of Claimants etc) Act 2004.

(2) Subject to subsection (3), the immigration officer must, as soon as is reasonably practicable after the power is exercised, notify a person who the immigration officer thinks has functions in relation to the investigation of the relevant offence.

(3) If the immigration officer has reasonable grounds for believing that the item referred to in subsection (1) has also been obtained in consequence of the commission of, or is evidence in relation to, an immigration offence, the immigration officer may notify a person who the immigration officer thinks has functions in relation to the investigation of the relevant offence.

(4) A person notified under this section of the exercise of a power mentioned in subsection (1) in relation to an item must, as soon as is reasonably practicable after being so notified, inform the immigration officer whether the person will accept the item.

(5) The person may inform the immigration officer that the person will not accept the item only if—

(a) the person does not think the item or information contained in it has been obtained in consequence of the commission of, or is evidence in relation to, an offence,

(b) the person does not have functions in relation to the investigation of the relevant offence, or

(c) the person thinks that it would be more appropriate for the relevant offence to be investigated by another person with such functions.

(6) If the person informs the immigration officer that the person will accept the item, the immigration officer must give it to the person as soon as is reasonably practicable.

(7) Once the item has been given as mentioned in subsection (6), any provision of an enactment which applies to items seized or taken away by the person applies to the item as if it had been seized or taken away by the person for the purposes of the investigation of the relevant offence.

(8) If the person informs the immigration officer that the person will not accept the item because subsection (5)(a) applies, the immigration officer must, as soon as is reasonably practicable, return the item in accordance with subsection (10).

(9) If the person informs the immigration officer that the person will not accept the item because subsection (5)(b) or (c) applies, the immigration officer must, as soon as is reasonably practicable—

(a) notify the exercise of a power mentioned in subsection (1) in relation to the item to another person (if any) who the immigration officer thinks has functions in relation to the investigation of the relevant offence, or

(b) if there is no such person, return the item in accordance with subsection (10).

(10) An item which must be returned in accordance with this subsection must be returned—

(a) to the person from whom it was seized, or

(b) if there is no such person, to the place from which it was seized or taken away.

(11) Where an item to which this section applies or information contained in such an item has been obtained in consequence of the commission of, or is evidence in relation to, more than one offence, references in this section to the relevant offence are to any of those offences.

(12) A function conferred or imposed by this section on an immigration officer may be exercised by any other immigration officer.

(13) In this section "enactment" includes—

(a) an enactment contained in subordinate legislation within the meaning of the Interpretation Act 1978,

(b) an enactment contained in, or in an instrument made under, an Act of the Scottish Parliament,

(c) an enactment contained in, or in an instrument made under, a Measure or Act of the National Assembly for Wales, and

(d) an enactment contained in, or in an instrument made under, Northern Ireland legislation.

Commencement: 12 July 2016, Immigration Act 2014 (Commencement No 1) Regulations 2016, SI 2016/603.

Definitions:

'immigration offence' an offence which relates to an immigration or nationality matter, s 48(11);

'enactment' s 49(13), includes subordinate legislation and legislation made, or made under, legislation made by the Scottish Parliament or an enactment made, or instrument made under, Northern Ireland legislation.

Guidance: *Search and Seizure*, v3, Home Office, Removals, enforcement and detention, general guidance, 16 December 2016. Available at: https://www.gov.uk/government/uploads/system/uploads/attachment_data/file/578886/Search-and-seizure_v3.pdf

Devolution: Applies throughout the UK.

3.5   *A Guide to the Immigration Act 2016*

An immigration officer must notify the relevant investigating authority, as soon as reasonably practicable, that they have seized items during a search. They have discretion to retain evidence where they have reasonable grounds to believe that it may be related to an immigration offence. Otherwise they must notify the relevant authority which will say whether or not it will accept the item. If so, they must hand it over as soon as reasonably practicable. If no investigating authority will accept it, it must be returned to the person from whom it was taken, or to the place from whence it was seized.

SECTION 50—RETENTION OF THINGS SEIZED UNDER PART 3 OF THE IMMIGRATION ACT 1971

Summary

Allows material seized to be retained for use as evidence at trial, for forensic examination or investigation, and to establish its lawful owner.

3.5

50 Retention of things seized under Part 3 of the Immigration Act 1971

After section 28H of the Immigration Act 1971 insert—

"**28 ZI Retention of seized material**

(1)   This section applies to anything seized by an immigration officer under this Part for the purposes of the investigation of an offence or on the basis that it may be evidence relating to an offence.

(2)   Anything seized as mentioned in subsection (1) may be retained so long as is necessary in all the circumstances and in particular—

   (a)   may be retained, except as provided for by subsection (3)—

      (i)   for use as evidence at a trial for an offence, or

      (ii)   for forensic examination or for investigation in connection with an offence, and

   (b)   may be retained in order to establish its lawful owner, where there are reasonable grounds for believing that it has been obtained in consequence of the commission of an offence.

(3)   Nothing may be retained for a purpose mentioned in subsection (2)(a) if a photograph or copy would be sufficient for that purpose."

Commencement: 12 July 2016, Immigration Act 2014 (Commencement No 1) Regulations 2016, SI 2016/603 (C.44)).

Amends: Immigration Act 1971, inserting s 28ZI *Retention of seized material*.

Devolution: Applies throughout the UK.

This section allows material seized to be retained for use as evidence at trial, for forensic examination or investigation, and to establish its lawful owner. Nothing may be retained where it would be sufficient for the purpose to retain a photograph or copy. The section aligns the framework for the retention of anything seized by an immigration officer for the purposes of a criminal investigation with that applying to police in England and Wales.[1]

---

1 See Public Bill Committee, 10th sitting (afternoon) *Hansard*, col 334 (3 November 2015).

SECTION 51—SEARCH FOR NATIONALITY DOCUMENTS BY DETAINEE CUSTODY OFFICERS ETC

> **Summary**
>
> Detainee custody officers, prison officers and prison custody officers can strip search a detained person or search their property for 'nationality' documents as very broadly defined.

3.6

51 Search for nationality documents by detainee custody officers etc

(1) The Secretary of State may direct a detainee custody officer, prison officer or prisoner custody officer to exercise any of the powers in subsection (6) in relation to—

    (a) a detained person who is detained in a removal centre, prison or young offender institution, or

    (b) a person who is detained in a short-term holding facility.

(2) The Secretary of State may direct a prison officer or prisoner custody officer to exercise any of the powers in subsection (6) in relation to a person detained in a prison or young offender institution—

    (a) who has been recommended for deportation by a court under section 3(6) of the Immigration Act 1971,

    (b) in respect of whom the Secretary of State has made a deportation order under section 5(1) of that Act,

    (c) to whom a notice has been given in accordance with regulations under section 105 of the Nationality, Immigration and Asylum

3.6 *A Guide to the Immigration Act 2016*

                 Act 2002 (notice of decision) of a decision to make a deportation order against that person, or

        (d)   in respect of whom the Secretary of State must make, or has made, a deportation order under section 32(5) of the UK Borders Act 2007.

(3) In this section and section 52 "relevant officer" means a detainee custody officer, prison officer or prisoner custody officer.

(4) The Secretary of State may give a direction in relation to a person detained as mentioned in subsection (1) or (2) only if the Secretary of State has reasonable grounds to believe a relevant nationality document will be found if a power in subsection (6) is exercised in relation to the person.

(5) A relevant officer to whom a direction is given under subsection (1) or (2) must (if able to do so) comply with it.

(6) The powers referred to in subsections (1), (2) and (4) are—

    (a)   to require the person to hand over to the relevant officer all relevant nationality documents in his or her possession,

    (b)   to search for such documents and to take possession of any that the relevant officer finds,

    (c)   to inspect any relevant nationality documents obtained in the course of the exercise of a power in paragraph (a) or (b), and

    (d)   to seize and retain any such documents so obtained.

(7) The power in subsection (6)(b) is a power to search any of the following—

    (a)   the person;

    (b)   anything the person has with him or her;

    (c)   the person's accommodation in the removal centre, short-term holding facility, prison or young offender institution;

    (d)   any item of the person's property in the removal centre, short-term holding facility, prison or young offender institution.

(8) A full search may be carried out under subsection (7)(a); but such a search may not be carried out in the presence of—

    (a)   another person detained as mentioned in subsection (1) or (2), or

    (b)   a person of the opposite sex.

(9) An intimate search may not be carried out under subsection (7)(a).

(10) A relevant officer may if necessary use reasonable force for the purposes of exercising a power in subsection (6)(a) or (b).

(11) A relevant officer must pass a relevant nationality document seized and retained under subsection (6)(d) to the Secretary of State as soon as is reasonably practicable.

Part 3—Enforcement **3.6**

(12) The Secretary of State may retain a relevant nationality document which comes into the Secretary of State's possession under subsection (11) while the Secretary of State suspects that—

  (a) a person to whom the document relates may be liable to removal from the United Kingdom in accordance with a provision of the Immigration Acts, and

  (b) retention of the document may facilitate the removal.

(13) If subsection (12) does not apply to a document which comes into the Secretary of State's possession under this section, the Secretary of State may—

  (a) arrange for the document to be returned in accordance with subsection (14), or

  (b) if the Secretary of State thinks that it would not be appropriate to return the document, dispose of the document in such manner as the Secretary of State thinks appropriate.

(14) A document which is required to be returned in accordance with this subsection must be returned to—

  (a) the person who was previously in possession of it, or

  (b) if it was not found in the possession of a person, the location in which it was found.

(15) In this section and section 52—

  "full search" means a search which involves the removal of an item of clothing which—

  (a) is being worn wholly or partly on the trunk, and

  (b) is being so worn either next to the skin or next to an article of underwear;

  "intimate search" means a search which consists of a physical examination of a person's body orifices other than the mouth;

  "nationality document" means a document which might—

  (a) establish a person's identity, nationality or citizenship, or

  (b) indicate the place from which a person has travelled to the United Kingdom or to which a person is proposing to go.

(16) For the purposes of this section and section 52 a nationality document is "relevant" if it relates to a person who is liable to removal from the United Kingdom in accordance with a provision of the Immigration Acts.

(17) In this section the following expressions have the same meaning as in Part 8 of the Immigration and Asylum Act 1999 (see section 147)—

  "detained person";

  "detainee custody officer";

3.6 *A Guide to the Immigration Act 2016*

"prisoner custody officer";

"removal centre";

"short-term holding facility".

Commencement: 12 July 2016, Immigration Act 2014 (Commencement No 1) Regulations 2016, SI 2016/603.

Definitions:

'detained person' Immigration and Asylum Act 1999 (IAA 1999), s 147;

'detainee custody officer' IAA 1999, s 147;

'full search' essentially a strip search, s 51(15);

'intimate search' physical examination of body orifices s 51(15);

'Immigration Acts' UK Borders Act 2007, s 61(2) (see s 91(5));

'nationality document' a document which might establish a person's identity, nationality or citizenship or indicate the place from which the person has travelled to the UK or the place to which a person is proposing to go s 51(15);

'prison custody officer' IAA 1999 s 147;

'*relevant*' in relation to a nationality document for the purposes of this section means that it relates to a person liable to removal under a provision of the Immigration Acts, s 51(16);

'relevant officer', a detainee custody officer, prison officer or a prison custody officer, s 51(3);

'removal centre' IAA 1999 s 147;

'short term holding facility' IAA 1999, s 147.

Devolution: Applies throughout the UK.

Detainee custody officers, prison officers and prison custody officers can search a person detained in a detention centre, short-term holding facility, prison or young offender institution, who is liable to removal or deportation, or search their property, when directed to do so by the Secretary of State if there are reasonable grounds to suspect that relevant 'nationality documents' will be found. The 'full' search may not be carried out in the presence of another detained person or a person of the opposite sex, including the persons conducting the search. An intimate search is not permitted. If documents are not retained by the Secretary of State, they must be returned to the person from whom they were taken, or disposed of if return is not appropriate. Although the name of the search was changed from 'strip' to 'full' at Commons' Report,[1] the extent of the powers was unchanged and the power is to conduct strip searches. 'Nationality documents' are broadly defined.

[1] Government amendments 3 and 4 at House of Commons' Report. Amendment 36 would have removed the power to strip search from the Bill: *Hansard* HC, col 223 (1 December 2015).

SECTION 52—SEIZURE OF NATIONALITY DOCUMENTS BY DETAINEE CUSTODY OFFICERS ETC

> **Summary**
>
> Permits the seizure and retention of nationality documents discovered in the course of other searches.

3.7

52 Seizure of nationality documents by detainee custody officers etc

(1) A relevant officer may seize a nationality document which the relevant officer finds in the course of the exercise of a power to search other than one conferred by section 51.

(2) Where a relevant officer seizes a nationality document under subsection (1), the relevant officer—

    (a) must seek the consent of the Secretary of State to retain the document, and

    (b) if the relevant officer obtains the Secretary of State's consent, must pass the document to the Secretary of State as soon as is practicable.

(3) The Secretary of State may give consent under subsection (2) only if the Secretary of State has reasonable grounds to believe that—

    (a) the document is a relevant nationality document, and

    (b) the document may facilitate the removal of the person to whom it relates from the United Kingdom in accordance with a provision of the Immigration Acts.

(4) If the Secretary of State does not give consent under subsection (2), the Secretary of State must—

    (a) direct the relevant officer to return the document as mentioned in subsection (5), or

3.7 *A Guide to the Immigration Act 2016*

(b) if the Secretary of State thinks that it would not be appropriate to return the document, direct the relevant officer to dispose of the document in such manner as the Secretary of State may direct.

(5) A document which is required to be returned in accordance with this subsection must be returned to—

(a) the person who was previously in possession of it, or

(b) if it was not found in the possession of a person, the location in which it was found.

(6) The Secretary of State may retain a relevant nationality document which comes into the Secretary of State's possession under this section while the Secretary of State suspects that—

(a) a person to whom the document relates may be liable to removal from the United Kingdom in accordance with a provision of the Immigration Acts, and

(b) retention of the document may facilitate the removal.

(7) If subsection (6) does not apply to a document which comes into the Secretary of State's possession under this section, the Secretary of State may—

(a) arrange for the document to be returned in accordance with subsection (5), or

(b) if the Secretary of State thinks that it would not be appropriate to return the document, dispose of the document in such manner as the Secretary of State thinks appropriate.

Commencement: 12 July 2016, Immigration Act 2014 (Commencement No 1) Regulations 2016, SI 2016/603.

Definitions:

'detained person' Immigration and Asylum Act 1999 (IAA 1999), s 147;

'detainee custody officer' IAA 1999, s 147;

'Immigration Acts' UK Borders Act 2007, s 61(2) (see s 91(5));

'intimate search' physical examination of body orifices, s 51(15);

'nationality document' a document which might establish a person's identity, nationality or citizenship or indicate the place from which a person has travelled to the UK or the place to which a person is proposing to go, s 51(15);

'prisoner custody officer' IAA 1999 s 147;

relevant in relation to a document for the purposes of this section means that it relates to a person liable to removal under a provision of the Immigration Acts, s 51(16);

'relevant officer' a detainee custody officer, prison officer or a prison custody officer, s 51(3);

'removal centre' IAA 1999 s 147;

'short term holding facility' IAA 1999 s 147.

Devolution: Applies throughout the UK.

This section permits detainee custody officers, prison officers and prisoner custody officers to seize and retain nationality documents which they encounter during other searches in detention centres and prisons. For example, under para 18A(1) of Schedule 2 to the IA 1971 immigration officers and constables have powers to search persons detained under para 16 of that Schedule for anything which might be used to cause physical injury to themselves or others, or to assist in effecting an escape.

Officers must obtain authorisation from the Secretary of State (SSHD) to exercise the power to retain a document. Such authorisation is to be given only if the SSHD suspects that the document relates to a person liable to removal and that retention of the document may facilitate the removal. The document may be retained only for so long as she has such suspicions. Where the SSHD gives an authorisation, the officers must pass the documents to her. If the authorisation is refused, they must return the documents to the person or location from whence they were seized unless the SSHD 'thinks that it would not be appropriate' (s 52(7)(b)) to return the document, it which case it must be disposed of as the SSHD directs.

SECTION 53—AMENDMENTS RELATING TO SECTIONS 51 AND 52

Summary
Expands the existing offences of assaulting or obstructing a detainee custody officer, prison officer or prisoner custody officer, to include where acting under s 51 of this Act.

3.8

53 Amendments relating to sections 51 and 52

(1) Schedule 11 to the Immigration and Asylum Act 1999 (detainee custody officers) is amended as follows.

3.8 *A Guide to the Immigration Act 2016*

(2) In paragraph 4 (offence of assaulting detainee custody officer)—

    (a) omit the "or" at the end of paragraph (b), and

    (b) at the end of paragraph (c) insert "or

        (d) performing functions under section 51 of the Immigration Act 2016 (search for nationality documents),".

(3) In paragraph 5 (offence of obstructing detainee custody officer)—

    (a) omit the "or" at the end of paragraph (b), and

    (b) at the end of paragraph (c) insert "or

        (d) performing functions under section 51 of the Immigration Act 2016 (search for nationality documents),".

(4) After paragraph 8 insert—

"9A A reference in paragraph 4(d) or 5(d) to a detainee custody officer performing functions under section 51 of the Immigration Act 2016 includes a reference to a prison officer or prisoner custody officer performing such functions."

Commencement: 12 July 2016, Immigration Act 2014 (Commencement No 1) Regulations 2016, SI 2016/603.

Amends: Schedule 11 *Detainee Custody Officers* of the Immigration Act 1999, amending paras 4 and 5, and inserting a new para 9.

Definitions: A reference in the Immigration and Asylum Act 1999 (IAA 1999), Schedule 11, paras (4)(d) and (5)(d) to '*a detainee custody officer performing functions under s 51 of the Immigration Act 2016*' includes a reference to a detainee custody officer performing functions under s 51 of this Act, s 53(4) inserting new para 9 into Schedule 11 *Detainee Custody Officers* to the IAA 1999.

Offences: Assaulting an immigration officer in the exercise of functions under s 51 of this Act (IAA 1999, Schedule 11, para 4); obstructing an immigration officer in the exercise of functions under s 51 of this Act (IAA 1999, Schedule 11, para 5).

Devolution: Applies throughout the UK.

This section expands the existing offences of assaulting or obstructing a detainee custody officer, prison officers or prisoner custody officers under para 4 of Schedule 11 to the (IAA 1999) to include where the officers are acting under s 51 of this Act.

SECTION 54—AMENDMENTS TO SEARCH WARRANT PROVISIONS AND SCHEDULE 8—AMENDMENTS TO SEARCH WARRANT PROVISIONS

Summary

Amends provisions on search warrants to give immigration officers the same powers as police officers, in particular making provision for multiple entry warrants.

3.9

54 Amendments to search warrant provisions

Schedule 8 (amendments to search warrant provisions) has effect.

Schedule 8

Section 54
Amendments to search warrant provisions

Immigration Act 1971 (c. 77)

1 The Immigration Act 1971 is amended as follows.

2(1) Section 28D (entry and search of premises) is amended as follows.

(2) In subsection (1)—

    (a) in paragraph (b) for "specified in the application" substitute " mentioned in subsection (1A) ", and

    (b) at the end of paragraph (e) insert " in relation to each set of premises specified in the application, ".

(3) After subsection (1) insert—

"(1A) The premises referred to in subsection (1)(b) above are—

    (a) one or more sets of premises specified in the application, or

    (b) subject to subsection (2A), any premises occupied or controlled by a person specified in the application, including such sets of premises as are so specified (in which case the application is for an "all premises warrant").

(1B) If the application is for an all premises warrant, the justice of the peace must also be satisfied—

3.9 *A Guide to the Immigration Act 2016*

        (a)   that because of the particulars of the offence referred to in paragraph (a) of subsection (1), there are reasonable grounds for believing that it is necessary to search premises occupied or controlled by the person in question which are not specified in the application in order to find the material referred to in paragraph (b) of that subsection, and

        (b)   that it is not reasonably practicable to specify in the application all the premises which the person occupies or controls and which might need to be searched.

  (1C)   Subject to subsection (2A), the warrant may authorise entry to and search of premises on more than one occasion if, on the application, the justice of the peace is satisfied that it is necessary to authorise multiple entries in order to achieve the purpose for which the justice issues the warrant.

  (1D)   If it authorises multiple entries, the number of entries authorised may be unlimited, or limited to a maximum."

(4)   In subsection (2) after "conditions" insert " referred to in subsection (1)(e) ".

(5)   After subsection (2) insert—

"(2A)   A justice of the peace in Scotland may not issue—

        (a)   an all premises warrant under this section, or

        (b)   a warrant under this section authorising multiple entries."

(6)   In subsection (7)—

        (a)   for "subsection (1)" substitute " this section ",

        (b)   in paragraph (a) for "the reference" substitute " references " and for "a reference" substitute " references ", and

        (c)   in paragraph (b) for "paragraph (d)" substitute " subsection (1)(d) ".

(1)   Section 28FB (search for personnel records with warrant) is amended as follows.

(2)   In subsection (1)—

        (a)   after "business premises" insert " mentioned in subsection (1A) ", and

        (b)   at the end of paragraph (c) insert " in relation to each set of premises specified in the application. "

(3)   After subsection (1) insert—

"(1A)   The premises referred to in subsection (1) above are—

        (a)   one or more sets of premises specified in the application, or

        (b)   subject to subsection (3C), any premises occupied or controlled by a person specified in the application, including such sets of

Part 3—Enforcement **3.9**

premises as are so specified (in which case the application is for an "all premises warrant").

(1B) If the application is for an all premises warrant, the justice of the peace must also be satisfied—

(a) that there are reasonable grounds for believing that it is necessary to search premises occupied or controlled by the person in question which are not specified in the application in order to find the records referred to in subsection (1)(b), and

(b) that it is not reasonably practicable to specify in the application all the premises which the person occupies or controls and which might need to be searched."

(4) In subsection (2) for "Those conditions are" substitute " The conditions referred to in subsection (1)(c) are ".

(5) After subsection (3) insert—

"(3A) Subject to subsection (3C), the warrant may authorise entry to and search of premises on more than one occasion if, on the application, the justice of the peace is satisfied that it is necessary to authorise multiple entries in order to achieve the purpose for which the justice issues the warrant.

(3B) If it authorises multiple entries, the number of entries authorised may be unlimited, or limited to a maximum.

(3C) A justice of the peace in Scotland may not issue—

(a) an all premises warrant under this section, or

(b) a warrant under this section authorising multiple entries."

4(1) Section 28J (search warrants: safeguards) is amended as follows.

(2) In subsection (2)—

(a) after paragraph (a) insert—

"(aa) if the application is for a warrant authorising entry and search on more than one occasion, state the ground on which the officer applies for such a warrant, and whether the officer seeks a warrant authorising an unlimited number of entries, or (if not) the maximum number of entries desired;", and

(b) for paragraph (b) substitute—

"(b) specify the matters set out in subsection (2A) below; and".

(3) After subsection (2) insert—

"(2A) The matters which must be specified pursuant to subsection (2)(b) above are—

3.9 *A Guide to the Immigration Act 2016*

- (a) if the application relates to one or more sets of premises specified in the application, each set of premises which it is desired to enter and search;
- (b) if the application relates to any premises occupied or controlled by a person specified in the application—
  - (i) as many sets of premises which it is desired to enter and search as it is reasonably practicable to specify;
  - (ii) the person who is in occupation or control of those premises and any others which it is desired to enter and search;
  - (iii) why it is necessary to search more premises than those specified under sub-paragraph (i);
  - (iv) why it is not reasonably practicable to specify all the premises which it is desired to enter and search."

(4) In subsection (6) at the end insert " unless it specifies that it authorises multiple entries ".

(5) After subsection (6) insert—

"(6A) If it specifies that it authorises multiple entries, it must also specify whether the number of entries authorised is unlimited, or limited to a specified maximum."

(6) In subsection (7) for paragraph (c) substitute—

"(c) each set of premises to be searched, or (in the case of an all premises warrant) the person who is in occupation or control of premises to be searched, together with any premises under the person's occupation or control which can be specified and which are to be searched; and".

(7) For subsection (9) substitute—

"(9) Two copies must be made of a warrant which specifies only one set of premises and does not authorise multiple entries; and as many copies as are reasonably required may be made of any other kind of warrant."

(8) After subsection (10) insert—

"(10A) All premises warrant" means a warrant issued in response to an application of the kind mentioned in section 24E(6)(b), 28D(1A)(b) or 28FB(1A)(b) or paragraph 25A(6AA)(b) of Schedule 2.

(10B) References in this section to a warrant authorising multiple entries is to a warrant of the kind mentioned in section 24E(8), 28D(1C) or 28FB(3A) or paragraph 25A(6AC) of Schedule 2."

5(1) Section 28K (execution of warrants) is amended as follows.

(2) After subsection (2) insert—

Part 3—Enforcement **3.9**

(2A) A person so authorised has the same powers as the officer whom the person accompanies in respect of—

(a) the execution of the warrant, and

(b) the seizure or detention of anything to which the warrant relates.

(2B) But the person may exercise those powers only in the company, and under the supervision, of an immigration officer."

(3) In subsection (3) for "one month" substitute " three months ".

(4) After subsection (3) insert—

"(3A) If the warrant is an all premises warrant, no premises which are not specified in it may be entered or searched unless an immigration officer of at least the rank of chief immigration officer has in writing authorised them to be entered.

(3B) No premises may be entered or searched for the second or any subsequent time under a warrant which authorises multiple entries unless an immigration officer of at least the rank of chief immigration officer has in writing authorised that entry to those premises."

(5) In subsection (4)(a) after "and" insert ", if not in uniform, ".

(6) After subsection (8) insert—

"(8A) Unless the warrant is a warrant specifying one set of premises only, the officer must comply with subsection (8) separately in respect of each set of premises entered and searched.

(8B) Subject to subsection (8C), a warrant must be returned in accordance with subsection (9)—

(a) when it has been executed, or

(b) in the case of a specific premises warrant which has not been executed, an all premises warrant or any warrant authorising multiple entries, on the expiry of the period of three months referred to in subsection (3) or sooner.

(8C) Subsection (8B) does not apply to a warrant issued by a justice of the peace in Scotland or by the sheriff if the warrant has been executed."

(7) In subsection (9) for the words from "A warrant" to "its execution," substitute " The warrant ".

(8) After subsection (13) insert—

"(13A) In subsection (8B)—

"specific premises warrant" means a warrant which is not an all premises warrant;

"all premises warrant" means a warrant issued in response to an application of the kind mentioned in section 24E(6)(b),

3.9 *A Guide to the Immigration Act 2016*

                28D(1A)(b) or 28FB(1A)(b) or paragraph 25A(6AA)(b) of Schedule 2.

      (13B) The reference in subsection (8B) to a warrant authorising multiple entries is to a warrant of the kind mentioned in section 24E(8), 28D(1C) or 28FB(3A) or paragraph 25A(6AC) of Schedule 2."

6(1) Paragraph 25A of Schedule 2 (search of premises for nationality documents) is amended as follows.

(2) In sub-paragraph (6A)—

      (a) for "specified in the application" substitute " mentioned in sub-paragraph (6AA) ", and

      (b) at the end of paragraph (b) insert " in relation to each set of premises specified in the application, ".

(3) After sub-paragraph (6A) insert—

"(6AA) The premises referred to in sub-paragraph (6A) above are—

      (a) one or more sets of premises specified in the application, or

      (b) subject to sub-paragraph (6BA), any premises occupied or controlled by a person specified in the application, including such sets of premises as are so specified (in which case the application is for an "all premises warrant").

(6AB) If the application is for an all premises warrant, the justice of the peace must also be satisfied—

      (a) that there are reasonable grounds for believing that it is necessary to search premises occupied or controlled by the person in question which are not specified in the application in order to find the relevant documents, and

      (b) that it is not reasonably practicable to specify in the application all the premises which the person occupies or controls and which might need to be searched.

(6AC) Subject to sub-paragraph (6BA), the warrant may authorise entry to and search of premises on more than one occasion if, on the application, the justice of the peace is satisfied that it is necessary to authorise multiple entries in order to achieve the purpose for which the justice issues the warrant.

(6AD) If it authorises multiple entries, the number of entries authorised may be unlimited, or limited to a maximum."

(4) In sub-paragraph (6B) after "conditions" insert " mentioned in sub-paragraph (6A)(b) ".

Part 3—Enforcement **3.9**

(5) After sub-paragraph (6B) insert—

"(6BA) A justice of the peace in Scotland may not issue—

(a) an all premises warrant under this paragraph, or

(b) a warrant under this paragraph authorising multiple entries."

(6) In sub-paragraph (6C) for "sub-paragraph (6A)" substitute " sub-paragraphs (6A) to (6BA) ".

UK Borders Act 2007 (c. 30)

7(1) Section 45 of the UK Borders Act 2007 (search of premises for nationality documents) is amended as follows.

(2) In subsection (2)—

(a) in paragraph (b) for "specified in the application" substitute " mentioned in subsection (2A) ", and

(b) at the end of paragraph (d) insert " in relation to each set of premises specified in the application, ".

(3) After subsection (2) insert—

"(2A) The premises referred to in subsection (2)(b) above are—

(a) one or more sets of premises specified in the application, or

(b) subject to subsection (3A), any premises occupied or controlled by a person specified in the application, including such sets of premises as are so specified (in which case the application is for an "all premises warrant").

(2B) If the application is for an all premises warrant, the justice of the peace must also be satisfied—

(a) that there are reasonable grounds for believing that it is necessary to search premises occupied or controlled by the person in question which are not specified in the application in order to find the nationality documents, and

(b) that it is not reasonably practicable to specify in the application all the premises which the person occupies or controls and which might need to be searched.

(2C) Subject to subsection (3A), the warrant may authorise entry to and search of premises on more than one occasion if, on the application, the justice of the peace is satisfied that it is necessary to authorise multiple entries in order to achieve the purpose for which the justice issues the warrant.

(2D) If it authorises multiple entries, the number of entries authorised may be unlimited, or limited to a maximum."

(4) In subsection (3) after "conditions" insert " mentioned in subsection (2)(d) ".

3.9 *A Guide to the Immigration Act 2016*

(5) After subsection (3) insert—

"(3A) A justice of the peace in Scotland may not issue—

(a) an all premises warrant under this section, or

(b) a warrant under this section authorising multiple entries."

Commencement: 1 December 2016, Immigration Act 2016 (Commencement No 2 and Transitional Provisions) Regulations 2016, SI 2016/1037.

Amends: The Immigration Act 1971 (IA 1971), s 28D *Entry and search of premises,* s 28FB *Search for personnel records: with warrant;* s 28J *Search warrants: safeguards;* s 28K *Execution of warrants;* para 25A of Schedule 2; UK Borders Act 2007, s 45 *Search for evidence of nationality: other premises.*

Guidance: *Warrants: procurement and use,* v1, Enforcement Instructions and Guidance: powers and operational procedure, Home Office, 1 December 2016. Available at: https://www.gov.uk/government/uploads/system/uploads/attachment_data/file/574036/Warrants-procurement-and-use-v1.pdf.

Definitions:

'premises' IA 1971, s 28L, see s 58.

Devolution: Applies throughout the UK. Provision is made to prevent a justice of the peace in Scotland from issuing multiple entry warrants.

Section 54 gives effect to Schedule 8 which makes multiple amendments to provisions of the IA 1971 concerning search warrant provisions. The Explanatory Notes to the Act state that when the IA 1971 was passed, powers of immigration officers to enter premises 'closely reflected' those available to the police in England and Wales, but over time changes to the Police and Criminal Evidence Act 1984 (PACE 1984) meant that the provisions are no longer aligned.[1] The new measures amend current laws to catch the immigration provisions up.

The Home Office has produced the first consolidated guidance on warrants to support the work of immigration officers in exercising powers under this section and Schedule.[2] Parts of the guidance have not been published and are marked 'official sensitive'.

Provision is made for warrants issued to immigration officers to be used to enter multiple premises on a number of different occasions (IA 1971, s 28D(1A)–(1D) as amended). This provision does not extend to Scotland where multiple entry warrants are not permitted (IA 1971, s 28D(2A) as amended).

Provision is made for a person accompanying an immigration officer to have the same powers as the officer in executing a warrant and in seizing items to which the warrant relates, but only where supervised (IA 1971, s 28K(2A) as amended). The guidance explains that anyone who is not an immigration or police officer who accompanies an arrest-trained or other immigration officer must be named separately on the warrant 'or by their company name' and their reasons for accompanying the visit must be provided to the court. It emphasises that where persons such as police, Her Majesty's Revenue and Customs, the Department of Work and Pensions and others wish to search for their own purposes they must use their own powers of entry or obtain warrants, and not rely on IA 1971, s 28K(2A) as inserted by this section. It suggests that interpreters and paramedics may also be among those listed as accompanying and refers to PACE Code B para 3.6(f) and notes for guidance 3C.

The guidance highlights that if a warrant is to be obtained by, or executed by, a police officer in England and Wales then the safeguards in ss 15 and 16 of PACE 1984 apply and that criminal and financial investigation officers applying for warrants under the Police and Criminal Evidence Act 1984 (Application to immigration officers and designated customs officials in England and Wales) Order 2013[3] must comply with PACE, ss 15–16.

The guidance sets out that warrants may be obtained by assistant immigration officers (who are warranted officers), and/or immigration officers who are not arrest-trained, but may only be executed by warranted immigration officers who are arrest trained. In England and Wales. Applications can be made online, but not in Scotland and Northern Ireland. The dedicated sections of the guidance on 'Applying for search warrants in Scotland', and 'Applying for search warrants in Northern Ireland' are very short. Applications in Scotland are made orally by evidence on oath direct to a sheriff in the Sheriff's Chambers. Applications for warrants in Northern Ireland are made by complaint by an immigration officer attending the home of a lay magistrate. Like the Police Service of Northern Ireland (PSNI), the immigration compliance and enforcement teams in Northern Ireland have their own forms, based on the PSNI templates.

The guidance specifies that where applications are made to a justice of the peace, the application must specify that there are no reasonable grounds for believing that the material sought consists of, or includes, items subject to legal privilege, excluded material and special procedure material. Excluded material is defined in PACE 1984, s 11 to include personal medical and counselling records; human tissue or tissue fluid and 'journalistic material', where the material is held in confidence. Special procedure material is defined in PACE, s 14 and includes journalistic material which is not held in confidence and

3.9 *A Guide to the Immigration Act 2016*

material created by an employee or employer, not excluded material and which is held in confidence. Sections 12–16 inclusive of the PACE (Northern Ireland) Order 1989 define the categories of legal privilege, excluded, journalistic, personal and special procedure material under that order. As PACE does not apply in Scotland, references to excluded and special procedure material do not apply in Scotland.

The guidance reminds immigration officers of the need to consider the Borders, Citizenship and Immigration Act 2009, s 55 and states:

> 'If there is reason to believe that a search might have an adverse effect on community relations between the police and the community, the officer in charge must consult the police before any visit takes place. In urgent cases the police must be informed as soon as practicable after the search.'

The validity of an immigration warrant is increased from one to three months (IA 1971, s 28K(3) as amended). The requirement for immigration search warrants obtained in Scotland to be returned after they have been executed is removed (IA 1971, s 28K(2A) as amended). The validity of an immigration warrant is increased from one to three months (IA 1971, s 28K(3) as amended).

The guidance provides that written authorisation from a Chief Immigration Officer will be required each time an immigration officer wishes to enter unspecified premises under an all premises warrant or, where permitted by the warrant, to search premises on a second or subsequent occasion. The authorisation must be recorded in the immigration officer's pocket notebook.

Paragraph 5(5) of Schedule 8 inserts the words 'if not in uniform' into s 28K(4)(a) of the Immigration Act 1971. The effect of this is summarised in the guidance:

> 'you are not required to show your warrant card to identify yourself when executing a warrant as long as you are in full Immigration Enforcement uniform. Your warrant number must be clearly visible. But if your Assistant Director (AD) has authorised you to execute the warrant out of uniform in plain clothes, you are still required to show your warrant card.'

---

1 Para 524.
2 *Warrants: procurement and use*, v1, Enforcement Instructions and Guidance: powers and operational procedure, Home Office, 1 December 2016. Available at: https://www.gov.uk/government/uploads/system/uploads/attachment_data/file/574036/Warrants-procurement-and-use-v1.pdf (accessed 15 December 2016).
3 SI 2013/1052.

Part 3—Enforcement **3.10**

SECTION 55—SUPPLY OF INFORMATION TO SECRETARY OF STATE AND SCHEDULE 9—DUTY TO SUPPLY NATIONALITY DOCUMENTS TO SECRETARY OF STATE: PERSONS TO WHOM DUTY APPLIES

> **Summary**
>
> Expands the existing information gateway in the Immigration and Asylum Act 1999, s 20 which enables the supply of information to the Secretary of State (SSHD) for immigration purposes. It is made a duty for specified persons, listed in new Schedule A1 to the 1999 Act, to provide the SSHD, when directed to do so, with a nationality document lawfully in their possession that may facilitate a person's removal from the UK.

3.10

55 Supply of information to Secretary of State

(1) Section 20 of the Immigration and Asylum Act 1999 (supply of information to Secretary of State) is amended in accordance with subsections (2) to (10).

(2) For the heading substitute " Power to supply information etc to Secretary of State ".

(3) In subsection (1) for paragraphs (a) to (f) substitute—

"(a) a public authority, or

(b) any specified person, for purposes specified in relation to that person."

(4) In subsection (1A) in each of paragraphs (a) and (b) for "a person listed in subsection (1) or someone acting on his behalf" substitute " a public authority or someone acting on behalf of a public authority ".

(5) After subsection (1A) insert—

"(1B) This section does not apply to—

(a) information which is held by the Crown Prosecution Service, or

(b) a document or article which comes into the possession of, or is discovered by, the Crown Prosecution Service, or someone acting on behalf of the Crown Prosecution Service,

if section 40 of the UK Borders Act 2007 applies to the information, document or article."

3.10 *A Guide to the Immigration Act 2016*

(6) After subsection (2A) insert—

"(2B) Subsection (2A)(a) does not affect any other power of the Secretary of State to retain a document or article."

(7) In subsection (3) after paragraph (d) insert—

"(da) anything else that is done in connection with the exercise of a function under any of the Immigration Acts;".

(8) After subsection (3) insert—

"(3A) Public authority" means a person with functions of a public nature but does not include—

(a) Her Majesty's Revenue and Customs,

(b) either House of Parliament or a person exercising functions in connection with proceedings in Parliament,

(c) the Scottish Parliament or a person exercising functions in connection with proceedings in the Scottish Parliament,

(d) the National Assembly for Wales or a person exercising functions in connection with proceedings in that Assembly, or

(e) the Northern Ireland Assembly or a person exercising functions in connection with proceedings in that Assembly."

(9) Omit subsection (4).

(10) After subsection (6) insert—

"(7) Nothing in this section authorises information, a document or an article to be supplied if to do so would contravene a restriction on the disclosure of information (however imposed)."

(11) After section 20 of the Immigration and Asylum Act 1999 insert—

"20A Duty to supply nationality documents to Secretary of State

(1) This section applies to a nationality document which the Secretary of State has reasonable grounds for believing is lawfully in the possession of a person listed in Schedule A1.

(2) The Secretary of State may direct the person to supply the document to the Secretary of State if the Secretary of State suspects that—

(a) a person to whom the document relates may be liable to removal from the United Kingdom in accordance with a provision of the Immigration Acts, and

(b) the document may facilitate the removal.

(3) A person to whom a direction is given must, as soon as is practicable, supply the document to the Secretary of State.

(4) If the document was originally created in hard copy form and the person possesses the original document, it must be supplied

Part 3—Enforcement **3.10**

to the Secretary of State unless it is required by the person for the performance of any of the person's functions.

(5) If the original document is required by the person for the performance of any of the person's functions—

(a) the person must, as soon as is practicable, supply a copy of the document to the Secretary of State, and

(b) if subsequently the person no longer requires the original document, the person must supply it to the Secretary of State as soon as is practicable after it is no longer required.

(6) Subsection (5)(b) does not apply if the Secretary of State notifies the person that the original document is no longer required.

(7) If subsection (5) applies the person may make a copy of the original document before supplying it to the Secretary of State.

(8) The Secretary of State may retain a nationality document supplied under this section while the Secretary of State suspects that—

(a) a person to whom the document relates may be liable to removal from the United Kingdom in accordance with a provision of the Immigration Acts, and

(b) retention of the document may facilitate the removal.

(9) Subsection (8) does not affect any other power of the Secretary of State to retain a document.

(10) The Secretary of State may dispose of a nationality document supplied under this section in such manner as the Secretary of State thinks appropriate.

(11) Nothing in this section authorises or requires a document to be supplied if to do so would contravene a restriction on the disclosure of information (however imposed).

(12) The Secretary of State may by regulations amend Schedule A1 so as to add, modify or remove a reference to a person or description of person.

(13) Regulations under subsection (12) may not amend Schedule A1 so as to apply this section to—

(a) either House of Parliament or a person exercising functions in connection with proceedings in Parliament,

(b) the Scottish Parliament or a person exercising functions in connection with proceedings in the Scottish Parliament,

(c) the National Assembly for Wales or a person exercising functions in connection with proceedings in that Assembly, or

3.10 *A Guide to the Immigration Act 2016*

> > (d) the Northern Ireland Assembly or a person exercising functions in connection with proceedings in that Assembly.
>
> (14) In this section "nationality document" means a document which might—
>
> > (a) establish a person's identity, nationality or citizenship, or
> >
> > (b) indicate the place from which a person has travelled to the United Kingdom or to which a person is proposing to go."
>
> (12) In section 166 of the Immigration and Asylum Act 1999 (regulations and orders)—
>
> > (a) after subsection (5) insert—
> >
> > "(5A) No regulations under section 20A(12) which amend Schedule A1 so as to—
> >
> > > (a) add a reference to a person or description of person, or
> > >
> > > (b) modify a reference to a person or description of person otherwise than in consequence of a change of name or transfer of functions,
> >
> > are to be made unless a draft of the regulations has been laid before Parliament and approved by a resolution of each House.", and
> >
> > (b) in subsection (6), before the "or" at the end of paragraph (a) insert—
> >
> > "(ab) under section 20A(12) and which falls within subsection (5A),".
>
> (13) Before Schedule 1 to the Immigration and Asylum Act 1999 insert the Schedule A1 set out in Schedule 9.

Schedule 9

Section 20A

Duty to supply nationality documents to Secretary of State: persons to whom duty applies

This is the new Schedule A1 to the Immigration and Asylum Act 1999 referred to in section 55—

"SCHEDULE A1

Section 20A

PERSONS TO WHOM SECTION 20A APPLIES

Law enforcement

1   The chief officer of police for a police area in England and Wales.

Part 3—Enforcement   **3.10**

2   The chief constable of the Police Service of Scotland.

3   The Chief Constable of the Police Service of Northern Ireland.

4   The Chief Constable of the British Transport Police Force.

5A Port Police Force established under an order made under section 14 of the Harbours Act 1964.

6   The Port Police Force established under Part 10 of the Port of London Act 1968.

7A Port Police Force established under section 79 of the Harbours, Docks and Piers Clauses Act 1847.

8   The National Crime Agency.

Local government

9A county council or district council in England.

10A London borough council.

11 The Greater London Authority.

12 The Common Council of the City of London in its capacity as a local authority.

13 The Council of the Isles of Scilly.

14A county council or a county borough council in Wales.

15A council constituted under section 2 of the Local Government etc (Scotland) Act 1994.

16A district council in Northern Ireland.

Regulatory bodies

17 The Gangmasters and Labour Abuse Authority.

18 The Security Industry Authority.

Health bodies

19 An NHS trust established under section 25 of the National Health Service Act 2006 or under section 18 of the National Health Service (Wales) Act 2006.

20 An NHS foundation trust within the meaning given by section 30 of the National Health Service Act 2006.

21 A Local Health Board established under section 11 of the National Health Service (Wales) Act 2006.

22A National Health Service Trust established under section 12A of the National Health Service (Scotland) Act 1978.

3.10 *A Guide to the Immigration Act 2016*

    23A   Health and Social Care trust established under Article 10 of the Health and Personal Social Services (Northern Ireland) Order 1991 (SI 1991/194 (NI 1)).

Education bodies

    24   The proprietor of a school or 16 to 19 Academy within the meaning of the Education Act 1996 (see sections 4 and 579(1) of that Act).

    25   The governing body of an institution within the further education sector within the meaning of the Further and Higher Education Act 1992 (see sections 90 and 91 of that Act).

    26   The governing body of a qualifying institution within the meaning of Part 2 of the Higher Education Act 2004 (see sections 11 and 21 of that Act).

    27   The proprietor or governing body of a school within the meaning of the Education (Scotland) Act 1980 (see section 135(1) of that Act).

    28   The proprietor or governing body of a post-16 education body within the meaning of the Further and Higher Education (Scotland) Act 2005 (see section 35 of that Act).

    29   The proprietor of a school within the meaning of the Education and Libraries (Northern Ireland) Order 1986 (SI 1986/594 (NI 3)) (see Article 2(2) of that Order).

    30   The governing body of an institution of further education within the meaning of the Further Education (Northern Ireland) Order 1997 (SI 1997/1772 (NI 15)) (see Article 2(2) of that Order).

    31   The governing body of a higher education institution as defined by Article 30(3) of the Education and Libraries (Northern Ireland) Order 1993 (SI 1993/2810 (NI 12)).

Registration officials

    32   The Registrar General for England and Wales.

    33   A superintendent registrar of births, deaths and marriages.

    34   A registrar of births, deaths and marriages.

    35   A civil partnership registrar within the meaning of Chapter 1 of Part 2 of the Civil Partnership Act 2004 (see section 29 of that Act).

    36   The Registrar General for Scotland.

    37A   district registrar within the meaning of section 7 of the Registration of Births, Deaths and Marriages (Scotland) Act 1965.

    38A   senior registrar within the meaning of that section.

39   An assistant registrar within the meaning of that section.

40   The Registrar General for Northern Ireland.

41   A person appointed under Article 31(1) or (3) of the Marriage (Northern Ireland) Order 2003 (SI 2003/413 (NI 3)).

42A person appointed under section 152(1) or (3) of the Civil Partnership Act 2004.

Other bodies: Northern Ireland

43   The Northern Ireland Housing Executive."

Commencement: 12 July 2016, Immigration Act 2014 (Commencement No 1) Regulations 2016, SI 2016/603.

Amends: Immigration and Asylum 1999 (IAA 1999), s 20 and renames it *Power to supply information etc to the Secretary of State;* inserts a new s 20A *Duty to supply nationality documents to the Secretary of State* into that Act. Amends s 166 *Regulations and Orders* of that Act to provide that regulations that add an individual or a class of persons to those under a duty to supply nationality documents to the Secretary of State, or modify such a person or class (other than when this is consequential), are subject to the affirmative procedure. Inserts new Schedule A1 *Persons to whom s 20A applies* into that Act.

Regulations: The Secretary of State may amend Schedule A1 by regulations to add, modify or remove a reference to a person or a description of person (IAA 1999, s 20A(12) as inserted by s 55(11)). There is protection against applying s 20A of the IAA 1999, as amended, to members of any of the parliaments or assemblies.

Regulations are subject to the negative resolution procedure (see s 93).

Definitions:

'Immigration Acts' UK Borders Act 2007, s 61(2) (see s 91(5));

'nationality document' a document which might establish a person's nationality or citizenship or indicate the place from which the person has travelled or to which the person is intending to go.

Devolution: Applies throughout the UK.

This section expands the existing information gateway in IAA 1999, s 20 which enables the supply of information to the Secretary of State (SSHD) for immigration purposes. The effect of the amendments to IAA 1999, s 20 is that the gateway encompasses all public authorities, and all persons acting on behalf of a public authority, other than Her Majesty's Revenue and Customs and those acting on its behalf. Persons exercising functions in relation to the

3.11 *A Guide to the Immigration Act 2016*

Westminster or devolved parliaments are also not within the scope of the provision.

Any public authority or any specified person, the latter for specified purposes, is empowered to supply information to the SSHD in connection with, *inter alia*, 'anything that is done in connection with the exercise of a function under any of the Immigration Acts' (IAA 1999, s 20(3)(da) as amended). In addition, a very wide range of bodies, connected with the police, local government, NHS trusts, registrars and the Northern Ireland Housing Executive, will be under a duty to supply 'nationality documents', which are very broadly defined, to the SSHD (IAA 1999, s 20A inserted by s 55(11)).

Prior to amendment, in addition to common law data sharing powers, s 20 of the 1999 Act only provided for the sharing of information, documents and articles from specified public authorities such as the police and the National Crime Agency. The effect of the amendments is to give other public authorities who hold information that they are willing to share for immigration purposes a clear statutory authority to do so.

It is made a duty for specified persons, listed in new Schedule A1 to the 1999 Act, to provide the SSHD, when directed to do so, with a nationality document which may facilitate a person's removal from the UK. The duty applies where the SSHD has reasonable grounds for believing that a document is already lawfully in the possession of the person or authority.

SECTION 56—DETENTION ETC BY IMMIGRATION OFFICERS IN SCOTLAND

> **Summary**
> Amends Scottish powers of detention prior to arrest, and of arrest without warrant, so that they apply to all immigration offences contained in, or for which an immigration officer has a power of arrest under, the Immigration Acts.

3.11

56 Detention etc. by immigration officers in Scotland

(1) The Criminal Law (Consolidation) (Scotland) Act 1995 is amended as follows.

Part 3—Enforcement **3.11**

(2) In section 24A (extension of period of detention under section 24) for subsection (7) substitute—

"(7) In this section and section 24B, "custody review officer" means—

(a) an officer who—

(i) is of a rank at least equivalent to that of police inspector, and

(ii) has not been involved in the investigation in connection with which the person is detained, or

(b) in relation to the detention of a person under section 24 by an immigration officer, a constable—

(i) of the rank of inspector or above, and

(ii) who has not been involved in the investigation in connection with which the person is detained."

(3) In section 26A(2) (power of arrest of authorised immigration officers) omit "or immigration enforcement offence".

(4) Section 26B(1) (interpretation of Part 3) is amended as follows.

(5) In the definition of "immigration offence"—

(a) after "means" insert " — (a) ", and

(b) at the end of paragraph (a) insert ", or

(b) (insofar as it is not an offence within paragraph (a)) an offence under the Immigration Acts or in relation to which a power of arrest is conferred on an immigration officer by the Immigration Acts;".

(6) Omit the definition of "immigration enforcement offence".

Commencement: 12 July 2016, Immigration Act 2014 (Commencement No 1) Regulations 2016, SI 2016/603.

Amends: The Criminal Law (Consolidation) (Scotland) Act 1995 (CL(C)(S)A 1995), s 24A, s 26A, s 26B.

Definitions:

'custody review officer' The CL(C)(S)A 1995, s 24A(7) as amended by s 56(2).

'Immigration Acts' UK Borders Act 2007, s 61(2) (see s 91(5));

The definition of an *immigration offence* in s 26B *Interpretation of Part 3* of the (CL(C)(S)A 1995 is amended.

Devolution: Applies to Scotland.

3.12 *A Guide to the Immigration Act 2016*

The effect of this section is that Scottish powers of detention prior to arrest, and of arrest without warrant, apply to all immigration offences contained in, or for which an immigration officer has a power of arrest under, the Immigration Acts. These include those offences that immigration officers encounter in the course of exercising a function under the Immigration Acts, listed in s 14 of the Asylum and Immigration (Treatment of Claimants etc.) Act 2004.

The brevity of the section results from the consolidation of Scottish law in the CL(C)(S)A 1995. The Explanatory Notes to the Immigration Act 2016 state that this: 'allows immigration officers to work effectively within the Scottish criminal justice system and ensures consistency in the immigration-related criminal investigation powers of immigration officers across the UK'.[1]

---

1 Para 274.

SECTION 57—POWERS TO TAKE FINGERPRINTS ETC FROM DEPENDANTS

> **Summary**
>
> Amends the definition of dependants in the Immigration and Asylum Act 1999 (IAA 1999), ss 141–142 *Fingerprints* and *Power to require attendance for fingerprinting*.

3.12

57 Powers to take fingerprints etc. from dependants

(1) Section 141 of the Immigration and Asylum Act 1999 (powers to take fingerprints from certain persons and their dependants) is amended as follows.

(2) In subsection (7) for paragraph (f) substitute—

"(f) any person ("F") who is—

(i) a member of the family of a person within any of paragraphs (a), (b) or (ca) to (e), or

(ii) a dependant of a person within paragraph (c)(i)."

(3) In subsection (8)(f) after "person" insert " of whose family he is a member or ".

Part 3—Enforcement   **3.12**

(4) In subsection (9)(f) after "person" insert " of whose family he is a member or ".

(5) After subsection (13) insert—

"(13A) For the purposes of subsection (7)(f)(i), a person is a member of the family of another person ("P") if—

    (a) the person is—

        (i) P's partner,

        (ii) P's child, or a child living in the same household as P in circumstances where P has care of the child,

        (iii) in a case where P is a child, P's parent, or

        (iv) an adult dependant relative of P, and

    (b) the person does not have a right of abode in the United Kingdom or indefinite leave to enter or remain in the United Kingdom.

(13B) In subsection (13A) "child" means a person who is under the age of 18."

(6) In subsection (14) for "(7)(f)" substitute " (7)(f)(ii) ".

(7) Section 142 of the Immigration and Asylum Act 1999 (attendance for fingerprinting) is amended as follows.

(8) In subsection (2) for "a dependant of" substitute " a member of the family of, or a dependant of, ".

(9) In subsection (2A) for "a dependant of" substitute " a member of the family of ".

(10) Until the commencement of the repeal of section 143 of the Immigration and Asylum Act 1999 (destruction of fingerprints) by paragraph 17(2) of Schedule 9 to the Immigration Act 2014, subsection (9) of that section has effect as if after "the person" there were inserted " of whose family he is a member or ".

(11) In section 144A(2) of the Immigration and Asylum Act 1999 (application of regulations about use and retention of fingerprints etc to dependants) after "the person" insert " of whose family F is a member or ".

Commencement: 12 July 2016, Immigration Act 2014 (Commencement No 1) Regulations 2016, SI 2016/603.

Amends: IAA 1999, s 141 *Fingerprinting*, s 142 *Attendance for fingerprinting* and s 144 *Other methods of collecting data about physical characteristics*.

Definitions:

Defines *when a person is a member of another person's family* for the purposes of s 141 of the IAA 1999: when the person is a partner; a child of; a child living in the same household as the principal of whom the principal has care; a parent of a minor child principal oran adult dependant relative of a principal.

Devolution: Applies throughout the UK.

This section amends the definition of dependants in s 141 *Power to take fingerprints* and 142 *Power to require attendance for fingerprinting* of the IAA 1999. The resultant definition is that of a family member in s 10 *Removal of certain persons unlawfully in the United Kingdom* as substituted by the Immigration Act 2014, s 1, specifically to include adult dependants other than spouses. The Explanatory Notes to the Act state that this alignment is the intention.[1] This was a late amendment to the Bill, made at Lords' Committee stage,[2] something forgotten at the time of the passage of the 2014 Act.

---

1 Para 276.
2 Amendment 214E, third sitting, *Hansard* HL, col 1648–1649 (1 February 2016).

SECTION 58—INTERPRETATION OF PART DETENTION AND BAIL

Summary

Definitions of 'immigration officer' 'premises' and 'subject to legal privilege' for the purposes of this part.

3.13

58 Interpretation of Part

(1) In this Part "immigration officer" means a person appointed by the Secretary of State as an immigration officer under paragraph 1 of Schedule 2 to the Immigration Act 1971.

(2) In this Part "premises" and "item subject to legal privilege" have the same meaning—

   (a) in relation to England and Wales, as in the Police and Criminal Evidence Act 1984;

   (b) in relation to Northern Ireland, as in the Police and Criminal Evidence (Northern Ireland) Order 1989 (SI 1989/1341 (NI 12));

   (c) in relation to Scotland, as in section 412 of the Proceeds of Crime Act 2002.

Commencement: 12 July 2016, Immigration Act 2014 (Commencement No 1) Regulations 2016, SI 2016/603.

Definitions:

'immigration officer' for the purposes of this Part: a person appointed by the Secretary of State as an immigration officer under the Immigration Act 1971 (IA 1971), Schedule 2, para 1;

'legal privilege' England and Wales, Police and Criminal Evidence Act 1984 (PACE 1984), s 10: communications between a professional legal adviser and his/her client or any person representing his/her client made in connection with the giving of legal advice to the client; communications between a professional legal adviser and his/her client or any person representing his client or between such an adviser or his/her client or any such representative and any other person made in connection with, or in contemplation of, legal proceedings and for the purposes of such proceedings; and items enclosed with or referred to in such communications and made in connection with the giving of legal advice; or with, or in contemplation of, legal proceedings and for the purposes of such proceedings; when they are in the possession of a person who is entitled to possession of them. Items held with the intention of furthering a criminal purpose are not items subject to legal privilege. Northern Ireland, Police and Criminal Evidence (Northern Ireland) Order 1989, SI 1989/1341 as for England and Wales, see Article 12. Scotland, as in s 412 of the Proceeds of Crime Act 2002: 'legal privilege' means protection in legal proceedings from disclosure by virtue of any rule of law relating to the confidentiality of communications and 'items subject to legal privilege' are communications between a professional legal adviser and his/her client or any person representing his/her client made in connection with, or in contemplation of, legal proceedings and for the purposes of those proceedings, which would be so protected;

'premises' England and Wales, PACE 1984, s 23 *Meaning of 'premises' etc*: 'premises' includes any place and, in particular, includes any vehicle, vessel, aircraft or hovercraft; any offshore installation ('offshore installation' has the meaning given to it by s 1 of the Mineral Workings (Offshore Installations) Act 1971 (MW (OI)A 1971)); any renewable energy installation ('renewable energy installation' has the same meaning as in Part 2, Chapter 2 of the Energy Act 2004); any tent or movable structure. Northern Ireland, Police and Criminal Evidence (Northern Ireland) Order 1989, as for England and Wales, see Article 25. Scotland, as in s 412 of the Proceeds of Crime Act 2002: any vehicle, vessel, aircraft or hovercraft, any offshore installation within the meaning given to it by s 1 of the MW (OI)A 1971 and any tent or moveable structure (IA 1971 s 28L).

Devolution: Applies throughout the UK.

3.14 A Guide to the Immigration Act 2016

DETENTION AND BAIL

SECTION 59—GUIDANCE ON DETENTION OF VULNERABLE PERSONS

> **Summary**
> Makes provision for statutory guidance to be taken into account in decisions to detain, or to continue to detain.

3.14

59 Guidance on detention of vulnerable persons

(1) The Secretary of State must issue guidance specifying matters to be taken into account by a person to whom the guidance is addressed in determining—

   (a) whether a person ("P") would be particularly vulnerable to harm if P were to be detained or to remain in detention, and

   (b) if P is identified as being particularly vulnerable to harm in those circumstances, whether P should be detained or remain in detention.

(2) In subsection (1) "detained" means detained under—

   (a) the Immigration Act 1971,

   (b) section 62 of the Nationality, Immigration and Asylum Act 2002, or

   (c) section 36 of the UK Borders Act 2007,

   and "detention" is to be construed accordingly.

(3) A person to whom guidance under this section is addressed must take the guidance into account.

(4) Before issuing guidance under this section the Secretary of State must lay a draft of the guidance before Parliament.

(5) Guidance under this section comes into force in accordance with regulations made by the Secretary of State.

(6) The Secretary of State may from time to time review guidance under this section and may revise and re-issue it.

(7) References in this section to guidance under this section include revised guidance.

Commencement: 12 July 2016, Immigration Act 2014 (Commencement No 1) Regulations 2016, SI 2016/603. SI 2016/847 provides that the *Guidance on adults at risk in immigration detention* comes into force on 12 September 2016.

Regulations: The Immigration (Guidance on Detention of Vulnerable Persons) Regulations 2016 (SI 2016/847).

Guidance: Statutory guidance on matters to be taken into account when deciding to detain, pertaining to 'vulnerability' as defined. The guidance must be laid before parliament in draft. Guidance was published as *Adults at risk in immigration detention: draft policy* on 26 May 2016. A revised version was laid before parliament on 21 July 2016 and updated on 23 August 2016.[1] This guidance came into effect on 12 September 2016. The Home Office issued new guidance to Home Office staff, *Enforcement Instructions and Guidance: Adults at Risk in immigration Detention.*[2] Chapter 55 of the Home Office Enforcement Instructions and Guidance: *Detention and Temporary Release* has been amended, in particular with the deletion of the guidance previously contained in para 55.10.[3]

Definitions:

'detained' detained under the Immigration Act 1971, the Nationality, Immigration and Asylum Act 2002, s 62 and the UK Borders Act 2007, s 36. Provides that 'detention' is to be construed accordingly.

Devolution: Applies throughout the UK.

This is the Government's response to the *Review into the welfare in detention of vulnerable persons* by Stephen Shaw CBE,[4] former Prisons and Probation Ombuds for England and Wales. Interestingly, given that his terms of reference explicitly excluded the decision to detain, it focuses on the decisions to detain and to continue to detain. The Ministerial Statement responding to Mr Shaw's review on 14 January 2016 said that the Government:

> 'will introduce a new "adult at risk" concept into decision-making on immigration detention with a clear presumption that people who are at risk should not be detained, building on the existing legal framework. This will strengthen the approach to those whose care and support needs make it particularly likely that they would suffer disproportionate detriment from being detained, and will therefore be considered generally unsuitable for immigration detention unless there is compelling evidence that other factors which relate to immigration abuse and the integrity of the immigration system, such as matters of criminality, compliance history and the imminence of removal, are of such significance as to outweigh the vulnerability factors'.[5]

The guidance specifies what is to be taken into account in determining whether a person is particularly at risk if detained and, if so, whether the person should be detained, or remain in detention. The guidance must be taken into account by those to whom it is issued.

3.14 *A Guide to the Immigration Act 2016*

During the passage of the Act, the Government published a sketch of what the guidance had to cover in the form of a draft 'adults at risk' policy.[6] Guidance was published as *Adults at risk in immigration detention: draft policy* on 26 May 2016. ILPA commented on this draft.[7] A revised version was laid before Parliament on 21 July 2016 and published in its final form on 23 August 2016.[8]

The ministerial statement made at the time of the publication of the review by Stephen Shaw CBE on 14 January 2016[9] indicated that the Government intended to balance the 'indicators of vulnerability' with the risk of immigration offending. This sounded very much the same as the intention behind para 55.10 of the Home Office Enforcement Instructions and Guidance, which the new approach was intended to replace. Paragraph 55.10 provided:

'The following are normally considered suitable for detention in only very exceptional circumstances, whether in dedicated immigration detention accommodation or prisons:

- those suffering from serious mental illness which cannot be satisfactorily managed within detention (in CCD [Criminal Casework Department] cases, please contact the specialist Mentally Disordered Offender Team). In exceptional cases it may be necessary for detention at a removal centre or prison to continue while individuals are being or waiting to be assessed, or are awaiting transfer under the Mental Health Act [1983];
- those where there is independent evidence that they have been tortured;
- people with serious disabilities which cannot be satisfactorily managed within detention;
- persons identified by the Competent Authorities as victims of trafficking unaccompanied children and young persons under the age of 18 (but see 55.9.3 above);
- the elderly, especially where significant or constant supervision is required which cannot be satisfactorily managed within detention;
- pregnant women, unless there is the clear prospect of early removal and medical advice suggests no question of confinement prior to this (but see 55.4 above for the detention of women in the early stages of pregnancy at Yarl's Wood);
- those suffering from serious medical conditions which cannot be satisfactorily managed within detention.'

The new statutory guidance points to a much more schematic approach to the decision although it does not make provision for better evidence to inform the decision, or for new tools with which to perform what the guidance very much treats as a balancing act. There is a shift away from whether a person's account of torture or ill-treatment is believed to the question of whether, even if it is, the person should be released. The statutory guidance provides:

'The clear presumption is that detention will not be appropriate if a person is considered to be "at risk". However, it will not mean that no one at risk will ever be detained. Instead, detention will only become appropriate at the point at which immigration control considerations outweigh this presumption. Within this context it will remain appropriate to detain individuals at risk if it is necessary in order to remove them. This builds on the existing policy and sits alongside the general presumption of liberty.'

This is arguably less protective in its approach than the former Home Office Enforcement Instructions and Guidance on *Detention and Temporary Release* para 55.10 – which used to contain its own list of those 'normally considered suitable for detention in only very exceptional circumstances'.[10] Paragraph 55.10 has been amended[11] so that it now does not contain any list of adults at risk, but instead cross-refers to the new guidance.

Further information and guidance on the operation of the adults at risk policy is provided in casework guidance, Enforcement Instructions and Guidance: *Adults at Risk in Immigration Detention.*[12]

The statutory guidance provides:

'The presumption will be that, once an individual is regarded as being at risk in the terms of this policy, they should not be detained. However, the risk factors for the individual, and the evidential weight that has been afforded to them, will then need to be balanced against any immigration control factors in deciding whether they should be detained.'

This is not repeated in the casework guidance.

The combined effect of the statutory and casework guidance is that being female, gay or lesbian is not regarded as an indicator of risk although being transsexual or intersex is. A 'more serious' learning difficulty, psychiatric illness or clinical depression 'depending on the nature and seriousness of the condition' is an indicator of risk as is a 'serious' physical disability or health condition. As to age, Mr Shaw's recommendation of an upper age limit is not followed but being over 70 is an indicator of risk.

There are three levels of evidence of risk. Pregnant women are automatically classified as meeting the highest level. Those over 70 will be classified as meeting at least the second level of evidence.

A person's own testimony gets them to the first level of evidence. Professional evidence that a person may be an adult at risk gets a person to the second

3.14 *A Guide to the Immigration Act 2016*

level. Professional evidence that the person is at risk and that detention will cause harm gets a person to the highest level. A report under Rule 35 of the Detention Centre Rules[13] as to a person's health or history of torture would appear to reach the second level.

As to the immigration factors to be weighed against risk, these are length of time in detention, public protection and 'compliance issues'.

Decisions on those with a positive 'reasonable grounds' decision that they are a potential victim of trafficking,[14] pending a conclusive decision, are dealt with on the basis of the modern slavery policy and not this guidance at all.[15]

The statutory guidance does not provide guidance as to how to weigh evidence of risk against immigration factors, although it purports to do so. The casework guidance includes a 'guide rather than a prescriptive template' on balancing risks against immigration control, indicating that each case must be decided on its own merits. It identifies the circumstances in which a person will be 'suitable for consideration for detention' by level of evidence of risk.

Where the evidence of risk is at the first level, a person will be considered suitable for detention only if:

- the date of removal can be forecast with some certainty and if this date is within a reasonable timescale given the logistics involved; or[16]
- public protection is at issue, for example, where the presence of the person in the UK is not considered conducive to the public good, ie a deportation case; or
- there are 'indicators of non-compliance' with immigration law which suggest that the individual will not be able to be removed unless they are detained.

Where the evidence of risk is at the second level, a person will be considered suitable for detention only if:

- the date of removal is fixed, or can be fixed quickly, and is within a 'reasonable timescale' and the person has failed to take 'reasonable' opportunities to make a voluntary return; or if the person is being detained at the border pending removal having been refused entry to the UK; or
- concerns about public protection would justify detention, for example the person is a 'foreign criminal', within the definition in s 19 of the immigration Act (IA 2014), or there is a relevant national security or other public protection concern; or
- there are 'indicators of non-compliance' which suggest that the individual is highly likely not to be able to be removed unless detained.

The guidance on the third category is that less compelling evidence of non-compliance should be taken into account if there are also public protection concerns and that the combination of such non-compliance and public protection concerns may justify detention in these cases. Under para 55.10, once there was independent evidence of torture, the burden shifted to the Home Office to demonstrate that there were very exceptional circumstances to justify detention, suggesting that the level of protection may be reduced in the new guidance. The reference to public protection appears broader and more general than the references to the risks of reoffending and of harm identified in para 55.10 as very exceptional circumstances which could justify detention. The casework guidance gives examples of criminal history, security risk, and a decision to deport for the public good. These are broader than the question of whether there will be a risk of re-offending or harm to the public, the test identified in Chapter 55 of the Enforcement Instructions and Guidance, and therein identified as one which should normally be assessed by the National Offender Management Service.

Where the evidence of risk is at the third level, a person will be considered suitable for detention only if:

- removal has been set for a date in the immediate future, there are no barriers to removal, and escorts and any other appropriate arrangements are, or will be, in place to ensure the safe management of the individual's return, and the individual has not complied with voluntary or ensured return; or

- there are significant concerns about publication protection; the person has had a four year or more custodial sentence; there is a 'serious relevant national security issue'; or the 'person presents a current public protection concern'.

The guidance on individuals within the latter category is that it is unlikely that questions of compliance on their own would warrant their detention, but non-compliance should be taken into account if there are also public protection concerns, or if the person can be quickly removed.

The guidance does not make express reference to para 55.1 of the Enforcement Instructions and Guidance which provides that 'there is a presumption in favour of temporary admission or release and, wherever possible, alternatives to detention are used', but this applies to adults at risk as to all persons detained under Immigration Act powers.

The UN Convention against Torture[17] definition of torture was adopted in the guidance. This is narrower than the definition that was used in para 55.10.[18] In *R (EO, RA, CE, OE & RAN) v SSHD* [2013] EWHC 1236 (Admin) it was held that previous determinations of the credibility of an individual's account are irrelevant to whether a medical report is independent evidence

3.14 *A Guide to the Immigration Act 2016*

of torture. Paragraph 10 of the guidance, however, stated that determinations of credibility may be taken into account in deciding the weight that should be afforded to evidence and into which of the three levels the individual falls. The charity Medical Justice brought a challenge to the change of definition which was linked to challenges by individuals.[19] The challenges alleged that the use of the narrower definition was contrary to the statutory purpose of s 59, that it disadvantaged those with protected characteristics, was discriminatory and was in breach of the duty to have regard to the equality obligations under the Equality Act 2010. On 22 November 2016, Ouseley J ordered an expedited hearing and granted interim relief pending a full judicial review in March 2017: the Home Office should revert to the *EO* definition of torture. The Home Office amended its casework guidance on 6 December 2016 to give effect to the order.[20] Among the documents amended, a new Detention Services Order 09/2016: *Detention Centre Rule 35*[21] on the preparation and assessment of reports, under Rule 35 of the Detention Centre Rules 2001,[22] about persons unsuitable for detention. It replaces the previous Detention Services Order 17/2012 and refers to the new casework guidance. The statutory guidance continued, as of 3 March 2017, to make reference to the UN Convention Against Torture definition.

In his review of immigration detention, Stephen Shaw paid special attention to the problems of short-term holding facilities and to the dreadful conditions in some of them. His concerns lead him to recommend that a discussion draft of the short-term holding facility rules be published as a matter of urgency.[23]

While regulations providing for the contracting out of short-term holding facilities were made in 2002,[24] it took until 2006 for draft rules to appear, covering similar ground for short-term holding facilities as do the Detention Centre Rules for immigration removal centres. In 2006 the Home Office consulted on draft rules.[25] In 2009 the Home Office consulted on another draft of the rules.[26]

On 30 April 2012,[27] Dr Julian Huppert MP asked why the rules had yet to be published. The then Minister, Damian Green MP, replied that, 'The Short-term Holding Facility Rules remain under development at present'.[28] In October 2013, Lord Ramsbotham asked the Parliamentary Under-Secretary of State for the Home Office, Lord Taylor of Holbeach, when the rules governing short-term holding facilities would be published. Lord Taylor replied that the rules had yet to be finalised and that there was no fixed date for their publication.[29]

On 3 March 2014, during the passage of the Bill which became the Immigration Act 2014, Lord Taylor of Holbeach gave Lord Avebury a commitment that rules governing the management and operation of short-term holding facilities, and the Cedars pre-departure accommodation, would be introduced before the summer recess.[30]

On 23 July 2014 the Home Office informed ILPA that Lord Taylor of Holbeach had written to Lord Avebury to say that the rules would not be introduced until after the summer recess. In a written answer of 24 October 2014 to a question by Lord Avebury on conditions in the short-term holding facilities at Heathrow, the Rt Hon Lord Bates for the Government indicated that rules on short-term holding facilities remained pending.[31]

The matter was raised during the Committee stage of the Bill where heavy reliance was placed on the Shaw report.[32] By the time that debate took place, the Home Office would have had in its possession the 9 March 2016 report from HM Inspectorate of Prisons on the conditions at Dover,[33] the account in which of the 'unacceptable' conditions in the Longport Freight Shed was to receive considerable media coverage when it was subsequently published on 9 March 2016.[34] Whether the prospect of the publication of that report acted as a spur or not, draft short-term holding facilities rules were published a mere 17 days later.[35] The new draft rules bear signs of haste; they largely resemble the draft published in 2009. The period for consultation on the draft rules ended in April 2016[36] but at the time of writing no rules have been published. Lord Ramsbotham asked a parliamentary question on the topic on 5 September 2016 and received the response that the rules would be published 'in due course'.[37] Baroness Williams of Trafford, the Minister who answered the question, has subsequently written to Lord Ramsbotham to say that the Home Office had so many replies to the consultation that it had not had time to sort them.[38]

---

1 See: https://www.gov.uk/government/publications/adults-at-risk-in-immigration-detention (accessed 10 November 2016).
2 Home Office, Enforcement Instructions and Guidance, *Adults at Risk in Immigration Detention*, v1, was published on 9 September 2016; v2, 6 December 2016. Version 2 is available at: https://www.gov.uk/government/publications/offender-management (accessed 10 November 2016). Chapter 55.10 of the Enforcement Instructions and Guidance refers to it as a new chapter 55b of the Enforcement Instructions and Guidance, but this chapter reference has not yet been given on the relevant guidance and it does not appear in the index to the Enforcement Instructions and Guidance at this point (as of 19 December 2016).
3 Amended 9 September 2016.
4 *Review into the welfare in detention of vulnerable persons: A report to the Home Office by Stephen Shaw*, published January 2016. Available at: https://www.gov.uk/government/publications/review-into-the-welfare-in-detention-of-vulnerable-persons (accessed 10 November 2016).
5 *Immigration Detention: Response to Stephen Shaw's Report into the welfare in detention of vulnerable persons*, Written Ministerial Statement HCWS470, 14 January 2016.
6 *Government note on detaining individuals for the purposes of immigration control – consideration of risk issues*, 1 March 2016. Available at: http://data.parliament.uk/DepositedPapers/Files/DEP2016-0190/Annex_B-Detaining_individuals_-_consideration_of_risk_issues.pdf (accessed 15 December 2016).
7 *ILPA comments to Immigration and Border Policy Directorate, Home Office, on the draft Adults at Risk in Immigration Detention policy*, 1 July 2016. Available at: http://www.ilpa.org.uk/resources.php/32274/ilpa-comments-to-immigration-and-border-policy-directorate-home-office-on-the-draft-adults-at-risk-i (accessed 10 November 2016).
8 Home Office, *Immigration Act 2016: Guidance on adults at risk in immigration detention*, 23 August 2016. Available at: https://www.gov.uk/government/publications/adults-at-risk-in-immigration-detention (accessed 10 November 2016). Changes were made to paras: 6 (additional

3.14 *A Guide to the Immigration Act 2016*

principles), 7 (examples of traumatic events), 9 (assessment of risk of harm), 11 (references to torture, sexual or gender based violence and post-traumatic stress disorder, 14 (compliance issues), 15 and 16 (restructuring of paras), and 19 (reports).
9 *Immigration Detention: Response to Stephen Shaw's Report into the welfare in detention of vulnerable persons*, Written Statement HCWS470, 14 January 2016.
10 See also *Das v SSHD* [2014] EWCA Civ 45 at para 68.
11 UK Visas and Immigration, Enforcement Instructions and Guidance: Chapter 55: *Detention and Temporary Release*, 9 September 2016. Available at: https://www.gov.uk/government/uploads/system/uploads/attachment_data/file/552478/EIG_55_detention_and_temporary_release_v21.pdf (accessed 10 November 2016).
12 Home Office, Enforcement Instructions and Guidance: *Adults at Risk in Immigration Detention*, v2, 6 December 2016. Available at: https://www.gov.uk/government/publications/offender-management (accessed 10 November 2016).
13 SI 2001/238.
14 See *Victims of Modern Slavery: competent authority guidance*, v3, Home Office, 21 March 2016.
15 Paragraph 18 of the statutory guidance, Home Office, Immigration Act 2016: *Guidance on adults at risk in immigration detention*, 23 August 2016. Available at: https://www.gov.uk/government/publications/adults-at-risk-in-immigration-detention. Filed, probably erroneously, under the *Offender Management* section of the Enforcement Instructions and Guidance (accessed 10 November 2016).
16 A restatement of the principles applicable to all detainees, see *R(Hardial* Singh*) v Governor of Durham Prison* [1983] EWHC 1 (QB) as applied in *Walumba Lumba & Kadian Mighty v SSHD* [2011] UKSC 12 and *Shepherd Masimba Kambadzi v SSHD* [2011] UKSC 23.
17 1465 UNTS 85.
18 See *R(EO, RA, CE, OE & RAN) v SSHD* [2013] EWHC 1236 (Admin).
19 *R (Medical Justice, JXL, et ors* CO/5386/2016, CO/5262/2016, CO/5630/2016, CO/5533/2016, CO/5529/2016, CO/5535/22016, CO/5534/2016, CO/5532/2016, CO/4835/2016, 21 November 2016.
20 *Adults at Risk in Immigration Detention*, Home Office Enforcement Instructions and Guidance, v2, 6 December 2016, at: https://www.gov.uk/government/publications/offender-management and Detention Services Order 09/2016: Detention Centre Rule 35, Home Office, v4, 6 December 2016. Available at: https://www.gov.uk/government/publications/application-of-detention-centre-rule-35.
21 Op. cit. First published on 12 September 2016.
22 SI 2001/236.
23 *Review into the welfare in detention of vulnerable persons: A report to the Home Office by Stephen Shaw*, January 2016. Available at: https://www.gov.uk/government/publications/review-into-the-welfare-in-detention-of-vulnerable-persons (accessed 10 November 2016), Executive Summary para 9.
24 The Immigration (Short-term Holding Facilities) Regulations 2002 (SI 2002/2538).
25 Immigration: the short-term holding facility rules, draft statutory instrument, January 2006. Available at: www.ilpa.org.uk/resources.php/14494/home-office-draft-short-term-holding-facilities-rules-2006, (accessed 10 November 2016). See also ILPA's response to the consultation on the draft rules, 13 February 2006. Available at: http://www.ilpa.org.uk/resource/14493/response-to-home-office-consultation-on-draft-short-term-holding-facilities-rules (accessed 10 November 2016), and Barbara Nicholson, Senior Policy Officer, Home Office to Elizabeth White, ILPA of 7 August 2006 responding to ILPA's comments on the consultation at: www.ilpa.org.uk/resources.php/1889/home-office-to-ilpa-of-7-august-2006-re-draft-short-term-holding-facility-sthf-rules (accessed 10 November 2016).
26 See Barbara Nicholson, Detention Services Policy Unit, UK Border Agency to Steve Symonds, ILPA, re further consultation on the draft short-term holding facility rules, 20 February 2009. Available at: www.ilpa.org.uk/resources.php/20183/uk-border-agency-ukba-to-ilpa-re-further-consultation-on-the-draft-short-term-holding-facility-sthf- (accessed 10 November 2016). See further ILPA's further response of 11 June 2009, at: www.ilpa.org.uk/resources.php/13062/uk-border-agency-further-consultation-of-the-draft-short-term-;yxcvbholding-facility-sthf-rules-ilpas-furt (accessed 10 November 2016). See also The Lord Brett, Parliamentary Under

Part 3—Enforcement 3.14

Secretary of State, to the Lord Avebury of 11 August 2009 re time limits for detention in short-term holding facilities at:www.ilpa.org.uk/resources.php/2919/the-lord-brett-parliamentary-under-secretary-of-state-to-the-lord-avebury-of-11-august-2009-re-time- (accessed 10 November 2016) and the Refugee Council to Kristian Armstrong, Children's Champion, UK Border Agency, of 5 August 2009 re short-term holding facilities and child protection. Available at: www.ilpa.org.uk/resources.php/2940/refugee-council-to-kristian-armstrong-childrens-champion-uk-border-agency-of-5-august-2009-re-short- (accessed 10 November 2016).

27 *Hansard* HC, col 1086W (30 April 2012).
28 *Op cit* Available at: http://www.publications.parliament.uk/pa/cm201212/cmhansrd/cm120430/text/120430w0001.htm#12043018000026 (accessed 10 November 2016).
29 Available at: http://www.publications.parliament.uk/pa/ld201314/ldhansrd/text/131030w0001.htm (accessed 10 November 2016).
30 *Hansard* HL, col 1140 (3 March 2014).
31 *Hansard*, Written Answer HL2190. Available at: http://www.parliament.uk/business/publications/written-questions-answers-statements/written-question/Lords/2014-10-20/HL2190 (accessed 10 November 2016).
32 *Hansard* HL cols 1679–1698 (1 February 2016).
33 *Report on an unannounced inspection of the short-term holding facilities at Longport freight shed, Dover Seaport and Frontier House* (7 September, 1–2 and 5–6 October 2015), HM Inspectorate of Prisons, 9 March 2016. Available at: https://www.justiceinspectorates.gov.uk/hmiprisons/inspections/longport-freight-shed-dover-seaport-and-frontier-house/ (accessed 10 November 2016).
34 See, eg, *Channel migrants detained in freight shed*, Dominic Casciani, BBC, 8 March 2016. Available at: http://www.bbc.co.uk/news/uk-35750968 (accessed 10 November 2016).
35 Simon Barrett, Removals, Enforcement and Detention, Immigration and Border Policy, Directorate, Home Office, Illegal Migration, Identity Security and Enforcement, letter (no named recipient) re consultation on Short Term Holding Facility Rules, 18 February 2016. Available at: http://data.parliament.uk/DepositedPapers/Files/DEP2016-0190/Annex_C_-_Letter_re_Short_Term_Holding_Facility_Rules_Consultation.pdf (accessed 10 November 2016); the Short-term Holding Facility Rules 2016, draft statutory instrument, 18 February 2016. Available at: http://data.parliament.uk/DepositedPapers/Files/DEP2016-0190/Annex_D_-_Short_Term_Holding_Facility_Rules_for_consultation.pdf (accessed 10 November 2016); Draft Short-term Holding Facility Rules 2016: Summary of provisions, Home Office, 18 February 2016. Available at: http://data.parliament.uk/DepositedPapers/Files/DEP2016-0190/Annex_E_-Short_Term_Holding_Facility_Rules_-_summary_of_provisions.pdf (accessed 10 November 2016).
36 See ILPA comments to Home Office on the draft rules for Short Term Holding Facilities, 14 April 2016. Available at: http://www.ilpa.org.uk/resource/32078/ilpa-comments-to-home-office-on-the-draft-rules-for-short-term-holding-facilities-sthfs-14-april-201 (accessed 10 November 2016).
37 *Hansard*, HL Written Question HL1512 (16 September 2016).
38 Communication from Lord Ramsbotham to Alison Harvey of ILPA, 17 October 2016.

SECTION 60—LIMITATION ON DETENTION OF PREGNANT WOMEN

Summary

Places a time limit, one-week with the authorisation of the Secretary of State (SSHD), and 72 hours in all other cases, on the detention of pregnant women and provides that the power to detain can only be used where the woman will shortly be removed from the UK, or where exceptional circumstances apply. A woman can be detained more than once using this power.

3.15

60 Limitation on detention of pregnant women

(1) This section applies to a woman if the Secretary of State is satisfied that the woman is pregnant.

(2) A woman to whom this section applies may not be detained under a relevant detention power unless the Secretary of State is satisfied that—

(a) the woman will shortly be removed from the United Kingdom, or

(b) there are exceptional circumstances which justify the detention.

(3) In determining whether to authorise the detention under a relevant detention power of a woman to whom this section applies, a person who, apart from this section, has power to authorise the detention must have regard to the woman's welfare.

(4) A woman to whom this section applies may not be detained under a relevant detention power for a period of—

(a) more than 72 hours from the relevant time, or

(b) more than seven days from the relevant time, in a case where the longer period of detention is authorised personally by a Minister of the Crown (within the meaning of the Ministers of the Crown Act 1975).

(5) In subsection (4) "the relevant time" means the later of—

(a) the time at which the Secretary of State is first satisfied that the woman is pregnant, and

(b) the time at which the detention begins.

(6) A woman to whom this section applies who has been released following detention under a relevant detention power may be detained again under such a power in accordance with this section.

(7) This section does not apply to the detention under paragraph 16(2) of Schedule 2 to the Immigration Act 1971 of an unaccompanied child to whom paragraph 18B of that Schedule applies.

(8) In this section—

"relevant detention power" means a power to detain under—

(a) paragraph 16(2) of Schedule 2 to the Immigration Act 1971 (detention of persons liable to examination or removal),

(b) paragraph 2(1), (2) or (3) of Schedule 3 to that Act (detention pending deportation),

(c) section 62 of the Nationality, Immigration and Asylum Act 2002 (detention of persons liable to examination or removal), or

(d) section 36(1) of the UK Borders Act 2007 (detention pending deportation);

"woman" means a female of any age.

(9) The Immigration Act 1971 is amended in accordance with subsections (10) and (11).

(10) In paragraph 16 of Schedule 2 (detention of persons liable to examination or removal) after sub-paragraph (2A) insert—

"(2B) The detention under sub-paragraph (2) of a person to whom section 60 (limitation on detention of pregnant women) of the Immigration Act 2016 applies is subject to that section."

(11) In paragraph 2 of Schedule 3 (detention or control pending deportation) after sub-paragraph (4) insert—

"(4ZA) The detention under sub-paragraph (1), (2) or (3) of a person to whom section 60 (limitation on detention of pregnant women) of the Immigration Act 2016 applies is subject to that section."

(12) In section 62 of the Nationality, Immigration and Asylum Act 2002 (detention by Secretary of State) after subsection (7) insert—

"(7A) The detention under this section of a person to whom section 60 (limitation on detention of pregnant women) of the Immigration Act 2016 applies is subject to that section."

(13) In section 36 of the UK Borders Act 2007 (detention) after subsection (2) insert—

"(2A) The detention under subsection (1) of a person to whom section 60 (limitation on detention of pregnant women) of the Immigration Act 2016 applies is subject to that section."

Commencement: 12 July 2016, Immigration Act 2014 (Commencement No 1) Regulations 2016, SI 2016/603.

Amends: Immigration Act 1971 (IA 1971), Schedule 2, para 16, Schedule 3, para 2; Nationality, Immigration and Asylum Act 2002 (NIAA 2002), s 62, UK Borders Act 2007 (UKBA 2007), s 36.

Definitions:

'relevant detention power' IA 1971, Schedule 2, para 16(2), Schedule 3, para 2(1)–(3); NIAA 2002 s 62,; UKBA 2007 s 36(1) (s 60(8));

'woman' female of any age (s 60(8)).

Devolution: Applies throughout the UK.

This section places a time limit, one-week with the authorisation of the SSHD, and 72 hours in all other cases, on the detention of pregnant women. It provides that the power to detain can only be used where the pregnant woman will shortly be removed from the UK or where exceptional circumstances apply. Time runs from the date on which the SSHD is satisfied that the woman is pregnant. A woman can be detained more than once using this power.

3.15 *A Guide to the Immigration Act 2016*

Neither the statement in s 60(2) that a pregnant woman may not be detained unless she will shortly be removed from the UK, or unless there are exceptional circumstances justifying the detention, nor the time limit, apply to all pregnant women. They apply only to those detained under a 'relevant detention power' (s 60(8)). Those outside the ambit of the provisions are those detained under subparas 16(1) and (1A) of Schedule 2 to the IA 1971; those detained pending examination under para 2 of that Schedule, pending a decision on whether to grant or refuse leave to enter; and those whose leave to enter has been suspended under para 2A pending completion of examination under that paragraph, and a decision on whether to cancel leave to enter.

For those protected by s 60, the test is in two stages. They may not be detained at all unless they will shortly be removed from the UK, or unless there are exceptional circumstances justifying the detention (s 60(2)). The subjective test that the SSHD is satisfied that the woman is shortly to be removed is vague. It cannot be simply about whether removal directions had been set; that is a matter of fact not of judgement. If there is no prohibition on the woman's detention under s 60(2) then a time limit is imposed under s 61(4).

In his review for the Government, Stephen Shaw CBE recommended a ban on the detention of pregnant women.[1] This recommendation was not accepted.[2] The matter was taken up in Parliament. At Lords' report an amendment was tabled, and accepted by the House of Lords, which focused specifically on pregnant women and imposed an outright ban on their detention.[3] On ping-pong, the Government tabled the text which is now this clause,[4] and it was accepted by the House of Commons.[5] The 'time limit' approach taken in this section is modelled on the provisions on the detention of families inserted by Part 1 of the Immigration Act 2014 (IA 2014). What is missing are provisions equivalent to those requiring families to be given notice of their removal, and thus of their detention, and provisions that require the involvement of an independent panel.[6] When the Bill returned to the House of Lords attempts were made to insert similar safeguards, but without success.[7]

In the dying hours of the Bill, on 10 May 2016, Baroness Lister of Burtersett tabled an amendment that would have inserted the word 'very' before 'exceptional', mirroring the wording of the Enforcement Instructions and Guidance at Chapter 55.10. Resisting the amendment, the Minister, Lord Keen of Elie, said:

> 'The provision does refer to "exceptional circumstances". The guidance as it exists talks of only "very exceptional circumstances" applying for the detention of pregnant women, and that will continue to be the policy that is applied in the context of the provision. I reiterate what was said in the other place last night: it is only in very exceptional circumstances that it will be considered appropriate for this provision on detention to be employed.'[8]

There followed an exchange in which peers pressed him to put the word 'very' on the face of the Act. The Minister's last word was:

> 'It is questionable whether there is any distinction to be drawn between exceptional, properly understood, and very exceptional or most exceptional. That is what lies behind the manner in which this provision has been drafted. Nevertheless, to dispel doubt in the minds of others, it has been said in the guidance that, as a matter of policy, the term "very exceptional" may be applied when approaching the application of this provision to the detention of pregnant women.'[9]

In *Pepper v Hart* [1992] UKHL 3 it was held that ministerial statements are an aid to statutory interpretation if they help to clarify an 'ambiguity' or 'obscurity' or to clarify wording the literal meaning of which leads to an 'absurdity'. These are significant restrictions on the statements to which reference can be made and it is difficult to find ambiguity in the word 'very' such as would allow recourse to the ministerial statement. It is, however, a statement of Government policy.

The new Chapter 55a of the Enforcement Instructions and Guidance on the *Detention of Pregnant Women*,[10] issued when the section came into force on 12 July 2016, provides further guidance and makes reference to 'very exceptional' circumstances:

> 'The "exceptional circumstances" that may justify detention of a pregnant woman who is not being removed shortly are likely to be confined to issues relating to risk of public harm (eg criminality or national security). The expectation is that detention other than where the pregnant woman's removal will take place shortly should be very exceptional. Examples of where this situation could arise may be where a pregnant woman is arrested and detained following a breach of bail conditions, or is detained under section 36(1) of the UK Borders Act 2007 pending a decision on whether the automatic deportation provisions of that Act apply or whether to make a deportation order. Detaining in order to facilitate a future removal (eg to obtain travel documents) or to prevent absconding would not, of themselves, be regarded as exceptional circumstances. Even where detention is based on exceptional circumstances, it will still be subject to the same time limits.'[11]

Since the IA 2014[12] it has been the case that a person gets three months' notice of liability to removal and to detention when refused. If not removed within those three months, they get another such notice. And so on. Pregnant women get notice that they are to be removed, but only once they are detained.

---

1   *Review into the welfare in detention of vulnerable persons: A report to the Home Office* by Stephen Shaw, January 2016. Available at: https://www.gov.uk/government/publications/review-into-the-welfare-in-detention-of-vulnerable-persons, p12 (accessed 16 December 2016).

2 Government response to Stephen Shaw's review into the welfare in detention of vulnerable persons, 14 January 2016.
3 Amendment 6, *Hansard* HL Vol 771, col 133–144 (12 April 2016).
4 *Motion* (b) substituting for Lords' amendment 85, see *Hansard* HC 25 April 2016, division 249.
5 Hansard HC Vol 608, cols 1251–1254.
6 IA 2014, s 2, inserting s 78 into the Nationality Immigration and Asylum Act 2002 (NIAA 2002) and s 3 of the 2014 Act inserting s 54A into the Borders, Citizenship and Immigration Act 2009.
7 *Hansard* HL Vol 771, cols 1663–1673 (10 May 2016).
8 *Hansard*, HL col 1669 (10 May 2016).
9 Col 1770.
10 *Detention of pregnant women*, v1, Enforcement Instructions and Guidance: Chapter 55a, Home Office, 12 July 2016. Available at: https://www.gov.uk/government/uploads/system/uploads/attachment_data/file/537066/Chapter_55a_Detention_of_pregnant_women_v1.pdf (accessed 15 December 2016).
11 Ibid p 5.
12 See s 1.

PART 1—MAIN PROVISIONS AND PART 2 AMENDMENTS TO OTHER ACTS

SECTION 61—IMMIGRATION BAIL POWER TO CANCEL LEAVE AND SCHEDULE 10 IMMIGRATION BAIL

Summary

Replaces temporary admission and bail under Immigration Act powers with a new single category of 'immigration bail'. Makes provision for (some) judicial oversight of detention. Makes provision for support for those released from detention. Gives the Secretary of State (SSHD) power to dictate to a court when it should impose an electronic monitoring condition. Amends the provisions of the IA2014 as to repeat bail hearings.

3.16

61 Immigration bail

(1) Schedule 10 (immigration bail) has effect.

(2) In that Schedule—

   (a) Part 1 contains the main provisions about immigration bail, and

   (b) Part 2 contains amendments to other Acts.

(3) A person may be released and remain on bail under paragraph 22 or 29 of Schedule 2 to the Immigration Act 1971 even if the person can no longer be detained under a provision of the Immigration Acts to which that paragraph applies, if the person is liable to detention under such a provision.

(4) The reference in subsection (3) to paragraph 22 or 29 of Schedule 2 to the Immigration Act 1971 includes that paragraph as applied by any other provision of the Immigration Acts.

(5) Subsections (3) and (4) are to be treated as always having had effect.

(6) Subsections (3) to (5) are repealed on the coming into force of the repeal of paragraphs 22 and 29 of Schedule 2 to the Immigration Act 1971 by paragraph 20 of Schedule 10.

Commencement: Sections 61(3)–(5), 12 May 2016. Other provisions are not yet in force.

Amends: The Immigration Act 1971 (IA 1971), s 11, s 24, s 28, Schedule 2, omitting paragraphs 21–25 and 29–34, Schedule 3, para 2 and omitting paras 3–10; the Special Immigration Appeals Act 1997, s 3, s 5 and substituting a new Schedule 3; the Immigration and Asylum Act 1999 (IAA 1999), s 10, s 53, s 95 and s 141; the Nationality, Immigration and Asylum Act 2002 (NIAA 2002), s 23, s 30, s 62, omitting ss 68–69, and ss 70–71; the Asylum and Immigration (Treatment of Claimants etc.) Act 2004, s 36; the Immigration, Asylum and Nationality Act 2006, s 24; the UK Borders Act 2007 (UKBA 2007), s 36 and the Criminal Justice and Immigration Act 2008, ss 132–133 (Schedule 10, Part 2).

Regulations: Schedule 10, para 12 makes provision as to what regulations under s 92(1) *Transitional and Consequential Provisions* of the Act may contain.

Definitions:

'appropriate judicial officer': a justice of the peace (England and Wales); a sheriff or a justice of the peace (Scotland); a lay magistrate (Northern Ireland) (Schedule 10, para 110(15));

'bail condition' Schedule 10, para 2(11);

References to *consideration of whether to grant immigration bail to a person* in Schedule 10, Part 1, para 11(3)(a) includes such consideration regardless of whether there is a hearing or whether the First-tier Tribunal makes a determination and includes the dismissal of an application by virtue of provision made under para 12(2) but does not include consideration in an elective bail hearing where the the First-tier Tribunal is prevented from granting bail to the person by Schedule 10, Part 1, para 3(4), ie where the Secretary of State withholds consent to bail under that para (Schedule 10, Part 1, paras 11(4)–(5));

'Convention Rights' Schedule 10, Part 1, para 2(10), to be construed in accordance with s 1 of the Human Rights Act 1998;

3.16 *A Guide to the Immigration Act 2016*

'detainee custody officer' for the purposes of Schedule 10: a person in respect of whom a certificate of authorisation is in force under s 154 of the IAA 1999 (Schedule 10, Part 1, para 10(7));

'electronic monitoring condition' Schedule 10, Part 1, para 4(1);

'financial condition' payment of a recognisance or payment by a surety, Schedule 10, Part 1, para 5;

References to *a grant of immigration bail to a person*, a grant of bail under Schedule 10, Part 1, paras 1(1)–(3), 10(12) or 10(13) (Schedule 10, Part 1, para 1(4));

A reference to *immigration bail granted or a condition imposed under Schedule 10* includes reference to immigration bail granted, or a condition imposed, by the court on granting bail (IA1971, Schedule 3, para 2(7)) (Schedule 10, Part 2, para 21); UKBA 2007 s 36(3C) (Schedule 10, Part 2, para 40);

'premises' the same meaning as in the Police and Criminal Evidence Act 1984 (Schedule 10, Part 1, para 10(15));

'relevant date' for the purposes of Schedule 10, Part 1, para 11(1)(b), the date on which the person's detention began, or the last date on which a 'relevant event' occurred in relation to the person, if later (Schedule 10, para 11(2));

'relevant event' consideration by the First-tier Tribunal of whether to grant immigration bail to the person; withdrawal by the person of an application for immigration bail treated as made by the person as the result of a reference under para 11 of Schedule 10 (ie a reference for an automatic bail hearing); withdrawal by the person of a notice that the person does not wish their case to be referred to the First-tier Tribunal under para 11 of Schedule 10 (ie for an automatic bail hearing), given under subpara 11(6)(b) of Schedule 10;

'search' for the purposes of Schedule 10, a search under para 2(1)(a) of Schedule 13 to the Immigration and Asylum Act 1999 (Schedule 10, Part 1, para 10(10));

'specified' for the purposes of para 4, pertaining to electronic monitoring conditions, means specified in the arrangements made for electronic monitoring in accordance with para 4(1). For the purposes of para 13 *Transitional Provision* of Schedule 10 it means specified in regulations made under s 92(1) of this Act.

Devolution: Applies throughout the UK. See reference to 'relevant court' above.

The provisions of this section and the schedule give the Home Office new powers to manage those without leave, be they refused or persons waiting (as in an asylum case) for an initial decision. Henceforth there will be no concept of 'temporary admission' to the UK while a decision is made on the case. Instead, anyone without leave who is waiting for a decision will be on 'immigration bail', the conditions of which will be managed by the Home Office or by the tribunal.

The notion of a single form of temporary permission has been a gleam in the Home Office's eye since the proposals for a simplification act back in 2008.[1] The provisions go beyond renaming. A person granted temporary admission would never normally come before the tribunal, so how to deal with the involvement of both the tribunal and the SSHD in immigration bail? Under Schedule 10 the tribunal manages immigration bail granted by the tribunal; the SSHD immigration bail granted by the SSHD. The tribunal can direct that the power to amend or remove conditions, or to impose new ones, may be exercised by the SSHD (Schedule 10, Part 1, para 6(3)) and see also comments on electronic monitoring below.

Subsections 61(3)–(5)

3.16.1 Subsections 61(3)–(5) were whisked into force the day the Act received Royal Assent. The House of Lords Committee on the Constitution[2] drew attention to these provisions under the heading 'retrospective legislation'.

In *R (B) v Secretary of State for the Home Department (No 2)* [2015] EWCA Civ 445, currently pending before the Supreme Court, the Court of Appeal held that while it is accepted that the power to impose bail conditions also extends to someone who could be detained even if they are not actually detained immediately prior to the grant of bail, the powers conferred by paras 22 and 29 of Schedule 2 to the IA 1971 should extend only to individuals who are, or who could lawfully be, subjected to immigration detention pending deportation. The court further held that where, as in the case it was considering, there was no realistic prospect of the person's deportation taking place, subjecting them to immigration detention pending deportation would not be lawful and that once the legal basis for detention falls away, so does the legal basis for imposing bail conditions; the power to impose such conditions being dependent upon the possibility of lawful detention. The effect of the Court of Appeal's judgment was to make the imposition of bail conditions unlawful in circumstances in which the person concerned could not lawfully be subject to immigration detention.

This is addressed by Schedule 10 which provides that bail conditions can be set for individuals who are either 'detained' or 'liable to detention' under relevant Immigration Act powers. A person is liable to detention if they could be detained were it not that a 'legal issue' or practical difficulty presently precludes or impedes their removal from the UK (NIAA 2002, s 67).

3.16.1 A Guide to the Immigration Act 2016

Pending the coming into force of Schedule 10, s 61(3) provides that the 1971 Act powers can be used 'even if the person can no longer be detained' provided that they are 'liable to detention'. Section 61(5) provides that: 'The amendment made by subsection (3) is to be treated as always having had effect'. This means that the provisions will have retrospective effect, as is acknowledged in the Explanatory Notes to the Bill:

> 'This clause is retrospective in its effect because it is intended to clarify the law following a recent Court of Appeal judgment ... on when immigration bail conditions can be imposed. The Court of Appeal judgment disturbed previously settled case law in this area. If the Court of Appeal's judgment stands (it is under appeal) then it will have a significantly limiting impact on judges' and the Home Office's ability to impose bail conditions and manage individuals, including those who pose a risk to the public where deportation is being pursued'.[3]

The House of Lords Select Committee on the Constitution questioned the use of the word 'clarify':

> '34. The statement that these provisions 'clarify' the law is questionable. The Court of Appeal has determined what the relevant provisions of the Immigration Act 1971 mean—and what, in law, they have always meant. The Government now wishes to revise what those provisions mean. The effect of clause 32(5) [now 63(5)] will therefore be to change the law and to do so retrospectively.... the rule of law requires government to act according to law, and from that perspective the retrospective provision of a legal basis for executive action is constitutionally suspect and calls for a clear justification. To the extent that such a justification is provided by the Government, it appears to turn upon considerations of administrative convenience and to rely upon the fact that the Court of Appeal's judgment disturbed what the Government considered to be a settled understanding of the legal position. We recognise that the Government was acting in accordance with its understanding of the law, but once that action has been judged to be unlawful we would expect a greater justification for changing the law with retrospective effect than simple administrative convenience.
>
> 35. As we have previously stated, there needs "to be a compelling reason in the public interest for a departure from the general principle that retrospective legislation is undesirable." ... The House may wish to assure itself that sufficient justification has been advanced for the use of retrospective legislation in this instance'.[4]

In the event, the House took little interest in the point.[5]

Schedule 10

3.16.2 Section 61(1)–(2) introduces Schedule 10. Schedule 10 replaces bail or temporary admission with a new single concept of immigration bail. A person liable to detention or detained under Immigration Act powers may be granted immigration bail by the SSHD (para 1(2)) or, if detained, by the First-tier Tribunal (para 1(3)).

Immigration bail must be granted subject to one or more of the following conditions (para 1(3)):

- appearance before the SSHD or First-tier Tribunal at a date and place specified;
- restrictions as to work, occupation or studies;
- restrictions as to residence;
- reporting requirements (to the SSHD or another person);
- electronic monitoring; and/or
- such other conditions as the person granting bail thinks fit.

A recognisance may be required, or a surety be required to put up a sum (para 5).

Whilst conditions of residence, reporting and restrictions on work are similar to the conditions to be imposed on temporary admission, the restriction on studies is new. During debates on the Bill, the Minister in the House of Lords stated: 'This existing power is used only in the context of a terrorism-related issue which is subject to SIAC provisions… I emphasise that this is an existing power used only in the most exceptional circumstances pertaining to terrorism'.[6]

A person must be given notice by the SSHD or First-tier Tribunal of when bail begins (para 3(5)) and of the conditions of that bail (para 3(7)). The notice is not required to specify when the bail ends.

Electronic monitoring conditions

3.16.3 The schedule as presented to Parliament[7] contained a power for the SSHD to change an electronic monitoring, or a residence, condition of bail imposed by the First-tier Tribunal.

This would have meant that the tribunal could have declined to impose such a condition; the Home Office could then have turned around and imposed it the next day. Following opposition from *inter alia* the House of

3.16.3 A Guide to the Immigration Act 2016

Lords' Select Committee on the Constitution[8] and the former Conservative Lord Chancellor Lord Mackay of Clashfern,[9] the Government amended the schedule[10] to replace the SSHD's proposed power to impose an electronic monitoring or residence condition, where the tribunal has not done so, with a duty on the SSHD or tribunal, when releasing on bail a person who has been the subject of deportation proceedings, to make such a person subject to an electronic monitoring condition unless it would be impractical or in breach of the European Convention on Human Rights (ECHR) so to do.

The House of Lords Select Committee on the Constitution, in its seventh report of session 2015–2016, said that:

> 'We are concerned that schedule 7, which would allow a Minister to override or alter independent judicial decisions about immigration bail conditions, is in tension with the principles of the rule of law. The usual process, should a Minister have concerns about a judicial decision, would be to appeal against it. The House may wish to ask the Government to clarify how their proposals comply with the rule of law. The House may also wish to ask the Government why, if the intention is to ensure the use of certain bail conditions for particular offenders (such as satellite monitoring for foreign nationals), they do not simply propose new criteria for the First-tier Tribunal to take into account when setting bail conditions.'[11]

The Minister, the Rt Hon Lord Bates, wrote to Lord Lang of Monkton, Chair of the Committee, on 1 March 2016 to say:

> 'I acknowledge the Committee's concerns regarding the potential conflict of the original drafting of the bail powers with the rule of law. I have thought carefully about this issue and today I have tabled amendments to remodel the relevant clause and schedule in the Bill to address these concerns. The new approach will introduce a statutory requirement that an electronic monitoring condition must be imposed on individuals subject to deportation proceedings unless the Secretary of State decides that this is inappropriate.'

When immigration bail is granted to a person detained pending deportation, including 'automatic deportation' under the UKBA 2007,[12] it must be granted subject to an electronic monitoring condition (Schedule 10, para 2 read with para 1). With two exceptions. The first is where the SSHD is granting bail and considers that an electronic monitoring condition would be impractical or contrary to a person's rights under the ECHR (Schedule 10, para 2(5)). The second exception is where bail is granted by the tribunal. Then, bail must not be granted subject to an electronic monitoring condition if the SSHD informs the tribunal that an electronic monitoring condition would be impractical or contrary to a person's rights under the ECHR (Schedule 10, para 2(7)).

In judging of impracticality or breaches of human rights, the SSHD may have regard to obstacles in making arrangements for electronic monitoring;

Part 3—Enforcement 3.16.3

resources; the likelihood of the person failing to comply with a bail condition; whether the person has been convicted; the likelihood of the person committing an offence while on bail; whether the person is a danger to public health; or a threat to public order; whether detention is necessary in the person's interests or for the protection of any other person; and such other matters as the SSHD or the tribunal deems relevant (Schedule 10, Part 1, para 2(9)). This appears to envisage that the tribunal can raise a consideration which the SSHD may, not must, take into account.

The First-tier Tribunal may not exercise its power to amend or remove conditions of bail to amend an electronic monitoring condition (Schedule 10, para 6(5)).

Where a person is on immigration bail pursuant to a grant of bail by the SSHD or a grant of by bail by the First-tier Tribunal in a case where the tribunal has directed that the power to amend or remove conditions, or impose new ones, may be exercised by the SSHD (Schedule 10, Part 1, para 6(3)), the SSHD may only remove an electronic monitoring condition if she concludes that it would be impractical for the person to continue to be subject to the condition or that it would be contrary to the person's rights under the ECHR for the person to be so subject (Schedule 10, Part 1, paras 7(3)–(4)).

If a person is not subject to an electronic monitoring condition then upon coming to the conclusion that it would not be impractical or a breach of a person's Convention rights to impose one, the SSHD must impose one (Schedule 10, Part 1, paras 7(3) and (5)).

Where a person formerly detained pending deportation is on bail and that bail is being managed by the tribunal, rather than by the SSHD, then the tribunal must not remove an electronic monitoring condition unless the SSHD notifies the Tribunal that she considers that it would be impractical or a breach of a person's Convention rights for them to continue to be subject to the condition (Schedule 10, Part 1, subparas 8(3)–(4)). If she notifies the tribunal to the contrary, it must impose the conditions (Schedule 10, subparas 8(3) and (5)). Thus although the SSHD is no longer seen to turn around and undermine what the tribunal is doing, she makes the decisions and the tribunal is not acting independently.

Regulations under section 92(1) *Transitional and Consequential provision* may make provision about the circumstances in which powers to impose an electronic monitoring condition may, or must, be exercised and enable the SSHD to exercise discretion in determining whether an electronic monitoring condition should be imposed on a person at a time, to be specified in regulations, when the person was at liberty but on temporary admission, temporary release, on bail or otherwise liable to be detained but not detained (Schedule 10, para 13).

3.16.4 *A Guide to the Immigration Act 2016*

The same regime applies to the Special Immigration Appeals Commission (SIAC) (Schedule 10, Part 1, paras 22–25).

The provisions do not describe any scope for the tribunal, or SIAC to disagree with the SSHD. If the tribunal or the commission considers that to impose such a condition will breach a person's human rights, despite the decision of the SSHD's representative to the contrary, the tribunal or commission will continue to be bound by s 6 of the Human Rights Act 1998 (HRA 1998) which, insofar as material, provides:

6 Acts of public authorities

(1) It is unlawful for a public authority to act in a way which is incompatible with a Convention right.

(2) Subsection (1) does not apply to an act if—

(a) as the result of one or more provisions of primary legislation, the authority could not have acted differently; or

(b) in the case of one or more provisions of, or made under, primary legislation which cannot be read or given effect in a way which is compatible with the Convention rights, the authority was acting so as to give effect to or enforce those provisions.

(3) In this section 'public authority' includes—

(a) a court or tribunal, and

(b) any person certain of whose functions are functions of a public nature.

The decision-making structure could also operate to allow the SSHD to declare a tag 'impractical' in circumstances in which the tribunal or commission considered that it should be imposed, or to advance human rights arguments against its imposition that the tribunal or commission considers to be without merit. Then the judge or immigration judge will be unable to impose the condition they wished to impose and will have to decide whether to grant bail without a tag, or that, without the tag, they will not grant bail.

Duty to arrange consideration of bail

3.16.4 The schedule contains provisions for automatic judicial oversight of detention. Powers to set up automatic judicial oversight of detention had been taken in Part III of the IAA 1999,[13] but the provisions were never brought into force and were repealed by the NIAA 2002.[14]

At Lords' Report on 15 March 2016 Amendment 84, proposing a new clause *Immigration detention: time limit and judicial oversight*, was tabled in the names

Part 3—Enforcement **3.16.4**

of Lord Ramsbotham, Lord Rosser, Baroness Hamwee and Lord Roberts of Llandudno.[15] This combined the notion of a time limit on detention with the principle of judicial oversight. It would have required that the SSHD make an application to the tribunal where she wished to detain a person, other than a person who had been sentenced to a term of imprisonment for 12 months or longer, or whom she had determined should be deported, for more than 28 days, at a stretch or in aggregate. On such an application the SSHD would have had to persuade the tribunal that the 'exceptional circumstances' of the case required detention beyond 28 days. The tribunal could then have extended detention for a further period, not limited to 28 days, and could have done so more than once, with no maximum.

Under the terms of the proposal, those sentenced to more than 12 months or whom the SSHD had determined should be deported would have had to bring an application for bail themselves. There would have been no automatic review of their detention. It is understood that this restriction, which was not a feature of amendments on bail and on a time limit on detention tabled at Lords' Committee,[16] was introduced so that the Labour front bench would support the amendment were it pressed to a vote. The detainee as ex-offender was not to escape detention by administrative fiat, without limit of time. The amendment was carried by 187 votes to 170.[17]

In the House of Commons, this amendment on judicial oversight was rejected and what became Schedule 10, Part 1, para 11 *Duty to arrange consideration of bail* was substituted in lieu of the Lords' proposal.[18] This provided for the SSHD to arrange a bail hearing before the tribunal when a person has been detained for six months from their first entry into detention or since their last bail hearing, whether automatic or a bail hearing they had instigated, save if the latter was a bail hearing taking place within 14 days of a proposed removal. In such cases the SSHD has, under Schedule 2 to the IA 1971, para 22(4),[19] power to refuse to consent to bail and therefore it is not an event that resets the clock. Instead, time runs from the bail hearing before it. Mirroring the amendment carried in the Lords, para 11 does not apply to those detained pending deportation (para 11(1)(a)). Nor does it apply to cases before SIAC, despite SIAC's being a specialist court of record presided over by a High Court judge and set up to hear national security cases (para 11(6)(a)). Nor does the section apply where a person waives, in writing, their right to the hearing (para 11(6)(a)). On 9 May 2016, the second time the Bill returned to the Commons on ping-pong, the Secretary of State tabled motion (a) in response to Lords' Motion 84B, reducing the interval between bail hearings from six months to four months.

The section is not phrased in terms of the SSHD justifying detention. The hearing is identical to an elective bail hearing. Nonetheless, given the presumption of temporary admission (henceforth immigration bail) set out in Chapter 55.1 of the Home Office Enforcement Instructions and Guidance, the SSHD will have to defend the decision to detain.

Section 62—Powers of Secretary of State to enable person to meet bail conditions

3.16.5 With the repeal of powers to support persons who have never claimed asylum (see Part 5 below), Schedule 10 makes new provision for the SSHD to provide support to a person bailed to an address of her choosing (Schedule 10, Part 1, para 9). It is provided, however, that the power is only to be used where the SSHD thinks that there are exceptional circumstances justifying the exercise of the power (para 9(3)) and the wording 'where a person is (a) on immigration bail' in para 9(1) creates doubt about whether an impecunious detainee could apply for an address to facilitate making a bail application. Without such an address they are unlikely to be granted bail and their rights to liberty under Article 5 of the ECHR risk being infringed.[20] The matter was discussed in the Public Bill Committee and the Minister, the Rt Hon James Brokenshire MP, gave the following assurances to Sir Keir Starmer KCB, QC MP for the official opposition:

> 'Schedule 5, paragraph 7 [now Schedule 10, Part 1, para 9] provides a power to allow the Secretary of State to meet accommodation costs and travel expenses for those granted immigration bail. That arrangement is designed to replace section 4(1)(c) of the Immigration and Asylum Act 1999, which ... to date has been used to provide accommodation for persons released on bail in the limited circumstances where we judge that that is appropriate ... in general, individuals seeking bail are expected to accommodate themselves or arrange accommodation through friends or relatives. This is no different from the way the section 4 power is currently used. It is clearly inappropriate to spend public money providing accommodation for people who do not need it. It should therefore only be in exceptional circumstances that the Secretary of State should pay for the accommodation of people seeking release from detention on bail. If the person is truly unable to arrange their own accommodation, the powers can be used to provide it on a case-by-case basis ... the concern expressed about the provision appears to be based on the assumption that there will be increased use of detention for a longer period, because bail can only be granted when an address is available. The new bail powers contain the concept of conditional bail, at paragraph 3(8). That will allow the tribunal to grant bail conditional on arrangements specified in the notice being in place to ensure that a person is able to comply with the conditions. Where a residence condition has been applied, it will be for the individual to find a suitable address during the period of conditional bail and, if a suitable address cannot be found, for them to go back to the tribunal for a further hearing. If the person is unable to find an address, consideration will be given to using the powers in paragraph 7 to provide one.
>
> **Keir Starmer:** As I understand the Minister, it is envisaged that the tribunal will use conditional bail to bail someone on the condition of a

residence, or an address, unspecified. There will then be a period during which the individual either finds an address or consideration will be given to supporting the individual to have an address so that they can be released. Is that how it is envisaged that this will work, when looked at in the round?'

James Brokenshire: That is how conditional bail can be used in these circumstances, as I think I described in my response to the hon. and learned Gentleman's points.'[21]

Just as there was doubt over whether para 9 could be used to obtain an address for bail, so its terms are not confined to the situation in which a person in detention is making an application for bail. It appears to be a power at large to support a person given immigration bail to a particular address, provided only that the person could not support him/herself at the address at which s/he is required to reside without that support and that the SSHD thinks that exceptional circumstances justify the exercise of the power. This is significant given that Part 5 of the Act removes powers of the SSHD to support persons who have never claimed asylum and limits her powers to support those whose claims for asylum have finally been determined and have not succeeded. Insofar as this Act contains a successor to s 4 of the IAA 1999, which is repealed by para 1 of Schedule 11 to this Act, para 11 would appear to be it.

Other provisions

3.16.6 Section 7 of the Immigration Act 2014 (IA 2014) requires rules to be made for the tribunal and for SIAC[22] to prohibit repeat bail hearings within 28 days, unless there is a material change in circumstances. Paragraph 12 of Schedule 11, Part 1, leaves unchanged para 22(4) of Schedule 2 to the IA 1971, inserted by s 7 of the 2014 Act and requiring the SSHD's consent for a person to be bailed where the person's removal is scheduled within the next 14 days. The prohibition on repeat bail hearings is re-enacted in para 12, but with a difference. While s 7 of the 2014 Act implicitly allowed a bail application to be heard, since all that is prevented is 'release' on bail within 14 days from the date on which bail has been granted, para 12(2) provides instead that a person must not be 'granted' immigration bail by the First-tier Tribunal without the consent of the SSHD. Equivalent provision is made for SIAC in paras 22–25 of Schedule 11, Part 2. The Tribunal Procedure Committee has indicated that it understands that the change in wording was not untended to make any substantive change in the law or in the way in which the tribunals and the Secretary of State approach these cases.[23]

Provision is made for bail granted by a criminal court, or court of criminal appeal, following a recommendation for deportation, to be treated in the same way as any other Schedule 10 bail (Schedule 10, Part 2, para 21(2) amending the IA 1971, Schedule 3, para 2(1)).

1 See *Simplifying Immigration Law: the draft Bill*, Cm 7730, Home Office, UK Border Agency, November 2009, para 3.9, and Part 6 of the Draft Bill.
2 House of Lords Select Committee on the Constitution, 7th Report, Session 2015–16, HL Paper 75, paras 29–34.
3 Explanatory Notes to the Immigration Bill, Bill 79, 2015–16–EN, para 168.
4 HL Paper 75, Session 2015–16, op.cit.
5 See the debate at *Hansard*, HL cols 1649–1659 (1 February 2016).
6 Lord Keen of Elie, Immigration Bill, House of Lords Committee, *Hansard*, col 1658 (1 Feb 2016). The existing power is contained in of Schedule 2 to the IA 1971. While this is applied, with modifications, in bail hearings before the SIAC by Schedule 3 to the Special Immigration Appeals Commission Act 1997, its use is in no way confined to cases before the commission. It may be that what was said is a garbled reference to imposing conditions equivalent to the requirements of the Academic Technology Approval Scheme contained in Part 15 of the Immigration Rules, HC 395.
7 HC Bill 74 of session 2015–2016, Schedule 5.
8 HL Paper 75 of session 2015–2016, op.cit.
9 *Hansard*, HL col 1787 (15 March 2016).
10 Amendment 82, House of Lords' Report stage, *Hansard* HL col 1787 (15 March 2016).
11 House of Lords Select Committee on the Constitution, 7th Report, Session 2015–16, HL Paper 75, paras 29–34.
12 Section 36.
13 Sections 44–50.
14 Schedule 9.
15 *Hansard* HL, col 1787 (15 March 2016).
16 Amendment 217 in the names of Lord Rosser, Lord Kennedy of Southwark, Baroness Hamwee and Lord Paddick and Amendment 218 in the names of Lord Ramsbotham, Baroness Hamwee and Lord Roberts of Llandudno. See also New Clause 9 *Review of Immigration Detention*, debated at Commons Report on 1 December 2015, see *Hansard* HC, cols 179–209.
17 *Hansard* HL, col 1804 (15 March 2016).
18 *Hansard* HC, Vol 608 (25 April 2016) and (9 May 2016).
19 As inserted by s 7 of the IA 2014.
20 See amendment 28 at Commons' Report.
21 Public Bill Committee, 10th sitting (morning) *Hansard* col 368 (3 November 2015).
22 See Schedule 9 to the IA 2014, Part 2, para 10 for similar provision for cases before SIAC.
23 *Consultation on Changes to the Tribunal Procedure (First-tier Tribunal) (Immigration and Asylum Chamber) Rules 2014 arising from the Immigration Act 2016* Tribunal Procedure Committee, 14 February 2017.

SECTION 62—POWER TO CANCEL LEAVE EXTENDED UNDER SECTION 3C OF THE IMMIGRATION ACT 1971

Summary

Gives the SSHD power to cancel s 3C leave for breach of conditions or use of deception in seeking leave to remain, whether successfully or not.

3.17

62 Power to cancel leave extended under section 3C of the Immigration Act 1971

(1) In section 3C of the Immigration Act 1971 (continuation of leave pending variation decision) after subsection (3) insert—

"(3A) Leave extended by virtue of this section may be cancelled if the applicant—

(a) has failed to comply with a condition attached to the leave, or

(b) has used or uses deception in seeking leave to remain (whether successfully or not)."

(2) In section 4(1) of that Act (persons by whom and means by which powers are to be exercised) after "conditions)" insert " or to cancel any leave under section 3C(3A) ".

Commencement: 1 December 2016, the Immigration Act 2016 (Commencement No 2 and Transitional Provisions) Regulations 2016, SI 2016/1037.

Amends: Immigration Act 1971 (IA 2014), ss 3 and 4.

Guidance: *Leave extended by section 3C (and leave extended by section 3D in transitional cases)*, Modernised Guidance: other cross-cutting guidance, Home Office, 1 December 2016. Available at: https://www.gov.uk/government/uploads/system/uploads/attachment_data/file/573995/3C_3D_Leave_v7.pdf.

Devolution: Applies throughout the UK.

At present, if a person makes an application for further leave before their leave expires, but the Home Office does not decide it until after that leave expires, leave continues on the same terms and conditions until the Home Office decision is made and any appeal against, or administrative review of, that decision is finally determined. Section 62 gives the Home Office power to cancel that leave so that the person would be left with no leave until such time as the Home Office made its decision and any appeals against, or administrative review of, that decision, are finally determined. There are two grounds for such a cancellation: that the person has failed to comply with a condition of their leave or that they have used deception in seeking leave to enter or remain. The deception need not have been successful and it is also not necessary for the deception to have been used in the most recent application for leave to remain. As the Home Office guidance, *Leave extended by section 3C (and leave extended by section 3D in transitional cases)*, makes clear, the powers to cancel in s 62 are strictly limited and '[s]ection 3C leave cannot be cancelled for any other reason.'[1]

3.17 *A Guide to the Immigration Act 2016*

Cancellation of section 3C leave under this provision operates to bring the period of leave to an end with immediate effect. The guidance provides:

'Where you are going to grant leave to remain despite the breach of conditions or deception you should not cancel section 3C leave.

When you are going to refuse an application, and the grounds for refusal include a breach of conditions or deception, you must decide whether to also cancel section 3C leave. The consequences of cancelling section 3C leave is that the person will not have section 3C leave while any appeal or administrative review against the refusal of the application is pending. This also means that any conditions associated with the previous immigration leave would no longer apply, for example a right to work or access public funds.'

The rationale for the section given in the guidance is:

'The power to cancel section 3C leave is intended to ensure that, where a person has practiced deception or failed to comply with the conditions of their leave, they are treated in the same way as people who have other types of leave and have that leave curtailed.'

But this fails to recognise the difference between s 3C leave and a grant of leave under the Immigration Rules. Section 3C leave protects a person's position until they have had the opportunity to challenge the decision under review. There may be circumstances in which to cancel s 3C leave would nullify the right to challenge the decision, for example, if the person could not afford to maintain themselves pending the hearing of an appeal. There may also be circumstances in which it would have irreversible consequences, for example, if the person then could not work and therefore lost their job, a consequence envisaged in that part of the guidance which deals with the effect of cancellation on children in the UK, and the assessment of whether cancellation is a proportionate response.

The guidance provides 'if you would not have refused the application solely because of the breach of conditions or use of deception then it will not normally be appropriate to cancel section 3C leave'.

Different aspects of s 3C leave were the subject of debate during the passage of the Bill. In the Public Bill Committee an amendment was tabled that would have reversed the effects of the judgment of the Court of Appeal in *R (Iqbal v SSHD)* [2015] EWCA 838, a judgment subsequently upheld by the Supreme Court.[2]

Mr Iqbal was granted entry clearance in January 2007 to come to the UK as a student. He had leave to remain until 30 April 2011. On 19 April, before leave had expired, Mr Iqbal made an application for further leave to remain as a Tier 4 Student. He did not submit the correct fee with his application because he had not appreciated that it had recently been increased by some £29. On 26 April the application and supporting documents were returned to him and he received them on 2 May, after leave had expired. He was informed that the failure to pay the proper fee meant that his application was invalid.

Mr Iqbal submitted a further application on 6 May 2012, after his leave had expired. The college at which he planned to study lost its licence before his application was considered and his application therefore fell for refusal because the college he had identified was no longer approved.

If he had been entitled to the automatic extension of leave under s 3C, then he would have been given 60 days in which to identify another approved institution which would accept him. He was not given that opportunity because the Secretary of State (SSHD) considered that he had no right to remain because the relevant application had been made after his leave had expired.

The Court of Appeal held that if a person such as Mr Iqbal makes an in-time application to vary their leave to remain which they reasonably think is a valid application, but, after their leave expires it turns out that the application was not valid, they have been in the UK without leave and without the protection of s 3C leave, even though they did not know this and had no reason to think it, between the expiry of the existing leave and the SSHD's decision that the application was invalid.

At the hearing, the SSHD was no more keen on this interpretation of the law than the claimant. The SSHD argued that an application which is invalid under the rules may nevertheless be an application that engages and brings into effect s 3C. She argued that when a person is notified that an application is invalid this constitutes a decision on the application within the meaning of s 3C. If that decision is made before leave has expired, the person's original leave will simply expire in the normal way and s 3C has no role to play (see s 3C(1)(c)). If it is decided after the expiry, leave will terminate at the date of the decision: s 3C(2)(a). She cited 'strong policy reasons' for this approach. First, that at the point at which the application is made neither the Secretary of State nor the applicant will know for sure whether or not the application, made in good faith and believed to be valid, is valid, and this could have consequences such as the applicant turning out to have been working unlawfully. Second, that the approach resulted in complexity and was difficult to understand both for applicants and caseworkers, giving rise to uncertainty, and third, that this complexity was exacerbated because, for example, obligations to enrol biometric information arose at a later date.

The Court of Appeal however, held that the section could not be interpreted in this way.

3.17 *A Guide to the Immigration Act 2016*

By the time the Bill reached Parliament the Home Office had decided that it could live with the effect of the judgment of the Court of Appeal in *Iqbal*. ILPA raised the matter directly with the Bill team and received the following response:

> 'the Court of Appeal stated in *Iqbal* that an invalid application did not trigger 3C leave and that this must be the way Parliament would have expected the legislation to work. The Court made the point that the power to enable regulations to be made prescribing the formal requirements of certain applications was first introduced by the Nationality, Immigration and Asylum Act 2002 (NIAA 2002) and that it is clear that an application must be validly made in accordance with the rules. In making these findings the Court of Appeal adopted the SSHD's secondary or alternative argument in *Iqbal*.
>
> The concern that the Home Office had in *Iqbal* was around certain practical consequences that would apply to people who would not know that they had made an invalid application. Having carefully considered the rules and processes the Home Office has on validity following *Iqbal*, we do not think that an amendment to section 3C is necessary or desirable.
>
> The Immigration Rules provide that in order for an application to be valid the applicant must enrol their biometric information (where required to do so), pay the correct fee and Immigration Health Surcharge (where required) and provide the mandatory documentation required for the application. Where a fee is omitted or the wrong fee paid, an applicant who has not made a valid application will be written to and advised what further action to take to ensure that their application is valid. Where people respond to that letter within the specified time limit (ten days) and provide the missing information they will have made a valid application and will be unaffected by the judgement in *Iqbal*. In addition we are improving our processes so that in the future it will be more difficult for people to submit an invalid application.
>
> Where a person has not made a valid application initially and despite having been contacted by the Home Office, has not corrected the errors in their application *Iqbal* confirms that the application does not operate to extend their leave under section 3C. Where that person commits an offence by working illegally, the question of whether to prosecute will be one for the CPS who, in applying the charging test, must be satisfied that prosecution would be in the public interest. The Home Office considers that where someone genuinely believed that they had made a valid application and thought they had leave to remain in the UK as a result of section 3C leave, it is very unlikely to be in the public interest to prosecute.
>
> Amending the legislation to reflect the alternative argument that an application is valid until the SSHD notifies the applicant that it is invalid, would mean that even where an applicant knowingly made an invalid

application their immigration leave would be extended. We do not think that would be a desirable outcome.

We believe that our processes and the public interest test strike the right balance in protecting an individual who has made a genuine error from being prosecuted while maintaining effective immigration control.'[3]

The Supreme Court agreed with the Court of Appeal. Applying ordinary principles of statutory interpretation, for no challenge was before it as to the legality or rationality of the rules and regulations, it found no ambiguity in the words of reg 37 of the Immigration and Nationality (Fees) Regulations 2011.[4] It upheld the Court of Appeal's rejection of Mr Iqbal's ground of alleged unfairness, holding that the comments of the tribunal in *Basnet v SSHD*[5] do not lay down a universal rule and the Secretary of State had not failed to publicise the fee change. In contrast, in the the joined case of *Ehsan*[7] it treated the failure to provide biometric information as giving rise to power to invalidate the application rather than rendering it invalid *ab initio*.

Before the Supreme Court the Secretary of State reverted to the position she had taken prior to the hearing before the Court of Appeal and had adopted in the correspondence with ILPA: that an invalid application did not result in leave being extended.

The Supreme Court reviewed the position that the Secretary of State had taken before the Court of Appeal.[7] Lord Carnwath said:

'I have found this a troubling case. It is particularly disturbing that the Secretary of State herself has been unable to maintain a consistent view of the meaning of the relevant rules and regulations. The public, and particularly those directly affected by immigration control, are entitled to expect the legislative scheme to be underpinned by a coherent view of their meaning and the policy behind them....

31. The problem is only too vividly demonstrated by the course of the arguments in this case. The policy concerns which underlay the Secretary of State's position in the Court of Appeal were and remain very real. They should have been apparent to the Department at least since 1996, when judgment was given in the *ILPA* case. Against that background, there was surely a need to introduce some measure of flexibility to ensure that bona fide applicants were not unduly penalised for simple mistakes which could be readily corrected.'[8]

A further amendment was also moved in Commons' Committee which would have replaced s 3C (2) of the IA 1971 'The leave is extended by virtue of this section' with 'The leave is extended from the day on which it would otherwise have expired'.[9]

3.17 *A Guide to the Immigration Act 2016*

Section 3C requires that the original leave has already expired when the SSHD makes her decision for the protection of s 3C to kick in for the period while an appeal can be brought or is pending. If the SSHD does manage to decide the application before the original leave expires, and refuses it, the applicant does not benefit from s 3C while the appeal or administrative review could be brought or is pending. The problem is with s 3C(1)(c):

'3C Continuation of leave pending variation decision

(1) This section applies if—

(a) a person who has limited leave to enter or remain in the United Kingdom applies to the Secretary of State for variation of the leave,

(b) the application for variation is made before the leave expires, and

(c) the leave expires without the application for variation having been decided.

(2) The leave is extended by virtue of this section'.

Thus persons refused before their original leave expires may have the right to appeal or to apply for administrative review, but run the risk of becoming overstayers if their leave expires before the conclusion of proceedings.

The amendment was rejected. ILPA took the matter up directly with the Bill Team, who said:

'As the Solicitor General set out in committee, it has always been the case that, where an application is refused and the applicant still has immigration leave, leave is not extended by section 3C while a challenge to the refusal can be brought. Section 3C applies only where an application remains undetermined at the point that the applicant's extant leave expires.

We do not think that paragraph 152 of the explanatory notes suggests otherwise. That paragraph sets out how section 3C operates, by way of background to the change to section 3C made by clause 30 of the Bill. The reference to leave being extended by section 3C while an appeal or administrative review against a refusal decision remains pending is in the context of the situation where the applicant finds that "their leave expires while their application remains undecided".

This is the intended position. People who still have extant immigration leave at the point of refusal are in a different position to those who are refused after their leave expires. People with extant immigration leave may be able to submit another in-time application for immigration leave. That is not an option for those whose application is refused after their leave has expired.

Furthermore the changes made by the Immigration Act 2014 to appeal rights means that where a person's application is refused while they still have extant leave, they are in a better position than they were previously. Before the Immigration Act 2014, a refusal made while a person still had leave would not result in a right of appeal. Following the changes made by that Act the availability of a right of appeal or administrative review is unaffected by whether a person has extant leave at the time of the decision.

Given this position we do not see any reason to change the long standing position on when 3C leave is triggered.'[10]

The reference to para 152 of the Explanatory Notes to the Bill[11] is to the following passage, highlighted by ILPA:

'A person who currently has leave and applies to extend their leave to enter or remain may well find that their leave expires while their application remains undecided, or while an appeal or administrative review against a refusal decision remains pending. To prevent people being left without leave, section 3C ... provides'.

ILPA continues to press the matter with the Home Office, for example, at meetings with its Complex Casework team and at its Business User Forum.

---

1 Certification under section 94B of the NIAA 2002, v7, Home Office, 1 December 2016. Available at: https://www.gov.uk/government/publications/section-94b-of-the-nationality-immigration-and-asylum-act-2002 (accessed 15 December 2016).
2 R (Mirza) v SSHD [2016] UKSC 63 and R (Iqbal) v SSHD [2016] UKSC 63 and R (Ehsan) v SSHD [2016] UKSC 63 (14 December 2016). See Amendment 217, debated Public Bill Committee, 10th sitting (morning) cols 371–374 (3 November 2015).
3 Andrew Eliot, Head of Bill Team, Home Office, to Alison Harvey, Legal Director, ILPA, 28 October 2015, by email.
4 SI 2011/1055.
5 [2012] UKUT 0113 (IAC).
7 R (Ehsan) v SSHD [2015] UKSC 0211 (14 December 2016).
7 Lord Carnwath, at paras 16 ff.
8 Lord Carnwath, at paras 30–31. The reference to the ILPA case is to R (Immigration Law Practitioners' Association) v SSHD [1997] Imm AR 189).
9 Amendment 216, debated Public Bill Committee, 10th sitting (afternoon) cols 371–374 (3 November 2015).
10 Andrew Elliot, Head of Bill Team, Home Office, to Alison Harvey, Legal Director, ILPA, 6 November 2015, by email.
11 Bill 74, EN 2015–2016.

Part 4—Appeals

SECTION 63—APPEALS WITHIN THE UK: CERTIFICATION OF HUMAN RIGHTS CLAIMS

> **Summary**
>
> Extends s 94B *Appeals from within the United Kingdom: certification of human rights claims made by persons liable to deportation* of the Nationality, Immigration and Asylum Act 2002 (NIAA 2002) to all appeals, and as a consequence, removes the reference to 'made by persons liable to detention' in the title.

4.1

63 Appeals within the United Kingdom: certification of human rights claims

(1) Section 94B of the Nationality, Immigration and Asylum Act 2002 (appeals from within the United Kingdom: certification of human rights claims made by persons liable to deportation) is amended in accordance with subsections (2) to (5).

(2) In the heading omit "made by persons liable to deportation".

(3) In subsection (1) omit the words from "who is liable" to the end of paragraph (b).

(4) In subsection (2) for the words from "removal" to "removed" substitute " refusing P entry to, removing P from or requiring P to leave the United Kingdom ".

(5) In subsection (3) for the words from "removed" in the first place it appears to "removed" in the second place it appears substitute " refused entry to, removed from or required to leave the United Kingdom ".

(6) In section 92(3)(a) of that Act (cases where human rights claim appeal must be brought from outside the United Kingdom) omit "made by persons liable to deportation".

Commencement: 1 December 2016, Immigration Act 2016 (Commencement No 2 and Transitional Provisions) Regulations 2016, SI 2016/1037.

4.1 A Guide to the Immigration Act 2016

Guidance: *Certification under section 94B of the Nationality, Immigration and Asylum Act 2002*, v7, Home Office, 1 December 2016. Available at: https://www.gov.uk/government/publications/section-94b-of-the-nationality-immigration-and-asylum-act-2002. See also *Leave extended by section 3C (and leave extended by section 3D in transitional cases), Modernised Guidance: other cross-cutting guidance*, Home Office, 1 December 2016. Available at: https://www.gov.uk/government/uploads/system/uploads/attachment_data/file/573995/3C_3D_Leave_v7.pdf

Amends: NIAA 2002, s 94B.

Devolution: Applies throughout the UK.

The Immigration Act 2014 (IA 2014) inserted s 94B *Appeals from within the United Kingdom: certification of human rights claims made by persons liable to deportation* into the NIAA 2002 to provide a power to certify deportation appeals, other than in cases based on fear of persecution or ill-treatment abroad, before these appeals began or while they were in train. The effect is that the appeal can only be pursued after the person has left the country. A person can be removed before the appeal is heard if to do so would not breach human rights and rights under EU law and in particular would not cause 'serious irreversible harm'. Section 63 extends these powers beyond deportation cases, where a person's presence in the UK is deemed 'not conducive to the public good', to all cases of persons appealing an immigration (non-asylum) decision.[1]

Section 63 amends s 94B of the 2002 Act to extend it to all appeals and, as a consequence, removes the reference in the title to 'made by persons liable to detention'. The wording of the provision leads to the conclusion that it covers persons with leave under s 3C of the Immigration Act 1971 (IA 1971) and this is the view taken by the Home Office; see the discussion below.

During the passage of the IA 2014, the Joint Committee on Human Rights expressed the view that judicial review was not an adequate means of challenging a certificate.[2] The 'deport first, appeal later' regime was challenged and the Court of Appeal gave judgment on it in *R (Kiarie) v SSHD* [2015] EWCA Civ 1020 (13 October 2015). The case has been appealed to the Supreme Court where it was heard in February 2017. Judgment is awaited.

Article 8 of the European Convention on Human Rights (ECHR) comprehends not only substantive rights but also procedural protection, as discussed in *R (Gudanaviciene) v Director of Legal Aid Casework* [2014] EWCA Civ 1622.

In *Kiarie* it was argued that an out-of-country appeal would result in unfairness in some cases because of the difficulties of obtaining evidence, preparing the appeal and presenting it. It was also argued that the process would create the appearance of unfairness. The Court of Appeal did not accept these arguments.

It accepted that an out-of-country appeal is not as good as an in-country appeal, but held that Article 8 did not demand access to the best possible appeal but to a procedure meeting the essential requirements of fairness and effectiveness. Entry clearance appeals were identified as an example of such fair and effective out-of-country appeals. Lord Justice Richards held:

> 'The Secretary of State is entitled ... to rely on the specialist immigration judges within the tribunal system to ensure that an appellant is given effective access to the decision-making process and that the process is fair to the appellant, irrespective of whether the appeal is brought in country or out of country.
>
> ... If particular procedures are needed in order to enable an appellant to present his case properly or for his credibility to be properly assessed, there is sufficient flexibility within the system to ensure that those procedures are put in place. That applies most obviously to the provision of facilities for video conferencing or other forms of two-way electronic communication or, if truly necessary, the issue of a witness summons so as to put pressure on the Secretary of State to allow the appellant's attendance to give oral evidence in person.'[3]

It was not accepted that preparation of the case presented particular difficulties. Although an appellant will be without legal aid because Article 8 appeals are not within the scope of legal aid[4] it was suggested that exceptional case legal aid funding[5] would be available in appropriate cases. The judgment recalls that of Sedley LJ in *R (Lim) v SSHD* [2007] EWCA Civ 77, where an out-of-country appeal was found to be good enough.

The Upper Tribunal has previously produced guidance on cases heard over video link[6] which may become relevant in such appeals.

The Court of Appeal judgment in *Kiarie* makes clear that the 'serious irreversible harm' test in s 94B of the NIAA 2002 is just one facet of the question of whether removal would breach human rights, not a stand-alone test.[7] This ought to have been clear from the wording of s 94B but Home Office guidance was misleading. The case law of the European Court of Human Rights (ECtHR) on this point was discussed in *De Souza Ribeiro v France*[8] in relation to Article 13 (the right to an effective remedy):

> '83. By contrast [with Article 3], where expulsions are challenged on the basis of alleged interference with private and family life, it is not imperative, in order for a remedy to be effective, that it should have automatic suspensive effect. Nevertheless, in immigration matters, where there is an arguable claim that expulsion threatens to interfere with the alien's right to respect with Article 8 of the Convention requires that States must make available to the individual concerned the effective possibility of challenging the deportation or refusal-of-residence order and of having the relevant issues examined with

sufficient procedural safeguards and thoroughness by an appropriate domestic forum offering adequate guarantees of independence and impartiality'

The original Home Office *Certification guidance in non-EEA deport cases*[9] took the approach of the ECtHR in *De Souza Ribeiro* as its starting point for understanding what is implied by the term 'serious irreversible harm' in s 94B(3) and for the contention that it implies a degree of permanence or very long-lasting effect. But in that case the term was used in the context of a discussion of why an admissible application to the court under Article 3 of the European Convention on Human Rights (ECHR) would normally be suspensive of removal. The court held that Mr De Souza Ribero's deportation had deprived him of an effective remedy against interference with his rights under Article 8 of the ECHR.

A similar reference to 'serious irreversible harm' was inserted by s 54 of the Crime and Courts Act 2013 as s 97A(2C) of the NIAA 2002. This also relates to deportation cases, but to those cases where the appeal is to be heard by the Special Immigration Appeals Commission (SIAC) by reason of a certificate that the decision to make a deportation order was taken on national security grounds.[10] During the passage of the Crime and Courts Bill, the then Immigration Minister said of that provision:

'[It] will support our ability to deport in future cases, in particular, where individuals raise less fundamental human rights issues, such as the right to a private life, or if their human rights claim is unfounded. For example, a person may suffer no serious irreversible harm in being away from their family for a few months while they appeal, even if they claim that permanent deportation would be contrary to the right to family or private life. The person will still have an appeal, and if they win they will be able to return to the UK. Nevertheless, having the individual out of the UK pending the appeal could be of real benefit in the context of the relatively small number of national security deportation cases. This measure is one of a number of reforms being explored by the Home Office and Ministry of Justice to support the Government's ability to deport foreign national terrorists more quickly than at present.'[11]

It cannot be assumed that judgments on deportation cases, where the Secretary of State (SSHD) has held that the person's presence in the UK is not conducive to the public good, transfer seamlessly to other immigration cases and the judgment of the Supreme Court in *Kiarie* will be scrutinised with care to ascertain the extent to which it is applicable in general immigration cases.

Neither the IA 2014 nor this Act amend s 78 *No removal while appeal pending* of the 2002 Act. That section operates to provide that an appeal brought in-country[12] shall have suspensive effect while it remains pending, with the consequence that the SSHD may neither remove the appellant nor require them to leave the UK.[13]

While many appellants will not have leave at the time of applying to stay, some will have made a 'human rights claim' within the meaning of s 82(1) of the NIAA 2002 at a time when they had leave, and will thus benefit from leave under s 3C of the Immigration Act 1971 (IA 1971) at the time of refusal. Will leave continue while the appeal is pending even though the appellant cannot pursue the appeal while they remain in the UK because it is suspended? The Home Office guidance takes the view that it will not and that '3C leave' will automatically be brought to an end by certification under s 94B, because a person will no longer have a pending appeal in the UK.[14]

The guidance on section 3C provides that:

'A person does not have section 3C leave during an appeal where the appeal can only be brought after the person has left the UK. In these cases section 3C leave will come to an end when their application is decided and certified. If the certificate is withdrawn the underlying decision should also be withdrawn. A new decision should be made which will generate a new right of appeal, which may be subject to recertification. Withdrawal of the decision does not mean that the person once again has section 3C leave. This is because section 3C leave can arise and exist only where it is a seamless continuation of leave, either extant leave or section 3C leave. Where there is a break in that leave, such that section 3C leave has come to an end, section 3C leave cannot be resurrected.'[15]

The IA 1971, s 3C provides:

'(2) The leave is extended by virtue of this section during any period when—

...

(b) an appeal under section 82(1) of the Nationality, Asylum and Immigration Act 2002 could be brought, while the appellant is in the United Kingdom against the decision on the application for variation (ignoring any possibility of an appeal out of time with permission),

(c) an appeal under that section against that decision, brought while the appellant is in the United Kingdom, is pending (within the meaning of section 104 of that Act) ...'.

Section 104 of the 2002 Act provides:

'**104 Pending appeal**

(1) An appeal under section 82(1) is pending during the period—

(a) beginning when it is instituted, and

(b) ending when it is finally determined, withdrawn or abandoned (or when it lapses under section 99).'

4.1 *A Guide to the Immigration Act 2016*

Section 99 of that Act provides:

'99 Section 97: appeal in progress

(1) This section applies where a certificate is issued under section 97 in respect of a pending appeal.

(2) The appeal shall lapse.'

Section 97 is concerned solely with national security appeals.

Nothing in s 92 of the NIAA 2002 disturbs the approach taken in s 104:

'...

(6) If, after an appeal under section 82(1)(a) or (b) has been brought from within the United Kingdom, the Secretary of State certifies the claim to which the appeal relates under section 94(1) or (7) or section 94B, the appeal must be continued from outside the United Kingdom.

(7) Where a person brings or continues an appeal under section 82(1)(a) (refusal of protection claim) from outside the United Kingdom, for the purposes of considering whether the grounds of appeal are satisfied, the appeal is to be treated as if the person were not outside the United Kingdom.

(8) Where an appellant brings an appeal from within the United Kingdom but leaves the United Kingdom before the appeal is finally determined, the appeal is to be treated as abandoned unless the claim to which the appeal relates has been certified under section 94(1) or (7) or section 94B.'

An appellant whose appeal is certified after it has been lodged, falls squarely with s 3C(2)(c) of the 1971 Act. Their appeal was brought while they were in the UK. It is pending within the definition in s 104 of the 2002 Act although it cannot be progressed. There is no support in s 3C for the contention that certification brings their appeal to an end. Consider also the drafting of Schedule 12 *Availability of Local Authority Support*, para 10, inserting new paras 10A and 10B into Schedule 3 to the NIAA 2002. In defining a 'relevant failed asylum seeker' who will be eligible for support, the drafters of that section found it necessary to particularise not only that a person could bring an appeal under s 82(1) of the 2002 Act, ignoring any possibility of an appeal out of time with permission,[16] but that 'if the person brought such an appeal, it would not be one that, by virtue of s 92(6), would have to be continued from outside the United Kingdom.'[17] Paragraph 10B is in identical terms. It is suggested that the drafting of Schedule 12, which also amends the 2002 Act, provides support for the interpretation contended for above.

The position is less clear where the certificate is issued at the point of refusal, before an appeal has been lodged. A comma appears to be missing after 'Kingdom' in s 3C(1)(b) of the 1971 Act. Does 3C(1)(b) mean that only where an appeal can be lodged while the person is in the UK does leave continue by virtue of the section, or that leave is continued by virtue of the section while a person, who has a right of appeal under s 82(1) of the 2002 Act, is in the UK? It is perhaps surprising that the point has yet to arise before the courts.

If the appellant leaves the UK, including to pursue the appeal, leave will lapse by operation of s 3C(3) and s 3D(3).

Confidence in its interpretation of s 3C may be the reason that the Government did not propose amendments to s 78 in either the IA 2014 or in this Act to address the possibility that persons remain in the UK, in limbo and unable to challenge the decision to refuse them until such time as they leave the UK. The Home Office guidance *Certification under section 94B of the Nationality, Immigration and Asylum Act 2002*,[18] like the guidance before it, *Certification guidance for non-EEA deportation cases: section 94B*[19] appears to assume that there is no barrier to removal:

> 'The result of section 94B certification is that any appeal can only be lodged and heard, or continued if the claim is certified after the appeal is lodged, while the person is outside the UK.'[20] This means the right of appeal against the decision to refuse the human rights claim is non-suspensive, meaning it is not a barrier to removal.'

The amendment effected to s 3C by s 62 *Power to cancel leave extended under section 3C of the Immigration Act 1971* of this Act, which has the same commencement date as this section, does not offer the Home Office an alternative approach because new s 3C(3A) of the IA 1971 inserted by s 62 only provides power to cancel leave where a person has breached the conditions of their leave, or has used deception and a person remaining in the UK and protected from removal by s 78 of the 2002 Act and/or s 3C of the 1971 Act will not necessarily have done either.

In the *Certification under section 94B of the Nationality, Immigration and Asylum Act 2002* guidance,[21] Home Office staff are instructed to consider using s 94B certification in all cases but provision is made for phased implementation in non-deportation cases from 1 December 2016. There are two criteria for certification during this period:

- the claimant did not have leave at the point that they made their human rights claim; and
- the claimant does not rely on their relationship with a British national family member.

4.1 A Guide to the Immigration Act 2016

'British national family member' is stated in the guidance to mean partner, parent or child. Thus it appears that a distinction is made between British citizens and the settled for these purposes. The guidance identifies that some cases may be suitable for certification under more than one power. It provides that a person should always be given the opportunity to provide reasons why their claim should not be certified prior to certification and experience from screening interviews for the detained fast track suggests that this could be as early as at the point of making an initial claim. The guidance provides that s 94B certification should not be used in cases in which the whereabouts of the claimant is unknown and the decision is placed on the file for service at a later date (in Home Office jargon 'served to file').

SS (Nigeria) [2014] 1 WLR 998 is relied on in the guidance as authority for the proposition that staff are not required to undertake additional research or make additional enquiries 'in the generality of cases'. This is, however, qualified by the statement that 'in some limited circumstances, the information provided by the claimant may suggest that further enquiries are necessary. Where that is the case, you should make those enquiries.' Home Office staff members are reminded that evidence on, for example, health conditions, may not be up to date.

The guidance states of claims made under Articles 2 or 3 of the ECHR that:

'if the claim has not been certified under section 94, or has met the threshold to be accepted as a fresh claim under paragraph 353, the claim is not clearly unfounded and therefore removal pending the outcome of the appeal may give rise to a risk of serious irreversible harm or breach human rights.'

The equating of not being clearly unfounded with not being suitable for certification may be of relevance to a wider swathe of cases.

It is provided in the guidance that where the protection elements of further submissions are not accepted as a fresh claim, but other parts of the submissions are accepted as a fresh human rights claim then consideration can be given to certification under s 94B.

It is identified in the guidance that certification as clearly unfounded under s 94 of the NIAA 2002 is to be preferred to certification under s 94B. The possibility of certifying those parts of a claim that could not be certified under s 94, whether other parts of the claim have been so certified, is identified.

The guidance provides that where a claimant is serving an indeterminate length sentence where release is at the discretion of the Parole Board[22] the case 'will not normally' be suitable for s 94B certification. This is stated to be because the Parole Board will have made a decision about release based on the claimant's deportation rather than on the possibility that they may return to the UK if any appeal is successful, with the result that there may be no provision to recall to prison in the event of such return, or to impose licence conditions.

Section 55 of the Borders, Citizenship and Immigration Act 2009 (BCIA 2009) requires the SSHD to have regard to the need to safeguard and promote the welfare of children. As discussed by the Supreme Court in *ZH (Tanzania) v Secretary of State for the Home Department* [2011] UKSC 4, by this route best interests considerations in respect of children under the 1989 UN Convention on the Rights of the Child are given domestic application.[23] Section 90 of this Act, which is in identical terms to s 71 of the IA 2014 before it, gives s 55 of the 2009 Act primacy over the provisions of the later Act. See the discussion of s 90 below. It is stated in the guidance that cases of unaccompanied children will not normally be suitable for certification and reference is made to the BCIA 2009, s 55. It is expressly provided, however, that such cases are not excluded from certification. The example given is 'if a child who is living in the UK with members of their wider family has made a human rights claim which has been refused, and they have parents in another country to whom they can return and who can support them with any appeal.' The guidance also provides that a child who has made a claim in their own right but is also part of a family group 'must be considered both in their own right and as an affected child in relation to the adult(s).' It does not elaborate on this. As to children in families, the separation of a family until the appeal is finally determined is for a lengthy, and unknown, period. It is stated that 'There may be positive benefits to children in experiencing a different educational system or culture, particularly in the country of a parent's nationality.' It is specifically stated in the guidance that:

> 'the evidence relied upon should be specific to the individual child, for example the Children Commissioner for England's 2015 report on the Skype family discussion paper talks about impacts of separation from parents in children generally and would not by itself constitute adequate evidence to demonstrate a significant impact on a specific child'[24]

Those whose cases involved allegations of trafficking or slavery benefit from greater protection and it is stated that certification should only be considered when the question of whether a person is a victim of human trafficking or slavery has been resolved. The guidance envisages that this question will be resolved under the National Referral Mechanism.

Provision is made in the Immigration (European Economic Area) Regulations 2006,[25] and has been made in the Immigration (European Economic Area) Regulations 2016,[26] for certification of EEA cases that do not involve deportation. The guidance does identify the possibility of certifying a human rights claim, made with an EEA claim, under s 94B. In such cases, the appellant would benefit from rights under the EEA Regulations to re-enter the UK to be present at the appeal.[27] Although it acknowledges that the Tribunal can consider human

4.1 *A Guide to the Immigration Act 2016*

rights claims raised in a 'section 120' notice[28] and that there is no need to bring two separate appeals, the guidance provides:

'If the claimant brings separate appeals under both regulation 26 of the EEA Regulations and section 82 of the 2002 Act, it is their responsibility to alert the First-tier Tribunal (Immigration and Asylum Chamber) that they will be lodging a regulation 26 appeal from within the UK, and a section 82 appeal from outside the UK, and that they should be linked for a single hearing'.

The guidance enjoins staff to proceed on the basis that the appeal will succeed. No guidance is given as to the length of separation that should be anticipated. The guidance envisages consideration of arguments about procedural unfairness as well as of the effects of separation on third parties. It is stated, however, that the Home Office is entitled to assume that proceedings will be fair unless representations are made by the claimant. The guidance suggests that representations that proceedings will be unfair because of the cost of internet or telephone use will not normally be sufficient. Examples given of the circumstances in which the powers of the Tribunal will be insufficient to secure a fair and effective appeal are:

- the claimant is disabled or otherwise personally not capable of giving instructions to legal representatives or communicating with family members or others who will give evidence in the appeal and there is no one who can assist the claimant with such instructions or communications in the country to which they are to be removed;

- the absence of a route by which the claimant could return to the UK if the Tribunal considered that their presence at the appeal was necessary for it to be fair.

The guidance remains confused on relevance of the 'serious irreversible harm' test. While correctly identifying that this is only one element of the test it at the same time manages to suggest that there must be evidence of serious irreversible harm if certification under s 94B is to be avoided.

A significant statement in the guidance is that:

'The test to be applied when considering whether temporary removal is proportionate in light of the public interest in removal differs between human rights claims in cases subject to deportation and other human rights claims.'

Not least because it acknowledges that the case of *Kiarie*[29] in the Supreme Court may not be determinative of the position in cases not involving deportation.

Examples given of cases in which certification may be appropriate include:

- a child or partner is undergoing treatment for a medical condition in the UK that can be satisfactorily managed through medication or other treatment and/or does not require the claimant to act as a carer; and
- a claimant has strong private life ties to a community that will be disrupted by removal (for example, a job, a mortgage, a prominent role in a community organisation).

Examples of cases in which it may not be appropriate to issue a s 94B certificate include 'if the child is seriously ill such that there is a risk (supported by appropriate evidence) that they could die or their condition could deteriorate significantly during a temporary separation and the claimant has a parental or similarly close relationship with them'.

No attempt is made in the examples to differentiate between deportation and other cases and examples used in previous versions of the guidance are included.[30] The section on public interest, however, does identify that the public interest in removal is strongest in deportation cases. It is stated that it is not a requirement that a person should have been in breach of the law or the Immigration Rules for certification to be appropriate.

The guidance states:

'Where a claimant could not depart voluntarily and is not currently removable, you should consider whether to exercise discretion not to certify under section 94B. It may be counterproductive to certify if the claimant would be unable to leave the UK to exercise a right of appeal.'

This is arguably unlawful. The effect of a certificate in such circumstances would be to keep an appellant from exercising a right of appeal. It could serve no other purpose unless and until removal or departure became possible. There was no suggestion in any of the debates in Parliament of using a s 94B certificate to keep a person from exercising their right of appeal.

It is suggested in the guidance that because a person has a passport or travel document it will be appropriate to certify because it can be assumed that they could make a voluntary departure.

As to the timing of certification, it is envisaged in the guidance that a claim will be certified at the time of refusal. The guidance suggests that it will be appropriate to consider certification at the stage of each subsequent appeal.

The guidance addresses the matters to be considered for the SSHD to decide to pay for a person's return to the UK.

4.1 A Guide to the Immigration Act 2016

1 The material date, see NIAA 2002, s 85(4). See *Certification under section 94B of the Nationality, Immigration and Asylum Act 2002* v8, 20 January 2017 for confirmation that human rights claims (initial claims or further submissions accepted as fresh claims under para 353) made on the basis of Article 2 and/or Article 3 of the ECHR, 'including medical claims', should not be certified under s 94B. See also the Public Bill Committee, 11th sitting (morning) *Hansard* col 380 (5 November 2016) per the Solicitor General, Robert Buckland QC MP.
2 Eighth Report of Session 2013–14, HL Paper 102/HC 935, December 2013.
3 Paragraph 65 of the judgment.
4 See the Legal Aid, Sentencing and Punishment of Offenders Act 2012 (LASPO 2012), s 9 and Sch 1.
5 Under s 10 of the LASPO 2012.
6 Upper Tribunal Immigration and Asylum Chamber Guidance, note 2013, no 2: *Video link hearings*, 30 September 2013.
7 See para 35 of the judgment.
8 [2012] ECHR 2066 (Appl No 22689/07) (13 December 2012).
9 *Certification guidance in non-EEA deport cases*, Home Office, 30 October 2014.
10 NIAA 2002, s 97.
11 *Hansard*, HC, Public Bill Committee, 12th sitting (morning): col 436 (12 February 2013) per Damian Green MP; a few lines earlier (also col 436), he also made reference to *Case of De Souza Ribeiro v France* [2012] ECHR 2066 (Appl No 22689/07), (13 December 2012).
12 Section 78(4).
13 Section 78(1).
14 *Certification under section 94B of the Nationality, Immigration and Asylum Act 2002*, v8, Home Office, 20 January 2017. Available at: https://www.gov.uk/government/publications/section-94b-of-the-nationality-immigration-and-asylum-act-2002 (accessed 20 January 2017).
15 *Leave extended by section 3C (and leave extended by section 3D in transitional cases)*, Modernised Guidance: other cross-cutting guidance, Home Office, 1 December 2016. Available at: https://www.gov.uk/government/uploads/system/uploads/attachment_data/file/573995/3C_3D_Leave_v7.pdf (accessed 15 December 2016).
16 Schedule 12, para 10 inserting new para 10A(4)(a) into Schedule 3 to the NIAA 2002.
17 Schedule 12, para 10 inserting new para 10A(4)(a) into Schedule 3 to the NIAA 2002.
18 Version 8, 20 January 2017.
19 *Certification guidance in non-EEA deport cases*, Home Office, 30 October 2014.
20 See also para 386 of the Immigration Rules, inserted by Statement of Changes in Immigration Rules HC 532 and removed from the rules by para 106 of Statement of Changes in Immigration Rules HC 693 at the time of changes to the appeals regime in immigration cases as a result of the coming into force of s 15 of the IA 2014.
21 *Certification under section 94B of the Nationality, Immigration and Asylum Act 2002*, v7, op.cit.
22 Identifying these as including cases where the person is sentenced in accordance with the discretionary conditional release scheme under the Criminal Justice Act 1991, given an extended sentence for public protection or given an extended determinate sentence.
23 The relevance of these considerations was expressly acknowledged by the Government at Lords' Report, *Hansard* HL, col 937 (1 April 2014) per the Lord Wallace of Tankerness.
24 The reference is to *Skype families: the effects of being separated from mum or dad because of recent immigration rules*, Office of the Children's Commissioner for England, JCWI and Middlesex University, September 2015. Available at: http://www.childrenscommissioner.gov.uk/sites/default/files/publications/SkypeFamilies-CCO.pdf (accessed 15 December 2016).
25 Immigration (European Economic Area) Regulations 2006, SI 2006/1003, reg 24AA.
26 Immigration (European Economic Area) Regulations 2006, SI 2016/1003, reg 33.
27 Immigration (European Economic Area) Regulations 2006, SI 2006/1003, regs 29AA and Immigration (European Economic Area) Regulations 2006, SI 2006/1003, reg 41.
28 NIAA 2002, s 120.
29 *R (Kiarie) v Secretary of State for the Home Department* [2015] EWCA 1020, judgment awaited from the Supreme Court.
30 *Certification under section 94B of the Nationality, Immigration and Asylum Act 2002*, vs, Home Office, 20 January 2017.

SECTION 64—CONTINUATION OF LEAVE: REPEALS

> **Summary**
> Repeals provisions which allow a person's leave to continue on the same terms and conditions pending an appeal or administrative review of a decision to revoke or cancel leave.

4.2

64 Continuation of leave: repeals

(1) In the Immigration Act 1971 omit section 3D (continuation of leave following revocation).

(2) In section 2(2)(a) of the Special Immigration Appeals Commission Act 1997 (jurisdiction: appeals) omit "or 3D".

(3) In section 120(4)(b) of the Nationality, Immigration and Asylum Act 2002 (requirement to state additional grounds for application etc) omit "or 3D".

(4) In consequence of the repeals made by this section, the following are repealed—

　(a) paragraph 14(b)(i) of Schedule 1 to the Immigration, Asylum and Nationality Act 2006, and

　(b) paragraph 22 of Schedule 9 to the Immigration Act 2014.

(5) The repeals made by this section do not apply in relation to a person ("P") where—

　(a) P's leave was extended by virtue of section 3D of the Immigration Act 1971 immediately before 6 April 2015, and

　(b) immediately before the coming into force of this section an appeal by P against the variation or revocation of P's leave to enter or remain in the United Kingdom was pending within the meaning of section 104 of the Nationality, Immigration and Asylum Act 2002.

Commencement: 1 December 2016, Immigration Act 2016 (Commencement No 2 and Transitional Provisions) Regulations 2016, SI 2016/1037.

Amends: Repeals 3D of the Immigration Act 1971 and makes consequential amendments to the Special Immigration Appeals Commission Act 1997 and to the Nationality, Immigration and Asylum Act 2002.

Devolution: Applies throughout the UK.

This section repeals provisions which allow a person's leave to continue on the same terms and conditions pending an appeal or administrative review of a decision to revoke or cancel leave. The Explanatory Notes to the Act contend that the provisions revoked 'have no continuing purpose'.[1] This is currently true, but for reasons that merit closer examination.

During the passage of the Immigration Act 2014 examples were given of where those losing rights of appeal would instead be given an administrative review. These included where leave is revoked or cancelled.[2] This example disappeared when the Explanatory Notes to the Bill became the Explanatory Notes to the 2014 Act. The subsequent Immigration Rules on administrative review[3] do not provide for administrative review where a person's leave is cancelled or revoked. Such a person has no right of appeal and no administrative review and thus becomes an overstayer from the moment leave is cancelled, whether or not the decision is subsequently successfully challenged by means of judicial review.

---

1 Explanatory Notes, para 298.
2 Explanatory Notes to Bill 206-EN 2013–2014 at para 73 'an administrative review may be sought when a person's leave is curtailed or is revoked'. See: http://www.publications.parliament.uk/pa/bills/cbill/2013-2014/0110/en/14110en.htm (accessed 11 November 2016) and see HL Bill 84-EN 2013–14, para 77. Available at: http://www.publications.parliament.uk/pa/bills/lbill/2013-2014/0084/en/14084en.htm (accessed 11 November 2016).
3 HC 395, Appendix AR.

SECTION 65—DEEMED REFUSAL OF LEAVE TO ENTER: REPEALS

> **Summary**
> Repeals provisions which allow a person's leave to continue on the same terms and conditions pending an appeal or administrative review of a decision to revoke or cancel leave.

4.3

65 Deemed refusal of leave to enter: repeals

(1) In the Immigration Act 1971 omit paragraph 2A(9) of Schedule 2 (deemed refusal of leave to enter).

(2) In consequence of the repeal made by this section, paragraph 23 of Schedule 9 to the Immigration Act 2014 is repealed.

(3) The repeals made by this section do not apply in relation to a person if, immediately before the coming into force of this section, the person's appeal by virtue of paragraph 2A(9) of Schedule 2 to the Immigration Act 1971 against the cancellation of the person's leave to enter under paragraph 2A(8) of that Schedule was pending within the meaning of section 104 of the Nationality, Immigration and Asylum Act 2002.

Commencement: 1 December 2016, Immigration Act 2016 (Commencement No 2 and Transitional Provisions) Regulations 2016, SI 2016/1037.

Amends: Repeals para 2A(9) of Schedule 2 to the Immigration Act 1971 and para 23 of Schedule 9 to the Immigration Act 2014.

Devolution: Applies throughout the UK.

This section repeals provisions that allow a person's leave to continue on the same terms and conditions pending an appeal or administrative review of a decision to revoke or cancel leave. Paragraph 2A(9) applies where a person arrives at port with entry clearance that constitutes leave to enter. It provides that where such a person's leave is cancelled at port, they are to be treated as if refused leave to enter at a time when they had current entry clearance under Part 5 of the Nationality, Immigration and Asylum Act 2002.

Following the changes made to the appeals regime by the Immigration Act 2014, neither refusal of leave to enter nor cancellation of entry clearance at port gives rise to a right of appeal. Accordingly, the provision has no continuing purpose and hence this repeal. See comments on s 64 above.

Rights of appeal of those with a pending appeal at the time of the coming into effect of the section are preserved.

Part 5—Support etc for Certain Categories of Migrant

SUPPORT

5.1 Part 5 makes substantial changes to support entitlements and provision. Section 66 and Schedule 11 in this Part make changes to Home Office support and accommodation for those at the end of the asylum process and for other migrants. Section 68 introduces Schedule 12 which makes changes to local authority support for families with children and local authority support for some groups of care leavers.

Much of the detail of these provisions is left to wide regulation-making powers. Following strong criticisms by the House of Lords Select Committee on Delegated Powers and Regulatory Reform,[1] these were made subject to the affirmative procedure so that they may be scrutinised in Parliament. The Committee noted that as 'the purpose of the regulations is to provide for relief from destitution, we consider that the House will wish to scrutinise very carefully the nature of the assistance to be provided and the terms on which it is to be made available'.[2] Schedules 11 and 12 will, therefore, not be brought into force until the regulations have been drafted and laid before Parliament.

The Home Office will commence the two Schedules at the same time. It is understood that they will not come into force before April 2017. There is likely to be an informal consultation on the draft regulations before they are laid before Parliament and debated. There is provision for transitional arrangements enabling those supported under the current system to continue to receive this support.

Schedule 11 on Home Office support and accommodation applies to the whole of the UK. The provisions of Schedule 12 are currently drafted as applicable to England with powers given the Secretary of State to extend provisions to the devolved administrations by regulations.

The then Minister, the Rt Hon James Brokenshire MP, wrote to the Rt Hon Nicola Sturgeon MSP giving her notice that the Immigration Bill was coming on 13 August 2015. He said in that letter that 'we remain conscious of our commitment to discuss ways of enabling different powers in Scotland in

5.1 *A Guide to the Immigration Act 2016*

relation to the provision of support and advice for asylum seekers, as agreed by the Smith Commission. We will take forward those discussions separately'.[3]

The Government has initiated dialogues with the devolved administrations about how provisions may be brought into effect in the devolved administrations. The Scottish administration expressed concern about the provisions in Schedule 12 in a strongly worded letter to the Minister. See the detailed discussion of devolution in the commentary on Schedule 12 below.

Section 67 Unaccompanied refugee children: relocation and support, and ss 69–73 on the transfer of relevant children sit separately from the other provisions of Part 5, both offering limited responses to the refugee crisis. Section 67 requires the Government to relocate to the UK a specified (but unstated) number of unaccompanied children from Europe, and results from the lobbying from Lord Dubs and others seeking to secure commitments to assist 3000 children. Sections 69–73 put in place a mechanism for transferring responsibility for an unaccompanied child from one Local Authority (LA) to another. This is aimed at sharing the responsibility for unaccompanied children arriving in the UK in need of protection among a wider range of Local Authorities to relieve pressures on Kent and other social services departments which typically receive larger numbers of newly arrived children.

---

1 Delegated Powers and Regulatory Reform Committee, *17th Report of Session 2015/16: Immigration Bill*, HL Paper 73, 22 December 2015. Available at: http://www.publications.parliament.uk/pa/ld201516/ldselect/lddelreg/73/73.pdf (accessed 15 November 2016).
2 Ibid.
3 Rt Hon James Brokenshire MP, Written Response 29521, *Hansard*, 9 March 2016.

SECTION 66—SUPPORT FOR CERTAIN CATEGORIES OF MIGRANT AND SCHEDULE 11—SUPPORT FOR CERTAIN CATEGORIES OF MIGRANT

Summary

Repeals the Immigration and Asylum Act 1999 (IAA 1999), s 4.

Amends the definition of an asylum seeker for the purpose of support so that individuals making further submissions on asylum or protection grounds may access support under IAA 1999, s 95.

Introduces new s 95A of the IAA 1999 making provision for support for failed asylum seekers who face a 'genuine obstacle' to leaving the UK;

Part 5—Support etc for Certain Categories of Migrant **5.2**

> regulations may place time limitations on applying for support under this provision.
>
> Ends the continuation of s 95 support for families with children who reach the end of the asylum process. Families will be required instead to qualify for s 95A support and, if they do not, apply for support under new Local Authority scheme (in Schedule 12, outlined below).

5.2

66 Support for certain categories of migrant

Schedule 11 (support for certain categories of migrant) has effect.

Schedule 11
Support for certain categories of migrant
Part 1
Amendments of the Immigration Acts

Abolition of power to support certain categories of migrant

1 Section 4 of the Immigration and Asylum Act 1999 (provision of accommodation for failed asylum-seekers, etc) is repealed.

2 In consequence of the repeal made by paragraph 1—

    (a) in section 26A of the Immigration Act 1971, omit subsection (1)(b)(ii);

    (b) in the following provisions, omit "section 4 or"—

        (i) section 3A(7A) of the Protection from Eviction Act 1977;

        (ii) paragraph 3A(1) of Schedule 2 to the Housing (Northern Ireland) Order 1983 (S.I. 1983/1118 (N.I. 15));

        (iii) section 23A(5A) of the Rent (Scotland) Act 1984;

        (iv) paragraph 4A(1) of Schedule 1 to the Housing Act 1985;

        (v) paragraph 11B of Schedule 4 to the Housing (Scotland) Act 1988;

        (vi) paragraph 12A(1) of Schedule 1 to the Housing Act 1988;

    (c) in section 99 of the Immigration and Asylum Act 1999, in subsections (1) and (4), omit "4,";

    (d) in section 103 of that Act—

        (i) omit subsection (2A), and

5.2 *A Guide to the Immigration Act 2016*

    (ii) in subsections (6) and (7), for "section 4 or 95" substitute "section 95";

 (e) in section 118(1)(b) of that Act, omit "4,";

 (f) in section 166(5) of that Act, omit paragraph (za);

 (g) in the Nationality, Immigration and Asylum Act 2002—

    (i) in section 23, omit subsection (5),

    (ii) in section 26, in subsection (3), omit "4,",

    (iii) omit section 49,

    (iv) in section 51, in subsection (2), omit paragraph (b), and

    (v) in section 55, in subsection (2)(a), omit "4,";

 (h) in the Asylum and Immigration (Treatment of Claimants, etc.) Act 2004, omit section 10;

 (i) in the Immigration, Asylum and Nationality Act 2006, omit section 43(1)(b), (2), (5), (6) and (7);

 (j) in the UK Borders Act 2007—

    (i) in section 17, in subsection (1)(a), omit "(and section 4)", and

    (ii) in section 40, in subsection (1), omit paragraph (e);

 (k) in section 134 of the Criminal Justice and Immigration Act 2008, omit subsection (5);

 (l) in Schedule 1 to the Legal Aid, Sentencing and Punishment of Offenders Act 2012, in paragraph 31(1)(a), omit "4 or" and "persons temporarily admitted and";

 (m) in paragraph 8 of Schedule 3 to the Immigration Act 2014, omit paragraph (a).

Power to support people making further submissions in relation to protection claims

3(1) Section 94 of the Immigration and Asylum Act 1999 (interpretation of Part 6) is amended as follows.

(2) In subsection (1)—

 (a) for the definition of "asylum-seeker" substitute—

   ""asylum-seeker" means a person falling within subsection (2A) or (2B) (but see also subsection (3C));";

 (b) omit the definition of "claim for asylum";

 (c) before the definition of "housing accommodation" insert—

   ""further qualifying submissions" has the meaning given by subsection (2C);";

Part 5—Support etc for Certain Categories of Migrant **5.2**

  (d) after the definition of "Northern Ireland authority" insert—

    ""protection claim" has the meaning given by section 82(2) of the Nationality, Immigration and Asylum Act 2002;".

(3) After subsection (2) insert—

"(2A) A person is an asylum-seeker for the purposes of this Part if—

  (a) the person is at least 18 years old,

  (b) the person has made a protection claim, and

  (c) the person's claim—

    (i) has been recorded by the Secretary of State, but

    (ii) has not been determined.

(2B) A person is also an asylum-seeker for the purposes of this Part if—

  (a) the person is at least 18 years old,

  (b) the person has made further qualifying submissions (see subsection (2C)), and

  (c) the person's submissions—

    (i) have been recorded by the Secretary of State, but

    (ii) have not been determined before the end of such period as may be prescribed.

(2C) A person makes "further qualifying submissions" if—

  (a) the person makes submissions to the Secretary of State that the person's removal from the United Kingdom would breach any of the obligations mentioned in section 82(2)(a)(i) or (ii) of the Nationality, Immigration and Asylum Act 2002 (protection claims), and

  (b) the submissions fall to be considered by the Secretary of State under paragraph 353 of the immigration rules."

(4) In subsection (3), for "claim for asylum" substitute " protection claim".

(5) After subsection (3) insert—

"(3A) For the purposes of this Part, further qualifying submissions made by a person are determined—

  (a) at the end of a prescribed period beginning with the relevant day (see subsection (3B)), or

  (b) in a case where no period is prescribed for the purposes of paragraph (a), at the end of the relevant day.

(3B) In subsection (3A) "the relevant day" means the day on which the Secretary of State notifies the person that the submissions made by the person are to be—

             (a)   accepted,

             (b)   rejected without being treated as a fresh protection claim, or

             (c)   treated as a fresh protection claim.

       (3C) If—

             (a)   further qualifying submissions made by a person are rejected without being treated as a fresh protection claim, and

             (b)   the person is granted permission to apply for judicial review of that rejection,

                   the person is to be treated as an asylum-seeker for the purposes of this Part during the review period (see subsection (3D)).

       (3D) In subsection (3C) "the review period" means the period—

             (a)   beginning with the day on which permission to apply for judicial review is granted, and

             (b)   ending with—

                   (i)   a prescribed period beginning with the day on which the judicial review is disposed of, or

                   (ii) in a case where no period is prescribed for the purposes of sub-paragraph (i), that day."

(6)   In subsection (8), after "subsection (3)" insert " or (3B) ".

4   In consequence of the repeal made by paragraph 3(2)(b)—

       (a)   in section 96 of the Immigration and Asylum Act 1999 (ways in which support may be provided), in subsection (1)(c), for "claim for asylum" substitute " protection claim ";

       (b)   in section 141 of that Act (fingerprinting)—

             (i)   in subsections (7)(e), (8)(e) and (9)(e), for "claim for asylum" substitute " protection claim ", and

             (ii) in subsection (15), for " "Claim for asylum"" substitute " "Protection claim" ";

       (c)   in section 167 of that Act (interpretation), in subsection (1), in the definition of "claim for asylum", for "Parts V and VI and section 141" substitute " Part 5 ";

       (d)   in Schedule 8 to that Act (provision of support: regulations), in paragraph 9(2)(b), for "claim for asylum" substitute "protection claim ";

       (e)   in section 135 of the Criminal Justice and Immigration Act 2008 (support: supplemental), in subsection (5), for "claim for asylum" substitute " protection claim ".

Part 5—Support etc for Certain Categories of Migrant **5.2**

Power to support failed asylum-seekers

5   Part 6 of the Immigration and Asylum Act 1999 (support for asylum-seekers) is amended as follows.

6   The heading of the Part becomes " Support for asylum-seekers, etc ".

7(1)   Section 94 (interpretation of Part 6) is amended as follows.

(2)   In subsection (1)—

    (a)   in the definition of "dependant", after "asylum-seeker" insert ", a failed asylum-seeker ";

    (b)   after the definition of "the Executive" insert—

        ""failed asylum-seeker" has the meaning given by subsection (2D);";

    (c)   for the definition of "supported person" substitute—

        ""supported person" means—

        (a)   in relation to support under section 95, an asylum-seeker, or a dependant of an asylum-seeker, who has applied for support and for whom support is provided under that section, and

        (b)   in relation to support under section 95A, a failed asylum-seeker, or a dependant of a failed asylum-seeker, who has applied for support and for whom support is provided under that section."

(3)   In subsection (2), after "section 95" insert " or 95A ".

(4)   After subsection (2C) (inserted by paragraph 3(3) above) insert—

    "(2D) A person is a failed asylum-seeker for the purposes of this Part if—

        (a)   the person is at least 18 years old,

        (b)   the person—

            (i)   was an asylum-seeker, or

            (ii)   would have been an asylum-seeker at any time if the person had been at least 18 years old at that time,

        (c)   the person's protection claim has been rejected, and

        (d)   the person is not an asylum-seeker."

(5)   Omit subsections (5) and (6).

8   In section 95 (persons for whom support may be provided), the heading becomes " Support for asylum-seekers, etc ".

9 After section 95 insert—

"95A Support for failed asylum-seekers, etc who are unable to leave UK

(1) The Secretary of State may provide, or arrange for the provision of, support for a person, for such period or periods as may be prescribed, if—

    (a) the person is a failed asylum-seeker, or a dependant of a failed asylum-seeker,

    (b) an application for support under this section is made in respect of the person which meets such requirements as may be prescribed,

    (c) it appears to the Secretary of State that the person is destitute, or is likely to become destitute within such period as may be prescribed, and

    (d) the person faces a genuine obstacle to leaving the United Kingdom.

(2) Subsections (3) to (8) of section 95 (meaning of "destitute") apply for the purposes of this section as they apply for the purposes of that section.

(3) Regulations made by the Secretary of State may make provision for determining what is, or is not, to be regarded as a genuine obstacle to leaving the United Kingdom for the purposes of this section.

(4) The Secretary of State may make regulations prescribing other criteria to be used in determining—

    (a) whether or not to provide support, or arrange for the provision of support, for a person under this section;

    (b) whether or not to continue to provide support, or arrange for the provision of support, for a person under this section.

(5) Regulations under subsection (4) may, in particular—

    (a) provide for the provision of support (or the continuation of the provision of support) to be subject to conditions;

    (b) provide for the provision of support (or the continuation of the provision of support) to be a matter for the Secretary of State's discretion to a prescribed extent or in cases of a prescribed description.

(6) A condition imposed by regulations under subsection (5)(a) may, in particular, relate to any of the following—

    (a) any matter relating to the use of the support provided;

    (b) compliance with a condition imposed under Schedule 10 to the Immigration Act 2016 (immigration bail);

    (c) the person's performance of, or participation in, community activities in accordance with arrangements made by the Secretary of State.

Part 5—Support etc for Certain Categories of Migrant **5.2**

(7) A copy of any conditions imposed by regulations under subsection (5)(a) must be given to the supported person.

(8) For the purposes of subsection (6)(c)—

(a) "community activities" means activities that appear to the Secretary of State to be beneficial to the public or a section of the public, and

(b) the Secretary of State may, in particular—

(i) appoint one person to supervise or manage the performance of, or participation in, activities by another person;

(ii) enter into a contract (with a local authority or any other person) for the provision of services by way of making arrangements for community activities in accordance with this section;

(iii) pay, or arrange for the payment of, allowances to a person performing or participating in community activities in accordance with arrangements under this section.

(9) Regulations by virtue of subsection (6)(c) may, in particular, provide for a condition requiring the performance of, or participation in, community activities to apply to a person only if—

(a) accommodation is to be, or is being, provided for the person under this section, and

(b) the Secretary of State has made arrangements for community activities in an area that includes the place where the accommodation is to be, or is being, provided.

(10) A local authority or other person may undertake to manage or participate in arrangements for community activities in accordance with this section.

(11) The powers conferred by Schedule 8 (supplementary regulation-making powers) are exercisable with respect to the powers conferred by this section as they are exercisable with respect to the powers conferred by section 95, but with the modification in subsection (12).

(12) Paragraph 9 of Schedule 8 (notice to quit) has effect with respect to the powers conferred by this section as if sub-paragraph (2)(b) were omitted."

10(1) Section 96 (ways in which support may be provided) is amended as follows.

(2) In subsection (1)—

(a) after "section 95" insert " or 95A ";

(b) in paragraph (c), for "the asylum-seeker" substitute " an asylum-seeker ";

5.2 A Guide to the Immigration Act 2016

(c) in paragraph (d)—

(i) for "the asylum-seeker" substitute " an asylum-seeker ", and

(ii) after "dependants" insert ", or a failed asylum-seeker and his dependants, ";

(d) in paragraph (e)—

(i) for "the asylum-seeker" substitute " an asylum-seeker ", and

(ii) after "dependants" insert ", or a failed asylum-seeker and his dependants, ".

(3) After subsection (1) insert—

"(1A) Support under section 95A may, in particular, be provided in the form of vouchers which may be exchanged for goods or services (as well as in the form of cash)."

(4) In subsection (2), after "section 95" insert " or 95A ".

11(1) Section 97 (supplemental) is amended as follows.

(2) In subsection (1)—

(a) after "section 95" insert " or 95A ";

(b) after "regard to" insert " the following ";

(c) in paragraph (a), at the beginning insert " in the case of the provision of accommodation under section 95, ".

(3) In subsections (4), (5) and (7), after "section 95" insert " or 95A ".

(4) After subsection (7) insert—

"(8) A tenancy is not a Scottish secure tenancy (within the meaning of the Housing (Scotland) Act 2001 (asp 10)) if it is granted in order to provide accommodation under section 95A.

(9) A tenancy which would be a Scottish secure tenancy but for subsection (8) becomes a Scottish secure tenancy if the landlord notifies the tenant that it is to be regarded as such."

12 In section 98, the heading becomes " Temporary support for asylum-seekers, etc ".

13 After section 98 insert—

"98A Temporary support for failed asylum-seekers, etc

(1) The Secretary of State may provide, or arrange for the provision of, support for persons within subsection (2) who it appears to the Secretary of State—

(a) may be destitute, and

(b) may face a genuine obstacle to leaving the United Kingdom.

(2) The persons referred to in subsection (1) are—

Part 5—Support etc for Certain Categories of Migrant **5.2**

        (a)   failed asylum-seekers, and

        (b)   dependants of failed asylum-seekers.

  (3)   Support may be provided under this section only until the Secretary of State is able to determine whether support may be provided under section 95A.

  (4)   Subsections (3) to (12) of section 95A apply for the purposes of this section as they apply for the purposes of that section."

14(1) Section 99 (provision of support by local authorities) is amended as follows.

  (2)   In subsection (1), for "or 98" substitute " 95A, 98 or 98A ".

  (3)   In subsection (3)—

        (a)   after "section 95" insert " or 95A ";

        (b)   for "section 96(1) and (2)" substitute " section 96(1) to (2) ".

  (4)   In subsection (4), for "or 98" substitute " 95A, 98 or 98A ".

15   In section 100 (local authority and other assistance for Secretary of State), in subsection (1), after "section 95" insert " or 95A ".

16   In section 101 (reception zones), in subsection (3), after "section 95" (in both places where it occurs) insert " or 95A ".

17   In section 112 (recovery of expenditure on support: misrepresentation etc), in subsections (1)(b) and (3), for "section 95 or 98" substitute " section 95, 95A, 98 or 98A ".

18   In section 113 (recovery of expenditure on support from sponsor), in subsections (1)(b), (4) and (5)(a), after "section 95" insert " or 95A ".

19(1) Section 114 (overpayments) is amended as follows.

  (2)   In subsection (1), for "section 95 or 98" substitute " section 95, 95A, 98 or 98A ".

  (3)   In subsection (4), for "section 95" substitute " section 95, 95A or 98A".

20   In section 118 (housing authority accommodation), in subsection (1)(b), for "or 98" substitute " 95A, 98 or 98A ".

21(1) Section 122 (support for children) is amended as follows.

  (2)   In subsection (1), after "section 95" insert " or 95A ".

  (3)   In subsection (2), after "section 95" insert " or (as the case may be) 95A ".

  (4)   In subsections (3) and (4), after "section 95" insert " or 95A ".

  (5)   In subsection (5)—

        (a)   in paragraph (b)(i), after "section 95" insert " or 95A ", and

        (b)   in paragraph (b)(ii), after "section 95" insert " or (as the case may be) 95A ".

5.2 *A Guide to the Immigration Act 2016*

22(1) Section 125 (entry of premises) is amended as follows.

  (2) In subsection (1), for "section 95 or 98" substitute " section 95, 95A, 98 or 98A ".

  (3) In subsection (2)—

    (a) in paragraph (b), at the beginning insert "in the case of accommodation provided under section 95 or 98, ";

    (b) after that paragraph insert—

      "(ba) in the case of accommodation provided under section 95A or 98A, the accommodation is being used for any purpose other than the accommodation of the failed asylum-seeker or any dependant of his,".

23 In section 127 (requirement to supply information about redirection of post), in subsection (1)(c), after "asylum-seekers" insert " or failed asylum-seekers".

24(1) Section 166 (regulations and orders) is amended as follows.

  (2) In subsection (5) (regulations subject to the affirmative procedure) for the "or" at the end of paragraph (c) substitute—

    "(ca) section 95A, or".

  (3) After subsection (5) insert—

    "(5A) No regulations under paragraph 1 of Schedule 8 which make provision with respect to the powers conferred by section 95A are to be made unless a draft of the regulations has been laid before Parliament and approved by a resolution of each House.

    (5B) Subsection (5A) does not apply to regulations under paragraph 1 of that Schedule which make provision of the kind mentioned in paragraph 3(a) of that Schedule."

  (4) In subsection (6) (regulations subject to the negative procedure) for the "or" at the end of paragraph (a) substitute—

    "(aa) under the provision mentioned in subsection (5A) and containing regulations to which that subsection applies, or".

25 In section 26A of the Immigration Act 1971 (registration card), in subsection (1)(b), after sub-paragraph (i) insert—

    "(ia) a claim for support under section 95A of the Immigration and Asylum Act 1999 (whether or not made by that person)."

26(1) The Nationality, Immigration and Asylum Act 2002 is amended as follows.

  (2) In section 18 (definition of asylum-seeker for purposes of Part 2), omit subsection (2).

  (3) In section 26 (withdrawal of support), in subsection (3)—

Part 5—Support etc for Certain Categories of Migrant **5.2**

    (a)   for "95 or 98" substitute " 95, 95A, 98 or 98A ";

    (b)   omit "(asylum-seeker)".

(4) In section 35—

    (a)   in subsection (2), for "section 95 or 98" substitute " section 95, 95A, 98 or 98A ";

    (b)   in subsection (3), after "section 95" insert " or 95A ".

(5) In section 43—

    (a)   in subsection (1), for "asylum-seeker" substitute " asylum-seekers and failed asylum-seekers, etc ";

    (b)   the heading of that section becomes " Form of support under Part 6 of the Immigration and Asylum Act 1999 ".

(6) In section 51 (choice of form of support), in subsection (2), omit the "and" after paragraph (b) and after paragraph (c) insert ", and

    (d)   sections 95A and 98A of that Act (support for destitute failed asylum-seekers)."

(7) In section 55 (late claim for asylum: refusal of support), in subsection (2), after paragraph (a) insert—

    "(aa)   sections 95A and 98A of that Act (support for failed asylum-seeker, & c),".

(8) In Schedule 3 (withholding and withdrawal of support)—

    (a)   omit paragraph 7A;

    (b)   in paragraph 14(1) and (2), for ", 7 or 7A" substitute " or 7 ".

27   In section 9 of the Asylum and Immigration (Treatment of Claimants, etc.) Act 2004 (failed asylum-seekers: withdrawal of support)—

    (a)   omit subsections (1) and (4);

    (b)   in subsection (3)(a) and (b), omit "other than paragraph 7A".

28   In the Immigration, Asylum and Nationality Act 2006, omit section 44 (power to repeal paragraph 7A of Schedule 3 to the Nationality, Immigration and Asylum Act 2002).

29   In section 40 of the UK Borders Act 2007 (supply of Revenue and Customs information), in subsection (1)(f), for "asylum-seekers and their dependants" substitute " persons ".

30   In Schedule 3 to the Immigration Act 2014 (excluded residential tenancy agreements), in paragraph 8 (accommodation provided by virtue of immigration provisions)—

    (a)   in paragraph (b) after "95" insert " or 95A ", and

    (b)   in paragraph (c) after "98" insert " or 98A ".

5.2 *A Guide to the Immigration Act 2016*

Accommodation centres: definition of "asylum-seeker" etc

31(1) Section 18 of the Nationality, Immigration and Asylum Act 2002 (definition of asylum-seeker for purposes of Part 2) is amended as follows.

(2) For subsection (1) substitute—

"(1) For the purposes of this Part a person is an "asylum-seeker" if—

(a) the person is at least 18 years old,

(b) the person has made a protection claim, and

(c) the person's claim—

(i) has been recorded by the Secretary of State, but

(ii) has not been determined.

(1A) A person is also an "asylum-seeker" for the purposes of this Part if the person is an asylum-seeker for the purposes of Part 6 of the Immigration and Asylum Act 1999 by virtue of section 94(2B) or (3C) of that Act."

(3) For subsection (3) substitute—

"(3) Protection claim" has the meaning given by section 82(2)."

32(1) In consequence of the amendment made by paragraph 31(3), section 26A of the Immigration Act 1971 (registration card) is amended as follows.

(2) In subsection (1)(b)(i), for "claim for asylum" substitute " protection claim".

(3) In subsection (2), for " "claim for asylum"" substitute " "protection claim"".

33 In consequence of the amendments made by paragraph 31, the Nationality, Immigration and Asylum Act 2002 is amended as follows.

34 In section 16 (establishment of accommodation centres), in subsection (3)(b), for "claims for asylum" substitute " protection claims ".

35 In section 21(3), for "claim for asylum" substitute " protection claim".

36 In section 29 (facilities), in subsection (1)(c), for "claim for asylum" substitute " protection claim ".

37(1) Section 55 (late claim for asylum: refusal of support) is amended as follows.

(2) In subsections (1)(a), (3)(a) and (6)(a), for "claim for asylum" substitute " protection claim ".

(3) In subsection (9), for " "claim for asylum"" substitute " "protection claim"".

(4) The heading of the section becomes " Late protection claim: refusal of support ".

38 In section 70 (induction), in the definition of "asylum-seeker" in subsection (3), after "section 18(1)(a)" insert " of this Act and section 94(2B)(a) of the Immigration and Asylum Act 1999 ".

Part 5—Support etc for Certain Categories of Migrant **5.2**

39(1) Section 71 (asylum-seeker: residence, etc restriction) is amended as follows.

  (2) In subsection (1)(a), for "claim for asylum" substitute " protection claim ".

  (3) In subsection (5), for " "claim for asylum"" substitute " "protection claim"".

40 In Schedule 3 (withholding and withdrawal of support), in paragraph 17(1), for the definition of "asylum-seeker" substitute—

""asylum-seeker" has the meaning given by section 18,".

Repeal of uncommenced provisions

41 The following provisions of the Nationality, Immigration and Asylum Act 2002, which contain amendments that have never been brought into force, are repealed—

  (a) section 44 (which amends sections 94 and 95 of the Immigration and Asylum Act 1999);

  (b) sections 45 and 46;

  (c) section 47 (which inserts a new section 122 into that Act);

  (d) section 53 (which inserts new sections 103, 103A and 103B into that Act).

42 In Schedule 15 to the National Health Service (Wales) Act 2006, in paragraph 2, for sub-paragraph (7) substitute—

"(7) Subsections (3) and (5) to (8) of section 95 of the Immigration and Asylum Act 1999, and paragraph 2 of Schedule 8 to that Act, apply for the purposes of sub-paragraph (6) as they apply for the purposes of that section, but with references in section 95(5) and (7) and that paragraph to the Secretary of State being read as references to a local social services authority."

43 In Schedule 3 to the National Health Service (Consequential Provisions) Act 2006, omit paragraph 9.

44 In section 21 of the Care Act 2014, for subsections (2) and (3) substitute—

"(2) For the purposes of subsection (1), section 95(3) and (5) to (8) of, and paragraph 2 of Schedule 8 to, the 1999 Act apply but with references in section 95(5) and (7) and that paragraph to the Secretary of State being read as references to the local authority in question."

45 In section 46 of the Social Services and Well-being (Wales) Act 2014, for subsections (2) and (3) substitute—

"(2) For the purposes of subsection (1), section 95(3) and (5) to (8) of, and paragraph 2 of Schedule 8 to, the 1999 Act apply but with references in section 95(5) and (7) and that paragraph to the Secretary of State being read as references to the local authority in question."

Part 2
Transitional and saving provision

46(1) The repeals made by paragraphs 1 and 2 do not apply in relation to—

   (a) any person for whom accommodation is being provided under section 4 of the Immigration and Asylum Act 1999 immediately before the day on which those paragraphs come into force,

   (b) any person who has made an application before that day for accommodation to be provided under that section and whose application has not been determined or withdrawn before that day,

   (c) any person who has appealed before that day against a decision not to provide accommodation for the person under that section, or a decision not to continue to provide accommodation for the person under that section, and whose appeal has not been determined or withdrawn before that day, and

   (d) any dependant of a person within paragraph (a), (b) or (c).

This is subject to sub-paragraph (2).

   (2) The repeals made by paragraph 2(d) (which remove the right to appeal against a decision not to continue to provide accommodation for a person under section 4 of the Immigration and Asylum Act 1999) apply in relation to any decision not to continue to provide accommodation under that section for any person within sub-paragraph (1) which is made on or after the day on which paragraph 2(d) comes into force.

   (3) On and after the day on which paragraphs 1 and 2 come into force, section 4 of the Immigration and Asylum Act 1999 has effect in relation to persons within sub-paragraph (1) as if in subsection (11)(b) the word "not" were omitted.

   (4) In this paragraph "dependant" has the same meaning as in Part 6 of the Immigration and Asylum Act 1999 (see section 94 of that Act).

47(1) The repeal made by paragraph 7(5) does not apply in relation to—

   (a) any person for whom support is being provided under section 95 of the Immigration and Asylum Act 1999 by virtue of section 94(5) of that Act immediately before the day on which paragraph 7(5) comes into force,

   (b) any person who has made an application before that day for support to be provided under section 95 of that Act and whose application has not been determined or withdrawn before that day,

   (c) any person who has appealed before that day against a decision not to provide support for the person under that section, or a decision not to continue to provide support for the person under that section, and whose appeal has not been determined or withdrawn before that day, and

   (d) any dependant of a person within paragraph (a), (b) or (c).

Part 5—Support etc for Certain Categories of Migrant **5.2**

(2) Where by virtue of sub-paragraph (1) a person is provided with support under section 95 of the Immigration and Asylum Act 1999 by virtue of section 94(5) of that Act on or after the day on which paragraph 7(5) comes into force, section 103 of that Act (appeals) does not apply in relation to any decision not to continue to provide that support for that person which is made on or after that day.

(3) In this paragraph "dependant" has the same meaning as in Part 6 of the Immigration and Asylum Act 1999 (see section 94 of that Act).

48 Schedule 3 to the Nationality, Immigration and Asylum Act 2002 (withholding and withdrawal of support) has effect as if—

(a) after paragraph 7C there were inserted—

"Eighth class of ineligible person: transitional cases

7D(1) Paragraph 1 applies to a person if—

(a) the person is a transitionally-supported person (see sub-paragraph (3)),

(b) the Secretary of State has certified that, in the Secretary of State's opinion, the person has failed without reasonable excuse to take reasonable steps—

(i) to leave the United Kingdom voluntarily, or

(ii) to place himself in a position in which he is able to leave the United Kingdom voluntarily,

(c) the person has received a copy of the Secretary of State's certificate, and

(d) the period of 14 days, beginning with the date on which the person receives the copy of the certificate, has elapsed.

(2) Paragraph 1 also applies to a dependant of a person to whom that paragraph applies by virtue of sub-paragraph (1).

(3) A person is a "transitionally-supported person" if—

(a) accommodation is provided for the person by virtue of section 4 of the Immigration and Asylum Act 1999 as that section has effect by virtue of paragraph 46 of Schedule 11 to the Immigration Act 2016, or

(b) support is provided for the person under section 95 of the Immigration and Asylum Act 1999 by virtue of section 94(5) of that Act, as that provision has effect by virtue of paragraph 47 of that Schedule.

(4) For the purpose of sub-paragraph (1)(d), if the Secretary of State sends a copy of a certificate by first class post to a person's last known address, the person is treated as receiving the copy on the second day after the day on which it was posted.

5.2 A Guide to the Immigration Act 2016

>   (5) The Secretary of State may by regulations vary the period specified in sub-paragraph (1)(d).", and
>
>   (b) in paragraph 14 (information), references to paragraph 7 included a reference to the paragraph 7D treated as inserted by this Schedule.

Commencement: Not yet in force.

Amends: Immigration and Asylum Act 1999 (IAA 1999); Nationality, Immigration and Asylum Act 2002 (NIAA 2002) and consequential amendments to numerous other statutes.

Regulations: may be made by the Secretary of State (SSHD) under the following provisions:

s 94(2B)(c)(ii) of the IAA 1999 prescribing the period after which a person's 'further qualifying submissions' have been recorded but not determined when they will be treated as an asylum seeker for the purpose of support, inserted by para 3(3);

s 94(3A)(a) of the IAA 1999 prescribing the period from the relevant day when further qualifying submissions are deemed to be determined, inserted by para 3(5);

s 94(3D)(b)(i) of the IAA 1999 prescribing the period after which a person ceases to be treated as an asylum seeker when a judicial review is disposed of, inserted by para 3(5);

s 95A(1) of the IAA 1999 prescribing the period or periods in which the Secretary of State may provide, or arrange for the provision of, support to a failed asylum seeker and their dependants meeting various conditions, inserted by para 9;

s 95A(1)(c) of the IAA 1999 prescribing the period in which a person is likely to become destitute for the purpose of qualifying for support, inserted by para 9;

s 95A(3) of the IAA 1999 to determine what is a genuine obstacle for leaving the UK, inserted by para 9;

s 95A(4) of the IAA 1999 to prescribe criteria for determining whether or not to provide or arrange to provide support, or to continue to do so;

all of which are subject to the affirmative procedure, s 166(5) of the IAA 1999, inserted by para 24(2).

Regulations may also be made under new para 7D(5) of Schedule 3 to the NIAA 2002 allowing the SSHD to vary the period when a transitionally-supported person ceases to become eligible for local authority services after receiving a certificate stating they have failed without reasonable excuse to

Part 5—Support etc for Certain Categories of Migrant **5.2.1**

take steps to leave the UK voluntarily, inserted by para 48, subject to the negative procedure in Parliament, para 16 of Schedule 3 to that Act.

Definitions:

'asylum-seeker', IA 1999, s 94(1), as amended by Schedule 11, paras 3(2)–(3); NIAA 2002, s 18(1) and (1A) as substituted by Schedule 11, para 31(2);

'community activities', activities that appear to the SSHD to be beneficial to the public or to a section of the public, IAA 1999, s 95A(8) as inserted by Schedule 11, para 9;

'dependant' IAA 1999, s 94(1);

'destitute' IAA 1999, s 95(3)–(8);

'determined' IAA 1999, s 94(3);

'failed asylum-seeker' IAA 1999, s 94(1) and (2D) as inserted by Schedule 11, para 7(2)(b) and 7(4);

'further qualifying submissions', IAA 1999, s 94(2C), as inserted by Schedule 11, para 3(3);

'genuine obstacle to leaving the United Kingdom' may be set out in regulations made under s 95A(3) of the IAA 1999 as inserted by Schedule 11, para 9;

'protection claim', IAA 1999, s 94(1) as amended by Schedule 11, para 3(2); NIAA 2002, s 18(3) as substituted by Schedule 11, para 31(3);

'relevant day' IAA 1999, s 94(3B) as inserted by Schedule 11, para 3(5);

'review period' IAA 1999, s 94(3D) as inserted by Schedule 11, para 3(5);

'Scottish secure tenancy' Housing (Scotland) Act 2001;

'supported person' IAA 1999, s 94(1) as substituted by Schedule 11, para 7(c);

'transitionally supported person' NIAA 2002, Schedule 3 para 7D(3), as substituted by Schedule 11, para 48.

Devolution: Applies throughout the UK.

Section 66 simply introduces the Schedule; all of the relevant provisions are in Schedule 11.

Repeal of section 4 of the Immigration and Asylum Act 1999

5.2.1 Paragraph 1 of Schedule 11 repeals s 4 of IAA 1999. Under IAA 1999, s 4, the Secretary of State has a broad power to provide support and accommodation to people who have temporary admission in the UK, or

5.2.1 A Guide to the Immigration Act 2016

are released from detention on temporary admission or bail. This is used to support those who reach the end of the asylum process and have lodged further submissions with the Home Office or who are unable to leave the UK due to a genuine obstacle. The power is also used to provide support to destitute migrants on temporary admission who have never claimed asylum, in order to prevent a breach of their human rights.

Following the repeal of IAA 1999, s 4, Schedule 11 makes separate provision for support and accommodation for people making further submissions on protection grounds (see below) but this does not include those who may make further submissions on Article 8 of the European Convention on Human Rights(ECHR) or on other grounds.

The Schedule makes separate provision under new s 95A of IAA 1999 for failed asylum seekers who are unable to leave the UK but the restrictions on access to this form of support that may be introduced through regulations may make this support available to a more limited group of people than is currently the case.

There is no power in Part 5 of the Act to support single adults who have never claimed asylum, with the exception of young people leaving care for whom there is a separate framework for support (see the commentary on Schedule 12). Examples of those affected include:

- stateless persons who have never claimed asylum;
- those who have never claimed asylum but who are attempting to return to their country of origin or former habitual residence and either their country will not admit them, they cannot be documented or there are delays in documenting them; and
- persons who have never claimed asylum but have a claim pending before the Home Office to regularise their status such as people brought to the UK as children who are found to have no lawful status or people applying to remain in the UK under Article 8 of the ECHR protecting the right to private and family life.

Currently, individuals in these circumstances, who have temporary admission but have never claimed asylum, are supported under the general power to accommodate under IAA 1999, s 4 that is due to be repealed.

There is a power under Part 3 of the Immigration Act 2016 (IA 2016) that could potentially be used to provide support and accommodation. Paragraph 9 of Schedule 10 provides powers for the Secretary of State to enable people to meet bail conditions. This includes a power at para 9(2) to provide support and accommodation to a person who is on immigration bail and subject to a condition requiring them to live at a specified address who would not be able to support themselves. This power may only be exercised where there are exceptional circumstances justifying its use (para 9(3)).

As those currently on temporary admission and temporary release will be deemed to be on immigration bail when Schedule 10 to IA 2016 comes into force, and will be subject to conditions of residence, this provides a general power that could potentially be used to provide support to those who are not asylum seekers who have temporary admission. The language of 'exceptional circumstances' in para 9(3) reflects the language of the current Home Office guidance on section 4 support.[1]

The use of this power may be limited by Home Office guidance as there is no power to make regulations in relation to the power to provide support under para 9(2). Challenges to guidance produced by the Home Office are likely to focus on using, or expanding the use of, this power.

There is no statutory right of appeal against the exercise of the power under para 9(2). Many persons who are not asylum seekers but access s 4 support have only been able to do so through exercising their right of appeal to the Asylum Support Tribunal against refusal of s 4 support in their case. Judicial review would be the available remedy against a decision to refuse support.

Transitional provision is made for those in receipt of support under IAA 1999, s 4 when Schedule 11 is commenced (see below).

---

[1] *Asylum support: section 4 policy and process*, UK Visas and Immigration, 4 April 2016. Available at: https://www.gov.uk/government/publications/asylum-support-section-4-policy-and-process (accessed 15 November 2016).

Support for people making further submissions in relation to protection claims

5.2.2 Currently persons who reach the end of the asylum process and make further submissions may access support under s 4 of the IAA 1999 while their submissions are being considered. If their further submissions are accepted as a fresh asylum claim (currently defined in s 94(1) of IAA 1999 as a claim that it would be contrary to the UK's obligations under the Refugee Convention, or under Article 3 of the ECHR for the claimant to be removed from, or required to leave, the UK), they may access support under s 95 of the IAA 1999.

The Home Office had conceded that those with outstanding claims under Article 8 of the ECHR claims may also be eligible for support under s 4 of IAA 1999, settling the case of *R (Mulumba) and First Tier Tribunal (Asylum Support) and the Secretary of State for the Home Department* (CO/2114/2014) where this issue

5.2.2 A Guide to the Immigration Act 2016

was raised. The First Tier Tribunal (Asylum Support) also held, in its decision in AS/14/11/32141 of Principal Judge Storey in August 2015, that *Birmingham County Council v Clue* [2010] EWCA Civ 460 applied to asylum support.[1] In that case, it was held that the local authority should not have refused assistance where the claimant was destitute and had a pending application to remain under Article 8 of the ECHR which was not abusive or hopeless.

Section 4 of the IAA 1999 will be repealed and para 3 of Schedule 11 makes new provision for those making further submissions on protection grounds to be supported under s 95 of the IAA 1999.

Paragraph 3(2) amends the definition in s 94(1) of the IAA 1999 of an asylum seeker to whom support is provided under the IAA 1999, s 95(1) to include:

- an adult who has made a protection claim that has been recorded but not determined by the Secretary of State (new s 94(2A) of the IAA 1999);
- an adult who has made further qualifying submissions that have been recorded by the Secretary of State and have not been determined by a prescribed period (new s 94(2B) of the IAA 1999); and
- an adult whose further qualifying submissions have been rejected without being treated as a fresh protection claim and who is granted permission to apply for judicial review of that rejection (new s 94(3C) of the IAA 1999).

A protection claim is defined (IAA 1999, s 94(1) as amended by para 3(2)(d)) with reference to NIAA 2002, s 82(2), that is as a claim that would breach the UK's obligations under the Refugee Convention or its obligations in relation to persons eligible for humanitarian protection. Further qualifying submissions are similarly defined as submissions that removal would breach the obligations mentioned in s 82(2)(a)(i) or (ii) of the NIAA 2002 (new s 94(2C) of the IAA 1999): removal would breach the UK's obligations under the Refugee Convention or its obligations in relation to persons eligible for a grant of humanitarian protection In its briefing paper to inform the House of Lords committee stage consideration of the Bill, the government stated that the Bill was not intended to alter the support framework for destitute asylum seekers but to expand it to include those lodging further submissions or granted permission to bring a judicial review in relation to their protection claim.[2]

No provision is made in this Part of the Act for those with outstanding applications or submissions on Article 8 of the ECHR grounds. See the above commentary on how the power in Schedule 10, para 9 could be used.

The drafting of new s 94(2B)(2)(c)(ii) of the IAA 1999, inserted by para 3 of Schedule 11, enables the Secretary of State to prescribe in regulations a period during which she may consider further qualifying submissions without being under a duty to provide support. During this period, the individual claimant would remain destitute. The Home Office indicated that the period would be two days where there are exceptional circumstances, or five days otherwise as in current guidance. This was confirmed by the Minister in the House of Commons:

> 'Once submissions are lodged, the person may seek support under section 4(2) of the 1999 Act, but that is normally provided only if a decision on the further submissions and accompanying support application is not made within five working days. Special consideration will continue to be given to cases in which the person is clearly in a vulnerable position, for example because of a disability or in the case of a pregnant woman. In such cases, support is usually granted if a decision on the further submissions is not made within two working days. We expect to continue those special provisions under the new arrangements and will reflect them in the regulations.'[3]

In *MK and AH and Refugee Action* [2012] EWHC 1896 (Admin) the Home Office policy of delaying 15 working days before making decisions on s 4 applications in further submissions cases was found to be unlawful. The policy was held to give rise to a significant risk of breaches of Article 3 of the ECHR and of the EU Reception Directive.[4]

New s 94(3A)(b) of the IAA 1999 makes provision for when further qualifying submissions are deemed to be determined for the purpose of support under Part 6 of the IAA 1999. They are deemed to be determined on the day on which the Secretary of State notifies the person that the submissions are accepted, rejected without being treated as a fresh protection claim, or treated as a fresh protection claim (new s 94(3B) of the IAA 1999) unless a longer period is prescribed (new s 94(3B)(a) of that Act).

In the case of a person granted permission to bring a judicial review of a decision not to accept further submissions as a fresh protection claim, they are treated as an asylum seeker for the purpose of support until the day on which the judicial review is disposed of, unless regulations prescribe a longer period (new s 94(3D)(b) of the IAA 1999). If no regulations are made, individuals risk their support being terminated immediately.

---

1 *Briefing note: Article 8 applications and eligibility for section 4 support*, Deborah Gellner, Asylum Support Appeals Project, February 2015 updated September 2016. Available at: http://www.asaproject.org/uploads/Feb_2015_ASAP_Briefing_Note-Article_8_application_and_eligibility_for_section_4_support_(updated_Sep_2016).pdf (accessed 15 December 2016).
2 Reforming support for migrants without immigration status: the new system contained in Schedules 8 and 9 to the immigration Bill, Home office, 21 January 2016. Available at: http://www.gov.uk/government/uploads/system/uploads/attachment_data/file/494240/support.pdf (accessed 15 November 2016), p5.

5.2.3 *A Guide to the Immigration Act 2016*

3 Rt Hon James Brokenshire MP, Minister for Immigration, House of Commons Public Bill Committee 13th sitting, *Hansard* cols 440–441, 10 November 2015. Available at: http://www.publications.parliament.uk/pa/cm201516/cmpublic/immigration/151110/am/151110s01.htm (accessed 1 December 2016).
4 Directive 2003/9/EC of the European Parliament of 27 January 2003 laying down minimum standards for the reception of asylum seekers.

Support for failed asylum seekers who face a genuine obstacle to leaving the United Kingdom

5.2.3 Paragraph 9 of Schedule 10 introduces new s 95A of the IAA 1999 making provision for support for failed asylum seekers and dependants of failed asylum seekers who are destitute/likely to become destitute and face a genuine obstacle to leaving the UK.

A 'failed asylum seeker' is defined in new s 94(2D) of the IAA 1999 introduced by para 4 of Schedule 11 as a person who was an asylum seeker for the purpose of asylum support, or would have been had they been an adult, whose protection claim has been rejected, and who is no longer an asylum seeker.

The meaning and tests for destitution apply in the same way as for IAA 1999, s 95 support (new s 95A(2) of that Act).

Genuine obstacle to leaving the United Kingdom

5.2.3.1 A 'genuine obstacle to leaving the United Kingdom' is not defined in the statute. Regulations under s 95A(3) of the IAA 1999 will make provision for determining what is, or is not, to be regarded as a genuine obstacle to leaving the UK for the purpose of support under s 95A of the IAA 1999. The Government has made the following statements about how a genuine obstacle to departure will be considered:

'34. The circumstances in which a genuine obstacle to departure will be considered to exist will be set out in regulations subject to Parliamentary approval and will include where:

- medical evidence shows that a person is unfit to travel (including cases where this is because they are in the late stages of pregnancy); or

- A person lacks the necessary travel document to leave the UK but is taking all reasonable steps to obtain this.

35. The regulations and guidance relating to section 95A support will also set out as clearly as possible the evidence a person will need to provide to obtain support. For example:

- A claim to be unable to depart the UK because of a medical reason will generally need to be supported by medical evidence that the person is unfit to travel by air. It will generally not be sufficient to show that they are receiving ongoing treatment for a medical condition. In rare cases, a person may be allowed to remain in the UK in order to continue to receive medical treatment, where a requirement to leave would breach the European Convention on Human Rights (ECHR), but any such factors will have been considered when the asylum claim was decided.

- A claim to be taking all reasonable steps to obtain a travel document will need to be supported by evidence appropriate to the documentation procedures of their country or origin. In the last three years the main nationalities of families on section 95 support, who have been refused asylum and exhausted their appeal rights but continued to be supported, are Pakistani, Nigerian and Chinese. The Home Office has established procedures for an application for an Emergency Travel Document to be made to the authorities of each of these countries and many others. Individuals can also apply for a travel document directly to the relevant authorities of their country of origin, generally via the High Commission or Embassy in the UK.

36. Section 95A support will be provided for as long as the obstacle to departure remains, subject, under the regulations, to any conditions placed on support, eg to comply with re-documentation procedures.'[1]

---

[1] *Reforming support for migrants without immigration status: the new system contained in Schedules 8 and 9 to the Immigration Bill*, Home Office, 21 January 2016. Available at: https://www.gov.uk/government/uploads/system/uploads/attachment_data/file/494240/Support.pdf (accessed 15 November 2016).

Time limitations on accessing section 95A support

5.2.3.2 Regulations setting out criteria for determining whether or not support may be provided or continue to be provided (new s 95A(4) of the IAA 1999) may also include conditions for accessing, or continuing to receive support under this provision (new s 95A(5) of the IAA 1999).

The Home Office document, *Reforming support for migrants without immigration status*[1] indicated its intention that it will not be possible to apply for s 95A support outside the prescribed 'grace' period for the termination of s 95 support. This would mean that it would only be possible to make an application for s 95A support during the period in which s 95 support is provided after

5.2.3.2 A Guide to the Immigration Act 2016

a final decision on the asylum claim, specifically within 21 days of the final decision for single adults and 90 days for families with children.

The Home Office states in the document that the regulations would create exceptions where the reason for applying outside that period was outside the person's control, for example, where they were not promptly notified of the refusal of their asylum appeal, or where they were hospitalised or otherwise too unwell to make an application for s 95A support during the grace period.[2]

ILPA raised that it would be impossible to apply for s 95A support if a person had not previously been in receipt of s 95 support from the Home Office, for example, because they were supported and accommodated by a friend, but are left destitute at a later stage where the friend finds that they are no longer able to provide support and accommodation, or where the person's s 95, or s 95A support was wrongly terminated by the Home Office. The Minister in the House of Lords addressed this point in his letter to Lord Rosser of 10 February 2016, stating that where an individual or family becomes destitute during the grace period from the date of the final decision on their claim, for example, because the accommodation provided by a friend ceases to be available, they will be able to apply for s 95 support for the remainder of that period and for s 95A support if they face a genuine obstacle to departure.[3]

Others for whom a genuine obstacle to leaving the UK arises outside the grace period for the termination of s 95 support, would be unable to access s 95A support. This may include, for example, pregnant women prevented from flying six weeks before their due date for the birth of the child, but who reach this advanced stage of pregnancy outside the grace period for termination of support.

The Government's stated aim is to prevent the creation of incentives for people to go underground after their asylum application is rejected by leaving open the possibility of accessing support at any later stage, but it is artificial to create a distinction between those who apply within the grace period for the termination of support under s 95 of the IAA 1999, and those who do not apply within this period. A person who is destitute and cannot leave the UK because they face a genuine obstacle to doing so will require support to prevent breaches of their human rights as they are not permitted to work in the UK, and have no access to mainstream benefits so that they would be unable to secure food or shelter.

The proposed limitation on access to support would affect large numbers of people. Home Office data shows that only 6 of the 105 people (5 per cent) needing s 4 support in 2015 due to being unable to return to their country as a result of late pregnancy, other medical reasons, or because they were taking all reasonable steps to return – made their application within the grace period and would qualify for support under the proposed system:

Part 5—Support etc for Certain Categories of Migrant **5.2.3.4**

A full breakdown of categories is given below:

(a) unable to leave the UK due to medical reasons – 42 (including six due to late pregnancy);

(b) taking all reasonable steps to leave the UK – 63;

(c) how many of these applications were made within 21 days of that person's appeal rights being exhausted:

- medical – 1; and
- steps to leave – 5.5.[4]

---

1 *Reforming support for migrants without immigration status: the new system contained in Schedules 8 and 9 to the Immigration Bill*, Home Office, 21 January 2016. Available at: https://www.gov.uk/government/uploads/system/uploads/attachment_data/file/494240/Support.pdf (accessed 15 November 2016).
2 Ibid, para 30.
3 Lord Bates to Lord Rosser, Immigration Bill – *Committee stage Day 4 (asylum support, section 95A right of appeal, 28-day grace period, local authority support, tuition fee support for care leavers, unaccompanied minors)*, 10 February 2016. Available at: http://data.parliament.uk/DepositedPapers/Files/DEP2016-0127/Lord_Rosser_letter_re_Lords_Committee_for_Immigration_Bill__3_Feb__.pdf (accessed 15 November 2016).
4 Rt. Hon. James Brokenshire MP, Written Response 29521, *Hansard*, 09 March 2016. Available at: http://www.parliament.uk/business/publications/written-questions-answers-statements/written-question/Commons/2016-03-02/29521/ (accessed 15 November 2016).

Other conditions of access to section 95A support

5.2.3.3 New s 95A(8) of the IAA 1999 provides that conditions of support may include involvement in community activities beneficial to the public. This replicates the conditions that were in force under s 4 of the IAA 1999 but which have never been operated.

No right of appeal against refusal/discontinuation of s 95A support

5.2.3.4 There is no provision providing a right of appeal to the Asylum Support Tribunal against refusal or discontinuation of s 95A support. The most recent statistics from the Asylum Support Tribunal indicate that in the year between September 2014 and August 2015, the Asylum Support Tribunal received 2067 applications for appeals against a Home Office refusal of asylum support. Of these appeal applications 62 per cent had a successful outcome, either through being allowed by the Tribunal (in 44 per cent of cases), through the case being remitted to the Home Office to make a new decision, or through the decision being withdrawn by the Home Office indicating that Home Office decisions on applications for s 4 IAA 1999 support are currently of very poor quality. Once

5.2.3.5 *A Guide to the Immigration Act 2016*

the ability of the Asylum Support Tribunal to scrutinise Home Office decisions is reduced, it is anticipated that refusals of asylum support will increase.[1]

---
1   Analysis of statistics received from the Asylum Support Tribunal, Asylum Support Appeals Project, 1 February 2016.

Nature of support under section 95A

5.2.3.5   New s 96(1A) of the IAA 1999 inserted by para 10(3) of Schedule 11 makes provision for support under s 95A to be provided in the form of cash, as well as in the form of vouchers. There is a prohibition on providing cash support for those supported under s 4 of the IAA 1999.

During the House of Lords Committee debate, the Minister stated, 'We expect that failed asylum seekers who move on to new Section 95A will continue to be supported as they were under s 95. This will generally be by way of accommodation and cash.'[1]

He further stated that cash support under s 95A will meet essential living needs and be provided at the same level as s 95 support.[2] The Government also envisages a seamless transition between ss 95 and 95A support enabling people to remain in their accommodation:

> 'Those granted section 95A support will generally have been in receipt of section 95 support at the point at which their asylum claim was refused and their appeal rights were exhausted. In such cases it will not be necessary for the Home Office to make a fresh assessment of whether they are destitute unless new information about this is received. In addition, it will generally be appropriate for the person or family to remain in the same accommodation and they will continue to receive a weekly cash allowance to cover their other essential living needs.'[3]

---
1   Rt Hon Lord Bates, Minister of State, Home Office, Immigration Bill 2015/16 House of Lords Committee, *Hansard* HL col 1831 (3 February 2016). Available at: http://www.publications.parliament.uk/pa/ld201516/ldhansrd/text/160203-0002.htm (accessed 15 November 2016).
2   Ibid, *Hansard HL* col 1832.
3   *Reforming support for migrants without immigration status: the new system contained in Schedules 8 and 9 to the Immigration Bill*, Home Office, 21 January 2016. Available at: https://www.gov.uk/government/uploads/system/uploads/attachment_data/file/494240/Support.pdf, para 37 (accessed 15 November 2016).

Families with children

5.2.4   Paragraph 7(5) of Schedule 11 will remove s 94(5) of the IAA 1999 which is the provision enabling families of children at the end of the asylum process to remain supported under s 95 of the IAA 1999 until they are removed from the UK. Adults with children whose asylum claims are finally determined must therefore qualify for support under new s 95A of the IAA 1999 in the same way as single adults. If they do not qualify for Home Office support under s 95A of the IAA 1999, they may qualify for support from their Local Authority (LA) under the provisions introduced by IA 2016, Schedule 12 (see further below).

Regulations will provide for s 95 support to be discontinued for families with children who reach the end of the asylum process after a grace period of 90 days:

> 'The consultation proposed a grace period of at least 28 days before section 95 support is discontinued in these family cases. Many respondents took the view that a 28-day grace period would be too short and suggested that a period of 90 days would be more appropriate and commensurate with the practical work to be done to engage with appeal rights exhausted families, including presenting them with clear information about their situation and its implications and persuading and enabling them to leave the UK where there is no genuine obstacle to them doing so. We have reflected carefully on these representations and have discussed the issue further with local authority colleagues and other partners. In light of that further consideration, we can confirm that the grace period before section 95 support is discontinued in family cases will be 90 days.'[1]

There will be a managed process of engagement by the Home Office, in tandem with the LA, with families whose asylum claim is finally determined to encourage voluntary returns, or to take families through the family returns process during this time.

Transitional provision is made for families with children at the end of the asylum process who are supported under s 95 of the IAA 1999 when Schedule 11 comes into force (see below).

---

1 *Reforming support for migrants without immigration status: the new system contained in Schedules 8 and 9 to the Immigration Bill*, Home Office, 21 January 2016. Available at: https://www.gov.uk/government/uploads/system/uploads/attachment_data/file/494240/Support.pdf, para 26 (accessed 15 November 2016).

Temporary support for failed asylum seekers

5.2.5 Paragraph 13 of Schedule 11 inserts new s 98A of the IAA 1999 enabling the Secretary of State to provide, or arrange temporary support for persons who she thinks may be destitute and facing a genuine obstacle to leaving the UK. It is unclear how this provision will operate in practice and it was not a focus of Parliamentary debates.

5.2.6   *A Guide to the Immigration Act 2016*

Transitional provision

5.2.6 Part 2 of Schedule 11 makes transitional arrangements for those supported under s 4 of the IAA 1999 when this provision is repealed. Transitional arrangements are also put in place for families with children accessing support at the end of the asylum process under s 95 of the IAA 1999 by virtue of s 94(5) of that Act when that provision is repealed.

Following para 46(1) of Schedule 11, the repeal of s 4 of the IAA 1999 will not apply to any person, or their dependants:

- for whom accommodation is being provided immediately before the day on which the repeal comes into force;
- who has made an application for s 4 support that has not been determined or withdrawn before that day; or
- any person who has appealed against a decision not to provide or to continue providing accommodation under s 4 and whose appeal has not been determined or withdrawn before that day.

After s 4 is repealed, however, there will be no appeal available against any decision not to continue to provide accommodation under s 4 of the IAA 1999 (para 46(2)).

Similar transitional provisions are made for families with children supported under s 95 of the 1999 Act by virtue of s 94(5) of that Act (para 47(1)) with a similar restriction on appeals against any decision not to continue to provide support under the provision after its repeal (para 47(2)).

SECTION 67—UNACCOMPANIED REFUGEE CHILDREN: RELOCATION AND SUPPORT

> **Summary**
>
> Requires the Secretary of State as soon as possible after the passing of the Act to make arrangements to relocate to the UK, and support a specified number of unaccompanied children from other countries in Europe.

5.3

67 Unaccompanied refugee children: relocation and support

(1)   The Secretary of State must, as soon as possible after the passing of this Act, make arrangements to relocate to the United Kingdom and

Part 5—Support etc for Certain Categories of Migrant **5.3**

support a specified number of unaccompanied refugee children from other countries in Europe.

(2) The number of children to be resettled under subsection (1) shall be determined by the Government in consultation with local authorities.

(3) The relocation of children under subsection (1) shall be in addition to the resettlement of children under the Vulnerable Persons Relocation Scheme.

Commencement: 31 May 2016, Immigration Act 2014 (Commencement No 1) Regulations 2016, SI 2016/603.

The provision requires the Secretary of State (SSHD), as soon as possible after the passing of the Act, to make arrangements to relocate to the UK and support a specified number of unaccompanied children from other countries in Europe. The section provides that the number of children to be resettled shall be determined by the Government in consultation with local authorities, and that the children shall be in addition to those resettled under the Vulnerable Persons Resettlement Scheme.

The duty to make arrangements to relocate to the UK a specific, but unstated, number of unaccompanied children was included by the Government following amendments pressed during the passage of the Bill by Lord Dubs aimed at requiring 3,000 unaccompanied children to be relocated in the UK. Lord Dubs was a holocaust survivor who reached safety in the UK as a child brought on the kindertransport and the Parliamentary debates recalled those that took place in Parliament leading to the kindertransport rescue efforts.[1]

The call for the UK to relocate 3,000 unaccompanied children was first made by the Save the Children and was taken up, for example, by the International Development Committee. The matter was debated in the House of Commons on 25 January 2016. The Government responded to the calls on 28 January 2016, making commitments to:

- work with UNHCR on a new initiative to resettle unaccompanied refugee children from conflict regions to the UK, complementing existing aid and resettlement programmes and not limited to children fleeing Syria;

- create a new fund of up to £10 million to support the needs of vulnerable refugee and migrant children in Europe; and

- provide further resources to the European Asylum Support Office to help Greece and Italy identify persons, including children, who could be reunited with family members in the UK under the Dublin III Regulation.[2]

The proposals were a step change from the UK's previous insistence on targeting its aid outside the European Union (EU) and the first indication that

5.3 *A Guide to the Immigration Act 2016*

the UK should show solidarity with other European States where refugees are arriving in need of protection.

The provision of resources to the European Asylum Support Office was directly linked to the UK's duties under the EU regulation known as the Dublin III regulation[3] that makes provision for identifying the EU Member State responsible for determining any application for international protection. This regulation is typically used by the UK to return asylum applicants to the first safe country of origin in the EU through which they passed, for their protection claim to be examined there. It places higher obligations on governments, however, to facilitate the consideration of protection claims from unaccompanied minors in Europe who have family members in the State,[4] applicants who have family members granted international protection in the State,[5] and, in certain circumstances those with family members who are asylum seekers with applications submitted close enough in time to be considered together.[6]

The case of *R (ZAT and others) v Secretary of State for the Home Department (Article 8 ECHR – Dublin Regulation – interface – proportionality)* (IJR) [2016] UKUT 61 (IAC) (22 January 2016) involved three separated children, plus the sibling of one of them who was dependent upon him and had special needs. Although there was not disagreement that the children's links in the UK, where they had family members ready and willing to care for them, meant that under the Dublin III Regulation the UK would ultimately be responsible for them, the Government argued, and continued to argue, for it appealed the case, that such responsibility only arose when the French authorities made a formal 'take charge' request to take the cases of the children. The evidence in the case was that such a request would take a year to materialize, during which period the children would be in danger in the camp in Calais. The Tribunal held that the children's rights to family life meant that the UK could not be required to wait for the request.

On 2 August 2016 the Court of Appeal allowed the SSHD's appeal against that judgment in *Secretary of State for the Home Department v ZAT and others* [2016] EWCA Civ 810 although the individuals were allowed to remain in the UK. The SSHD argued that the Tribunal had not given sufficient weight to the need to follow the Dublin III Regulation process. She also submitted fresh evidence as to the situation for children in France.

The Court of Appeal did not accept the SSHD's fresh evidence that there were no obstacles to children claiming asylum and family reunion in France, and held that in the light of the evidence submitted by ZAT and the other claimants, and given their mental health, it was understandable that the Tribunal had concluded that refusing to admit them until they had applied for asylum in France was a disproportionate interference with their rights under Article 8 of the ECHR. The court held, however, that the Tribunal had erred in the legal test it had applied in that it did not reflect the principal that only in especially compelling cases could individuals apply direct to the UK to seek family reunion without using the Dublin III Regulation or established entrance clearance procedures. Had the cases remained live, they would have been remitted. Lawyers representing individuals who wish to bypass established routes must show why established procedures cannot be followed and must provide the SSHD with all the information she would have had if the Dublin III process or entry clearance process had been used. Consideration is being given as to whether those representing ZAT and the other individuals will apply for permission to appeal to the Supreme Court.

Whilst the case was ongoing, pressure continued both inside and outside Parliament for the Government to take on more responsibility towards unaccompanied children in Europe in the context of the refugee crisis. Lord Dubs successfully pressed his amendment calling for the relocation of 3,000 children to a vote in the House of Lords on 21 March 2016. The Minister subsequently issued a statement on 21 April 2016, essentially describing steps towards the commitments made on 28 January 2016.[7]

Lord Dubs' amendment was subsequently defeated by the Government in the House of Commons on 25 April 2016. The House of Lords was constitutionally unable to press an amendment concerning 'financial privilege', the expenditure of money, and this was the reason given to the House of Lords for rejecting its amendment, when the Bill returned to the Lords. Lord Dubs responded by taking out the explicit reference to '3,000 children' and putting forward an amendment which was accepted in the House of Lords on 26 April 2016 and is now s 67 of the Immigration Act 2016 (IA 2016).

On 4 May 2016, the Government issued a press release[8] indicating that it would accept Lord Dubs' revised amendment. It announced an initiative to resettle in the UK unaccompanied asylum seeking children from Greece, Italy and France. It stated that in order not to encourage new and dangerous crossings to Europe, it would make the scheme retrospective, restricting resettlement to children registered before the EU migration agreement with Turkey came into force on 20 March 2016. The Government stated that it would work with UNHCR and non-governmental organisations (NGOs) such as Save the Children to deliver the scheme, and that the scheme would be separate from any EU-administered resettlement schemes. It further stated that those at risk of trafficking or exploitation would be prioritised for resettlement, and that existing family reunion routes would be accelerated.

The scheme was debated in Parliament during the consideration of Lords' amendments to the Bill in the House of Commons on 9 May 2016. Concerns were raised that children who had gone missing in Europe would not have been registered before the proposed limitation date of 20 March 2016. The Minister gave the following assurance:

5.3 A Guide to the Immigration Act 2016

> 'I will come on to the issue of registration, which has been highlighted by a number of people, in a moment. To be clear, we are not seeking to impose an over-burdensome or legalistic requirement on children to prove that they have been formally registered, but we will need to see some evidence that they were present in Europe before 20 March. This will avoid creating a new and perverse incentive for families to entrust their children to people traffickers. Our focus will be on reunifying children with families in the UK, but we will also consider cases of children at risk of exploitation or abuse.'[9]

The Minister indicated that the Government intended to be flexible in its interpretation and approach when implementing the amendment. This also applied in relation to the language of 'refugee' children within the text of the amendment adopted:

> 'I would like to reassure the House that we intend to be flexible in our interpretation and approach when implementing this amendment, to ensure that it is practical and supports the most vulnerable children, as intended. We believe the amendment, as currently drafted, enables us to do that. The use of the term "refugee" can be interpreted to include certain asylum seekers and avoid the requirement of a child having to go through a full refugee determination process before being admitted to the UK. Our Syrian resettlement scheme already operates in a not dissimilar way, and we do not believe any clarifications are necessary.'[10]

The lack of progress towards relocating unaccompanied children in the UK was criticised in a report by the House of Lords Select Committee on the EU.[11] In response to enquiries by a journalist from *The Guardian* newspaper, the Home Office stated:

> 'More than 20 children have been accepted for transfer to the UK since the Act was given Royal Assent and the majority of these have already arrived. We are consulting with local authorities across the country to confirm available capacity and ensure appropriate support systems are in place.
>
> We are also in active discussions with the UNHCR and the Italian, Greek and French governments to strengthen and speed up mechanisms to identify, assess and transfer children to the UK and ensure this in their best interests.'[12]

The statement was ambiguous. At least some of the children coming to the UK had entitlements to come, for example, under the Dublin III Regulation, independently of the provision in s 67. It did little to assuage concerns that the Government was not acting quickly enough to respond to the ongoing risks faced by children in the camps in Calais and Greece, both through its duty to facilitate relocation under s 67 of the IA 2016, or through the acceleration of Dublin III procedures.

Large numbers of children were still in the Calais camp when it was due to be closed by the French authorities, despite assurances by both the UK and

Part 5—Support etc for Certain Categories of Migrant **5.3**

French authorities that provision would be made for them before the closure occurred. The UN Committee on the Rights of the Child strongly criticised the protection failures that followed:

> 'The events of the past week have shown clearly that political and other considerations prevailed over the initial promises by both Governments that the situation of unaccompanied children would be their priority. The best interests of the child have been completely disregarded.'

> Disagreements between the French and UK Governments over who should take responsibility for the majority of these children have led to major violations of these children's rights. Hundreds of children have been subjected to inhumane living conditions, left without adequate shelter, food, medical services and psychosocial support, and in some cases exposed to smugglers and traffickers.'[12]

In a written statement of 8 February 2017, Robert Goodwill MP, Minister of State for Immigration stated that the government had brought over 200 children from Calais under s 67 of the IA 2016 and that it intended to bring 350 children under the scheme before bringing it to a close. Concern has been expressed about the low numbers of children assisted and the government is currently facing parliamentary pressure to continue the scheme.[13]

---

1   See for example, *Hansard* HL Vol 113 cc1011-6810 (5 July 1939). Available at: http://hansard.millbanksystems.com/lords/1939/jul/05/refugee-problem#S5LV0113P0_19390705_HOL_20 (accessed 15 November 2016) HC Report 1 February 1949.
2   *Resettlement of unaccompanied refugee children*, Rt Hon James Brokenshire MP, Written Ministerial Statement HCWS497, 28 January 2016. Available at: http://www.parliament.uk/written-questions-answers-statements/written-statement/Commons/2016-01-28/HCWS497 (accessed 15 November 2016).
3   Regulation (EU) No 604/2013 of the European Parliament and of the Council of 26 June 2013, establishing the criteria and mechanisms for determining the Member State responsible for examining an application for international protection lodged in one of the Member States by a third-country national or a stateless person (recast). Available at: http://eur-lex.europa.eu/LexUriServ/LexUriServ.do?uri=OJ:L:2013:180:0031:0059:EN:PDF (accessed 15 November 2016).
4   Ibid, Article 8.
5   Ibid, Article 9.
6   Ibid, Article 11.
7   *Resettlement of unaccompanied refugee children*, Rt Hon James Brokenshire MP, Written Ministerial Statement HCWS497, 28 January 2016. Available at: http://www.parliament.uk/written-questions-answers-statements/written-statement/Commons/2016-01-28/HCWS497 (accessed 15 November 2016).
8   *Unaccompanied asylum-seeking children to be resettled from Europe*, Prime Minister's Office press release, 4 May 2016. Available at: https://www.gov.uk/government/news/unaccompanied-asylum-seeking-children-to-be-resettled-from-europe (accessed 15 November 2016).
9   Rt Hon James Brokenshire, MP, Immigration Bill 2015/16, Commons consideration of Lords' messages, House of Commons, *Hansard* col 487 (9 May 2016). Available at: https://hansard.parliament.uk/Commons/2016-05-09/debates/16051030000001/ImmigrationBill (accessed 15 November 2016).
10 Ibid, col 489.
11 *Children in crisis: unaccompanied migrant children in the EU*, 2nd Report of Session 2016–17, House of Lords Select Committee on the European Union, HL Paper 34, 26 July 2016.

5.3.1 A Guide to the Immigration Act 2016

Available at: http://www.publications.parliament.uk/pa/ld201617/ldselect/ldeucom/34/3402.htm (accessed 15 November 2016).
12 *Calais camp: French and UK Governments fell well short of their child rights obligations*, UN Committee on the Rights of the Child, 2 November 2016. Available at: http://www.ohchr.org/EN/NewsEvents/Pages/DisplayNews.aspx?NewsID=20815&LangID=E (accessed 15 December 2016).
13 Robert Goodwill MP, Minister of State for Immigration, written statement HCWS, 8 February 2017. Available at: https://www.parliament.uk/business/publications/written-questions-answers-statements/written-statement/commons/2017-02-08/HCWS467 (accessed 1 March 2017).

Other issues debated in Parliament

5.3.1 The refugee crisis provided the context for a number of amendments proposed during the passage of the Act aimed at improving the protection available to those fleeing persecution. The amendments were not adopted by the Government, in certain cases because debates continued late into the night when votes were taken.

Protection of locally engaged staff in Afghanistan and Iraq

5.3.1.1 At Lords' Report, Lord Dubs and Baroness Hamwee tabled an amendment which would have made provision for those who worked with Her Majesty's Government in Iraq or Afghanistan and who are now refugees so that they could be resettled in the UK or come to the UK to claim asylum.

The amendment was modelled on the UK's policy for staff with whom it worked in Iraq, as set out in the then Secretary of State for Foreign and Commonwealth Affairs, the Rt Hon David Miliband MP's statement to Parliament,[1] both in terms of eligible persons and the dependants whom they can bring with them. The Iraq policy was preferred to policies for locally engaged staff in Afghanistan as it was more inclusive. Under the Afghanistan Intimidation Policy, as far as it has been possible to establish, at most one person has been resettled in the UK. There was a separate redundancy scheme including a resettlement policy for Afghanistan but resettlement was limited to a small subset of locally engaged staff working in Helmand outside protected bases, and to seriously injured staff whose only reason for failing to qualify under the policy was that the termination of their employment was due to injuries sustained in combat.

The Afghan policies were the subject of a legal challenge in *R (Hottak & anor) v Secretary of State for Foreign and Commonwealth Affairs & anor* [2016] EWCA Civ 438 (09 May 2016) on the grounds that they discriminate unlawfully by treating Afghan locally engaged staff less favourably, than Iraqi locally engaged staff were treated in a comparable situation. The challenge failed subsequent to the debates on the Bill.

Lord Dubs, who moved the amendment, sought an assurance that the Government would include the provision in the Act or otherwise make other provision to help those who worked for the UK armed forces in Iraq and Afghanistan, some of whom were in the camps in Calais. Lord Ashton of Hyde for the Government said in response:

> 'In answer to the noble Lord, Lord Dubs, I cannot accept the amendment. However, I can go some way towards what he was asking for as his second alternative. If he can give me examples of where the existing schemes are not working, I am happy to take them to the MoD and explain why they are not working. However, I submit that the schemes which are operating do fulfil our moral and legal obligations.'[2]

---

1 *Iraq: Assistance to Locally Employed Staff*, Written Statement, Rt Hon David Miliband MP, Secretary of State for Foreign and Commonwealth Affairs, *Hansard* col 27WS, (9 October 2007). Available at: http://www.publications.parliament.uk/pa/cm200607/cmhansrd/cm071009/wmstext/71009m0001.htm (accessed 15 November 2016).
2 Lord Ashton of Hyde, Immigration Bill Report Stage 2015/16, 3rd sitting, House of Lords, *Hansard* HL, col 2188 (21 March 2016). Available at: http://www.publications.parliament.uk/pa/ld201516/ldhansrd/text/160321-0003.htm (accessed 15 November 2016).

Humanitarian visas for those fleeing genocide

5.3.1.2 Lord Alton of Liverpool tabled amendments that would have made provision for the granting of humanitarian visas to those fleeing genocide. These received strong support, especially on the grounds that that they could benefit Christian minorities in Syria, but the vote on the amendments was unsuccessful, probably because of the late hour at which the vote was taken.

Refugee family reunion

5.3.1.3 Amendments were tabled during the passage of the Bill which would have made provision to:

- broaden the criteria for refugee family reunion, including to make provision for minor children recognised as refugees to be reunited in the UK with their parents;
- allow British citizens to sponsor family members recognized as persons in need of international protection without having to meet all the requirements of Appendix FM; and
- provide legal aid for refugee family reunion.

Different versions of the amendments were tabled at different stages. They were particularly important as they would have created safe and legal routes under which refugees who had family members in the UK would be able to access protection without the need to make dangerous journeys to reach safety.

5.3.1.4 *A Guide to the Immigration Act 2016*

The amendment lost momentum as attention focused on attempts to secure the relocation in the UK of 3,000 children from Europe, but support was starting to build. Unfortunately, the debate at Lords' report came at a late hour and the vote was lost. Ministers did not offer any concessions or assurances.

Family reunion policies

5.3.1.4 The Liberal Democrats tabled amendments challenging the requirements of Appendix FM and the rules in respect of refugee family reunion. Ministerial responses were negative, however.

SECTION 68—AVAILABILITY OF LOCAL AUTHORITY SUPPORT, AND SCHEDULE 12—AVAILABILITY OF LOCAL AUTHORITY SUPPORT

Summary

Amends Schedule 3 to the Nationality, Immigration and Asylum Act 2002 (NIAA 2002).

Makes provision for Local Authority (LA) support under certain conditions for migrant families with children, including those at the end of the asylum process, who do not qualify for Home Office support.

Removes certain categories of young people from the mainstream leaving care provisions under the Children Act 1989 and introduces a new framework for support for those who will no longer qualify for mainstream leaving care support.

Prevents LAs paying higher education tuition fees for care leavers who have no leave to remain, who have pending applications for leave to remain or who have limited leave to remain.

5.4

68 Availability of local authority support

Schedule 12 (availability of local authority support) has effect.

Part 5—Support etc for Certain Categories of Migrant **5.4**

Schedule 12

Section 68

Availability of local authority support

1   Schedule 3 to the Nationality, Immigration and Asylum Act 2002 (withholding and withdrawal of support) is amended as follows.

2(1)   Paragraph 1 (ineligibility for support) is amended as follows.

(2)   In sub-paragraph (1) (excluded support or assistance) after paragraph (g) insert—

"(ga)   in relation only to a person in England to whom this paragraph applies by virtue of paragraph 4, 5 or 7B—

    (i)   section 23CZA of that Act (arrangements for certain former relevant children to continue to live with former foster parents), or

    (ii)   regulations under section 23D of that Act (personal advisers),".

(3)   In that sub-paragraph, in paragraph (h) for "or 36" substitute ", 35A or 35B ".

(4)   After sub-paragraph (2) insert—

"(2A)   In the case of the provisions referred to in sub-paragraph (1)(ga), sub-paragraph (2) applies only in relation to a person in England to whom this paragraph applies by virtue of paragraph 4, 5 or 7B."

3   After paragraph 1 insert—

"1A(1)   A person to whom this paragraph applies is not eligible for assistance under section 23C(4)(b), 23CA(4) or 24B(2)(b) of the Children Act 1989 (grants to meet expenses connected with education or training) which consists of a grant to enable the person to meet all or part of the person's tuition fees.

(2)   The duty in section 23C(4)(b) or 23CA(4) of that Act and the power in section 24B(2)(b) of that Act may not be exercised or performed in respect of a person to whom this paragraph applies so as to make a grant to enable the person to meet all or part of the person's tuition fees.

(3)   This paragraph applies to a person in England who is aged 18 or over and who—

(a)   has leave to enter or remain in the United Kingdom which has been granted for a limited period,

(b)   is an asylum-seeker, or

(c)   has made an application for leave to enter or remain in the United Kingdom which has not been withdrawn or determined.

(4) In this paragraph "tuition fees" means fees payable for a course of a description mentioned in Schedule 6 to the Education Reform Act 1988."

4(1) Paragraph 2(1) (exceptions) is amended as follows.

(2) In paragraph (c) for "or 10" substitute ", 10, 10A or 10B ".

(3) After the "or" at the end of paragraph (c) insert—

"(ca) under section 95A or 98A of the Immigration and Asylum Act 1999 (support for failed asylum-seekers etc), or".

5 After paragraph 2 insert—

"2A(1) Paragraph 1(1)(g) or (ga) does not prevent the provision of support or assistance under a relevant provision to a person to whom paragraph 1 would otherwise apply by virtue of paragraph 7B if—

(a) conditions A and B are satisfied in relation to that person, and

(b) condition C, D or E is satisfied in relation to that person.

(2) In sub-paragraph (1) "relevant provision" means—

(a) section 23C, 23CZA or 23CA of the Children Act 1989,

(b) regulations under section 23D of that Act, or

(c) section 24A or 24B of that Act.

(3) Condition A is that—

(a) the person has made an application for leave to enter or remain in the United Kingdom, and

(b) where regulations made by the Secretary of State require that the application must be of a kind specified in the regulations for this condition to be satisfied, the application is of that kind.

(4) Condition B is that—

(a) the application is the first application for leave to enter or remain in the United Kingdom that the person has made, or

(b) where regulations under sub-paragraph (3)(b) require that the application must be of a kind specified in the regulations for condition A to be satisfied, the application is the first application of that kind that the person has made.

(5) Condition C is that the application has not been determined or withdrawn.

(6) Condition D is that—

Part 5—Support etc for Certain Categories of Migrant **5.4**

(a) the application has been refused,

(b) the person could bring an appeal under section 82(1) against the refusal (ignoring any possibility of an appeal out of time with permission), and

(c) if the person brought such an appeal, it would not be one that, by virtue of section 92(6), would have to be continued from outside the United Kingdom.

(7) Condition E is that—

(a) the application has been refused,

(b) the person has appealed under section 82(1) against the refusal,

(c) the appeal is not one that, by virtue of section 92(6), must be continued from outside the United Kingdom, and

(d) the appeal is pending within the meaning of section 104.

(8) For the purposes of sub-paragraph (3) the Secretary of State may by regulations provide for circumstances in which—

(a) a person is to be treated as having made an application for leave to enter or remain in the United Kingdom (despite not having made one), or

(b) a person is to be treated as not having made such an application where the Secretary of State is satisfied that the application made is vexatious or wholly without merit."

6 After paragraph 3 insert—

"3A Notwithstanding paragraph 3, paragraph 1(1)(g) prevents a local authority in England from providing support or assistance under section 17 of the Children Act 1989 to a person in respect of a child if —

(a) the support or assistance is of a type that could be provided to the person by virtue of paragraph 10A (see paragraph 10A(11)), and

(b) support is being provided to the person by virtue of paragraph 10A or there are reasonable grounds for believing that support will be provided to the person by virtue of that paragraph.

3B Notwithstanding paragraph 3, paragraph 1(1)(g) prevents a local authority in England from providing support or assistance under section 23C, 23CA, 24A or 24B of the Children Act 1989 to a person if—

(a) support is being provided to the person by virtue of paragraph 10B or section 95A of the Immigration and Asylum Act 1999, or

5.4 *A Guide to the Immigration Act 2016*

(b) there are reasonable grounds for believing that support will be provided to the person by virtue of that paragraph or section.

3C Notwithstanding paragraph 3, paragraph 1(1)(ga) prevents a local authority in England from providing support or assistance under a provision mentioned in paragraph (ga) to a person if—

(a) support is being provided to the person by virtue of paragraph 10B or section 95A of the Immigration and Asylum Act 1999, or

(b) there are reasonable grounds for believing that support will be provided to the person by virtue of that paragraph or section."

7 In paragraph 6 (third class of ineligible person: failed asylum-seeker), in sub-paragraph (1), in the words before sub-paragraph (a), after "person" insert " in Wales, Scotland or Northern Ireland ".

8 In paragraph 7 (fourth class of ineligible person: person unlawfully in United Kingdom), in the words before sub-paragraph (a), after "person" insert " in Wales, Scotland or Northern Ireland ".

9 Before paragraph 8 insert—

"Sixth class of ineligible person: person in England without leave to enter or remain

7B(1) Paragraph 1 applies to a person in England if—

(a) under the Immigration Act 1971, he requires leave to enter or remain in the United Kingdom but does not have it, and

(b) he is not an asylum-seeker.

(2) Paragraph 1 also applies to a dependant of a person to whom that paragraph applies by virtue of sub-paragraph (1).

Seventh class of ineligible person: primary carer without leave to enter or remain

7C(1) Paragraph 1 applies to a person in England ("P") if—

(a) P is the primary carer of a British citizen ("the relevant British citizen"),

(b) the relevant British citizen is residing in the United Kingdom,

(c) the relevant British citizen would be unable to reside in the United Kingdom or in another EEA State if P were required to leave the United Kingdom,

(d) if circumstances were not as mentioned in paragraphs (a) to (c), under the Immigration Act 1971 P would require leave to enter or remain in the United Kingdom but would not have such leave, and

(e) P is not an asylum-seeker.

Part 5—Support etc for Certain Categories of Migrant **5.4**

(2) Paragraph 1 also applies to the dependant of a person to whom that paragraph applies by virtue of sub-paragraph (1).

(3) In making for the purposes of this Schedule or regulations made under it a determination as to whether sub-paragraph (1)(c) applies in relation to P, a person may rely on—

- (a) a document of a kind specified in regulations made by the Secretary of State, or
- (b) information or guidance provided by the Secretary of State for the purposes of such a determination."

10   After paragraph 10 insert—

"Accommodation and subsistence etc: England

10A(1) The Secretary of State may make regulations providing for arrangements to be made for support to be provided to a person to whom paragraph 1 applies by virtue of paragraph 7B(1) or 7C(1) and—

- (a) who is destitute,
- (b) who has with him a dependent child,
- (c) who is not a relevant failed asylum seeker, and
- (d) in relation to whom condition A, B, C, D or E is satisfied.

(2) A person is a "relevant failed asylum seeker" for the purposes of sub-paragraph (1)(c) if the person is a failed asylum seeker within the meaning of Part 6 of the Immigration and Asylum Act 1999 and—

- (a) the person is receiving support under section 95A of that Act,
- (b) the person has made an application for such support which has not been refused, or
- (c) there are reasonable grounds for believing such support would be provided to the person if an application by the person for such support were made.

(3) Condition A is that—

- (a) the person has made an application for leave to enter or remain in the United Kingdom and has not withdrawn the application,
- (b) where regulations under this paragraph require that the application must be of a kind specified in the regulations for this condition to be satisfied, the application is of that kind, and
- (c) the application has not been determined.

(4) Condition B is that—

  (a) the person could bring an appeal under section 82(1) (ignoring any possibility of an appeal out of time with permission), and

  (b) if the person brought such an appeal, it would not be one that, by virtue of section 92(6), would have to be continued from outside the United Kingdom.

(5) Condition C is that—

  (a) the person has appealed under section 82(1),

  (b) the appeal is not one that, by virtue of section 92(6), must be continued from outside the United Kingdom, and

  (c) the appeal is pending within the meaning of section 104.

(6) Condition D is that—

  (a) the person's appeal rights are exhausted, and

  (b) he has not failed to cooperate with arrangements that would enable him to leave the United Kingdom.

(7) Condition E is that a person specified in regulations under this paragraph is satisfied that the provision of support is necessary to safeguard and promote the welfare of a dependent child.

(8) Regulations under this paragraph may specify—

  (a) factors which a person specified by virtue of sub-paragraph (7) may or must take into account in making a determination under that sub-paragraph;

  (b) factors which such a person must not take into account in making such a determination.

(9) The Secretary of State may make regulations providing for arrangements to be made for support to be provided to a person ("P")—

  (a) to whom paragraph 1 applies by virtue of paragraph 7B(1) or 7C(1), and

  (b) who it appears to a person specified in the regulations may be destitute,

until a person by whom support may be provided under arrangements by virtue of sub-paragraph (1) is able to determine whether such support should be provided to P.

(10) Arrangements for a person by virtue of this paragraph may include arrangements for a dependant.

(11) The support that may be provided under arrangements by virtue of this paragraph may take the form of—

  (a) accommodation;

Part 5—Support etc for Certain Categories of Migrant **5.4**

(b) subsistence in kind, or cash or vouchers to pay for subsistence.

(12) Subsections (3) to (8) of section 95 of the Immigration and Asylum Act 1999 (meaning of "destitute") apply for the purposes of this paragraph as they apply for the purposes of that section.

(13) For the purposes of sub-paragraph (3) regulations under this paragraph may provide for circumstances in which—

(a) a person is to be treated as having made an application for leave to enter or remain in the United Kingdom (despite not having made one);

(b) a person is to be treated as not having made such an application where the Secretary of State is satisfied that the application made is vexatious or wholly without merit.

(14) For the purposes of sub-paragraph (6) a person's appeal rights are exhausted at the time when—

(a) he could not bring an appeal under section 82 (ignoring any possibility of an appeal out of time with permission), and

(b) no appeal brought by him is pending within the meaning of section 104.

10B(1) The Secretary of State may make regulations providing for arrangements to be made for support to be provided to a person to whom paragraph 1 applies by virtue of paragraph 7B(1) and—

(a) who would otherwise be eligible for support or assistance under section 23C, 23CZA or 23CA of the Children Act 1989, under regulations under section 23D of that Act or under section 24A or 24B of that Act, and

(b) in relation to whom condition A, B, C or D is satisfied.

(2) Condition A is that—

(a) the person is destitute,

(b) the person has made an application for leave to enter or remain in the United Kingdom and has not withdrawn the application,

(c) where regulations under this paragraph require that the application must be of a kind specified in the regulations for this condition to be satisfied, the application is of that kind, and

(d) the application has not been determined.

(3) Condition B is that—

(a) the person is destitute,

(b) the person could bring an appeal under section 82(1) (ignoring any possibility of an appeal out of time with permission), and

5.4 A Guide to the Immigration Act 2016

- (c) if the person brought an appeal under section 82(1), it would not be one that, by virtue of section 92(6), would have to be continued from outside the United Kingdom.

(4) Condition C is that—

- (a) the person is destitute,
- (b) the person has appealed under section 82(1),
- (c) the appeal is not one that, by virtue of section 92(6), must be continued from outside the United Kingdom, and
- (d) the appeal is pending within the meaning of section 104.

(5) Condition D is that—

- (a) the person's appeal rights are exhausted, and
- (b) a person specified in regulations under this paragraph is satisfied that support needs to be provided to the person.

(6) Regulations under this paragraph may specify—

- (a) factors which a person specified by virtue of paragraph (b) of sub-paragraph (5) may or must take into account in making a determination under that paragraph;
- (b) factors which such a person must not take into account in making such a determination.

(7) The Secretary of State may make regulations providing for arrangements to be made for support to be provided to a person ("P")—

- (a) to whom paragraph 1 applies by virtue of paragraph 7B(1), and
- (b) who it appears to a person specified in the regulations may be destitute,

until a person by whom support may be provided under arrangements by virtue of sub-paragraph (1) is able to determine whether such support should be provided to P.

(8) The support that may be provided under arrangements by virtue of this paragraph may, in particular, take the form of—

- (a) accommodation;
- (b) subsistence in kind, or cash or vouchers to pay for subsistence.

(9) Subsections (3) to (8) of section 95 of the Immigration and Asylum Act 1999 (meaning of "destitute") apply for the purposes of this paragraph as they apply for the purposes of that section.

(10) For the purposes of sub-paragraph (2) regulations under this paragraph may provide for circumstances in which—

- (a) a person is to be treated as having made an application for leave to enter or remain in the United Kingdom (despite not having made one);

Part 5—Support etc for Certain Categories of Migrant   5.4

(b) a person is to be treated as not having made such an application where the Secretary of State is satisfied that the application made is vexatious or wholly without merit.

(11) For the purposes of sub-paragraph (5) a person's appeal rights are exhausted at the time when—

(a) he could not bring an appeal under section 82 (ignoring any possibility of an appeal out of time with permission), and

(b) no appeal brought by him is pending within the meaning of section 104."

11   In paragraph 11 (assistance and accommodation: general), in the words before sub-paragraph (a), for "or 10" substitute ", 10, 10A or 10B ".

12   In paragraph 13 (offences), in sub-paragraphs (1)(b) and (2)(a), for "or 10" substitute ", 10, 10A or 10B ".

13   In paragraph 14 (information), in sub-paragraphs (1) and (2), for "or 7" (as substituted by paragraph 26(8)(b) of Schedule 11) substitute ", 7, 7B or 7C".

14(1) Paragraph 15 (power to amend Schedule 3) is amended as follows.

(2) After paragraph (a) insert—

"(aa) to modify any of the classes of person to whom paragraph 1 applies;".

(3) In paragraph (c) after "remove" insert ", or modify the application of,".

(4) After paragraph (c) insert—

"(d) to enable regulations to be made by the Secretary of State providing for arrangements to be made for support to be provided to a class of person to whom paragraph 1 applies;

(e) to apply paragraph 1A in relation to Wales;

(f) to make provision which has a similar effect to paragraph 1A and which applies in relation to Scotland or Northern Ireland."

15(1) Paragraph 16 (orders and regulations) is amended as follows.

(2) In sub-paragraph (2)(d) after "amending" insert ", repealing or revoking ".

(3) In sub-paragraph (3) after "2(1)(d) or (e)" insert ", 2A(3)(b), 10A or 10B ".

16   In Schedule 3 to the Immigration Act 2014 (excluded residential tenancy agreements) after paragraph 8 insert—

"8A An agreement under which accommodation is provided to a person under arrangements made by virtue of paragraph 10A or 10B of Schedule 3 to the Nationality, Immigration and Asylum Act 2002 (support for certain persons who are otherwise ineligible for support by virtue of that Schedule)."

5.4 A Guide to the Immigration Act 2016

Commencement: Not yet in force.

Amends: Schedule 3 to the Nationality, Immigration and Asylum Act 2002 (NIAA 2002).

Regulations: may be made under the following powers:

Paragraph 2A(8) of Schedule 3 to the NIAA 2002 prescribing persons who may be treated as having made an application for leave to enter or remain for the purpose of qualifying for leaving care support under the Children Act 1989, inserted by para 5;

Paragraph 7C(1)(a) of Schedule 3 to the NIAA 2002 specifying the kind of document that may be relied on to determine whether a child cared for by a non-EEA national would be unable to reside in another EEA state if the carer were required to leave the UK, inserted by para 9;

Paragraph 10A(1) of Schedule 3 to the NIAA 2002 for the SSHD to provide for arrangements for support under this paragraph to be provided to a person who meets the relevant criteria, inserted by para 10;

Paragraph 10A(3) of Schedule 3 to the NIAA 2002 for the SSHD to prescribe the kind of application for leave to enter or remain that enables the person to meet the condition for support under para 10A, inserted by para 10;

Paragraph 10A(7) of Schedule 3 to the NIAA 2002 specifying a person who may be satisfied that support is necessary to safeguard and promote the welfare of the child in order for support to be provided under para 10A, inserted by para 10;

Paragraph 10A(9) of Schedule 3 to the NIAA 2002 providing for arrangements to be made for support under para 10A whilst determining whether support should be provided, inserted by para 10;

Paragraph 10A(13) of Schedule 3 to the NIAA 2002 to provide for circumstances in which a person may be treated as having made an application for leave to enter or remain to qualify for support under para 10A or for circumstances where a person is to be treated as not having made an application, inserted by para 10;

Paragraph 10B(1) of Schedule 3 to the NIAA 2002 to provide for arrangements to be made for support under para 10B, inserted by para 10;

Paragraph 10B(2)(c) of Schedule 3 to the NIAA 2002 for the SSHD to prescribe the kind of application for leave to enter or remain that enables the person to meet the condition for support under para 10B, inserted by para 10;

Paragraph 10B(5) of Schedule 3 to the NIAA 2002 specifying persons who may be satisfied that support needs to be provided the person in order to qualify for support under para 10B, inserted by para 10;

Part 5—Support etc for Certain Categories of Migrant 5.4

Paragraph 10B(6) of Schedule 3 to the NIAA 2002 prescribing factors to be taken into account by a person who may be satisfied that support needs to be provided to a person, inserted by para 10;

Paragraph 10B(7) of Schedule 3 to the NIAA 2002 providing for arrangements to be made for support under parag 10B whilst determining whether support should be provided, inserted by para 10;

Paragraph 10B(10) of Schedule 3 to the NIAA 2002 providing for circumstances in which a person may be treated as having made an application for leave to enter or remain to qualify for support under para 10B or for circumstances where a person is to be treated as not having made an application, inserted by para 10;

Paragraph 15(d) of Schedule 3 to the NIAA 2002 to provide for arrangements to be made for support to a class of person ineligible for local authority services, inserted by para 14(4) and subject to the negative procedure in Parliament;

All the other powers above are subject to the affirmative procedure in parliament, para 16 of Schedule 3 to the NIAA 2002, inserted by para 15(3).

Definitions:

For the definition of when a person's appeal rights are *exhausted* see the NIAA 2002, Schedule 3 para 10A(14) and 10B(14) as inserted by Schedule 12 para 10.

For the definition of when a person is treated as *having made an application for leave to enter or remain in the UK*, see the NIAA 2002, Schedule 3, para 10A(13) as inserted by Schedule 12, para 10.

'asylum-seeker' an adult who has made a claim for asylum within the meaning of s 18(3) of the NIAA 2002 that has been recorded but not determined, NIAA 2002, Schedule 3, para 17(1);

'dependant' NIAA 2002, Schedule 3, para 17(1);

'destitute' Immigration and Asylum Act 1999 (IAA 1999), s 95(3)–(8);

'failed asylum-seeker' IAA 1999, s 94(1) and (2D) as inserted by Schedule 11, para 7(2)(b) and 7(4);

'relevant failed asylum-seeker' NIAA 2002, s 10A(2) inserted by Schedule 12, para 10;

'relevant provision', s 23, 23ZA, 23CA, 24A or 24B of the Children Act 1989 (CA 1989), or regulations made under s 23D of that Act, NIAA 2002 Schedule 3, para 2A(2) as inserted by Schedule 12, para 5;

'relevant British citizen' NIAA 2002, Schedule 3, para 7C(1)(a) inserted by Schedule 12, para 9;

5.5 *A Guide to the Immigration Act 2016*

'tuition fees', fees payable for a course of a description mentioned in Schedule 6 to the Education Reform Act 1988, NIAA 2002, Schedule 3, para 1A(4), as substituted by Schedule 12, para 3.

Devolution: Applies throughout the UK but Schedule 12 as currently drafted applies only to England. The Government may extend provisions under Schedule 3 of the NIAA 2002 to devolved administrations by regulations under new para 15(d) of that Schedule (inserted by para 14(4) Schedule 12 to the IA 2016). Specific provisions relating to payment of tuition fees of care leavers may be extended to Wales under new para 15(e) of, and to Scotland and Northern Ireland under new para 15(f) of, Schedule 3 to the NIAA 2002, both inserted by para 14(4) of Schedule 12 to the Immigration Act 2016 (IA 2016). Paragraph 16 of Schedule 3 to the NIAA 2002 also contains powers to use regulations to make certain changes to provisions and amend legislation in consequence. These are extended to include powers to repeal or revoke legislation by new para 16(2)(d) Schedule 3 to the NIAA 2002, inserted by para 15(2) of the IA 2016.

Section 68 simply introduces the Schedule; all of the relevant provisions are in Schedule 12. Schedule 12 was introduced to the Bill on the last day of its consideration by the Public Bill Committee in the House of Commons and was amended significantly by the government at later stages. As the Schedule makes a range of different changes affecting different groups of people and new provisions were inserted at different places within the Schedule, it is difficult to read the Schedule sequentially and a preferred approach may be to analyse the provisions thematically according to how Schedule 3 to the NIAA 2002 is amended by Schedule 12 to make provision for the different groups affected.

SCHEDULE 3—NATIONALITY, IMMIGRATION AND ASYLUM ACT 2002

5.5 Schedule 12 principally amends Schedule 3 to the NIAA 2002. It is helpful to understand how Schedule 3 to that Act works in order to analyse the amendments made by the IA 2016.

Schedule 3 to the NIAA 2002 sets out a list of provisions in para 1(1) that create powers or duties, mostly for Local Authorities (LAs), to provide support and assistance. These include, for example, support and assistance under Part 1 of the Care Act 2014, under s 21 of the National Assistance Act 1948 (NAA 1948) and under ss 17, 23C, 24A or 24B of the CA 1989. Paragraph 1(1) provides that a person to whom that paragraph applies shall not be eligible for support and assistance under those provisions. The Schedule then identifies classes of people to whom the paragraph applies, and who are, therefore, ineligible for support under the listed provisions, as well as some exceptions.

The Schedule makes explicit that the provisions do not prevent support or assistance to British citizens (para 2(1)(a)) or to children (para 2(1)(a)(b)). The classes of ineligibility for services are therefore only applicable to adults and not children. There is also an exception where the exercise of the power or duty under the relevant provision is necessary to avoid a breach of the person's rights under the European Convention on Human Rights (ECHR) or their rights under the EU Treaties (para 3). It is under this exception, for example, that LAs are able to exercise their powers under the CA 1989, s 17 to support migrant families with children who would otherwise be ineligible for assistance.

Paragraph 9 of Schedule 12 to the IA 2016 inserts two new classes of ineligibility for support and assistance into Schedule 3 to the NIAA 2002. Paragraph 7B inserted into Schedule 3 to the 2002 Act identifies as ineligible for support and assistance a person who requires but does not have leave to enter or remain in the UK under the Immigration Act 1971 (IA 1971) and is not an asylum seeker (defined in para 17(1) of Schedule 3 as an adult who has made a claim for asylum within the meaning of s 18(3) of the NIAA 2002 that has been recorded but not determined). The category of ineligibility in new para 7B replaces three current categories of ineligibility: failed asylum seekers co-operating with removal directions (para 6); persons unlawfully in the UK (in breach of immigration laws defined in s 50A of the British Nationality Act 1981); and failed asylum seekers with children (para 7A). The Government has stated that this is to simplify the definition of those excluded from LA provision.

New paragraph 7C of Schedule 3 to the NIAA 2002, inserted by paragraph 9 of Schedule 12, identifies *Zambrano* carers[1] as a further class of persons identified as normally ineligible for the local authority services set out in Schedule 3 to the NIAA 2002.

Schedule 3 to the NIAA 2002 is further amended to prevent the the exercise of LA powers to provide support and assistance to prevent a breach of human rights under para 3 of that Schedule in circumstances where support could instead be provided by two new frameworks of support provision established within the Schedule. New paras 3A and 10A inserted into Schedule 3 to the NIAA 2002 relate to the provision of support and assistance to families with children and new paras 3B and 10B relate to the provision of LA support and assistance to certain groups of young people leaving care. The provision in para 3 of Schedule 3 to the NIAA 2002 enabling LAs to exercise their powers to prevent a breach of human rights remains available as a residual safeguard where a person is not eligible for support or assistance under the new frameworks for support created.

A new paragraph 1A is inserted into Schedule 3 to the NIAA 2002 and deals with the provision of higher education tuition fees by LAs affecting a wider group of young people in care. These provisions are dealt with separately and discussed in further detail below.

---

1   Non-EEA nationals lawfully present in the UK on account of being the primary carer of a British citizen child, commonly named *Zambrano* carers after the case that established the principle of their right of residence under EU law: *Ruiz Zambrano* [2011] EUECJ C-34/09 (8 March 2011).

FAMILIES WITH CHILDREN

5.6 The amendments to Schedule 3 to the NIAA 2002 making provision for families with children are a response to concerns raised during the passage of the IA 2016 that the removal of support under s 95 of the IAA 1999 from families with children at the end of the asylum process would lead to destitution and LAs having to take responsibility for supporting families under their duties to promote and safeguard the welfare of children under the CA 1989, s 17.

As discussed above, para 3 of Schedule 3 to the NIAA 2002 creates an exception to the categories of ineligibility for LA support by permitting LAs to exercise their powers or duties to prevent breaches of rights under the ECHR. In this way, LAs may provide support to adults with children under the CA 1989, s 17 to safeguard and promote the welfare of the child even where migrant families might otherwise be ineligible for support because of their immigration status.

Paragraph 6 of Schedule 12 to the IA 2016 limits the exercise of LA powers under this human rights exception by introducing new para 3A to Schedule 3 to the NIAA 2002, which prevents a LA from providing support or assistance to a family under the CA 1989, s 17 if they would qualify for a type of support under the new Home Office regulated framework established under new para 10A of Schedule 3 to the NIAA 2002. Under para 3A, support may not be provided under the CA 1989, s 17 if it is of a type that could be provided by virtue of para 10A, and either support is being provided under para 10A or there are reasonable grounds for believing that support will be provided under that paragraph.

Local Authority duties under the CA 1989, s 17 are not removed or restricted altogether by these provisions. The provision in para 3 of Schedule 3 to the NIAA 2002 enabling LAs to exercise their powers to prevent a breach of human rights and thereby provide support under the CA 1989, s 17 to promote and safeguard the welfare of the child remains as a residual safeguard where a person is not eligible for support or assistance under the new frameworks for support created.

Support for families with children under new para 10A

5.6.1 The framework for support under new para 10A is not limited to failed asylum seekers with children, but encompasses other migrant families who do not qualify for mainstream support provision, for example, migrant families currently supported under the CA 1989, s 17 due to the risk of destitution.

Under new para 10A the SSHD may make regulations providing for support for a person who would otherwise be ineligible for LA services because they do not have leave to enter or remain or are a *Zambrano* carer (the two new classes of ineligibility inserted into Schedule 3 to the NIAA 2002). Support may be provided under this provision where the person is destitute, has a dependent child and does not meet the criteria for support under new section 95A of the IAA 1999 (paras 10A(1)–(2)). This means that families with children must first consider if they qualify for support under new section 95A, and access support and accommodation from the Home Office under that provision where applicable. If they do not qualify for s 95A support, for example, because they do not have a genuine obstacle to returning to their country, or because they were not previously an asylum seeker, the family may access support under para 10A provided they meet one of the following conditions:

A   they have a pending application for leave to enter or remain of a type to be specified in regulations (10A(3));

B   they could bring a statutory appeal (10A(4));

C   they have a pending statutory appeal (10A(5));

D   they have exhausted their appeal rights and are cooperating with removal (10A(6)); or

E   support is necessary to promote and safeguard the welfare of the child (10A(7)).

Under para 10A(13), the SSHD may also, by regulations, provide for other persons to be treated as having made an application for leave to enter, or remain for the purpose of accessing support under this provision. She may also identify persons as not to be treated as having made an application for leave to enter or remain where she is satisfied that the application is vexatious or wholly without merit.

New para 10A(4)(a) provides the Home Office with a power to support families who have a pending statutory appeal. This would be a pending appeal against the refusal of a human rights claim that does not engage protection grounds (eg under Article 8 of the ECHR), or an appeal against revocation of refugee status since those with a pending appeal on protection grounds (on the basis that removal would breach the UK's obligations under the Refugee

5.6.2 *A Guide to the Immigration Act 2016*

Convention, or Article 3 of the ECHR) qualify for support under s 95 of the IAA 1999. Under new para 10A(4)(b) however, support will not be provided on the basis of the pending appeal if the Secretary of State has certified the claim such that the person cannot appeal from within the UK, for example, under the 'remove first appeal later' provisions inserted by IA 2016, s 63. In such circumstances, a person who wishes to challenge their removal will have to bring a judicial review. Unless regulations provide otherwise, there is no specific provision under para 10A ensuring support while applying for judicial review or, indeed, while the family make other representations to the Home Office. The family might qualify instead, under new para 10A(6), for support necessary to safeguard and promote the welfare of the child.

Support necessary to promote and safeguard the welfare of the child

5.6.2 New para 10A(6) provides a residual category for support to promote and safeguard the welfare of the child where the family do not otherwise qualify for support. Under new para 10A(7) the SSHD may make regulations to specify the person who must take the decision on whether this support is required and may specify what they must, or may take into account in so doing.

This allows the SSHD to prescribe for LAs what is necessary to safeguard and promote the welfare of children even though it is LA departments rather than the Home Office that have specialist expertise in relation to children and families. It may also have the effect of LAs undertaking more limited assessments of children and families under this provision than they might otherwise have undertaken under the CA 1989, s 17.

Nature of support under para 10A

5.6.3 It is the Government's intention that it will be LAs who support families under this provision, though the drafting of new para 10A(1) which allows the Secretary of State to make regulations providing for 'arrangements to be made' for support, does not make this explicit. The Government stated that LAs were not referenced on the face of para 10A because this follows the existing drafting of Schedule 3 to the 2002 Act, which takes account, for example, of the fact that there are not LAs in Northern Ireland.[1]

The Minister in the House of Lords also gave the assurance in correspondence that support under section 10A would meet essential living needs.[2]

---

1 *Reforming support for migrants without immigration status: the new system contained in Schedules 8–9 to the Immigration Bill,* Home Office, 21 January 2016. Available at: https://www.gov.uk/government/uploads/system/uploads/attachment_data/file/494240/Support.pdf, p 12, footnote 6 (accessed 15 November 2016).

Part 5—Support etc for Certain Categories of Migrant   5.6.5

2   Lord Bates to Lord Rosser, *Immigration Bill – Committee stage Day 4 (asylum support, section 95A right of appeal, 28-day grace period, local authority support, tuition fee support for care leavers, unaccompanied minors)* 10 February 2016. Available at: http://data.parliament.uk/DepositedPapers/Files/DEP2016-0127/Lord_Rosser_letter_re_Lords_Committee_for_Immigration_Bill__3_Feb__.pdf (accessed 15 November 2016).

Potential for gaps in support and destitution

5.6.4 New para 10A(9) was inserted into Schedule 3 to the NIAA 2002 to allow for support to be provided by a LA to a family who appears to be destitute whilst it is determining whether support should be provided. This was in response to concerns raised by ILPA and others at an earlier stage of the Bill that LAs would be prevented from providing support to a family under the provision that prevented it from providing support under the CA 1989, s 17, where there were reasonable grounds to believe that the family would be eligible for Home Office support under s 95A of the IAA 1999 (as provided by new para 10A to Schedule 3 to the NIAA 2002) even if the family was not in practice receiving this support. The circumstances in which the LA will be able to provide support to families who may be destitute will be determined in regulations, giving rise to the risk that there will remain gaps through which families with children may fall.

Despite the insertion of this provision enabling LAs to provide support in emergencies, for example, the risk of destitution will remain as the new process for supporting families established under Schedules 11–12 relies on families understanding the complexities and criteria of three different systems of support, how to access these and on their having the ability, confidence and English language skills to advocate effectively for themselves. Families risk falling through the gaps between the three different systems of support: s 95 provision, s 95A support and support under para 10A of Schedule 3 to the NIAA 2002 which itself has different sets of eligibility criteria under its different paragraphs.

It is also likely that the Home Office regulations will enable LAs to conduct more limited assessments than they might have otherwise undertaken under the CA 1989, s 17.

Children with additional welfare needs

5.6.5 The Government stated that the Schedule 'enables local authorities to provide under s 17 of the CA 1989 for any other needs of a child or their family which must be addressed to safeguard and promote the child's welfare'.[1]

During the passage of the Bill, ILPA expressed concerns as to whether this would be achieved. New paragraph 3A prevents LAs from providing support and assistance where the support is of a type that could be provided under para 10A. This could be interpreted as preventing LAs from providing for the welfare of a child, if the child were being provided with support under para 10A, but this was inappropriate for their needs, for example, Home Office accommodation under s 95A of the IAA 1999 may be a type of support that could be provided under para 10A, but the particular accommodation provided might not be suitable for the needs of a particular child.

The nature and the extent of support that can be provided under para 10A to children and families are not defined in the Act and secondary legislation has not yet been made. It may, therefore, be unclear to LAs whether and at what point their duties under the CA 1989, s 17 to provide additional support would take effect. This could be clarified by making reference in regulations to para 10 of the Asylum Support Regulations 2000, SI 2000/704 (as amended) which specifies the level and nature of support for essential living needs under s 95 of the IAA 1999, following the assurance that support under para 10A would meet essential living needs.

Ministers were clear, however, that LAs would be required to meet social care needs that were additional to accommodation and subsistence support to prevent destitution through their powers under the CA 1989, s 17:

'We are simplifying the basis on which the principal need of families without immigration status can be met by local authorities. That need is for accommodation and subsistence support to prevent destitution, as is clearly shown by the study I have highlighted and previously referred to. In respect of family groups, we are clear that section 17 of the Children Act will remain the basis on which local authorities will meet any other social care needs beyond destitution – that is, what they consider to be necessary to safeguard or promote the welfare of a child pending resolution of a family's immigration status or their departure from the UK.'[2]

---

1 Clive Peckover, Asylum and Family Policy Unit, Immigration and Border Policy Directorate, Home Office to National Asylum Stakeholder Forum, *Immigration Bill – support for certain categories of migrant (new Schedule on local authority support)*, 12 November 2015. Available at: http://www.ilpa.org.uk/resources.php/31560/immigration-bill-ilpa-briefing-for-house-of-commons-committee-government-new-clause-17-and-governmen (accessed 15 November 2016).
2 Rt Hon James Brokenshire MP, Minister for Immigration, Immigration Bill 2015/16 Public Bill Committee, 15th sitting, *Hansard* HC, col 529 (10 November 2015). Available at: http://www.publications.parliament.uk/pa/cm201516/cmpublic/immigration/151117/am/151117s01.htm (accessed 15 November 2016).

CARE LEAVERS: LEAVING CARE SUPPORT

5.7 Under the CA 1989, local authorities have continuing duties to young people who leave their care.[1] These duties continue until the young person reaches the age of 21 years, or until 25 years if they are in full-time education, in recognition of the fact that young people need support to make the transition to adulthood.

For young people who were 'looked after' by the local authority for at least 13 weeks since the age of 14 years, including some period after the age of 16 years ('former relevant children')[2] the local authority has a duty to remain in contact with the young person, to allocate a personal adviser and regularly to review their 'pathway plan'. A 'pathway plan' provides an assessment of the young person's need for advice, assistance and support and sets how those needs will be addressed. Local authorities also need to provide financial support and accommodation, including the option of remaining in an existing foster placement, and to provide advice and assistance with education, training and employment. For young people who were looked after for shorter periods or who were privately fostered after the age of 16 years ('qualifying young people'), there are more limited duties but these include the provision of support and accommodation and assistance with education, training and employment.

Leaving care provisions under ss 23C, 24A and 24B of the CA 1989 are listed within para 1(1) of Schedule 3 to the NIAA 2002. Currently children at the end of the asylum process who reach the age of 18 years (and who therefore become an adult who does not have leave to enter or remain and who would normally not be eligible for services) may be supported by LAs where it would breach their rights under the ECHR not to provide support (for example, because they would otherwise be destitute), by operation of para 3 of Schedule 3 to the NIAA 2002. Following *R (SO) v London Borough of Barking and Dagenham* [2010] EWCA Civ 1101, support under this provision is provided under the LA's leaving care duties under the CA 1989.[3]

Schedule 12 to the IA 2016 amends para 1(1) of Schedule 3 to the NIAA 2002 to include additional leaving care provisions within the scope of services that those classified as ineligible may not access. Paragraph 2(2) of Schedule 12 to IA 2016 inserts new para 1(1)(ga) into Schedule 3 to the NIAA 2002. This prevents those classed as ineligible within the Schedule from being allowed to remain in their existing foster placement whilst they make the transition to adulthood, a major reform[4] introduced by the Government in 2013. The provision also prevents the allocation of a personal adviser,[5] a role established in regulations to provide advice, and support to young people leaving care in place of a parent.[6]

Schedule 12 para 6 of the IA 2016 inserts new para 3B into Schedule 3 to the NIAA 2002 which prevents a LA from providing support under s 23C, 23CA, 24A or 24B (leaving care provisions) of the CA 1989 to a person normally ineligible for services if support is provided, or there are reasonable grounds to believe it will be provided, under new para 10B of Schedule 3 to

5.7.1 *A Guide to the Immigration Act 2016*

the 2002 Act or under new s 95A of the IAA 1999. A separate para 3C was also inserted preventing the provision of assistance under s 23ZA (remaining in a foster placement) and s 24D (allocation of a personal adviser) of the CA 1989 where support is provided under new para 10B of Schedule 3 to the 2002 Act or under new s 95A of the IAA 1999.

Through these provisions, Schedule 12 to IA 2016 has the effect of removing access to mainstream leaving care support provided by social services under the CA 1989 from care leavers currently classed as normally ineligible for services but supported under para 3 of Schedule 3 to the NIAA 2002 to prevent a breach of their human rights. Following the changes made by Schedule 12 to IA 2016, young people who will be prevented from accessing mainstream leaving care provision are those who:

- reach the age of 18 years:
- require leave to enter or remain in the UK but do not have it (new para 7B(1)(a));
- are not asylum seekers (new para 7B(1)(b)); and
- do not have a pending immigration application that is their first application for leave to enter or remain (new para 2A).

It introduces a new Home Office regulated framework of support under new para 10B of Schedule 3 to the 2002 Act and new s 95A of the IAA 1999 in place of the mainstream leaving care provisions of the CA 1989 for these young people.

1 CA 1989, ss 23C, 23CA, 23CZA, 23D, 24A and 24B.
2 See The Care Leavers (England) Regulations 2010, SI 2010/2571.
3 *R (SO) v London Borough of Barking and Dagenham* [2010] EWCA Civ 1101.
4 Inserting section 23CZA into CA 1989.
5 Under CA 1989, s 23D.
6 Care Leavers (England) Regulations 2010, SI 2010/2571, reg 8.

Young people not affected by the changes on access to leaving care support

5.7.1 It is helpful to clarify which groups of young people are not affected by the provisions on access to LA leaving care support and will continue to be able to mainstream provision in the normal way.

Young people under the age of 18 years are not affected by the provisions because they are children and para 1 of Schedule 3 to the NIAA 2002 does not prevent the provision of support or assistance to a child, by operation of para 2(1)(a) of that Schedule.

Part 5—Support etc for Certain Categories of Migrant   5.7.1

Young people with leave to enter or remain are not affected by the provisions. This is because they do not fall within a class of ineligibility under Schedule 3 to the NIAA 2002. They are not a person, included within new para 7A, who does not have leave to enter or remain. Young people with continuing leave under s 3C of the IA 1971 because they applied to extend or vary the leave granted within the period of their leave are also not affected by the provisions for the same reason.

Young people who are asylum seekers are not affected by the provisions on access to LA leaving care support because para 7B of Schedule 3 of the NIAA 2002 excludes asylum seekers from the class of ineligibility.

Young people who make further qualifying submissions on asylum or protection grounds that have not been determined, or who have those submissions accepted as a fresh asylum or protection claim will also continue to be supported by LAs because the definition of 'asylum seeker' follows that in section 18 of the NIAA 2002, (para 17(1) to Schedule 3 to the NIAA 2002 amended by para 40 to Schedule 11, IA 2016), which is amended to reflect the new definition used for Part 6 of the IAA 1999 (para 31 to Schedule 11, IA 2016).

Young people with a pending immigration application that is their first application for leave to enter or remain are also not affected, by operation of new para 2A of Schedule 3 to the NIAA 2002 inserted by para 5 of Schedule 12 to IA 2016. The drafting and position of this provision is awkward because it was added to the Schedule at a later stage following a Government amendment. It was inserted by the Government in response to submissions made by the ILPA during the passage of the Bill that the provisions would exclude from mainstream leaving care support those young people who had a pending immigration application, for example, on the basis that return to their country of origin would breach Article 8 of the ECHR protecting the right to private and family life, an application that may be made by victims of trafficking. The amendment brought forward by the Government is limited to where a young person has a pending immigration application that is their first application for leave to enter or remain (Condition B, para 2A(4) Schedule 3 to the NIAA 2002).

New para 2A(8) of Schedule 3 to the NIAA 2002 allows the SSHD to make regulations determining persons who may be treated as having made an application for leave to enter or remain for the purpose of continuing to access mainstream leaving care support under the CA 1989 despite not having made one but this is subject to delegated legislation and it therefore remains unclear how this provision might be used. It would allow for regulations to make provision for young people who would otherwise be excluded from mainstream leaving care support under these provisions.

5.7.2 *A Guide to the Immigration Act 2016*

Young people affected by the changes on access to leaving care support in Schedule 12

5.7.2 The Government's intention was for Schedule 12 to affect only young people who have not established a lawful basis to remain and whose long-term future will not be in the UK: '[T]he changes made by Schedule 9 of the Bill affect only those adults leaving local authority care who have not established a lawful basis on which to remain here and will generally have exhausted their appeal rights against the refusal of their asylum claim or leave to remain application.'[1]

The changes in Schedule 12 may, however, affect other categories of young people, with pending applications or entitlements, whose future may well be in the UK. Young people affected by the provisions include:

- young people who have not been supported by their LA to regularise their status and have no leave when they reach the age of 18 years as a result;

- young people with a pending immigration application (or appeal arising from this) which is not their first application for leave to enter or remain;

- young people who have an outstanding application to register as a British citizen but have not made an application for leave to enter or remain;

- young people applying for judicial review of an incorrect decision on their claim prior to permission for judicial review being granted;

- young people who cannot return to their country due to a genuine obstacle to removal, which may in certain cases persist for lengthy periods of time;

- young people who have exhausted their appeal rights but have grounds for a further application; and

- young people who have exhausted their appeal rights.

There were specific debates in Parliament on the injustice that would be caused to young people who reach the age of 18 years without the LA having taken steps to regularise their status. Lord Alton of Liverpool pressed amendments during the passage of the Bill that would have disapplied the provisions of Schedule 12 altogether for young people in this position.[2] He provided compelling examples of young people who had lived most of their lives in the UK in foster care without their insecure immigration status having been identified by the LA until they turned 18 years-old. The amendments were rejected, the Minister stating:

Part 5—Support etc for Certain Categories of Migrant 5.7.3

'The Department for Education's statutory guidance for this group is clear that social workers need to support these children to engage with the immigration authorities to resolve their immigration status. This work should be done as an integral part of their pathway plan, which must address the support they will need if they are granted leave to remain in the UK and their long-term future is here.'[3]

The statutory guidance in place, however, has not prevented young people from falling through the gaps, as the examples of young people given by Lord Alton during the debate illustrated.

---

1   Lord Bates to Lord Rosser, *Immigration Bill – Committee stage Day 4 (asylum support, section 95A right of appeal, 28-day grace period, LA support, tuition fee support for care leavers, unaccompanied minors)* 10 February 2016. Available at: http://data.parliament.uk/DepositedPapers/Files/DEP2016-0127/Lord_Rosser_letter_re_Lords_Committee_for_Immigration_Bill__3_Feb__.pdf (accessed 15 November 2016).
2   Lord Alton of Liverpool, Immigration Bill 2015/16, House of Lords Committee, 4th sitting, *Hansard* HL, col 1845 (3 February 2016). Available at: http://www.publications.parliament.uk/pa/ld201516/ldhansrd/text/160203-0002.htm#st_150 (accessed 15 November 2016).
3   Rt Hon Lord Bates, Minister of State, Home Office, Immigration Bill 2015/16, House of Lords Committee, 4th sitting, *Hansard* col 1858 (3 February 2016). Available at: http://www.publications.parliament.uk/pa/ld201516/ldhansrd/text/160203-0002.htm#st_150 (accessed 15 November 2016).

Support for care leavers under Schedule 12, para 10B

5.7.3   The effect of Schedule 12 is to exclude the above categories of young people from the principal leaving care provisions of the CA 1989, which place duties on LAs to continue to provide support and assistance to young people leaving their care and to continue to act as their 'corporate parent' by keeping in touch with the young person, appointing a personal adviser, keeping their pathway plan under review, and making specific provision to meet their educational and training needs.

Young people may qualify instead for more limited support under paragraph 10B of Schedule 3 to the NIAA 2002 provided they meet the necessary conditions (paragraph 10B(1) to (6)):

- they are destitute and have made an application for leave to enter or remain, of a type specified in regulations, which has not been determined;

- they are destitute and could bring a statutory appeal under s 82(1) that is not certified as one that must be continued from outside the UK under s 96(2) of the NIAA 2002;

- they are destitute and have a pending statutory appeal under s 82(1) of the NIAA 2002 that is not certified as one that must be continued outside the UK under s 96(2) of that Act; or

5.7.3 *A Guide to the Immigration Act 2016*

- their appeal rights are exhausted and a person specified in regulations under this paragraph is satisfied that support needs to be provided. The SSHD may also make regulations specifying what may or must be taken into account in making this determination.

The types of provision necessary for meeting the needs of children leaving care are given such a high priority that these are set out as duties on the LA and specified in detail in the CA 1989. They include the requirement to develop a pathway plan setting out a personalised plan for the young person's welfare, regularly review this pathway plan, allocate a personal adviser able to maintain contact with the young person and provide guidance and support, and provide assistance to meet their health, welfare, education and training needs. The nature of support that will be provided to young people under para 10B is principally left to be determined in regulations, albeit subject to the affirmative procedure in Parliament, and the exact nature of provision remains unclear.

Local authorities will be empowered to provide a care leaver who has exhausted their appeal rights with any additional support they consider appropriate, including the possibility of young people remaining in their foster placement.[1] Support to young people may, however, include being moved to adult support and accommodation provided by the Home Office under IAA 1999, s 95A. Ministers have indicated that LAs will be able under regulations to meet any other social care needs of the young person.[2] However, as adult dispersal accommodation provided under IAA 1999, s 95A could potentially provided in any part of the country, this could remove young people from their established support structures.

Ministers suggested that such additional support from a LA, where it was satisfied it needed to be provided to a young person, could allow for a managed transition process:

> 'This will enable the local authority to ensure that support does not end abruptly, so that there can be a managed process of encouraging and enabling departure from the UK. The local authority will be able to provide accommodation, subsistence and, by virtue of paragraph 11 of Schedule 3, such other social care support as it considers necessary in individual circumstances. This might, for example, include social worker support in coming to terms with the requirement to leave the UK and making arrangements for that. Where appropriate, it might involve remaining in a foster placement for that period.'[3]

The clear duties placed on LAs under the CA 1989 are replaced by regulations made by the SSHD, where the extent to which LAs will be under duties or a discretion to provide support under para 10B is unclear. In the light of the resource constraints on LAs, it is likely that provision for young people leaving care will not be made where the LA has no clear duties in relation to the provision of support in accordance with an assessment of welfare need. A key rationale given by Edward Timpson, now Minister for the Department of Education, for placing a legal duty on LAs to make provision for 'staying put' arrangements that enable young people to remain in foster care placements makes this clear:

> 'A growing number of local authorities already offer young people the choice to stay but with little financial support it can be challenging for their foster families. Now all councils will have to follow their example, and we are giving them £40 million towards the cost.'[4]

In the absence of a clear duty and funding of provision, local authorities are unlikely to provide the additional support that this vulnerable group of young people leaving care will require when making the transition to adulthood.

The Government has committed to consulting with leaving care organisations on the detail of the regulations.[5]

---

1 Lord Bates to Lord Rosser, *Immigration Bill – Committee stage Day 4 (asylum support, section 95A right of appeal, 28-day grace period, LA support, tuition fee support for care leavers, unaccompanied minors)* 10 February 2016. Available at: http://data.parliament.uk/DepositedPapers/Files/DEP2016-0127/Lord_Rosser_letter_re_Lords_Committee_for_Immigration_Bill__3_Feb__.pdf (accessed 15 November 2016); Rt Hon James Brokenshire MP to Emma Smale and Enver Solomon, co-chairs, Alliance for Children in Care and Care Leavers, *Immigration Bill – care leavers*, 10 March 2016 Asylum – Housing, Rt Hon James Brokenshire MP, WA29521, 9 March 2016. Available at: http://www.i/pa.org.uk/resource/31952/rt-hon-james-brokenshire-mp-immigration-minister-to-co-chairs-alliance-for-children-in-care-and-care/ (accessed 15 November 2016).
2 Ibid.
3 Rt Hon Lord Bates, Minister of State, Home Office, Immigration Bill 2015/16, House of Lords Committee, 4th sitting, *Hansard* HL col 1858 (3 February 2016). Available at: http://www.publications.parliament.uk/pa/ld201516/ldhansrd/text/160203-0002.htm#st_150 (accessed 15 November 2016).
4 *Children to stay with foster families until 21*, Department for Education, news article, 4 December 2013 https://www.gov.uk/government/news/children-to-stay-with-foster-families-until-21 (accessed 15 November 2016).
5 Rt Hon James Brokenshire MP to Emma Smale and Enver Solomon, co-chairs, Alliance for Children in Care and Care Leavers, *Immigration Bill – care leavers*, 10 March 2016. Available at: http://www.i/pa.org.uk/resource/31952/rt-hon-james-brokenshire-mp-immigration-minister-to-co-chairs-alliance-for-children-in-care-and-care/ (accessed 15 November 2016).

CARE LEAVERS: TUITION FEES

5.8 The Education (Student Support) Regulations 2011, SI 2001/1986 provide, *inter alia*, for categories of people eligible for student finance (and therefore home fees) for higher education study. Those with refugee status, humanitarian protection or indefinite leave to remain are eligible for student

5.8 A Guide to the Immigration Act 2016

finance, although those with humanitarian protection or indefinite leave to remain additionally need to have had a period of lawful residence in the UK for three years. Since an amendment to the regulations made by the Department of Business, Innovation and Skills, young people with limited leave to remain were no longer eligible for student finance. This prevented many young people from being able to access higher education due to the high costs of both tuition fees and their living expenses.

Local authorities have continuing duties to young people leaving their care, including under the CA 1989, s 24B which provides for LAs to provide assistance with education, training and employment including by making grants to enable them to meet expenses connected with their education and training (CA 1989, s 24B(2)(b)). In the case of *R (Kebede) v Newcastle City Council* [2013] EWCA Civ 960, it was held that the cost of higher education tuition was an expense that fell within the scope of a LA's duties under the CA 1989, s 24B. Local authorities were therefore obliged to fund at a local level the higher education of young people in their care who were not entitled to student finance when provision had formally been made available centrally for young people with limited leave to remain under the student finance regulations. Whilst this was a significant expense for LAs, particularly since tuition fees were often set at the overseas rate for asylum seekers, those with limited leave to remain and others unable to access student finance, it ensured that young people were able to continue their education helping them to rebuild their lives after periods of trauma and difficulty and enabled LAs to meet their obligations to these young people.

Schedule 12 Paragraph 3 of to the IA 2016 inserts new para 1A into Schedule 3 to the NIAA 2002. This prevents LAs from providing grants to meet expenses connected to education and training for young people leaving their care. The provisions are applied to a wider category of young people than those affected by the limitation on access to leaving care support, and will affect young people with limited leave to remain and young people who are asylum seekers, or have other pending applications for leave to enter or remain as well as young people who have exhausted their appeal rights in the UK. Though refugee leave is a limited form of leave to enter or remain, young people with refugee status will not be affected by the provision as they qualify for a student loan as soon as they are recognised as a refugee, however, young people with limited leave to remain, or pending applications will face difficulty accessing funding for higher education and may not be able to pursue this.' No alternative provision was made or promised during the passage of the IA 2016 for those young people who will no longer be able to access support from their LA to access higher education.

Part 5—Support etc for Certain Categories of Migrant **5.9**

DEVOLUTION

5.9 The provisions of Schedule 12 are currently drafted as applicable to England. The Government is empowered to extend provisions under Schedule 3 of the NIAA 2002 to devolved administrations by operation of regulations under new para 15(d) of that Schedule (inserted by para 14(4) of Schedule 12 to the IA 2016) which enables the SSHD to make support available to different classes of persons.

Specific provisions relating to payment of tuition fees of care leavers may be extended to Wales under new para 15(e) and to Scotland and Northern Ireland under new para 15(f) of Schedule 3 to the NIAA 2002, both inserted by para 14(4) of Schedule 12 to the IA 2016.

Paragraph 16 of Schedule 3 of the NIAA 2002 also contains powers to use regulations to make certain changes to provisions and amend legislation in consequence. These are extended to include powers to repeal or revoke legislation by new para 16(2)(d) Schedule 3 to the NIAA 2002 inserted by para 15(2) of Schedule 12 to the IA 2016.

The Government's position on devolution with respect to the provisions inserted into Schedule 3 to the NIAA 2002 is as follows:

'The amendments make changes to the availability of local authority support in England for certain categories of migrant. As immigration is a reserved matter and immigration legislation makes provision for migrants' access to local authority services, the government has in mind to amend the Bill at a later stage to extend these provisions to the rest of the UK once we have had further dialogue with the Devolved Administrations.'[1]

Whilst immigration control is a reserved matter, the provisions impact on social care provision which is devolved. Proposed amendments to the Bill seeking the requirement that the Government obtain legislative consent from the devolved administration before making changes to social care systems were, defeated.

The Government has initiated dialogues with the devolved administrations about how provisions may be brought into effect in the devolved administrations. The Scottish administration expressed concern about the provisions in a strongly worded letter to the Minister:

'I have noted the changes to Schedule 3 of the 2002 Act on local authority support for asylum seekers, which you plan to extend to Scotland. Once again, I am extremely concerned about the impact this will have, particularly

5.10 *A Guide to the Immigration Act 2016*

on children and young adults. Care leavers face some of the most difficult challenges in our society. To cut off their support at a time, when they are at their most vulnerable is both morally wrong and also places them at serious risk of harm. Furthermore, I also believe it is wrong to seek to remove young adults who may have spent the majority of their lives in the UK and may no longer have any connection with their countries of origin.... I hope that you will seriously consider and take on board the comments I have made believe the proposals in the Bill will not achieve their objectives, are wrong in principle and undermine our ambition to build a fairer Scotland.'[2]

The extension of the provisions through secondary legislation will mean that they are not subject to the same detailed scrutiny by Parliament as the provisions for England. If the measures made in secondary legislation are found to be incompatible with the UK's obligations under the Human Rights Act 1998 (HRA 1998) they may be struck down rather than simply declared incompatible as is the case for primary legislation.

---

1 Clive Peckover, Asylum and Family Policy Unit, Immigration and Border Policy Directorate, Home Office to National Asylum Stakeholder Forum, *Immigration Bill – support for certain categories of migrant (new Schedule on LA support)*, 12 November 2015. Available at: http://www.ilpa.org.uk/resources.php/31560/immigration-bill-ilpa-briefing-for-house-of-commons-committee-government-new-clause-17-and-governmen (accessed 15 November 2016).
2 Letter from Alex Neil MSP, Cabinet Secretary for Social Justice, Communities and Pensioners' Rights to Rt Hon James Brokenshire MP, 8 December 2015. Available at: http://data.parliament.uk/DepositedPapers/Files/DEP2016-0300/2015-12-OS_Alex_Neil_to_JB_-_support.pdf (accessed 15 November 2016).

TRANSFER OF RESPONSIBILITY FOR RELEVANT CHILDREN

5.10 Sections 69–73 on the transfer of responsibility for relevant children were introduced to the Immigration Bill by the Government at Report stage in the House of Commons. They create a mechanism in England under which responsibility for caring for unaccompanied children may be transferred from one LA to another, either on a voluntary basis or under an enforced scheme.

The proposals were developed in the context of the refugee crisis, during which increased numbers of unaccompanied asylum seeking children seeking protection in the UK led to Kent County Council, where many children arrived, voicing concerns about the pressure on the local authority.[1] In July 2015, the Association of Directors of Children's Services and Kent County Council wrote to all LAs in England requesting their help in providing suitable foster, or residential care placements to unaccompanied children arriving in Kent. The provisions in IA 2016 put the voluntary arrangements established at that time on a statutory footing and introduce a compulsory transfer scheme which would be used where LAs did not come forward in sufficient numbers to volunteer to take on the responsibility for newly arrived children. Ministers stated that they hoped that the voluntary arrangements would succeed and that the power to require LAs to co-operate with the transfer of unaccompanied children would not need to be used.[2]

---

1 Letter of James Brokenshire MP Immigration Minister to Sir Keir Starmer MP, 25 November 2015. Available at: http://data.parliament.uk/DepositedPapers/Files/DEP2015-0916/2015-11-25_JB_to_Keir_Starmer_-_support_amendments.pdf (accessed 15 November 2016).
2 For example, Lord Bates, Minister of State, Home Office, Immigration Bill 2015/16 Report stage, House of Lords, 2nd sitting, *Hansard* HL, col 1759 (15 March 2016). Available at: http://www.publications.parliament.uk/pa/ld201516/ldhansrd/text/160315-0001.htm#16031556000351 (accessed 15 November 2016).

SECTION 69—TRANSFER OF RESPONSIBILITY FOR RELEVANT CHILDREN

> **Summary**
>
> Creates a mechanism in England under which responsibility for caring for unaccompanied children may be transferred from one local authority to another on a voluntary basis.

5.11

69 Transfer of responsibility for relevant children

(1) This section applies in relation to a local authority in England ("the first authority") if—

    (a) the authority has functions under any of the provisions of or made under Part 3, 4 or 5 of the Children Act 1989 (support for children and families and care, supervision and protection of children) ("the relevant provisions") in relation to a relevant child, or

    (b) functions under any of the relevant provisions may be conferred on the authority in relation to a relevant child.

(2) The first authority may make arrangements with another local authority in England ("the second authority") under which—

    (a) if this section applies to the authority by virtue of paragraph (a) of subsection (1), the functions mentioned in that paragraph become functions of the second authority in relation to the relevant child, and

(b) if this section applies to the authority by virtue of paragraph (b) of subsection (1), the functions mentioned in that paragraph become functions that may be conferred on the second authority in relation to the relevant child.

(3) The effect of arrangements under this section is that, from the time at which the arrangements have effect in accordance with their terms—

  (a) functions under the relevant provisions cease to be functions of, and may not be conferred on, the first authority in relation to the relevant child ("C"),

  (b) any of the relevant provisions which immediately before that time applied in relation to C as a result of C's connection with the first authority or the area of the first authority have effect as if C had that connection with the second authority or the area of the second authority (if that would not otherwise be the case), and

  (c) C is to be treated for the purposes of the relevant provisions as if C were not and had never been ordinarily resident in the area of the first authority (if that would otherwise be the case).

(4) Subsection (3)(b) is subject to any change in C's circumstances after the time at which the arrangements have effect.

(5) Nothing in subsection (3) affects any liability of the first authority in relation to C for any act or omission of the first authority before the time at which the arrangements have effect.

(6) The Secretary of State may by regulations make further provision about the effect of arrangements under this section.

(7) Arrangements under this section may not be brought to an end by the first or second authority once they have come into effect.

(8) In this section "local authority" means a local authority within the meaning of the Children Act 1989 (see section 105(1) of that Act).

(9) In this section "relevant child" means—

  (a) a person under the age of 18 who is unaccompanied and has made a protection claim which has not been determined,

  (b) a person under the age of 18 who is unaccompanied and who—

    (i) requires leave to enter or remain in the United Kingdom but does not have it, and

    (ii) is a person of a kind specified in regulations made by the Secretary of State, or

  (c) a person under the age of 18 who is unaccompanied and who—

    (i) has leave to enter or remain in the United Kingdom, and

    (ii) is a person of a kind specified in regulations made by the Secretary of State.

Part 5—Support etc for Certain Categories of Migrant **5.11**

(10) The Secretary of State may by regulations make provision about the meaning of "unaccompanied" for the purposes of subsection (9).

(11) In subsection (9)—

(a) "protection claim" has the meaning given by section 82(2) of the Nationality, Immigration and Asylum Act 2002, and

(b) the reference to a protection claim having been determined is to be construed in accordance with section 94(3) of the Immigration and Asylum Act 1999.

Commencement: 31 May 2016, Immigration Act 2016 (Commencement No 1) Regulations 2016, SI 2016/603.

Regulations: May be made by the Secretary of State (SSHD) under s 69(6) to make further provision about the effect of arrangements under this section dealing with voluntary transfer arrangements between local authorities; under s 69(9) to specify kinds of unaccompanied children with, and without leave to remain, within the scope of the scheme; and under s 69(10) to make provision about the meaning of 'unaccompanied'.

Guidance: *Interim National Transfer Protocol for Unaccompanied Asylum Seeking Children 2016–17*, v0.8, Department for Education, Home Office, Department for Communities and Local Government, 1 July 2016.

Definitions:

'C' the relevant child (see below), s 69(3);

'first authority' the local authority making an arrangement to transfer a child to another local authority, s 69(1);

'local authority' a local authority within the meaning of the Children Act 1989 (CA 1989) (see s 105(1) of that Act), s 69(8);

'protection claim' has the meaning given by s 82(2) of the Nationality, Immigration and Asylum Act 2002 (NIAA 2002), s 69(11)(a);

'protection claim having been determined' is to be construed in accordance with s 94(3) of the Immigration and Asylum Act 1999, s 69(11)(b);

'the relevant provisions' Parts 3, 4 or 5 of the CA 1989 on support for children and families and care, supervision and protection of children, s 69(1);

'relevant child' an unaccompanied person under 18 years who has made a protection claim which has not been determined; an unaccompanied person under 18 years who requires leave to enter or remain in the UK but does not have it and is of a kind specified in regulations made by the SSHD; or an unaccompanied person under 18 years who has leave to enter or remain in the UK and is of a kind specified in regulations made by the SSHD, s 69(9);

5.11 A Guide to the Immigration Act 2016

'second authority' the local authority with whom an arrangement is made or sought to transfer a child from another local authority, s 69(2);

'unaccompanied' the meaning may be provided for in regulations by the Secretary of State, s 69(10);

Devolution: Currently applies to England, but can be extended by regulations made by the devolved administrations, at which point the SSHD has power under s 73 to make enabling legislation.

Section 69 establishes the voluntary mechanism under which a LA may transfer responsibility for a relevant child to another LA. This is modelled on the voluntary transfer arrangements that were in place between Kent social services and other LAs offering placements to newly arrived children from July 2015.

Under the voluntary mechanism established, a LA may make arrangements with another LA to transfer responsibility for a 'relevant child' (s 69(2)). The child then becomes the responsibility of the second LA and any local connections apply as if the second LA had always had responsibility for the child (s 69(3)).

The transfer mechanism was broadly welcomed because transferring responsibility with the relocation of the child was considered preferable to placing a child in an out-of-area placement with more limited access to support where there is pressure on services within a LA.

A 'relevant child' is defined in s 69(9) as an unaccompanied person under 18 years who has made a protection claim which has not been determined. A protection claim is one which would breach the UK's obligations under the Refugee Convention or its obligations in relation to those eligible for a grant of humanitarian protection (NIAA 2002, s 82).

The provisions may also be applied to unaccompanied children under 18 years who require leave to enter or remain in the UK, but do not have it and are of a kind specified in regulations made by the SSHD. They may also be applied to unaccompanied children who have been granted leave to enter or remain in the UK and are of a kind specified in regulations made by the SSHD, s 69(9). Regulations have so far not been made under this section and so the provisions currently only apply in relation to unaccompanied children who have made a protection claim.

Whilst the intention of the scheme is to make provision for newly arrived children, the legislation is drafted broadly creating a risk it could be improperly applied to unaccompanied children established in a LA, whether they are an asylum seeker, have limited leave to remain, humanitarian protection or refugee status, to be transferred to another LA at any point in time during their care. The scope of the scheme is currently limited through guidance to unaccompanied children seeking asylum (see below).

The Government stated that its reason for including children with leave to remain was so that the provisions could also cover children who arrive in the UK with refugee status, as the Government had announced its intention to work with UNHCR to lead a new initiative to identify and resettle unaccompanied refugee children from conflict regions where it is in the best interests of the child. This would enable the scheme to be used where voluntary arrangements with LAs were not sufficient.[1]

Transferring children to another LA under the scheme after they are established in the care of a LA has the potential to undermine the duties of LAs towards looked after children in their care, including the duty to promote permanence and stability in their care,[2] and to ensure placements do not disrupt the child's education or training.[3] The stage at which the child is moved to another LA will be relevant to whether this is in their best interests, which must be taken into account. Whilst it might be possible to contemplate the transfer to a second LA of an unaccompanied child who has newly arrived in the UK, it is unlikely to be in a child's best interests to move them once they have spent any length of time in the first LA, developed relationships with carers or other individuals important to the child, become established in education or oriented themselves within the area. Local authorities also have duties under the CA 1989 to ascertain the child's wishes and feelings[4] and give due consideration to those wishes and feelings in any decision concerning the child.[5]

Another concern raised in Parliament was the lack of time limits within the provisions for the transfer of responsibility for a child from one LA to a receiving LA. This risks delay or 'drift' in establishing or enforcing the transfer arrangements, contrary to children's best interests, particularly as situations of limbo or uncertainty may increase the risk of children going missing. Statutory guidance on *Working Together to Safeguard Children* provides that a LA social worker should make a decision about the type of response that is required for a child within one working day of a referral being received.[6]

Guidance issued on the operation of the scheme in the form of an interim protocol has addressed these concerns to some extent.[7] The guidance makes clear that the transfer mechanism only applies to unaccompanied children who have applied for asylum.[8] It indicates that the transfer decision should be made as soon as practicable and ideally within 48 hours of the arrival of the child into care, unless it would be in the child's best interests to defer that decision.[9] It further states that where children are settled and established in a LA area, that LA may make the decision that it is not in the best interests of the child for them to be moved.[10] The protocol includes guidance on assessing the best interests of the child, including their views and matters relating to

5.11 *A Guide to the Immigration Act 2016*

their personal identity, their care, protection and safety, their health needs, their education and their access to legal representation.[11]

Children may be transferred from Kent social services, or any other LA where the number of unaccompanied children from abroad exceeds the threshold of 0.07 per cent of the numbers of children in the LA area. This may currently include some LAs in London.

---

1 Rt Hon Lord Bates, Minister of State, Home Office, Immigration Bill 2015/16 Report stage, House of Lords, 2nd sitting, *Hansard* HL, col 1840 (15 March 2016). Available at: http://www.publications.parliament.uk/pa/ld201516/ldhansrd/text/160315-0001.htm#16031556000351 (accessed 15 November 2016).
2 *The Children Act 1989 Guidance and Regulations Volume 2: Care planning, placement and case review* (statutory guidance), Department for Education, June 2015. Available at: https://www.gov.uk/government/uploads/system/uploads/attachment_data/file/441643/Children_Act_Guidance_2015.pdf (accessed 15 November 2016).
3 CA 1989, s 22C(7) and (8)(b), see also above statutory guidance and regulations.
4 CA 1989, s 22(4), see also above statutory guidance and regulations.
5 CA 1989, s 22(5), see also above statutory guidance and regulations.
6 *Working Together to Safeguard Children: A guide to inter-agency working to safeguard and promote the welfare of children*, HM Government, March 2015. Available at: https://www.gov.uk/government/uploads/system/uploads/attachment_data/file/419595/Working_Together_to_Safeguard_Children.pdf, para 38.
7 *Interim National Transfer Protocol for Unaccompanied Asylum Seeking Children 2016–17*, v0.8, Department for Education, Home Office, Department for Communities and Local Government, 1 July 2016. Available at: https://www.gov.uk/government/publications/naccompanied-asylum-seeking-children-interim-national-transfer-scheme (accessed 15 November 2016).
8 Ibid, p 7.
9 Ibid, p 9.
10 Ibid, p 7.
11 Ibid, Annex A.

SECTION 70—DUTY TO PROVIDE INFORMATION FOR THE PURPOSES OF TRANSFER OF RESPONSIBILITY

Summary

Facilitates the mechanism in England under which responsibility for caring for unaccompanied children may be transferred from one local authority to another by placing duties on local authorities to provide relevant information.

5.12

70 Duty to provide information for the purposes of transfers of responsibility

(1) The Secretary of State may direct a local authority in England to provide information of the kind specified in subsection (2) to the Secretary of State for the purposes of enabling—

    (a) arrangements to be made under section 69, or

    (b) the Secretary of State to exercise functions under section 72.

(2) The information mentioned in subsection (1) is—

    (a) information about the support or accommodation provided to children who are looked after by the local authority within the meaning of the Children Act 1989;

    (b) such other information as may be specified in regulations made by the Secretary of State.

(3) A local authority which is directed to provide information under this section must provide it—

    (a) in such form and manner as the Secretary of State may direct, and

    (b) before such time or before the end of such period as the Secretary of State may direct.

(4) In this section "local authority" has the same meaning as in section 69.

Commencement: 31 May 2016, Immigration Act 2016 (Commencement No 1) Regulations 2016, SI 2016/603.

Definitions:

'local authority' a local authority (LA) within the meaning of the Children Act 1989 (see s 105(1) of that Act), s 69(8), s 70(4).

Devolution: Currently applies to England, but can be extended by regulations made by the devolved administrations, at which point the Secretary of State has power under s 73 to make enabling legislation.

This section facilitates both the voluntary arrangements (under s 69) and the scheme enforced by the SSHD (s 72) for transferring responsibility for relevant children by requiring LAs to provide relevant information if directed to do so by the SSHD for the purpose of either mechanism. A LA might be asked, for example, to provide the SSHD with the numbers of its available foster carers. The LA is required to provide the information in the format directed by the SSHD and within the time frame directed.

SECTION 71—REQUEST FOR TRANSFER OF RESPONSIBILITY FOR RELEVANT CHILDREN

> **Summary**
>
> Facilitates the mechanism in England under which responsibility for caring for unaccompanied children may be transferred from one local authority to another by requiring a local authority to provide written reasons for not complying with a transfer request.

5.13

71 Request for transfer of responsibility for relevant children

(1) Subsection (2) applies if—

    (a) a local authority in England ("the first authority") requests another local authority in England ("the second authority") to enter into arrangements under section 69, and

    (b) the second authority does not comply with the first authority's request.

(2) The Secretary of State may direct the second authority to provide the first authority and the Secretary of State with written reasons for its failure to comply with the request.

(3) In this section "local authority" has the same meaning as in section 69.

Commencement: 31 May 2016, Immigration Act 2016 (Commencement No 1) Regulations 2016, SI 2016/603.

Regulations: May be made by the Secretary of State (SSHD) under s 69(6) to make further provision about the effect of arrangements under this section dealing with voluntary transfer arrangements between local authorities (LAs).

Guidance: *Interim National Transfer Protocol for Unaccompanied Asylum Seeking Children 2016-17*, v0.8, Department for Education, Home Office, Department for Communities and Local Government, 1 July 2016.

Definitions:

'first authority' the local authority making an arrangement to transfer a child to another local authority, s 69(1);

'local authority' a LA within the meaning of the Children Act 1989 (see s 105(1) of that Act), s 69(8);

'second authority' the LA with whom an arrangement is made or sought to transfer a child from another LA, s 69(2);

Devolution: Currently applies to England, but can be extended by regulations made by the devolved administrations, at which point the SSHD has power under s 73 to make enabling legislation.'

The provision facilitates the statutory mechanism under which responsibility for unaccompanied children may be transferred from one LA to another LA in England. A LA which does not comply with a request to accept a voluntary transfer of responsibility from another LA may be directed to provide written reasons for doing so by the SSHD.

SECTION 72—SCHEME FOR TRANSFER OF RESPONSIBILITY FOR RELEVANT CHILDREN

> **Summary**
>
> Creates a mechanism in England under which responsibility for caring for unaccompanied children may be transferred from one local authority to another under a scheme enforced by the Secretary of State.

5.14

72 Scheme for transfer of responsibility for relevant children

(1) The Secretary of State may prepare a scheme for functions of, or which may be conferred on, a local authority in England ("the transferring authority") to become functions of, or functions which may be conferred on, one or more other local authorities in England (a "receiving authority") in accordance with arrangements under section 69.

(2) A scheme under this section—

   (a) must specify the local authorities to which it relates, and

   (b) unless it relates to all relevant children who may be the subject of arrangements under section 69 between the transferring authority and each receiving authority, must specify the relevant child or children, or descriptions of relevant children, to which it relates.

(3) The Secretary of State may direct the transferring authority and each receiving authority under a scheme under this section to comply with the scheme.

(4) A direction may not be given under subsection (3) unless the Secretary of State is satisfied that compliance with the direction will not unduly prejudice the discharge by each receiving authority of any of its functions.

(5) Before giving a direction under subsection (3) to a local authority, the Secretary of State must give the authority notice in writing of the proposed direction.

(6) The Secretary of State may not give a direction to a local authority before the end of the period of 14 days beginning with the day on which notice under subsection (5) was given to it.

(7) The local authority may make written representations to the Secretary of State about the proposed direction within that period.

(8) The Secretary of State may modify or withdraw a direction under subsection (3) by notice in writing to the local authorities to which it was given.

(9) A modification or withdrawal of a direction does not affect any arrangements made under section 69 pursuant to the direction before it was modified or withdrawn.

(10) Subsections (5) to (7) apply to the modification or withdrawal of a direction as they apply to the giving of a direction, but as if—

(a) the reference to the proposed direction were to the proposed modification or proposal to withdraw the direction, and

(b) subsection (6) permitted the Secretary of State to withdraw the direction before the end of the 14 day period with the agreement of the local authorities to which it applies.

(11) In this section "local authority" and "relevant child" have the same meanings as in section 69.

Commencement: 31 May 2016, Immigration Act 2016 (Commencement No. 1) Regulations 2016, SI 2016/603.

Guidance: *Interim National Transfer protocol for Unaccompanied Asylum Seeking Children*, version 0.8, draft operational from 1 July 2016, Home Office, Department for Education and Department for Communities and Local Government.

Definitions:

'local authority' a local authority (LA) within the meaning of the Children Act 1989 (see s 105(1) of that Act), s 69(8), s 72(11);

'receiving authority' one or more LAs on which the SSHD may confer functions from another LA under the scheme, s 72(1);

'relevant child' an unaccompanied person under 18 years who has made a protection claim which has not been determined; an unaccompanied person under 18 years who requires leave to enter or remain in the UK but does not have it and is of a kind specified in regulations made by the SSHD; or an unaccompanied person under 18 years who has leave to enter or remain in the UK and is of a kind specified in regulations made by the SSHD, s 69(9), s 72(11);

Part 5—Support etc for Certain Categories of Migrant **5.14**

'transferring authority' a local authority from which the SSHD may confer functions on one or more other LAs;

'unaccompanied' the meaning may be provided for in regulations by the SSHD, s 69(10);

Devolution: Currently applies to England, but can be extended by regulations made by the devolved administrations, at which point the SSHD has power under s 73 to make enabling legislation.

This section allows the SSHD to establish a scheme under which responsibility for unaccompanied children may be transferred from a LA to one or more other LAs (s 72(1)) and to direct that LAs comply with the scheme (s 72(3)).

Ministers stated that they hoped that the voluntary arrangements would succeed and that the power to require LAs to co-operate with the transfer of unaccompanied children would not need to be used, but they were seeking to ensure there was a mechanism in place to deal with difficulties similar to those experienced by Kent social services following the refugee crisis.[1]

The SSHD is only able to give a direction to comply with the scheme if it is satisfied that it will not unduly prejudice the discharge of functions by the LAs concerned (s 72(4)). She must also give written notice of the proposed direction to comply (s 72(5)) and allow a 14-day period in which the LA may make representations (ss 72(6)–(7)). The Secretary of State may modify or withdraw the direction in response (s 72(8)).

---

[1] Lord Bates, Minister of State, Home Office, Immigration Bill 2015/16 Committee stage, House of Lords, 1st sitting, *Hansard* HL, col 632, (18 January 2016). Available at: http://www.publications.parliament.uk/pa/ld201516/ldhansrd/text/160118-0001.htm#1601184000412 (accessed 15 November 2016).

SECTION 73—EXTENSION TO WALES, SCOTLAND AND NORTHERN IRELAND

Summary

Provides for the mechanism under ss 69–72 for the transfer of responsibility of relevant children to be extended by regulations made by the devolved administrations and empowers the Secretary of State to make enabling legislation to facilitate this.

5.15 A Guide to the Immigration Act 2016

5.15

73 Extension to Wales, Scotland and Northern Ireland

(1) The Secretary of State may by regulations make such provision as the Secretary of State considers appropriate for enabling any of the provisions of sections 69 to 72 to apply in relation to Wales, Scotland or Northern Ireland.

(2) The Secretary of State may by regulations make provision which—

   (a) has a similar effect to—

      (i) any of the provisions mentioned in subsection (1), or

      (ii) provision which may be made under section 69(6) or (10), and

   (b) applies in relation to Wales, Scotland or Northern Ireland.

(3) Regulations under subsection (1) may amend, repeal or revoke any enactment (including an enactment contained in this Act).

(4) Regulations under subsection (1) or (2) may not confer functions on—

   (a) the Welsh Ministers,

   (b) the Scottish Ministers,

   (c) the First Minister and deputy First Minister in Northern Ireland,

   (d) a Northern Ireland Minister, or

   (e) a Northern Ireland department.

(5) In this section "enactment" includes—

   (a) an enactment contained in subordinate legislation within the meaning of the Interpretation Act 1978;

   (b) an enactment contained in, or in an instrument made under, an Act or Measure of the National Assembly for Wales;

   (c) an enactment contained in, or in an instrument made under, an Act of the Scottish Parliament;

   (d) an enactment contained in, or in an instrument made under, Northern Ireland legislation.

Commencement: 31 May 2016, Immigration Act 2016 (Commencement No 1) Regulations 2016, SI 2016/603.

Regulations: Under s 73(1) to make such provision as the Secretary of State considers appropriate for enabling any of the provisions of ss 69–72 to apply in relation to Wales, Scotland and Northern Ireland.

Definitions:

'enactment' includes secondary legislation, an enactment contained in, or in an instrument under, an Act or Measure of the National Assembly for Wales, an Act of the Scottish Parliament or Northern Ireland legislation.

Devolution: this is the subject matter of the section.

The statutory mechanism for the transfer of relevant children under ss 69–72 only applies in England. The provisions do not apply to the devolved administrations and may not be conferred on them by regulations. They may only be extended through regulations made by the devolved administrations. The Secretary of State is empowered under this section to make enabling legislation to facilitate this if the devolved administrations choose to act.

Part 6—Border Security

SECTION 74—PENALTIES RELATING TO AIRPORT CONTROL AREAS AND SCHEDULE 13—PENALTIES RELATING TO AIRPORT CONTROL AREAS

> **Summary**
> Creates a civil penalty regime targeting airlines and airport officers who allow passengers to disembark without being presented to immigration control where a control zone has been designated.

6.1

74 Penalties relating to airport control areas

(1) In paragraph 26 of Schedule 2 to the Immigration Act 1971 (supplementary duties of those connected with ships or aircraft or with ports) after sub-paragraph (3A) insert—

"(4) Part 1A of this Schedule makes provision for and in connection with the imposition of a penalty for certain breaches of sub-paragraph (2) or (3)."

(2) In that Schedule after Part 1 insert the Part 1A set out in Schedule 13.

Schedule 13

Section 74

Penalties relating to airport control areas

This is the Part 1A of Schedule 2 to the Immigration Act 1971 referred to in section 74(2)—

6.1 *A Guide to the Immigration Act 2016*

"PART 1A PENALTY FOR BREACH OF PARAGRAPH 26(2) OR (3)

Penalty for breach of paragraph 26(2) or (3)

28(1) Sub-paragraph (2) applies where the Secretary of State has given written notice under paragraph 26(2) to the owner or agent of an aircraft—

    (a) designating a control area for the embarkation or disembarkation of passengers in an airport in the United Kingdom, and

    (b) specifying conditions or restrictions to be observed in the control area.

(2) The Secretary of State may impose a penalty on the owner or agent if the owner or agent fails to take all reasonable steps to secure that—

    (a) passengers embarking on or disembarking from the aircraft at the airport do not embark or disembark at the airport outside the control area, or

    (b) the conditions or restrictions specified in the notice are observed.

(3) Sub-paragraph (4) applies where the Secretary of State has given written notice under paragraph 26(3) to a person concerned with the management of an airport in the United Kingdom—

    (a) designating a control area in the airport, and

    (b) specifying conditions or restrictions to be observed in the control area.

(4) The Secretary of State may impose a penalty on the person if the person fails to take all reasonable steps to secure that the conditions or restrictions specified in the notice are observed.

(5) The Secretary of State may impose a separate penalty under sub-paragraph (2) or (4) in respect of each failure of the kind mentioned in that sub-paragraph.

(6) The amount of a penalty imposed under sub-paragraph (2) or (4) may be such an amount as the Secretary of State considers appropriate; but the amount of each penalty must not exceed the prescribed maximum.

Codes of practice

28A(1) The Secretary of State must issue a code of practice to be followed by—

    (a) agents and operators of aircraft to whom notices under paragraph 26(2) have been given, and

Part 6—Border Security **6.1**

- (b) persons concerned with the management of airports in the United Kingdom to whom notices under paragraph 26(3) have been given.

(2) The Secretary of State must have regard to the code (in addition to any other matters the Secretary of State thinks relevant)—

- (a) when deciding whether to impose a penalty under paragraph 28, and
- (b) when considering a notice of objection under paragraph 28C.

(3) The Secretary of State must issue a code of practice specifying matters to be considered in determining the amount of a penalty under paragraph 28.

(4) The Secretary of State must have regard to the code (in addition to any other matters the Secretary of State thinks relevant)—

- (a) when imposing a penalty under paragraph 28, and
- (b) when considering a notice of objection under paragraph 28C.

(5) Before issuing a code under this paragraph the Secretary of State must lay the code before Parliament.

(6) A code under this paragraph comes into force in accordance with provision made by regulations made by the Secretary of State.

(7) The Secretary of State may from time to time review a code under this paragraph and may revise and re-issue it following a review.

(8) References in sub-paragraphs (5) and (6) to a code include a revised code.

Penalty notices

28B(1) If the Secretary of State decides that a person is liable to a penalty under paragraph 28, the Secretary of State must notify the person of that decision.

(2) A notice under sub-paragraph (1) (a "penalty notice") must—

- (a) be in writing,
- (b) state why the Secretary of State thinks the recipient is liable to the penalty,
- (c) state the amount of the penalty,
- (d) specify the date on which the penalty notice is given,
- (e) specify the date, at least 28 days after the date specified in the notice as the date on which it is given, before which the penalty must be paid,

6.1 *A Guide to the Immigration Act 2016*

    (f)   specify how the penalty must be paid,

    (g)   include an explanation of the steps that the person may take if the person objects to the penalty (including specifying the manner and form in which any notice of objection must be given to the Secretary of State), and

    (h)   include an explanation of the steps the Secretary of State may take to recover any unpaid penalty.

Objections

28C(1)   The recipient of a penalty notice ("the recipient") may object to the penalty notice by giving a notice of objection to the Secretary of State.

(2)   A notice of objection must—

    (a)   be in writing,

    (b)   give the reasons for the objection,

    (c)   be given in the manner and form specified in the penalty notice, and

    (d)   be given before the end of the period of 28 days beginning with the date specified in the penalty notice as the date on which it is given.

(3)   Where the Secretary of State receives a notice of objection, the Secretary of State must consider it and—

    (a)   cancel the penalty,

    (b)   reduce the penalty,

    (c)   increase the penalty, or

    (d)   determine not to alter the penalty.

(4)   After reaching a decision as to how to proceed under sub-paragraph (3), the Secretary of State must notify the recipient of the decision in writing.

(5)   A notification under sub-paragraph (4) must be given before the end of the period of 70 days beginning with the date specified in the penalty notice as the date on which it is given, or such longer period as the Secretary of State may agree with the recipient.

(6)   A notification under sub-paragraph (4), other than one notifying the recipient that the Secretary of State has decided to cancel the penalty, must—

    (a)   state the amount of the penalty following the Secretary of State's consideration of the notice of objection,

Part 6—Border Security **6.1**

- (b) state the Secretary of State's reasons for the decision under sub-paragraph (3),
- (c) specify the date, at least 28 days after the date on which the notification is given, before which the penalty must be paid,
- (d) specify how the penalty must be paid,
- (e) include an explanation of the recipient's rights of appeal, and
- (f) include an explanation of the steps the Secretary of State may take to recover any unpaid penalty.

Appeals

28D(1) A person ("the appellant") may appeal to the court against a decision to require the person to pay a penalty under paragraph 28.

(2) An appeal may be brought only if the appellant has given a notice of objection and the Secretary of State has—

- (a) reduced the penalty under paragraph 28C(3)(b),
- (b) increased the penalty under paragraph 28C(3)(c), or
- (c) determined not to alter the penalty under paragraph 28C(3)(d).

(3) An appeal must be brought within the period of 28 days beginning with the date on which the appellant is notified of the Secretary of State's decision on the notice of objection under paragraph 28C(4).

(4) On appeal, the court may—

- (a) allow the appeal and cancel the penalty,
- (b) allow the appeal and reduce the penalty, or
- (c) dismiss the appeal.

(5) An appeal is to be a re-hearing of the Secretary of State's decision to impose a penalty and is to be determined having regard to—

- (a) any code of practice under paragraph 28A(1) which had effect at the time of the events to which the penalty relates,
- (b) any code of practice under paragraph 28A(3) which has effect at the time of the appeal, and
- (c) any other matters which the court thinks relevant (which may include matters of which the Secretary of State was unaware).

(6) Sub-paragraph (5) has effect despite any provision of rules of court.

6.1 *A Guide to the Immigration Act 2016*

(7) In this paragraph "the court" means—

(a) the county court, if the appeal relates to a penalty imposed under paragraph 28 in relation to an airport in England and Wales;

(b) the sheriff, if the appeal relates to a penalty imposed under paragraph 28 in relation to an airport in Scotland;

(c) a county court in Northern Ireland, if the appeal relates to a penalty imposed under paragraph 28 in relation to an airport in Northern Ireland.

(8) But—

(a) the county court in England and Wales, or a county court in Northern Ireland, may transfer proceedings under this paragraph to the High Court, and

(b) the sheriff may transfer proceedings under this paragraph to the Court of Session.

Enforcement

28E(1) This section applies where a sum is payable to the Secretary of State as a penalty under paragraph 28.

(2) In England and Wales the penalty is recoverable as if it were payable under an order of the county court in England and Wales.

(3) In Scotland the penalty may be enforced in the same manner as an extract registered decree arbitral bearing a warrant for execution issued by the sheriff court of any sheriffdom in Scotland.

(4) In Northern Ireland the penalty is recoverable as if it were payable under an order of a county court in Northern Ireland.

(5) Where action is taken under this paragraph for the recovery of a sum payable as a penalty under this Chapter, the penalty is—

(a) in relation to England and Wales, to be treated for the purposes of section 98 of the Courts Act 2003 (register of judgments and orders etc) as if it were a judgment entered in the county court;

(b) in relation to Northern Ireland, to be treated for the purposes of Article 116 of the Judgments Enforcement (Northern Ireland) Order 1981 (S.I. 1981/226 (N.I. 6)) (register of judgments) as if it were a judgment in respect of which an application has been accepted under Article 22 or 23(1) of that Order.

(6) Money paid to the Secretary of State by way of a penalty under paragraph 28 must be paid into the Consolidated Fund.

Service of documents

28F(1) A document which is to be issued or served on a person outside the United Kingdom for the purposes of paragraph 28B or 28C or in the course of proceedings under paragraph 28E may be issued or served—

    (a) in person,

    (b) by post,

    (c) by facsimile transmission,

    (d) by e-mail, or

    (e) in any other prescribed manner.

(2) The Secretary of State may by regulations provide that a document issued or served in a manner listed in sub-paragraph (1) in accordance with the regulations is to be taken to have been received at a time specified by or determined in accordance with the regulations.

Interpretation of this Part of this Schedule

28G In this Part of this Schedule—

"penalty notice" has the meaning given by paragraph 28B(2);

"prescribed" means prescribed by regulations made by the Secretary of State.

Regulations under this Part of this Schedule

28H(1) Regulations under this Part of this Schedule are to be made by statutory instrument.

(2) A statutory instrument containing (whether alone or with other provision) regulations under paragraph 28(6) may not be made unless a draft of the instrument has been laid before, and approved by a resolution of, each House of Parliament.

(3) A statutory instrument containing any other regulations under this Part of this Schedule and to which sub-paragraph (2) does not apply is subject to annulment in pursuance of a resolution of either House of Parliament.

(4) Regulations under this Part of this Schedule—

    (a) may make different provision for different purposes;

    (b) may make incidental, supplementary, consequential, transitional, transitory or saving provision."

6.1 A Guide to the Immigration Act 2016

Commencement: Not yet in force.

Amends: Immigration Act 1971 (IA 1971), Schedule 2, para 26 and inserts a new Part 1A *Penalties relating to airport control areas* into that Act.

Regulations: The code of practice is brought into effect by regulations subject to the negative procedure (IA 1971, Schedule 2 Part 1A, para 28A(6) read with s 93 of this Act). The Secretary of State must prescribe a maximum penalty for the owner, agent or person concerned with the management of an airport.

Guidance: The Secretary of State must issue a code of practice to be followed by agents and operators of aircraft and by those concerned with the management of airports. She must have regard to the code when considering imposing a penalty or when considering an objection to a penalty. She must also issue a code specifying matters to be considered in determining the amount of the penalty. This she must have regard to when imposing a penalty and when considering a notice of objection. Both codes, and any revisions, must be laid before parliament.

Definitions:

'the appellant' a person appealing against a penalty, IA 1971, Schedule 2, Part 1A, para 28D(1);

'the court' IA 1971, Schedule 1, Part 1A, para 28D(7): a county court in England and Wales, a sheriff in Scotland and a county court in Northern Ireland. Provision is made for transfer of proceedings to the High Court or Court of Session;

'penalty notice' IA 1971, Schedule 2, Part 1A, para 28B(2);

'prescribed' prescribed in regulations by the Secretary of State, IA 1971, Schedule 2, Part 1, para 28G;

'the recipient' the recipient of a penalty notice, IA 1971, Schedule 2, Part 1A, para 28C(1).

Devolution: Extends throughout the UK. There are references to the different courts to which an appeal may be made.

Section 74 and Schedule 13 create a civil penalty regime targeting airlines and airport officers who allow passengers to disembark without being presented to immigration control where a control zone has been designated. Zones are designated in statutory instruments laid before Parliament and are subject to the negative procedure.[1]

Unlike the case of landlords/landladies in IA 1971, Part 2, s 37 *Offence of leasing premises*, who will be subject to criminal offences because civil penalties are considered insufficient, this conduct is already a criminal offence. The Explanatory Notes offer no explanation of why a civil penalty is needed other than that this will make the legislation 'simpler to enforce'.[2] The criminal offence, set out in s 27 of the IA 1971, requires that the person act 'knowingly' or fail without reasonable excuse to comply with a direction given. The civil penalty uses a test of the person having taken 'reasonable steps'. The criminal offence carries a penalty of a fine of not more than level 5 on the standard scale, imprisonment for not more than six months, or both.

1   IA 1971, Sch 2, para 26(3A).
2   Explanatory Notes to HL Bill 79, 2015–16, para 27.

SECTION 75—MARITIME ENFORCEMENT AND SCHEDULE 14—MARITIME ENFORCEMENT

Summary
Allow immigration officers to exercise their powers on ships in territorial waters and where they are in hot pursuit of ships onto the High Seas.

6.2

75 Maritime enforcement

Schedule 14 (maritime enforcement) has effect.

Schedule 14
Maritime enforcement

1   The Immigration Act 1971 is amended as follows.

2   In section 25(1) (offence of assisting unlawful immigration to member State), in paragraphs (a) and (b) after "breach" insert " or attempted breach ".

3   In section 25A (helping an asylum-seeker to enter United Kingdom) in subsection (1)(a)—

   (a)   after "arrival" insert " or attempted arrival ", and

   (b)   after "entry" insert " or attempted entry ".

4   In section 25B (assisting entry to United Kingdom in breach of deportation or exclusion order)—

   (a)   in subsection (1), in paragraphs (a) and (b) after "breach" insert " or attempted breach ",

   (b)   for subsection (2) substitute—

      "(2)   Subsection (3) applies where the Secretary of State has made an order excluding an individual from the United Kingdom on the grounds of public policy, public security or public health, other than a temporary exclusion order.",

6.2 A Guide to the Immigration Act 2016

  (c) in subsection (3)—

    (i) in paragraphs (a) and (b) after "remain" insert ", or attempt to arrive in, enter or remain, ", and

    (ii) in paragraph (c) for the words from "personally" to the end substitute " made an order excluding the individual from the United Kingdom on the grounds of public policy, public security or public health ", and

  (d) after subsection (4) insert—

    "(5) In this section a "temporary exclusion order" means an order under section 2 of the Counter-Terrorism and Security Act 2015."

5 In section 28 (proceedings) after subsection (2) insert—

  "(2A) Section 3 of the Territorial Waters Jurisdiction Act 1878 (consent of Secretary of State for certain prosecutions) does not apply to proceedings for an offence under section 25, 25A or 25B."

6 In section 28A(3) (arrest without warrant) in paragraphs (a) and (b) after "committed" insert " or attempted to commit ".

7 After Part 3 insert—

"Part 3A
Maritime enforcement

28M Enforcement powers in relation to ships: England and Wales

(1) An immigration officer, an English and Welsh constable or an enforcement officer may exercise the powers set out in Part 1 of Schedule 4A ("Part 1 powers") in relation to any of the following in England and Wales waters—

  (a) a United Kingdom ship;

  (b) a ship without nationality;

  (c) a foreign ship;

  (d) a ship registered under the law of a relevant territory.

(2) But Part 1 powers may be exercised only—

  (a) for the purpose of preventing, detecting, investigating or prosecuting an offence under section 25, 25A or 25B, and

  (b) in accordance with the rest of this section.

(3) The authority of the Secretary of State is required before an immigration officer, an English and Welsh constable or an enforcement officer may exercise Part 1 powers in relation to a foreign ship, or a ship registered under the law of a relevant territory, within the territorial sea adjacent to the United Kingdom.

Part 6—Border Security **6.2**

(4) Authority for the purposes of subsection (3) may be given in relation to a foreign ship only if the Convention permits the exercise of Part 1 powers in relation to the ship.

28N Enforcement powers in relation to ships: Scotland

(1) An immigration officer, a Scottish constable or an enforcement officer may exercise the powers set out in Part 2 of Schedule 4A ("Part 2 powers") in relation to any of the following in Scotland waters—

    (a) a United Kingdom ship;

    (b) a ship without nationality;

    (c) a foreign ship;

    (d) a ship registered under the law of a relevant territory.

(2) But Part 2 powers may be exercised only—

    (a) for the purpose of preventing, detecting, investigating or prosecuting an offence under section 25, 25A or 25B, and

    (b) in accordance with the rest of this section.

(3) The authority of the Secretary of State is required before an immigration officer, a Scottish constable or an enforcement officer may exercise Part 2 powers in relation to a foreign ship, or a ship registered under the law of a relevant territory, within the territorial sea adjacent to the United Kingdom.

(4) Authority for the purposes of subsection (3) may be given in relation to a foreign ship only if the Convention permits the exercise of Part 2 powers in relation to the ship.

28O Enforcement powers in relation to ships: Northern Ireland

(1) An immigration officer, a Northern Ireland constable or an enforcement officer may exercise the powers set out in Part 3 of Schedule 4A ("Part 3 powers") in relation to any of the following in Northern Ireland waters—

    (a) a United Kingdom ship;

    (b) a ship without nationality;

    (c) a foreign ship;

    (d) a ship registered under the law of a relevant territory.

(2) But Part 3 powers may be exercised only—

    (a) for the purpose of preventing, detecting, investigating or prosecuting an offence under section 25, 25A or 25B, and

    (b) in accordance with the rest of this section.

6.2 *A Guide to the Immigration Act 2016*

(3) The authority of the Secretary of State is required before an immigration officer, a Northern Ireland constable or an enforcement officer may exercise Part 3 powers in relation to a foreign ship, or a ship registered under the law of a relevant territory, within the territorial sea adjacent to the United Kingdom.

(4) Authority for the purposes of subsection (3) may be given in relation to a foreign ship only if the Convention permits the exercise of Part 3 powers in relation to the ship.

28P Hot pursuit of ships in United Kingdom waters

(1) An immigration officer, an English and Welsh constable or an enforcement officer may exercise Part 1 powers in relation to a ship in Scotland waters or in Northern Ireland waters if—

   (a) the ship is pursued there,

   (b) immediately before the pursuit of the ship, the ship was in England and Wales waters, and

   (c) the condition in subsection (7) is met.

(2) Part 1 powers may be exercised under subsection (1) only—

   (a) for the purpose mentioned in subsection (2)(a) of section 28M, and

   (b) (if relevant) in accordance with subsections (3) and (4) of that section.

(3) An immigration officer, a Scottish constable or an enforcement officer may exercise Part 2 powers in relation to a ship in England and Wales waters or in Northern Ireland waters if—

   (a) the ship is pursued there,

   (b) immediately before the pursuit of the ship, the ship was in Scotland waters, and

   (c) the condition in subsection (7) is met.

(4) Part 2 powers may be exercised under subsection (3) only—

   (a) for the purpose mentioned in subsection (2)(a) of section 28N, and

   (b) (if relevant) in accordance with subsections (3) and (4) of that section.

(5) An immigration officer, a Northern Ireland constable or an enforcement officer may exercise Part 3 powers in relation to a ship in England and Wales waters or in Scotland waters if—

   (a) the ship is pursued there,

Part 6—Border Security **6.2**

      (b)   immediately before the pursuit of the ship, the ship was in Northern Ireland waters, and

      (c)   the condition in subsection (7) is met.

(6)   Part 3 powers may be exercised under subsection (5) only—

      (a)   for the purpose mentioned in subsection (2)(a) of section 28O, and

      (b)   (if relevant) in accordance with subsections (3) and (4) of that section.

(7)   The condition referred to in subsection (1)(c), (3)(c) and (5)(c) is that—

      (a)   before the pursuit of the ship, a signal is given for it to stop, and

      (b)   the pursuit of the ship is not interrupted.

(8)   The signal referred to in subsection (7)(a) must be given in such a way as to be audible or visible from the ship.

(9)   For the purposes of subsection (7)(b), pursuit is not interrupted by reason only of the fact that—

      (a)   the method of carrying out the pursuit, or

      (b)   the identity of the ship or aircraft carrying out the pursuit,

    changes during the course of the pursuit.

(10)   Nothing in this Part affects any other legal right of hot pursuit that a constable or an enforcement officer may have.

28Q   **Interpretation of Part 3A**

(1)   In this Part—

"the Convention" means the United Nations Convention on the Law of the Sea 1982 (Cmnd 8941) and any modifications of that Convention agreed after the passing of this Act that have entered into force in relation to the United Kingdom;

"enforcement officer" means—

      (a)   a person who is a commissioned officer of any of Her Majesty's ships, or

      (b)   a person in command or charge of any aircraft or hovercraft of the Royal Navy, the Army or the Royal Air Force;

"England and Wales waters" means the sea and other waters within the seaward limits of the territorial sea adjacent to England and Wales;

"English and Welsh constable" means only a person who is—

(a) a member of a police force in England and Wales,

(b) a member of the British Transport Police Force, or

(c) a port constable, within the meaning of section 7 of the Marine Navigation Act 2013, or a person appointed to act as a constable under provision made by virtue of section 16 of the Harbours Act 1964;

"foreign ship" means a ship which—

(a) is registered in a State other than the United Kingdom, or

(b) is not so registered but is entitled to fly the flag of a State other than the United Kingdom;

"Northern Ireland constable" means only a person who is—

(a) a member of the Police Service of Northern Ireland,

(b) a member of the Police Service of Northern Ireland Reserve, or

(c) a person appointed as a special constable in Northern Ireland by virtue of provision incorporating section 79 of the Harbours, Docks, and Piers Clauses Act 1847;

"Northern Ireland waters" means the sea and other waters within the seaward limits of the territorial sea adjacent to Northern Ireland;

"Part 1 powers" means the powers set out in Part 1 of Schedule 4A;

"Part 2 powers" means the powers set out in Part 2 of that Schedule;

"Part 3 powers" means the powers set out in Part 3 of that Schedule;

"relevant territory" means—

(a) the Isle of Man;

(b) any of the Channel Islands;

(c) a British overseas territory;

"Scottish constable" means only a person who is a constable, within the meaning of section 99 of the Police and Fire Reform (Scotland) Act 2012 (asp 8);

"Scotland waters" means the sea and other waters within the seaward limits of the territorial sea adjacent to Scotland;

"ship" includes every description of vessel (including a hovercraft) used in navigation;

"ship without nationality" means a ship which—

(a) is not registered in, or otherwise entitled to fly the flag of, any State or relevant territory, or

(b) sails under the flags of two or more States or relevant territories, or under the flags of a State and relevant territory, using them according to convenience;

"United Kingdom ship" means a ship which—

(a) is registered under Part 2 of the Merchant Shipping Act 1995,

(b) is a Government ship within the meaning of that Act,

(c) is not registered in any State or relevant territory but is wholly owned by persons each of whom has a United Kingdom connection, or

(d) is registered under an Order in Council under section 1 of the Hovercraft Act 1968.

(2) For the purposes of paragraph (c) of the definition of "United Kingdom ship" in subsection (1), a person has a "United Kingdom connection" if the person is—

(a) a British citizen, a British overseas territories citizen or a British Overseas citizen,

(b) an individual who is habitually resident in the United Kingdom, or

(c) a body corporate which is established under the law of a part of the United Kingdom and has its principal place of business in the United Kingdom."

8 After Schedule 4 insert—

"Schedule 4A

Sections 28M, 28N and 28O

Enforcement powers in relation to ships

Part 1
England and Wales

Introductory

1(1) This Part of this Schedule sets out the powers exercisable by immigration officers, English and Welsh constables and enforcement officers (referred to in this Part of this Schedule as "relevant officers") under sections 28M and 28P(1).

(2) In this Part of this Schedule—

"items subject to legal privilege" has the same meaning as in the Police and Criminal Evidence Act 1984 (see section 10 of that Act);

"the ship" means the ship in relation to which the powers set out in this Part of this Schedule are exercised.

6.2 *A Guide to the Immigration Act 2016*

Power to stop, board, divert and detain

2(1) This paragraph applies if a relevant officer has reasonable grounds to suspect that—

    (a) an offence under section 25, 25A or 25B is being, or has been, committed on the ship, or

    (b) the ship is otherwise being used in connection with the commission of an offence under any of those sections.

(2) The relevant officer may—

    (a) stop the ship;

    (b) board the ship;

    (c) require the ship to be taken to a port in the United Kingdom and detained there.

(3) The relevant officer may require the master of the ship, or any member of its crew, to take such action as is necessary for the purposes of sub-paragraph (2)(c).

(4) A relevant officer must give notice in writing to the master of any ship detained under this paragraph.

(5) The notice must state that the ship is to be detained until the notice is withdrawn by the giving of a further notice in writing signed by a relevant officer.

Power to search and obtain information

3(1) This paragraph applies if a relevant officer has reasonable grounds to suspect that there is evidence on the ship (other than items subject to legal privilege) relating—

    (a) to an offence under section 25, 25A and 25B, or

    (b) to an offence that is connected with an offence under any of those sections.

(2) The relevant officer may search—

    (a) the ship;

    (b) anyone on the ship;

    (c) anything on the ship (including cargo).

(3) The relevant officer may require a person on the ship to give information about himself or herself or about anything on the ship.

(4) The power to search conferred by sub-paragraph (2)—

    (a) is only a power to search to the extent that it is reasonably required for the purpose of discovering evidence of the kind mentioned in sub-paragraph (1), and

Part 6—Border Security **6.2**

- (b) in the case of a search of a person, does not authorise a relevant officer to require the person to remove any clothing in public other than an outer coat, jacket or gloves.

(5) In exercising a power conferred by sub-paragraph (2) or (3) a relevant officer may—

- (a) open any containers;
- (b) require the production of documents, books or records relating to the ship or anything on it (but not including anything the relevant officer has reasonable grounds to believe to be an item subject to legal privilege);
- (c) make photographs or copies of anything the production of which the relevant officer has power to require.

(6) The power in sub-paragraph (5)(b) to require the production of documents, books or records includes, in relation to documents, books or records kept in electronic form, power to require the provision of the documents, books or records in a form in which they are legible and can be taken away.

(7) Sub-paragraph (5) is without prejudice to the generality of the powers conferred by sub-paragraphs (2) and (3).

(8) A power conferred by this paragraph may be exercised on the ship or elsewhere.

Power of arrest and seizure

4(1) This paragraph applies if a relevant officer has reasonable grounds to suspect that an offence under section 25, 25A or 25B has been, or is being, committed on the ship.

(2) The relevant officer may arrest without warrant anyone whom the constable or officer has reasonable grounds for suspecting to be guilty of the offence.

(3) The relevant officer may seize and retain anything found on the ship which appears to the officer to be evidence of the offence (but not including anything that the constable or officer has reasonable grounds to believe to be an item subject to legal privilege).

(4) A power conferred by this paragraph may be exercised on the ship or elsewhere.

Protective searches of persons

5(1) A relevant officer may search a person found on the ship for anything which the officer has reasonable grounds to believe the person might use to—

- (a) cause physical injury,

(b) cause damage to property, or

(c) endanger the safety of any ship.

(2) The power conferred by sub-paragraph (1) may be exercised—

(a) only if the officer has reasonable grounds to believe that anything of a kind mentioned in that sub-paragraph is concealed on the person; and

(b) only to the extent that it is reasonably required for the purpose of discovering any such thing.

(3) The relevant officer may seize and retain anything which the officer has reasonable grounds to believe might—

(a) cause physical injury,

(b) cause damage to property, or

(c) endanger the safety of any ship.

(4) If the person is detained, nothing seized under sub-paragraph (3) may be retained when the person is released from detention.

(5) A power conferred by this paragraph to search a person does not authorise a relevant officer to require the person to remove any clothing in public other than an outer coat, jacket or gloves, but it does authorise the search of a person's mouth.

(6) A power conferred by this paragraph may be exercised on the ship or elsewhere.

Search for nationality documents

6(1) A relevant officer may require a person found on the ship to produce a nationality document.

(2) The relevant officer may search a person found on the ship where the officer has reasonable grounds to believe that a nationality document is concealed on the person.

(3) The power conferred by sub-paragraph (2) may be exercised—

(a) only if the officer has reasonable grounds to believe that a nationality document is concealed on the person; and

(b) only to the extent that it is reasonably required for the purpose of discovering any such document.

(4) Subject as follows, the officer may seize and retain a nationality document for as long as the officer believes the person to whom it relates will arrive in the United Kingdom by virtue of the exercise of the power in paragraph 2.

Part 6—Border Security **6.2**

(5) The power to retain a nationality document in sub-paragraph (4) does not affect any other power of an immigration officer to retain a document.

(6) Where the nationality document has been seized and retained by a relevant officer who is not an immigration officer, the document must be passed to an immigration officer as soon as is practicable after the ship has arrived in the United Kingdom.

(7) The power conferred by this paragraph to search a person does not authorise a relevant officer to—

(a) require the person to remove any clothing in public other than an outer coat, jacket or gloves, or

(b) seize and retain any document the officer has reasonable grounds to believe to be an item subject to legal privilege.

(8) In this paragraph a "nationality document", in relation to a person, means any document which might—

(a) establish the person's identity, nationality or citizenship, or

(b) indicate the place from which the person has travelled to the United Kingdom or to which the person is proposing to go.

(9) A power conferred by this paragraph may be exercised on the ship or elsewhere.

Assistants

7(1) A relevant officer may—

(a) be accompanied by other persons, and

(b) take equipment or materials,

to assist the officer in the exercise of powers under this Part of this Schedule.

(2) A person accompanying a relevant officer under sub-paragraph (1) may perform any of the officer's functions under this Part of this Schedule, but only under the officer's supervision.

Reasonable force

8A A relevant officer may use reasonable force, if necessary, in the performance of functions under this Part of this Schedule.

Evidence of authority

9A A relevant officer must produce evidence of the officer's authority if asked to do so.

Protection of relevant officers

10A A relevant officer is not liable in any criminal or civil proceedings for anything done in the purported performance of functions under this Part of this Schedule if the court is satisfied that—

    (a)   the act was done in good faith, and

    (b)   there were reasonable grounds for doing it.

Offences

11(1) A person commits an offence under the law of England and Wales if the person—

    (a)   intentionally obstructs a relevant officer in the performance of functions under this Part of this Schedule, or

    (b)   fails without reasonable excuse to comply with a requirement made by a relevant officer in the performance of those functions.

(2) A person who provides information in response to a requirement made by a relevant officer in the performance of functions under this Part of this Schedule commits an offence under the law of England and Wales if—

    (a)   the information is false in a material particular, and the person either knows it is or is reckless as to whether it is, or

    (b)   the person intentionally fails to disclose any material particular.

(3) A relevant officer may arrest without warrant anyone whom the officer has reasonable grounds for suspecting to be guilty of an offence under this paragraph.

(4) A person guilty of an offence under this paragraph is liable on summary conviction to imprisonment for a term not exceeding 51 weeks, to a fine or to both.

(5) In the application of sub-paragraph (4) in relation to an offence committed before the coming into force of section 281(5) of the Criminal Justice Act 2003 the reference to 51 weeks is to be read as a reference to 6 months.

Part 2
Scotland

Introductory

12(1) This Part of this Schedule sets out the powers exercisable by immigration officers, Scottish constables and enforcement officers (referred to in this Part of this Schedule as "relevant officers") under sections 28N and 28P(3).

Part 6—Border Security **6.2**

(2) In this Part of this Schedule—

"items subject to legal privilege" has the same meaning as in Chapter 3 of Part 8 of the Proceeds of Crime Act 2002 (see section 412 of that Act);

"the ship" means the ship in relation to which the powers set out in this Part of this Schedule are exercised.

Power to stop, board, divert and detain

13(1) This paragraph applies if a relevant officer has reasonable grounds to suspect that—

(a) an offence under section 25, 25A or 25B is being, or has been, committed on the ship, or

(b) the ship is otherwise being used in connection with the commission of an offence under any of those sections.

(2) The relevant officer may—

(a) stop the ship;

(b) board the ship;

(c) require the ship to be taken to a port in the United Kingdom and detained there.

(3) The relevant officer may require the master of the ship, or any member of its crew, to take such action as is necessary for the purposes of sub-paragraph (2)(c).

(4) A relevant officer must give notice in writing to the master of any ship detained under this paragraph.

(5) The notice must state that the ship is to be detained until the notice is withdrawn by the giving of a further notice in writing signed by a relevant officer.

Power to search and obtain information

14(1) This paragraph applies if a relevant officer has reasonable grounds to suspect that there is evidence on the ship (other than items subject to legal privilege) relating—

(a) to an offence under section 25, 25A or 25B, or

(b) to an offence that is connected with an offence under any of those sections.

(2) The relevant officer may search—

(a) the ship;

(b) anyone on the ship;

(c) anything on the ship (including cargo).

(3) The relevant officer may require a person on the ship to give information about himself or herself or about anything on the ship.

(4) The power to search conferred by sub-paragraph (2)—

    (a) is only a power to search to the extent that it is reasonably required for the purpose of discovering evidence of the kind mentioned in sub-paragraph (1), and

    (b) in the case of a search of a person, does not authorise a relevant officer to require the person to remove any clothing in public other than an outer coat, jacket or gloves.

(5) In exercising a power conferred by sub-paragraph (2) or (3) a relevant officer may—

    (a) open any containers;

    (b) require the production of documents, books or records relating to the ship or anything on it (but not including anything the relevant officer has reasonable grounds to believe to be an item subject to legal privilege);

    (c) make photographs or copies of anything the production of which the relevant officer has power to require.

(6) The power in sub-paragraph (5)(b) to require the production of documents, books or records includes, in relation to documents, books or records kept in electronic form, power to require the provision of the documents, books or records in a form in which they are legible and can be taken away.

(7) Sub-paragraph (5) is without prejudice to the generality of the powers conferred by sub-paragraphs (2) and (3).

(8) A power conferred by this paragraph may be exercised on the ship or elsewhere.

Power of arrest and seizure

15(1) This paragraph applies if a relevant officer has reasonable grounds to suspect that an offence under section 25, 25A or 25B has been, or is being, committed on the ship.

(2) The relevant officer may arrest without warrant anyone whom the officer has reasonable grounds for suspecting to be guilty of the offence.

(3) The relevant officer may seize and retain anything found on the ship which appears to the officer to be evidence of the offence (but not including anything that the officer has reasonable grounds to believe to be an item subject to legal privilege).

(4) A power conferred by this paragraph may be exercised on the ship or elsewhere.

Protective searches of persons

16(1) The relevant officer may search a person found on the ship for anything which the officer has reasonable grounds to believe the person might use to—

(a) cause physical injury,

(b) cause damage to property, or

(c) endanger the safety of any ship.

(2) The power conferred by sub-paragraph (1) may be exercised—

(a) only if the officer has reasonable grounds to believe that anything of a kind mentioned in that sub-paragraph is concealed on the person; and

(b) only to the extent that it is reasonably required for the purpose of discovering any such thing.

(3) The relevant officer may seize and retain anything which the officer has reasonable grounds to believe might—

(a) cause physical injury,

(b) cause damage to property, or

(c) endanger the safety of any ship.

(4) If the person is detained, nothing seized under sub-paragraph (3) may be retained when the person is released from detention.

(5) A power conferred by this paragraph to search a person does not authorise a relevant officer to require the person to remove any clothing in public other than an outer coat, jacket or gloves, but it does authorise the search of a person's mouth.

(6) A power conferred by this paragraph may be exercised on the ship or elsewhere.

Search for nationality documents

17(1) The relevant officer may require a person found on the ship to produce a nationality document.

(2) The relevant officer may search a person found on the ship where the officer has reasonable grounds to believe that a nationality document is concealed on the person.

(3) The power conferred by sub-paragraph (2) may be exercised—

(a) only if the officer has reasonable grounds to believe that a nationality document is concealed on the person; and

(b) only to the extent that it is reasonably required for the purpose of discovering any such document.

6.2 *A Guide to the Immigration Act 2016*

(4) Subject as follows, the officer may seize and retain a nationality document for as long as the officer believes the person to whom it relates will arrive in the United Kingdom by virtue of the exercise of the power in paragraph 13.

(5) The power to retain a nationality document in sub-paragraph (4) does not affect any other power of an immigration officer to retain a document.

(6) Where the nationality document has been seized and retained by a relevant officer who is not an immigration officer, the document must be passed to an immigration officer as soon as is practicable after the ship has arrived in the United Kingdom.

(7) The power conferred by this paragraph to search a person does not authorise a relevant officer to—

(a) require the person to remove any clothing in public other than an outer coat, jacket or gloves, or

(b) seize and retain any document the officer has reasonable grounds to believe to be an item subject to legal privilege.

(8) In this paragraph a "nationality document", in relation to a person, means any document which might—

(a) establish the person's identity, nationality or citizenship, or

(b) indicate the place from which the person has travelled to the United Kingdom or to which the person is proposing to go.

(9) A power conferred by this paragraph may be exercised on the ship or elsewhere.

Assistants

18(1) A relevant officer may—

(a) be accompanied by other persons, and

(b) take equipment or materials,

to assist the officer in the exercise of powers under this Part of this Schedule.

(2) A person accompanying a relevant officer under sub-paragraph (1) may perform any of the officer's functions under this Part of this Schedule, but only under the officer's supervision.

Reasonable force

19A relevant officer may use reasonable force, if necessary, in the performance of functions under this Part of this Schedule.

Evidence of authority

20A relevant officer must produce evidence of the officer's authority if asked to do so.

Part 6—Border Security **6.2**

Protection of relevant officers

21 A relevant officer is not liable in any criminal or civil proceedings for anything done in the purported performance of functions under this Part of this Schedule if the court is satisfied that—

(a) the act was done in good faith, and

(b) there were reasonable grounds for doing it.

Offences

22(1) A person commits an offence under the law of Scotland if the person—

(a) intentionally obstructs a relevant officer in the performance of functions under this Part of this Schedule, or

(b) fails without reasonable excuse to comply with a requirement made by a relevant officer in the performance of those functions.

(2) A person who provides information in response to a requirement made by a relevant officer in the performance of functions under this Part of this Schedule commits an offence under the law of Scotland if—

(a) the information is false in a material particular, and the person either knows it is or is reckless as to whether it is, or

(b) the person intentionally fails to disclose any material particular.

(3) A relevant officer may arrest without warrant anyone whom the officer has reasonable grounds for suspecting to be guilty of an offence under this paragraph.

(4) A person guilty of an offence under this paragraph is liable on summary conviction to imprisonment for a term not exceeding 12 months, to a fine not exceeding level 5 on the standard scale or to both.

Part 3
Northern Ireland

Introductory

23(1) This Part of this Schedule sets out the powers exercisable by immigration officers, Northern Ireland constables and enforcement officers (referred to in this Part of this Schedule as "relevant officers") under sections 28O and 28P(5).

(2) In this Part of this Schedule—

"items subject to legal privilege" has the same meaning as in the Police and Criminal Evidence (Northern Ireland) Order 1989 (SI 1989/1341 (NI 12)) (see Article 12 of that Order);

"the ship" means the ship in relation to which the powers set out in this Part of this Schedule are exercised.

Power to stop, board, divert and detain

24(1) This paragraph applies if a relevant officer has reasonable grounds to suspect that—

(a) an offence under section 25, 25A or 25B is being, or has been, committed on the ship, or

(b) the ship is otherwise being used in connection with the commission of an offence under any of those sections.

(2) The relevant officer may—

(a) stop the ship;

(b) board the ship;

(c) require the ship to be taken to a port in the United Kingdom and detained there.

(3) The relevant officer may require the master of the ship, or any member of its crew, to take such action as is necessary for the purposes of sub-paragraph (2)(c).

(4) A relevant officer must give notice in writing to the master of any ship detained under this paragraph.

(5) The notice must state that the ship is to be detained until the notice is withdrawn by the giving of a further notice in writing signed by a relevant officer.

Power to search and obtain information

25(1) This paragraph applies if a relevant officer has reasonable grounds to suspect that there is evidence on the ship (other than items subject to legal privilege) relating—

(a) to an offence under section 25, 25A or 25B, or

(b) to an offence that is connected with an offence under any of those sections.

(2) The relevant officer may search—

(a) the ship;

(b) anyone on the ship;

(c) anything on the ship (including cargo).

(3) The relevant officer may require a person on the ship to give information about himself or herself or about anything on the ship.

Part 6—Border Security **6.2**

(4) The power to search conferred by sub-paragraph (2)—

    (a)   is only a power to search to the extent that it is reasonably required for the purpose of discovering evidence of the kind mentioned in sub-paragraph (1), and

    (b)   in the case of a search of a person, does not authorise a relevant officer to require the person to remove any clothing in public other than an outer coat, jacket or gloves.

(5) In exercising a power conferred by sub-paragraph (2) or (3) a relevant officer may—

    (a)   open any containers;

    (b)   require the production of documents, books or records relating to the ship or anything on it (but not including anything the officer has reasonable grounds to believe to be an item subject to legal privilege);

    (c)   make photographs or copies of anything the production of which the officer has power to require.

(6) The power in sub-paragraph (5)(b) to require the production of documents, books or records includes, in relation to documents, books or records kept in electronic form, power to require the provision of the documents, books or records in a form in which they are legible and can be taken away.

(7) Sub-paragraph (5) is without prejudice to the generality of the powers conferred by sub-paragraphs (2) and (3).

(8) A power conferred by this paragraph may be exercised on the ship or elsewhere.

Power of arrest and seizure

26(1) This paragraph applies if a relevant officer has reasonable grounds to suspect that an offence under section 25, 25A or 25B has been, or is being, committed on the ship.

(2) The relevant officer may arrest without warrant anyone whom the officer has reasonable grounds for suspecting to be guilty of the offence.

(3) The relevant officer may seize and retain anything found on the ship which appears to the officer to be evidence of the offence (but not including anything that the constable or officer has reasonable grounds to believe to be an item subject to legal privilege).

(4) A power conferred by this paragraph may be exercised on the ship or elsewhere.

6.2 *A Guide to the Immigration Act 2016*

Protective searches of persons

27(1) The relevant officer may search a person found on the ship for anything which the officer has reasonable grounds to believe the person might use to—

    (a) cause physical injury,

    (b) cause damage to property, or

    (c) endanger the safety of any ship.

(2) The power conferred by sub-paragraph (1) may be exercised—

    (a) only if the officer has reasonable grounds to believe that anything of a kind mentioned in that sub-paragraph is concealed on the person; and

    (b) only to the extent that it is reasonably required for the purpose of discovering any such thing.

(3) The relevant officer may seize and retain anything which the officer has reasonable grounds to believe might—

    (a) cause physical injury,

    (b) cause damage to property, or

    (c) endanger the safety of any ship

(4) If the person is detained, nothing seized under sub-paragraph (3) may be retained when the person is released from detention.

(5) A power conferred by this paragraph to search a person does not authorise a relevant officer to require the person to remove any clothing in public other than an outer coat, jacket or gloves, but it does authorise the search of a person's mouth.

(6) A power conferred by this paragraph may be exercised on the ship or elsewhere.

Search for nationality documents

28(1) The relevant officer may require a person found on the ship to produce a nationality document.

(2) The relevant officer may search a person found on the ship where the officer has reasonable grounds to believe that a nationality document is concealed on the person.

(3) The power conferred by sub-paragraph (2) may be exercised—

    (a) only if the officer has reasonable grounds to believe that a nationality document is concealed on the person; and

    (b) only to the extent that it is reasonably required for the purpose of discovering any such document.

Part 6—Border Security **6.2**

(4) Subject as follows, the officer may seize and retain a nationality document for as long as the officer believes the person to whom it relates will arrive in the United Kingdom by virtue of the exercise of the power in paragraph 24.

(5) The power to retain a nationality document in sub-paragraph (4) does not affect any other power of an immigration officer to retain a document.

(6) Where the nationality document has been seized and retained by a relevant officer who is not an immigration officer, the document must be passed to an immigration officer as soon as is practicable after the ship has arrived in the United Kingdom.

(7) The power conferred by this paragraph to search a person does not authorise a relevant officer to—

(a) require the person to remove any clothing in public other than an outer coat, jacket or gloves, or

(b) seize and retain any document the officer has reasonable grounds to believe to be an item subject to legal privilege.

(8) In this paragraph a "nationality document", in relation to a person, means any document which might—

(a) establish the person's identity, nationality or citizenship, or

(b) indicate the place from which the person has travelled to the United Kingdom or to which the person is proposing to go.

(9) A power conferred by this paragraph may be exercised on the ship or elsewhere.

Assistants

29(1) A relevant officer may—

(a) be accompanied by other persons, and

(b) take equipment or materials,

to assist the officer in the exercise of powers under this Part of this Schedule.

(2) A person accompanying a relevant officer under sub-paragraph (1) may perform any of the officer's functions under this Part of this Schedule, but only under the officer's supervision.

Reasonable force

30 A relevant officer may use reasonable force, if necessary, in the performance of functions under this Part of this Schedule.

6.2 *A Guide to the Immigration Act 2016*

Evidence of authority

31 A relevant officer must produce evidence of the officer's authority if asked to do so.

Protection of relevant officers

32 A relevant officer is not liable in any criminal or civil proceedings for anything done in the purported performance of functions under this Part of this Schedule if the court is satisfied that—

(a) the act was done in good faith, and

(b) there were reasonable grounds for doing it.

Offences

33(1) A person commits an offence under the law of Northern Ireland if the person—

(a) intentionally obstructs a relevant officer in the performance of functions under this Part of this Schedule, or

(b) fails without reasonable excuse to comply with a requirement made by a relevant officer in the performance of those functions.

(2) A person who provides information in response to a requirement made by a relevant officer in the performance of functions under this Part of this Schedule commits an offence under the law of Northern Ireland if—

(a) the information is false in a material particular, and the person either knows it is or is reckless as to whether it is, or

(b) the person intentionally fails to disclose any material particular.

(3) A relevant officer may arrest without warrant anyone whom the officer has reasonable grounds for suspecting to be guilty of an offence under this paragraph.

(4) A person guilty of an offence under this paragraph is liable on summary conviction to imprisonment for a term not exceeding 6 months, to a fine not exceeding level 5 on the standard scale or to both."

Commencement: 31 May 2016, the Immigration Act 2016 (Commencement No 1) Regulations 2016, SI 2016/603, reg 2(c).

Amends: The Immigration Act 1971 (IA 1971), s 25, 25A, 25B, 28 and 28A and inserts a new Part 3A *Maritime Enforcement* (sections 28M–28Q) and a new Schedule 4A *Enforcement Powers in relation to ships*.

Part 6—Border Security 6.2

Definitions:

'the Convention' IA 1971, s 28Q(1) (inserted by Schedule 14, para 7);

'enforcement officer' IA 1971, s 28Q(1) (inserted by Schedule 14, para 7);

'England and Wales waters' IA 1971, s 28Q(1) (inserted by Schedule 14, para 7);

'English and Welsh constable' IA 1971, s 28Q(1) (inserted by Schedule 14, para 7);

'foreign ship' IA 1971, s 28Q(1) (inserted by Schedule 14, para 7);

'items subject to legal privilege' IA 1971, Schedule 4A: England and Wales, Police and Criminal Evidence Act 1984, s 10 (Schedule 4A, Part 1, para 1(2)); Scotland, Proceeds of Crime Act 2002, s 412 and Part 8, Chapter 3 (Schedule 4A, para 12(2)); Northern Ireland: Police and Criminal Evidence (Northern Ireland) Order 1989 (SI 1989/1341 (N 12)), Article 12 (Schedule 4A, Part 3, para 23(2)) (all inserted by Schedule 14, para 8);

'Northern Ireland constable' IA 1971, s 28Q(1) (inserted by Schedule 14, para 7);

'Northern Ireland waters' IA 1971, s 28Q(1) (inserted by Schedule 14, para 7);

'Part 1 powers' IA 1971, s 28Q(1) (inserted by Schedule 14, para 7);

'Part 2 powers' IA 1971, s 28Q(1) (inserted by Schedule 14, para 7);

'Part 3 powers' IA 1971, s 28Q(1) (inserted by Schedule 14, para 7);

'relevant officers' in IA 1971, Schedule 4A, Part 1, IA 1971, Schedule 4A, Part 1, para 1;

'relevant territory' IA 1971, s 28Q(1) (inserted by Schedule 14, para 7);

'Scottish constable' IA 1971, s 28Q(1) (inserted by Schedule 14, para 7);

'Scotland waters' IA 1971, s 28Q(1) (inserted by Schedule 14, para 7);

'ship' in IA 1971, Part 3A, IA 1971s 28Q(1) (inserted by Schedule 14, para 7);

'the ship' in IA 1971, Schedule 4A, IA 1971, IA 1971, Schedule 4A, para 1(2): the ship in relation to which powers are exercised;

'ship without nationality' IA 1971, s 28Q(1) (inserted by Schedule 14, para 7);

'United Kingdom connection' IA 1971, s 28Q(2) (inserted by Schedule 14, para 7);

'United Kingdom ship' IA 1971, s 28Q(1) (inserted by Schedule 14, para 7)

Offences: Of obstructing immigration officers and constables exercising powers under this part, IA 1971, Schedule 4A, ss 11, 22 and 33.

6.2 *A Guide to the Immigration Act 2016*

Devolution: The new Schedule 4A to the IA 1971 is in three parts, the first pertaining to England and Wales, the second to Northern Ireland and the third to Scotland. The Schedule builds on the concept of 'English, Welsh, Northern Irish and Scots waters' introduced in the Modern Slavery Act 2015 (MSA 2015), s 39.

Section 75 and Schedule 14 extend the powers of immigration officers onto the sea. They allow immigration officers and their 'assistants' to stop, board, divert and detain ships. Immigration officers and their assistants are given powers of search, arrest without warrant, and seizure. They can prevent persons from landing. The Schedule sets out the powers for England and Wales, then for Scotland and then for Northern Ireland.

The powers build on Part 3 of, and Schedule 2 to, the MSA 2015 in respect of offences under ss 1–2 of that Act.[1] In this Act the powers are concerned with offences under ss 25 and 25A–25B of the IA 1971: assisting unlawful immigration to an EU Member State, helping an asylum-seeker enter the UK, and assisting entry to the UK in breach of a deportation or exclusion order.

Paragraphs 5 (England and Wales), 7 (Scotland) and 16 (Northern Ireland) of the new Schedule 4A to the IA 1971 are concerned with 'protective' searches. An officer can search a person, without warrant, for anything which the officer has reasonable grounds to believe the person might use to cause physical injury, to cause damage to property, or to endanger the safety of any ship. There is no requirement that the officer need have reasonable grounds to believe that such an item is concealed on the person.

Paragraphs 7, 18 and 29 of new Schedule 4A to the IA 1971 permit a relevant officer to be accompanied by other persons, as assistants. The persons concerned may perform any of the officer's functions, under the officer's supervision. The Minister, the Rt Hon James Brokenshire MP, said:

> 'The provision permitting powers to be exercised by accompanying officers reflects existing powers under other legislation—most notably, the powers recently considered by the House in the Modern Slavery Act 2015. The extension of powers to assistants also exists in general for those working alongside customs officers under section 8 of the Customs and Excise Management Act 1979.
>
> … We have therefore sought to ensure that there is no mismatch between customs powers and immigration powers…
>
> The reason why such powers may be given to assistants is not to permit untrained individuals to exercise those powers, but to ensure effective joint working with partner agencies that have at least a basic level of law enforcement training. The measure permits officers from partner

organisations who may be working alongside enforcement officers, such as fisheries inspection officers, to assist immigration officers. It is important to emphasise the requirement that such persons must still be supervised'.[2]

Powers of search, arrest and seizure can be exercised on the ship 'or elsewhere'. The Home Office Enforcement Instructions and Guidance at Chapter 31 rely on *Singh v Hammond* [1987] 1 All ER 829, [1987] Crim LR 332 as authority for its stop and search operations, for example, at tube stations. The Home Office takes the case as authority for the proposition that powers in statute to examine persons 'who have arrived in the United Kingdom' can be used not only at port but in-country. The Home Office Enforcement Instructions and Guidance provided at Chapter 31.10[3] as available until 7 October 2016:

'In *Singh v Hammond*, the court held that:

"An examination [under paragraph 2 of Schedule 2 to the IA 1971] ... can properly be conducted by an immigration officer away from the place of entry and on a later date after the person has already entered ... if the immigration officer has some information in his possession which causes him to enquire whether the person being examined is a British citizen and, if not, ... whether he should be given leave and on what conditions.'"

It is suggested that *Singh v Hammond* is not correctly decided. Schedule 2 is concerned with the examination of persons arriving in or leaving the UK (see IA 1971 s 4(2)) and read in context the paragraph appears concerned with the port of entry.[4]

The Minister, the Rt Hon James Brokenshire MP, appeared confused in his defence of the power:

'***James Brokenshire:*** ... the hon. and learned Gentleman ... was rightly probing and testing as to the intent of the term 'elsewhere'. In part, it ensures that there is provision to arrest a person should they jump overboard to evade enforcement officers ... or, if the vessel is in more inland waters, on to land ... I reassure the Committee that the test ... connects the exercise of the powers with suspicion regarding the ship.

Keir Starmer: ... there is no power of arrest in the paragraph; there is only a power of search. So sub-paragraph (8) would not help in the circumstance where someone jumps overboard and needs to be arrested ...

James Brokenshire: That is connected to sub-paragraph (3), which states: "The relevant officer may require the master of the ship, or any member of its crew, to take such action as is necessary for the purposes of sub-paragraph (2)(c)."

Obviously, the officer would require the ship to be taken to a port. That is connected to the ability to search .... There may be circumstances, for

6.2 *A Guide to the Immigration Act 2016*

example, in which someone jumps off a ship and is rescued by officers where a search may be appropriate under the exercise of that power'.[5]

Immunity from both prosecution and civil suit is given by paras 10, 21 and 32 of Schedule 4A to the IA 1971 to immigration officers, constables and 'enforcement officers' for anything done in the purported performance of functions under the relevant part of that Schedule if the court is satisfied that the act was done in good faith and that there were good grounds for doing it. This is not only immunity from suit when performing functions under the relevant part of the Schedule, but immunity when acting 'in purported performance of functions under this part'. The Explanatory Notes to the Act say only 'to carry out their functions, relevant officers require some protection from prosecution'.[6] The immunity was debated and the Minister, the Rt Hon James Brokenshire MP said:

> 'On the protection of officers against civil and criminal liability, the measure extends only to personal liability; it does not prevent a claim for which an employer may be vicariously liable.... There are many other examples of where law enforcement officers are given equivalent protection'.[7]

Paragraphs 11, 22 and 33 of the new Schedule 4A, inserted by para 8 of Schedule 14, make it a criminal offence to obstruct an official in the exercise of these powers or to fail without reasonable excuse to comply with a requirement made by a relevant officer. A Master may be able to defend him/herself from prosecution for refusing to comply with an unsafe order, such as ordering a ship to stop in traffic separation schemes, or in circumstances where the ship might be stranded on an ebbing tide; orders to divert to unsuitable ports, for example, ports which are too small for merchant ships, or excessively difficult for yachts to reach in the prevailing weather conditions; and about costs associated with unwanted port calls, by arguing that s/he had a 'reasonable excuse' not to do so.[8]

In debates on this Act, Ministers emphasised that all those intercepted on board ship would be brought to the UK and that there was thus no risk of *non-refoulement* of persons in need of international protection.[9] Subsequently, the Policing and Crime Act 2017 builds on these powers in ways which raise again the question of such risk. Part 4, Chapter 5 *Maritime enforcement: English and Welsh offences*, Chapter 6 *Maritime enforcement: Scottish offences* and Chapter 7 *Maritime enforcement: Northern Irish offences* of that Act give the SSHD powers to require UK ships intercepted in English and Welsh, Scottish, Northern Irish, foreign or international waters, and ships of any nationality intercepted in UK waters, to be stopped, detained and/or sent to a port outside the UK.[10]

The powers differ from those contained in this Act and in the MSA 2015 which only permit the diversion of ships to UK ports rather than to ports

Part 6—Border Security **6.2**

anywhere in the world. Concerns were raised during debates of a risk of *refoulement* of refugees and persons in need of international protection on those ships.[11] Article 33 of the 1951 UN Convention Relating to the Status of Refugees provides:

> 'No Contracting State shall expel or return ("refouler") a refugee in any manner whatsoever to the frontiers of territories where his life or freedom would be threatened on account of his race, religion, nationality, membership of a particular social group or political opinion.'

In *Hirsi Jamaa and others v Italy*[12] a case concerning 'pushbacks' of refugees in the Mediterranean to Libya, the European Court of Human Rights found Italy to owe all obligations under the to European Convention on Human Rights those in need of international protection that it had taken onto a ship flying its flag and which was under control of its personnel. Under the Policing and Crime Bill, however, officials will be boarding ships that fly other flags. They will have powers to control the ship;[13] although, as with paras 11, 22 and 33 of new Schedule 4A to the IA 1971, a person is not guilty of the offence in Clause 94 (of HL Bill 84) of obstructing an officer in England and Wales if they have 'reasonable excuse' not to do so, and this would appear to give some control back to the Master of the vessel.

It was said in debates on this Act that the provisions are unobjectionable because similar powers had been taken in the Modern Slavery Act 2015[14] and the Explanatory Notes to the Bill highlighted the specificity of the offences, and the targeted nature of the provisions.[15] The argument that maritime enforcement powers are unobjectionable because similar provision has already been made in other legislation appears in the Explanatory Notes to the Policing and Crime Act.[16]

---

1 MSA 2015, Sch 2 para 2.
2 Immigration Bill, Public Bill committee, 13th sitting (afternoon), *Hansard* cols 475–476 (10 November 2015).
3 Chapter 31 *Enforcement Visits* was withdrawn on 7 October 2016. See now Home Office General Instructions, Immigration Removal, Enforcement and Detention, *Enforcement Interviews*, vl, 12 July 2016.
4 See Public Bill Committee, 10th sitting (afternoon) *Hansard* cols 327–328 (3 November 2016).
5 Immigration Bill, Public Bill committee, 13th sitting (afternoon) *Hansard* cols 475–476 (10 November 2015).
6 Paragraph 434.
7 Immigration Bill, Public Bill committee, 13th sitting (afternoon) *Hansard* cols 475–476 (10 November 2015).
8 Paragraphs 11(1)(b), 22(1)(b) and 33(1)(b) of the new Sch 4A inserted by para 8 of Sch 14.
9 Public Bill Committee, 13th sitting (am), 10 November 2015, col 468.
10 HL Bill 84 of session 2016–2017.
11 See, eg *Hansard* HL Vol 774, cols 449–450 (18 July 2016) per Lord Paddick.
12 Application no 27765/09, judgment of 23 February 2012.
13 Sections 84, 86, 88, 96, 98, 100, 107, 109.
14 For example, Immigration Bill Public Bill Committee, 13th sitting (afternoon) *Hansard*, col 475 (10 November 2015) per the Rt Hon James Brokenshire MP 'The provision permitting powers

to be exercised by accompanying officers reflects existing powers under other legislation—most notably, the powers recently considered by the House in the Modern Slavery Act 2015'.
15 Explanatory Notes to HL Bill 79 of session 2016–2017, paras 413–415.
16 Explanatory Notes, para 127.

SECTION 76—PERSONS EXCLUDED FROM THE UNITED KINGDOM UNDER INTERNATIONAL OBLIGATIONS

Summary

Provides for certain persons' exclusion from the UK, pursuant to the UK's international obligations under UN Security Council resolutions and EU Council decisions, to be automatic and not to require statutory instruments. Makes provision as to the effect of an exclusion.

6.3

76 Persons excluded from the United Kingdom under international obligations

(1) In section 8 of the Immigration Act 1971 (exceptions for seamen, aircrews and other special cases) in subsection (5) after "expired" insert " or otherwise ceased to be in force ".

(2) In section 8A of that Act (persons ceasing to be exempt) after subsection (3) insert—

"(4) References in this section to a person who ceases to be exempt do not include a person who ceases to be exempt by virtue of section 8B(3)."

(3) Section 8B of that Act (persons excluded from the United Kingdom under international obligations) is amended as follows.

(4) In subsection (1) after paragraph (b) insert—

"(and any leave given to a person who is an excluded person is invalid)".

(5) For subsection (3) substitute—

"(3) Any exemption of a person from the provisions of this Act under section 8(1), (2) or (3) does not apply while the person is an excluded person."

(6) In subsection (4) for "a designated instrument" substitute " an instrument falling within subsection (5) ".

(7) In subsection (5) for "The Secretary of State may by order designate an instrument" substitute "An instrument falls within this subsection".

(8) After subsection (5) insert—

Part 6—Border Security   6.3

"(5A) Subsection (1), (2) or (3) does not apply to a person if—

    (a) the application of that subsection to that person would be contrary to the United Kingdom's obligations under—

        (i) the Human Rights Convention (within the meaning given by section 167(1) of the Immigration and Asylum Act 1999), or

        (ii) the Refugee Convention (within the meaning given by that provision), or

    (b) the person has been exempted from the application of that subsection under a process applying by virtue of the instrument falling within subsection (5)."

(9) Omit subsections (6) to (8).

Commencement: 12 July 2016, Immigration Act 2016 (Commencement No 1) Regulations 2016, SI 2016/603.

Definitions:

'excluded person' Immigration Act 1971 (IA 1971), s 8B(4): a person named by or under, or of a description specified in, an instrument falling with s 8B(5) of the IA 1971 as amended by this Act.

Amends: IA 1971, ss 8, 8A, 8B.

Devolution: Applies throughout the UK.

This section provides for the exclusion of certain persons from the UK, pursuant to the UK's international obligations under UN Security Council resolutions and EU Council decisions, to be automatic and not to require statutory instruments. It amends s 8B of the IA 1971 to consolidate UK legislation relating to international travel bans and to provide that once a person is listed by the UN, or by the Council of the European Union, as being subject to a travel ban he or she becomes an 'excluded person' within the meaning of s 8B(4). No longer will it be necessary to amend the Immigration (Designation of Travel Bans) Order 2000, SI 2000/2724, to give effect to the bans. Instead the bans will have automatic effect in the UK. It makes provision as to the effect of s 8B of the IA 1971.

The section provides that where an excluded person is given leave, that leave is invalid. The exemption from immigration control under the IA 1971 for seacrews, aircrews and other special cases does not apply whilst the person continues to be an excluded person.

An exclusion will not apply if it would be contrary to the UK's obligations under the European Convention on Human Rights or the 1951 Refugee Convention, or if the EU or UN has allowed an exemption to apply.

Part 7—Language Requirements for Public Sector Workers

PART 7

7.1 Part 7 imposes a specific duty upon public authorities to ensure that their workers in customer-facing roles speak sufficient English to perform these roles effectively. In doing so, public authorities must have regard to a code of practice issued by the Secretary of State dealing with processes for recruitment, complaints from members of the public, and other matters.

This Part of the Act came into force on 21 November 2016.[1] The Government issued a draft code of practice for consultation on 13 October 2015 and its report of findings from the consultation on 19 February 2016.[2] The Government subsequently published the draft *Code of Practice on the English Language Requirement for Public Sector Workers* on 21 July 2016 and laid this before Parliament.[3] The government stated that the draft code of practice was made available in advance of the provisions coming into force to help public authorities be ready comply with the duty on the date the legislation entered into force.[4] The finalised version of the code was published on 29 November 2016.[5] Regulations laid before Parliament on 30 November 2016 brought the code of practice into force on 22 December 2016.[6]

The introduction of the English language requirement for public sector workers was a commitment made in the Conservative Party manifesto, among other commitments to 'promote British values within society'. The need for legislation in this area was questioned during the debates in Parliament, particularly since many professions within the public sector already applied standards for spoken English.

Workers may face bullying, harassment or discrimination at work in the context of complaints about their level of ability in speaking English. Whilst employment law is generally out of scope of Legal Aid, cases involving discrimination remain within scope: para 43(1) of Schedule 1, Part 1 to the Legal Aid, Sentencing and Punishment of Offenders Act 2012.

---

1 Immigration Act 2016 (Commencement No. 2 and Transitional Provisions) Regulations 2016, SI 2016/1037.

7.2 A Guide to the Immigration Act 2016

2   *Consultation on draft language requirements for public sector workers*, Cabinet Office, 13 October 2015; *Consultation report on draft English language requirements for public sector workers Code of Practice*, Cabinet Office, 19 February 2016; both available at: https://www.gov.uk/government/consultations/language-requirements-for-public-sector-workers (accessed 16 December 2016).
3   *Code of Practice on the English language requirement for public sector workers: Part 7 of the Immigration Act 2016*, October 2016, v1.0, Cabinet Office and Home Office, 21 July 2016. Available at: https://www.gov.uk/government/publications/english-language-requirement-for-public-sector-workers-code-of-practice (accessed 14 November 2016).
4   English language requirement, Written Statement HCWS112 Rt Hon Ben Gummer MP, Minister of State for Cabinet Office and Paymaster General, 21 July 2016. Available at: https://www.parliament.uk/business/publications/written-questions-answers-statements/written-statement/Commons/2016-07-21/HCWS112/ (accessed 14 November 2016).
5   *Code of Practice on the English Language Requirement for Public Sector Workers*, Cabinet Office and Home Office, 29 November 2016. Available at: https://www.gov.uk/government/publications/english-language-requirement-for-public-sector-workers-code-of-practice (accessed 1 December 2016).
6   The Code of Practice (English Language Requirements for Public Sector Workers) Regulations 2016, SI 2016/1157.

SECTION 77—ENGLISH LANGUAGE REQUIREMENTS FOR PUBLIC SECTOR WORKERS

> **Summary**
>
> Requires a public authority to ensure that each person who works for it in a 'customer-facing' role speaks sufficient English to enable the effective performance of their role.

7.2

77 English language requirements for public sector workers

(1)   A public authority must ensure that each person who works for the public authority in a customer-facing role speaks fluent English.

(2)   In determining how to comply with subsection (1), a public authority must have regard to the code of practice under section 80 that is for the time being applicable to that authority.

(3)   A public authority must operate an adequate procedure for enabling complaints to be made to the authority about breaches by the authority of subsection (1) and for the consideration of such complaints.

(4)   In determining whether a procedure is adequate for the purposes of subsection (3), a public authority must have regard to the code of practice under section 80 that is for the time being applicable to that authority.

(5)   For the purposes of this Part a person works for a public authority if the person works—

Part 7—Language Requirements for Public Sector Workers 7.2

        (a)   under a contract of employment with the public authority,

        (b)   under a contract of apprenticeship with the public authority,

        (c)   under a contract to do work personally with the public authority,

        (d)   in England and Wales or Scotland, as an agency worker within the meaning of the Agency Workers Regulations 2010 (SI 2010/93) in respect of whom the public authority is the hirer within the meaning of those regulations,

        (e)   in Northern Ireland, as an agency worker within the meaning of the Agency Workers Regulations (Northern Ireland) 2011 (SR 2011/350) in respect of whom the public authority is the hirer within the meaning of those regulations,

        (f)   for the public authority as a constable, or

        (g)   for the public authority in the course of Crown employment.

(6)   In subsection (5) "Crown employment"—

        (a)   in relation to England and Wales and Scotland, has the meaning given by section 191(3) of the Employment Rights Act 1996,

        (b)   in relation to Northern Ireland, has the meaning given by Article 236(3) of the Employment Rights (Northern Ireland) Order 1996 (SI 1996/1919 (NI 16)), and

        (c)   includes service as a member of the armed forces of the Crown and employment by an association established for the purposes of Part 11 of the Reserve Forces Act 1996.

(7)   References in this Part to a person who works in a customer-facing role are to a person who, as a regular and intrinsic part of the person's role, is required to speak to members of the public in English.

(8)   For the purposes of this Part a person speaks fluent English if the person has a command of spoken English which is sufficient to enable the effective performance of the person's role.

(9)   This section applies in relation to a person who is working in a customer-facing role for a public authority when this section comes into force as well as to a person who begins to work in such a role after that time.

(10)   This section does not apply in relation to a person whose work is carried out wholly or mainly outside the United Kingdom.

Commencement: 21 November 2016, The Immigration Act 2016 (Commencement No 2 and Transitional Provisions) Regulations 2016, SI 2016/1037.

Guidance: In determining how to meet its obligation, and in operating an adequate complaints procedure that allows complaints to be made about

7.2 A Guide to the Immigration Act 2016

breach of the obligation, a public authority must have regard to the applicable code of practice issued under s 80.

Definitions:

'contract' a contract in writing whether express or implied, written or oral, s 83;

'Crown employment' England, Wales and Scotland: Employment Rights Act 1996, s 191(3); Northern Ireland: Northern Ireland Employment Rights (Northern Ireland) Order 1996, SI 1996/1919 (NI 16); includes service as a member of the armed forces of the crown and employment by an association established for the purposes of Part 11 of the Reserve Forces Act 1996 (s 77(6));

'customer facing role' where 'as a regular and intrinsic part of the person's role' the person is required to speak to members of the public in English, s 77(7);

'fluent English' a command of spoken English which is sufficient to enable the effective performance of the person's role, s 77(7);

'public authority' s 78, s 83;

'works for a public authority' s 77(5).

Devolution Extends throughout the UK but public authorities in Wales, Scotland and Northern Ireland are only under the duty insofar as reserved matters are concerned, s 78(3)–(8).

The section imposes a duty on the public authority to ensure that each person who works for the authority in a customer-facing role speaks 'fluent' English (s 77(1)). The authority must have regard to the code of practice issued under s 80 in complying with this duty.

The duty applies throughout the UK but public authorities in Wales, Scotland and Northern Ireland are only under the duty insofar as reserved matters are concerned (ss 78(3)–(8)). In Wales, the duty may be met by public sector workers speaking Welsh (s 82(3)).

The language requirement may also be met through the use of a sign language interpreter. This was placed in the code of practice following concerns raised in Parliament about discrimination on the basis of disability.[1] Public authority employers are also under a duty to make reasonable adjustments for people with disabilities under the Equality Act 2010.

The use of the term 'fluent' for describing the required level of English or Welsh is misleading as 'fluent English' is defined in the Act as 'a command of spoken English which is sufficient to enable the effective performance of the person's role' (s 77(8)). The standard of English required will therefore vary according to the nature of the role performed. The standard also refers only to spoken English so ability in reading or writing English is not required to meet the standard.

The public authority is required to operate a complaints procedure to enable members of the public to make complaints about breaches of the language requirement by the authority (s 77(3)). The authority is required to have regard to the code of practice issued under s 80 to ensure its complaints procedure, and the steps it takes to consider complaints, are adequate.

The duty applies to customer-facing roles. These are defined as roles in which a worker is required to speak to members of the public in English as a regular and intrinsic part of their role (s 77(8)). Further guidance on this is provided in the code of practice.[2] The circumstances in which a person 'works' for a public authority are set out at s 77(5). The definition is broad and encompasses employees and apprentices working under a contract with the public authority as well as agency workers where the public authority is the hirer and contracts for personal services. It does not include circumstances where the public authority contracts services from another body which hires the staff. See the commentary on s 79. The provisions do not apply with respect to employees who work outside the UK (s 77(10)).

The provisions apply to those already working for the public authority when this Part of the Act came into force as well as to those recruited after that date (s 77(9)). The public authority must, therefore, ensure that both new and existing staff members meet the language requirement.

---

[1] *Code of Practice on the English language requirement for public sector workers: Part 7 of the Immigration Act 2016*, Cabinet Office and Home Office, 29 November 2016. Available at: https://www.gov.uk/government/publications/english-language-requirement-for-public-sector-workers-code-of-practice, para 1.6 (accessed 1 December 2016).

[2] Ibid, paras 1.9–1.13.

SECTION 78—MEANING OF 'PUBLIC AUTHORITY'

> **Summary**
> Defines a 'public authority' for the purposes of this Part, in particular to provide that it applies to authorities in the exercise of reserved, not devolved, functions. Provides a power to amend the list of authorities excluded from the definition of a public authority by regulations.

7.3   *A Guide to the Immigration Act 2016*

7.3

78 Meaning of "public authority"

(1) Subject as follows, in this Part "public authority" means a person with functions of a public nature.

(2) A person is not a public authority for the purposes of this Part if, apart from this subsection, the person would be a public authority for those purposes merely because the person exercises functions on behalf of another public authority.

(3) A person who exercises functions in relation to Scotland is a public authority for the purposes of this Part in relation to those functions only if and to the extent that those functions relate to a reserved matter.

(4) In subsection (3) "Scotland" and "reserved matter" have the same meanings as in the Scotland Act 1998.

(5) A person who exercises functions in relation to Wales is a public authority for the purposes of this Part in relation to those functions only if and to the extent that those functions relate to a matter which is outside the legislative competence of the National Assembly for Wales.

(6) A person who exercises functions in relation to Northern Ireland is a public authority for the purposes of this Part in relation to those functions only if and to the extent that those functions relate to an excepted matter.

(7) In subsection (6) "Northern Ireland" and "excepted matter" have the same meanings as in the Northern Ireland Act 1998.

(8) The following are not public authorities for the purposes of this Part—

   (a) the Security Service;

   (b) the Secret Intelligence Service;

   (c) the Government Communications Headquarters.

(9) The relevant Minister may by regulations amend subsection (8) so as to add, modify or remove a reference to a person or description of person with functions of a public nature.

Commencement: 21 November 2016, The Immigration Act 2016 (Commencement No 2 and Transitional Provisions) Regulations 2016, SI 2016/1037.

Regulations: A Minister may make regulations to amend the list of authorities excluded from the definition of a public authority under s 78(8) which so far lists three security services. Regulations are subject to the affirmative procedure (s 78(9) and s 93(2)(h)).

Guidance: In determining how to meet its obligation, and in operating an adequate complaints procedure that allows complaints to be made about breach of the obligation, a public authority must have regard to the applicable code of practice issued under s 80.

Definitions:

'contract' a contract in writing whether express or implied, in writing or oral, s 83;

'excepted matter' for the purposes of s 78(6), Northern Ireland Act 1998;

'Northern Ireland' for the purposes of s 78(6), Northern Ireland Act 1998;

'public authority' a person with functions of a public nature, s 83;

'relevant Minister' the Secretary of State or the Chancellor of the Duchy of Lancaster (s 83);

'reserved matter' has the same meaning as in the Scotland Act 1998 (s 78(3));

'Scotland' has the same meaning as in the Scotland Act 1998 (s 78(3));

'Wales' has the same meaning as in the Government of Wales Act 2006 (s 83).

Devolution: Extends throughout the UK but public authorities in Wales, Scotland and Northern Ireland are only under the duty insofar as reserved matters are concerned (s 78(3)–(8)).

The section defines a 'public authority' and therefore those who are subject to the duty in s 77(1) to ensure that their workers speak sufficient English to enable the effective performance of their role. A public authority is defined as a person with functions of a public nature (s 78(1)).

The report of the findings of the consultation on the draft code of practice for the English language requirement for public sector workers identified that many organisations were unclear whether they were a public authority for the purpose of this Part.[1] The Government indicated that further guidance would be issued in the code of practice but that this would not provide a list of public authorities subject to the duty.[2] Guidance in the code issued subsequently invites bodies to consider the following factors when assessing whether they are a public authority: the extent to which the organisation has assumed responsibility for the function in question; the nature and extent of the public perception as to whether the function in question is public rather than private; the nature and extent of any statutory power or duty in relation to the function in question; and the extent to which the State pays for the function in question.[3]

7.4 *A Guide to the Immigration Act 2016*

Respondents to the consultation on the draft code of practice expressed concern that members of the public would not know which organisations were public authorities and which were outsourced to private contractors, causing confusion and customer dissatisfaction.[4] It is the Government's intention to extend the duty to private contractors in due course under its powers in s 79 below.[5]

One of the main purposes of the definitions section is to make clear that the provisions only apply in respect of matters within the competence of the Westminster Parliament rather than within the competence of the Scots, Welsh and Northern Ireland assemblies. This may prove problematic where competence is shared.

Section 78(9) excludes the Security Service, the Secret Intelligence Service and Government Communications Headquarters (GCHQ) from the definition of a public authority. It is unclear what might have constituted a 'customer-facing' role in the case of these services in any event.

---

1 *Consultation on draft language requirements for public sector workers*, Cabinet Office, 13 October 2015. Available at: https://www.gov.uk/government/consultations/language-requirements-for-public-sector-workers, p 19 (accessed 14 November 2016).
2 Ibid.
3 *Code of practice on the English language requirement for public sector workers: Part 7 of the Immigration Act 2016*, Cabinet Office and Home Office, 29 November 2016. Available at: https://www.gov.uk/government/publications/english-language-requirement-for-public-sector-workers-code-of-practice (accessed 1 December 2016).
4 *Consultation on draft language requirements for public sector workers*, Cabinet Office, 13 October 2015. Available at: https://www.gov.uk/government/consultations/language-requirements-for-public-sector-workers, p 19 (accessed 14 November 2016).
5 Ibid.

SECTION 79—POWER TO EXPAND MEANING OF PERSON WORKING FOR PUBLIC AUTHORITY

Summary

A power to extend the provisions to contractors by regulations.

7.4

79 Power to expand meaning of person working for public authority

(1) The relevant Minister may by regulations amend section 77 with the effect that a person who works for a contractor of a public authority is a person who works for the authority for the purposes of this Part.

Part 7—Language Requirements for Public Sector Workers 7.4

(2) In subsection (1) "contractor", in relation to a public authority, means a person who—

    (a) provides a service to members of the public as a result of an arrangement made with a public authority (whether or not by that person), but

    (b) is not a public authority.

(3) For the purposes of subsection (1) a person works for a contractor if the person works—

    (a) under a contract of employment with the contractor,

    (b) under a contract of apprenticeship with the contractor,

    (c) under a contract to do work personally with the contractor,

    (d) in England and Wales or Scotland, as an agency worker within the meaning of the Agency Workers Regulations 2010 (SI 2010/93) in respect of whom the contractor is the hirer within the meaning of those regulations, or

    (e) in Northern Ireland, as an agency worker within the meaning of the Agency Workers Regulations (Northern Ireland) 2011 (SR 2011/350) in respect of whom the contractor is the hirer within the meaning of those regulations.

Commencement: 21 November 2016, The Immigration Act 2016 (Commencement No 2 and Transitional Provisions) Regulations 2016, SI 2016/1037.

Amends: Creates a power to amend s 77.

Regulations: A Minister may by regulations amend s 77 so that a contractor of a public authority is a person who works for the authority for the purposes of this part. Regulations are subject to the affirmative procedure (s 93(2)(i)).

Definitions:

'contract' a contract in writing whether express or implied, in writing or oral, s 83;

'contractor' a person who is not a public authority but provides a service to members of the public as a result of an arrangement made by a public authority, s 79(2);

'public authority' a person with functions of a public nature, s 83;

'relevant Minister' the Secretary of State or the Chancellor of the Duchy of Lancaster, s 83;

'Wales' has the same meaning as in the Government of Wales Act 2006 (s 83).

Devolution: Extends throughout the UK but public authorities in Wales, Scotland and Northern Ireland are only under the duty insofar as reserved matters are concerned (s 78(3)–(8)).

This section provides a power to extend the duty, to ensure that workers speak 'fluent' English, to contractors by regulations (s 79(1)). A contractor is a person who is not a public authority but provides a service to members of the public as a result of an arrangement by a public authority (s 79(2)). This includes private and voluntary sector providers undertaking functions outsourced by the public authority. They are not currently covered by the duty to ensure those working for them in customer-facing roles speak sufficient English to enable the effective performance of their role. The Secretary of State may make regulations under this section bringing private and voluntary sector providers within the scope of the duty.

A person works for a contractor if the relationship with the contractor is the same as those set out in s 77(7) concerning persons working for a public authority. This includes agency workers within the meaning of the Agency Workers Regulations 2010, SI 2010/93 where the contractor is the hirer within the meaning of those Regulations (England, Wales and Scotland) and agency workers within the meaning of the Agency Workers Regulations (Northern Ireland) 2011, SR 2011/350 (s 79(3)(d)–(e)).

Respondents to the consultation on the draft code expressed concern that members of the public would not know which organisations were public authorities and which were outsourced to private contractors, causing confusion and customer dissatisfaction.[1] In the report on the consultation, the Government indicated that it was minded to extend the duty to private and voluntary sector providers of public services within this Parliament.[2]

---

1 *Consultation on draft language requirements for public sector workers*, Cabinet Office, 13 October 2015. Available at: https://www.gov.uk/government/consultations/language-requirements-for-public-sector-workers, p 19 (accessed 14 November 2016).
2 Ibid.

SECTION 80—DUTY TO ISSUE CODES OF PRACTICE

Summary
Places the relevant Minister under an obligation to issue a code or codes of practice with respect to the English language requirements.

7.5

80 Duty to issue codes of practice

(1) The relevant Minister must issue a code or codes of practice for the purposes of section 77.

(2) A code of practice must include provision about the following matters—

   (a) the standard of spoken English to be met by a person working for a public authority to which the code applies in a customer-facing role;

   (b) the action available to such a public authority where such a person does not meet that standard;

   (c) the procedure to be operated by such a public authority for enabling complaints to be made to the authority about breaches by the authority of section 77(1) and for the consideration of such complaints;

   (d) how the public authority is to comply with its other legal obligations as well as complying with the duty in section 77(1).

(3) A code of practice may make such other provision as the relevant Minister considers appropriate for securing that a person who works for a public authority to which the code applies in a customer-facing role speaks fluent English.

(4) A code of practice may make provision in relation to—

   (a) all public authorities,

   (b) particular descriptions of public authority, or

   (c) particular public authorities.

(5) But the relevant Minister must ensure that there is at all times a code of practice in force which applies to each public authority.

(6) A code of practice may make different provision for different purposes, including different provision for different public authorities or descriptions of public authority.

Commencement: 21 November 2016, The Immigration Act 2016 (Commencement No 2 and Transitional Provisions) Regulations 2016, SI 2016/1037.

Guidance: Requires the relevant Minister to issue a code or codes of practice for the purposes of s 77.

Definitions:

'public authority' a person with functions of a public nature, s 83;

'relevant Minister' the Secretary of State or the Chancellor of the Duchy of Lancaster, s 83.

7.5 A Guide to the Immigration Act 2016

Devolution: Extends throughout the UK but public authorities in Wales, Scotland and Northern Ireland are only under the duty insofar as reserved matters are concerned (s 78(3)–(8)).

This section places the relevant Minister under an obligation to issue a code or codes of practice with respect to the English language requirements. The relevant Minister may issue more than one code.

The code of practice must deal with: the standards of English to be met by those working for public authorities; what the authority should do if the person does not meet the relevant standard; the complaints procedure; and adherence with other legal duties (such as non-discrimination, human rights, protection of staff from bullying and harassment, and other employment law obligations) in complying with the duty. The code can make other relevant provision and can make different provisions for different public authorities but a code of practice must be in force at all times in respect of each public authority.

The finalised version of the code of practice was published on 29 November 2016.[1] Regulations made under s 81(3) and laid before parliament on 30 November 2016 will bring the code into force on 22 December 2016.[2] For the procedure for issuing codes of practice see s 81.

The code of practice states that public authorities must give members of staff a reasonable opportunity to reach the necessary standard of fluency in English or Welsh.[3] Authorities should consider providing training or re-training to support staff to meet the language requirements.[4] It further states that a public authority should only consider dismissing an employee as a last resort, after all reasonable alternatives have been considered.[5]

Following concerns raised in Parliament about the potentially discriminatory impact of the duty on Black and Minority Ethnic groups who may be the subject of complaints based on racism, the guidance identifies that a complaint about a staff member's accent, dialect, manner or tone of communication, origin or nationality would not be considered a legitimate complaint about fluency and that public authorities should make this clear in their complaints policies.[6] Public authorities should also not take forward complaints that are vexatious, oppressive, threatening or abusive. These include complaints which are without foundation, and/or which are intended to result in harsh or wrongful treatment of the person who is the subject of the complaint.[7] The guidance also refers to duties under the Equality Act 2010 and human rights legislation.

---

1   Code of Practice on the English Language Requirement for Public Sector Workers, Cabinet Office and Home Office, 29 November 2016. Available at: https://www.gov.uk/government/

Part 7—Language Requirements for Public Sector Workers **7.6**

publications/english-language-requirement-for-public-sector-workers-code-of-practice (accessed 1 December 2016).
2 The Code of Practice (English Language Requirements for Public Sector Workers) Regulations 2016, SI 2016/1157.
3 *Code of practice on the English language requirement for public sector workers: Part 7 of the Immigration Act 2016*, Cabinet Office and Home Office, 29 November 2016. Available at: https://www.gov.uk/government/publications/english-language-requirement-for-public-sector-workers-code-of-practice, para 3.10 (accessed 1 December 2016).
4 Ibid, para 3.3.
5 Ibid, paras 3.10–3.11.
6 Ibid, para 4.4.
7 Ibid, paras 4.5–4.6.

SECTION 81—PROCEDURE FOR CODES OF PRACTICE

> **Summary**
>
> Makes provision for drawing up codes of practice and for bringing them into effect.

7.6

81 Procedure for codes of practice

(1) In preparing a code of practice the relevant Minister must consult such persons as the relevant Minister thinks appropriate.

(2) Before issuing a code of practice the relevant Minister must lay a draft of the code before Parliament.

(3) A code of practice comes into force in accordance with provision made by regulations made by the relevant Minister.

(4) After a code of practice has come into force the relevant Minister must publish it in such manner as the relevant Minister thinks appropriate.

(5) The relevant Minister may from time to time review a code of practice and may revise and re-issue it following a review.

(6) References in subsections (1) to (4) to a code of practice include a revised code.

Commencement: 21 November 2016, The Immigration Act 2016 (Commencement No 2 and Transitional Provisions) Regulations 2016, SI 2016/1037.

Regulations: The code is brought into effect by regulations subject to the negative procedure, s 81(3) read with s 93.

Definitions:

'relevant Minister' the Secretary of State or the Chancellor of the Duchy of Lancaster, s 83.

Devolution: Extends throughout the UK but public authorities in Wales, Scotland and Northern Ireland are only under the duty insofar as reserved matters are concerned, s 78(3)–(8).

The section makes provision for drawing up codes of practice and bringing them into effect. There is an obligation on the relevant Minister to consult on the code but only with 'such persons as the relevant Minister thinks appropriate'. A code of practice is laid before Parliament in draft and comes into force by means of regulations. There is then an obligation to publish the code of practice but it may be published 'in such manner as the relevant Minister thinks appropriate'. Codes can be reviewed and reissued; this is a power not an obligation, but if a code of practice is reviewed and reissued then all the obligations in the section apply.

SECTION 82—APPLICATION OF PART TO WALES

> **Summary**
>
> Makes special provision for Wales, specifically that public authorities in Wales must ensure that the person concerned speaks Welsh or English.

7.7

82 Application of Part to Wales

(1) Subsection (2) makes provision about the application of this Part in relation to—

    (a) a public authority that exercises functions only in Wales, and

    (b) a public authority that exercises functions outside Wales and in Wales, to the extent that it exercises functions in Wales.

(2) In the provisions of this Part listed in subsection (3) references to English are to be read as references to English or Welsh.

(3) Those provisions are—

    (a) section 77(1), (7) and (8), and

    (b) section 80(2)(a) and (3).

Part 7—Language Requirements for Public Sector Workers **7.8**

Commencement: 21 November 2016, The Immigration Act 2016 (Commencement No 2 and Transitional Provisions) Regulations 2016, SI 2016/1037.

Definitions:

'public authority' s 83;

'Wales' Government of Wales Act 2006, s 83.

Devolution: Makes special provision for Wales.

This section provides that public authorities exercising functions in Wales (whether solely or not) must ensure that those working for them in customer-facing roles speak fluent Welsh or English. The recognition of both Welsh and English for the purpose of the duty is in line with the requirements of language schemes made pursuant to the now-repealed Welsh Language Act 1993 (WLA 1993) and the standards in the Welsh Language (Wales) Measure 2011 mccc 1 / 2011 nawm 1.

Under s 78, however, the duty on public authorities in Wales only applies in respect of devolved matters.

SECTION 83—INTERPRETATION OF PART

Summary

Contains definitions for the purposes of this Part.

7.8

83 Interpretation of Part

In this Part—

"contract" means a contract whether express or implied and, if express, whether oral or in writing;

"public authority" has the meaning given by section 78;

"relevant Minister" means the Secretary of State or the Chancellor of the Duchy of Lancaster;

"Wales" has the same meaning as in the Government of Wales Act 2006.

Commencement: 21 November 2016, The Immigration Act 2016 (Commencement No 2 and Transitional Provisions) Regulations 2016, SI 2016/1037.

7.9   *A Guide to the Immigration Act 2016*

Definitions:

'contract' a contract in writing whether express or implied, in writing or oral, s 83

'public authority' s 78, s 83;

'relevant Minister' the Secretary of State or the Chancellor of the Duchy of Lancaster, s 83.

'Wales' Government of Wales Act 2006, s 83.

Devolution: Extends throughout the UK but public authorities in Wales, Scotland and Northern Ireland are only under the duty insofar as reserved matters are concerned, s 78(3)–(8).

This section contains definitions for the purpose of Part 7. The relevant Minister who must issue a code or codes of practice on the public sector English language requirement is defined in this section as the Secretary of State or the Chancellor of the Duchy of Lancaster. It is likely that the Chancellor of the Duchy of Lancaster was selected because this postholder is in overall charge of the Cabinet Office and would be able to make codes of practice for departments under different Ministries.

SECTION 84—CROWN APPLICATION

Summary

Provides that this Part binds the Crown.

7.9

84 Crown application

This Part binds the Crown.

Commencement: 21 November 2016, The Immigration Act 2016 (Commencement No 2 and Transitional Provisions) Regulations 2016, SI 2016/1037.

Devolution: Extends throughout the UK but public authorities in Wales, Scotland and Northern Ireland are only under the duty insofar as reserved matters are concerned, s 78(3)–(8).

This section provides that this Part binds the Crown. This means that the Government must also comply with the provisions and cannot claim an exemption through the exercise of a prerogative power. The devolved administrations are only bound insofar as reserved matters are concerned.

Part 8—Fees and Charges

IMMIGRATION

SECTION 85—IMMIGRATION SKILLS CHARGE

> **Summary**
> Makes provision for an immigration skills charge to be levied on those hiring third-country nationals as skilled workers.

8.1

85 Immigration skills charge

(1) The Immigration Act 2014 is amended as follows.

(2) After section 70 insert—

"70A Immigration skills charge

(1) The Secretary of State may by regulations provide for a charge to be imposed on—

    (a) persons who make immigration skills arrangements, or

    (b) any description of such persons.

(2) "Immigration skills arrangements" are arrangements made by a person ("the sponsor") with the Secretary of State with a view to securing that an individual who is not exempt for the purposes of this section is granted entry clearance or leave to remain in the United Kingdom to enable the individual to work for the sponsor in the United Kingdom.

(3) Regulations under this section may in particular—

    (a) impose a separate charge on a sponsor in respect of each individual in relation to whom the sponsor makes immigration skills arrangements;

    (b) specify the amount of any charge (and different amounts may be specified for different purposes);

8.1 A Guide to the Immigration Act 2016

        (c)   make provision about when or how a charge may or must be paid to the Secretary of State;

        (d)   make provision about the consequences of a sponsor failing to pay a charge;

        (e)   provide for exemptions from a charge;

        (f)   provide for the reduction, waiver or refund of part or all of a charge (whether by conferring a discretion or otherwise).

(4)   Sums paid by virtue of regulations under this section must—

        (a)   be paid into the Consolidated Fund, or

        (b)   be applied in such other way as the regulations may specify.

(5)   Regulations under this section may be made only with the consent of the Treasury.

(6)   An individual is exempt for the purposes of this section if he or she is—

        (a)   a British citizen;

        (b)   a national of an EEA State other than the United Kingdom;

        (c)   a national of Switzerland;

        (d)   otherwise entitled to enter or remain in the United Kingdom by virtue of an enforceable EU right or of any provision made under section 2(2) of the European Communities Act 1972.

(7)   In this section "entry clearance" has the meaning given by section 33(1) of the Immigration Act 1971."

(3)   In section 74(2) (orders and regulations which are subject to affirmative resolution procedure) after paragraph (j) insert—

        "(ja)   regulations under section 70A;".

Commencement: 12 July 2016 (s 94(4)). For transitional provision see the regulations.

Amends: Immigration Act 2014 (IA 2014), inserts a new s 70A *Immigration skills charge.*

Regulations: Power for the Secretary of State to make regulations for the imposition of the charge (IA 2014, s 70). These are subject to the affirmative procedure (IA 2014, s 74(2)(ja) inserted by s 85(2)). The Immigration Skills Charge Regulations 2017 were published in draft on 10 February 2017 and intended to come into effect on 6 April 2017.

Definitions:

An individual is *exempt for the purposes of s 70 of the Immigration Act 2014* if the person is a British citizen, a national of another EEA State, a Swiss national or

Part 8—Fees and Charges 8.1

otherwise entitled to remain in the UK in exercise of an EU right (IA 2014, s 70(6) inserted by s 85(2)). Further exemptions are proposed in the draft regulations;

'immigration skills arrangements' arrangements made by a sponsor with the Secretary of State 'with a view to securing' that an individual not exempt is granted entry clearance or leave to remain to work for the 'sponsor' IA 2014, s 70(2) inserted by s 85(2).

Devolution: Extends throughout the UK.

An immigration skills charge will require an employer sponsoring a skilled worker from outside the European Economic Area (EEA) to pay an additional charge, which could then be used to fund apprenticeships. The charge will be experienced by sponsors simply as a fee increase.

On 24 March 2016, the Rt Hon James Brokenshire MP made a statement on changes to Tier 2 of the points-based system.[1] This confirmed that that the immigration skills charge would be introduced in April 2017 and would be levied on Tier 2 employers that employ skilled migrant workers. The charge will, therefore, be applied to certificates of sponsorship issued by employers after that date. The statement also confirmed that the charge will be set at £1000 per certificate of sponsorship per year. Draft regulations and explanatory material were published on 10 February 2017.[2]

A reduced rate of £364 will apply to small and charitable sponsors as defined in the Immigration and Nationality (Fees) Regulations 2006, SI 2006/226. Under these Regulations, a small sponsor is either a company subject to the small companies' regime under ss 381–383 of the Companies Act 2006.[3]

In brief, the small companies regime applies to companies meeting at least two of three qualifying conditions:

- an annual turnover of £10.2 million or less;
- a balance sheet of £5.1 million or less; and/or
- having 50 employees or fewer.

Charitable sponsors under the regulations[4] are charities within the meaning of s 1 of the Charities Act 2011 (CA 2011), s 1 of the Charities Act (Northern Ireland) 2008 (CA(NI) 2008), or a body entered in the Scottish Charity Register, which includes universities.

The charge will not apply to:

- specified PhD-level posts defined in the draft regulations by reference to the Standard Occupational Classification 2010 Index;

8.1 *A Guide to the Immigration Act 2016*

- the Intra-company Transfer Graduate Trainee category;
- international students switching from a Tier 4 student visa to a Tier 2 visa;
- Tier 2 Ministers of Religion and Sportspersons; and
- Out of country applications where the entry clearance is six months or less.

Apprenticeships are jobs offered by employers, under a Government scheme that combines employment with study towards a recognized qualification ranging from the equivalent of five GCSE passes to a degree-level qualification. The Government supports these through a framework of national standards, contributions toward training costs, exemptions from employer contributions to national insurance for certain apprentices, and through grants to small employers to set up apprenticeships.

An employer who pays the immigration skills charge will not receive the money for their own apprenticeship scheme; instead the money will go into a general Government fund for apprenticeships. The Government has introduced separate measures to fund apprenticeships through an automatic levy on large employers with annual wage bills of over £3 million that will be applied through the pay-as-you-earn scheme from April 2017.[5] Some employers will, therefore, pay both levies, the levy on large employers and the immigration skills charge, when employing skilled workers from outside the EEA.

Transitional provision is made in the draft regulations. The charge does not apply when the worker has already been assigned a Tier 2 Certificate of Sponsorship at the time when the regulations come into force (proposed for 6 April 2017) or where a Tier 2 worker already in the UK on that date subsequently extends their leave or changes job or employer.

The charge will be calculated according to the length of employment on the Certificate of Sponsorship. The charge must be paid before the sponsor can assign a Certificate of Sponsorship and can be refunded where the application is refused or withdrawn.

---

1 Tier 2 (Skilled workers), Rt Hon James Brokenshire MP, Written Ministerial Statement HCWS660, 24 March 2016. Available at: https://www.parliament.uk/business/publications/written-questions-answers-statements/written-statement/Commons/2016-03-24/HCWS660/ (accessed 14 November 2016).
2 Immigration and Nationality (Fees) Regulations 2006, SI 2006/226, Schedule 4, para 1.
3 The Immigration Skills Charges Regulations were published together with a letter *Immigration Skills Charge* from the Rt Hon Robert Halfon MP, Minister for Apprenticeships and Skills, to Gordon Marsden MP, Shadow Minister (Education) *Immigration Skills Charge: Summary of draft regulations*.
4 Immigration and Nationality (Fees) Regulations 2006, SI 2006/226, Schedule 4, para 1.
5 See *Apprenticeship funding: how it will work*, Department for Education guidance, October 2016, at: https://www.gov.uk/government/publications/apprenticeship-levy-how-it-will-work.

See also *Apprenticeship levy: employer-owned apprenticeship training: Government response to consultation*, Department for Business Innovation and Skills, November 2015, available at: https://www.gov.uk/government/uploads/system/uploads/attachment_data/file/482049/apprenticeship_levy_response_25112015.pdf and *Apprenticeship funding: pprenticeship funding in England from May 2017*, Department for Education, October 2016, at: https://www.gov.uk/government/uploads/system/uploads/attachment_data/file/562401/Apprenticeship_funding_from_May_2017.pdf (accessed 14 November 2016).

PASSPORTS AND CIVIL REGISTRATION

8.2 The first chapter of Part 8 is headed 'Immigration' which is an indication that this chapter, on passports and civil registration, is not about immigration. It will affect British citizens just as much as persons under immigration control.

SECTION 86—POWER TO MAKE PASSPORT FEES REGULATIONS

> **Summary**
>
> Power for the Secretary of State (SSHD) to make regulations setting out the fees to be charged in respect of applications for the issue of passports or other travel documents.

8.3

86 Power to make passport fees regulations

(1) The Secretary of State may by regulations provide for fees to be charged in respect of the exercise by the Secretary of State of such functions in connection with applications for the issue of a passport or other travel document as may be specified.

(2) Regulations under subsection (1) are referred to in this section and section 87 as "passport fees regulations".

(3) Passport fees regulations must provide for the fee in respect of the exercise of each specified function to comprise one or more amounts each of which is—

　　(a) a specified fixed amount, or

　　(b) an amount calculated by reference to a specified hourly rate or other specified factor.

(4) Provision made under subsection (3) may be intended to result in a fee in respect of a specified function which exceeds the costs of exercising the function.

(5) In specifying the amount of any fee, or hourly rate or other factor, the Secretary of State may have regard only to the costs of exercising—

    (a) the function;

    (b) any other function of the Secretary of State in connection with United Kingdom passports or other UK travel documents;

    (c) any consular function.

This is subject to section 87(5).

(6) In respect of any fee provided for under this section, passport fees regulations may—

    (a) provide for exceptions;

    (b) provide for the reduction, waiver or refund of part or all of a fee (whether by conferring a discretion or otherwise);

    (c) make provision about—

        (i) the consequences of failure to pay a fee;

        (ii) enforcement;

        (iii) when a fee may or must be paid.

(7) In this section—

"consular function" means—

    (a) any of the functions described in Article 5 of the Vienna Convention on Consular Relations set out in Schedule 1 to the Consular Relations Act 1968;

    (b) any function in the United Kingdom which corresponds to a function mentioned in paragraph (a);

in each case regardless of whether the function is exercised by a consular officer or by another person authorised by the Secretary of State;

"costs" includes—

    (a) the costs of the Secretary of State, and

    (b) the costs of any other person (whether or not funded from public money);

    "function" includes a power or a duty;

    "specified" means specified in passport fees regulations;

    "travel document" means a document which enables or facilitates travel from one state to another and a "UK travel document" means such a document issued by the Secretary of State;

    "United Kingdom passport" has the same meaning as in the Immigration Act 1971 (see section 33 of that Act).

(8) Any reference in this section to the exercise of a function includes a reference to its exercise in particular circumstances, including its exercise—

(a) at particular times or in a particular place;

(b) under particular arrangements;

(c) otherwise in particular ways,

and, for this purpose, "arrangements" includes arrangements for the convenience of applicants or persons making requests for the exercise of a function.

Commencement: 12 July 2016, Immigration Act 2016 (Commencement No 1) Regulations 2016, SI 2016/603.

Regulations: Empowers the Secretary of State to make regulations for the fees to be charged in connection with applications for passports or travel documents. Regulations will be subject to the negative procedure (s 86 read with s 93).

Definitions:

'consular function' a function described in Article 5 of the Vienna Convention on Consular Relations 1963 set out in the Consular Relations Act 1968 (s 86(7));

'costs' includes the costs of the Secretary of State and those of other persons whether or not the latter are funded by public money;

'function' includes a power or duty;

'specified' specified in passport fees regulations;

'travel document' a document enabling or facilitating travel from one State to another;

'UK travel document' a document enabling or facilitating travel from one state to another issued by the Secretary of State;

'United Kingdom Passport' as in Immigration Act 1971, s 33 (a current passport issued by the Government of the United Kingdom, the Lieutenant-Governor of any of the Islands, or the Government of any territory which is for the time being a British overseas territory).

Devolution: Extends throughout the UK.

This section creates a power for the SSHD to make regulations setting out the fees to be charged in respect of applications for the issue of passports or other travel documents. The functions in respect of which fees can be charged may be specified in regulations. The fees must be a fixed amount specified in the regulations, or an amount that is to be calculated by reference

8.4   A Guide to the Immigration Act 2016

to the hourly rate, or other factor specified in the regulations (s 86(3)). The fee charged may exceed the cost of exercising the function (s 86(4)).

The functions that can be considered by the SSHD when fixing a fee include not only functions in connection with the issue of the individual passport but the costs of issuing passports and travel documents more generally (s 86(5)).

The regulations can provide for exceptions and the reduction, waiver or refund of part, or all, of a fee including by conferring a discretion or otherwise. The SSHD may make provision about the failure to pay a fee, time limits for payment and enforcement (s 86(6)).

The structure of the provisions bears a striking resemblance to the Immigration Act 2014, Fees: ss 68–70 and Schedule 9, Part 11.

SECTION 87—PASSPORT FEES REGULATIONS: SUPPLEMENTAL

> **Summary**
>
> Provides that fees regulations may be made only with the consent of the Treasury, that fees may relate to something done outside the UK and that fees may be recovered as a debt due.

8.4

87 Passport fees regulations: supplemental

(1)   Passport fees regulations may be made only with the consent of the Treasury.

(2)   A fee under section 86 may relate to something done outside the United Kingdom.

(3)   Fees payable by virtue of section 86 may be recovered as a debt due to the Secretary of State.

(4)   Fees paid to the Secretary of State by virtue of section 86 must be—

   (a)   paid into the Consolidated Fund, or

   (b)   applied in such other way as passport fees regulations may specify.

(5)   Section 86 is without prejudice to—

   (a)   section 1 of the Consular Fees Act 1980 (fees for consular acts etc),

   (b)   section 102 of the Finance (No 2) Act 1987 (government fees and charges), or

   (c)   any other power to charge a fee.

Commencement: 12 July 2016, Immigration Act 2016 (Commencement No 1) Regulations 2016, SI 2016/603.

Devolution: Extends throughout the UK.

This section provides further detail on the power to charge fees for passports through regulations.

Fees regulations may be made only with the consent of the Treasury. Fees may relate to something done outside the UK and may be recovered as a debt due to the Secretary of State. Fees paid under the regulations must be paid into the Consolidated Fund (the Government's general bank account at the Bank of England) or be applied in such other way as is specified in fees regulations. In other words, the passport authority cannot keep the money. Subsection 80(5) sets out that these provisions are without prejudice to the existing powers to charge passport fees, namely those in the Consular Fees Act 1980 (CFA 1980), the Finance Act (No 2) 1987 or in any other legislation.

Again, the resemblance to the fees provisions of the Immigration Act 2014 in respect of immigration fees is striking. See notes to s 86.

SECTION 88—POWER TO CHARGE FOR PASSPORT VALIDATION SERVICES

Summary

Provides a power to charge fees for the provision of passport validation services.

8.5

88 Power to charge for passport validation services

(1) The Secretary of State may charge a fee in respect of the provision of passport validation services to persons on request.

(2) "Passport validation services" are services in connection with confirming the validity of United Kingdom passports or the accuracy of the information contained in them which are provided for the purpose of preventing or detecting crime.

(3) In this section "United Kingdom passport" has the same meaning as in the Immigration Act 1971 (see section 33 of that Act).

(4) A fee payable under this section may be recovered as a debt due to the Secretary of State.

8.5 A Guide to the Immigration Act 2016

(5) Fees paid to the Secretary of State under this section must be—

    (a) paid into the Consolidated Fund, or

    (b) applied in such other way as the Secretary of State may by regulations specify.

(6) Regulations under subsection (5) may be made only with the consent of the Treasury.

(7) This section is without prejudice to—

    (a) section 1 of the Consular Fees Act 1980 (fees for consular acts etc),

    (b) section 102 of the Finance (No 2) Act 1987 (government fees and charges), or

    (c) any other power to charge a fee.

Commencement: 12 July 2016, Immigration Act 2016 (Commencement No 1) Regulations 2016, SI 2016/603.

Regulations: Regulations may be made with the consent of the Treasury (s 88(6)), specifying how the fees paid under this section are to be applied (s 85(5));

Definitions:

'United Kingdom passport' as in the Immigration Act 1971 (IA 1971), s 33 (a current passport issued by the Government of the United Kingdom, the Lieutenant-Governor of any of the Islands, or the Government of any territory which is for the time being a British overseas territory).

Devolution: Extends throughout the UK.

This provides a power to charge fees for confirming the validity of a UK passport, or the accuracy of the information in it. Again, fees can only be made with the consent of the Treasury, must be paid into the Consolidated Fund or be applied in such other way as is specified in fees regulations, and the provisions are without prejudice to existing powers to charge passport fees, namely those in the Consular Fees Act 1980, the Finance Act (No 2) 1987, or in any other legislation.

SECTION 89—CIVIL REGISTRATION FEES AND SCHEDULE 15—CIVIL REGISTRATION FEES

Summary

Makes provision for fees in connection with certificates of births, marriages and deaths, and other functions of registrars.

Part 8—Fees and Charges **8.6**

8.6

89 Civil registration fees

(1) Schedule 15 (civil registration fees) has effect.

(2) In that Schedule—

  (a) Part 1 amends enactments about civil registration in connection with powers to make regulations for the charging of fees, and

  (b) Part 2 makes consequential and related amendments.

SCHEDULE 15

CIVIL REGISTRATION FEES

PART 1 POWERS TO MAKE REGULATIONS FOR THE CHARGING OF FEES

1   Before section 72 of the Marriage Act 1949 (but after the heading of Part 6 of that Act) insert—

"71A Fees

(1) The Secretary of State may by regulations provide for fees to be payable to such persons as may be prescribed in respect of—

  (a) the giving of notice of a marriage to a superintendent registrar;

  (b) an application for the reduction of the waiting period in relation to a notice of marriage (see section 31(5A));

  (c) the registration for the solemnization of marriages of a building certified as required by law as a place of religious worship, or the cancellation of such a registration;

  (d) the authorisation of a person to be present at the solemnization of marriages in such a building;

  (e) the presence of a superintendent registrar or registrar at a marriage (except in a case falling within section 51(1A));

  (f) the delivery under section 57(1) of a certified copy of entries in a marriage register book;

  (g) the carrying out of a search of—

    (i) any marriage register book,

    (ii) any index kept in relation to such a book, or

    (iii) certified copies of entries in such a book;

  (h) the provision of a certified copy, or other record of information, relating to an entry in a marriage register book;

  (i) the issue of the Registrar General's licence under section 7 of the Marriage (Registrar General's Licence) Act 1970;

  (j) such other marriage services as may be prescribed.

(2) Regulations under this section may—

    (a) specify the amount of any fee payable under the regulations, or

    (b) set out how such a fee is to be determined.

(3) Subsection (4) applies where the regulations provide for a fee to be payable to a superintendent registrar or registrar.

(4) The regulations may provide for such part of the fee as may be specified by or determined in accordance with the regulations to be payable by the superintendent registrar or registrar to the Registrar General in prescribed circumstances.

(5) The regulations may provide for the reimbursement, reduction, waiver or refund of part or all of a fee whether by conferring a discretion or otherwise.

(6) Regulations under this section must be made by statutory instrument.

(7) Regulations under this section may—

    (a) provide for exemptions from any of the provisions of the regulations;

    (b) contain such consequential, incidental, supplemental and transitional provision as the Secretary of State considers appropriate.

(8) A statutory instrument containing regulations under this section is subject to annulment in pursuance of a resolution of either House of Parliament.

(9) In this section—

"marriage services" means services in connection with marriages which are provided by or on behalf of the Registrar General, a superintendent registrar or registrar;

"prescribed" means prescribed in regulations made under this section."

Commencement: 12 July 2016, Immigration Act 2016 (Commencement No 1) Regulations 2016, SI 2016/603.

Amends: Marriage Act 1949, inserting new s 71A *Fees*; Births and Deaths Registration Act 1953 (BDRA 1953), inserting new s 38A *Fees*; Registration Service Act 1953, inserting new s 19B *Fees in respect of provision of copies of records etc*; Civil Partnership Act 2004, s 34; Marriage (Same Sex Couples) Act 2013, s 9; Places of Worship Registration Act 1855, substituting a new s 5 *Fees*; Savings Banks Act 1887, s 10; Marriage Act 1949, ss 27, 31, 41, 43D, 51, 57, 63–65A, 74 and 78; BDRA 1953, ss 13, 30–33A, 34A, 39, 39A, 41; Registration Service Act 1953 (RSA 1953), removing s 16; Factories Act 1961, s 178; Public Expenditure and Receipts Act 1968, Schedule 3; Marriage (Registrar General's

Licence) Act 1970, removing s 17; Social Security Administration Act 1992, s 124; Education Act 1996, s 564.

Regulations: Regulations prescribing fees may be made under the Marriage Act 1949, s 71A (negative procedure); the BDRA 1953, s 38A *Fees* (negative procedure, BDRA 1953, s 39); the RSA 1953, s 19B *Fees in respect of provision of copies of records* (negative procedure); an order can be made under the Civil Partnership Act 2004, s 34; regulations can be made under the Marriage (Same Sex Couples) Act 2013, s 9; Places of Worship Registration Act 1855, s 5 *Fees* (negative procedure).

Definitions:

'the appropriate fee' Factories Act 1961, s 178(3) as inserted by Schedule 15, para 33; Social Security Administration Act 1992, s 124(5)(a) as inserted by Schedule, 15 para 36; Education Act 1996, s 564(4) as inserted by Schedule 15, para 37;

'birth or death registration services' services in connection with the registration of births or deaths provided by or on behalf of the Registrar General, superintendent registrar, registrar or any other person, BDRA 1953, s 38A(6), inserted by Schedule, 15 para 2;

'marriage services' Marriage Act 1949, s 71A (9) inserted by Schedule 15, para 1;

'prescribed' Marriage Act 1949, s 71A (9) inserted by Schedule 15, para 1; BDRA, s 38A(6) inserted by Schedule 15, para 2; BDRA 1953, s 41 as amended by Schedule 2, para 31; see further the Marriage Act 1949, s 78(1) as amended by Schedule 15, para 20.

Devolution: Extends throughout the UK.

Part 1 of Schedule 15 enables fees to be set through regulations for a number of specified functions of the Registrar General, superintendent registrars and registrars, covering a range of registration services related to births, deaths, adoptions, parental orders, marriages, gender recognition and similar.

Fees can be set for services previously provided without charge. Regulations can be made to provide for the reduction, waiver, or refund of part or all of a fee, whether by conferring a discretion or otherwise.

The Marriage Act 1949 is amended to enable fees to be set in connection with marriages, including the giving of notice of a marriage, marriage services provided by, or on behalf of, superintendent registrars or registrars, and marriage services under other enactments.

Similarly, regulations under the BDRA 1953 can be made to set fees for birth and death registration services (including those performed under other enactments).

8.6   *A Guide to the Immigration Act 2016*

The Registrar General holds a wide range of records, both modern and historic. The Secretary of State is empowered to prescribe fees for the provision of copies or other records of any information held by the Registrar General under a new power inserted into the RSA 1953. Other services under this Act for which fees can be charged include the verification of divorces obtained overseas. The provision for fees in connection with conversions of civil partnerships into marriages in the Marriage (Same Sex Couples) Act 2013 is aligned with that made for births, deaths, marriages and civil partnerships.

Part 2 of Schedule 15 makes provision for consequential and related amendments to other enactments.

Part 9—Miscellaneous and General

WELFARE OF CHILDREN

SECTION 90—DUTY REGARDING THE WELFARE OF CHILDREN

> **Summary**
>
> Provides that any conflict between any section of Immigration Act 2016 (IA 2016) with s 55 of the Borders, Citizenship and Immigration Act 2009 (BCIA 2009) is to be resolved in favour of the latter.

9.1

90 Duty regarding the welfare of children

For the avoidance of doubt, this Act does not limit any duty imposed on the Secretary of State or any person by section 55 of the Borders, Citizenship and Immigration Act 2009 (duty regarding welfare of children).

Commencement: 12 May 2016 (s 94(5)).

Devolution: Extends throughout the UK.

This section replicates the Immigration Act 2014 (IA 2014), s 71. That section was intended to be a sop to concerns expressed as to whether the IA 2014, s 19 was compatible with the duty to safeguard and promote the welfare of children set out in s 55 of the Borders, Citizenship and Immigration Act 2009 (BCIA 2009).[1] The ILPA training notes at the time commented that it was in many ways an unhappy provision, and asked whether it would be inserted into all immigration acts henceforth. The trigger for the insertion of the section into this Act was concerns at the impact of s 63 on children.

9.1 *A Guide to the Immigration Act 2016*

The section has the potential to be used to 'read down' any provisions of the Act that risk giving rise to breaches of s 55. It reverses the normal principle of statutory interpretation: the doctrine of implied repeal *leges posteriores priores contrarias abrogant.*

Statement of Changes in Immigration Rules HC 532 nodded to s 71 of the IA 2014, amending para Gen 1.1 in Appendix FM to HC 395 to read as follows:

> 'GEN.1.1. This route is for those seeking to enter or remain in the UK on the basis of their family life with a person who is a British Citizen, is settled in the UK, or is in the UK with limited leave as a refugee or person granted humanitarian protection (and the applicant cannot seek leave to enter or remain in the UK as their family member under Part 11 of these rules). It sets out the requirements to be met and, in considering applications under this route, it reflects how, under Article 8 of the Human Rights Convention, the balance will be struck between the right to respect for private and family life and the legitimate aims of protecting national security, public safety and the economic well-being of the UK; the prevention of disorder and crime; the protection of health or morals; and the protection of the rights and freedoms of others (*and in doing so also reflects the relevant public interest considerations as set out in Part 5A of the Nationality, Immigration and Asylum Act 2002*). It also takes into account the need to safeguard and promote the welfare of children in the UK, in line with the Secretary of State's duty under section 55 of the Borders, Citizenship and Immigration Act 2009.' (New words in italic text.)

Home Office guidance on the issuing of 'deport first; appeal later' certificates under s 98B of the Nationality, Immigration and Asylum Act 2002 (NIAA 2002) reminds us that the case of a child can itself be certified: 'children are not excluded from the scope of certification under section 94B and consideration must be given to all such cases on an individual basis'.[2] It sets out the sorts of cases in which the interests of a child would not trump deportation prior to an appeal being heard:

> 'this is an indicative list and not prescriptive or exhaustive:
>
> ...
>
> - a child or partner is undergoing treatment for a medical condition in the UK that can be satisfactorily managed through medication or other treatment and/or does not require the claimant to act as a carer;'

It then gives examples of cases which might meet the threshold. These include cases where the child is seriously ill and requires full-time care 'by the claimant'.

The examples suggest a high threshold and are difficult to reconcile with a 'best interests' test, and a duty to safeguard and promote the welfare of children. For example, they suggest that if a child is seriously ill but does not require full-time care or does not require that the claimant provide the care, the threshold would not be met.

The IA 2014, s 19 inserts an interpretation of Article 8 of the European Convention on Human Rights (ECHR) into the NIAA 2002 as ss 117A–117D of that Act. Section 71 of IA 2014 applies to those provisions but Chapter 13 of the Home Office Immigration Directorate Instructions,[3] which describes how the Article 8 provisions are to be applied, takes a restrictive view of the interests of the child:

> When considering the public interest statements, words must be given their ordinary meanings. The *Oxford English Dictionary* defines 'unduly' as 'excessively' and 'harsh' as 'severe, cruel'.
>
> 2.5.3 The effect of deportation on a qualifying partner or a qualifying child must be considered in the context of the foreign criminal's immigration and criminal history. The greater the public interest in deportation, the stronger the countervailing factors need to be to succeed. The impact of deportation on a partner or child can be harsh, even very harsh, without being unduly harsh, depending on the extent of the public interest in deportation and of the family life affected.'

The Supreme Court considered the nature and extent of the duty under s 55 of the 2009 Act in *MM (Lebanon) and others v SSHD et another* [2017] UKSC 10, a case dealing with requirements of the Immigration Rules specific to families, and held that the immigration rules and the Secretary of State's guidance on the application of s 55 were both unlawful and failed to give effect to the judgment of the European Court of Human Rights in *Jeunesse v The Netherlands* (2015) 60 EHRR 789. The best interests of the child must be determined on a case by case basis.

---

1 *Hansard* HL, col 936 (1 April 2014).
2 Home Office, *Section 94B of the Nationality, Immigration and Asylum Act 2002*, v8, 20 January 2017. Available at: https://www.gov.uk/government/publications/section-94b-of-the-nationality-immigration-and-asylum-act-2002 (accessed 20 January 2017).
3 *Immigration directorate instructions Chapter 13: criminality guidance in Article 8 ECHR cases*, v5.0, 28 July 2014. Available at: https://www.gov.uk/government/uploads/system/uploads/attachment_data/file/337253/Article_8_ECHR_Guidance_-_v5_0_-Version__2_.pdf (accessed 27 November 2016).

FINAL PROVISIONS

SECTION 91 FINANCIAL PROVISION

> **Summary**
>
> Provision for expenditure to be incurred to give effect to the provisions of the Act.

9.2

91 Financial provisions

The following are to be paid out of money provided by Parliament—

(a) any expenditure incurred under or by virtue of this Act by a Minister of the Crown, a person holding office under Her Majesty or a government department, and

(b) any increase attributable to the Act in the sums payable under any other Act out of money so provided.

Commencement: 12 May 2016 (s 94(5)).

Devolution: Extends throughout the UK.

This section makes provision for expenditure to be incurred to give effect to the provisions of the Act.

SECTION 92—TRANSITIONAL AND CONSEQUENTIAL PROVISION

> **Summary**
>
> Power to make transitional and saving provision, including power to amend primary legislation.

9.3

92 Transitional and consequential provision

(1) The Secretary of State may by regulations make such transitional, transitory or saving provision as the Secretary of State considers appropriate in connection with the coming into force of any provision of this Act.

Part 9—Miscellaneous and General **9.3**

(2) The Secretary of State may by regulations make such provision as the Secretary of State considers appropriate in consequence of this Act.

(3) The provision that may be made by regulations under subsection (2) includes provision amending, repealing or revoking any enactment.

(4) "Enactment" includes—

  (a) an enactment contained in subordinate legislation within the meaning of the Interpretation Act 1978;

  (b) an enactment contained in, or in an instrument made under, an Act of the Scottish Parliament;

  (c) an enactment contained in, or in an instrument made under, a Measure or Act of the National Assembly for Wales;

  (d) an enactment contained in, or in an instrument made under, Northern Ireland legislation.

(5) In section 61(2) of the UK Borders Act 2007 (meaning of "the Immigration Acts")—

  (a) omit the "and" at the end of paragraph (i), and

  (b) at the end of paragraph (j) insert ", and

    (k) the Immigration Act 2016."

Commencement: 12 May 2016 (s 94(5)).

Amends: UK Borders Act 2007, s 61(2) *Citation* (definition of 'Immigration Acts') to include this Act.

Definitions:

'enactment' to include subordinate legislation and enactments made in or under acts of the Scottish Parliament, measures or acts of the National Assembly for Wales and instruments made under Northern Ireland legislation.

Orders and Regulations: Powers to make transitional, 'transitory', saving and consequential provision, including to amend primary legislation. These orders and regulations are not subject to any parliamentary procedure. The Immigration Act 2016 (Consequential Amendments) Regulations 2016, SI 2016/655, the Immigration Act 2016 (Transitional Provisions) Regulations, SI 2016/712 and the Immigration Act 2016 (Commencement No 2 and Transitional Provisions) Regulations 2016, SI 2016/1074 have so far been made.

Devolution: Extends throughout the UK. Can be used by the Westminster Parliament to amend enactments of the devolved administrations.

The section provides power to make transitional, 'transitory', consequential and saving provision. See for example, the Immigration Act 2016 (Consequential Amendments) Regulations 2016, SI 2016/655, which came into force on

9.4 A Guide to the Immigration Act 2016

12 July 2016. These make amendments to secondary legislation consequential on changes made by Part I of the Act. See the notes to s 34 for a discussion of the Immigration Act 2016 (Transitional Provision) Regulations 2016, SI 2016/712 and the notes to s 37 and Schedule 5 and s 38 and Schedule 6 for a discussion of the transitional provisions of the Immigration Act 2016 (Commencement No 2 and Transitional Provisions) Regulations 2016, SI 2016/1074.

SECTION 93—REGULATIONS

Summary

Sets out the parliamentary procedure in respect of order- and regulation-making powers provided for in the Act.

9.4

93 Regulations

(1) Regulations made by the Secretary of State or the Chancellor of the Duchy of Lancaster under this Act are to be made by statutory instrument.

(2) A statutory instrument containing (whether alone or with other provision) any of the following regulations may not be made unless a draft of the instrument has been laid before, and approved by a resolution of, each House of Parliament—

(a) regulations under section 3 which amend or repeal primary legislation,

(b) regulations under section 6,

(c) regulations under section 11 which amend or repeal primary legislation,

(d) regulations under section 14, 15 or 21,

(e) regulations under section 36(2),

(f) regulations under section 42(1) or (2),

(g) regulations under section 73(1) or (2),

(h) regulations under section 78(9),

(i) regulations under section 79(1),

(j) passport fees regulations within the meaning of section 86 which include provision specifying functions as mentioned in subsection (1) of that section,

Part 9—Miscellaneous and General **9.4**

- (k) regulations under section 92(2) which amend or repeal primary legislation,
- (l) regulations under paragraph 1(13) of Schedule 6, and
- (m) regulations under paragraph 2(7) of that Schedule.

(3) Primary legislation means any of the following—
- (a) an Act of Parliament;
- (b) an Act of the Scottish Parliament;
- (c) a Measure or Act of the National Assembly for Wales;
- (d) Northern Ireland legislation.

(4) A statutory instrument—
- (a) containing any other regulations made by the Secretary of State or the Chancellor of the Duchy of Lancaster under this Act, and
- (b) to which subsection (2) does not apply,

is subject to annulment in pursuance of a resolution of either House of Parliament.

(5) Subsection (4) does not apply to regulations under section 92(1) or 94(1).

(6) Regulations made by the Secretary of State or the Chancellor of the Duchy of Lancaster under this Act—
- (a) may make different provision for different purposes or areas,
- (b) may make provision which applies generally or for particular purposes or areas,
- (c) may make transitional, transitory or saving provision, or
- (d) may make incidental, supplementary or consequential provision.

Commencement: 12 May 2016 (s 94(5)).

Devolution: Extends throughout the UK.

Sets out the parliamentary procedure in respect of order-, and regulation-making powers for which provision is made in the Act. These are dealt with under the relevant sections above. The affirmative procedure requires that both Houses of Parliament approve an instrument before it can come into force. The negative procedure, the same procedure as is used for the Immigration Rules, means that the instrument comes into force on the day appointed, but if one House of Parliament votes against it, it will be annulled, whether or not it has already come into force. Commencement orders (s 94) and transitional and consequential provision orders do not require any parliamentary procedure to come into effect.

9.5   A Guide to the Immigration Act 2016

SECTION 94—COMMENCEMENT

> **Summary**
> Makes provision for different parts and sections of, and schedules to, the Act to be brought into force.

9.5

94 Commencement

(1) Subject to subsections (3) to (5) this Act comes into force on such day as the Secretary of State appoints by regulations.

(2) Regulations under subsection (1) may appoint different days for different purposes or areas.

(3) Subsections (3) to (5) of section 61 come into force on the day on which this Act is passed.

(4) Section 85 comes into force at the end of the period of two months beginning with the day on which this Act is passed.

(5) This Part comes into force on the day on which this Act is passed.

Commencement: 12 May 2016 (s 94(5)).

Orders and Regulations: Power to appoint commencement dates by order. The Immigration Act 2016 (Commencement No 1) Regulations 2016, SI 2016/603 and the Immigration Act 2016 (Commencement No 2 and Transitional Provisions) Regulations 2016, SI 2016/1074 have so far been made.

Devolution: Extends throughout the UK.

This section It allows different dates to be appointed for commencement in different areas, or for different purposes. The sections with an appointed commencement date are 61(3)–(5), and this Part – Part 9 *Miscellaneous and General*, which came into force on the day the Act was passed, 12 May 2016, and s 85 *Immigration Skills Charge*, which came into force on 12 July 2016 (s 95(4)), lining-up with the second commencement date in SI 2016/603. No skills charge was introduced on that date, see notes to s 85.

SECTION 95—EXTENT

> **Summary**
>
> Sets out to which parts of the United Kingdom the Immigration Act 2016 will apply, and makes provision for its extension to the Channel Islands and the Isle of Man.

9.6

95 Extent

(1) This Act extends to England and Wales, Scotland and Northern Ireland, subject as follows.

(2) Sections 69 to 72 extend to England and Wales only.

(3) Any amendment, repeal or revocation made by this Act has the same extent within the United Kingdom as the provision to which it relates.

(4) But subsection (3) does not apply to the amendments made to the Modern Slavery Act 2015 by paragraphs 30 and 35 of Schedule 3 (for the extent of which, see the amendments to section 60 of that Act made by paragraph 33 of that Schedule).

(5) Her Majesty may by Order in Council provide for any of the provisions of this Act to extend, with or without modifications, to any of the Channel Islands or the Isle of Man.

(6) A power under any provision listed in subsection (7) may be exercised so as to extend (with or without modifications) to any of the Channel Islands or the Isle of Man any amendment or repeal made by or under this Act of any part of an Act to which the provision listed in subsection (7) relates.

(7) Those provisions are—

   (a) section 36 of the Immigration Act 1971,

   (b) section 52(2) of the Civil Jurisdiction and Judgments Act 1982,

   (c) section 9(3) of the Special Immigration Appeals Commission Act 1997,

   (d) section 170(7) of the Immigration and Asylum Act 1999,

   (e) section 163(4) of the Nationality, Immigration and Asylum Act 2002,

   (f) section 49(3) of the Asylum and Immigration (Treatment of Claimants, etc) Act 2004,

   (g) section 63(3) of the Immigration, Asylum and Nationality Act 2006,

   (h) section 60(4) of the UK Borders Act 2007,

   (i) section 76(6) of the Immigration Act 2014, and

   (j) section 60(6) of the Modern Slavery Act 2015.

9.6 *A Guide to the Immigration Act 2016*

Commencement: 12 May 2016 (s 94(5)).

Orders and Regulations: Power to extend any provisions of the Act not already applying to them (by virtue of being a modification of existing legislation) by Order in Council, with or without modification, to the Channel Islands and Isle of Man.

Devolution: Extends throughout the UK.

This section sets out to which parts of the UK the Act will apply and makes provision for its extension to the Channel Islands and to the Isle of Man. It applies the Act to the whole of the UK with exceptions for ss 69–72 *Transfer of responsibility for relevant children*, which extend only to England and Wales. The section must, however, be read with provisions of the Act limiting the extent of particular sections. The approaches to modifications in respect of the devolved administrations in the Act are:

- The provisions apply without modification.

- The provisions apply with modifications on the face of the Act to reflect existing structures and differences. For example, Schedule 8 para 2 inserts a new s 28D(2A) into the the Immigration Act 1971 so that provisions for multi-entry warrants for immigration officers do not extend to Scotland, where multi-entry warrants are not permitted. This typifies the approach: the Act makes provision that reflects the situation in England, and then separate provision is made for the devolved administration in which the law is different, rather than the situation being reviewed across the UK as a whole and a decision taken as to which approach to prefer. Very often, as here, the need for a modification was only spotted at a late stage and the Act was amended during its passage.[1]

- The provisions extend across the UK but only in respect of reserved matters (eg the requirement that public sector workers in a customer-facing role speak 'fluent' English set out in Part 7). It would be open to the devolved administrations to make similar provision for matters within their competence.

- Specific provision is made for a devolved administration, see for example, s 56 *Detention by immigration officers in Scotland*.

- The provisions extend to England (or to England and Wales) only but can be extended further by regulations made by the Westminster Parliament. This is the case for the *Residential Tenancies* provisions scheme set out in ss 39–41. This is in contrast to the approach in Part 2, Chapter 3 *Residential Tenancies* of the Immigration Act 2014 where, on the face of the Act,[2] the provisions were stated to apply throughout the UK, but in the event were limited to England by the commencement order).[3]

The use of secondary legislation to implement certain provisions in the devolved administrations means that where provisions are found to be incompatible with the Human Rights Act 1998 (HRA 1998) the regulations could be struck down, whereas provisions of primary legislation can only be declared incompatible. Add to this the question of the borderline between devolved and reserved matters and we can anticipate litigation, in particular in Scotland. The UK Government has indicated that it does not consider that legislative consent motions are required for extensions to the devolved administrations. See, for example, the letter of the Rt Hon James Brokenshire MP, Minister for Immigration and Security, to Margaret Bruges MSP, Minister for Housing and Welfare in the Scottish Government, on the residential tenancies provisions.[4]

Devolution featured heavily in the report on the Bill by the House of Lords Select Committee on the Constitution[5] and was extensively debated in the Lords. Lord Hope of Craighead proposed amendments to provisions of the Bill dealing with illegal working in licenced premises, residential tenancies, and support under Part 5, saying:

> 'It is a feature of the Bill that the provisions which apply to England and Wales are set out in full and we are debating them, line by line, as we ordinarily do; but although the Bill applies to Scotland, Wales and Northern Ireland, it does not set out the measures which deal with certain devolved matters relating to those Administrations. That has three consequences. First, this House – or, indeed, this Parliament – is not able to debate the detail of the legislation …
>
> Secondly, as I understand the purpose of these provisions, it is not intended that the devolved legislatures should legislate on these matters either …. Thirdly, the measures which seek to apply these provisions in relation to Wales, Scotland and Northern Ireland are to be contained in a statutory instrument.
>
> Here the Minister is proposing to take measures in relation to Scotland with regard to devolved matters. If he was not to seek the consent of the Scottish Parliament, there may be really considerable consequences.'[6]

The then Minister, the Rt Hon Lord Bates, said in reply:

> 'I concur with the view that these are very important issues: they are not trivial issues but are very substantial…. In respect of illegal working in licensed premises, to which the noble and learned Lord referred, we have not had time to amend the Bill but have published draft regulations so that our method and intent are clear.
>
> … As with the right-to-rent scheme in the 2014 Act, we believe that the extension of these provisions to the whole of the UK has only consequential impact on devolved legislation and remains for an immigration purpose.

9.7 *A Guide to the Immigration Act 2016*

We have not sought to put the residential tenancies provisions for Scotland or Wales in the Bill or to publish draft regulations. This is because both the Scottish Parliament and the Welsh Assembly have been legislating in this space.... With the law in flux in Wales and Scotland, we had to decide whether it was worth amending the law only to need to re-amend it a few months later, and we thought that once was better.

... the dispersal of migrant children is not an area in which Wales, Scotland or Northern Ireland have competence to legislate, and their consent is therefore, in our opinion, not required for the UK Government to legislate in this area.'[7]

Amendments to other acts made by this Act extend as far as the provisions amended extend (s 95(3)) – with the exception of the new s 54A *Gangmasters and Labour Abuse Authority: information gateways*, and the new Schedule 4A *Information Gateways: specified persons* as inserted into the Modern Slavery Act 2015 (MSA 2015) by Schedule 3, paras 30 and 35. These extend only to England and Wales (Schedule 3, para 33, amending s 60(1) *Extent*, of the MSA 2015).

Section 95(7) makes provision for a range of existing powers to be used to extend the provisions of the Act, with or without modification, to the Channel Islands, or the Isle of Man.

1 Amendment 197 in the name of the Rt Hon Lord Bates, at Lords' Committee stage.
2 Section 76.
3 Immigration Act 2014 (Commencement No 6) Order 2016, SI 2016/11.
4 On 13 October 2015. Available at: http://data.parliament.uk/DepositedPapers/Files/DEP2016-0300/2015-10-13_JB_to_Margaret_Burgess_MSP.pdf (accessed 14 November 2016).
5 HL Select Committee on the Constitution, seventh report of session 2015–2016, HL Paper 75. *Immigration Bill*, see: http://www.publications.parliament.uk/pa/ld201516/ldselect/ldconst/75/7502.htm (accessed 14 November 2016).
6 *Hansard* HL, cols 1754 ff (15 March 2016).
7 *Hansard* HL, cols 1758–9 (15 March 2016). The Rt Hon Lord Bates resigned during the passage of the Act to walk across Latin America to raise funds for UNICEF.

SECTION 96—SHORT TITLE

Summary

Sets out the name of the Act.

9.7

96 Short title

This Act may be cited as the Immigration Act 2016.

Commencement: 12 May 2016 (s 94(5)).

Devolution: Extends throughout the UK.

This gives the name of the Act. The long title was amended during the passage of the Act. At Lords' Committee stage, Government amendment 246, in the name of the Rt Hon Lord Bates, broadened the long title of the Bill to substitute reference to its making provision about 'enforcement of certain legislation relating to the labour market' for reference to making provision about the 'Director of Labour Market Enforcement'.[1] The short title was the subject of debate[2] since provisions pertaining to labour market enforcement in Part 1, and provisions on civil registration fees in Part 8, do not pertain to immigration.

---

1 See HL Committee col GC190 (9 February 2016). The amendment followed on from the changes made by Government amendments laid at that stage.
2 Amendment 154 in the names of Baroness Hamwee and Lord Paddick, Lords' Report. HL col 1300 (9 March 2016).

Appendix

Materials

Within subsections below, materials are arranged in reverse chronological order.

(All websites verified as accessible as at 20 November 2016.)

WHOLE ACT

All debates and copies of Bills, Explanatory Notes to Bills and amendments are available at: http://services.parliament.uk/bills/2015-16/immigration.html – with links to:

- all debates http://services.parliament.uk/bills/2015-16/immigration/stages.html;
- all documents (save letters): http://services.parliament.uk/bills/2015-16/immigration/documents.html; and
- letters: http://www.parliament.uk/depositedpapers.

The Government published copious material when the Bill was presented to Parliament, including a detailed human rights memorandum. Subsequent material was produced during the passage of the Bill. This can be found at: https://www.gov.uk/government/collections/immigration-bill-2015-16#documents. Details are given below.

ILPA Immigration Bill briefings, and briefings promoted by ILPA are available at: http://www.ilpa.org.uk/pages/immigration-bill-2015.html

Rt Hon Amber Rudd MP, Home Secretary, Speech to Conservative Party Conference 2016, 4 October 2016. Available at: http://press.conservatives.com/post/151334637685/rudd-speech-to-conservative-party-conference-2016

Immigration Act: overview, Home Office, 12 July 2016 (first published 9 December 2015). Available at: https://www.gov.uk/government/publications/immigration-bill-2015-overarching-documents/immigration-bill-201516-overview-factsheet

Appendix   Materials

Rt Hon Lord Bates to Lord Hope of Craighead and others, *Immigration – Lords' Report – Second Day* (re Scotland Bill) 18 March 2016. Available at: http://data.parliament.uk/DepositedPapers/Files/DEP2016-0300/2016-03-18_Lord_Bates_to_Lord_Hope_Immigration_Bill_Lords_Rep_2_Day.pdf

Rt Hon Lord Bates to Baroness Fookes, chair, House of Lords' Select Committee on Delegated Powers and Regulatory Reform, re the committee's 17th and 18th reports, 1 March 2016, Annex 3 to the committee's 23rd report of session 2015–2016, HL Paper 111, 9 March 2016. Available at: http://www.publications.parliament.uk/pa/ld201516/ldselect/lddelreg/111/111.pdf

Rt Hon Lord Bates to Rt Hon Harriet Harman MP, chair, Joint Committee on Human Rights, 1 March 2016, published 9 March 2016. Available at: http://www.parliament.uk/documents/joint-committees/human-rights/Lord_Bates_re_Immigration_Bill_010316.pdf

Rt Hon Lord Bates to Lord Lang of Monkton, chair, House of Lords' Select Committee on the Constitution re the Committee's 7th Report, 1 March 2016 (on file at ILPA).

Rt Hon Lord Bates to Baroness Lister of Burtersett and others, *Immigration Bill – Day 5* (European migration, dual nationality, general aviation, English language & Tier 1 investors) 1 March 2016. Available at: http://data.parliament.uk/DepositedPapers/Files/DEP2016-0189/Letter_from_Lord_Bates_-_Immigration_Bill_Committee_Stage_Day_5.pdf

Rt Hon Lord Bates to Lord Rosser, *Immigration Bill – Lords' Report – Government Amendments* (Parts 1–5 and the recommendations of the House of Lords' Select Committee on Delegated Powers and Regulatory Reform) 1 March 2016. Available at: http://data.parliament.uk/DepositedPapers/Files/DEP2016-0190/letter_fr_Ld_Bates_to_Ld_Rosser-_Immigration_Bill_Amendments_RS.pdf with Annex A: Explanatory Table of Government Amendments (Parts 1–3 and 5 (transfer of children) and 8 (welfare of children) and delegated powers); 1 March 2016. Available at: http://data.parliament.uk/DepositedPapers/Files/DEP2016-0190/Annex_A_-_2016-03-01_Explanatory_table_of_Gov_amendments.pdf

Immigration Bill: third supplementary delegated powers memorandum, Home Office, 1 March 2016. Available at: http://data.parliament.uk/DepositedPapers/Files/DEP2016-0190/Immigration_Bill_2015-6_DPRRC_Third_Supplementary_Memorandum-1-3-16.pdf

Immigration Bill: second supplementary delegated powers memorandum, Home Office, 21 January 2016. Available at: http://www.parliament.uk/documents/lords-committees/delegated-powers/ImmigrationBill2ndSuppDelegatedPowersMemo.pdf

Materials Appendix

Immigration Bill: Government amendments, House of Lords' Select Committee on Delegated Powers and Regulatory Reform, 18th Report, HL Paper 83,15 January 2016. Available at: http://www.publications.parliament.uk/pa/ld201516/ldselect/lddelreg/83/83.pdf

Rt Hon Lord Bates, to Baroness Fookes, chair, House of Lords' Select Committee on Delegated Powers and Regulatory Reform, re initial response to the committee's 17th Report, 12 January 2016, published as Appendix 2 to the committee's 19th report of session 2015–2016, HL Paper 85, 21 January 2016. Available at: http://www.publications.parliament.uk/pa/ld201516/ldselect/lddelreg/85/8505.htm

Immigration Bill: Supplementary delegated powers memorandum, Home Office, 12 January 2016. Available at: http://www.parliament.uk/documents/lords-committees/delegated-powers/ImmigrationBillSuppDelegatedPowersMemo.pdf

Rt Hon Lord Bates to Lord Rosser, *Immigration Bill – Issues raised at second reading*, 8 January 2016. Available at: http://data.parliament.uk/Deposited Papers/Files/DEP2016-0028/Letter_from_Lord_Bates_to_Lord_Rosser_RE_Immigration_Bill.pdf

Michael Matheson MSP to Rt Hon James Brokenshire MP, 6 January 2016 (*nb* wrongly dated 2015). Available at: http://data.parliament.uk/DepositedPapers/Files/DEP2016-0300/2016-01-06_Michael_Matheson_to_JB_-_licensing.pdf

Immigration Bill, House of Lords' Select Committee on the Constitution, 7th report of session 2015–2016, HL Paper 75, 21 December 2015. Available at: http://www.publications.parliament.uk/pa/ld201516/ldselect/ldconst/75/7502.htm

Immigration Bill: delegated powers memorandum, Home Office, 1 December 2015. Available at: https://www.gov.uk/government/uploads/system/uploads/attachment_data/file/482043/2015-12-01_Immigration_Bill_Delegated_powers_memo_-_Lords.pdf

Immigration Bill: European Convention on Human Rights, supplementary memorandum, Home Office, 26 November 2015. Available at: https://www.gov.uk/government/uploads/system/uploads/attachment_data/file/481280/Immigration_Bill_ECHR_Supplementary_memo.pdf

Overarching Impact Assessment: Immigration Bill, IAHO0214, Home Office, 25 November 2015. Available at: https://www.gov.uk/government/uploads/system/uploads/attachment_data/file/482041/2015-11-30_revised_overarching_IA_-_Lords.pdf

Immigration Bill: European Convention on Human Rights memorandum, Home Office, 17 September 2015. Available at: https://www.gov.uk/government/uploads/system/uploads/attachment_data/file/462206/Immigration_Bill_ECHR_Memo.pdf

Appendix Materials

Rt Hon James Brokenshire MP to Rt Hon Nicola Sturgeon MSP, 16 September 2015. Available at: http://data.parliament.uk/DepositedPapers/Files/DEP2016-0300/2015-09-16_JB_to_Nicola_Sturgeon_Immigration_Bill_notice_of_intro.pdf

Rt Hon James Brokenshire MP to Rt Hon Nicola Sturgeon MSP, *Immigration Bill* (re Scotland, right to rent, support and English language), 13 August 2015. Available at: http://data.parliament.uk/DepositedPapers/Files/DEP2016-0300/2015-08-13_JB_to_Rt_Hon_Nicola_Sturgeon_MSP_RE_Immigration_Bill.pdf

Rt Hon David Cameron MP, Prime Minister, speech of 21 May 2015. Available at: https://www.gov.uk/government/speeches/pm-speech-on-immigration

MULTIPLE PARTS

Lord Keen of Elie QC to Lord Rosser, re issues raised during Committee: follow-up points from committee consideration on 1 February (immigration officer training, nationality documents, complaints, restrictions on studies, pregnant women in detention, review of detention, police registration), 23 February 2016. Available at: http://data.parliament.uk/DepositedPapers/Files/DEP2016-0237/Letter_to_Lord_Rosser_RE_Committee_Consideration_of_Immigration_Bill.pdf

Rt Hon Lord Bates to Baroness Lister of Burtersett *Immigration Billl – Report Stage – Day 2* (re the right to rent scheme, and an amendment to extend the grace period of Home Office asylum support), 21 March 2016. Available at: http://data.parliament.uk/DepositedPapers/Files/DEP2016-0289/L_Bates_to_Bns_Lister_of_Burtersett_-_Immigration_Bill_Report_2nd_Day.pdf

Rt Hon Lord Bates to Lord Rosser, *Immigration Bill – Government amendments* (re Government amendments Parts 3–7), 21 January 2016 with appendix: Home Office, Further explanation of government amendments tabled regarding Parts 3 and 5–7 and 21 January 2016 (Appendix on file at ILPA). Available at: http://data.parliament.uk/DepositedPapers/Files/DEP2016-0084/Letter_from_Lord_Bates_to_Lord_Rosser.pdf

Rt Hon Harriet Harman MP, chair, Joint Committee on Human Rights to Rt Hon Theresa May MP, Home Secretary (re immigration bail, bank accounts, human rights claims and housing, and support to migrants), 20 January 2016, published 21 January 2016. Available at: http://www.parliament.uk/documents/joint-committees/human-rights/correspondence/JCHR_Immigration_Bill_Letter_200116.pdf

Rt Hon Lord Bates to Lord Rosser, Immigration Bill – Government Amendments (re Part 1 LME and illegal working, and Part 2 Eviction and Driving) 12 January

2016. Available at: http://data.parliament.uk/DepositedPapers/Files/DEP2016-0033/Immigration_Bill_letter_regarding_committee_amendments.pdf

Further explanation of Government amendments tabled on 21 January 2015 (Parts 1–2), Home Office, 12 January 2016. Available at: http://data.parliament.uk/DepositedPapers/Files/DEP2016-0084/Further_explanation_of_Gov_amendments_To_immigration_bill.pdf

PART 1—LABOUR MARKET AND ILLEGAL WORKING

Independent Review of the Overseas Domestic Worker Visa, James Ewins, 6 November 2015 (published 17 December 2015). Available at: https://www.gov.uk/government/uploads/system/uploads/attachment_data/file/486532/ODWV_Review_-_Final_Report__6_11_15_.pdf

Chapter 1—Labour Market

Tackling exploitation in the Labour Market: government response to consultation, Home Office and Department for Business, Innovation and Skills, January 2016. Available at: https://www.gov.uk/government/uploads/system/uploads/attachment_data/file/491260/BIS-160-11-government-response-to-tackling-exploitation-in-the-labour-market.pdf

ILPA response to Department for Business Innovation and Skills Consultation: Tackling Exploitation in the Labour Market, ILPA, 7 December 2015. Available at: http://www.ilpa.org.uk/resources.php/31617/ilpa-response-to-department-for-business-innovation-and-skills-consultation-tackling-exploitation-in

Tackling exploitation in the labour market: consultation document, Home Office and Department for Business, Innovation and Skills, 13 October 2015. Available at: https://www.gov.uk/government/consultations/labour-market-exploitation-improving-enforcement

Trafficking in Persons Report 2015, Country Narratives: United Kingdom, US Department of State. Available at: https://www.state.gov/documents/organization/243562.pdf

Director of Labour Market Enforcement

Immigration Act 2016 factsheet 1: Labour Market Enforcement, Home Office, July 2016 (first published 9 December 2015). Available at: https://www.gov.uk/government/uploads/system/uploads/attachment_data/file/483755/Immigration_Bill_Factsheet_02_-_labour_market__report_.doc

Appendix Materials

ILPA response to the consultation on the role of the Director of Labour Market Enforcement, 7 December 2015. Available at: http://www.ilpa.org.uk/resources.php/31617/ilpa-response-to-department-for-business-innovation-and-skills-consultation-tackling-exploitation-in

Rt Hon James Brokenshire MP to Peter Bone MP and Albert Owen MP, chairs, Public Bill Committee considering the Immigration Bill, (definition of a worker) 28 October 2015. Available at: http://www.publications.parliament.uk/pa/cm201516/cmpublic/immigration/memo/ib38.pdf

Gangmasters and Labour Abuse Authority

House of Lords Select Committee on Delegated Powers and Regulatory Reform, HL Paper 83, 15 January 2016 see *Whole Act* above.

Labour exploitation of migrants, A/HRC/26/35, Report of the [United Nations] Special Rapporteur on the human rights of migrants, François Crépeau, 3 April 2014.

Labour Market Enforcement Undertakings and Orders

Code of Practice on Labour Market Enforcement Undertakings and Orders, Home Office and Department for Business, Energy and Industrial Strategy, 29 November 2016. Available at: https://www.gov.uk/government/publications/labour-market-enforcement-undertakings-and-orders-code-of-practice

Chapter 2: Illegal working

Immigration Act 2016 factsheet 2: Illegal working (sections 34 to 38), Home Office, July 2016 (first published 9 December 2015). Available at: https://www.gov.uk/government/uploads/system/uploads/attachment_data/file/483754/Immigration_Bill_Factsheet_03_-_illegal_working__report_.doc

Philippa Rouse, Head of Illegal Migration, Identity Security and Enforcement, Immigration and Border Policy Directorate (IBPD), Home Office, to Alison Harvey, Legal Director ILPA, email re transitional provision, 3 June 2016 at 12.30pm.

Alison Harvey, Legal Director, ILPA to Sally Weston, Immigration and Border Policy Directorate, Home Office, email re transitional provision, 2 June 2016 at 12.33pm.

An inspection of how the Home Office tackles illegal working: October 2014–March 2015, Independent Chief Inspector of Borders and

Immigration, 17 December 2015. Available at: http://icinspector.independent.gov.uk/wp-content/uploads/2015/12/ICIBI-Report-on-illegal-working-17.12.2015.pdf

Cities and Local Government Bill; Education and Adoption Bill; Immigration Bill, House of Lords' Select Committee on Delegated Powers and Regulatory Reform, 17th Report of session 2015–16, HL Paper 73, 22 December 2015. Available at: http://www.publications.parliament.uk/pa/ld201516/ldselect/lddelreg/73/7303.htm#a3

Offence of Employing Illegal Worker

An Employer's Guide to Right to Work Rent Checks, Home Office, 12 July 2016. Available at: https://www.gov.uk/government/uploads/system/uploads/attachment-data/file/571001/Employer_s_guide_to_right_to_work_checks/

Proceeds of Crime, Rt Hon Lord Bates, Written Answer HL 5291, 28 January 2016. Available at: http://www.parliament.uk/business/publications/written-questions-answers-statements/written-question/Lords/2016-01-20/HL5291

Worker Registration Scheme, Written Answer 12752, Rt Hon James Brokenshire MP, 21 October 2015. Available at: http://www.parliament.uk/business/publications/written-questions-answers-statements/written-question/Commons/2015-10-21/12752

Proceeds of Crime Guidance, Crown Prosecution Service, undated. Available at: http://www.cps.gov.uk/legal/p_to_r/proceeds_of_crime_act_guidance/

Illegal working in licensed premises

The [Draft] Immigration (Alcohol Licensing) (Northern Ireland) Regs, 9 March 2016. Available at: https://www.gov.uk/government/uploads/system/uploads/attachment_data/file/506393/sw_20160304_draft_alcohol_licensing_northern_ireland_regulations_v2.pdf

The [Draft] Immigration (Alcohol Licensing) (Scotland) Regs 9, March 2016. Available at: https://www.gov.uk/government/uploads/system/uploads/attachment_data/file/506394/sw_he_draft_immigration_alcohol_licensing_scotland_regulations_2.pdf

The [Draft] Immigration (Late Hours Catering) (Scotland) Regs, 9 March 2016. Available at: https://www.gov.uk/government/uploads/system/uploads/attachment_data/file/506392/sw_20160304__draft_late_hours_catering_scotland_regulations__v3.pdf

Appendix   Materials

Michael Matheson MSP to Rt Hon James Brokenshire MP, 6 January 2016, see *Whole Act* above.

Home Office, Regulatory triage assessment: introduction of immigration status check to alcohol and late night refreshment licence applications, 9 October 2015. Available at: https://www.gov.uk/government/uploads/system/uploads/attachment_data/file/471590/Illegal_working_licensing_impacts_assess.pdf

Illegal working in relation to private hire vehicles etc

Guidance for licensing authorities to prevent illegal working in the taxi and private hire sector in England and Wales, Home Office, 1 December 2016. Available at: https://www.gov.uk/government/publications/licensing-authority-guide-to-right-to-work-checks

Guidance for licensing authorities in Scotland to prevent illegal working in the taxi and private hire car sector, Home Office, 1 December 2016, https://www.gov.uk/government/uploads/system/uploads/attachment_data/file/574067/Guidance-for-licensing-authorities-to-prevent-illegal-working-in-the-taxi-and-private-hire-car-sector-in-Scotland.pdf

Guidance for the department for infrastructure to prevent illegal working in the taxi sector in Northern Ireland, Home Office, 1 December 2016, https://www.gov.uk/government/uploads/system/uploads/attachment_data/file/574123/Guidance-for-licensing-authorities-to-prevent-illegal-working-in-the-taxi-and-private-hire-car-sector-in-Northern-Ireland.pdf

Guidance on examining identity documents, National Document Fraud Unit, Home Office, 12 July 2016 https://www.gov.uk/government/publications/recognising-fraudulent-identity-documents

An employer's guide to right to work checks, Home Office, 12 July 2016. Available at: https://www.gov.uk/government/uploads/system/uploads/attachment_data/file/571001/Employer_s_guide_to_right_to_work_checks.pdf

Rt Hon James Brokenshire MP to Michael Matheson MSP, *Taxi and private hire vehicle licensing*, 9 February 2016. Available at: http://data.parliament.uk/DepositedPapers/Files/DEP2016-0300/2016-02-09_JB_to_Michael_Matheson_MSP.pdf

Michael Matheson MSP letter to Rt Hon James Brokenshire MP, 6 January 2016, see *Whole Act* above.

Regulatory triage assessment: illegal working in relation to private hire vehicles etc, Home Office, 24 November 2015. Available at: https://www.gov.uk/government/uploads/system/uploads/attachment_data/file/482061/2015-11-24_Illegal_working_taxis_impact_assessment.pdf

Rt Hon James Brokenshire MP to Michael Matheson MSP, *Immigration Bill – taxi and private hire licensing*, 6 November 2015. Available at: http://data.parliament.uk/DepositedPapers/Files/DEP2016-0300/2015-11-06_JB_to_Michael_Matheson_-_taxis.pdf

An employer's guide to acceptable right to work documents, Home Office, May 2015. Available at https://www.gov.uk/government/uploads/system/uploads/attachment_data/file/441957/employers_guide_to_acceptable_right_to_work_documents_v5.pdf

Guidance for employers on preventing illegal working in the UK: Croatian nationals, Home Office, July 2013, https://www.gov.uk/government/uploads/system/uploads/attachment_data/file/257339/guidance-croation.pdf

Illegal working notices and orders

Illegal working closure notices and compliance orders: Guidance for frontline professionals, Home Office, 1 December 2016. Available at: https://www.gov.uk/government/publications/illegal-working-closure-notice-and-compliance-orders

Rt Hon Lord Bates to Lord Alton of Liverpool et ors, *Immigration Bill – issues raised at Lords' Committee*, 20 January, 28 January 2016. Available at: http://data.parliament.uk/DepositedPapers/Files/DEP2016-0091/Letter_from_Lord_Bates_RE_issues_raised_on_Immigration_Bill.pdf

PART 2—ACCESS TO SERVICES

Immigration Bill 2015 – Access to services, Home Office, Policy statement, 23 October 2015. Available at: https://www.gov.uk/government/uploads/system/uploads/attachment_data/file/471627/PES_-_Access_to_Services.pdf

Residential tenancies

Immigration Act 2014: Guidance on taking reasonable steps to end a residential tenancy agreement within a reasonable time frame, Home Office, 1 December 2016. Available at: https://www.gov.uk/uploads/system/uploads/attachment-date/file/5272477/statutory_Guidance_-_Defence_to_Offence_Against_Landlords_v1_._.pdf

Thirteenth Report of Session, 2016-17, HL Paper 68, Joint Committee on Human Rights, 18 November 2016. Available at: http://www.publications.parliament.uk/pa/jt201617/jtselect/jtstatin/68/68.pdf

Appendix   Materials

Immigration Act 2016: factsheet 3: Residential tenancies (sections 39–42), Home Office, July 2016 (first published 9 December 2015). Available at: https://www.gov.uk/government/uploads/system/uploads/attachment_data/file/483757/Immigration_Bill_Factsheet_04_-_residential_tenancies__report_.doc

A short guide on right to rent, Home Office, 14 June 2016. Available at: https://www.gov.uk/government/publications/landlords-right-to-rent-checks-guide

Rt Hon James Brokenshire MP to Margaret Burgess MSP, (Scotland and right to rent), 13 October 2015. Available at:http://data.parliament.uk/DepositedPapers/Files/DEP2016-0300/2015-10-13_JB_to_Margaret_Burgess_MSP.pdf

Margaret Burgess MSP to Rt Hon James Brokenshire MP (Scotland and right to rent), 24 September 2015. Available at: http://data.parliament.uk/DepositedPapers/Files/DEP2016-0300/2015-09-24_Margaret_Burgess_MSP_to_James_Brokenshire.pdf

Evaluation of right to rent scheme, Full evaluation report of phase one, research report 83, Home Office, 20 October 2015. Available at: https://www.gov.uk/government/publications/evaluation-of-the-right-to-rent-scheme

Right to rent: private landlords' duty to carry out immigration status checks, SN07025, House of Commons library, 12 February 2016. Available at: http://researchbriefings.files.parliament.uk/documents/SN07025/SN07025.pdf

'No passport equals no home': An Independent evaluation of the right to rent scheme, Joint Council for the Welfare of Immigrants, 3 September 2015. Available at: https://www.jcwi.org.uk/sites/jcwi/files/documets/No%20Passport%20Equals%20No%20Home%20Right%20to%20Rent%20Independent%20Evaluation_0.pdf

Driving

An inspection of the 'hostile environment': measures relating to driving licences and bank accounts, January to July 2016, Independent Chief Inspector of Borders and Immigration, October 2016 [sent to the Home Secretary on 29 July 2016]. Available at: http://icinspector.independent.gov.uk/wp-content/uploads/2016/10/Hostile-environment-driving-licences-and-bank-accounts-January-to-July-2016.pdf

Immigration Act 2016: factsheet 4: Driving licenses, Home Office, July 2016 (first published 9 December 2015). Available at: https://www.gov.uk/government/uploads/system/uploads/attachment_data/file/483758/Immigration_Bill_Factsheet_05_-_driving__report_.doc

Bank Accounts

Baroness Williams of Trafford, Minister of State for the Home Office, Pilot of the powers to search for and seize driving licences held by illegal migrants,

Materials   Appendix

14 February 2017. Available at: http://data.parliament.uk/DepositedPapers/Files/DEP2017-0136/Williams_to_LordRosserUK_driving_licences_held_illegal_migrants.pdf

See *Driving licences* above for: *An inspection of the 'hostile environment': measures relating to driving licences and bank accounts*, January–July 2016, Independent Chief Inspector of Borders and Immigration, October 2016.

Immigration Act 2016: factsheet 5: Bank accounts, Home Office, July 2016 (first published 9 December 2015). Available at: https://www.gov.uk/government/uploads/system/uploads/attachment_data/file/483759/Immigration_Bill_Factsheet_06_-_banks__report_.doc

Robert Buckland QC MP to Albert Owen MP, chair, Public Bill Committee, Immigration Bill – measures on bank accounts, 4 November 2015. Available at: http://data.parliament.uk/DepositedPapers/Files/DEP2015-0855/Ltr_to_Albert_Owen_-_Immigration_Bill_Committee_-_Bank_accounts.pdf

Immigration Bill – tackling existing current accounts held by illegal migrants, impact assessment, RPC-15- HMT-3042, HM Treasury, Home Office, Ministry of Justice, Financial Conduct Authority, 3 August 2015. Available at: https://www.gov.uk/government/uploads/system/uploads/attachment_data/file/462233/Immigration_Bill_bank_accounts_impact_assessment.pdf

PART 3—ENFORCEMENT

Powers of immigration officials etc

Search and Seizure, v3, Home Office, Removals, enforcement and detention: general guidance, 16 December 2016. Available at: https://www.gov.uk/government/uploads/system/uploads/attachment_data/file/578886/Search-and-seizure_v3.pdf

Warrants: procurement and use, v1, Enforcement Instructions and Guidance: powers and operational procedure, Home Office, 1 December 2016. Available at: https://www.gov.uk/government/uploads/system/uploads/attachment_data/file/574036/Warrants-procurement-and-use-v1.pdf

Operational enforcement visits Version 2.0, Home Office General Instructions, Immigration Removal, Enforcement and Detention, 19 January 2017. Available at: https://www.gov.uk/government/uploads/system/uploads/attachment_data/file/557153/operational-enforcement-visits_v1.pdf

Enforcement Interviews Version 1.0, Home Office General Instructions, Immigration Removal, Enforcement and Detention, 12 July 2016. Available at: https://www.gov.uk/government/uploads/system/uploads/attachment_data/file/537358/Enforcement-interviews-v1.pdf

Appendix Materials

Immigration Act 2016: factsheet 6: Enforcement officer powers, Home Office, July 2016 (first published 9 December 2015). Available at: https://www.gov.uk/government/uploads/system/uploads/attachment_data/file/483800/Immigration_Bill_Factsheet_07_-_enforcement__report_.doc

Enforcement visits, Home Office Enforcement Instructions and Guidance, Chapter 31, version until 7 October 2016, when it was withdrawn.

Police and Criminal Evidence Act 1984 (Pace) Code B: Revised Code of practice for searches of premises by police officers and the seizure of property found by police officers on persons or premises, Home Office, 23 October 2013

Detention and bail

Consultation on changes to the Tribunal Procedure (First-tier Tribunal) (Immigration and Asylum Chamber) Rules 2014 arising from the Immigration Act 2016, Tribunal Procedure Committee, 9 February 2017.

Adults at Risk in Immigration Detention, Home Office Enforcement Instructions and Guidance, v2 (elsewhere referred to as Chapter 55b of those instructions but not so entitled), 6 December 2016. Available at: https://www.gov.uk/government/publications/offender-management,

Detention Services Order 09/2016: Detention Centre Rule 35, v4, Home Office, 6 December 2016. Available at: https://www.gov.uk/government/publications/application-of-detention-centre-rule-35

Bail, Enforcement Instructions and Guidance, Chapter 57, 5 December 2016. Available at https://www.gov.uk/government/uploads/system/uploads/attachment_data/file/574666/Chapter_57_EIG_v9.pdf

'Immigration detention in the UK: recent developments', Alison Harvey [2016] *Journal of Immigration, Asylum and Nationality Law* (2016) Vol 30 No 3, 222–251.

Care and Management of Pregnant Women in Detention, Detention Services Order 06/2016, Home Office, 1 November 2016. Available at https://www.gov.uk/government/publications/pregnant-women-in-detention (Detention Services Order 02/2013 *Pregnant women* of April 2013 was withdrawn in July 2016. It was stated that a new version would appear in August 2016 but the 1 November 2016 version was the first to appear).)

Detention and Temporary Release, Enforcement Instructions and Guidance, Chapter 55, last updated 9 September 2016. Available at: https://www.gov.uk/government/uploads/system/uploads/attachment_data/file/552478/EIG_55_detention_and_temporary_release_v21.pdf

Immigration Act 2016: Guidance on adults at risk in immigration detention, Home Office, 23 August 2016 (laid before parliament in draft on 21 July 2016; updated 23 August 2016 and came into effect 12 September 2016. see SI 2016/847). Available at: https://www.gov.uk/government/publications/

Materials Appendix

adults-at-risk-in-immigration-detention *ILPA comments on Draft Detention Services Order 05/2016: Care and management of pregnant women in detention*, 11 August 2016. Available at: http://www.ilpa.org.uk/resource/32391/ ilpa-comments-on-draft-detention-services-order-052016-care-and-management-of-pregnant-women-in-dete

Detention of pregnant women, v1, Enforcement Instructions and Guidance: Chapter 55a, Home Office, 12 July 2016. Available at: https://www.gov.uk/government/ uploads/system/uploads/attachment_data/file/537066/Chapter_55a_ Detention_of_pregnant_women_v1.pdf

Immigration Act: factsheet 7: immigration bail, Home Office, July 2016 (first published 9 December 2015). Available at: https://www.gov.uk/government/ uploads/system/uploads/attachment_data/file/483804/Immigration_Bill_ Factsheet_08_-_bail__report_.doc

ILPA comments to Immigration and Border Policy Directorate, Home Office, on the draft adults at risk in immigration detention policy, 1 July 2016. Available at: http:// www.ilpa.org.uk/resources.php/32274/ilpa-comments-to-immigration-and-border-policy-directorate-home-office-on-the-draft-adults-at-risk-i

ILPA comments to Home Office on the draft rules for Short-term Holding Facilities, 14 April 2016. Available at: http://www.ilpa.org.uk/resource/32078/ ilpa-comments-to-home-office-on-the-draft-rules-for-short-term-holding-facilities-sthfs-14-april-201

Lord Keen of Elie QC to Baroness Hamwee and Baroness Lister of Burtersett (detention and appeals), 21 March 2016 (on file at ILPA).

Victims of Modern Slavery: competent authority guidance, v3, Home Office, 21 March 2016. Available at: https://www.gov.uk/government/uploads/system/ uploads/attachment_data/file/521763/Victims_of_modern_slavery_-_ Competent_Authority_guidance_v3_0.pdf

Rt Hon Lord Bates to Lord Ramsbotham, *Immigration Bill – Lords' Report – Detention Amendments* (time limit on detention and detention of vulnerable persons) 11 March 2016. Available at: http://data.parliament.uk/ DepositedPapers/Files/DEP2016-0260/L_Ramsbotham_L_Rosser_Bns_ Hamwee_-_Immigration_Bill__Amendments.pdf

Report on an unannounced inspection of the short-term holding facilities at Longport freight shed, Dover Seaport and Frontier House (7 September, 1–2 and 5–6 October 2015), HM Inspectorate of Prisons, 9 March 2016. Available at: https://www.justiceinspectorates.gov.uk/hmiprisons/inspections/longport-freight-shed-dover-seaport-and-frontier-house/

Channel migrants detained in freight shed, Dominic Casciani, BBC, 8 March 2016. Available at: http://www.bbc.co.uk/news/uk-35750968

Immigration Detention, Written statement HCWS679, Rt Hon Theresa May MP, 18 April 2016. Available at: http://www.parliament.uk/business/publications/

Appendix Materials

written-questions-answers-statements/written-statement/Commons/2016-04-18/HCWS679/

Government note on detaining Individuals for the purposes of immigration control – consideration of risk issues, 1 March 2016. Available at: http://data.parliament.uk/DepositedPapers/Files/DEP2016-0190/Annex_B-Detaining_individuals_-_consideration_of_risk_issues.pdf

Simon Barrett, Removals, Enforcement and Detention, Immigration and Border Policy Directorate, Home Office Illegal Migration, Identity Security and Enforcement letter (no named recipient) re consultation on Short Term Holding Facility Rules, 18 February 2016. Available at: http://data.parliament.uk/DepositedPapers/Files/DEP2016-0190/Annex_C_-_Letter_re_Short_Term_Holding_Facility_Rules_Consultation.pdf, with:

- the Short-term Holding Facility Rules 2016, draft statutory instrument, 18 February 2016. Available at: http://data.parliament.uk/DepositedPapers/Files/DEP2016-0190/Annex_D_-_Short_Term_Holding_Facility_Rules_for_consultation.pdf;

- the draft Short-term Holding Facility Rules 2016: Summary of provisions, Home Office, 18 February 2016: http://data.parliament.uk/DepositedPapers/Files/DEP2016-0190/Annex_E_-Short_Term_Holding_Facility_Rules_-_summary_of_provisions.pdf.

Government response to Stephen Shaw's review into the welfare in detention of vulnerable persons, 14 January 2016. Available at: https://www.gov.uk/government/publications/government-response-to-the-review-on-welfare-in-detention-of-vulnerable-persons

Immigration detention: response to Stephen Shaw's report into the welfare in detention of vulnerable persons, Rt Hon James Brokenshire MP, Written Statement HCWS470, 14 January 2016. Available at: https://www.parliament.uk/business/publications/written-questions-answers-statements/written-statement/Commons/2016-01-14/HCWS470/

Stephen Shaw CBE, *A review into the welfare in detention of vulnerable persons*, published 14 January 2016. Available at: https://www.gov.uk/government/publications/review-into-the-welfare-in-detention-of-vulnerable-persons

Simplifying Immigration Law: the draft Bill, Cm 7730, Home Office, UK Border Agency, November 2009. Available at: https://www.gov.uk/government/uploads/system/uploads/attachment_data/file/238514/7730.pdf

Lord Brett, Parliamentary Under-Secretary of State to the Lord Avebury, 11 August 2009, re time limits for detention in short-term holding facilities. Available at: www.ilpa.org.uk/resources.php/2919/the-lord-brett-parliamentary-under-secretary-of-state-to-the-lord-avebury-of-11-august-2009-re-time-

The Refugee Council to Kristian Armstrong, Children's Champion, UK Border Agency, re short-term holding facilities and child protection, 5 August 2009.

Materials   Appendix

Available at: www.ilpa.org.uk/resources.php/2940/refugee-council-to-kristian-armstrong-childrens-champion-uk-border-agency-of-5-august-2009-re-short-

ILPA further response to draft short-term holding facilities rules, 11 June 2009. Available at: www.ilpa.org.uk/resources.php/13062/uk-border-agency-further-consultation-of-the-draft-short-term-;yxcvbholding-facility-sthf-rules-ilpas-furt

Barbara Nicholson, Detention Services Policy Unit, UK Border Agency to Steve Symonds, ILPA, re further consultation on the draft short-term holding facility rules, 20 February 2009. Available at: www.ilpa.org.uk/resources.php/20183/uk-border-agency-ukba-to-ilpa-re-further-consultation-on-the-draft-short-term-holding-facility-sthf-

Barbara Nicholson, Senior Policy Officer, Home Office to Elizabeth White, ILPA re ILPA's response to the consultation on the short-term holding facilities draft rules, 7 August 2006. Available at: www.ilpa.org.uk/resources.php/1889/home-office-to-ilpa-of-7-august-2006-re-draft-short-term-holding-facility-sthf-rules

ILPA response to the consultation on the short-term holding centre rules, 13 February 2006. Available at: http://www.ilpa.org.uk/resource/14493/response-to-home-office-consultation-on-draft-short-term-holding-facilities-rules and

Immigration: the short-term holding facility rules, draft statutory instrument, January 2006. Available at: www.ilpa.org.uk/resources.php/14494/home-office-draft-short-term-holding-facilities-rules-2006

Power to cancel leave

Leave extended by section 3C (and leave extended by section 3D in transitional cases), Modernised Guidance: other cross-cutting guidance, Home Office, 1 December 2016. Available at: https://www.gov.uk/government/uploads/system/uploads/attachment_data/file/573995/3C_3D_Leave_v7.pdf

ILPA response (RH comments), Andrew Eliot, Head of Bill Team, Home Office, to Alison Harvey, Legal Director, ILPA, 28 October 2015, by email.

PART 4—APPEALS

Certification under section 94B of the Nationality, Immigration and Asylum Act 2002, v8, Home Office, 20 January 2017. The previous versions were, v6, issued on 9 May 2016 and v 7 issued on 1 December 2016. Available at: https://www.gov.uk/government/publications/section-94b-of-the-nationality-immigration-and-asylum-act-2002

Appendix Materials

Immigration Act: factsheet 8: Appeals, Home Office, July 2016 (first published 9 December 2015). Available at: https://www.gov.uk/government/uploads/system/uploads/attachment_data/file/483837/Immigration_Bill_Factsheet_09_-_appeals__report_.doc

Section 94B of the Nationality, Immigration and Asylum Act 2002, v6, Home Office, 9 May 2016. Available at: https://www.gov.uk/government/publications/section-94b-of-the-nationality-immigration-and-asylum-act-2002 (replacing *Certification guidance in non-EEA deport cases*, Home Office, 30 October 2014).

Immigration Bill: Clause 34: appeals within the UK: certification of human rights claims, Home Office, January 2016. Available at: https://www.gov.uk/government/uploads/system/uploads/attachment_data/file/494241/Clause_34_-_Briefing_for_Lords_Committee_-_January_2016.pdf

Keeling schedule: Nationality, Immigration and Asylum Act 2002, Schedule 3 Withholding and withdrawal of support, showing changes which would be effected by the Immigration Bill local authority support measures in Schedules 8 and 9. (HL Bill 79, ordered to be printed, 2 December 2015), Home Office, 2 December 2015. Available at:https://www.gov.uk/government/uploads/system/uploads/attachment_data/file/487540/2015-12-09_2002_Act_Sch3_Keeling_Schedule.pdf

Keeling schedule: Immigration and Asylum Act 1999, Part 6: Support for Asylum-seekers etc, showing changes which would be effected by the Immigration Bill support measures in Schedule 8, paragraphs 1 to 15. (Bill 96, ordered by the House of Commons to be printed, 17 November 2015), 17 November 2015. Available at: https://www.gov.uk/government/uploads/system/uploads/attachment_data/file/480026/2015-11-20_1999_Act_Part_6_Keeling_Schedule.pdf

Immigration Bill 2015 – Appeals: Policy equality statement, Home Office, 27 October 2015. Available at: https://www.gov.uk/government/uploads/system/uploads/attachment_data/file/472711/PES_-_appeals.pdf

Skype families: the effects of being separated from mum or dad because of recent immigration rules, Office of the Children's Commissioner for England, JCWI and Middlesex University, September 2015, at http://www.childrenscommissioner.gov.uk/sites/default/files/publications/SkypeFamilies-CCO.pdf.

Criminality guidance in Article 8 ECHR cases, v6.0, Chapter 13, Immigration Directorate Instructions, Home Office, 27 February 2017. Available at: https://www.gov.uk/government/uploads/system/uploads/attachment_data/file/594709/Article_8_Criminality_cases_v6.0.pdf

Video link hearings: Guidance note 2013, no 2:, Hon Mr Justice Blake, President, Upper Tribunal Immigration and Asylum Chamber, 30 September 2013. Available at: https://www.judiciary.gov.uk/wp-content/uploads/JCO/Documents/Guidance/Presidential+Guidance+note+2013+No+2+-+Video+link+hearings.pdf

Materials Appendix

PART 5—SUPPORT ETC FOR CERTAIN CATEGORIES OF MIGRANTS

Support

Robert Goodwill MP, Minister of State for Immigration, Written Statement HCWS 467, 8 February 2017. Available at: https://www.parliament.uk/business/publications/written-questions-answers-statements/written-statement/commons/2017-02-08/HCWS 467

Calais camp: French and UK Governments fell well short of their child rights obligations, UN Committee on the Rights of the Child, 2 November 2016. Available at: http://www.ohchr.org/EN/NewsEvents/Pages/DisplayNews.aspx?NewsID=20815&LangID=E

Briefing note: Article 8 applications and eligibility for section 4 support, Deborah Gellner, Asylum Support Appeals Project, February 2015 updated September 2016. Available at: http://www.asaproject.org/uploads/Feb_2015_ASAP_Briefing_Note-Article_8_application_and_eligibility_for_section_4_support_(updated_Sep_2016).pdf

Children in crisis: unaccompanied migrant children in the EU, 2nd Report of Session 2016–17, House of Lords Select Committee on the European Union, HL Paper 34, 26 July 2016. Available at: http://www.publications.parliament.uk/pa/ld201617/ldselect/ldeucom/34/3402.htm

'Migrant children are being failed by UK, says Lords Committee report', Amelia Gentleman, *The Guardian*, 26 July 2016. Available at: https://www.theguardian.com/world/2016/jul/26/unaccompanied-migrant-children-failed-uk-government-lords-eu-committee

Immigration Act 2016 factsheet 10: Availability of local authority support, Home Office, July 2016 (first published 9 December 2015). Available at: https://www.gov.uk/government/uploads/system/uploads/attachment_data/file/483845/Immigration_Bill_Factsheet_11_-_Local_Authority_support__report_.doc

Immigration Act 2016 factsheet 9: Support for certain categories of migrants (section 66), Home Office, July 2016 (first published 9 December 2015). Available at: https://www.gov.uk/government/uploads/system/uploads/attachment_data/file/483838/Immigration_Bill_Factsheet_10_-_Support__report_.doc

Unaccompanied asylum-seeking children to be resettled from Europe, Prime Minister's Office press release, 4 May 2016. Available at: https://www.gov.uk/government/news/unaccompanied-asylum-seeking-children-to-be-resettled-from-europe

Refugees and Resettlement, Written Ministerial Statement HCWS687, Rt Hon James Brokenshire MP, 21 April 2016. Available at: http://www.parliament.

Appendix Materials

uk/business/publications/written-questions-answers-statements/written-statement/Commons/2016-04-21/HCWS687

Asylum support: section 4 policy and process, v7, UK Visas and Immigration, 4 April 2016. Available at: https://www.gov.uk/government/publications/asylum-support-section-4-policy-and-process

Revised transcript of evidence taken before the EU Sub-Committee on Home Affairs, Inquiry into unaccompanied minors in the EU, evidence session no 1, Alison Harvey, Kathryn Cronin and Baljeet Sandhu, 16 March 2016. Available at: http://data.parliament.uk/writtenevidence/committeeevidence.svc/evidencedocument/eu-home-affairs-subcommittee/unaccompanied-minors-in-the-eu/oral/30989.html

Rt Hon Lord Bates to the Earl of Listowel *Immigration Bill – care leavers*, 11 March 2016. Available at:http://data.parliament.uk/DepositedPapers/Files/DEP2016-0259/LBatestoEarlofListowelImmigrationBill.pdf

Rt Hon James Brokenshire MP to Emma Smale and Enver Solomon, co-chairs, Alliance for Children in Care and Care Leavers, Immigration Bill – care leavers, 10 March 2016.

Asylum – Housing, WA29521, 9 March 2016, Rt Hon James Brokenshire MP. Available at:http://www.parliament.uk/business/publications/written-questions-answers-statements/written-question/Commons/2016-03-02/29521/

ILPA written evidence to the House of Lords European Union Select Committee for its enquiry into unaccompanied children in Europe, 10 March 2016, (with supplementary evidence of 6 April 2016). Available at: http://www.ilpa.org.uk/resources.php/31951/ilpas-evidence-to-the-house-of-lords-eu-select-committee-for-its-enquiry-into-unaccompanied-children

Rt Hon Lord Bates, to Baroness Kennedy of the Shaws (student support for care leavers), 8 March 2016, referenced in the debate by the Rt Hon Lord Bates Hansard HL col 1782 (col 15 March 2016).

Rt Hon James Brokenshire MP to Alex Neil MSP, Immigration Bill (support and asylum seeking children), 1 February 2016. Available at: http://data.parliament.uk/DepositedPapers/Files/DEP2016-0300/2016-02-01_JB_to_Alex_Neil_-_asylum.pdf

Resettlement of unaccompanied refugee children, Written Ministerial Statement HCWS497, Rt Hon James Brokenshire MP, 28 January 2016. Available at: http://www.parliament.uk/written-questions-answers-statements/written-statement/Commons/2016-01-28/HCWS497

Lord Bates to Lord Rosser *Immigration Bill – Committee stage* Day 4 (asylum support, section 95A right of appeal, 28-day grace period, local authority support, tuition fee support for care leavers, unaccompanied minors), 10 February 2016. Available at: http://data.parliament.uk/DepositedPapers/

Files/DEP2016-0127/Lord_Rosser_letter_re_Lords_Committee_for_ Immigration_Bill__3_Feb__.pdf

Analysis of statistics received from the Asylum Support Tribunal, Asylum Support Appeals Project, 1 February 2016.

Impact Assessment: reforming support for failed asylum-seekers and other migrants without immigration status, IA: HO0195, Home Office, 28 January 2016. Available at: https://www.gov.uk/government/uploads/system/uploads/attachment_data/file/497333/2016-01-29_Immigration_Bill_-_support_-_revised_impact_assessment.pdf

Reforming support for migrants without immigration status: the new system contained in Schedules 8 and 9 to the Immigration Bill, Home Office, 21 January 2016. Available at: https://www.gov.uk/government/uploads/system/uploads/attachment_data/file/494240/Support.pdf

Alex Neil MSP to Rt Hon James Brokenshire MP (support and children), 16 December 2015. Available at: http://data.parliament.uk/DepositedPapers/Files/DEP2016-0300/2015-12-16_Alex_Neil_to_JB_-_support.pdf

Alex Neil MSP to Rt Hon James Brokenshire MP (support and care leavers), 8 December 2015. Available at: http://data.parliament.uk/DepositedPapers/Files/DEP2016-0300/2015-12-08_Alex_Neil_to_JB_-_support.pdf

Clive Peckover, Asylum and Family Policy Unit, Immigration and Border Policy Directorate, Home Office to National Asylum Stakeholder Forum, *Immigration Bill – support for certain categories of migrant* (new schedule on local authority support), 12 November 2015. Available at: http://www.ilpa.org.uk/resources.php/31560/immigration-bill-ilpa-briefing-for-house-of-commons-committee-government-new-clause-17-and-governmen

Reforming support for failed asylum seekers and other illegal migrants: response to consultation, Home Office, 3 November 2015. Available at: https://www.gov.uk/government/uploads/system/uploads/attachment_data/file/473231/Response_to_Consultation.pdf

Reforming support for failed asylum seekers and other illegal migrants, policy equality statement, Home Office, 30 October 2015. Available at: https://www.gov.uk/government/uploads/system/uploads/attachment_data/file/473234/Policy_Equality_Statement.pdf

ILPA evidence to the House of Lords European Union Select Committee for its enquiry into migrant smuggling, 21 August 2015. Available at: http://www.ilpa.org.uk/resources.php/31315/ilpa-submission-to-house-of-lords-select-committee-on-the-european-union-home-affairs-sub-committee-

Impact Assessment: reforming support for failed asylum-seekers and other illegal migrants, IA: HO0195, 1 July 2015 (see 28 January 2016 above for the Impact Assessment of that date which bears the same number and a slightly modified

Appendix Materials

name). Available at: http://www.parliament.uk/documents/impact-assessments/IA15-008C.pdf

The Children Act 1989 Guidance and Regulations Vol 2: *Care planning, placement and case review* (statutory guidance), Department for Education, June 2015. Available at: https://www.gov.uk/government/uploads/system/uploads/attachment_data/file/441643/Children_Act_Guidance_2015.pdf

Working Together to Safeguard Children: A guide to inter-agency working to safeguard and promote the welfare of children, HM Government, March 2015. Available at: https://www.gov.uk/government/uploads/system/uploads/attachment_data/file/419595/Working_Together_to_Safeguard_Children.pdf

The Children Act 1989 Guidance and Regulations Volume 3: planning transition to adulthood for care leavers, Department for Education, January 2015 (revision). Available at: https://www.gov.uk/government/uploads/system/uploads/attachment_data/file/397649/CA1989_Transitions_guidance.pdf

Children to stay with foster families until 21, Department for Education, news article, 4 December 2013. Available at: https://www.gov.uk/government/news/children-to-stay-with-foster-families-until-21

Iraq: Assistance to Locally Employed Staff, Written Statement, Rt Hon David Miliband MP, Secretary of State for Foreign and Commonwealth Affairs, *Hansard* col 27WS (9 October 2007). Available at: http://www.publications.parliament.uk/pa/cm200607/cmhansrd/cm071009/wmstext/71009m0001.htm

1930s debates on the Kindertransports are available on the Hansard millbanksystems website, see for example, *HL* Deb 05 July 1939, vol 113 cc1011-6810. Available at: http://hansard.millbanksystems.com/lords/1939/jul/05/refugee-problem#S5LV0113P0_19390705_HOL_20

Transfer of responsibility for relevant children

Interim National Transfer Protocol for Unaccompanied Asylum Seeking Children 2016–17, v0.8, Department for Education, Home Office, Department for Communities and Local Government, 1 July 2016. Available at: https://www.gov.uk/government/publications/unaccompanied-asylum-seeking-children-interim-national-transfer-scheme

Rt Hon James Brokenshire MP to Sir Keir Starmer MP, KCB, QC, *Immigration Bill – Support for migrant care leavers and dispersal of unaccompanied asylum-seeking children*, 25 November 2015. Available at: http://data.parliament.uk/DepositedPapers/Files/DEP2015-0916/2015-11-25_JB_to_Keir_Starmer_-_support_amendments.pdf

Materials Appendix

Rt Hon Theresa May MP, Home Office, Rt Hon Nicky Morgan MP, Department for Education and Rt Hon Greg Clark MP, Department for Communities and Local Government to council leaders (dispersal of unaccompanied asylum seeking children), 24 November 2015. Available at: http://data.parliament.uk/DepositedPapers/Files/DEP2016-0127/Joint_Ministerial_Ltr_to_Local_Councils_re_Kent_Dispersal_Scheme.pdf

PART 6—BORDER SECURITY

Operational enforcement visits Version 1.0, Home Office General Instructions, Immigration Removal, Enforcement and Detention, 26 September 2016. Available at: https://www.gov.uk/government/uploads/system/uploads/attachment_data/file/557153/operational-enforcement-visits_v1.pdf

Enforcement Interviews Version 1.0, Home Office General Instructions, Immigration Removal, Enforcement and Detention, 12 July 2016. Available at: https://www.gov.uk/government/uploads/system/uploads/attachment_data/file/537358/Enforcement-interviews-v1.pdf

Immigration Act: Factsheet 11: Border security, Home Office, 9 December 2015 (first published July 2016). Available at: https://www.gov.uk/government/uploads/system/uploads/attachment_data/file/483849/Immigration_Bill_Factsheet_12_-_border_security__report_.doc

Policing and Crime Bill: European Convention on Human Rights memorandum, Home Office, HM Treasury, and Ministry of Justice, 25 February 2016. Available at: http://www.parliament.uk/documents/joint-committees/human-rights/ECHR_memo_Policing_and_Crime_Bill_Feb_2016.pdf

PART 7—LANGUAGE REQUIREMENTS FOR PUBLIC SECTOR WORKERS

Code of Practice on the English Language Requirement for Public Sector Workers, Cabinet Office and Home Office, 29 November 2016. Available at: https://www.gov.uk/government/publications/english-language-requirement-for-public-sector-workers-code-of-practice

Code of practice on the English language requirement for public sector workers: Part 7 of the Immigration Act 2016, October 2016, v1.0, Cabinet Office and Home Office, 21 July 2016 (draft). Available at: https://www.gov.uk/government/publications/english-language-requirement-for-public-sector-workers-code-of-practice

Appendix   Materials

English language requirement, Written Statement HCWS112, Rt Hon Ben Gummer MP, Minister of State for Cabinet Office and Paymaster General, 21 July 2016. Available at: https://www.parliament.uk/business/publications/written-questions-answers-statements/written-statement/Commons/2016-07-21/HCWS112/

Immigration Act 2016: factsheet 12: English language, Home Office, July 2016 (first published 9 December 2015). Available at: https://www.gov.uk/government/uploads/system/uploads/attachment_data/file/483867/Immigration_Bill_Factsheet_13_-_English_language__report_.doc

Consultation report on draft English language requirements for public sector workers: Code of Practice, Cabinet Office, 19 February 2016. Available at: https://www.gov.uk/government/consultations/language-requirements-for-public-sector-workers

Alex Neil MSP to Rt Hon Matthew Hancock MP (Scotland and English language), 3 November 2015. Available at: http://data.parliament.uk/DepositedPapers/Files/DEP2016-0300/2015-11-03_Alex_Neil_to_Matthew_Hancock_-_English_language.pdf

Consultation on draft language requirements for public sector workers, Cabinet Office, 13 October 2015. Available at: https://www.gov.uk/government/consultations/language-requirements-for-public-sector-workers

Rt Hon Matthew Hancock MP to Humza Yousaf MSP, *Immigration Bill: language provision for public sector workers,* 16 September 2015. Available at: http://data.parliament.uk/DepositedPapers/Files/DEP2016-0300/2015-09-16_Matthew_Hancock_to_Hamza_Yousef_MSP.pdf

Rt Hon James Brokenshire MP letter to Rt Hon Nicola Sturgeon MSP, 16 September 2015 see *Whole Bill* above.

Impact Assessment: English language requirement for public sector workers, Cabinet Office and Home Office (omitted ref no), 20 May 2015. Available at: https://www.gov.uk/government/publications/english-language-requirement-for-public-sector-workers-impact-assessment

UK Immigration Bill: Language requirements for Welsh public sector workers, Legislative consent resolution NDM5593, Carwyn Jones AM (Brigend), Welsh Assembly 15 March 2016. Available at: http://www.parliament.uk/documents/commons-public-bill-office/2015-16/legislative-consent-resolutions/Immigration-Bill-LCM-160317.pdf – with legislative consent memorandum: Immigration Bill: Language requirements for public sector workers, Legislative consent memorandum, Carwyn Jones AM, First Minister, Welsh Assembly February 2016. Available at: http://www.assembly.wales/laid%20documents/lcm-ld10557/lcm-ld10557-e.pdf

PART 8—FEES AND CHARGES

Immigration

Rt Hon Robert Halfon MP, Minister of State for Apprenticeships and Skills to Gordon Marsden MP, Shadow Minister for Education et ors, *Immigration Skills Charge*, 10 February 2017, enclosing The Immigration Skills Charge Regulations 2017 (draft) and *Immigration Skills Charge: Summary of Draft Regulations*, Department for Education

Apprenticeship funding: how it will work, guidance, Department for Education,, October 2016. Available at: https://www.gov.uk/government/publications/apprenticeship-levy-how-it-will-work

Apprenticeship funding: apprenticeship funding in England from May 2017, Department for Education, October 2016. Available at: https://www.gov.uk/government/uploads/system/uploads/attachment_data/file/562401/Apprenticeship_funding_from_May_2017.pdf

Tier 2 (Skilled workers), Written Ministerial Statement HCWS660, Rt Hon James Brokenshire MP, 24 March 2016. Available at: https://www.parliament.uk/business/publications/written-questions-answers-statements/written-statement/Commons/2016-03-24/HCWS660/

Rt Hon Lord Bates to Lord Rosser, *Immigration Bill – Committee stage consideration – immigration health charge*, 3 February 2016. Available at: http://data.parliament.uk/DepositedPapers/Files/DEP2016-0096/Lord_Rosser_letter_RE_Immigration_Bill_Committee_Stage.pdf

Apprenticeship levy: employer-owned apprenticeship training: Government response to consultation, Department for Business Innovation and Skills, November 2015. Available at https://www.gov.uk/government/uploads/system/uploads/attachment_data/file/482049/apprenticeship_levy_response_25112015.pdf

Passports and civil registration

Immigration Act 2016: Factsheet: Fees and charges (sections 85 to 89), July 2016 (first published 17 September 2015). Available at: https://www.gov.uk/government/uploads/system/uploads/attachment_data/file/461708/Fees.pdf

PART 9—MISCELLANEOUS AND GENERAL

Section 94B of the Nationality, Immigration and Asylum Act 2002, v8, Home Office, 20 January 2017. The previous versions were v6, issued on 9 May 2016 and

Appendix   Materials

v7, issued on 1 December 2016. Available at: https://www.gov.uk/government/publications/section-94b-of-the-nationality-immigration-and-asylum-act-2002

Criminality guidance in Article 8 ECHR cases, v5.0, Immigration Directorate Instructions, Chapter 13, Home Office, 28 July 2014. Available at: https://www.gov.uk/government/uploads/system/uploads/attachment_data/file/337253/Article_8_ECHR_Guidance_-_v5_0_-Version__2_.pdf

Index

[*all references are to paragraph number*]

Access to services
  residential tenancies
    commencement provisions, 2.2
    eligibility for services, 2.3
    eviction of disqualified
      occupiers, 2.5
    excluded agreements, 2.1
    housing and homelessness
      services, 2.3
    introduction, 2.1
    leasing premises offence, 2.4
    Northern Ireland, in, 2.7
    order for possession of
      dwelling-house, 2.6
    relevant agreements, 2.1
    relevant tenants, 2.1
    Scotland, in, 2.7
    transitional provisions, 2.2
    Wales, in, 2.7
Accommodation
  failed asylum seekers facing genuine
    obstacle to leaving the UK, 5.2.4
Airport control areas
  penalties, 6.1
Annual reports
  generally, 1.4
  publication, 1.5
Appeals
  certification of human rights
    claims, 4.1
  continuation of leave, 4.2
Asylum seekers
  categories of migrant, 5.2
  facing genuine obstacle to leaving
    the UK
    accommodation, 5.2.4
    cash, 5.2.4
    community activity condition,
      5.2.3.3
    effect of refusal or discontinuation,
      5.2.3.4
    'failed asylum seeker', 5.2.3

Asylum seekers – *contd*
  facing genuine obstacle to leaving the
    UK – *contd*
    families with children, 5.2.4.1
    generally, 5.2.3
    'genuine obstacle to leaving the
      UK', 5.2.3.1
    nature, 5.2.4
    no right of appeal, 5.2.3.4
    other conditions of access, 5.2.3.3
    temporary arrangements, 5.2.5
    time limitations, 5.2.3.2
    transitional arrangements, 5.2.6
  family reunion
    generally, 5.3.4
    policies, 5.3.5
  introduction, 5.1
  making further submissions as to
    protection claims, 5.2.2
  persons fleeing genocide, 5.3.3
  repeal of s 4 IAA 1999, 5.2.1
  support provision
    categories of migrant, 5.2
    facing genuine obstacle to leaving
      the UK, 5.2.3–5.2.3.3
    introduction, 5.1
    making further submissions as to
      protection claims, 5.2.2
    other debated issues, 5.3.1–5.3.5
    relocation of children, 5.3
    repeal of s 4 IAA 1999, 5.2.1
    unaccompanied refugee children, 5.3

Bail
  address of person bailed, 3.16.5
  commencement of provisions, 3.16.1
  conditions, 3.16.2–3.16.3
  definitions, 3.16
  duty to arrange consideration, 3.16.4
  electronic monitoring, 3.16.3
  general provision, 3.16
  other provisions, 3.16.6

Index

Bail – *contd*
   prohibition on repeat hearings, 3.16.6
   support for person bailed, 3.16.5
Bank accounts
   carrying out immigration checks, 2.10
Births, marriages and deaths
   fees and charges, 8.6
Border security
   airport control areas
     penalties, 6.1
   maritime enforcement
     exercise of powers by officers, 6.2
     hot pursuit onto High Seas, 6.2
   persons excluded from the UK
     international obligations, under, 6.3
Bullying at work
   language requirements for public sector workers, and, 7.1

Care leavers
   affected young people, 5.7.1.2
   devolution, and, 5.9
   general provision, 5.4
   leaving care support, 5.7
   support under Sch 12 Para 10B, 5.7.2
   tuition fees, 5.8
   unaffected young people, 5.7.1.1
Certification of human rights claims
   appeals within the UK, 4.1
Charges and fees
   births, marriages and deaths, 8.6
   civil registration, 8.6
   immigration skills arrangements, 8.1
   passport validation services, 8.5
   passports
     regulation-making powers, 8.2–8.3
     supplemental provision, 8.4
Child welfare
   general duty, 9.1
Citation
   general provision, 9.7
Civil registration
   fees and charges, 8.6
Closure notices
   illegal working, 1.38
Codes of practice
   English language requirements for public sector workers
     duty to issue, 7.5
     introduction, 7.1
     procedure, 7.6

Commencement
   general provision, 9.5
Community activities
   failed asylum seekers facing genuine obstacle to leaving the UK, 5.2.3.3
Compliance orders
   illegal working, 1.38
Consequential provisions
   generally, 9.3
'Contract'
   English language requirements, 7.8
'Contractor'
   English language requirements, 7.4
Crown application
   English language requirements, 7.9
'Crown employment'
   English language requirements, 7.2
Custody officers
   amendment to related provisions, 3.8
   search for nationality documents, 3.6
   seizure of nationality documents, 3.7
'Customer facing role'
   English language requirements, 7.2

'Deport first, appeal later'
   certification of human rights claims, 4.1
Detention
   immigration officers, by
     Scotland, in, 3.1
   pregnant women, of
     limitation, 3.15
   Scotland, in
     immigration officers, by, 3.11
   vulnerable persons, of
     guidance, 3.14
Devolution
   care leavers, and, 5.9
Director of Labour Market Enforcement (DLME)
   annual reports
     generally, 1.4
     publication, 1.5
   appointment, 1.1.1
   enforcement strategy, 1.2–1.3
   establishment, 1.1.1
   functions
     annual reports, 1.4–1.5
     enforcement strategy, 1.2–1.3
     generally, 1.1.1

Director of Labour Market Enforcement (DLME) – *contd*
functions – *contd*
information gateways, 1.6–1.7
information requests, 1.8
restriction on exercise, 1.9
funding, 1.1.1
information gateways, and
general provisions, 1.6
GLAA, and, 1.31
limits on disclosure, 1.7
persons to whom disclosure may be made, 1.6
specified persons, 1.31
supplementary, 1.7
information requests, and, 1.8
introduction, 1.1
labour market enforcement strategy, and
definitions, 1.3
general provision, 1.2
non-compliance in the labour market, 1.3
publication, 1.5
publication of strategy and reports, 1.5
reports
generally, 1.4
publication, 1.5
requests for information, 1.8
restriction on exercising functions as to individual cases, 1.9
staffing, 1.1.1

Disqualification from renting by immigration status
children, 2.1
commencement provisions, 2.2
disqualified persons, 2.1
eligibility for services, 2.3
eviction of disqualified occupiers, 2.5
excluded agreements, 2.1
housing and homelessness services, 2.3
introduction, 2.1
leasing premises offence, 2.4
'limited right to rent', 2.1
Northern Ireland, in, 2.7
order for possession of dwelling-house, 2.6
reasonable steps defence, 2.4
'relevant national', 2.1
relevant tenants, 2.1

Disqualification from renting by immigration status – *contd*
'residential tenancy agreement', 2.1
Scotland, in, 2.7
transitional provisions, 2.2
Wales, in, 2.

Driving
driving when unlawfully in the UK, 2.9
searches relating to licences, 2.8

Electronic monitoring
immigration bail, 3.16.3

Employing illegal workers
illegal working, 1.35

Enactment
definition, 9.3

Enforcement
custody officers
amendment to related provisions, 3.8
search for nationality documents, 3.6
seizure of nationality documents, 3.7
definitions, 3.13
detention
immigration officers, by, 3.1
pregnant women, 3.15
Scotland, in, 3.11
vulnerable persons, 3.14
detention in Scotland
immigration officers, by, 3.11
detention of pregnant women
limitation, 3.15
detention of vulnerable persons
guidance, 3.14
examination by immigration officers, 3.1
fingerprinting
certain persons and their dependants, 3.12
immigration bail
address of person bailed, 3.16.5
commencement of provisions, 3.16.1
conditions, 3.16.2–3.16.3
definitions, 3.16
duty to arrange consideration, 3.16.4
electronic monitoring, 3.16.3
general provision, 3.16
other provisions, 3.16.6
prohibition on repeat hearings, 3.16.6
support for person bailed, 3.16.5

Index

Enforcement – *contd*
  immigration officers
    definition, 3.13
    powers, 3.1–3.12
  immigration officers' powers
    detention in Scotland, 3.11
    examination, detention and
      removal, 3.1
    fingerprinting, 3.12
    retention of seized materials, 3.5
    search for nationality documents, 3.6
    search of premises, 3.1–3.2
    search warrants, 3.9
    seizure and retention, 3.3–3.4
    seizure of nationality documents, 3.7
  interpretation, 3.13
  leave extended under s 3C
    Immigration Act 1971
    power to cancel, 3.17
  'legal privilege', 3.13
  nationality documents
    search by custody officers, 3.6
    seizure by custody officers, 3.7
    supply to Secretary of State, 3.10
  PACE
    search warrants, 3.9
    seizure and retention, 3.3
  pregnant women
    limitation on detention, 3.15
  'premises', 3.13
  prison officers
    search for nationality
      documents, 3.6
  questioning by immigration
    officers, 3.1
  retention of seized materials, 3.5
  search for nationality documents, 3.6
  search of premises
    connection with imposition of civil
      penalty, in, 3.2
    connection with removal, in, 3.1
  search warrants
    amendment to provisions, 3.9
  seizure and retention
    duty to pass on items taken away, 3.4
    general powers, 3.3
    retention of seized materials, 3.5
  seizure of nationality documents, 3.7
  supply of information to Secretary
    of State

Enforcement – *contd*
  supply of information to Secretary of
    State – *contd*
    general provision, 3.10
    nationality documents, 3.10
    temporary admission, 3.16
English language requirements for public sector workers
  Codes of Practice
    duty to issue, 7.5
    introduction, 7.1
    procedure, 7.6
  'contract', 7.8
  'contractor', 7.4
  Crown application, 7.9
  'Crown employment', 7.2
  'customer facing role', 7.2
  definitions, 7.8
  'fluent', 7.2
  general provision, 7.2
  introduction, 7.1
  person working for public authority,
    7.2, 7.4
  'public authority', 7.3
  'relevant Minister', 7.8
  Welsh public authorities, and, 7.7
Examination of persons with leave
  immigration officers, by, 3.1
Extent
  general provision, 9.6

Failed asylum seekers facing genuine obstacle to leaving the UK
  support provision
    accommodation, 5.2.4
    cash, 5.2.4
    community activity condition, 5.2.3.3
    effect of refusal or discontinuation,
      5.2.3.4
    'failed asylum seeker', 5.2.3
    families with children, 5.2.4.1
    generally, 5.2.3
    'genuine obstacle to leaving the
      UK', 5.2.3.1
    nature, 5.2.4
    no right of appeal, 5.2.3.4
    other conditions of access, 5.2.3.3
    temporary arrangements, 5.2.5
    time limitations, 5.2.3.2
    transitional arrangements, 5.2.6

Families with children
   availability of local authority support
      additional welfare needs of child, 5.6.5
      amendments to Sch 3 NIAA 2002, 5.5
      care leavers, 5.7–5.9
      destitution, 5.6.4
      general provision, 5.4
      nature, 5.6.3
      new paragraph 10A, under, 5.6.1
      potential for gaps, 5.6.4
      promote and safeguard welfare of the child, 5.6.2
      purpose, 5.6
   care leavers
      affected young people, 5.7.1.2
      devolution, and, 5.9
      general provision, 5.4
      leaving care support, 5.7
      support under Sch 12 Para 10B, 5.7.2
      tuition fees, 5.8
      unaffected young people, 5.7.1.1
   failed asylum seekers facing genuine obstacle to leaving the UK, 5.2.4.1
   transfer of responsibility for relevant children
      extension to rest of UK, 5.15
      general provision, 5.11
      introduction, 5.10
      provision of information, 5.12
      request, 5.13
      scheme mechanism, 5.14

Family reunion
   generally, 5.3.4
   policies, 5.3.5

Fees and charges
   births, marriages and deaths, 8.6
   civil registration, 8.6
   immigration skills arrangements, 8.1
   passport validation services, 8.5
   passports
      regulation-making powers, 8.2–8.3
      supplemental provision, 8.4

Final provisions
   commencement, 9.5
   consequential, 9.3
   extent, 9.6

Final provisions – *contd*
   financial, 9.2
   regulations, 9.4
   short title, 9.7
   transitional, 9.3

Financial provisions
   generally, 9.2

Fingerprinting
   certain persons and their dependants, 3.12

'Fluent'
   English language requirements, 7.2

Freezing orders
   carrying out immigration checks on bank accounts, 2.10

Gangmasters and Labour Abuse Authority (GLAA)
   appointment of officers, 1.11
   enforcement, 1.11
   functions in the labour market, 1.11
   introduction, 1.1
   investigatory functions, 1.11
   labour abuse prevention officers, 1.12
   naming, 1.10
   PACE-related investigative and enforcement powers, 1.12
   relationship with other agencies, 1.13
   requests for assistance, 1.13
   role, 1.10

Gangmasters Licensing Authority (GLA)
   generally, 1.10

Genocide
   support for persons fleeing, 5.3.3

Harassment at work
   language requirements for public sector workers, and, 7.1

Hot pursuit onto High Seas
   maritime enforcement, 6.2

Humanitarian visas
   persons fleeing genocide, and, 5.3.3

Illegal working
   closure notices, 1.38
   compliance orders, 1.38
   definitions, 1.34
   employing illegal workers, 1.35
   general offence, 1.34

Index

Illegal working – *contd*
   licensed premises, in, 1.36
   private hire vehicles, 1.37
   transitional provision, 1.34
Immigration Act 2014
   immigration skills charges, 8.1
Immigration bail
   address of person bailed, 3.16.5
   commencement of provisions, 3.16.1
   conditions, 3.16.2–3.16.3
   definitions, 3.16
   duty to arrange consideration, 3.16.4
   electronic monitoring, 3.16.3
   general provision, 3.16
   other provisions, 3.16.6
   prohibition on repeat hearings, 3.16.6
   support for person bailed, 3.16.5
Immigration officers
   detention of persons in Scotland, 3.11
   definition, 3.13
   examination, detention and removal, 3.1
   fingerprinting, 3.12
   powers, 3.1–3.12
   retention of seized materials, 3.5
   search for nationality documents, 3.6
   search of premises, 3.1–3.2
   search warrants, 3.9
   seizure and retention, 3.3–3.4
   seizure of nationality documents, 3.7
Immigration skills arrangements
   charges and fees, 8.1
Information gateways
   general provisions, 1.6
   GLAA, and, 1.31
   limits on disclosure, 1.7
   persons to whom disclosure may be made, 1.6
   specified persons, 1.31
   supplementary, 1.7
Information hub
   generally, 1.8

Labour abuse prevention officers
   generally, 1.12
Labour market
   consequential amendments, 1.31
   definitions, 1.33

Labour market – *contd*
   Director of Labour Market Enforcement (DLME)
   annual reports, 1.4–1.5
   appointment, 1.1.1
   enforcement strategy, 1.2–1.3
   establishment, 1.1.1
   functions, 1.1.1
   funding, 1.1.1
   introduction, 1.1
   publication of strategy and reports, 1.5
   reports, 1.4
   staffing, 1.1.1.
   Gangmasters and Labour Abuse Authority
   appointment of officers, 1.11
   enforcement, 1.11
   functions in the labour market, 1.11
   introduction, 1.1
   investigatory functions, 1.11
   labour abuse prevention officers, 1.12
   naming, 1.10
   PACE-related investigative and enforcement powers, 1.12
   relationship with other agencies, 1.13
   requests for assistance, 1.13
   role, 1.10
   Gangmasters Licensing Authority, 1.10
   illegal working
   closure notices, 1.38
   compliance orders, 1.38
   definitions, 1.34
   employing illegal workers, 1.35
   general offence, 1.34
   licensed premises, in, 1.36
   private hire vehicles, 1.37
   transitional provision, 1.34
   information gateways
   general provisions, 1.6
   GLAA, and, 1.31
   limits on disclosure, 1.7
   persons to whom disclosure may be made, 1.6
   specified persons, 1.31
   supplementary, 1.7

Index

Labour market – *contd*
  information hub, 1.8
  interpretation, 1.33
  introduction, 1.1
  labour abuse prevention officers, 1.12
  'labour market enforcement functions', 1.3
  labour market enforcement strategy
    definitions, 1.3
    general provision, 1.2
    non-compliance in the labour market, 1.3
    publication, 1.5
  labour market enforcement orders
    appeals, 1.24
    applications, 1.19
    code of practice, 1.25
    conviction, on, 1.20
    discharge, 1.23
    failure to comply, 1.27
    further provision, 1.22
    investigative functions, 1.26
    measures available, 1.21
    offences by bodies corporate, 1.28
    partnerships, 1.30
    power to make on application, 1.18
    supplementary, 1.25
    unincorporated associations, 1.29
    variation, 1.23
  labour market enforcement undertaking
    code of practice, 1.25
    duration, 1.16
    giving of notice, 1.17
    introduction, 1.14
    investigative functions, 1.26
    measures, 1.15
    power to request, 1.14.1
    supplementary, 1.25
  labour market offence, 1.3
  non-compliance in the labour market, 1.3
  overseas domestic workers, 1.33.1
  regulations, 1.32
  restriction on exercising functions as to individual cases, 1.9
  unincorporated associations, 1.29
Labour market enforcement orders
  appeals, 1.24
  applications, 1.19

Labour market enforcement orders – *contd*
  code of practice, 1.25
  conviction, on, 1.20
  discharge, 1.23
  failure to comply, 1.27
  further provision, 1.22
  investigative functions, 1.26
  measures available, 1.21
  offences by bodies corporate, 1.28
  partnerships, 1.30
  power to make on application, 1.18
  supplementary, 1.25
  unincorporated associations, 1.29
  variation, 1.23
Labour market enforcement strategy
  definitions, 1.3
  general provision, 1.2
  non-compliance in the labour market, 1.3
  publication, 1.5
Labour market enforcement undertaking
  code of practice, 1.25
  duration, 1.16
  giving of notice, 1.17
  introduction, 1.14
  investigative functions, 1.26
  measures, 1.15
  power to request, 1.14.1
  supplementary, 1.25
Language requirements for public sector workers
  Codes of Practice
    duty to issue, 7.5
    introduction, 7.1
    procedure, 7.6
  'contract', 7.8
  'contractor', 7.4
  Crown application, 7.9
  'Crown employment', 7.2
  'customer facing role', 7.2
  definitions, 7.8
  'fluent', 7.2
  general provision, 7.2
  introduction, 7.1
  person working for public authority, 7.2, 7.4

Index

Language requirements for public sector workers – *contd*
'public authority', 7.3
'relevant Minister', 7.8
Welsh public authorities, and, 7.7
Leave extended under s 3C Immigration Act 1971
power to cancel, 3.17
Leave to enter
deemed refusal, 4.3
Legal privilege
generally, 3.13
Licensed premises
illegal working, 1.36
Local authority support
care leavers
affected young people, 5.7.1.2
devolution, and, 5.9
general provision, 5.4
leaving care support, 5.7
support under Sch 12 Para 10B, 5.7.2
tuition fees, 5.8
unaffected young people, 5.7.1.1
families with children
additional welfare needs of child, 5.6.5
amendments to Sch 3 NIAA 2002, 5.5
care leavers, 5.7–5.9
destitution, 5.6.4
general provision, 5.4
nature, 5.6.3
new paragraph 10A, under, 5.6.1
potential for gaps, 5.6.4
promote and safeguard welfare of the child, 5.6.2
purpose, 5.6
Locally engaged staff in Afghanistan and Iraq
generally, 5.3.2

Maritime enforcement
exercise of powers by officers, 6.2
hot pursuit onto High Seas, 6.2
Maritime officers
exercise of enforcement powers, 6.2

Nationality documents
search by custody officers, 3.6
seizure by custody officers, 3.7
supply to Secretary of State, 3.10
Northern Ireland
extent of Act, 9.6

Overseas domestic workers
generally, 1.33.1

PACE
search warrants, 3.9
seizure and retention, 3.3
Passport validation services
fees and charges, 8.5
Passports
fees and charges
regulation-making powers, 8.2–8.3
supplemental provision, 8.4
validation services, 8.5
Penalties
airport control areas, 6.1
Persons excluded from the UK
international obligations, under, 6.3
Persons fleeing genocide
generally, 5.3.3
Persons working for public authority
English language requirements
extended meaning, 7.4
generally, 7.2, 7.4
Pregnant women
limitation on detention, 3.15
Premises
generally, 3.13
Presence not conducive to the public good
certification of human rights claims, 4.1
Penalties
airport control areas, 6.1
Persons excluded from the UK
international obligations, under, 6.3
Primary legislation
meaning, 9.4
Prison officers
search for nationality documents, 3.6
Private hire vehicles
illegal working, 1.37

526

'Public authority'
English language requirements, 7.3
Public sector workers
English language requirements
Codes of Practice, 7.5–7.6
'contract', 7.8
'contractor', 7.4
Crown application, 7.9
'Crown employment', 7.2
'customer facing role', 7.2
definitions, 7.8
'fluent', 7.2
general provision, 7.2
introduction, 7.1
person working for public authority, 7.2, 7.4
'public authority', 7.3
'relevant Minister', 7.8
Welsh public authorities, and, 7.7
recruitment, 7.1

Questioning of persons with leave
immigration officers, by, 3.1

Refugee children
relocation and support, 5.3
Regulations
general provision, 9.4
'Relevant Minister'
English language requirements, 7.8
Relocated unaccompanied refugee children
generally, 5.3
Repeal provisions
continuation of leave, 4.2
deemed refusal of leave to enter, 4.3
Residential tenancies
disqualification from renting by immigration status
children, 2.1
commencement provisions, 2.2
disqualified persons, 2.1
eligibility for services, 2.3
eviction of disqualified occupiers, 2.5
excluded agreements, 2.1
housing and homelessness services, 2.3
introduction, 2.1

Residential tenancies – *contd*
disqualification from renting by immigration status – *contd*
leasing premises offence, 2.4
'limited right to rent', 2.1
Northern Ireland, in, 2.7
order for possession of dwelling-house, 2.6
reasonable steps defence, 2.4
'relevant national', 2.1
relevant tenants, 2.1
'residential tenancy agreement', 2.1
Scotland, in, 2.7
transitional provisions, 2.2
Wales, in, 2.7
Retention of seized materials
generally, 3.5

Scotland
extent of Act, 9.6
Searches
driving licences, for, 2.8
nationality documents, for, 3.6
premises, of
connection with imposition of civil penalty, in, 3.2
connection with removal, in, 3.1
Search warrants
amendment to provisions, 3.9
Seizure and retention
duty to pass on items taken away, 3.4
general powers, 3.3
retention of seized materials, 3.5
Seizure of nationality documents
generally, 3.7
Serious irreversible harm
certification of human rights claims, 4.1
Short title
general provision, 9.7
Statutory instruments
meaning, 9.4
Supply of information to Secretary of State
general provision, 3.10
nationality documents, 3.10

527

Index

Support provision
- asylum seekers, for
  - categories of migrant, 5.2
  - facing genuine obstacle to leaving the UK, 5.2.3–5.2.3.3
  - introduction, 5.1
  - making further submissions as to protection claims, 5.2.2
  - other debated issues, 5.3.1–5.3.5
  - repeal of s 4 IAA 1999, 5.2.1
  - unaccompanied refugee children, 5.3
- failed asylum seekers facing genuine obstacle to leaving the UK, for
  - accommodation, 5.2.4
  - cash, 5.2.4
  - community activity condition, 5.2.3.3
  - effect of refusal or discontinuation, 5.2.3.4
  - 'failed asylum seeker', 5.2.3
  - families with children, 5.2.4.1
  - generally, 5.2.3
  - 'genuine obstacle to leaving the UK', 5.2.3.1
  - nature, 5.2.4
  - no right of appeal, 5.2.3.4
  - other conditions of access, 5.2.3.3
  - temporary arrangements, 5.2.5
  - time limitations, 5.2.3.2
  - transitional arrangements, 5.2.6
- family reunion, and
  - generally, 5.3.4
  - policies, 5.3.5

Support provision – *contd*
- locally engaged staff in Afghanistan and Iraq, and, 5.3.2
- persons fleeing genocide, and, 5.3.3
- persons on immigration bail, for, 3.16.5
- relocated unaccompanied refugee children, for, 5.3

Temporary admission
- generally, 3.16

Transfer of responsibility for relevant children
- extension to rest of UK, 5.15
- general provision, 5.11
- introduction, 5.10
- provision of information, 5.12
- request, 5.13
- scheme mechanism, 5.14

Transitional provisions
- generally, 9.3

Unaccompanied refugee children
- relocation and support, 5.3

Unincorporated associations
- generally, 1.29

Wales
- English language requirements for public sector workers, 7.7
- extent of Act, 9.6

Welfare of children
- general duty, 9.1

Welsh public authorities
- English language requirements, 7.7